Frommer's®

Suzy Gershman's

where to buy the best of everything

The Outspoken Guide
for World Travelers and
Online Shoppers

1st Edition

D1534043

WILEY

Wiley Publishing, Inc.

For ETM,
with all my heart and all my love and all my best wishes

Published by:

WILEY PUBLISHING, INC.

111 River St.
Hoboken, NJ 07030-5774

ISBN: 978-0-470-04304-2
Editor: Stephen Bassman
Special thanks to Marc Nadeau, Alexia Travaglini and Jennifer Reilly
Production Editor: Katie Robinson
Photo Editor: Richard Fox
Cartographer: Guy Ruggiero
Production by Wiley Indianapolis Composition Services

For information on our other products and services or to obtain technical support, please contact our Customer Care Department within the U.S. at 800/762-2974, outside the U.S. at 317/572-3993 or fax 317/572-4002.

Wiley also publishes its books in a variety of electronic formats. Some content that appears in print may not be available in electronic formats.

Manufactured in the United States of America

5 4 3 2 1

Contents

Map List

About the Authors

Suzy Gershman is a journalist, author, and global-shopping goddess who has worked in the fashion and fiber industry for more than 25 years. Her essays on retailing have been used by the Harvard School of Business; her reportage on travel and retail has appeared in *Travel & Leisure, Travel Holiday, Travel Weekly,* and most of the major women's magazines. She is translated into French for Condé Nast's *Air France Madame* magazine. The *Born to Shop* series, now over 20 years old, is translated into eight languages.

Gershman is also the author of *C'est La Vie* (Viking and Penguin Paperback), the story of her first year as a widow living in Paris. She divides her time between her new home in San Diego, a small house in Provence and the airport.

Sarah Lahey retired from her career in home style to raise a family and recently rejoined the work force as editorial director for the *Born to Shop* series. Sarah also shows and sells English smalls at several Northern California antiques fairs. She lives with her husband and dogs, Bentley and Bex, outside San Francisco.

To Start With

I grew up in Texas where, during my childhood, stores advertised that they were the "biggest store in the biggest state." When Alaska was admitted to the Union, they modified to say they were simply the "best stores in the best state."

I learned then that *best* is a very subjective word.

Over 25 years of writing the Born to Shop guides has convinced me even further that not only is *best* a matter of opinion, but it's also a matter of perspective. The *best of what* is a far more productive inquiry.

Best is used in lists and magazine covers and guidebooks and door medallions—actually, the best barbeque in Texas (Rudy's in San Antonio) is behind a sign that reads "Worst Bar-B-Que in Texas." Some like to claim that the major brands are therefore the best brands—they have the reputation and the track record—while others claim that the best is always a secret passed on to rich people who know which craftsmen to use. Sometimes the *best* is—to me, anyway—simply where you are guaranteed to get value for your money, find what you are looking for in the first place, and have a great time in the hunting and gathering game of life.

"When you buy the best, you only cry once."

—Chinese proverb

While I understand and appreciate luxury brands and the concept of luxe, I don't believe that the best things in life have designer tags on them. In fact, during the early parts of the creation of this book, I called it *Best Wishes* because that seems to be the only thing the world can agree on when it comes to the best.

A discussion of the best things in life has little to do with shopping, but stores, bargains, and heart-stopping shopping adventures are indeed my expertise. In this guide, I have tried to create a workbook of exceptional stores in all price categories— the stores most notable for what they do or how they sell merchandise, the best stores for serving a specific purpose. They are by no means the fanciest stores in the world or the most expensive.

I've also looked at what some other people consider the best stores to assess how they fit into the shopper's community of excellence. For example, I don't think that Neiman Marcus is one of the best stores in America. It might have been at one time, but it has changed. (Haven't we all?) Neiman Marcus was best at starting something new in American retail—bringing style and designers to the American South—but it continues to be among the best at something else: their information services that help clients shop. So I have covered the store from its historic as well as its present position in the world of retail, as I see it.

THE ORIGINS OF THIS BOOK

All literature, it is said, derives from two simple truths: Somebody comes to town; somebody leaves town.

While this book is nonfiction, and surely not literature, it began from the same roots. Shortly after my late husband's death in 2000, I gave up my home in the U.S. and moved to France.

Somebody leaves town.

Cleaning out—and selling—my large house in the suburbs was pure torture, like enduring another death in the family. I still shudder when I think of the indignities of a tag sale. Yet I was able to part with my things and not my research materials. When I moved to France, I took with me files and maps and notebooks and all the workbooks I had piled up in not only twenty years of *Born to Shop* reporting, but countless cruise itineraries, tours, and research trips for magazine articles.

Six years later, I bought a house in Texas, as my father was then 87 years old and suddenly ailing. (I spent 2 years near him before he died. Then I moved to San Diego.)

Somebody comes to town.

I did not give up my French residency, but I did put a full office into the San Antonio house and shipped over all my files from Paris. When I first contacted shippers and saw the cost of sending books and paper, I decided I'd better evaluate exactly what I had stashed in my *cave* in Paris and spread all over my house in Provence. Should I pay the high costs of shipping everything back and forth across the Atlantic, or should I trash the stuff? Perhaps the names and addresses and stores stored up were no longer useful. On the other hand, perhaps they were gold. Hmmm.

I decided to test a few of my resources. It didn't take long to realize I had a gigantic accumulation of what I consider important information, ranging from notes on how to buy jewelry (taken in Rio at an interview with the late Hans Stern, founder of H. Stern jewellers), to where to buy reindeer soap in Oslo. My notes had phone numbers and websites. I realized it would be pretty easy to check old information, update it, and add new insights . . . and websites. The germ of this book was born.

Of course, with the decision to write this book came the need to make several trips around the world to make sure I was totally up to date. There were also a few dirty little secrets I didn't want revealed on a chat show: I had never been to Sydney or Delhi. (That's been fixed.)

Texas is great, but hey—a woman with wanderlust can't stay one place fer long (pardner). Since I was continually traveling back to my house in Provence and keeping up with ongoing research for the Born to Shop series and for other print projects, I made some detours along the way. Yeah, I did gain ten pounds and travel 100,000 extra miles in the last year and a half, but I couldn't give you better info if we sat down to lunch together, just you and I.

AND . . . VOILA

The book you are now holding has been in gestation in the attic, across the sea, under the bed and in the bamboo armoire, awaiting the electronic age and a million frequent flyer miles, waiting for me to be ready. It is a thoroughly fact-checked rendition of my Rolodex, my Filofax, my hard drive, and a million miles of international travel—and possibly $1 million worth of shopping expeditions. Sorry you missed the tag sale, but this is more useful, I think.

This book is for everyone who is interested in shopping, in the retail business, or the ways products are marketed and merchandised. I cover everything from couture to cut-rate, so you needn't be a high-end shopper to successfully use these pages. I've always thought that I write for and serve people with more imagination than money. It doesn't take much to walk into a fancy store and buy something you like—or something a clever sales person tells you to buy—it only takes money. This book is for people who have the curiosity to try new brands, to get out and see, to order online, to travel to a foreign destination, or to explore a shopping experience as a whole.

This is a travel log, an everyday blog, and an exploration into the marketing and sale of merchandise the world over. My publisher calls it "outspoken"; I call it honest. The book is as much for those with wanderlust as it is for the armchair shopper. It was created not to reflect your fantasy life but instead to be practical, to make your life and your shopping easier.

I've tried to incorporate information throughout that reflects our current lifestyle and the cultural trends that brought us to the kind of shopping and products we have today, with a nod to why we buy certain things. This is the book I have worked much of my career to write.

HOW TO USE THIS BOOK

This guide is divided into 12 chapters. There are also several indexes, divided by category of goods and destinations. If we did our job right, the book is fairly simple to use, and versatile. If you're in the market for new furniture, read through "Chapter Nine: Home Style & Tabletop." If you're travelling to Tokyo, see my suggestions in "Chapter Twelve: The Best Shopping Destinations & Adventures"—and consult the Index for Tokyo in the back of this book. Or simply open this book to any page, and I hope you'll find a store or travel tip that will inspire you to plan your next shopping vacation.

All listings are divided into four parts, starting with **the very top line of the review,** which includes the name of the store or brand and some very simple icons, including 🛒, which means that this is a store I single out in "Chapter Two: The World's Best: The Short List." The VALUE tag doesn't mean the items are inexpensive; it means you get good value for what you pay.

The top line also includes nationality, and all listings have one (sometimes two) attached to them. I distinguish between the store brand's nationality and the designer's with a slash mark. (So a Stella McCartney listing for Adidas would say GERMAN/BRITISH because Adidas is a German-based brand but McCartney is English.) Since I am from the state of Texas, stores that originate or are anchored in Texas are marked as TEXAN. As any Texan can tell you, Texas may be part of the U.S. and proud of it, but Texas is also a place unto itself. (Hook 'em.) One-of-a-kind stores will note the location, not the nationality. So Elegant Linens (p. 307) is labelled PARK CITY, UTAH (not USA).

At the end of the top line you'll find pricing information, which is against my better judgement because prices change constantly and currency fluctuates. But you know this, so I know you can cope. We have used this scale:

$$\begin{aligned}
\$ &= \text{up to } \$25 \\
\$\$ &= \text{up to } \$50 \\
\$\$\$ &= \text{up to } \$100 \\
\$\$\$\$ &= \text{up to } \$1,000 \\
\$\$\$\$\$ &= \text{over } \$1,000
\end{aligned}$$

Prices in the book are in U.S. dollars, and the basic rate of exchange used was:

$$\begin{aligned}
\pounds 1 &= \$2 \\
1\euro &= \$1.40 \\
\text{HK}\$7 &= \$1 \\
7 \text{ yuan} &= \$1 \\
\yen 100 &= \$1
\end{aligned}$$

The bulk of each listing consists of my thoughts on the subject matter and why I think this store or product is among the best in the world.

Below that you'll find my recommendations for **"Best Bets,"** or my favourite products at that particular store. Then, onto **"Web Tips,"** a section I took seriously; I am not sure this book would even exist today if it wasn't, in a small way, somewhat about online shopping. Without the Web, this would be a travel guide. With it, it's a practical guide. As a result, most reviews include some tips for ordering online. So you don't have to go to Provence to buy Joël Durand chocolates (p. 382).

Each review ends with what I call the nitty-gritty, or **"Where to Buy."** Here, I've tried to list the number of stores worldwide, other stores where you'll find the brand, and information about the flagship stores—both in the home country and again in the U.S. (if there are two). As anyone who has ever gone online already knows, to find the store nearest to you, go to the "store locator" feature on the appropriate website.

Finally, you may see a tip embedded in a review in bold for emphasis. **"World Traveler"** gives you tips you'll need if you're travelling and shopping ("don't miss these other stores on this block in Tokyo's Gaza district," and so on); **"Buyer Beware"** points out the drawbacks or restrictions of some otherwise fine brands; and **"Shop Talk"** injects a bit of celebrity and fashion culture into the book. If Madonna is shopping there or Oprah is told she cannot shop there, I've noted it here. Bon appétit.

FINAL CONFESSIONS

I have suffered more or less the same nightmare for well over three years. I wake up screaming, "LouLou."

The LouLou in question is LouLou de la Falaise who now has one very charming, very interesting, very exciting store in Paris (p. 51). In my nightmare, I have left her—and her store—out of this book. I live in fear that there are stores I know very well—and admire dearly—which for some reason or another escaped me at the crucial moment of organization and did not end up in this book. Oh God, where's my heart medicine?

There is a second part to the anxiety dream. This part is not as frantic but concerns me nonetheless.

I worry that you will enjoy a listing in this book and specifically seek out that store. You look around and mutter to yourself, "Is she nuts?"

It's not that I worry that we don't share the same taste. I worry that the store has changed, that there's been a bad season or that somehow you've seen another side of the store (or used another entrance). Send me your tales of stores gone wrong and other comments and candidates for a future edition at suzy@suzygershman.com.

This book is woven with dreams and hopes and visions and ideas. It's my most fervent wish that some of the truths herein touch your soul and give you a new view on retail and the world—and that the fishing is good no matter where you roam.

ACKNOWLEDGMENTS

This book has been a labor of love and psychosis for over three years. I never would have gotten through it without the help of Sarah Lahey, *Born to Shop* Editorial Director, who held me together and also did research and lots of work on these pages.

Sarah flew around the world with me a few times, endured the French Internet café and spent enormous effort birthing this book.

I've also had a lot of support from my partner Ed, who let me whine and financed many of the explorations needed to complete these pages.

A number of personal friends not only helped me, but got their families involved—Pamela Mullin gave me a few listings and brought in her daughter and son-in-law, Darcy and Matt Cobb, to teach me how the young, rich and gorgeous of Los Angeles are shopping these days.

The editorial team, especially editor Steve Bassman, has been supportive and patient—I thank them for many years of wisdom and hard work. My agent, Alice Martell, and her daughter, Katie, have been invaluable—as always. Katie joined the Board of Advisors as our Teen Queen.

Indeed, the Board of Advisors has been a great resource to help me work out raw edges and refine geographical boundaries.

I thank all of you from the bottom of my heart.

Board of Advisors:
Gaby Atherton, Rio
Stephen Bassman, New York
Paul Baumrind, New York
Elana Berlin, American Girl
Trude G. Boodt, Scottsdale & Paris
Spencer Christian, San Francisco
Sally Shelton Colby, Paris & Provence
Karen Fawcett, Paris & D.C.
Michele Geddes Peck, New York
Peter Greenberg, Mastertrav himself
Dorie Greenspan, New York & Paris
Betty Murray Halff, Queen of Catalogs
Ruth Jacobs, London
Aaron James, Los Angeles
Mira Jarvinen, Philadelphia & Palm Beach
Diane Johnson, San Francisco & Paris
Johanne Killeen, Providence, Boston & Provence
Sarah Lahey, Editorial Director *Born to Shop*
Alexander Lobrano, Paris
Carolyn Logan, Atlanta
Katie Martell, Teen Queen
Jennifer McCormick, Los Angeles
Robert Price, San Antonio & Paris
Maggie Sheerin, R.I.P.
Craig Smith, Atlanta
Richard Sungaila, Orange County
Hans Stern, Rio, R.I.P.
Leonard Rabinowitz, Los Angeles
Janelle Wang, San Francisco
Kimberly Zenz, Shipping Goddess

Chapter One

*How to Be a Shopping
God or Goddess*

*Y*ou would know if you were meant to be a Shopping God or Goddess—it's an innate skill that comes not from shopping, but from shopping well. But like any natural talent, it doesn't mean you are born with a complete set of skills or can't improve yourself. Didn't mother tell you that practice makes perfect?

Mere mortals may ask how to get to Carnegie Hall (practice, practice, practice), but a Shopping God or Goddess wants to know how to get to Woodbury Common.

Many were born to shop; few have the historical perspective to be a Shopping God or Goddess.

We always hold hands. If I let go, she shops.

—Henny Youngman

Over 25 years ago, when I first had the idea for the Born to Shop series of travel guides, I went to my then agent and said something like "Voilà!"

She was not impressed with my book outline and refused to handle the proposal or the series—she said I was a serious journalist who worked for *Time* magazine and I would ruin my reputation by writing about a silly subject like shopping. I took the proposal to my husband's agent, who sold it in 2 days.

I tell this story because I have always been convinced that it is my training as a serious journalist that took me—and the guides I write—where I am now and is what makes me different from the man in the street or the woman in the mall.

This is a serious book; I consider shopping to be as good an indication of sociological and psychological statements about the times and the population as any other medium. I did not spend 3 years of my life writing this book to consider it frivolous, so stop sniggering.

How to move from being Born to Shop into the strata of Shopping God or Goddess? Herewith, my tips and secrets.

BE CURIOUS

Maybe curiosity killed the cat, but it rarely kills the shopper. (I don't mean to be glib here—curiosity can kill the shopper—don't go down any alleys in search of a fake Vuitton handbag.)

Intellectual curiosity is part of many professions, and it is vitally important to the Shopping Goddess. But I'm also talking motivational curiosity—you have to *want to know* what's up those stairs, around the bend, at the far corner of the mall or just up yonder in that little hut there.

Very often I feel like the Indian scout in all those cowboy and Indian movies I watched as a child. I ride ahead to see what's out there, to make sure it's safe for the rest of you guys. That's my job. I walk the extra flight of stairs; I climb every mountain.

The scouting part of curiosity is driven by physical strength, but you must also be willing to ask a lot of questions. You have to listen, not talk. One of my favorite ways to gain information is to play the game I call "Dumb American"—this works best outside of America—but I thrill to walking up to the desk and saying something like, "I don't know anything about this brand. Can you tell me about the designer? Where's this made? Who owns this company?"

This is not to say I believe what I am told, but it's a start. Then you can do more research. You can't move beyond the mall without doing a good bit of research.

DO YOUR RESEARCH

Research is part of curiosity, of course, but at a certain point it takes you way past being merely curious and into being educated. Online research is good—and easy for anyone with a computer—but in-person research is the most valuable. If you watch as many police dramas as I do, you know that walking a beat is important and face-to-face interviews are even more important.

As they say in the opening number of the Broadway musical *The Music Man,* "you've gotta know the territory." If you like to be a smart shopper (I frankly like being an emotional shopper), you will learn everything you can about the product and the company that makes it before you dive in. The higher the price tag, the more need for serious research. Pretend you are a market analyst for a Wall Street firm.

Comparison shopping is another part of research. You don't know if you've been smart until you know what's out there—and where. I once led a shopping tour in Hong Kong and noticed that one of my guests took notes everywhere we went and then went online in the hotel lounge each afternoon to compare Hong Kong prices to those available back in the U.S. Now there's a Shopping God in the making.

While I do research online, I don't find it very rewarding; yes, the Internet is a miracle and is a source of facts, when you can find them—but the Internet is lacking in soul. Most of my work is done with magazines—and then followed up in person. My home looks like the waiting room of a dentist's office.

They know me at the seniors' residence around the corner because I drop off a valise full of magazines every other month. I hope that the seniors do not notice how much has already been torn from these magazines.

I subscribe to zillions of magazines, but I also buy them in airports—great for regional publications—and load up on foreign magazines whenever I can. If I have guests coming from faraway destinations and they ask what they can bring me, I always request magazines. When I arrive in any city on a road trip, the first thing I do after check-in is check out the room for available free magazines and then head to the nearest newsagent to load up. Yes, this is expensive.

While foreign languages are not my strong suit, I have discovered you don't need to be Henry Higgins to delight in foreign magazines, especially if they have pictures. Ones in an alphabet you can quickly read are more easily digested, but in a pinch I will decipher Greek and Russian. (I am lost with Asian and Arabic languages.) If the picture has a name and address and looks worth checking out, I will translate.

I get a lot of tips and a lot of information from magazines; I tear and clip and save and follow up. I subscribe to the *Washington Post* rule of three hard checks—when I have found one mention of the same source from three different publications, I put it on the list for personal inspection. In the end, it's only after personal inspection that I know anything. To make sure you understand the need to touch and feel the merchandise, let me quickly tell you the story of a pair of navy trousers.

I love the brand Territory Ahead. They have only a handful of retail stores, and none are near where I live. I must shop by catalog or online. So, in my trusty catalog I find a pair of trousers I love and plan to order them. I never get anything done when I plan to, so the order form sits on the floor next to my desk for a few weeks. By chance, I get to the store in Berkeley and find the trousers in the flesh. They are awful. Who could have known that from the picture in the catalog or online? Instead, I choose others that I adore.

No matter how good the brand, you never know anything until you've seen it, touched it and in some cases smelled and tasted it before you can pass judgment. Nothing, but nothing, replaces personal reconnaissance.

GO TO MUSEUMS

People laugh at me whenever I say that all good shopping sprees begin in a museum. I'm not trying to be funny.

If you are at all interested in merchandise (of any quality or price), you can't judge it accurately until you know what the best looks like, until you've learned the elements that make the best be the best.

Especially seek out museums of art, folk art and industrial and product design. And going to the gift shop doesn't count; you need to peruse the collections.

TRUST NO ONE

I rarely follow up on personal tips. I have spent years following other people's advice and recommendations and found that as much as I like or trust the person, I rarely agree with his opinions on what makes a good store or a worthwhile shopping adventure. Don't accept anyone's opinions (including mine) as gospel without checking them out for yourself.

In the long run, no one else's opinion matters except for yours. Nothing replaces personal reconnaissance.

BE SKEPTICAL

I guess skepticism goes with trust, but I put it into a different category because I have many levels on which I am skeptical.

Let me tell you about my first job in New York. I was a guest editor at a major magazine, spending 1 month working in their offices in New York. I was 20 years old and very sophisticated for my age. Although I came to New York from Texas, I was not just off the ranch or out of the dust bowl. Nonetheless, I believed in magazines.

Then one day, while at a photo shoot, I saw the assistant— a young woman a few years older than me—fix the model's hair and apply her makeup from whatever tools were laid out on the table. When the photos ran, the makeup credits included all major brands and specific colors that were new to the season and being touted in the advertising. I was shocked, horrified and fascinated. You mean it's all a sham?

Well, yes—a lot of it is a sham; not all of it, but a lot of it. Sham, however, is too harsh a word. It's merely business. It's not personal; it's just business. Magazines exist by selling advertising. All editorial is merely packaging to bring you a bevy of ads.

Do you remember the day you found out there was no Santa Claus? How about the day you found out the truth about a Cadillac? I actually took the news about Santa a lot more calmly—but when I discovered that there was no "Best Car in America" created specifically as a Cadillac but that it was merely an amalgam of upscale General Motors parts, well, I

10 Shopping Scams & How to Avoid Them

1. **The price miscalculation:** The clerk calculates a price in U.S. dollars, but uses the wrong exchange rate, making the price appear quite attractive. *Avoid It:* Know your exchange rate, and mention it to the clerk while he or she calculates.

2. **The sketchy shop referral:** "My cousin owns this shop. You can trust him." Right. *Avoid It:* Disregard all unsolicited referrals.

3. **The classic bait & switch:** This one's been around for centuries. That great deal in the ad (the bait) turns out to be "no longer available" so you're stuck browsing for other items that are "just as good" (the switch). *Avoid It:* Call the shop to confirm the deal before you go.

4. **The floor sample bait & switch:** You buy an item but are told you have taken the sample and you will be brought a fresh one "from the back." The new item is not the same quality. *Avoid It:* Inspect all "items from the back," and never let a clerk pack or wrap your items out of sight.

5. **The can't-get-it-in-the-U.S. pitch:** "This item is okay but you can get it in United States. This *other* model is brand new, costs a little more but is much better and you can only buy it here." *Avoid It:* Ignore the pitch, and try to talk the price down; assume both items are worth the same.

6. **The gift-card wipeout:** You answer an online ad for a discounted luxury gift card (say $350 for a $500 card) and verify the card's value at the store before paying the seller. When you go to use the card a few days or weeks later you learn that the seller has wiped out the value online. (Sad but true: The editor of this guide has firsthand research for this one.) *Avoid It:* Know

felt as if I'd been kicked inside. Nowadays I hear a Toyota and a Lexus are the same car. What's a consumer to do?

A lot of research and a lot of quiet reflection.

The next time you believe someone's opinion on what's best, remember that photo shoot and your grandmother's Cadillac. Consider all editorial and advertorial information with a grain of salt.

As an amusing aside, I want you to know that the young woman I mentioned went on to become the president of a major makeup firm and is one of the most powerful women in beauty today.

To further make my point, let's take this one more step. In my research I find a magazine article that says the hottest new which stores allow you to use gift card codes online. If you still insist on buying the card, have your purchases ready at the store cashier and use the card immediately before you pay the seller.

7. **The "handcrafted" lie:** You are assured that this charming item was handcrafted by local artisans when in fact it is a mass-produced item made in a factory in China. *Avoid It:* If you cannot verify craftsmanship, assume that all products are factory-made, and pay accordingly.

8. **The blank shipping fees voucher ("sign here"):** You allow the very nice shopkeeper to mail the item for you, and she admits that she doesn't know exactly what the shipping will cost because the item must be packed and weighed at the post office (this makes sense)—so you must sign a second credit card voucher, with the price to be filled in once the post office supplies the information. Ha. *Avoid It:* Always agree on a specific fee before you pay for shipping.

9. **The refund empty promise:** "If you change your mind about this, I will give you a full refund." *Avoid It:* Always assume otherwise.

10. **Online auction scams:** This is reportedly the most common Internet scam: You buy that antique bike on eBay for $300, pay, then never hear from the seller again. *Avoid It:* Beware of fake eBay websites and emails that don't contain "ebay.com/" or "ebay.co.uk/". (Make sure the slash mark is in the right place.) Also beware of sellers with zero feedback or numerous feedback/bids from a single source. For more eBay scam tips, try the blog www.trevorginn.com.

designer with the must-have item of the season is so and so and suggests I rush right out and buy one of his handbags for $800 to $1,200. For that kind of money, I can have just about any handbag in the store (as long as the store isn't Chanel or Fendi). Why would I spend my hard-earned bucks on a name-less newcomer just because someone else told me he was hot? And what if that someone at the magazine was this year's version of the girl I knew in 1969 who threw together the hair and makeup for the photo shoots?

You always doubt.

Because you are skeptical, you don't fall—even if tempted—when the sales clerk tells you that the VAT is 19% so the million-dollar handbag you are considering will actually be 20% less.

You know that while VAT may indeed be levied at 19%, it is refunded at 12%. You are skeptical of sales pitches, no matter how attractive they seem. You doubt editorial and even advertorial. You trust advertising only in countries where it's against the law to lie in adverts.

So you already know that the store on Fifth Avenue, the one with the giant handwritten banner, is not really Going Out Of Business.

NETWORK

The Shopping Goddess is proud of her shopping and bargaining skills, but more importantly, she loves information (as does any curious person). She is happy to pass on what she's learned. When the passing only goes one direction, she may become mildly annoyed or even passive-aggressive. But when she has like-minded friends, she develops a network.

Many of the people listed on the Board of Advisors page of this book make up my personal network. We share serious shopping information. Yesterday Trude wrote me that she found Ahava products at Bath & Body Works. My friend Elana told me about the American Girl sale (p. 282).

A few weeks ago, Richard sent me the address of the TSE Cashmere factory in Southern California. Richard and I have been sharing shopping tips for about 20 years. We don't have much of a social fabric—we get together whenever we're in the same town at the same time, which is rare, and we e-mail only when we have a winner. But that's the kind of network that makes you a God, not a shopper. And Richard is a God.

Because of the trust factor, the network does not include informational or advertorial services provided online. The Shopping Goddess's network is personal, as is trust.

LEARN THE BUSINESS SIDE OF RETAIL

The Shopping Goddess is not just interested in a new blusher or a flashy new trinket at an enticing price. The entire pie that contributes to the buying and selling of goods fascinates. Most Gods and Goddesses are interested in marketing, architecture and retail, even when there's nothing to buy. When I travel and read the local paper, I rip out pages and adverts that mention stores I have never heard of or branches of chains I've never seen. I am just plain curious.

So picture me in my hotel room in Dallas, working on this very book. I take a break to read the paper. In the business section—usually the best source for retail information—I see an article about the new Madewell 1937 store that opened the day before in North Park Center. This is an experimental chain being broken out by J.Crew, so there are just a handful of these stores in existence. Naturally, I've never seen one. Before you can sing "The Eyes of Texas," I am on the train and speeding toward the mall.

The Shopping Goddess has no peace without exploration and adventure. She cannot sit home and read a book, especially when the business pages have spelled out something new and interesting. Without marketing, there is no capitalism, and capitalism is what makes shopping fun.

Throughout my career as a woman with wanderlust, I have had a moving list of hotels I must stay in before I die. The list moves because I get to some and learn of new ones; the skies widen and my interests broaden. Often the dream hotel is not what I hoped it would be. That's life. I also have a dream list of stores and markets to visit before I die. More often than not, the stores on my dream list do live up to expectations. That could be because my dream list of retail is invariably related to architecture and design and because I have usually read enough in business features to pique my curiosity. Part of being a Shopping God or Goddess is understanding the whole.

SHOP YOUR PERSONAL INTERESTS

I do own some designer merchandise; I may have even paid full price for it. But for the most part I am not the customer who shops in designer boutiques. I haunt these stores merely out of curiosity—I want to see the design and decor. I travel specifically to see a certain store or the work of an architect if it is related to retail.

Remember that line from *Being There*, "I like to watch"? Well, that also applies to the Shopping God. Curiosity flows into window-shopping, merchandise-stroking and traveling all over the world just to see stores and feel the vibe. Being a skilled shopper is not about buying things; it's about observing things and grasping the big picture.

I can tell you outright that if you are interested in architecture and design, you owe yourself a trip to Tokyo. You need to leave home and travel just to see and to be. Me? I've been to Tokyo several times and while I will continue to revisit, I'm now planning a trip to Fukuoka to check out The Canal City Mall. I don't really know where Fukuoka is, but never mind.

I like new and novel retail, especially if it's been designed by a clever architect (I Brake for Architecture). I like designer clothes but mostly to look at; I shop alternative retail. When I plan a Born to Shop & Spa Tour, I do not take people to designer boutiques. I create the tour in the image of my own shopping style. As you reach for your merit badges in shopping, remember they are only worth having when you place your own interests in the equation.

SHOP THE CIRCLES OF LIFE

If architecture, window-shopping, supermarkets that sell fashion and souks that keep the good stuff stashed away are the light side of this business, then my philosophy of the circle of life is heavier. But there is a moral to this story and a shopping lesson to remember.

Maybe I think about this because I have suffered so much loss in my own life, but I very often think that the cycles of retail are related to the circle of life, that this is a factor few people take into account when looking at the whole of what is available out there. I'll give you a personal example.

My late husband was in the sports information business and loved to watch his games. For Father's Day, I gave him a large-screen television. That September he fell ill; he died 3 months later. The TV was virtually new, yet no longer had very much resale value. I was going to move to France and didn't need the TV since the electricity is different in Europe. A perfectly good, top-brand, $1,000 TV set was sold for $250. Somebody got a very good deal. Are you open to deals like that? The Shopping Goddess is. But the beat goes on; the circle and the cycle continue.

My husband dies, I move to France and am forced to leave behind most of my beloved belongings. I hire a tag sale producer (big mistake). My office has been decorated with tole trays and a large collection of red and white transfer wares, collected from England. There are numerous big soup tureens with lids and ladles. I decide to take the trays to France with me and sell the transfer ware.

I expect to get a nice price for it since it's a gorgeous collection. Not so, says the tag sale producer—you always make more money if items are sold individually. Urrrgggghhhhh. At auction houses collections are often sold as lots.

Life lesson: At tag sales, collections are broken apart so that the circle of collecting can begin again for someone else. If your collection is so important, donate it to a museum.

Remember the tole trays I just told you about? (Yeah, yeah, I tole you so.) Well, they are now in France. Some day my son will inherit that house. He doesn't know that those trays are worth thousands of dollars. He probably sees them as junk Mom collected over the years and threw onto the walls to add a little color. He could toss them or give them away or sell them for $25 each.

Life lesson: One man's junk is another man's treasure.

Now let's complete the circle. I move back to the United States. I want a big-screen TV. I had a perfectly good big-screen TV that would still be valuable today, but no, I sold it for $250. I buy a new one for $899. All things go round—life, death, Infinity TV.

Life lessons: 1) Try to buy perfectly good, hopefully new merchandise when someone is forced to relocate or when the owner has died; 2) The same person will buy and sell (or give away) the same things time after time—this is part of what keeps the economy growing. Nothing is forever. Circumstances change. Life changes. Keep on shopping.

Retail and the economy that supports retail depend on the circle of life. People perish. Merchandise endures. And so disaster and death contribute to the retail cycles of the world. Perfectly good products are dumped once the sell-by date has been passed; many have not really expired but must be sold for a fraction of their retail value, or destroyed.

Destinations cannot sell their hotel rooms because of fears of an epidemic—air fares plunge and a perfectly nice trip is yours if you plan to wash your hands a lot. Somebody comes to town, somebody leaves town, and all sorts of shopping experiences ensue.

UNDERSTAND ALL ASPECTS OF VALUE

On to other business and money matters. I always say it takes only money to go shopping. To be a smart shopper, it takes many of the skills already mentioned. Among those skills is the ability to manage your finances and to judge value in product, because the two really are interlinked. The world would be an easier place to shop if you got what you paid for, but you often don't. That's why we need to be educated shoppers in the first place.

To me, price is not the object—it's about value. While I think it's obscene that a modern "it" bag costs over $1,000 these days and part of my brain says I would never pay that for a handbag, I can also tell you that one of the best things I ever bought was a Chanel handbag for $1,500 in the Chanel store in the InterContinental Hotel in Hong Kong. It was in the window of the store; I certainly was not searching out such a bag. But it stood up and waved at me from the window, I rationalized my way home with it and guess what—I still love it 4 years later and a similar bag now costs $2,200. Who knew that a $1,500 bag could be a bargain? The value of this bag is in the combination of the status and the escalating price teamed with the fact that in this price range you get a product that is so well made that it lasts for enough years to pay for itself.

Granted, you need to have $1,500 to play the game in the first place, but choosing to spend that money wisely is far more important than merely buying everything in sight. And depending on your personal needs, one $1,500 handbag could be smarter than three $500 handbags. That depends on you and your lifestyle.

Is the Chanel bag made any better than a similar bag? No, it is not. The value to me comes in other factors. There's real value and there's perceived value, both important to consider.

Unfortunately, many people equate designer brand with value and with quality. These are two different subjects. An item of low quality can have high value and unfortunately the reverse is also true. And then there's private label—one of the most terrifying business aspects of the real world, because it proves that you don't get what you pay for, which rattles our core theories.

Let's say I own a factory that makes pantyhose and it is cheaper to keep the machinery running 24 hours a day and to staff my factories with three 8-hour shifts than it is to stop and start and open and close the factory. I make the premium pantyhose in the world that sells for a high price in department stores, and I advertise, and shoppers all over the world know and respect my pantyhose. But because I run my shop 24 hours a day, I have far more product than I can sell at these high prices. So I put the identical pantyhose into other boxes under other brand names, I sell the pantyhose to grocery stores and big box stores that call it their house brand, and I even let my pantyhose be shipped around the world and sold at deep discounts.

As a business person I have broken no laws and done nothing wrong.

As a shopper, I am screwed if I can't trust my own judgment that the pantyhose from the supermarket are identical to the pantyhose with the fancy name.

As a shopper, you have two choices:

- Learn to judge products by the way they are made, not by the way they are sold; or
- Understand that a splurge is often related to perceived value or to psychological perks, not to innate value.

🖱 The Amazon.com Rule of Shopping

I used to just use Amazon.com for buying books. Silly me. I knew they sold other things, but I thought you should rely on a site for what it does best and to me, Amazon means books. I've learned (okay, Sarah taught me) to go first to Amazon, and then cruise the Web for comparisons. I don't like to spend a lot of time with research and comparisons, so I consider Amazon as my baseline and then take it from there. And let's face it, free shipping is a very attractive form of persuasion. I've heard of someone who bought her TV from Amazon—no tax, free delivery, and they brought it right in the door. I investigated that idea, but didn't find great prices for the kind of TV I wanted.

When I decided I couldn't live another day without a Kitchen-Aid, I spent a week looking at print ads and researching online. I did indeed buy from Amazon and got the Artisan model delivered to my door for $249. Sales in various stores had the same model for $269, and then I would have had to pay tax and schlep the thing home with me. And I saved on time and gas as well.

LEARN THE VALUE OF GOOD SERVICE

This is one of the most important marketing lessons in capitalism, so I will start off by telling you a story.

Once upon a time I went on a trip and booked into a fancy hotel. Internet access at this hotel was a fair-enough 5€ ($6.50) an hour which was charged as you signed on. Although the Internet setup was right there on my very stylish desk, the cable did not work. This also meant that the hotel business center was down. We are so sorry, madame.

In need of information from my e-mail, I began to walk around town in search of an Internet café. The one I found had four phone cabins to one side and four computer stations to the other. The one computer with a QWERTY keyboard was taken, but I decided I'd suffer through AZERTY. I did my e-mail, using the Internet for 1 hour.

I paid 1€.

I got the exact same e-mail from the Internet café as I would have gotten in my room. I saved 4€. I had a different experience but the same product.

For people who have the money to make a purchase, where price is not the immediate issue, service and attitude become a profound part of the perception of value.

Another story: Sarah (Born to Shop Editorial Director) and I walk into Hermès in Paris. We are well dressed. Sarah explains it's her birthday and her husband always buys her an enamel bangle bracelet for each birthday. They cost about $500, which is a nice enough sale. Sarah is basically begging the woman to take her money. After giving Sarah a thorough once-over, the saleswoman suggests she go to the end of the line. There is no line.

In fact, we leave.

Oprah Winfrey had a similar experience in this same store.

So when we talk about value, we have to talk about the combination of attitude and service. Bad attitude equals bad business practices to me, and bad attitude diminishes value.

I walk into a store in Napa that has merchandise I know from a small corner of France. I feel elated, as if seeing an old friend.

"Is this from the Jean Vier factory?" I ask the proprietor.

"It is from France," he sniffs, and turns away.

When salespeople go out of their way to help you, the value of the brand increases. That's why Gap sales clerks are given lessons in how to smile as customers enter the store. That's why hotel personnel are trained to call you by your name.

One member of the Board of Advisors of this book explained that it wasn't the cost or the designer that interested him, it was the unparalleled service. He especially wanted to acknowledge that while Ralph Lauren is a good brand and an obvious choice for this book, the service from Dwayne Nichols in the Ralph Lauren Beverly Hills store was what made him loyal to that store and actually made him buy more. All politics are local; all brand loyalty comes down to how you are treated in the store or at the point of purchase.

KNOW THE RULE OF THE JUNGLE

As any savvy shopper can tell you, the best merchandise in the market (or the store) is always put away. This is a fact that is as old—older—than time. This is a fact that is related to human nature and the nature of shopping.

This merchandise is not even in view for mere mortals to consider buying. The merchant does not need its reflected glory to draw in shoppers or to dazzle would-be buyers. The merchant keeps it for just the right buyer or just the right moment. The best things in the world are put away—sometimes hidden—and must be sought. Embroider that fact on your heart or your hand and keep it handy.

And here's a cute story to go with it. I was just discussing life and shopping with my friend Carol who along with her husband Fred was recently in India. She explained to me that

"When they like you they let you go to the back room." I didn't have the heart to explain to her that when they smell money they let you go to the back room.

In Carol's descriptions of her shopping adventures there were two to three rooms—nothing up front, a few things in the middle and then the treasure trove. Or, after inspecting Room Two, her husband Fred would announce to the owner "This is junk, we're leaving" and the owner would say "Wait, wait, wait" and would then scurry to a back, back room and bring out things wrapped in newspaper.

Trust me on this, the good stuff is always hidden.

KNOW WHEN TO QUIT

Sure you can shop 'til you drop, but why would you? On the way down, you'll make mistakes and buy the wrong things. Think about it for a minute: What percentage of items in your closets are never worn because they turned out to be uncomfortable? What percentage aren't worn because your office went to casual dress or you changed jobs or lifestyles? What percentage of the items were plain old mistakes? How many were bargains that were too good to pass up? And here's one of my favorites: How many items have flaws that you swore you'd fix but haven't gotten around to yet?

I estimate that at least 30% of my clothes were bought on the road when the weather changed. I also admit that I have fat clothes and thin clothes and I refuse to believe that I will never wear those thin clothes again. I have high heels because they go with suits, and the suits are hanging there, but frankly, I haven't worn a suit in years. Well, better safe than sorry.

A few days ago, I was in a discount store and came upon a camel-colored, pure cashmere, label-intact, genuine Zegna sports coat, men's size 44. My partner wears a 42. The coat was on sale for $45 because it had a tiny, iddy bitty, barely visible dot of a hole on the cuff. I started to buy the jacket because it was too good a buy to leave it there. And then I had to remember that it didn't fit anyone I knew. That we didn't need it. That triumph falls short when you wonder why you have so much stuff in your closet and not a thing to wear.

REMEMBER THE ALAMO

Well you don't have to remember the Alamo if you don't want to, but whatever you do, do not forget the bottom line—your bottom line. One of the most important, and least-talked-about, parts of the act of good shopping is staying within your own budget. There is nothing in this world that is worth going into debt for. Especially a handbag.

Chapter Two

The World's Best:
The Short List

*T*his chapter could have been called "Personal Best." The listings on these pages are the best for me on a personal level—the ones I keep going back to in between testing other brands. Most selections here have full listings in the body text of this book (see page references), where they are marked with the 🛍 icon. If, for whatever reason, a store did not fit into a chapter or category elsewhere in the book, I list contact information here.

We are what we repeatedly do. Excellence is not just an act we perform but a habit.

— Aristotle

The 11 Best One-of-a-Kind Stores

Some of these stores are chains, but in those cases I am only swooning over a particular store or flagship. I chose 11 because 10 was not enough.

ABC Carpet & Home NYC

The most ethereally beautiful, interesting and exciting lifestyle store in the world: It's an old-fashioned New York department store cum warehouse space draped with fluttery fabrics and done to perfection with room sets and made-up beds, piles of silken pillows, stacks of dishes and pots and pans, and gifts galore. See p. 36.

Ashneil HONG KONG

Every inch of space, even breathing space of this store, is piled with handbags that mimic the latest designer styles at somewhat reasonable prices. These handbags are not illegal copies but are inspired by the greats. You can find the latest "It" knockoff for about $300. See p. 120.

Comme des Garçons TOKYO

Many comme des garçons "guerilla" stores go into oddball locations (Warsaw, Beirut, Reykjavik) and stay open for a year and then leave town—not the Tokyo location, which showcases the artful, expensive wear in a large, bright, modern space that always reeks of the company's various adventurous scents. See p. 218.

Dries van Noten ANTWERP

Taste both the candy box decor of the store itself and then the work of design king van Noten, who does quirky, drapey mix-n-max and get outta here topped with chiffon and delight. See p. 82.

Fred Segal LOS ANGELES

Fred Segal is a classic temple to the culture of L.A., where skinny jeans were relaunched recently and where art meets fashionista with some cult makeup on the side. Even if you buy nothing here, a prowl through the store will teach you how to get The Look. Bring your black AmEx. See p. 99.

John Derian NYC

Derian must have been running with scissors to an art class and woke up in a dream—his decoupage plates first showed up at Bergdorf's as a cross between whimsy and art. Derian opened his own visual feast of a store in Lower Manhattan, where he sells intricate tabletop, bedtime and gift wares. 6 E. 2nd St., NYC. ☎ 212/677-3917. www.johnderian.com.

Louis Vuitton PARIS

When this flagship was under construction, Vuitton built a giant LV monogram suitcase around it. Now they have a store so complete it comes with a museum inside it. The vintage luggage hanging on the walls and up into the skylights is a nice touch. See p. 267.

Prada SoHo NYC

So discreet is this store that it has no sign—it just looks like an architectural wonder, which it is. See p. 227.

Shiatzy Chen SHANGHAI

The Shanghai store of this chain is otherworldly in its presentation of handcrafted clothes for men and women, with accessories that merge classical Chinese art form with high heels and lizard handbags. Think Mink Dynasty. I was so impressed I actually called Eva Air and booked a ticket to Taipei to see the flagship. See p. 91.

10 Corso Como MILAN

One of the first lifestyle stores in the world, created by an important Italian fashionista who bought a sprawling industrial complex with courtyard and from it sells fashion and home style, along with books and desire. Upstairs there's even a little hotel. See p. 60.

TopShop LONDON

The London flagship is mind-boggling, with three floors of stuff for the would-be fashion victim and a maternity shop for the happy few. This is a department store with an ability to crank out new merchandise every few days so that the latest catwalk styles are available, often for less than $100. See p. 296.

The 10 Best Chains or Multiples

Anthropologie USA

When I lived full time in France, I used to say that the only thing that would bring me back to America was a job at Anthropologie. I simply identify with this hodge-podge store of clothes, home style and stuff. This U.S. lifestyle store of BoHo and Rich Hippie delights me for home and closet and bath and wall and floor, with a rustic twist and an ability to cash in on what I call the ABC Carpet phenom in a more mass market environment. See p. 37.

Big Lots USA

Stop by to see what's new in the ever-changing parade of mark-downs and end-of-range goods. Stock changes with whatever bargains have been acquired so you can furnish your home, load up on gift wrap and buy things you never knew you needed, but at everyday low, low prices. 1,500 stores in the U.S. www.biglots.com.

British India MALAYSIAN

This Asian fashion house has beaded linens for women and British Colonial style for gents; also home style. While many styles (for men and women) feature banded collars, the styles tend to be Western and in current fashion rather than Asian or costumey. Think cocktails at the officers' club or sundowners over croquet before the sunset on the Empire. Several stores in Asia. 50 Jalan Sultan Ismail; Lot 10, Kuala Lumpur, Malaysia. ☎ 603/2142-2127.

Chanel FRENCH/GERMAN

This is the most focused designer look in the world, expert at making its logo of interlocked C's the most desirable brand on earth. You can buy nail polish or couture from the same store, which is dripping in beige, mirrors, lilies and lust. To say that

Karl Lagerfeld, who relaunched this brand, is a genius is not really doing either of them (the man or the brand) justice. You could say he's a God. See p. 123.

H&M SWEDISH

Hennes & Mauritz stands for fashion-forward, low-cost apparel sold from a lifestyle firm with the latest fashion inspirations arriving every week for men, women, kids and home. Street fashion meets the High Street for those on limited budgets who are into this season's must-have looks. Barbara Walters shops here, too. See p. 290.

Hermès FRENCH

This luxury-defining house makes the rules and doesn't need to follow others due to distinct styles in silks, leathers and enamel that let the public know who's on first without flashing obvious logos. One accessory from this brand can define an entire persona. See p. 122.

Hema DUTCH & Monoprix FRENCH

These are two different stores, in two different countries with two different owners. Yet they are very similar so I am making them one listing. Abracadabra.

Hema is more or less the Dutch version of Monoprix. The stores have hip clothing at low prices, often designed in limited-edition collections by big names. Monoprix stores usually have supermarkets and are a bit more like full-service department stores; Hema is more like a dime store with organic touches. See p. 45 for Hema and p. 53 for Monoprix.

Tokyu Hands JAPANESE

This store is five to eight floors (depends on which branch you visit) of Japanese inventions and gadgets and toys and crafts supplies and yes, hardware. You can stock up on items that you could not even imagine existed or buy little things that tickle your fancy. It's just stuff, but oh, what stuff. See p. 325.

Shanghai Tang CHINESE

Focus, humor, color and whimsy carry these Chinese inspirations from the world of Suzie Wong and onto the must-have list for stylish shoppers. In the beginning this line was all mandarin-collared Mao shirts in lime green or hot pink with a lot of the Duchess of York thrown in. Now the line has become an international luxury line and is much more cosmopolitan. See p. 90.

5 Best Concept Stores

Container Store USA

Who ever heard of getting organized as a selling concept? But this chain of stores doesn't stop with closets and drawers. They sell all sorts of containers from wastebaskets to bathroom shelves to gift wrap and school backpacks. See p. 42.

Disney Stores USA

If you don't think that Minnie Mouse made into the Statue of Liberty and selling for under $10 isn't genius, then you are Goofy. Walt Disney taught the world that the movie was a small piece of the pie—the characters can be spun into theme parks and merchandise and live forever, especially in the bank. See p. 43.

H. Stern BRAZILIAN

Maybe this is the original concept store—this giant jewelry store and world-famous brand has workrooms in the flagship building, as well as a museum and a tour of the process of how stones go from mine to wrist. Coffee is served. See p. 138.

Jim Thompson THAI

The story is just as legendary as the merchandise. This rumored CIA agent turned the silk business into a lifestyle business, with everything from bedding to ties, robes and kimonos available. See p. 203.

Nike Stores USA

Whether you are in a Niketown, a Nike outlet store or NikeParis, you get entertainment plus the art gallery form of merchandising. This concept store gave birth to many interactive sports-oriented merchandise stores (such as the NBA stores) and also to brand workshop stores (such as Sony and Apple). See p. 210.

King of the Concept Stores

Ralph Lauren USA

If I listed Ralph Lauren and/or the Polo empire every place it belongs in this book, you'd be very bored, very quickly. So RL, as he is known in print (but never called in person) gets this

The World's Best: Highlights

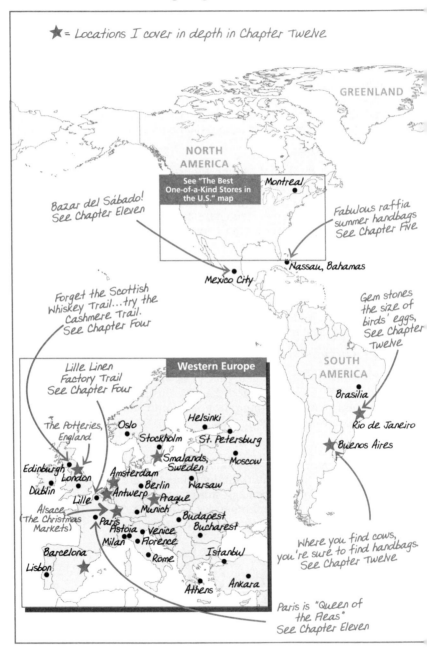

★ = Locations I cover in depth in Chapter Twelve

GREENLAND

NORTH AMERICA

See "The Best One-of-a-Kind Stores in the U.S." map

Montreal

Bazar del Sábado! See Chapter Eleven

Fabulous raffia summer handbags See Chapter Five

Nassau, Bahamas

Mexico City

Forget the Scottish Whiskey Trail...try the Cashmere Trail. See Chapter Four

Gem stones the size of birds' eggs, See Chapter Twelve

SOUTH AMERICA

Lille Linen Factory Trail See Chapter Four

Western Europe

Brasilia

Rio de Janeiro

The Potteries, England

Oslo

Helsinki

Stockholm

St. Petersburg

Smalands, Sweden

Moscow

Buenos Aires

Edinburgh

London

Amsterdam

Berlin

Warsaw

Dublin

Antwerp

Prague

Lille

Munich

Where you find cows, you're sure to find handbags. See Chapter Twelve

Alsace (The Christmas Markets)

Paris

Pistoia

Budapest

Bucharest

Venice

Barcelona

Milan

Florence

Istanbul

Lisbon

Rome

Ankara

Athens

Paris is "Queen of the Fleas" See Chapter Eleven

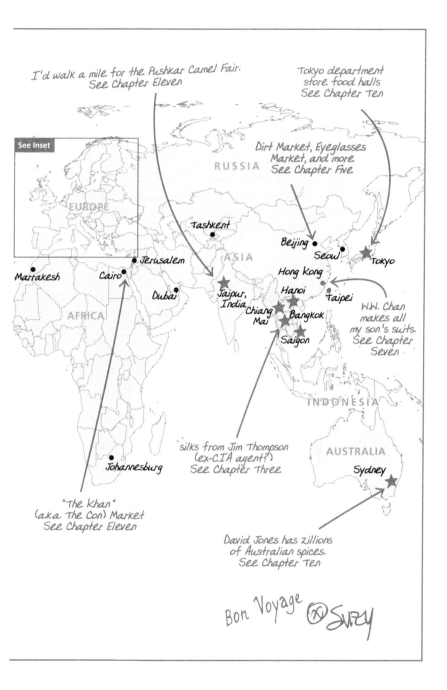

category unto himself. He practically created the American concept store as we know it today; he absolutely created the factory outlet business as it exists today. His ability to turn a look into a lifestyle and to re-create it constantly and yet within the boundaries of exquisite taste is miraculous. See p. 49.

3 Best Department Stores

Bergdorf Goodman NYC

The small store deftly handles fashion, beauty and home style with a separate but equally glam mens store across the street. This is why you eat Breakfast at Tiffany's, and then spend the day shopping here. See p. 40.

Liberty LONDON

This Mock Tudor institution has floor after floor of goods that represent what treasure hunters would have packed into the *Pinta, Nina* and *Santa Maria*, if only Columbus had been a merchant. See p. 50.

Marks & Spencer BRITISH

Maybe Napoleon was right after all—this British value-for-money chain has come back from the dead to offer hot fashion at fair prices. See p. 53.

5 Best Grocery & Gourmet Food Stores

Auchan FRENCH

This French *hypermarché* is so large the clerks wear roller skates. Come for the excellent selection of merchandise at the best prices; also good for home, garden, fashion, office, electronics and the like. This is what Wal-Mart or Super Target would be if they were French. 1,000+ stores worldwide. www.group-auchan.com.

City Super CHINESE

This supermarket chain in Hong Kong reflects the needs of the upper-middle-class, busy shopper who wants a cool-looking store, interesting one-stop shopping capabilities, cooked gourmet food and sophistication in a convenient-to-the-office environment for big city living. See p. 374.

Fortnum & Mason BRITISH

This is one of the few places in the UK where I don't care what the USD/BPS exchange rate is—though most of my most extreme splurges usually do not cost more than £20 ($40). I buy jams and lime curd, also tea and coffee and gifts of tastes not seen on the shelves of other supermarkets. There are days when I know I would kill for a jar of lime curd. See p. 370.

L'Epicerie FRENCH

Of Paris's many gourmet grocery stores, this one, uh, takes the cake because of what's on offer. Prices are high, but there's a little of everything, from pastries to wines to cheeses and olives, fruits, vegs and a large variety of kinds of salt. See p. 371.

Trader Joe's USA

This cost-conscious gourmet food store offers a nod toward health foods and organic products and all the salted soy beans you can eat. Some stores sell wine, but others simply put out a nice selection between bulk and gourmet that is more funky than Whole Foods, and therefore more fun. See p. 378.

5 Best Malls

Forum at Caesar's Palace LAS VEGAS

It's the world's silliest mall (but hey, it's in Las Vegas, so it's okay) and is delicious in its combination of Ye Olde Roman decor with luxury brands. Come to gawk. See p. 44.

Kierland Commons SCOTTSDALE, AZ

This is a newer mall concept in Scottsdale, Arizona—it's an open-air mall structured as an entire village, with a hotel and residential lofts and sidewalk water spritzers to keep you cool. This is the future. I have seen it, and I have shopped it. See p. 48.

North Park Center TEXAN

This Dallas mall is where many brands test new concepts in their attempts to reach sophisticated real people who don't have big hair. There's an excellent mix of the multiples you love to shop plus stores you have never seen before. 8687 N. Central Expressway, Dallas. ☎ 214/361-6345. www.northpark center.com.

Best of the USA: Highlights

Adkins Antiques **15**
Amba **6**
Archie McPhee **1**
Architectural Artifacts **17**
Architecture Kids Store **10**
Arizona Mills **14**
Barbwire **10**
Bed Balloon Company **17**
Berings **15**
Bodega **25**
Brentwood Country Mart **5**
Britex **4**
Brownes & Co. Apothecary **18**
Caesar's Palace **8**
Carlsbad Factory Outlet **6**
Charles Street Hardware **25**
Cleaning Ideas **14**
Dancing Ladies **11**
Desert Passage Mall **8**
DiBruno Bros. **22**
E & J Designer Shoe Outlet **10**
Edelweiss Kitchen **5**
El Redegral Outlets **10**
Elegant Linens **9**
Ferry Building Marketplace **4**
Forgotten Shanghai **4**

Forum at Caesar's **8**
Fred Segal **5**
Frugal Fannie's **25**
Gilbert Ortega **1**
Gilman Outlets **3**
Great Stuff by Paul **21**
Gump's **4**
HD Buttercup **5**
Heath **3**
Hejfina **17**
Hu's **20**
Indigo Seas **5**
Jade **17**
Kierland Commons **10**
Kitson **5**
Larchmont Beauty Supply **5**
Let's Do Lunch **5**
Lily et Cie **5**
Lisa Kline **5**
Liz's Antique Hardware **5**
Lori's Designer Shoes **17**
Lucchesse **12**
Maverick Fine Western Wear **13**
Nancy Boy **4**
Nancy Brown **11**
Nantucket Looms **24**

Old Plank Road **17**
Origins **4**
Ortega's **11**
Packards **11**
Pike's Place **1**
Pinto Ranch **15**
Ragazzi's Flying Shuttle **1**
Reading Terminal Market **22**
ReBuilding Center **2**
Replacements, Ltd. **19**
Rolo **4**
Saba **1**
Santa Fe Dry Goods **11**
Scottsdale Fashion Square **10**
Solo **6**

26

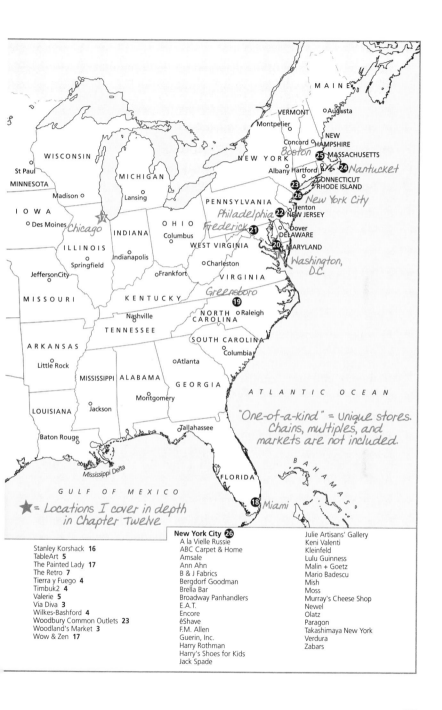

MAINE

Augusta

VERMONT

Montpelier

NEW HAMPSHIRE

Concord

Boston **25** MASSACHUSETTS

NEW YORK

Albany   Hartford   **24** *Nantucket*

23 CONNECTICUT

RHODE ISLAND

New York City **26**

PENNSYLVANIA   **22** Trenton   NEW JERSEY

Philadelphia   Dover   DELAWARE

Frederick   **21**

OHIO   Columbus   **20** MARYLAND

WEST VIRGINIA

Washington, D.C.

WISCONSIN

St Paul

MINNESOTA

MICHIGAN

Madison   Lansing

I O W A

Des Moines   *Chicago*   INDIANA

ILLINOIS   Indianapolis

Springfield

JeffersonCity

MISSOURI   KENTUCKY   *Greensboro*   **19**

Nashville   NORTH CAROLINA   Raleigh

TENNESSEE

ARKANSAS   SOUTH CAROLINA

Little Rock   Columbia

MISSISSIPPI   ALABAMA   GEORGIA

LOUISIANA   Jackson   Montgomery

Baton Rouge

Mississippi Delta

GULF OF MEXICO

Tallahassee

FLORIDA

B A H A M A S

A T L A N T I C   O C E A N

"One-of-a-kind" = Unique stores.
Chains, multiples, and
markets are not included.

18 *Miami*

★ *= Locations I cover in depth*
in Chapter Twelve

Charleston

Frankfort

VIRGINIA

Atlanta

Jackson

Stanley Korshack **16**
TableArt **5**
The Painted Lady **17**
The Retro **7**
Tierra y Fuego **4**
Timbuk2 **4**
Valerie **5**
Via Diva **3**
Wilkes-Bashford **4**
Woodbury Common Outlets **23**
Woodland's Market **3**
Wow & Zen **17**

New York City **26**
A la Vielle Russie
ABC Carpet & Home
Amsale
Ann Ahn
B & J Fabrics
Bergdorf Goodman
Brella Bar
Broadway Panhandlers
E.A.T.
Encore
êShave
F.M. Allen
Guerin, Inc.
Harry Rothman
Harry's Shoes for Kids
Jack Spade

Julie Artisans' Gallery
Keni Valenti
Kleinfeld
Lulu Guinness
Malin + Goetz
Mario Badescu
Mish
Moss
Murray's Cheese Shop
Newel
Olatz
Paragon
Takashimaya New York
Verdura
Zabars

Siam Paragon BANGKOK

This enormous mall prides itself on the high number of international designer labels sold in the boutiques here. There's also a department store; a floor devoted to local Thai brands of crafts, beauty and fashion; many restaurants and eateries and an entire lifestyle all under much glitz and sparkle. See p. 58.

Woodbury Common CENTRAL VALLEY, NY

At the world's largest outlet mall, located 90 minutes from Manhattan, golf carts or track shoes should be issued so you can get around to the many buildings that have stores representing every big brand—at discounted prices, of course. See p. 433.

3 Best Off-Price Stores

Century 21 NYC

This is the best department store for deals, discounts, big names and all manner of fashion for home, men, women, children and especially those who crave big names. Racks are so crammed with merchandise that you have to be strong enough to take the stress. See p. 427.

Il Salvagente ITALIAN

This is a hidden source for discounted fashion and some accessories specializing in Italian designer brands. Of course it's hit or miss, but for the most part you'll find the names if not the sizes that you want. See p. 430.

Moda di Andrea FRENCH

Here's a dream shop for shoe addicts who want French and Italian big name brands such as Tod's, Hogans, Prada, at discount prices. It's conveniently located behind the flagship Galeries Lafayette in Paris so you don't need to stray too far to find shoe nirvana. See p. 430.

3 Best Flea Markets

Brimfield MASSACHUSETTS

This dealers' market is held six times a year in the middle of Massachusetts where during a 10-day period a variety of open fields are turned into a tented village of vendors. Shipping available. See p. 414.

Chatou PARIS

Held twice a year outside of Paris, the Chatou fair sells antiques in a village setting, with plenty of food stalls thrown in. It's big enough to be wonderful fun, but not so big as to be overwhelming. Low prices, and shipping available. See p. 415.

Newark NOTTINGHAMSHIRE

This dealers' market in Nottinghamshire is held six times a year, open to anyone willing to schlep out there and pay the admission. It's an enormous affair with indoor and outdoor vendors who, in times of financial difficulty, will adjust prices to suit the weaker U.S. dollar. Market Square, Nottinghamshire, England.

4 Best Baths

Dr. Hauschka Lemon Bath GERMAN

There's also a good rose bath, but the lemon has more wake-up factor. Be careful when you use this stuff; it's slick. Enter and exit tub with care or you could feel bad about your (broken) neck. See p. 178.

Jo Malone BRITISH

This is your source for outrageously expensive and delicious lotions, potions, oils and aromatherapy. See p. 165.

Kiss My Face Cold & Flu USA

A blend of herbs and spices will steam out your aches and pains while you soak in the therapeutic bath water. See p. 163.

Original Source BRITISH

Flavorful UK drugstore brand of bath and shower gel also has a full range of health and beauty aids. All scents bear testing, but the tea tree and mint, if you can take the tingle, will change bath rituals forever. See p. 166.

5 Best Treatment Brands & Products

Amore Pacific KOREAN

This is one of those skin care lines with an entire regimen—if I could afford it, I would probably switch to this brand. I bought a $150 starter kit just to understand what it was all about and fell in love with the easy process and the purity of the cleansing process. See p. 179.

Cils Demasq FRENCH

This is, without doubt, the best eye-makeup remover ever invented. *Cils* is French for eyelashes. Find it in French dime stores or duty-free shops. See p. 410.

Durance FRENCH

This Provençale brand makes an especially yummy lavender hand cream. See p. 162.

June Jacobs USA

These spa treatment products can be found at specific spas or online and are great for face and body; they're made with fruit and botanical extracts. See p. 180.

Sisley FRENCH

If I were to pick one overall brand that I thought was best for everything for the face—treatment and color cosmetics—I would pick the French brand Sisley. The ingredients are natural, the shades are soft and natural, while the treatment products are rich and smell very, very good. See p. 181.

8 Makeup Essentials

Bourjois FRENCH & *Chanel* FRENCH

I buy lipstick from both these brands even though you can argue that they come from the same factory. I also splurge on Chanel makeup and treatments occasionally; this is simply a great brand. See p. 174.

MAC CANADIAN/USA

With good quality, excellent colors and no combos with shades you hate, MAC makes good eye shadows at the price you want to pay. It's a division of Estee Lauder. See p. 174.

Makeup Forever FRENCH

A small tube of the concealer from this French brand will last you until your next face-lift but will blow your mind with the quality of the cover in the meantime. See p. 175.

Nars USA/FRENCH

This French makeup artist has excellent color cosmetics, but the most important item he makes is called The Multiple Stick—a cream stick for eyes, lips and cheeks. Make mine Malibu, Palm Beach and/or Cannes. See p. 176.

Shu Uemura JAPANESE

He was the Japanese grandfather of international big name makeup artists, of color for all facial expressions and uses, of silky eyelashes and sea water treatments. I like everything this brand does but do wish I could unload some of the yellow and green shadows I bought when having jungle fever. See p. 177.

Sue Devitt AUSTRALIAN

I use the fat crayon eye pencils from this Australian line and swear that Kenya (a dark brown shade) is the best eyeliner pencil of my life. www.suedevittstudios.com.

Yves Saint Laurent FRENCH

This is the best mascara I've ever used, ever. When I am in one of my drama queen moods, I use the dark red mascara, which I find very alluring. They also make excellent foundation and tints. See p. 411.

5 Must Haves for My Guy

Armani blazer ITALIAN

I buy them at the factory outlet stores, natch. See p. 252.

British India banded collar shirts MALAYSIAN

They're 100% cotton, long sleeve (of course). See p. 19.

Nick & Nora pajamas USA

He wears the bottom, I wear the top. We buy 'em at Target. See p. 61.

Tommy Bahama sports shirts USA

He wears the silk and cotton mix, short sleeve. See p. 217.

W.W.Chan bespoke suits CHINESE

Sure, he's a 42R, but he still looks better in a handmade suit.
See p. 254.

5 Baby Gifts I Give Regularly

Basq Belly Oil USA

This is actually for the new mom or mom to be. See p. 191.

Christian Dior baby bottle FRENCH

It might be silly, but it's always applauded at the baby shower.
See p. 277.

Diaper bag for Dad USA

Jack Spade probably makes a nice one, too, but I buy online
from this diaper bag source with bags for guys. See p. 203.

Porthault baby bib FRENCH

Let baby drool on fabric from the famed French linen company. See p. 310.

Snugli USA

This is a tote for the baby, but I've used it for a geriatric cat,
too. See p. 266.

9 Foodstuffs I Can't Live Without

Fralinger's salt water taffy USA

I'll take the black and white (chocolate and vanilla) taffy,
please. See p. 381.

Thornton's toffee BRITISH

Even my dog is named Toffee. See p. 385.

Garrett Popcorn USA

I go for the caramel corn, without nuts. See p. 392.

Maille Provencale Mustard FRENCH

My favorite of their bevy of flavored mustards is spicy and
tangy. See p. 390.

Joël Durand Letter "L" chocolates FRENCH

"L" is for Lavender. See p. 382.

Lamme's Chewy Pecan Pralines TEXAN

Soft and nutty, these are fattening enough to turn you into Bevo. See p. 382.

Super Ginger Tea CHINESE

There doesn't seem to be much tea in this hot ginger beverage. Buy 20 sachets for $4.99. www.asiachi.com.

Carambar FRENCH

Mass market, hard-to-chew caramels hail from France. www.carambar.com.

Starbucks Mocha USA

I don't smoke, but I am addicted to this brew and spend more on my fix than I want to imagine. See p. 387.

5 It's-Not-Home-Without-It Items

Le Creuset cookware FRENCH

These cast iron pots and pans are heavy, but they make me cook well. See p. 342.

Pratesi bed linen ITALIAN

I've had some of these linens for over 25 years and they keep on washing and looking divine. See p. 311.

Tempur-Pedic mattress USA

It molds to your body. See p. 303.

Tupperware USA

I'm not a desperate housewife; I'm an international Tupperware hostess. I like to throw parties in Paris. See p. 318.

Wedgwood dishes BRITISH

I have more dishes than most stores, but this is my newest selection—a matte finish set from Replacements. See p. 351.

Chapter Three

Lifestyle & Department Stores

*I*n the beginning, shortly after God created retail (but before He created the mall), there were small stores that catered to the guild trades and then, eventually, department stores that sold a variety of items. The most successful department stores were based on the concept that bigger was best; they strived to carry as many brands and categories of merchandise as possible, making it simple for the consumer to outfit his life from one emporium.

Brands sold to department stores or eventually opened their own stores, to better showcase their work. Then, an odd thing happened—store executives realized that the longer the shopper stayed in a store, the more he bought. The more he bought, the less disposable income he had for another brand.

So brands began line extensions to sell every possible need under one roof and one conceptual umbrella, unified by a store or brand philosophy and/or united by the creator's touch. These stores were soon called lifestyle stores. If you liked the dress, you are sure to love the sheets. Line extensions are a way of growing a brand, making more money and reinforcing the original brand all at the same time. Various types of brands aim to become lifestyle icons, not just brands or labels. Look at the difference between Gap, Old Navy and Banana Republic—all divisions of the same firm but each geared to a different audience and lifestyle.

In the '70s and '80s, lifestyle stores began to blossom at the same time that department stores began to flounder. To be successful, the lifestyle store must provide a focus that is honed in advertising, presentation and design. Frequently, the lifestyle is further extended through multi-media presentation, most likely print catalog or online. Yet nothing replaces the actual feel of setting foot into the best stores for a total look because they are created to touch all your senses.

The odds of going into a store for a loaf of bread and coming out with only a loaf of bread are about 3 billion to one.

—Erma Bombeck

Among the hottest entries into the field are French couturiers and luxury brands. Fewer than 10 years ago, Christian Dior was considered very old chapeau and almost dead. Now it is a lifestyle brand, not because there are so many more couture customers in the world (there aren't), but because the spicy John Galliano–infused couture gave the house a new look and new energy and the line extension people came up with everything from custom licenses to baby bottles. At one time, couture existed mostly to sell perfume. Now, it is the dog that wags the designer baby bottle.

You can probably argue that there is little difference between a lifestyle store and a concept store or a department store and a specialty store. It is pretty confusing, which is why I have mixed and mingled them into this one chapter. You may think I've gone lightly on the subject of department stores. That reflects my personal opinion that few department stores are among the best of anything in the world.

I have chosen to put malls into this chapter because they offer a look at a lifestyle and concept all rolled into one package. For the most part, I rarely send people to malls and like them only for the convenience they offer. Nonetheless, my senior prom was held in a mall and the mall has become a lifestyle to people all over the world. Amen.

This is the only chapter in the book that is not divided into subcategories, because there is enormous crossover (and confusion) in what it takes to create good malls, concept stores, specialty and department stores. Stores are listed alphabetically.

ABC Carpet & Home NYC $–$$$$

World's Best

If this isn't a concept then I'd better join the convent— vavavavroom. Yeah, they do have carpet (actually, the carpet store is across the street from the home store), but the killer part of the store is the aura that knocks you senseless with the overwhelming selection of color, texture, tchotchkes and home needs in stunning windows and displays of ethereal elegance. Hell, even the ad campaigns are stunning.

No matter what part of the store you shop—outlet or regular flagship—you will see room sets and heaps of merchandise strewn around in artful heaps as if you has just discovered Ali Baba's cave of delights. Often the merchandise is ethnic in origin or appearance, so you get an even more exotic flair. Sometimes there are promotional events that tie the merchandise to a destination.

The store (pictured on p. 34) is somewhat expensive, but does have good sales and several outlet stores, although the outlets are in out-of-the-way places that require a car.

BEST BETS   The main foyer of the ground floor—you walk into the store and realize you've gone to visual heaven and your heart skips a beat with glee. **WEB TIPS**   The website's easy to use, but merchandise isn't sold online; you really must visit in person.

Anthropologie flagship store in Manhattan.

WHERE TO BUY   1 store. Also outlets in the Bronx, NY; Hacken-sack, NJ; and Delray Beach, FL. **FLAGSHIP**   888 & 881 Broadway, NYC. ☎ **212/473-3000.** Mon–Fri 10am–8pm; Sat 10am–7pm; Sun 11am–6:30pm. Subway: Union Sq. Harrod's location: 87–135 Brompton Rd., 2nd floor, London. Mon–Sat 10am–8pm; Sun noon–6pm. MC, AE, DISC, V. Tube: Knights-bridge. www.abchome.com.

Anthropologie USA $–$$$$

World's Best

We have all walked into a store at one time or another and known we are home—emotionally, visually, fashionably, simply and forever—at home. This is how I feel about the Anthropologie chain. Although the flagship NYC store is indeed the best, just about any branch I hang in is my home. This is one of the best lifestyle stores in the world because of its clear and unwavering focus. The merchandise changes constantly, but the philosophy does not.

It pays to visit as many branches as possible since all stores were not created equally and store size does matter—the bigger, the better. The new flagship, recently opened in Rockefeller Plaza in midtown Manhattan, is so large and so complete it has the chain's first—and so far, only—art gallery.

This is a store that caters not only to women's fashion and home style, but to an entire lifestyle of Boho (bohemian) wisdom, where clothes are droopy and drapey and possibly made with vintage fabrics, where home items are a little bit Venetian and a little bit country French, and the two actually mix together—with also a 1930s Americana beat and a nice selection of books, soaps, beauty routines and bed linen. Oh yeah, you can buy the bed, too. It's cast iron, of course, and looks best with zillions of pillows and scads of dusty colors.

Home style has no age limits. I am crazy about the mix of Indian, Chinese and French-style merchandise that all works together in a merry jumble of pattern, color and texture. The bed linens are dreamy, although I confess that $48 for a pillow sham is beyond me. The stemless wine glasses at $12 are a better deal.

BEST BETS   The best thing about the store is that it teaches you how to mix periods and styles and layers and looks and come out looking fabulous and not like a bag lady.

WEB TIPS   You can shop online, but don't miss the catalog, which is almost as much fun as a magazine. In fact, maybe I want to create a magazine for these guys and be the first editor. (Do I get paid in clothes? Dishes? Bedspreads? Bring it on!)

WHERE TO BUY   84 stores in U.S. including NYC; Berkeley, CA; San Diego, CA; San Antonio, TX; and Westport, CT. **FLAGSHIP** Rockefeller Center, NYC. Mon–Sat 10am–7pm; Sun 11am–6pm. AE, DISC, MC, V. Subway: B, D, F, V at 50th St. Philadelphia: 1801 Walnut St. ☎ **215/568-2114.** Mon–Sat 11am–7pm; Sun 11am–7pm. Subway: Broad St. www.anthropologie.com.

Asprey BRITISH $$$$–$$$$$

Years ago, I asked my friend Maggie why she shopped at Asprey because I thought it was such a stuffy, old-fashioned, non-creative place to shop. "Oh," she explained, "I once had to buy a gift for Prince Charles for a charity committee I was on and it was the perfect place. I got him a picture frame."

Indeed, Asprey has been traditionally that kind of place: okay for royalty but not very sexy. All that has changed. Enter the new century, c'mon down, Jade Jagger, and bring on the team from Tiffany & Co. Now this store is young and fun and jazzy and very sophisticated. While many think of it as a jewelry store, it actually sells a lifestyle.

Asprey pendant.

The interior of the flagship store has been created as the courtyard of a very fancy British neighborhood, with brick walls running in a half circle, welcoming you into your own private village. It was built by Sir Norman Foster and is very different from his other work: If you buy nothing, it is worth it just to stand and gawk. This is not a jewelry store, it is a monument.

Note that the handbags here start at 1,000 pounds ($2,000). Everything is so expensive that you know this is the kind of place where money is not discussed.

BEST BETS   You can still find just the right picture frame for Chuck and Cam. There's handbags and luggage and clothing; lifestyle items for the person who has everything and is looking for quiet understatement and cultish elegance.

WEB TIPS   The website is gorgeous—you are immediately hit in the face with flying luxury goods—earrings, handbags, watches. You can see them so well that you may drool on your keyboard, but you cannot buy online. Getting prices online is difficult.

WHERE TO BUY   3 stores in U.S. (NYC, Beverly Hills, Honolulu), 10 worldwide and expanding. **FLAGSHIP**   167 New Bond St., London, W1. ☎ **44207/493-6767.** Mon–Sat 10am–6pm. AE, MC, V. Tube: Bond St. www.asprey.com.

Barneys USA $–$$$$$

The Barneys' woman is possibly a character from a Plum Sykes novel, a Bergdorf Blonde over east 1 block to the store "the boys" built—a tribute to Barneys' grandsons, who made the leap from fairly priced men's suiting to Manolo's and a tearoom. In keeping with the drama of much of today's young, fast and very new dollars, the store has risen and fallen in financial crisis and is now rebounding in its own image but without the original owners to add their very refined perspective of fashion edginess. The Barneys man is beyond dapper—he may use the store as a meeting place for friends or pickups. As a lifestyle store, Barneys is both uptown and downtown, physically and emotionally. This time, downtown means hip, not discount.

What Barneys sells is what can't be bought: attitude. In fashion, there are little-known brands in jewelry, there are one-of-a-kind pieces. The makeup tends to be cult resources. Because it's just so hard to prowl too many stores in a pair of stilettos and life is so full with the children's activities, and lunch and the manicure and, oh yes, tea, well, it's just easier to pick from a well-selected source that reinforces the notion that you are cutting edge.

BEST BETS   The tabletop department and giftwares. Avoid the outlets; they bring in cheaper merchandise to beef up the stock.

WHERE TO BUY   7 stores, 10 Co-Ops, and 12 outlets in the U.S. **FLAGSHIP**   660 Madison Ave., NYC. ☎ **212/826-8900.** Mon–Fri 10am–8pm; Sat 10am–7pm; Sun 11am–6pm. AE, DISC, VC, V. Subway: W to Fifth Ave. www.barneys.com.

Bergdorf Goodman NYC $–$$$$$

World's Best   Continually creative with a sophisticated edge, Bergdorf has many lines that do not have their own stores but come to BG to test the waters and later become internationally famous in their own right. It's all about the new and exclusive merch.

The jewelry department is excellent; the basement is devoted to beauty. The home-style floor has zillions of small salons selling merchandise and gift items in a setting that looks like the pages of a magazine. The Men's Store across the street is a tribute and a temple to rich men everywhere (p. 223). What makes this store work is that it has charm. It feels small; it feels like each visit here is an opportunity to discover something new, something special.

BEST BETS   The little-known but sublime brands in jewelry, fashion and accessories. Don't miss the Home floor, especially before Christmas.

WEB TIPS   Google "Bergdorf coupon code" and you should be able to find codes for free shipping.

WHERE TO BUY   1 store: 754 Fifth Ave. at 58th St., NYC. ☎ **800/558-1855.** Mens Store: 745 Fifth Ave. at 58th St., NYC. Mon–Fri 10am–8pm; Sat 10am–7pm; Sun noon–6pm. AE, DISC, MC, V. Subway: F at 57th St. www.bergdorfgoodman.com.

Brentwood Country Mart SANTA MONICA $–$$$$

This isn't even a mall, it's a lesson in what rich people want and enjoy. This so-called country mart is a barnlike structure that houses stores and foods serving the wealthy communities west of Beverly Hills. The shops are unique and often one of a kind, although there is a branch of Calypso (from St. Barth's and New York City). There are also a number of events and charity drives that attract locals and celebs. Most of the people who shop here wouldn't be caught dead in Beverly Hills.

WEB TIPS   You can get the lay of the land online but cannot shop.

WHERE TO BUY   1 store: 225 26th St., Santa Monica, CA. ☎ **310/ 451-9877.** Mon–Sat 10am–6pm; Sun noon–5pm. AE, DISC, MC, V. www.brentwoodcountrymart.com.

Bulgari ITALIAN $$$$–$$$$$

Bulgari once made very expensive watches and jewelry, and in fact, they still do. Was there ever anything more gotta-have-it than that snake watch? But they've added to and expanded their expertise. It's not just about the diamonds.

About 15 years ago, Bulgari wanted to bring in an aspirational customer and some younger money, so they created a line of not-as-expensive jewelry made with ceramics and 18kt gold. After that, the hits kept coming with ideas to do luxury work at affordable prices, so handbags ($1,000) and sunglasses ($400) were born. Sure, you can still get a $75,000 limited-edition watch but the more normal range is $10,000 to $15,000 for watches and $200 for ties. This is an attainable luxury brand. To make it even hotter, before you could say *"Arrivederci, Roma"* the brand had amenities in luxury hotels (free), fragrance ($135) and then, *voilà,* their own chain of hotels (villas $1,400+ a night). This is one of the most remarkable extension stories in the world.

There are some outlet stores. The one I just visited was as nice as any boutique: Ties were $50 and earrings were marked down to $4,000. Phew.

BEST BETS   I'll take the free shampoo and conditioner at participating hotel partners. They are about the best hotel amenities you'll ever beg, borrow or steal.

WHERE TO BUY   200+ stores worldwide. **FLAGSHIP**   Via Condotti 10, Rome. ☎ **3906/679-3876.** Mon–Fri 10am–6pm; Sat 10am–5pm. AE, MC, V. Metro: Spanish Steps. Outlet store: Via Aurelia 1052, Rome. ☎ **3906/661-7071.** www.bulgari.com.

Compagnie Française de l'Orient et Chine (CFOC)
FRENCH $–$$$$

The French lost Indochine but were quick to grasp Chinese clothing and home style in a way that is subtle enough to mix into fashion classics. CFOC, as it is called, was begun in 1966, a significant date because few were into Chinese retail at that time. This line is the antithesis of Shanghai Tang (p. 57). The clothes are made in solid colors and represent understated fashion; there's nothing glitzy here. Home furnishings are sometimes sold in separate stores from clothes.

WHERE TO BUY   6 stores in Paris; also Brussels and Barcelona. **FLAGSHIP**   170 blvd. Haussmann, Paris, 8e. ☎ **331/4260-6532.**

Mon–Sat 10am–7pm. Métro: St. Philippe du Roule. www.cfof. com.

The Container Store USA `VALUE` $–$$

World's Best

The Container Store can make you resolve to be organized. What amazes me about the success of this store is that its concept is so American: Where else in the world does anyone have the space to be this organized? This anal? This compulsive? This downright yummy? Where else would a neat closet be considered sexy?

Shop Talk

Tom Ford says he stays up at night ordering from the Container Store online.

Containers is right—all kinds of containers. There's gift wrap, mailing tubes and boxes; hangers and travel sets; home care items; units for organizing closets, bathrooms, kitchens, cars. There's stuff to make the house smell better; there's vases (because they "contain" flowers). Every space and situation lends itself to the concept.

BEST BETS   I buy the big plastic bins in which I organize each chapter of my books. I like the fashion-colored plastic hangers and the air purifer gel balls.

WEB TIPS   The website is clean and clear, with some editorial information on how to organize yourself before you move into your dorm room, how to set up your office and so on.

WHERE TO BUY   37 stores in U.S., including NYC, Pasadena, Rockville, Miami, Chicago, more. **FLAGSHIP**   7700 W. Northwest Hwy., Dallas, TX. ☎ **214/373-3131.** Mon–Sat 9am–9pm; Sun 10am–4pm. AE, DISC, MC, V. www.containerstore.com.

The Corner Berlin BERLIN $$–$$$$$

Berlin has been chockablock with good shopping ever since the Wall came down and East Berlin—once shut off from capitalism—has made up for it with a number of galleries, shopping districts and interesting stores. Top of the heap is The Corner, as it is called, which sells clothes from not the usual designers (they carry LouLou de la Falaise) and a little of everything else. The store is open, bright and moderne, with paving stones that lead the way through the various departments. There's vintage furniture, books, music, clothes—think vases ($50) on top of coffee tables ($500) with hanging, upside-down light fixtures.

BEST BETS   This is a gallery store, something like Colette in Paris; the architecture is interesting, as are the display units which shift in elevation.

WEB TIPS   Despite its German domain, the site is in English.

WHERE TO BUY   1 store: 17 Driesener Strasse (Gendarmenmarkt), Berlin. ☎ **4930/4373-4363.** 11am–8pm. AE, MC,V. www.thecornerberlin.de.

H.D. Buttercup LOS ANGELES $–$$$$

Once upon a time, Paulette Cole, the woman who is mostly responsible for the thunder at ABC Carpet, divorced her husband—Mr. Cole. Mr. Cole subsequently moved to LA and began his own version of the concept . . . in an old bakery near Culver City. And so H.D. Buttercup was born.

I like this store enormously, but it is not in the same category of *grand* as ABC in New York. A lot of this has to do with the space. It's vendor leased, which dictates the showroom-like ambiance; there can't be any cross-merchandising because each area represents a different store or brand.

Dubbed "manu-tailing" by Mr. Cole, the concept allows (over 50) individual furniture manufacturers to become retailers, displaying their goods and selling directly to the consumer. By cutting out the middle man or designer or retail outlet, manufacturers can offer their latest designs at reduced prices. You can wander around and get an eyeful of style and wonder and have a good time shopping.

BEST BETS   Vary from dealer to dealer. The best bet is the fact that it's not far from LAX so if you have a layover and are bored, you can visit and still get back to the airport.

WEB TIPS   Sales and events are announced on the site; you cannot buy.

WHERE TO BUY   1 store: 3225 Helms Ave., Los Angeles, CA. ☎ **310/945-5440.** Mon–Sat 10am–7pm; Sun 11am–6pm. Credit cards depend on each dealer. www.hdbuttercup.com.

Disney Stores USA $–$$$$

World's Best   The first time I went into a Disney store, I was thinking to myself, "Yeah, yeah, yeah, give me a break." I was expecting coonskin caps and Snow White apples. I happened to be inspecting the newly opened flagship on Fifth Avenue and when I came to a plush toy of the Statue of Liberty with a Minnie Mouse head for $5, I knew I was in the midst of genius. Walt Disney understood that movies were nice but characters were money in the bank. With a constant flow of new characters, there's constantly new merchandise and creativity at various prices.

BEST BETS   The character merch is brilliant.

WEB TIPS   You might as well be the roadrunner to figure out which website to use since there are sites for various countries, for online shopping and for Disney.

WHERE TO BUY   104 stores in Europe; 58 stores in the UK, also stores across USA. **FLAGSHIP**   711 Fifth Ave., NYC. ☎ **212/702-0702.** Mon–Sat 10am–8pm; Sun 1am–6pm. AE, DISC, MC, V. Subway: E, V to Fifth Ave./53rd St. www.disneyshopping.com.

Forum at Caesar's LAS VEGAS

It's not an exceptionally large mall (160 stores), but you have never seen anything like this, even in Disney World. Created as a Las Vegas version of an ancient Roman village, the mall is adjacent to Caesar's Palace on the Las Vegas Strip. Along with the upmarket stores and fancy chef eateries, there are mimes, statues, water shows and much entertainment. Stores include Bulgari, Burberry, Dior, Versace, Valentino.

BEST BETS   A new annex has great stores but not so much razzmatazz.

WEB TIPS   If you Google the Forum, you'll end up on www.simon.com. Instead, go to www.harrahs.com and search for "shopping."

WHERE TO BUY   3500 Las Vegas Blvd. S., Las Vegas, NV. ☎ **702/893-4800.** Sun–Thurs 10am–11pm; Fri–Sat 10am–midnight. www.simon.com or www.harrahs.com.

Gump's SAN FRANCISCO $–$$$$

This is a specialty store that acts like a concept store. Many items are unique, handcrafted and/or made exclusively for the store. The ground floor of the store—especially the jewelry department—is almost in art gallery format. All items reflect the store's strong bias as to who it is and what is right for them. Even Scandinavian art glass—which has nothing to do with Asia—looks right when Gump's says so. In fact, a lot of what Gump's sells is authority—although part of the success of the store has to be its location right off Union Square.

Because the merchandise is so varied, prices are all over the place. This is a good place to buy the Agraria line of potpourri which began in San Francisco ($30 and up).

BEST BETS   One-of-a-kind jewelry such as a black jade necklace by Lynn Nakamura, $3,750. I have fallen in love with a Tibetan chest of drawers which I don't find overpriced at $985.

WEB TIPS   The site in no way reflects the glamour of the store. Still, if you know what you want, you may be able to find and buy it online. Born to Shop Editorial Director Sarah Lahey got a

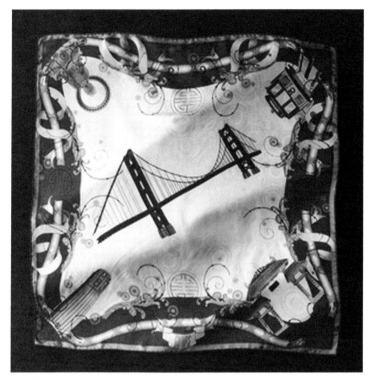

Gump's "San Francisco scarf."

deal worth celebrating: a set of three bamboo nesting tables for $175 plus $18 for local shipping.

WHERE TO BUY   1 store: 135 Post St., San Francisco, CA. ☎ **415/ 982-1616.** Mon–Sat 10am–6pm. AE, DISC, MC, V. BART: Market/ Powell. www.gumps.com.

Hema DUTCH ⟨VALUE⟩ $–$$

World's Best   Hema (say Hay-ma) just may be worth a trip to Amsterdam. The store graphics and packaging are clean and simple; the look is more fashionable than Gap's, but not overly cute or prissy. This is a one-stop-suits-all resource with clothing, home style, some food items and a large selection of personal grooming items, many of them private label and green (ecologically oriented). Hema is where you just go and wander and find things that are useful, well designed and well priced. Obviously, the larger the store, the better the selection.

BEST BETS   The minty dandruff shampoo and house line of shampoos/conditioners and bath products are great, even if you don't have dandruff; the fashion is color-fully Dutch and very affordable.

WEB TIPS   The site is in Dutch, so you can actually muddle through it and pretend you are on *Saturday Night Live*, but you can't order merchandise.

Hermès narrow enamel bracelet.

WHERE TO BUY   320 stores worldwide, including Amsterdam. **FLAGSHIP**   Kalvertoren Mall, Kalverstraat 212, Amsterdam. ☎ **3120/422-8988.** Mon 11am–6:30pm; Tues and Wed 9:30am–6:30pm; Thurs 9:30am–9pm; Fri and Sat 9:30am–6:30pm; Sun noon–6:30pm. MC, V. Transportation: Muntplein. www.hema.nl.

World's Best

Hermès FRENCH $$–$$$$

Very few of the international luxury brands are excellent in several categories of wares. Hermès is the exceptional exception, known for their handbags, leather goods, silk scarves, ties, enamel bangle bracelets and fragrances. The store design is dramatic—the windows of the flagship store in Paris are worth pressing your nose to while breathing deeply. Few brands say "status" in as many different categories of goods, all of which can be visually identified—no need for a logo or visible label. Did you see the Hermès Harley in the downtown NYC store? Now that's entertainment!

The original part of the Paris flagship store has a very rarefied atmosphere and a constant herd surrounding the scarf ($325) cases. Nonetheless, there's a museum on the top floor and a lot to enjoy here. Don't forget to stand back when you are outside so you can see the man on horseback on the roof.

Shop Talk

This is the store that turned away Oprah Winfrey during a private event. A store rep apologized on her show: "You did meet up with one very, very rigid staffperson." Oprah retorted, "Rigid or rude?"

BEST BETS   The men's ties are the most perfect gift in the world. But wait, there's also the enamel bracelets, which Sarah and I collect.

WHERE TO BUY   57 stores, including NYC, London, Seoul, Tokyo, more; some department stores and airports. **FLAGSHIP**   24 rue du faubourg St. Honoré, Paris, 8e. ☎ **331/4017-4717.** Mon–Sat 10am–7pm. AE, MC, V. Métro: Concorde. www.hermes.com.

Indigo Seas LOS ANGELES $–$$$

Despite the name, this is not a way-faring store or one that has to do with ships that go down to the sea. The water refers to deepwater trade and the treasure comes from all over Asia, with a lot of American vintage beachwares thrown in. There's table-cloths from the fifties and shell-encrusted picture frames and batik hand-dyed fabrics. The entire collection feeds off itself and gives energy to create a whole look.

BEST BUYS   Vintage tabletop from the fifties.

WHERE TO BUY   1 store: 123 N. Robertson Blvd., Los Angeles, CA. ☎ **310/550-8758.** Mon–Fri 10am–5pm; Sat 10am–4pm. AE, DISC, MC, V. No website.

Jeffrey USA $$$$–$$$$$

Jeffrey rose to retail fame as the shoe buyer for Barneys. His family is in shoes (see Bob Ellis on p. 142), so he comes to it with expertise and flair and a lot of, uh, sole. On leaving Bar-neys, Jeffrey opened a store in Atlanta and then tackled Manhattan with a totally outré store in the Meatpacking Dis-trict. When Jeffrey arrived, there was little there save the old warehouses and the notion of less expensive real estate. In no time at all, the limos brought the customers. In a few years, the entire area was awash in stores, galleries, trendy restaurants and the In Crowd in search of the It destination. Jeffrey is a museum to what's cool and hip.

Jeffrey carries the same big name designers that other stores carry, but he buys their lines differently and always has merchandise that no one else has. His salespeople were wooed from the best luxury brands and came to him complete with Filofaxes of names and numbers. My vendeuse, whom I had to sharply remind I was always broke, used to call me on the eve of every sale to ask if she could set aside products for me. Now that's selling.

BEST BUYS   There's no price tag on the cutting edge. Some-times there's a DJ. Sometimes there's celebrities. There's buzz all of the time. Jeffrey is the specialty store of the New Age.

WEB TIPS   The website sucks. Don't waste your time. And no, you can't buy online nor can you get any feel for the store or what it sells.

WHERE TO BUY   2 stores, NYC and Atlanta, GA. NYC: 449 W. 14th St. ☎ **212/206-1272.** Mon–Wed and Fri 10am–8pm; Thurs 10am–9pm; Sat 10am–7pm; Sun 12:30–6pm. AE, DISC, MC, V. Subway: A, C, E to 14th St. Atlanta: 3500 Peachtree Rd. NE. ☎ **404/237-9010.** Same hours as NYC store. www.jeffrey newyork.com.

Jim Thompson THAI $–$$$

World's Best   When I worked at QVC I was told that any merchandise with a good story could be sold. Therefore, I am not sure whether the subsequent success of this line is related to the great story behind it or simply brilliant merchandising. Regardless, this is a great total product, based on the Thai silk business.

Here's the story: Jim Thompson was an American living in Bangkok after World War II. In the fifties he got involved in the re-introduction of Thai silk as a cottage industry. Rumor has it, he was a CIA agent. No one knows for sure, but one day he disappeared and has never been heard from since.

World Traveler

Thompson's original house in Bangkok is now a museum, at 6 Soi Kasemsan 2, Rama 1 Rd. (☎ 662/216-7368; www.jim thompsonhouse.com). You can tour all six buildings of his exquisite estate, and admission is only $1.

Now Thompson's business is run by a team as clever as the owners of LVMH, and the silk business has turned into a lifestyle business. You'll find sheets and bedding, clothes, men's ties (of course), silk robes and kimonos some yard goods, plush animals, fashions and accessories and anything else you can think of. Many of the motifs incorporate elephants; some are a tad touristy to transcend into fashion. Nonetheless, a visitor will be bitten and smitten and will need to buy a lot of this stuff. In fact, visitors to Bangkok may find they need to go into every Jim Thompson store they pass—and they are strewn around hotel lobbies, airports and major commercial districts.

There is a wholesale silk business that caters to the international design trade; the stores are mostly based in Thailand and southern Asia. There are outlet stores, although the fabric outlet that I visited has marginal savings. This line is represented to the trade in design showrooms around the world.

WEB TIPS   The website's quick and easy, with good graphics and lots of info, but you cannot order online. Check eBay for sales.

WHERE TO BUY   43 stores. Bangkok, including Bangkok International Airport, several hotels, outlets, Siam Paragon (p. 448); also Singapore, Tokyo, Melbourne, and Paris. **FLAGSHIP** 9 Surawong Rd., Bangkok. ☎ 662/632-8100. AE, MC, V. Daily 9am–9pm. www.jimthompson.com.

Kierland Commons SCOTTSDALE, AZ

World's Best   This is one of those new-fangled malls that doesn't even resemble a mall. It's not enclosed and has been created as an artificial village. You get the pleasures of walking in a downtown-like village area and shopping all your favorite stores and multiples while served by one parking space. There are several restaurants and all the "real people" needs any shopper might want. There's even a hotel and residential loft apartments on-site to complete the community feel.

In hot weather, the walkways are misted so you don't suffer heat stroke. This is the living habitat of the future. I swear it.

BEST BETS   The "village" feel that makes you want to wander, shop, eat, enjoy life in a small and safe town environment. This is the un-mall mall.

WEB TIPS   The website gives you tourist tips such as: "Take your out-of-state driver's license to the concierge desk and get a free info and coupon book."

WHERE TO BUY   Greenway Parkway, Scottsdale, AZ. ☎ **480/ 348-1577.** Mon–Sat 10am–7pm; Sun noon–6pm. www.kierland commons.com.

Stanley Korshak TEXAN $–$$$$$

The most shocking thing about this store is that it co-exists and even thrives in the same town as Neiman Marcus. Aside from the fact that Stanley Korshak did not evolve into an internationally recognized brand name or even sprout branch stores across America, the store is very, very similar in spirit to NM and serves the same new-money client. Neither a department store nor a specialty shop, this is a lifestyle store of the most true fashion since it serves the clients who need service as tall as their oil wells.

Of course there's valet parking and private shoppers and lots of "Hey, y'all." To attract the younger set—and to offer up goods that are more moderately priced—there's a few boutiques called The Shak (get it?). These are mostly in hotels dotted around Dallas.

BEST BUYS   Lots of unique merchandise, especially in men's novelty gadgets and shave/beauty items.

WEB TIPS   You can shop online, though selection is limited. The section called Gift Rapt gets points for the clever title alone.

WHERE TO BUY   1 store: 500 Crescent Court, Dallas, TX. ☎ **214/ 871-3600.** Mon–Sat 10am–6pm. Shak: 600 Crescent Court, Dallas. AE, DISC, MC, V. www.stanleykorshak.com.

Ralph Lauren USA $–$$$$$

World's Best   In the beginning, Ralph created ties. But he didn't like the shirts and suits that were being sold with his ties, so he went into menswear. Then he didn't like the way the stores were showcasing the brand, so he went into retail. Then he got rich and invested in personal interests, such as cars and cowboys and active sports. Then he saw holes in the marketplace for all these items—to say nothing about the need for a home style and lifestyle integration—and before you could say *Ohmigod,* Ralph Lauren had created his universe. This is a total cradle-to-grave line; if you had to pick one style for dress and home, you could do worse than think of Ralph and his empire.

To further prove what a marketing genius this man is, he pretty much invented the factory outlet business as we know it today. There have been factory sales and ways to unload damaged and excess merchandise for over 100 years but Ralph Lauren said, "Bring it on." At a time when many major brands were afraid that outlets would hurt their image or their relationship with department stores, Lauren not only opened freestanding, attractive stores but began to make merchandise to be sold in these outlets.

The Polo line is one of the most copied in the world of faux—if tempted by a fake, be sure to count how many legs the pony has. Ralph Lauren is a national treasure.

BEST BETS   The weaving of quality, architecture, goods and attitude; plus the elegant and dramatic custom and couture lines, as stylish as any European brand—and as costly, of course. You can spend $25 or $2,500 and look good.

WEB TIPS   The site is good but doesn't begin to give you the whole experience.

WHERE TO BUY   150+ stores worldwide. **FLAGSHIP**   Rhinelander Mansion, 867 Madison Ave., NYC. ☎ **212/606-2100.** Mon–Wed 10am–6pm; Thurs 10am–7pm; Fri and Sat 10am–6pm; Sun noon–5pm. AE, DISC, MC, V. Subway: 1 to 72nd St. www. ralphlauren.com.

Liberty LONDON VALUE $–$$$$

World's Best   Each time I enter Liberty of London, you can hear me mutter, "Give me Liberty or give me death." Liberty is simply one of the best stores in the world. But wait—note that when I enter the store, I come around to the rear of the store, to the old Tudor building. This is the good part.

You'll find tiers of wooden arcades surrounding an atrium; miles of style pushed into vignettes, boutiques, sales areas, corridors and nooks (or crannies). When I call this store value oriented, I only mean that the price seems to justify the show-biz

Tiebacks and tassels in a Liberty display window.

experience. The handbag of my dreams, a tote made from Liberty fabric, costs $800. That is no bargain, especially for a fabric and seasonal tote bag. But if I were made of money, I'd have that bag and every other one in the range—the wow factor is astonishing.

BEST BETS   The Liberty Room featuring items made from Liberty fabrics (agenda, $22); Liberty bath products (grapefruit bath oil, $12). I also like the knitting and crafts department. I've bought Etro fabrics off the bolt and taken them to my tailor in Hong Kong (p. 216).

WEB TIPS   The merchandise featured is minimal and you can't order online. In fact, you can't even get an idea of what Liberty is all about from this site.

WHERE TO BUY   1 store: Great Marlborough St., London W1. ☎ 4420/7734-1234. Mon–Wed 10am–7pm; Thurs 10am–8pm; Fri and Sat 10am–7pm; Sun noon–6pm. AE, MC, V. Tube: Oxford Circus. www.liberty.co.uk.

LouLou de la Falaise PARIS $$$$

LouLou is the daughter of a famous fashion mother and the former muse to no other than Yves Saint Laurent. When YSL retired, LouLou decided to open a small store selling off her collection of everything from 30 years of musing. You could sort of call it a private eBay sale offered live on the Left Bank of Paris. The store became so successful that LouLou opened a second one and had to begin designing and buying merchandise, since her closets were soon depleted of vintage YSL. Yet the concept was always the same—this is the merchandise that was in, or really would have been in, LouLou's private closets. The left bank store is now closed; c'est la vie.

BEST BETS   Pieces with humor and style.

WHERE TO BUY   1 store. Also select department stores, The Corner Berlin (p. 42), more. **FLAGSHIP**   21 rue Cambon, 1er, Paris. ☎ **33142/600-266.** Mon–Sat 10am–7pm. Metro: Concorde. AE, MC, V. www.loulou-de-la-falaise.com.

Macy's USA $–$$$$

Although my first job in retail was at Macy's, this is not one of my favorite stores and I find the NYC flagship too large to be the best of anything. However, I am knocked silly by the job Macy's has done with a 2,000-item product launch of Martha Stewart merchandise exclusive to the store. This is a lifestyle offering within a department store that is so strong you may stop shopping your former haunts to try Macy's.

BEST BETS   The bedding isn't as well made as Ralph Lauren but the kitchenwares are to die for.

WEB TIPS   You can create a wedding registry online here or even just a "wish list" for other occasions.

WHERE TO BUY   800+ stores in U.S.; **FLAGSHIP**   Herald Sq., 151 W. 34th St., NYC. ☎ **212/695-4400.** Mon–Sat 10am–9:30pm; Sun 11am–8:30pm. All major credit cards. Subway: 34th St. www. macys.com.

Maison Michel Biehn PROVENCE $$$$

Built into a private mansion on the main shopping street of the Provençal village Isle-sur-Sorgue, Michel Biehn's store specializes in ethnic design. He once sold Provençal regional dress and tabletop, but when that became scarce, he branched out into Indian textiles and exotic goods because of the way they once influenced Provençal fabric via *les tissues indiennes*. Wander the rooms and touch everything. There's also numerous books about style, all by Biehn with some translated into English. What makes this one of the best stores in the world is that each time you visit, it's different, yet at heart, still focused on the same thing. The eye, the heart and the soul of the store stay the same while the look and the featured items change.

BEST BETS   The Indian twirly skirts are pricey (about $350) but have a drape to them that no other crinkly skirt comes near replicating. Most are reversible.

WEB TIPS   Although you cannot buy, the website gives you such detailed photos that you get a good feel for the store and its charms.

WHERE TO BUY   1 store: 7 av. des 4 Otages, L'Isle-sur-Sorgue, France. ☎ **334/9020-8904.** Sat–Sun 10am–1pm and 2:30–6:30pm and by appointment; no appointments Tues–Wed. AE, CB, MC, V. www.michel-biehn.com.

World's Best *Marks & Spencer* BRITISH ⟨VALUE⟩ $–$$$$

Originally created to offer value for money, Marks has been reborn as one of the hottest department stores in the UK—there's clothes, supermarket and now home in what are called Life stores. The first is opening in Manchester as we go to press.

The most successful part of their stores has always been the supermarket and the private label foodstuffs business, but the clothing lines are coming up in the world. The St. Michael brand of underwear has been retired, but the Per Una line of young fashions is scorching. Autograph is the most expensive line here, made by big-name British designers who do special collections. Life stores also have tech centers and restaurants. Additionally, there are a few dozen M&S outlet stores where goods are sold for 30% less; many of these have full price supermarkets downstairs and outlet prices upstairs. (There are none in London.)

BEST BETS   Basics at fair prices, well cut and well made. There's plus sizes, petites and generous sizes in everything from shoes to lingerie.

WEB TIPS   Extraordinarily detailed website. You can shop online with UK delivery—the site is in conjunction with Amazon.

WHERE TO BUY   450+ stores in UK. **FLAGSHIP**   458 Oxford St., London W1. ☎ **4420/7935-7954.** Daily 10am–6pm. AE, MC, DISC, V. Tube: Marble Arch or Bond St. www.marksand spencer.co.uk.

World's Best *Monoprix* FRENCH ⟨VALUE⟩ $–$$

Although Monoprix was created after its founder—who married a member of the Galeries Lafayette family from Paris—visited Woolworth's stores in the U.S. (on his honeymoon, no less), Monoprix has thrived and Woolworth's has disappeared. Maybe Target became what Woolworth's should have been; maybe we need lessons from the French on how to provide mass market style with fashionista chic. *Ici, la.*

Billed as your "city *marché*," Monoprix serves the urban city center of every trading area in Paris and most major

French cities. There are some international stores, but not many. Most Monoprix stores have a supermarket as well as aisles of choice featuring clothing, health and beauty aids and home style. Monoprix is where you go for a liter of milk and end up buying a bathing suit, some Bourjois makeup, fish-net tights, a string bikini and a few bottles of wine.

Fashion merchandise is introduced every 8 weeks; the store carries a 50/50 mix of classics and trendy fashion items. Their children's clothing is outstanding. There are assorted lines by famous French designers done on a limited edition basis. The designers are never the Karl Lagerfeld type but are more casual.

BEST BETS Fashion at a price; even French aristo ladies shop here. The children's clothing is also fabulous. I just bought a five-piece wardrobe of mix and match clothes for $200.

WEB TIPS The site is in French, and you cannot order merchandise.

WHERE TO BUY 250+ stores in France. Cannes, Lyon, Lille, Aix-en-Provence. **FLAGSHIP** 52 av. des Champs Elysees, Paris, 8e.☎331/5377-6565. Mon–Sat 9am–midnight in summer, 9am–10pm in winter. MC, V. Metro: FD Roosevelt. www.monoprix.fr.

Muji JAPANESE ⌂VALUE $–$$

Muji is what Gap should have or could have been. It is the no-nonsense design capital of simplicity and functional yet chic and cosmopolitan design. The Tokyo flagship is three stories of easy to shop, easy to wear, easy to afford everything for your life. There's a cafe and gourmet grocery mart in the flagship also.

There are many stores in the UK, several around the world and only one in the U.S.—the one in the U.S. is actually part of the MoMA Design Store in Manhattan. But wait! As we go to press, Muji is poised to open two stores in Manhattan. Watch this space.

BEST BETS Everything is plain but perfect, from the T-shirt that comes in a square wrap the size of a postcard ($20) to the simple bed linen ($60), to makeup or desktop accessories (beginning at $2).

WEB TIPS Go to www.muji.co.uk and access the British English language website (with prices in sterling). You'll also find a full list of websites at www.muji.net/eng.

WHERE TO BUY 34 stores. **FLAGSHIP** 3-8-3 Marunouchi, Chiyoda-hu, Tokyo. ☎ 813/5208-8241. NYC: 451 Broadway. Subway: N, Q, R, W to Canal. www.muji.net.

Nantucket Looms NANTUCKET, MA $–$$$$

Begun in the late sixties as a weaving studio and showcase for local talent in the heart of Nantucket, Nantucket Looms is true to its original concept but has surrendered its original location to Ralph Lauren and moved to smaller digs where they still sell the island lifestyle. The store is famous for their throws but they also sell furniture and tabletop. More importantly, this store is an icon representing the soul of Nantucket: simple, modern meets colonial, windswept, rich in textures, natural and expensive.

BEST BETS   Throws and shawls that are hand-woven right there in the studio. Prices depend on size and fiber—cotton, wool and cashmere are used.

WEB TIPS   There are a limited number of items available for sale online; consider the cotton baby blanket for $175.

WHERE TO BUY   1 store: 16 Federal St., Nantucket. ☎ 508/228-1908. Mon–Sat 10am–5pm in winter and 10am–10pm in summer. AE, DISC, MC, V. www.nantucketlooms.com.

Neiman Marcus TEXAN $–$$$$$

When I was a girl growing up in Texas, Neiman Marcus was not the name of a store: it was a prayer. "Dear God, please make Momma take me to Dallas to buy a dress."

Ultimately, Neiman brought brands and style to the South and to Texas; Neiman created marketing concepts for the oil rich and made national news with their Christmas catalogue and his/hers gifts—his/hers safaris, his/hers jet skis, his/hers hot-air balloons. In a world where Macy's didn't tell Gimbel's, no one had to be reminded that Neiman Marcus represented the fantasy aspects of retail married to show business in a time when that notion was otherwise unheard of. But times have changed. Nowadays NM is best served by its information services and the ways they entice loyal customers to succumb to the ease of shopping Neiman.

BEST BETS   The range of small luxe brands such as Eskander; an excellent string of outlet stores dotted across America (named **Last Call**), a fairly good sales and markdown policy and an unerring eye for novelty merchandise for people who have more money than taste.

WEB TIPS   It's easy to order from the website—quick links, large photos, good descriptions. I found a skirt on sale online that was full price in the store, same day.

WHERE TO BUY   60+ stores in the U.S. **FLAGSHIP**   1618 Main St., Dallas, TX. ☎ 214/741-6911; 800/937-9146. Mon–Wed

10am–6pm; Thurs 10am–8pm; Fri 10am–6pm. AE, DISC, MC, V. www.neimanmarcus.com.

Nordstrom USA $–$$$$

Nordstrom serves the population as the poor man's Neiman Marcus. Once upon a time, Nordstrom was a shoe store. This is important to remember because they still have one of the best shoe selections in any department store in the world—and because the store has grown to what it is today by careful design and purpose.

Many department stores grow, or die, higgledy piggledy. Not Nordstrom. The store is known for its customer service. If the item you want isn't in stock, the sales staff will search every store in the chain to find it for you. And you can return anything at any time after you purchase it for a full refund, no questions asked. You don't even need a receipt.

BEST BETS   The shoe department. Outlets are good, too.

WEB TIPS   The website is much like Neiman's—easy to use with good graphics. You'll find a good selection of sale items online.

WHERE TO BUY   43 stores in U.S. **FLAGSHIP**   500 Pine St., Seattle, WA. ☎ **206/628-2111.** Mon–Sat 9:30am–9pm; Sun 11am–7pm. AE, DISC, MC, V. www.nordstrom.com.

Oriental Bazaar TOKYO $–$$$$

As the name implies, this large store sells all things Oriental. It is run like an American store and sells everything you want, need or didn't know you needed as souvenirs, gifts and decorative touches. On the ground floor you might think this is a TT (Tourist Trap) or a glorified Pier 1, but the higher you ascend (up 3 flights), the better the merchandise. The good stuff is always put away.

BEST BETS   This is one of the few places to buy used kimonos without going to a dealer or a temple sale.

WHERE TO BUY   1 store: 5-9-13 Jingumae, Tokyo. ☎ **813/3400-3933.** Daily 9:30am–6:30pm. AE, MC,V. Metro: Omotosando. No website.

Oviesse ITALIAN `VALUE` $–$$$

This is a lifestyle store that has become a way of life for me—I don't fit into French clothes so I go over to Italy to buy from the plus-size range of these highly fashionable but very inexpensive clothes. This store might be the Italian version of Target although the style is much more on-focus. The store is a division of the Coin department-store chain in Italy.

Naturally, some seasons are better than others and some stores are better than others. I pay $35 for a linen dress, $55 for a two-piece pants outfit and $15 for a handbag.

BEST BET   The best plus-size clothes for the price in the world. I bought an ivory linen trouser suit for $100.

WEB TIPS   You cannot buy online so who cares if the site is only in Italian?

WHERE TO BUY   70+ stores in Italy. Opening soon in Germany. www.oviesse.it.

Saks Fifth Avenue USA $–$$$$$

You could argue whether Saks is a department store or a specialty store, but why waste your time? The flagship on Fifth Avenue (hence the name, Saks Fifth Avenue) is by far the store to visit, but branch stores are very good at catching the local vibe with merchandise needed in that locale.

Saks is a great store because it's neither too big nor too small. Everything has been bought with a target customer in mind. When that merchandise doesn't move, there are fantastic sales. The home collection isn't that large, but the pieces are great and Saks is one of the few U.S. stores to sell Lisa Corti (p. 346). Each Saks adapts itself to the locale; some Saks stores have separate Mens Stores. (Saks prides itself on its menswear; see p. 224.)

WEB TIPS   There's strong information easily placed on the home page about sales and promotional deals; when you click on each particular store, you can get a map and all info needed for that store.

WHERE TO BUY   100+ stores in U.S., in Beverly Hills, Chicago, San Antonio, more; Saks, Saks Mens Stores and Off Fifth outlet stores. **FLAGSHIP**   611 Fifth Ave., NYC. ☎ **212/753-4000.** Mon–Fri 10am–7pm; Sun noon–7pm. Subway: Rockefeller Center or 54th St. www.saks.com.

Shanghai Tang CHINESE $$–$$$$

World's Best   I am not sure if I am correct in saying that David Tang, who created this firm, is the genius behind it; or if the people who run it now are the genius guys—perhaps it's the synergy between them.

Tang's concept was to take original Chinese clothing styles and do them in neon colors of high quality silk. From there an empire of high style and Chino chic was born, with stores all over the world. Since then, a highly motivated design team has taken high color, Chinese heritage design and modern concepts and gone mad with the kind of classical clothes and

accessories you can't live without. There's everything from fragrance to stuffed animals to yard goods (with private tailoring available in the flagship store) to cashmeres and coasters and even note cards.

BEST BETS   The silk shirts and (for whimsy) the handbags. Personally, I'm dreaming of the silk pj's, which they happen to give away in first class on Cathay Pacific.

WHERE TO BUY   20 stores worldwide, including London, Paris, Beijing, Shanghai. **FLAGSHIP**   12 Pedder St., Central, Hong Kong. ☎852/2525-

Shanghai Tang "silk road print doctor's bag."

7333. Mon–Sat 10am–8pm; Sun 11am–7pm. NYC: 600 Madison Ave. at 58th St. ☎ 212/888-0111. Mon–Sat 10am–6pm; Sun noon–6pm. Subway: R, W, Fifth Ave. AE, DISC, MC, V. www.shanghaitang.com.

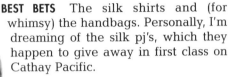

Shiatzy-Chen TAIWANESE $$$$–$$$$$

There are some stores that are religious experiences. When you walk into this store in Shanghai, you may get goose bumps, burst into tears or just feel your heart turn over. The store is gorgeous and the merchandise almost seems worth the outrageous prices. And they do have sales.

There are clothes for men and women as well as accessories for women and furs. This is one-stop shopping for the rich, the famous, the glam and the rock star. Most styles have a Chinese influence in the cut. The prices have Italian influences—a jacket costs $1,200 and a suit is $3,400. But wait, I just got a jacket on sale for $450. Double happiness!

BEST BETS   The swank clothes in the same caliber as Armani, such as the hand-stitched satin Mao jacket for $965.

WEB TIP   You may need to turn off your pop-up blocker to access the English version of this site.

WHERE TO BUY   10 stores worldwide. **FLAGSHIP**   No. 49-1, Sec. 2, Chongshan N. Rd. ☎ 886/2-2542-5508. Taipei; other stores: Bund no. 9, 9 Zhong Shan Rd., Shanghai. ☎ 86/21-6321-9155. Also in Paris, Beijing, Qingdao, and Hong Kong. www.shiatzy-chen.com.

Siam Paragon BANGKOK $–$$$$.

Very, very fancy Bangkok mall with brand-name designer stores, brand-name chefs and restaurants, gourmet food shops, a local department store, a 21-screen multiplex and, best yet, an entire floor devoted to Thai-made products, fashion, beauty and home style. Even the food court is fabulous.

BEST BETS   The fourth floor with all the Thai flagships, from the department store Paragon to the spa and beauty brand Thann & Harn.

WEB TIPS   Get information about the "prestige cards" and their benefits online to see if you qualify or want to apply for the perks.

WHERE TO BUY   991/1 Rama l Rd., Bangkok. ☎ **662/610-9000.** Daily 10am–10pm. Restaurants on ground floor open until 11pm. www.siamparagon.co.th.

Takashimaya New York NYC/JAPANESE $$–$$$$$

| World's Best |

True, Takashimaya began in Japan as a department store in the tradition of old-fashioned department stores, no question. However, the Manhattan location is no branch store— here Takashimaya has out-created any specialty store that ever existed. A visit to this store makes you under-stand why it is traditional to bow on entering.

The store sells expensive things to people who have everything. Takashimaya sells style from a well-chosen array of brands, *Takashimaya body care set.*

including many brands that other stores do not have, many of which are French. This is by no means a Japanese department store.

BEST BETS   There is emphasis on quality and simplicity as well as unique merchandise. The packaging—shopping bags and gift boxes—is among the most dramatic in the world. Unique accessories are the thing to home in on, such as a flower choker made of pale green feathers ($250), or silk-covered navy blue pearls ($99).

WEB TIPS   There's a website for the NYC branch with helpful information, but you can only order select items online.

WHERE TO BUY   1 store in U.S. 693 Fifth Ave., NYC. ☎ **212/ 350-0100.** Mon–Sat 10am–7pm; Sun noon–5pm. Subway: Fifth Ave. AE, DISC, MC, V. www.takashimaya-ny.com.

10 Corso Como MILAN $$–$$$$

Take two very talented and stylish Italian sisters who look a lot like twins and you get either a Greek tragedy . . . or the most talked-about team in a generation of fashion talent. One sister became the editor of *Italian Vogue;* the other opened the most important store in town with worldwide ripples of influence.

10 Corso Como is named for its address, which, a decade on, has become trendy—but in the beginning, this was nowhere land, and real estate was cheap so owner Carla Sozzani could afford to be large and to sprawl through garage and warehouse space. Here you might find an embroidered pashmina shawl for $600 or a pair of sneakers for $150. I bought an embroidered tote bag from the outlet store for $35.

World Traveler

Don't miss out on one of Carla's newest additions—a three-suite B&B called 3 Rooms (☎ 03902/626-163) on the top floor of the store, designed by Carla in her classical ethnic urban style. Walk a few blocks over to the outlet: Via Tazoli 3 Milan, ☎ 3902/2901-5130.

Part of the charm of the store is its evolution—sometimes there's a restaurant, sometimes not. A bookstore rests upstairs. The gift wrap and paper goods freely given away eat into store profits. The place spells class, adventure and high style.

BEST BETS   This is one of the few stores in town that is open on Sundays, and it's such a great store that it can be the kingpin of your plans—a total destination.

WEB TIPS   For now, look at galleriacarlasozzani.com.

WHERE TO BUY   1 store: 10 Corso Como, Milan, Italy. ☎ 3902/2900-2674. Subway: Girabaldi. AE, MC, V. www.10corscomo.com.

Target USA VALUE $–$$$

Originally created as a discount division of Dayton Hudson and their department stores, Target has moved into the fast lane as the mass culture provider of, well, everything. In many ways the store is a metaphor for America—fast and trendy and disposable and cheap.

The perception is that Target offers everyday low prices. But on comparison tests I made, the prices were exactly the same as at other stores—when you can find a match-up in the merchandise. Therein lies the catch. Target has rather unique merchandise, aimed at a marketing niche.

Guest designers have provided the snap, and the stores have created a cult aura that makes you revisit if only to see what's new. Merchandise by Michael Graves (architect), Isaac Mizrahi (fashion bad boy), Liz Lange (maternity clothes), Cynthia Rowley (teens), 🚗 **Nick & Nora** (fabulous pajamas) and Sonia Kashuk (makeup artist) have made the chain look smart, even if you are still shrugging your shoulders and saying to yourself, "Just who is Mossimo anyway? Proenza who?"

Shop Talk
Those who question the skills required of models might have enjoyed "Target's Model-less Fashion Show" held in New York in November 2007; it used hologram technology in place of models.

BEST BETS   Weekend clothes at affordable prices.

WEB TIPS   Sign up for the newsletter and trend alerts; you'll also get coupons.

WHERE TO BUY   1,300 stores in U.S. First store ("Super Target"): 1515 County Rd. BW, Roseville, MN. ☎ **651/631-0330.** This was just remodeled and is now a Super Target, replacing the notion of flagship. Minneapolis: 900 Nicolet Mall. Mon–Sat 8am–9pm; Sun 10am–6pm. AE, DISC, MC, V. www.target.com.

Tiffany & Co. USA $$–$$$$$

They do not serve breakfast at Tiffany. They don't have a snack bar, there's no latte, nor do they sell clothes or furniture. What they sell is the whiff of success, the Tiffany Experience.

The stores, and the very exclusive Tiffany robin's-egg blue box, have become legends. Nothing says you care like something in a blue box. Preferably a small blue box, since this is primarily a jewelry store. An engagement ring from Tiffany & Co. is thought to be the ultimate love token. In fact, anything that comes in that box says you cared enough to send the very best.

It's the trifles that help define the Tiffany Experience and have made this firm a player—they have had signature jewelry collections from a handful of cutting-edge designers, each with his own distinctive style and contribution to jewelry—be it Elsa Peretti (who created some of the most iconic pieces Tiffany has ever sold) to the newer pieces of Frank Gehry.

BEST BETS   The gift certificates never, ever expire. I've been holding onto one for 18 years and they assure me it's still good. Unfortunately, $118 credit doesn't buy much here anymore.

WEB TIPS   The home page is a Tiffany robin's-egg blue box, of course. They now list jewelry prices online.

WHERE TO BUY   80+ stores in US; 20 more locations in London, Paris, San Francisco, Austin, more. **FLAGSHIP**   727 Fifth Ave., NYC. ☎ **212/755-8000.** Mon–Fri 10am–7pm; Sat 10am–6pm; Sun noon–5pm. AE, DISC, MC, V. Subway: N, R, W to Fifth Ave. www.tiffany.com.

Urban Outfitters USA ⟨VALUE⟩ $–$$$

Back in the day when there were hippies, Urban Outfitters was the fashionable hippie's main squeeze. Hippies grew up and went middle class, but their kids still needed someplace to shop so Urban Outfitters modified itself and morphed into the hippest . . . without the hippie.

The store sells a complete lifestyle with just enough trendiness to it to appeal to teens and tweens and just enough of a price break to be affordable for college co-eds, young professionals and young couples starting their exploration of home style. On the other hand, don't be fooled into thinking this is a bargain resource—prices aren't any less than at Anthropologie; the style is just younger and the marketing skews the brand to seem accessible.

BEST BETS   Home style for the dorm or first apartment.

WEB TIPS   The site's complicated and takes some time to maneuver; however, you'll find lots of merchandise marked "online only."

WHERE TO BUY   Over 100 stores in the U.S., Canada and Europe. **FLAGSHIP**   1627 Walnut St., Philadelphia, PA. ☎ **215/569-3131.** Mon–Sat 10am–8pm; Sun 11am–7pm. AE, DISC, MC, V. www.urbanoutfitters.com.

Venetia Studium ITALIAN $–$$$$$

Take ten million teeny weeny Fortuny pleats and turn them into an incredible fashion business turned concept store and you get this small chain of Venetian stores that only sell oriental-style printed and pleated velvets and silks made into accessories and chandeliers. The colors are husky and dusky; the mood is very Gustav Klimt—these are exotics that would make Marco Polo proud. Mariano Fortuny was actually born in Spain but became Venetian by choice. He ruled the 1920s with his exotic designs and technological advances—the way he made pleats (today called Fortuny pleats) is said to have died with him. He worked in silk and velvet, often hand stamped with patterns in gold leaf and finished off with beads from Murano. Chandeliers are still being made and sold here.

BEST BETS   The velvet flowers are so gorgeous you want to pray; the tassel-laden handbags for evening and wraps are beyond compare. Flowers are $35.

WEB TIPS   The site has lots of slow intros and fade-ins and -outs; save time by logging on to www.venetiastudium/shop.

WHERE TO BUY   6 stores in Venice, 1 in London. **FLAGSHIP** Calle Largo xxii, San Marco 2403, Venice. ☎ **3941/522-9281.** www.venetiastudium.com.

Chapter Four

Women's Clothing

To me, clothing is only one part of the whole when it comes to a life or a lifestyle. And like many shoppers (as statistics have proven), I'm not as interested in clothing as I once was. What does interest me is the way people mix clothes nowadays—they shop at Louis Vuitton and Wal-Mart.

If you were to catch me today in my local supermarket, I'm wearing a pair of Gloria Vanderbilt stretch jeans from TJMaxx, a big linen Eileen Fisher shirt from the Neiman Marcus outlet and some slip-on shoes from the Aerosoles outlet; and I'm carrying an ancient Hermès Birkin handbag. I think this mélange represents the new "now."

> I like my money right where I can see it: hanging in my closet.
> —Carrie Bradshaw, Sex & The City

Who would imagine that the average price for a pair of jeans would get to be $200? That the inexpensive handbags now cost $300, the average bag costs $500 and the run-of-the-mill designer bag is over $1,000? Killer IT bags cost over two grand. Money is funny and fashion is fleeting. We're all just trying to get by and feel good about the way we look. I understand that the way I look influences the way I feel, about myself and my day. So the best clothes in the world—the best wardrobe around—is the one that makes you feel confident.

Nothing else matters.

Activewear

Danskin USA (VALUE) $–$$

Let's ignore the men's part of this brand unless you are Billy Elliot or a professional dancer. However, therein lies the brand's fame—Danskin makes professional ballet gear used by real dancers and wannabes alike.

It was easy for Danskin to move into active and exercise wear because they had a, uh, leg up in the category early on. By the 1970s—partly thanks to Donna Karan's introduction of the bodysuit, leotards became a fashion item. Colored tights and footless tights (leggings) have come and gone on fashion horizons. With prices far below the average fashion and designer brand, Danskin provides not only the bodywear, but

Womenswear on the Web

Bluefly.com
Everything from this fashion discounter is first quality, brand new and straight off the runways. Hundreds of new styles are introduced every day and prices vary from 20% off top name designer goods like Chanel to 40% discount on other brands. Watch for promotional sales, that is "Saturday only." For many, this is a way of life.

Laredoute.com
Pronounced "la ruh doot", this site is like a French Spiegel catalog. It is extremely popular in France and in the UK, where Brits like to hate the French but love their merchandise. Offering a wide selection of French labels, La Redoute also sells basics as well as glam. The Jean Paul Gautier exclusive-to-La-Redoute line is a good buy; his five pocket denim skirt was $40. Goods may be returned within 14 days for any reason.

Net-a-porter.com
This designer label site offers high fashion lines such as Chloe, Jimmy Choo, Bottega Veneta and Proenza Schouler, all presented in magazine style. Your purchase will arrive in a ribbon tied box and should you have second thoughts, everything can be returned within 14 days. Shipping is expensive, beginning at $25 for the first item and going up from there. Goods are shipped from New York where local taxes are added.

all keys for a fashion alternative and a professional range for all active sports and dance. Kickboxing, anyone?

Oh yes, plus sizes are available.

BEST BETS   The tights ($12) and leggings ($16–$40) *never* bag at the knees and come in many styles and colors.

WEB TIPS   You'll get a 10% discount off your first Web order; enter ORDER1 in the coupon box at checkout. (For more on coupons, see p. 406.)

WHERE TO BUY   3 stores and 17 outlet stores in U.S. and Canada; department stores. **FLAGSHIP**   159 Columbus Ave., NYC. ☎ **212/724-2992.** AE, DISC, MC, V. Mon–Thurs 10am–7pm; Fri–Sat 10am–8pm; Sun 11am–7pm. Subway: 1, 9 at 66th St. www.danskin.com.

Stella McCartney for Adidas GERMAN/BRITISH $–$$$$
I have become a reluctant fan of Stella McCartney, mostly an intellectual fan because this woman has style, creativity and a finger in every pie. It's no surprise that she makes some of the

best designs in activewear, created for the
German shoe brand Adidas. Her success
with this line is due to an understanding of
body movement that she works into the
clothes, rendering them stellar. Her
cachet is enormous, but so is the fact that
the clothes work for workout.

Prices are indicative of the amount of
technology involved and the brand's
name so that a pair of shoes may seem
reasonable at $100, but a windbreaker
costs closer to $200. A tennis line is
launching as we go to press.

*Stella McCartney "run
winter jacket."*

If the prices are too high for your budget, note that the line
is sold in the 48 Adidas outlet stores (internationally) and that
sale items are available on the website.

BEST BETS   Turns out Stella is a genius in technology, fabric and
problem solving. Check out Asheni silver ballet slippers for
$85.

WEB TIPS   You can view the entire line at once, or shop by
category—apparel, shoes, accessories. There's a good zoom
feature to see details.

WHERE TO BUY   20 stores in the U.S., over 200 worldwide. **FLAG-
SHIP**   22 av. des Champs Elysées, Paris 8e. ☎ **331/5659-3280.**
AE, MC, V. Mon–Thurs 10am–8pm; Fri–Sat 10am–10pm. Métro:
Franklin Roosevelt. NYC: 610 Broadway. ☎ **212/529-0081.**
Mon–Sat 10am–8pm; Sun 11am–7pm. AE, DISC, MC, V. Sub-
way: Broadway/Lafayette St. www.shopadidas.com/stella.

Puma GERMAN [VALUE] $$–$$$

Once considered an almost dead brand, Puma came back into
vogue about the same time as Adidas, emerging with designer
duds such as Alexander McQueen and getting seriously into
international sports—they support Japanese golf, Moroccan
football, cricket and so forth. There is a special division of the
firm for sports and serious athletes, but this is also a very hot
street brand.

Check out the ever-changing parade of hot-colored sneakers. The line has a retro sixties' feel to it and is now very
cutting edge; the accessories easily cross over from activewear
to fashion to collectibles.

BEST BETS   The line has a very good sense of humor which is
probably why it appeals to young people. There's a shoe
called The Bee which actually folds into a bee shape (I swear).
They have a jacket called the Storm Trooper ($75) and a line

of travel running clothes called Train Away. These guys are clever. Did I tell you about the Mongolian BBQ line, which lets you play designer (http://mongolianshoebbq.puma.com)?

WEB TIPS   The website is also clever, with a separate online site (www.pumashop.com). Puma has a lower-priced division named Nuala designed by model Christy Turlington (http://nuala.puma.com).

WHERE TO BUY   50+ stores worldwide, including 17 in U.S.; also department and specialty stores in 56 countries. **FLAGSHIP** Zeil 72-82, Frankfurt. ☎ **4969/2199-7636.** Mon–Sat 10am–8pm. AE, MC, V. NYC: 33 Union Sq. W. ☎ **212/206-7761.** Mon–Sat 10am–8pm; Sun 11am–7pm. AE, DISC, MC, V. Subway: Union Sq. www.puma.com.

Basic Tops & T's

Anne Fontaine FRENCH $$$–$$$$

Beginning with the basic white shirt, Anne Fontaine has built an international business selling white and black blouses with, every now and then, an oddball pastel thrown into the mix. The concept has been so popular that several copycat brands co-exist on the high street. Fontaine remains the best because of the mix of dressy, traditional and fashion looks attributed to a variety of white shirts in various fabrications.

The size system is based on a size 1 as the smallest and size 4 as the largest. Fontaine creates approximately 300 new designs each year. This is a lifestyle, a concept, a niche.

You'll have the most fun shopping in one of the freestanding stores, but the line is carried in some department stores. Some pieces can be bought online. There are outlet stores. Because she has so many copycats after her, Anne Fontaine is evolving her business, so no one can really catch her. She has just opened a new concept store in Paris.

BEST BETS   The white shirts. Prices hover around $100 to $145 for basic blouses and go much higher, *bien sur*. In the flagship Paris store, check out the new spa downstairs with 77 different treatment options.

WEB TIPS   The website requires a Flash Player 8 plug-in; If you don't have it, you can install the software. Good luck. On my last visit, the site was under new construction. *Merde.*

WHERE TO BUY   70 stores worldwide; 22 in U.S. **FLAGSHIP**   370 rue Saint Honore, Paris, 1er. ☎ **331/4261-0370.** Mon–Sat

10am–7pm. AE, DISC. MC, V. Métro: Tuileries. NYC: 687 Madison Ave., at 62nd St. ☎ **212/688-4362.** Mon–Fri 10am–7pm; Sat 11am–6pm; Sun noon–5pm. AE, DISC, MC, V. Subway: Fifth Ave./59th St. www.annefontaine.com.

Linq USA $$–$$$$

The perfect T-shirt is indeed a basic staple but one that enhances your figure, which is why the Linq shirt is the best in the world. Okay, why is this shirt different from every other T-shirt out there? Well, it's long, lean and makes you look thin. The color range changes with the season but is fabulous and there are little fashion twists that embellish without getting in the way—shorn silk and such. Even a basic white T-shirt is suddenly stunning with a little silk on the edges.

BEST BETS   Styles vary with the season—there's the long sleeve (a long, lean sleeve), the traditional T-shirt, the cami and other styles. Retail ranges from $58 to $148.

WHERE TO BUY   Major department stores in the U.S. include Bloomingdale's, Nordstrom, also Searle NYC. No website.

Uniqlo JAPANESE VALUE $–$$

Uniqlo is to Japan as Gap is to the U.S.—only the merchandise is more basic and less expensive. Quality is high. There are over 700 stores worldwide, so they are obviously doing something right, and the new flagship in New York's SoHo has hit the district with a huzza. As Gap becomes more diluted in scope, Uniqlo burns vibrantly.

There is some fashion and a soupçon of style, but mostly this is the line the T-shirt built. This is sort of a good news, bad news concept in that we have all been weaned on inexpensive fashion and expect it from a variety of sources. Uniqlo doesn't do fashion, a situation that may change now that they have hired a fashion director from Barneys.

The very nature of Uniqlo's success is that it is plain Jane, that the basics are not affected by trend. This brand is similar to the **Muji** concept (p. 54), another Japanese phenom.

BEST BETS   T-shirt for $6; sweater for $13 and down coat for $98.

WEB TIPS   The collection is shown on a scrolling link—you must click fast and accurately to see an individual item.

WHERE TO BUY   700+ stores worldwide; pop-up store is being tested in Barker Arcade at Kensington High St.; also vending machines in Japan. **U.S. FLAGSHIP**   546 Broadway, at Prince, NYC. ☎ **917/237-8800.** Mon–Sat 10am–8pm; Sun 11am–7pm. AE, DISC, MC, V. Subway: Broadway Lafayette or Prince. www.uniqlo.com.

Bridal

With wedding gowns more than any other type of fashion, I am of the opinion that it only takes money to have the wedding gown of your dreams. If you haven't got much money, then you need to be clever.

If you are not a tiny bride, don't fret—there are many sources for queen-sized gowns. After all, it's your day, be you princess or queen. Even JCPenney has plus-size gowns in their catalogs and for sale at their outlets.

No matter what size you are, I pass on my sister's trick: With a limit to her budget and a desire for simple chic (teamed with not much time or patience), she went to the end-of-summer sales (she had a winter wedding) and found a white silk suit she liked on the racks at Neiman Marcus. The suit had a lovely jacket and a simple skirt. My sister tossed the skirt and had a new one—long—made by her regular seamstress. She was such a beautiful bride, I wept. Total cost: $345 for the jacket and $125 for the skirt.

Another trick: The so-called **Bridal Building** at 1385 Broadway is in the heart of Manhattan's Garment District. Flyers are given away on the weekends, announcing who is open for business. Often the elevator man knows of sales or has suggestions. (Honest.) The best time to go, especially if you are a sample size (6) is after market in April and October. Prices are about half of those in department stores and wedding shops. (Cash is preferred, but some take checks.)

Amsale NYC/ETHIOPIAN $$$$$

Although she also does evening gowns and now has a very nice list of celebrity clients, Ethiopian-born Amsale (say "Am–sal-eh") Aberra is really just the gal behind the wedding dress—the sleek, elegant wedding dress that is devoid of froufrou excess. She calls herself a bridal designer; her gowns hang from the ceiling of her Madison Avenue boutique like pieces of art in a gallery.

BEST BETS   As wedding confections go, the prices are reasonable—under $5,000 for the whole shebang. While well known, Amsale remains a less obvious choice than Vera Wang yet serves the same clientele.

WEB TIPS   The gowns are shown in large photos on the website with several views—front, side and back, with close-up attention to detail.

WHERE TO BUY   1 store: 625 Madison Ave., at 58th St., NYC.
☎ **212/583-1700.** AE, DISC, MC, V. By appointment only.
Subway: Fifth Ave./59th St. www.amsale.com.

Kleinfeld NYC $$$$$

Kleinfeld offers a huge selection of designer gowns and a variety of price points. Therefore, brides from all over make the pilgrimage and begin their wedding journey with a big "Aaaahhhh." I just saw the store featured on *Regis & Kelly;* indeed, the store is considered *the* source for brides-to-be.

BEST BETS   The store sells not only bridal gowns—traditional and nontraditional styles—but mother-of-the-bride and wedding-party finery. Bridal gowns begin at $1,800.

WEB TIPS   You'll save time before your appointment by previewing the gowns on the website. There's a good selection of plus-size gowns and eveningwear—great for mothers and bridesmaids. Click on "gift registry" to link to Bloomingdale's.

WHERE TO BUY   2 stores, in Manhattan and Brooklyn. 110 W. 20th St., NYC. ☎ **646/633-4300.** Tues and Thurs 12:30–8pm; Fri 11:30am–6pm; Sat 9:30am–5pm; Sun 10am–5pm. AE, DISC, MC, V. Subway: F, V at 23rd St. www.kleinfeld bridal.com.

Kleinfeld store interior.

The Recycled Bride

For the bride with lots of style but little cash, there are ways around plunking down the cost of a new car on a wedding gown. On a TV show I was asked where I would buy a wedding gown. When I admitted that I'd first take a look at the offerings at Goodwill, a gasp rose from the audience.

There are also specialty stores that sell used wedding gowns—hell, they've only been worn once—but I am fond of the spectacle and sideshow elements involved in sample sales and discount wedding gown events.

Resale Gowns: Perhaps the most interesting resale choice is **The Bridal Garden,** 54 W. 21st St., NYC (☎ **212/252-0661;** www.thebridalgarden.com), which takes bridal gowns as a charitable donation on behalf of needy children. When you buy from them, 100% of the money actually goes to the charity. **Michael's,** 1041 Madison Ave. at 79th St., NYC (☎ **212/737-7273;** www.michaels consignment.com), the Manhattan resale shop, also has an atelier that sells only wedding gowns.

Factory Outlet Bargains: There are factory outlets around the U.S. that carry wedding gowns. Eight **JCPenney** (☎ **800/322-1189;** www.jcpenny.com) catalog outlets in the U.S. have gowns; call for the nearest location. Designer **Jessica McClintock** (☎ **800/711-8717;** www.jessicamcclintock.com), who makes the Gunne Sax line, has bridal and wedding wear at her outlet stores; the website has a store locator and shows all styles. **Alfred Angelo** (☎ **866/826-4356;** www.alfredangelo.com), a large manufacturer of wedding gowns, has an outlet in SawGrass Mills, in Boca Raton, FL (☎ **561/241-7755**).

Barneys Bridal Sample Sale: As these things go, the bridal sale that **Barneys Co-Op,** 255 W. 17th St., NYC (☎ **212/716-8860;** www.barneys.com), puts on is a very sedate and civilized affair. It has proved more interesting now that Vera Wang has ceased her independent wedding gown sample sale and merged with Barneys. The gowns are upmarket, fancy and expensive. They are just less expensive than if you bought them under normal circumstances. This is an annual event, usually held the last 2 weeks of August through the first week of September.

Filene's Basement "Running of the Brides": Before we go any further with this, I am going to tell you that there is a survival trick that makes the difference between triumph and failure in this bride-eat-bride shop-a-thon. Since designer wedding gowns go for as little as $249, and competition is fierce—herewith the secret: It's all about swapping.

You race in there with the herd and you grab anything, or as many anythings as you can get your paws on. Don't worry about style or size or, for heaven's sake, the color (they're pretty much all white). Then, once you have something, you slow down and see what other people have. Then you begin to trade with them. If you have nothing to trade, you are out of business.

Originally held just in the Boston flagship **Filene's Basement,** 426 Washington St., Boston (☎ **617/542-2011**), the wedding sales are now held in several major cities. The number of sales per year varies with the venue; there are three a year in Boston. Yes, the event is worth flying into town for. Yes, there is a long line to get in, although you do not need to overnight on the pavement. Yes, you'd better be the kind of person who likes this sort of thing. There can be kicking and screaming.

The lines usually include the bride and her party, or at least a mother and/or sister or a best friend or partner, as you need as much help as possible with the grabbing, the trading and the trying on. Expect to strip right there to fit into the dress. If you're shy, forget it. Why would anyone go through all this? Well, you can find a $2,000 gown for $250. In fact, gowns go for $249 to $499, with most expensive designers priced at $699 (retail up to and over $9,000). Get dates of the sales online at www.filenesbasement. com/bridal.jsp.

Filene's Basement "Running of the Brides."

Vera Wang USA $$$$$

After training with Ralph Lauren, Vera Wang went out on her own, first designing wedding gowns and then building an empire focused on the needs of the bride. In reality, she's now moved into mass market with a full line for Kohls, but right now, the subject is roses.

Wang can provide not only the wedding gown and the clothes for attendants and mothers of bride and groom but also the lingerie, the shoes, the jewelry, the accessories and the perfume for the bride. Oh yes, did I mention that she'll even offer you the wedding bed? The dishes? The household items you may want or need? The stationery for thank yous?

BEST BETS   The one-stop-serves-all-needs concept wins. Gowns start at $2,000, though most are over $5,000.

WEB TIPS   Wang sometimes has sample sales at Barneys. Call or check the website for dates and times. For images, the website is slow; you might request a catalog instead.

WHERE TO BUY   3 stores. Bridal store and bridesmaids' boutique in New York, lifestyle store in Hawaii; also at Saks, Neiman Marcus, Barneys and select bridal boutiques. **FLAGSHIP**   991 Madison Ave., in the Carlyle Hotel, NYC. ☎ **212/628-3400.** By appointment only. AE, DISC, MC, V. Subway: 6 at 77th St. www.verawang.com.

Cashmere

If all cashmere were created equally (which it is not), there would be nothing wrong with buying your cashmere at Costco and various other big-box stores that sell cashmere sweaters, usually for well under $100. Ply—the number of threads in the knit—allows for bulk or weight but not quality, although you don't want a one-ply sweater.

So here's the difference between a $400 cashmere sweater and a $100 sweater: the combing and the production. Shorter fibers are combed out of high-priced cashmere, so it lasts longer and doesn't pill. It's not where it comes from but where's it's finished that matters: The good stuff comes from Scotland or Italy. In fact, I am somewhat partial to the offerings from Lands' End (☎ **800/960-9432;** http://landsend.com), especially Mongolian cashmere sweaters ($120–$140) and T's ($90). J.Crew (www.jcrew.com) also uses famous factories in Italy.

Cruising Cashmere Country

You've heard of Scotland's Whisky Trail? I take you on the Cashmere Trail where there are mills and sometimes even bargains to be had. While every now and then you can latch onto a tour out of Edinburgh, the tours are often sponsored by specific mills and are therefore limited or biased. Rent a car instead. In the countryside alongside the River Tweed, you'll find a half dozen or more villages such as Peebles, Galashiels, Kelso, Innerleithen, Berwick upon Tweed, Jedburgh and Selkirk. The capital of it all is the village of Hawick, about an hour's drive from Edinburgh.

Hawick (say Hawk) is filled to bursting with cashmere factories and outlet shops, although many of the smaller mills have been bought up by bigger firms. Try **Hawick Cashmere Limited,** Trinity Mills, Duke Street, (☎ **441450/372-510;** www.hawickcashmere. com); and **Lovat Mill,** Commercial Rd. (☎ **441450/373-231**). Note that most of these mills sell cashmere at factory prices online as well; also try www.hawickknitwear.com and www.peterscott. co.uk. For general information see www.iknow-scotland.co.uk or write to scottishcashmere@aol.com.

Brora BRITISH $$$$

Scottish cashmere in women's and children's designs that are witty and unique. Also accessories and a funky BoHo look that can't be taken too seriously even though the elements are serious—such as the cashmere itself.

BEST BETS   The cardigan sweaters are available in over a dozen styles; most are in the $300 to $400 range.

WEB TIPS   Select one of 20 colors from the chart, then choose a style in that shade. They'll ship to the U.S., but shipping charges begin at $28.

WHERE TO BUY   7 stores in London area. **FLAGSHIP**   81 Marylebone High St., London. ☎ **4420/7229-1515.** Mon–Sat 10am–6pm; Sun noon–5pm. AE, MC, V. Tube: Baker St. or Bond St. www.brora.co.uk.

Kinross Cashmere USA $$$$

Scottish cashmere sweaters that never pill and continue to look brand new, even after washing. (I put them in the washer on a delicate cold cycle, then air dry.) The color palette is fab—most are available in more than 15 choices—and they're made in both traditional and trendy styles. The dye lots remain

Loro Piana cashmere cape.

constant from year to year, so you can always add a new piece to go with what you already own. Kinross makes men's sweaters as well.

BEST BETS   Twin sets—both hoodies and cardigans paired with a sleeveless, low-cut tank. Prices are reasonable for the high quality (all under $300 and most under $200).

WEB TIPS   All styles and colors are shown online, but you can't order from the website. Some of the links are slow to load, but each style is shown in detail, including the available colors. Le Sportif boutique in Tiburon, CA, holds a Kinross trunk show every August where you can order with a 10% discount.

WHERE TO BUY   Specialty boutiques; 6 Sportif (www.6-sportif. com). Tiburon, CA: 1550 Tiburon Blvd. ☎ **415/435-2220.** Mon–Sat 10am–5pm. AE, MC, V. www.kinrosscashmere.com.

Loro Piana ITALIAN $$$$

Italians—well, Northern Italians—love quality and they love a look that is very similar to the English Country style. No firm combines them better than Loro Piana. It's casual but rich, filled with the nuances of upper-crust style. Besides all those luxe stores, there's also a slew of factory outlet stores in various outlet malls and, even better, a flagship outlet—called the factory store—right in the main factory in Romagnano, west of Milan.

World Traveler

Fewer than 500 meters from Loro Piana in Romagnano, Italy, stands the **Colombo factory store,** via Novara 263 (☎ 3901/6383-2373; www.lanificiocolombo.it), another source of premium cashmere more classical in style.

BEST BETS   A cashmere scarf at the factory store costs $150 yet retails for $450 in regular stores.

WEB TIPS   The English version is slow to load, but with patience, you can scroll through the collection.

WHERE TO BUY   37 stores worldwide. **FLAGSHIP**   Via Montenapoleone 27/C, Milan. ☎ **3902/777-2901.** Mon–Sat 10am–7pm. AE, MC, V. Romagnano Factory store: Via Novara 484. ☎ **3901/6382-6875.** www.loropiana.com.

N. Peal BRITISH $$$$

This firm offers the most perfect combination of talents: quality fibers, traditional styles and fashion colors (there are more than 55 hues). They also sell their own line of cashmere shampoo products—a great gift item. With the high cost of British goods, N. Peal has closed its U.S. stores and now does trunk shows, most often as charity benefits.

BEST BETS   This venerable firm now has a lower-priced line called Pure. A sweater will cost about $225 and a camisole is $115. Regularly, sweaters are $400 and up.

WEB TIPS   The online shop has good sales, sometimes up to 20% off.

WHERE TO BUY   London, New York, Chicago, more. **FLAGSHIP** 37 & 71 Burlington Arcade, London W1. ☎ **4420/7493-5378.** Mon–Sat 9:30am–6pm. AE, MC, V. Tube: Green Park. www. npeal.com.

Pringle BRITISH $$$$

If you are thinking argyles and Perry Como sweaters or Queen Elizabeth style twin sets, well, forget it right now—this is the house with the dachshund knit into the sweater and items made with colors and crazy giddiness. In a recent past season, Pringle took a traditional fisherman's sweater and shortened and widened it into a new cult classic. This line has leapt from has-been to one of the best in the world in a matter of a year or two.

   The new flagship on Bond Street lets you know that this is not for little old ladies who may catch a chill. There is also seasonal ready-to-wear.

BEST BETS   The elegant classics done with a twist that makes them very now, such as the fisherman's sweater mentioned above. All are pricey; expect to pay from $500 to $1,000 for a sweater. The line is too new to be discounted much, but there are a few outlets.

WEB TIPS   The collections are presented online in a runway/fashion-show format. No prices and no Web orders.

WHERE TO BUY   4 stores in UK, also Taiwan and Japan; outlet in Hawick, see p. 75. **FLAGSHIP**   112 New Bond St., London W1. ☎ **44-020/7297-4580.** Mon–Sat 10am–5pm; Sun noon–5pm. AE, MC, V. Tube: Bond St. www.pringle-of-scotland. co.uk.

Chic & Simple

There are some fashion lines that defy fashion by offering simple and classical style. Whether the clothes are cut and sewn or knit, the drape and fit are made for comfort but the look is utter simplicity and charm—always appropriate. Some of these lines offer a total lifestyle (like Eileen Fisher), while others may be sold at stores that represent a statement but carry various lines.

Ann Ahn NYC/LAOTIAN $$$$

Teeny, weeny Madison Avenue boutique filled with subtle clothes at staggeringly high prices (Japanese crinkle dress, $800) that are worn by those who cherish big beads and craftsy or handmade coats. Simple, often baggy styles, comfortable and always timeless.

BEST BETS   One-stop shopping with accessories as well as clothes and coats. Can provide a "look."

WHERE TO BUY   1 store: 961 Madison Ave. at 75th St., NYC. ☎ 212/288-6068. Mon–Sat 10am–6pm. AE, MC, V. Subway: 68th St. Hunter College. No website.

Eskandar BRITISH/PERSIAN $$$$–$$$$$

Alas, this is a look I would wear exclusively if I could only afford it. Eskandar is the sophisticated Eileen Fisher with a slightly Korean-Zen touch—although it is a British line with a Persian creator headquartered in London.

The clothes do not come in regular sizes and tend to be boxy and drapey, always casual but elegant; they're classic in the timeless precision of ethnic dressing. The high quality of the fabrics put the clothes into their own category of luxe. They're all natural and tend to be in neutral or earth shades; there are tweeds in the winter wools. Trousers usually have elastic waists, and none of the clothes are too fitted.

BEST BETS   Works well on women with figure flaws or who look better in clothes than without them. An embroidered linen tunic costs $650; simple white shirts are $440.

WEB TIPS   You cannot buy from the website, but there are several sites, including eBay, that offer the brand online. I didn't think $500 for a used sweater was a bargain, but whatchagonna do?

WHERE TO BUY   3 stores worldwide; also at Neiman Marcus and NM outlets and Bergdorf-Goodman, NYC. **FLAGSHIP**   134 Lots Rd., London. ☎ 4420/7351-7333. Mon–Fri 10am–6pm; Sat

10:30am–5:30pm. AE, MC, V. Paris: 7 rue Princesse, Paris 6e.
☎ **331/4326-1010.** Mon 11:30am–7pm; Tues–Sat 10:30am–
7pm. AE, MC, V. NYC: 33 E. 10th St. ☎ **212/533-4200.** Mon–
Sat 10:30am–7pm. AE, MC, V. www.eskandar.com.

Eileen Fisher USA $$–$$$$

If the world ever bans fashion and switches to uniforms, I vote
for Eileen Fisher as Queen of Style. You can live a comfortable,
stylish and classical life in her clothes and not go broke. Furthermore, a lot of the pieces have elastic waists and are droopy
or stretchy. The line is designed in color groups so you can mix
and match various pieces to create your own look or choose if
you want a skirt or trousers with that top, a jacket or a sweater.
I travel in these clothes because there are a lot of knits in the
line and the clothes are casual but always stylish so you arrive
looking like a million bucks, even in a coach seat. There is a
travel line; also petite and plus sizes.

BEST BETS   The line is considered an affordable designer brand
in the mid-range. Expect to pay $75 to $300; clothes go on sale
for perhaps $109 for trousers, $200 for a silk pleated skirt.
There's also a fidelity card that rewards frequent shoppers—if
you buy enough in the regular stores, you get a discount and,
sometimes, a free tote bag.

WEB TIPS   There's a "pack your bag" section on the Eileen
Fisher website where you can put together everything for a
weekend getaway. Garnet Hill (www.garnethill.com) sells an
exclusive line of Eileen Fisher linens. See p. 307.

WHERE TO BUY   35 stores in the U.S., including Chicago,
Boston, Costa Mesa, Scottsdale and Seattle; also department
stores worldwide. **FLAGSHIP**   395 W. Broadway, SoHo, NYC.
☎ **212/431-4567.** Mon–Thurs 11am–7pm; Fri and Sat 11am–
8pm; Sun noon–6pm. AE, DISC, MC, V. www.eileenfisher.com.

Designer Boutiques

For other notable designer boutiques see "Chapter Three:
Lifestyle & Department Stores."

Armani ITALIAN $$$$–$$$$$

Giorgio Armani is one of the most important forces in international design; he has several different branches in retail for
different lifestyles, be it his most expensive and couture lines
(Giorgio Armani Black Label is the most expensive; Collezzioni
is also pricey) or his bridge line Emporio or his jeans line AJ.

There's also Armani Exchange. The wide range of Armani lines allows you to "do" Armani your way, within your budget.

World Traveler

Even if you don't normally buy this line, the flagship in Milan is a must-see. It's got the Armani makeup and fragrance, a restaurant by Nobu, the Armani chocolates, home style, and the entire Armani Casa line. It's Armani's only concept store.

There's also housewares, makeup and perfume; there's chocolates; there's caffes (that's how he spells it); and hotels are coming—this guy should meet Vera Wang.

I often joke that Armani is for women who don't know how to dress or who don't like fashion, who like to play it safe. The fabrics and cuts are sumptuous and distinct—everyone can tell you are wearing expensive clothes, which is part of the subtext that goes with the brand. If you wear Armani, you must be someone. You have arrived. *Insider tip:* Armani goes up to size 50, which is far larger than most designer lines.

BEST BETS   When you don't know what's appropriate to wear for an event, don't moan while looking through your closet, just put on an Armani pantsuit. Of course, a trouser suit will set you back over $2,000. But that's why God created resale shops. You will never go wrong wearing Armani.

WEB TIPS   The only online shopping on the Armani site is for Armani Exchange, from the U.S. only.

WHERE TO BUY   350+ stores in 39 countries; includes Armani boutiques, Collezioni stores, Emporio Armani, A/X Exchange, Armani Jeans, Armani Junior, more. **FLAGSHIP**   via Manzoni 31, Milan. ☎ **392/7231-8630.** Mon–Sat 11am–7pm. AE, MC, V. www.armani.com.

Brown's LONDON $$–$$$$$

Brown's single-handedly brought fashion and designer names to London. Most of the designers introduced here have since gone on to open their own freestanding stores, yet this fashion icon has just enough clout to sell Jan Muir after the late designer's death. The main store remains an icon on South Molton Street—it is the main reason you go to South Molton Street now. There's some menswear, too.

BEST BETS   Best for the sheer scope of designers represented—over 150. During sale periods, prices are slashed about 30%. Think Antwerp designers and Japanese unknowns.

WEB TIPS   The online shop is a great source for designer handbags. If you can't find what you're looking for in-store, try Brown's website. There's a currency converter on the site.

Lanvin display at the Dover Street Market.

WHERE TO BUY   1 store: 24–27 S. Molton St., London W1.
☎ **44020/7514-0016.** Mon–Sat 10am–6:30pm; Thurs 10am–7pm; closed Sun. AE, MC, V. Tube: Bond St. Outlet: Browns Labels 4 Less, 50 S. Molton St., London. ☎ **44020/7514-0052.** Mon–Sat 10am–6:30pm; Thurs 10am–7pm. www.browns fashion.com.

Dover Street Market (DSM) LONDON $$$$

This is a street market like I am Santa Claus. What the name really means is this is a designer market place located on Dover Street. It's a gorgeous London town house that works on the open format and showcases both big-name designers and the kind of people you are waiting to discover. There's lotsa Japanese designer clothing, which makes sense since this is the brain child of Rei Kawakubo from Comme des Garçons, but there's also many of the Antwerp designers and people like Maria Cornejo and Alber Elbaz.

The best way to tackle the store is to start at the top floor (4F) and walk down the staircase. You might not buy anything, but you'll at least enjoy it as a museum of cool.

BEST BETS   The audacity of the creativity. Prices start at over $300 for a simple white shirt, and sizes are truly tiny, but you'll find unique one-of-a kind styles here.

WEB TIPS   The website is sharp and sells small items such as fragrance, watches and wallets—but it's not worth it otherwise.

To understand what DSM really means, you have to be in the space.

WHERE TO BUY   1 store: 17 Dover St., London, W1. ☎ **4420/ 7493-2342.** Mon–Sat 11am–6pm; Thurs 11am–7pm. AE, MC, V. Tube: Green Park. www.doverstreetmarket.com.

Dries van Noten BELGIAN $$$$–$$$$$

World's Best   You know about stars who are known only by their first names: Liza, Goldie, Gwyneth. This Belgian designer is known to fashionistas simply as Dries (say Dreez).

Wearing his avant-garde clothing is like wearing the Victoria Cross of style—it says not only that you have money, but that you have know-how. The clothes feature unique fabrics and cuts; drape can be important in many of the pieces. There's also an expansive (and expensive) use of beading and embroidery in much of the work.

The store in Antwerp—his home town—is one of the best stores in the world. (See p. 445 for more on Antwerp and the design scene there.) Het Modepalais is set into a corner property, so the store fits into a cake slice–sized space of restored finesse, trimmed with polished wooden cabinets and populated by ethereal clothing.

Because this line is expensive and sometimes oddball, you may find Dries on sale at affordable prices.

BEST BETS   The strangely cut clothing, so unusual it defies fashion seasons and modes, therefore can be worn forever; prices hover in the high hundreds and do cross over $1,000, especially if you are buying in euros.

WEB TIPS   Entire collection is shown; no Web orders.

WHERE TO BUY   2 stores, also in 500+ retail outlets such as Barneys and Jeffrey. **FLAGSHIP**   Het Modepalais, Nationalstraat 18, Antwerp. ☎ **323/470-2510.** AE, MC, V. Quai Malaquai, Paris, 6m. ☎ **331/4427-0040.** Mon–Sat 11am–7pm. AE, MC, V. www.driesvannoten.be.

Jeffrey USA $$$$–$$$$$

See listing on p. 47.

Joyce HONG KONG $$–$$$$$

Joyce Ma brought big-name designers to Hong Kong by installing them in shops in upmarket malls but soon opened her own department store. She's since had several stores, but her current store on Canton Road in the heart of Hong Kong's designer shopping is a temple to design and beauty. Even if the brands now have their own shops, Joyce's blending of brands makes her sublime eye the one to trust.

If you can't afford the prices, there is an outlet store in Aberdeen. *Insider's tip:* I never find anything here—the prices aren't as low as I like and the sizes tend to run very small.

BEST BETS   The makeup department is amazing.

WHERE TO BUY   5 stores. Soon opening in China. **FLAGSHIP**   Shop G106 Gateway, Canton Rd., Kowloon, MTR: TST. ☎ 852/2367-8128. Outlet: Horizon Plaza, 2 Li Wing St., Floor 21, Ap Lei Chau. ☎ 852/2814-8313. www.joyce.com.

LouLou de la Falaise PARIS $$-$$$$$

See listing on p. 51.

Marc Jacobs FRENCH/USA $$$-$$$$$

Jacobs is an American in Paris who came up through the garmento racks of Seventh Avenue. He transformed fashion history when he went to work for Louis Vuitton in Paris and created the signature Speedy tote in pastel patent leather. Since then there's been no stopping his creative genius, although the things he makes for his own line are more funky than what he creates for Vuitton.

BEST BETS   Handbags and clothes in hot colors, interesting fabrics and with retro looks that are funky and fun while being trendsetting and cool. My giant splashy print tote was $250 and a sixties-style swing coat was $250 on sale.

WEB TIPS   You can view runway fashion photos online but cannot order. You can also view pics of the fun store window displays (usually political). Try Bluefly.com or Bizrate.com for discounts.

WHERE TO BUY   In NYC, Paris, Moscow, UAE, more; Bloomingdale's, Barneys, Neiman Marcus, Louis Vuitton (separate line) and eBay everywhere. **FLAGSHIP**   403 Bleecker St., NYC. ☎ 212/924-0026. Mon–Sat noon–8pm; Sun noon–7pm. AE, MC, V. Subway: 8th Ave./14th St. or Christopher St. www.marcjacobs.com.

Maria Luisa PARIS $$$-$$$$$

One of the most extraordinary stores in the world in that it offers a closed world of shopping to those with the money and the manners to shop here. This is the kind of store where Madame is known, where Madame is called to see certain things when they come in, where Madame may be seated while clothes and accessories are brought out. The business has grown so much that there are several boutiques in a cluster in the 1er between the Hotel Meurice and the Hotel de Crillon.

BEST BETS   The staff will put you together by mixing various designer items to give you a drop-dead and very one-of-a-kind look. It only takes money. This is for the ladies who lunch, their daughters and exotic eurotrash fashionistas (or Russians). Forget it if you are larger than size 8.

WHERE TO BUY   1 store, 2 rue du Cambon, Paris 1er. ☎ 331/ 4703-9615. Mon–Sat 10:30am–7pm. AE, MC, V. Métro: Concorde. 3 other shops (one for men) around the corner on rue du Mont Thabor.

Missoni ITALIAN $$–$$$$$

Few brands have done better than the Missoni family when it comes to focus. The colorful, stripey, squiggly, ziggy and zaggy lines of the famed Missoni look is very specific, yet able to change seasonally. There's men's, women's, kids', home and a sport line. Sometimes you can find it on sale or discounted at an outlet mall or off-pricer; I've bought pieces at Century 21 in New York City and my local Neiman's Last Call.

BEST BETS   The Missoni knits use technology to striate a design with colors, be it stripes, intarsia or pucker power. The fabrics change, but the use of color and the imaginative signature are constant, making each piece a classic. Expect to pay over $2,500 for a signature knit jacket.

WEB TIPS   The Missoni website online shopping link will direct you to net-a-porter.com, where you can find about half of the current collection.

WHERE TO BUY   22 stores in 15 countries; major department stores and fashion boutiques worldwide. **FLAGSHIP**   Via Montenapoleone 8, Milan. ☎ 392/7600-3555. Mon–Sat 10am–7pm. AE, MC, V. NYC: 1009 Madison Ave. at 78th St. ☎ 212/ 517-9339. Mon–Sat 10am–6pm; closed Sun. AE, MC, V. Subway: 6 at 77th St. www.missoni.com; www.missonihome.com.

Pucci ITALIAN $$$$–$$$$$

Marquis Emilio Pucci, the jet-setter, started his line of geometric prints and began an empire that spawned a zillion copies. He was part of the post–World War II *dolce vita,* good life, that burst into public view. Pucci was born in Naples and brought the southern, Mediterranean sense of color into his work. By the sixties, Pucci designs were everywhere, the printed silk jersey dress was the must-wear dress of American and European ladies who lunch. Soon the line was licensed to bath towels, lingerie, bathing suits, sunglasses and more.

In recent years the line has staged a comeback due to investment and guidance from LVMH. The count's daughter Laudomia also keeps a hand in. Some of the prints are archival; others are new creations. Creative director is Englishman Matthew Williamson.

BEST BETS   The vintage clothing is less money than the new, but note, the vintage Pucci runs small. Also make certain you aren't buying a nightie that you think is a dress. Dresses are about $1,200, handbags are $800 and up; bathing suit $575. The travel kit is $300.

WEB TIPS   The website is designed for high-bandwidth connections. It's very fast and features animation, video and music, so you must click quickly.

WHERE TO BUY   26 stores worldwide; discounts at DSW stores and Loehmann's in U.S. **FLAGSHIP**   via Montenapoleone 14, Milan. ☎ **392/7631-8356.** Mon 2–7pm; Tues–Sat 10am–7pm. AE, MC V. NYC: 701 Fifth Ave., at 54th St. ☎ **212/230-1135.** Mon–Sat 10am–6pm. Subway: 51st St.; 24 E. 64th St., NYC. ☎ **212/752-4777.** Mon–Sat 10am–6pm. AE, MC, V. Subway: 6 at 68th St. www.emiliopucci.com.

Sonia Rykiel FRENCH $$$$$

Any fashionista can spot a Sonia sweater at 10 meters. (Fashionistas always use the metric system.) They're droopy yet cling-to-the-body knits that whisper Sonia. She is another designer who made her mark with focus and while her line changes with the seasons, she remains true to her trademarks—plenty of sweaters, stripes, knitted rosettes and her SR monogram in rhinestones.

There is an outlet store right in Paris in the 14e; the resale shop Reciproque (p. 435) has a selection of vintage Sonia.

BEST BETS   The average sweater is $200 to $500 but will be less at the outlet and maybe less at the resale. Vintage Sonia is a hot ticket; you never know what it will go for.

WHERE TO BUY   32 stores worldwide. **FLAGSHIP**   194 blvd. St. Germain des Pres, Paris, 6e. ☎ **331/4954-6060.** Tues 11am–7pm; Wed–Sat 10:30am–7pm. Métro: St. Germain des Pres. SR Stock (outlet): 64 and 112 rue d'Alesia, Paris, 14e. ☎ **331/4395-0631.** Mon–Sat 11am–7pm. AE, MC, V. Métro: Alesia. www.soniarykiel.com.

Yohji Yamamoto & Y's JAPANESE $$$$–$$$$$

One of the most creative designers in the world, Yohji is a mastermind of shape and form and invention and the color black. Sure, black existed since the time of fire, but black as the ruler of the chic universe is very much related to the Yohji touch. Yohji designs for men and women, although many items fall into the unisex category.

Both lines work with simple colors that are pure Yohji: black (of course), navy, white, beige and sometimes a plaid or two. Edges may be raw, hems are surely uneven, shirts may have a limited number of sleeves and safety pins may be part of the get-up. With fashion this raw, it never goes out of style.

BEST BETS   Anything without a size and with a droopy enough shape to flatter any height and any figure. Comfort is a big factor in Yohji-land. His high-end line is expensive (think over $1,000 per item), so there is a lower-priced line called Y's, which is just now getting its own series of boutiques around the world. Items in the Y's line fall into the $250 to $500 price range.

WEB TIPS   This is a slow, dramatic website with a black background. No online orders. You can sometimes buy at Yoox. com.

WHERE TO BUY   Department stores worldwide; cutting-edge boutiques and freestanding stores representing YY line as well as Y, Y-3, Y-3 Lifestyle and so on. **FLAGSHIP**   5-3-6 Minamiaoyama Minato-ku, Tokyo. ☎ **033/40-6006.** AE, MC, V. NYC: 103 Grand St. ☎ **212/966-9066.** Mon–Sat 11am–7pm. AE, MC, V. Subway: N, Q, R, W to Canal. www.yojhiyamamoto.co.jp. Outlet store at The Mall, outside Florence, see p. 432.

Ethnic, International & BoHo Looks

Blanc de Chine CHINESE $$$$–$$$$$

Think Giorgio Armani meets Shanghai Tang and you've got Blanc de Chine (pictured on p. 64), a Hong Kong–based luxury label for men's and women's clothing and home style. None of the bright colors or brash combinations of Shanghai Tang—coincidentally located downstairs from the Blanc de Chine mother store—are used here; the palette is soft pastels and neutrals. While there are some traditional Suzie Wong–style dresses for sale, most of the clothing is Chinoise but classic—neither costumey nor dated. Because the sizes tend to run small (think Asian fit), some women may want to try the men's jackets.

Fabrics are top-of-the-line silks, wools and velvets; finishing is often by hand.

The bed linen is in the same palette, made of silk or satin. A duvet may cost $2,500. There are bed sets, travel throws, pajamas and even little travel quilts and pillows that roll up into a bedroll unlike any ever seen on a camping expedition. If you travel in the first-class cabin, you most certainly already snuggle down with your Blanc de Chine.

Architecture is part of the schtick. The New York store especially is very moderne and swank with a swirly staircase and a Zen-like studied ambiance of cool luxe.

BEST BETS   The unisex nature of Chinese style means that women who aren't as tiny as the traditional Chinese body can try the menswear. While the jackets cost an average of $500, they are made with exquisite details and the promise of lasting chic. The clothes cost even more in the U.S., where jackets begin at $700.

WEB TIPS   You can view the collections online; however, the photos don't do justice to the clothing. Book a flight to Hong Kong or NYC, now, if possible.

WHERE TO BUY   5 stores, in Hong Kong, Beijing, NYC. **FLAGSHIP** 12 Pedder St., Hong Kong. ☎ **852/2524-7934,** or 852/2524-7934. MTR: Central. Mon–Sat 10am–7pm; Sun noon–5pm. NYC: 673 Fifth Ave. at 51st St. ☎ **212/308-8688.** Mon–Sat 10am–7pm; Sun noon–6pm. AE, MC, V. Subway: Fifth Ave. www.blancdechine.com.

Calypso FRENCH WEST INDIAN $$-$$$$

The look is what you might call island-chic but also fits into the category of rock-and-roll glamour or BoHo classics. You can wear your own jeans with a top or fashion accessory from Calypso and feel not only the sand between your toes, but the money in your wallet. (Although your wallet will be significantly depleted after your purchase.)

BEST BETS   The colors will make you feel like dancing, and the resort looks define all that is sunny. A floaty cotton dress will cost $200.

WEB TIPS   This website is a dream—it's quick and gorgeous, and features several views of each item.

WHERE TO BUY   33 stores worldwide. **FLAGSHIP** Route de Saline, Saint Jean, St Barth's. ☎ **590/59027-7839.** Daily 9am–8pm. AE, MC, V. **U.S. FLAGSHIP** 9815 Madison Ave., NYC. ☎ **212/585-0310.** Mon–Sat 10am–7pm; Sun noon–6pm. AE, MC, V. Subway: 6 at 68th St. www.calypso-celle.com.

Cleo's DUBLIN $$$$

At first glance Cleo's may resemble a tourist store laden with handknits and tweeds, but inspection reveals one of the world's best sources for hand-knit Irish woolens.

The sweaters are at once classic and trendy, hearty yet sophisticated—while things such as the cloaks have a more old-fashioned and romantic feel. There is a catalog but no website; they will ship to the U.S.

BEST BETS   Gorgeous tweedy handknits you'll wear forever. One of my favorite sweaters ever is a nubby olive-green thing for which I happily paid $300.

WHERE TO BUY   1 store. 18 Kildare St., Dublin. ☎ **353/01-676-1421.** Mon–Sat 10:30am–7pm. AE, MC, V.

Cleo's brushed wool cardigan.

Lilly Pulitzer USA $$$–$$$$

Yeah, it's the same family as the prize, but in this case the prize goes not only to the original creator, but to the team that resurrected the Palm Beach resort prints and made them oh-so-chic all over again. This brand is ethnic if you believe in a "WASP look" or a "forever summer" state of mind.

Everyone knows it's hard to be fashionable in hot weather and even harder to look good in pink and green, yet a Lilly signature print—invariably on a white cotton ground—immediately tells the world you were born of the country club set. There's clothes for men, women and children as well as some home style. There's even maternity wear. You can still find vintage Lilly out there, but not in the Lilly Pulitzer stores.

BEST BETS   The signature print dresses, of course—$150 to $300. Watch for home style.

WEB TIPS   You can shop online by season or by category. There's also a good selection of handbags at the website.

WHERE TO BUY   17 stores in U.S.; also in over 80 clothing shops in U.S.; Bloomingdales, Nordstrom, Saks, Neiman Marcus, more. **FLAGSHIP**   600 Front St., Key West, FL. ☎ **305/295-0995.** Mon–Sat 10am–6pm; Sun noon–5pm. AE, MC, V. www.lillypulitzer.com.

Mia Zia FRENCH/MOROCCAN $$–$$$$

Inspired by the look and feel of the North African lifestyle, Mia Zia has luxury goods in desert colors—T-shirts, shoes, and home style in the colors of sand and clay. It sounds costumey or silly but it's very, very chic. Imagine heavily embroidered twin sets, or striped linens—the inspirations of the *medina* made modern.

The line is created by Valerie Barkowski, who opened her first concept store in Paris—in a country with rich connections to North Africa. Mia Zia offers the same resort glam you might find at Calypso, but woven in the colors of the Atlas Mountains and pronounced with the accent of an ancient souk. The most classic of the pieces is created from Berber style stripes in dark colors against a burnt orange background.

BEST BETS   Exotic style lasts for more than 1,001 nights.

WEB TIPS   You cannot order from the website but the minute you see the background color of the home page—a burnt dusty orange—you will understand everything about this line and how it crosses from Africa into real life.

WHERE TO BUY   6 stores worldwide. **FLAGSHIP**   4 rue Caumartin, Paris, 9e. ☎ **331/4451-9445.** Mon–Sat 10am–7pm. MC, V. Métro: Opera. Other cities include Antwerp, Geneva, St. Barths and Ibiza. www.maroussia.be/miazia/FR/intro.htm.

Nitya   INDIAN/FRENCH $$$–$$$$

Take a lesson from the Maharaja then marry it with the current rage for embroidery, fine stitchery and flowing clothes; throw in perhaps a Nehru jacket and some European charm and you have the Nitya brand, which I have never found in the U.S. to my utter disappointment.

This line has several things to offer that you won't find elsewhere—they make chic sleeveless clothing and lightweight cotton clothing that you can wear layered in summer and still look good, which is a feat. They make clothes with elastic waists and things that flow enough to cover figure flaws. Clothes are often handwashable.

While there are items in black, mostly the line is in tropical colors, lots of white and beige and soft pastels, some reds and grays for winter. The items are light and gauze-y, meant to be worn in layers. There are some wool knits for winter but mostly this is a line that floats in the air.

Note that there's a store in Paris that sells old merchandise at 20% to 30% off, so you don't have to schlep out to the official Nitya outlet in Marne La Vallee. This store, Vidna, 9 rue St. Placide (☎ **331/4548-9575**), is 1 block from Bon Marche department store.

BEST BETS   Flowing clothes worn over trousers with elastic waists for those with less than perfect figures. Prices are in the bridge category—$150 to $300—but there are outlet stores and good sales. Last summer I fell into a sale in the outlets in which every item was 50€ ($65). Why didn't I buy more?

WEB TIPS   The website features beautiful photography, but there's not much information available. No prices, no descriptions, no shopping.

WHERE TO BUY   9 stores worldwide. **FLAGSHIP**   40 rue Bonaparte, Paris, 6e. ☎ **331/4051-7743.** Mon–Sat 11am–7pm. AE, MC, V. Métro: Saint Germain des Pres. Other cities include Kuala Lumpur, Kuwait City, Bahrain, Riyadh and London. www.nitya-paris.com.

Origins SANTA FE $$–$$$$

In some parts of the U.S., ethnic dress is simply what is worn— you look like an idiot if you arrive in what was suitable in your home town. Of course, if you overdo it, you can also look like an idiot. That's why I shop at Origins in Santa Fe where I get what I term "the Santa Fe" look, but what is in fact a version of the ethnic/rich hippie/BoHo glam worn by a certain style of woman all over the world. In winter there's velvets; in summer there's linens. The clothes come from various area artisans and assorted ethnic markets in Asia and the subcontinent—it's a jumble of colors and textures and sizes and shawls. Then you pick beads and hats and bags to go with the ensemble. In winter, there are coats. In fact, there's everything in this store and it never goes out of style.

BEST BETS   Comfy clothes that have individual style and pizazz. Prices range from $100 to $500.

WEB TIPS   The website doesn't do much of anything, but it does list about two dozen artists and artisans who sell their clothing at this store in the wearable art program.

WHERE TO BUY   1 store: 135 W. San Francisco St., Santa Fe. ☎ **505/988-2323.** Mon–Sat 10am–6:30pm; Sun 11am–6:30pm. AE, DISC, MC, V. www.originssantafe.com.

Shanghai Tang CHINESE $$$–$$$$

World's Best   The brilliant thing about this line is that it has managed to reinvent itself each season with fashion items that are à la mode and not at all Chinese-y. With clothing collections for men, women and children and a full range of gift items with some home style. *Note:* the U.S. stores aren't great.

BEST BETS   The cashmere tops with mandarin collars are stunning; they begin at $385 for a short-sleeve version.

WEB TIPS   There's a size chart on the website (www.shanghai tang.com); order carefully, as this clothing runs very small. I

The French Fisherman Shirt

Classic Irish fisherman's knits were originally created by each family in a distinctive stitch so that a body tossed to sea might be more easily identified. French fisherman's shirts offer no such distinctions except for the fact that they are most traditionally navy and white horizontal stripes. They were created so that a man lost at sea might be more easily spotted in the water. The shirt became an official part of the French seaman's uniform in 1858. It hails from Brittany on the Atlantic coast of France.

As a fashion cut, the shirt, named a mariniere or sailor shirt, usually features a boat neck and a long sleeve, often worn at three-quarters. Adopted by Pablo Picasso and subsequently Coco Chanel as a uniform in the south of France in the 1920s, the shirts became a fashion statement and today are made in a myriad combination of colors—but always two. More than two colors and you have a striped shirt.

Two French brands that make the shirts: **Amor-Lux,** 16 rue Vavin, Paris 6e (☎ **331/4407-0077;** www.amorlux.com; 1,500+ stores worldwide), has a range of over two dozen color combinations and makes uniforms for several French sports teams and for the French Post Office; and **St. James,** which opened in NYC, 1045 Madison Ave. (☎ **212/535-1470**), remains more staid but nonetheless somewhat with it. The cream and hot pink combos, for example, run $62. Buy both brands at French department stores and the occasional French market. Expect to pay about $50 for a shirt, or $38 on sale.

bought a denim jacket online and had to return it; fortunately, although it was shipped from China, I could mail it back to the New York store.

See p. 57 for a full listing.

World's Best *Shiatzy Chen* CHINESE/TAIWANESE $$$$–$$$$$
Shiatzy Chen is a woman's name—she has been a major designer in Taiwan for the last 25 years and has recently exploded onto the international front. The look is known as Neo-Chinese. This is not your father's Made in Taiwan.

Fabrics are sumptuous, and much is embroidered. We're talking cashmere mandarin-collar jackets and beaded or mink-trimmed Suzie Wong dresses. The fabrics, the colors, the workmanship will make you weep (unfortunately, so will the prices). Although the brand originated in Taipei, there are stores in Paris and throughout China. Just don't drool on the clothes; this is considered rude, even in China.

BEST BUYS   The prices are very high. Still, $3,000 for a little woven mink jacket might be worth it to you. It's all a matter of what's in your wallet. A simple blouse will cost $600 and a dress $2,000.

WEB TIPS   The website is difficult to use—you must click to allow pop-ups and then go to the English version, unless you read Chinese. You cannot shop online nor can you easily retrieve store addresses. Be patient; click again.

WHERE TO BUY   There are stores in the major Chinese cities, including Hong Kong. By 2010 the brand expects to have 50 stores in China alone; currently, there are 10 stores worldwide. **FLAGSHIP**   49–1 Zhongshan N. Rd., Sec. 2, Taipei. ☎ **8862/2542-5506.** Mon–Sat 10am–9pm. **CHINESE FLAGSHIP**   9 the Bund, Shanghai, China. ☎ **8621/6321-9155.** Mon–Sun 10am–9pm. AE, MC, V. www.shiatzychen.com.

Ventilo FRENCH $$$$

The clothes are clever, ethereal and possessed of a specific look that is timeless and somewhat in the Rich Hippie cate-

gory. Who else but Armand Ventilo would mix black-and-white polka dots, stripes and lace, beading and embroidery in one outfit and get away with it? Don't fret; there are some simple items too.

This is a total lifestyle line with home style as well as fragrance and a cafe in some stores. There are outlet stores in French outlet malls. Prices at outlets tend to be about half regular retail although the clothes are a year old. In this age of the $1,000 "it" bag, I just found a hip and hot handbag at the outlet for $300. The outlets are named **Ventistock.**

BEST BETS   The timeless classics with beading, about $300 to $500.

WHERE TO BUY   European department stores; 35 freestanding stores worldwide + 27 more in France; concept store with tearoom. Paris: 27 bis rue du Louvre,

An outfit from Ventilo's Fall 2007 collection.

Paris 2e. ☎ **331/4476-8297.** Mon–Sat 10:30am–7pm; Marais branch Sun 11:30am–5pm. AE, MC, V. Métro: Etienne Marcel. www.ventilo.fr.

Green/Eco-Friendly

American Apparel USA $–$$

This firm is revolutionary for many reasons—they are environmentally and ecologically concerned, they do not run sweatshops, everything is produced in America, pay is fair as are bonuses, garments are engineered for function and comfort. That understood, the line is mostly cotton knits—leggings, underwear, T-shirts, tops and even little dresses.

BEST BETS   Merchandise in stores is organized by color; some of it is shrink wrapped. T's are under $20; dresses under $40.

Shop Talk

American Apparel founder Dov Charney openly admits to sleeping with his employees (who are featured in his scantily clad ads). Google search for an eye-opening article in *Jane* magazine.

WEB TIPS   The website's somewhat confusing with lots of links to useless info; "store locations" and "online store" are top, centered. There's free shipping with orders over $50.

WHERE TO BUY   140 stores worldwide, including L.A., NYC, London, Paris, more. **FLAGSHIP**   104 S. Robertson, Los Angeles, CA. ☎ **310/274-6292.** Mon–Sat 10am–8pm; Sun 11am–6pm. AE, DISC, MC, V. www.americanapparel.net.

Santa Fe Hemp USA $–$$

Hemp is a natural fiber much like linen—it can be made into clothes, twine, yarn and just about anything else; it can be woven or knit. Yes, it is vaguely related to the marijuana plant, but not significantly so. Still, you will get high on the shopping here. The clothes are casual, sturdy and, well, chic.

BEST BETS   I like banded collar shirts and baggy trousers with drawstring waists. Most separates cost $59. The trousers I buy cost $69 and are a blend of hemp and organic cotton and have been clay dyed into funky earth tones.

WEB TIPS   You can shop easily online although the computer screen cannot do justice to texture and variations in dye that you enjoy from shopping in person. The store is only 1 block from the main plaza and is worth finding when you wander Santa Fe (p. 472).

WHERE TO BUY   3 Stores in New Mexico. **FLAGSHIP**   105 E. Water St., Santa Fe. ☎ **505/984-2599.** Sun–Thurs 10am–7pm; Fri and Sat 10am–9pm. MC, V. www.santafehemp.com.

Jeans

....

Acne SWEDISH $$$$

Forget the Clearasil or the dermatologist; this is a Swedish brand of jeans that is so cool the brand did a store swap with Browns Focus of London. Acne is actually an anagram for Ambition to Create Novel Expression, so there. This is the jean that started the skinny revolution.

BEST BETS Whatever fits. All are in the $300 range.

WEB TIPS The jeans are shown both front and back on the website; models' tummies are bare, so you can get a good idea of the cut.

WHERE TO BUY 400 stores in 25 countries; also at Fred Segal in LA; see p. 99. **FLAGSHIP** Hamngatan 10–14, Stockholm. ☎ **468/203-455.** Mon–Sat 10am–7pm. MC, V. www.acnejeans.com.

Antik Denim USA $$$$

This is an American firm with French designers, which is kinda cute when you see how Wild West the store and the brand are. Each pair of jeans is individually decorated. Unlike other brands, the decorations are not necessarily embroidery or glitter but heat transferred.

BEST BETS Jeans with unique embroidery; most are "reasonably priced" under $200.

WEB TIPS I could have flown to LA in the time it took to open the online store. Try www.revolveclothing.com instead.

WHERE TO BUY Distributed worldwide (mostly west of the Mississippi). **FLAGSHIP** 8013 Melrose Ave., Los Angeles. ☎ **323/782-8333.** Mon–Sat 11am–7pm. AE, DISC, MC, V. www.antik denim.com.

Diesel & Diesel Design Lab ITALIAN $$$$

The success of this brand is due to one thing—the fit in the tush. Add to that the ability to stay on top of trends and technology with customized jeans, various washes and stores all over the world. The decor of the stores is also very hot and was when Diesel first set up shop, at a time before other brands were doing up their stores so extravagantly. One Diesel shop is finished off with a dozen washing machines.

Diesel is in the process of becoming a lifestyle source—they make underwear and jewelry and sell far more than jeans in their stores.

WEB TIPS   The jeans styles are featured online; views are slow to load and there's no online shopping. Retailing at $160 to $200, the jeans are also available on Bluefly.com for under $80.

WHERE TO BUY   13 flagship stores worldwide, including Milan, London, Barcelona, Amsterdam. **U.S. FLAGSHIP**   Union Sq. W., NYC. ☎ **646/336-8552.** Mon–Sat 11am–9pm; Sun 11am–8pm. AE, DISC, MC, V. Subway: Union Sq. www.dieseljeans.com.

An Earnest Cut & Sew USA $$$$$

Customized jeans, anyone? The master tailor will work with you to create the perfect jeans, which will be sewn on-site and ready in about 4 or 5 hours. You can designate all details and finishes from buttons to stitching to pockets to textures and fades. Of course, all this comes at a price; custom jeans run $700 to $850. Thankfully there are less expensive options.

BEST BET   Select a pair of jeans already in stock, have them altered to fit and walk away for under $350.

WEB TIPS   You can order some styles from the website; however, I couldn't find detailed size info such as rise and inseam measurements.

WHERE TO BUY   2 stores in NYC; also at Barneys, Saks, Bloomingdales, more. **FLAGSHIP**   821 Washington, between Gansevoort and Little W. 12th, NYC. ☎ **212/242-3414.** Sun–Fri 11am–7pm; Sun noon–5pm. AE, DISC, MC, V. Subway: A, C, E to 14th St. or L to 8th Ave. www.earnestsewn.com.

Levi-Strauss USA VALUE $–$$$

You might say it all started here with the Levi jeans, first made of canvas and then denim. Levis are constantly evolving, not just their jeans in terms of cut and style but the way they sell their product—there's customized jeans fitted to your bum in some stores and a new concept of stores that is slowly rolling out all over the country. This new world has more than jeans and offers jackets, leather clothing and accessories. The idea is to come on strong with history and simplicity so that people simply scratch their heads and wonder why they pay several hundred dollars for designer jeans when the original costs $35 to $65.

WEB TIPS   The shopping website is www.levistore.com. Levi Straus Signature, at www.levistraussSignature.com, is meant for all figure types.

WHERE TO BUY   44 Stores in the U.S. **FLAGSHIP**   25 W. 14th St., NYC. ☎ **212/242-2128.** Daily 11am–9pm. AE, MC, V. www.levi.com.

Price Check: Designer Jeans

Accounting for 3% of the $11-billion jeans market, premium denim is here to stay. What exactly makes a pair of jeans "premium"? Is it Price? Fabric? Style? Celebrity endorsement? Ask any manufacturer and you'll get the same answer: fit. It's how your bum looks from behind. It's how the pants skim your hips. No matter what the label, if the rear view isn't great, the jeans won't sell.

Visit 15 premium jeans' websites and you'll read 15 gimmicks—There's ring-spun denim, triple needle stitching, bleach "whiskers," distress and special fading. There's seam detail, special leg cuts, pocket placement . . . the hype goes on and on.

- The one common denominator of these high-end jeans? Price. Premium brands begin at $150 (**7 for all Mankind;** www.7forallmankind.com); and go way up from there. For $625, **Evisu**'s jeans (www.evisu.com) are given as many as 30 "dips" to achieve the ultimate shade of indigo. **Rock & Republic** (www.rockandrepublic.com) stresses fit (long and lean). **True Religion** (www.truereligionbrandjeans.com) is popular with the college crowd and offers varied styles, all in the $250 range. Other leaders of the premium pack include **Serfontaine** (www.serfontaine.com), **Ksubi;** ($300+; www.ksubi.com), **Blue Blood** ($275; www.bluebloodbrand.com) and **Chip and Pepper** ($275; www.chipandpepper.com).
- The reason there are so many lines of jeans—and they keep coming—is that they fit the body in different ways and few people have the same body structure.
- There's a thriving business in vintage jeans, which tend to be lesser brands worn and washed to perfection.
- Watch out for fake designer jeans. Shop carefully—especially if you are buying online.

Not Your Daughter's Jeans USA $$–$$$$

Created for women over 40, these jeans are meant to deliver the same fashion knockout as other jeans but fit a body that may have settled a bit due to forces of gravity. After this line became a big hit, the firm introduced Tummy Tuck jeans.

The jeans cost $88, which is a bargain in the world of jeans these days. They're also made in the U.S., which is far different from mass-marketed jeans.

BEST BETS   The jeans run one to two sizes larger than standard. This is no doubt a marketing gimmick, but who doesn't want to think she's a smaller size?

WEB TIPS   Read all about the jeans online—but no shopping. Use the map to find a store near you.

WHERE TO BUY   Major department stores including Nordstrom and Dillard's. www.tummytuckjeans.com.

Paper Denim USA $$$$

With a focus on fit and quality, Paper Denim's women's low-rise jeans feature a two-piece contour waistband, eliminating the dreaded "back gap." They also incorporate flat pressed and selvedge side seams for comfort, along with reinforced riveting and oversized belt loops.

BEST BETS   The combination of comfort, style and price makes these jeans a best bet. All are in the $100 to $150 range.

WEB TIPS   The website has slow links and information is limited. No online orders, though I also found the jeans online at Revolveclothing.com for between $88 and $98.

WHERE TO BUY   Department and specialty stores including Barneys, Fred Segal, Bloomingdale's and Saks in the U.S.; Selfridges and Harvey Nichols in London. www.paperdenim.com.

Maternity

You've come a long way, baby—and mom to be. Some women shun maternity clothes totally; others just buy the few pieces they need and make do with others. By the time fashion began to creep into maternity wear—in the 1970s—the most important ingredient in marketing clothing for the mom-to-be was that the garments were inexpensive, because no one thought a pregnant woman would spend much on something she would wear during a 6-month period and perhaps never again. Those with specialty needs should note that any online search will provide sources for plus size maternity clothes, tall gal maternity clothes, petite size maternity clothes and yes, maternity scrubs (www.smartscrubs.com). For maternity beauty products, see p. 191.

Formes FRENCH $$$–$$$$

Sometimes written as Formes Paris, this line is more chic than your average American mall brand, yet not so out there as to be silly. The fashion instincts lean toward the BoHo. This is a chic, versatile collection with a full range of styles and relatively fair prices. There are flirty looks, monotone separates for a more sleek presentation and clothes for all occasions.

BEST BETS   BoHo maternity! A simple, wrap dress is about $150; trousers cost $200 and sweaters are $160.

WEB TIPS   The site is in French, but you can click on "English."

WHERE TO BUY   90 stores in 23 countries (none in U.S.; 2 in Canada). **FLAGSHIP**   22 rue Cambon, Paris 1. ☎ **331/4926-0066.** Mon–Sat 10:30am–7pm. Métro: Concorde. 2185 rue Crescent, Montreal, Canada. ☎ **514/843-6996.** Mon–Wed 10am–5:30pm; Thurs and Fri 10am–7pm; Sat 10am–5pm; Sun 1–5pm. www.formes.com.

IsabellaOliver.com BRITISH $$$$

Isabella Oliver is a website from a British firm but thankfully has offices in the U.S. so that shipping does not cause an international dilemma nor does belly have to travel on the wrong

side of the bump. Most importantly, the firm is conceptual so that you either love it and have to have it . . . or are not interested.

The clothes remind me of the early Donna Karan lifestyle clothes with the sleek bodysuit and wrap-ups—not that anyone would put a pregnant woman in a bodysuit, but these clothes have the same monochromatic sleekness that makes them almost a uniform and clearly a way of life.

BEST BETS   The knit wrap dresses are $150 to $180.

Isabella Oliver bandeau wrap top.

WEB TIPS   Click on "maternity no-no's" for great fashion tips. Call ☎ **866/614-9387** for customer service in the U.S.

Liz Lange USA VALUE $–$$$

Liz Lange is the pioneer who brought maternity wear into this century. She has been rewarded not only with national recognition but a contract with Target stores. You can buy expensive Liz or cheap Liz.

First into business in 1997, Lange hit on a turn-of-the-21st-century need—chic, well-designed maternity clothes for the modern woman who didn't mind paying for the privilege. She was a hit in fewer than 9 months, tackling Manhattan's Upper

East Side and soon becoming the maven on maternity. She literally wrote the book on maternity style, sells her clothes through other stores and brings it home to real people via Target stores.

Among Lange's most interesting concept is the idea of a Fourth Trimester—the 3 months after giving birth as a time with special needs and special clothes.

BEST BETS   Target. Most everything in the line is under $35. Her "starter kit" and "office chic" combos are good choices.

WHERE TO BUY   Maternity boutiques, department stores and Target. **FLAGSHIP**   958 Madison Ave. at 76th St., NYC. ☎ **212/879-2191.** www.lizlange.com; www.target.com.

Trendsetters

Fred Segal LOS ANGELES $$–$$$$

World's Best
You do not need to understand how to get the LA Look. You just have to have enough money to shop at Fred Segal. There's trends galore and much of it is appropriately casual, slouchy and comfortable. If the prices don't make you itch, you're home free.

There are other branches of this store and its creator, Ron Herman, has some stores in his name, but the flagship on Melrose is where you want to worship. Remember some of the rules: You do not stare at celebs; you do not grab your cell phone to call your mom and tell her who you just spotted; you pay for small items with a credit card and pay cash for big items; you may shop with your entourage but not your parents.

This was the home of $300 jeans before everyone had $200 jeans. Now you get $600 jeans here.

Insider's tips: Each year, usually end of September, there's a big sale when everything is half off. Also, Segal will open an enormous store in Las Vegas in 2008.

BEST BETS   The total look, feel and concept—from Cosabella lingerie to jeans, this is all you need to make a statement. Oh yeah, and some big bucks. OK, big boobs help too. But what else is new?

WEB TIPS   This website is under construction as we go to print.

WHERE TO BUY   1 store: 8100 Melrose Ave. at Crescent Heights. ☎ **323/651-4129.** Mon–Sat 10am–7pm; Sun noon–6pm. AE, DISC, MC, V. www.fredsegal.com.

Kitson LOS ANGELES $–$$$$

Shoppers note that Kitson Men is across the street from plain old Kitson which is a women's clothing, accessories, gift and lifestyle store. There's also a kids' store.

The look is more developed than Fred Segal (see above); it's more of a *Sex & the City* goes Paris Hilton look. Fred Segal is old Hollywood; this is new. Don't look now, but isn't that Nicole Ritchie featured on the website? Find everything from short skirts you wear with patent leather bowling shoes to Japanese publishing trends. Valley girls need not apply.

BEST BETS   Trucker hats $38; Kitson hoodie for $108 or a leather charm bracelet for $295.

WHERE TO BUY   1 store in 3 parts: 115 S. Robertson Blvd. ☎ **310/ 859-2652.** Kitson Kids: 108 S. Robertson Blvd. ☎ **310/246-3829.** Kitson Men: 146 N. Robertson. ☎ **310/358-9550.** Mon–Fri 10am–7pm; Sat 9am–7:30pm; Sun 11am–6pm. AE, DISC, MC, V. www.shopkitson.com.

Lilith FRENCH $$$–$$$$

Lilith offers a look that is uniquely hers—baggy and droopy and layered and extravagant and even a little bit rock-and-roll. Her clothes are considered cult favorites and are rarely found by those who aren't specifically seeking the brand.

BEST BETS   The palette and layers and whimsy and funk factor. Dresses usually cost around $400 to $500.

WHERE TO BUY   Some French department stores such as Printemps and Galerie Lafayette. 2 freestanding stores in Paris; 1 in Berkeley, Ca. **FLAGSHIP**   5 rue Cambon, Paris, 1er ☎ **331/ 4296-8954.** Daily 11am–7pm; AE, MC,V. Métro: Concorde. No website.

Pleats Please JAPANESE $$–$$$$

When I say this line is hot, I really mean it—it's hot because it's cool, but it's also hot on the body because of the fabrics. I do not suggest this line in summer unless you will be in air-conditioning. Then again, it's these very fabrics that make the clothes so perfect.

Designed by Issey Miyake, the line features geometrically shaped clothes that are permanently crinkled into tiny knife pleats that expand according to your body type and the fit. They don't wrinkle; they are both casual and dressy; they don't age; they are classical and timeless.

BEST BETS   Travel separates that mix and match: clothes range from $150 for a top to $500 for an outfit. The line is known for its solid colors that can mix and match but there are sometimes seasonal prints. Avoid the prints and stick to travel colors (that is, black).

WEB TIPS   You may not be able to open this website if you have a pop-up blocker.

WHERE TO BUY   4 stores; department and specialty stores worldwide. NYC: 128 Wooster St., New York. ☎ **212/226-3600.** Mon–Sat 11am–7pm; Sun 11am–6pm. AE, DISC, MC, V. Other cities include Paris, London, and Tokyo. www.pleatsplease.com.

Underwear & Lingerie

Agent Provocateur BRITISH $$$$

This is one of those brands that has grabbed the world by the imagination and brought garter belts (called suspenders in Britspeak) back into fashion. It's a nice girls can be naughty sort of line, titillating and expensive. If you aren't looking for the sex kitten bit, fear not—just gander by the windows, they are usually very hot. It's a free peep show to entice you to come in and shop. They also have some accessories.

BEST BETS   Catch me if you can. This is not where you run in for a pair of knickers but rather a total ensemble, which will cost you $200.

WEB TIPS   Stunning soft porn. Click on "web exclusives" for Web-only deals.

WHERE TO BUY   26 freestanding worldwide. **FLAGSHIP**   6 Broadwick St., London W1. Mon, Tues, Wed, Fri, Sat 11am–7pm; Thurs 11am–8pm; Sun noon–5pm. AE, MC, V. Tube: Piccadilly Circus. www.agentprovocateur.com.

Bravissimo BRITISH $$–$$$$$

About a dozen stores dotted around the UK and an online store to give you, as they say, the Big Picture. This firm specializes in—their words—"big-boobed ladies." They have just launched a size K cup, larger than a size G cup.

You can pre-book fitting appointments at the shops.

BEST BETS   Big bras. Duh. $60 to $80 each.

WEB TIPS   Click on "fitting advice" for tips on buying comfortable large-size lingerie.

WHERE TO BUY   Stores: 12 in UK. **FLAGSHIP**   20 Tavistock St., London. ☎   44845/408-1907. Mon–Sat 10am–7pm; Sun 11am–5pm. Tube: Covent Garden. www.bravissimo.com.

Cadolle PARIS $$$$

First a word about the French language: Cadolle is the family name of one of the women credited with inventing the brassiere, back in 1889. But the word *cadolie* means pushcart in French. Thought you'd get a kick out of that.

This business is over 100 years old and now has two parts, a regular store where you can buy yummy underpinnings and a couture division, which requires an appointment. For those who aren't versed in the beauties of a French bra, they are constructed to lift and separate.

BEST BETS   Anything dripping with lace; prices begin at around $200.

WEB TIPS   The website keep reminding you to be patient, as it's very, very slow. It's as much Paris travelogue as lingerie presentation.

WHERE TO BUY   1 store. 4 rue Cambon, Paris 1er. ☎ **331/4260-8422.** Mon–Sat 10am–6:30pm. Métro: Concorde. Atelier: 255 rue Saint Honore, Paris 1er, by appointment only. ☎ **331/4260-9494.** Mon–Fri 10am–1pm and 2–6:30pm. MC. Métro: Concorde. www.cadolle.fr.

Eres FRENCH $$$-$$$$

In France, bathing suits and underwear are sold in the same stores, as they are considered the same thing. Therefore it's no surprise that Eres—an upmarket brand owned by Chanel—makes both bathing suits and lingerie. Eres is best known for having created the sheer gauze underwear craze, which is still the staple of the underwear empire. Their bathing suits come in basic designs created in perhaps as many as a dozen different cuts so that one can find the right fit to flatter the figure.

BEST BETS   The gauzy lingerie, prices $125 to $200.

WEB TIPS   There's only one swimsuit and one bra and panty combo shown. No online shopping.

WHERE TO BUY   4 Stores U.S.; 6 worldwide. **FLAGSHIP**   2, rue Tronchet, Paris 8e. ☎ **331/4742-2882.** Daily 10am–7pm. AE, MC, V. Métro: Madeleine. www.eresparis.com.

La Perla ITALIAN $$$$

La Perla has long been known as one of the most elegant lingerie lines in the world. Capitalizing on their international image, they moved into clothing—starting with boudoir-wear and now with ready to wear. But you shop here for the sexy, the lacy, the strategically see-through.

BEST BETS   The bras are to die for. Unfortunately, they're in the $200 price range.

WEB TIPS   You can shop online everywhere but the U.S.

WHERE TO BUY   Stores in Chicago, Las Vegas (Caesar's Forum Shops), Costa Mesa Shopping Center, Miami and NYC; department stores worldwide. **FLAGSHIP**   Via Manzoni 17, Milan. ☎ **3902/805-3092.** Mon–Sat 10am–7pm. Also 250 Boylston St., Boston. ☎ **617/423-5709.** Mon–Sat 10am–7pm; Sun noon–5pm. www.laperla.com.

Pompea ITALIAN   VALUE $

I have always bought my underwear in dime stores, so it was a special day when I discovered this brand at Upim, the Italian version of Target. They make stretch underwear without specific sizes; the bras are soft. Colors are white, nude and black.

BEST BETS   This is the thong to make you love wearing a thong ($6).

WEB TIPS   No online shopping, but great photos.

WHERE TO BUY   Department and mass market stores such as Upim, Auchan and Carrefour all over Italy. www.pompea.com.

Buyer Beware

I found a Pompea outlet store at a mall once and rushed over. Tragedy! There were colors like orange and purple and ugly, horrible leftovers. At $6 for a bra, we can probably all afford to go first class and shop at Upim.

Sabia Rosa PARIS $$$$

If you are wondering who in the world would spend $400 (or more) for a pair of knickers, let me put this in context—women who wear couture and very, very expensive designer clothing feel that they have to honor the integrity of the clothes with the proper underwear—which is not Jockey for Her. This is the kind of store where a man takes his mistress.

Sabia Rosa underthings are made by hand with the best of materials in the world. Madonna shops here.

WHERE TO BUY   1 store. 73 rue sts. Peres, Paris, 6e. ☎ **331/4548-8837.** Mon–Sat 10am–7pm. MC, V. Métro: Sevres Babylone. No website.

Tezenis Intimo ITALIAN   VALUE $

A stroll through one of these stores define the reasons we travel—to see something you can't find at home, to learn, to get some zing and even to buy something, because this line

Underwear Online

Both **www.barenecessities.com** and **www.figleaves.com** claim to be the world's leading online retailer of intimate apparel for women and men. Both stock inventory from all leading manufacturers and both will pass on manufacturers' sale prices. Neither is necessarily less expensive than regular retailers, but you'll pay no sales tax on items shipped to US destinations.

Figleaves charges $4.50 for standard shipping; there's no shipping charge on orders over $75 from Barenecessities. My preference is Barenecessities just because they always have a better selection (more colors) of the bra I wear. This DKNY bra is $30 on both sites, but I go with selection and all this stuff is subjective. Since you aren't saving much money, the best advantage is availability of items not stocked in retail stores.

really is affordable. They do not advertise; their flagship store in Rome isn't their best store; they appeal to teens, tweens and grown-ups. This underwear maker does cotton sleepwear and intimates in mix-and-match styles, some prints and some solids. Expect to pay about $75 for a five-piece collection of items.

BEST BETS   The solids are sweet, but boring—it's the prints that are really the heart of the line.

WEB TIPS   The collection is shown in tiny photos on the website; no online orders.

WHERE TO BUY   90 stores in 13 countries, but not in the U.S.
FLAGSHIP   148 via del Corso, Rome. Mon–Sat 10am–7pm. MC, V. There is a store in every major city in Italy, usually in the thick of the high street. www.tezenis.com.

Vintage (Designer)

Decades and Decades Two   USA $$$$$

Do you know who Peggy Moffit is? If yes, then Decades is for you. If not, well, you can still shop here but you might not be sophisticated (or old) enough. (Peggy Moffit was Rudi Gernreich's fit model.) This vintage couture store specializes in the sixties and seventies and sells to many, many celebs. They are the leading source of clothing from this particular time period.

While Decades carries upscale vintage designs from the 1930s to 1990s, its sister store, Decades Two, concentrates on contemporary clothing from the 1990s to the present day.

Both boutiques are highly selective, accepting only 20% of what consignors bring in.

BEST BETS Designer goods including Balenciaga, Chanel, Marc Jacobs and Chloe. All are up to 80% off.

WHERE TO BUY 3 stores. **FLAGSHIP** 8214½ Melrose Ave., LA. ☎ **323/655-0223.** Mon–Sat 11:30am–6pm. London: Dover Market, 17 Dover St. ☎ **207/493-2342.** Mon–Sat 11am–6pm; Sun 11am–7pm. AE, MC, V. Tube: Green Park. Decades Two: 8214 Melrose Ave. (just east of Harper). ☎ **3232/655-1960.** Mon–Sat 11:30–6pm, or by appointment. MC, V. www.decades inc.com.

Didier Ludot PARIS $$$$–$$$$$

This man single-handedly brought vintage out of the closet in Europe, first by specializing in vintage Chanel suits and then moving into vintage French luxury names and couture. The store is crammed with clothes and accessories and sometimes luggage; even the windows are worth the visit just to take in the atmosphere.

BEST BETS A Chanel suit, *bien sur,* if you've got $3,500.

WEB TIP My pop-up blocker made it difficult to enter this site; however, by holding down the "control" key as I clicked, I was able to access everything.

WHERE TO BUY 1 store: 24 passage de la galerie Montpensier, Jardin de Palais Royal, Paris, 1er. ☎ **331/4296-0656.** Mon–Sat 11am–7pm. AE, MC, V. Métro: Palais Royal. www.didierldot. com.

Keni Valenti NYC $$$$$

Valenti calls it "retro-couture" and, considering the quality of what he sells, he can call it anything he wants. His collection includes designer dresses, suits, casual clothes, shoes and accessories.

BEST BETS It's all fab. Chanel suits begin at $2,200; designer dresses are in the $1,500 to $3,000 range.

WEB TIPS Call to order.

World Traveler

You'll find more vintage clothing in New York at the Manhattan Vintage Show, held two to three times a year at the Metropolitan Pavillion, 125 W. 18th St. (www. manhattanvintage.com; $20). Peruse 80 to 100 booths of clothing, textiles and some fur.

WHERE TO BUY   1 store. 155 W. 29th St., 3F, Room C5, NYC. ☎ **917/686-9553.** Mon–Fri 10am–6pm, by appointment only. AE, MC, V. Subway: Penn Station. www.kenivalenti.com.

Lily et Cie BEVERLY HILLS, CA $$$$$

You may not know the name but you know the clothes—this Beverly Hills store provides most of the vintage evening gowns worn to the big awards show, and no she doesn't lend them out—the stars pay, often $15,000 for a dress. Conveniently located across the street from the Four Seasons Beverly Hills, this store is light and airy and stocked with big names.

BEST BETS   The owner works hands-on with her clients and knows the dresses and the women who wear them. She will search for a dress or a certain style for you.

WEB TIPS   Website coming soon.

WHERE TO BUY   1 store. 9044 Burton Way, Beverly Hills, CA. ☎ **310/724-5757.** Tues–Fri 10am–6pm; Sat 11am–5pm. AE, MC, V. www.lilyetcie.com.

Steinberg & Tolkein LONDON $$–$$$$$

This is a jumble of mostly designer but some simply period clothing; don't miss the downstairs. It's thought to be Europe's largest collection of vintage clothing and one of the best stashes of secondhand couture in the world. The prices range from high to outrageous. That hasn't stopped the celebs and the models from shopping here. One of the house specialties is costume jewelry but you'll also find clothes, shoes and bags.

Everything is arranged in alphabetical order by designer.

BEST BETS   Selection. There are over 10,000 garments. Chanel prices start at around $500 for a top.

WHERE TO BUY   1 store: 193 King's Rd., London SW3. ☎ **4420/ 7376-3660.** Mon–Sat 11am–7pm; Sun noon–6pm. MC, V. No website.

Virginia LONDON $$$$

Nestled in a retail honeyspot in Holland Park, this small vintage clothing store is run by a former movie queen and is chock-packed with glam clothes.

BEST BETS   Gowns from the '40s, for hundreds of dollars.

WHERE TO BUY   1 store. 98 Portland Rd., London W11. ☎ **4420/ 7727-9908.** Mon–Sat noon–6pm. MC, V. Tube: Holland Park. No website.

Wearable Art

Jilli Blackwood GLASGOW $$$$–$$$$$

Essentially a textile artist, Jilli does art for walls and bodies—she weaves, embroiders and fits together all the threads and fabric shreds to make clothing. She has done a hanging for the U.S. consulate in Edinburgh, has some ready made at Conran's in Tokyo and does shows. Mostly she likes to work one on one with her customer to create something totally unique. I have seen her things and they are heart-attack gorgeous.

She began with vests for men and women, then went to hats, now does some kilts as well as evening wear, shawls and one-of-a-kind silk organza

Jilli Blackwood silk-and-leather top hat.

(hand-dyed, gray, stitched squares with antique gold mesh thread and crosses merged into a fairy dress kind of thing). She has also worked with the kimono shape and form.

BEST BETS   Each piece is a one of a kind; a kimono coat costs $4,500 to $5,000.

WEB TIPS   Click on the "fabrics" link to see the intricate detail of her designs.

WHERE TO BUY   1 store; also at some galleries and crafts shops in U.S. and UK. 24 Cleveden Rd., Glasgow. ☎ 44141/334-6180. Hours vary; call before you visit. www.jilliblackwood.com.

Julie Artisan's Gallery NYC $$$$–$$$$$

First opened in 1973, Julie's is not only the first gallery of wearable art but an astonishing business to have stayed alive in such a high-rent district for so many years. She does some invitational shows but mostly showcases a variety of textile artists who do clothing and accessories, be they loomed, hand painted, quilted or embroidered.

BEST BETS   The collections change, as do prices.

WEB TIPS   You can see what's available in the gallery by logging on to the website; no online shopping.

WHERE TO BUY   1 store. 762 Madison Ave. at 65th St., NYC. ☎ **212/717-5959.** Mon–Sat 11am–6pm. AE, MC, V. Subway: 68th St/Hunter College. www.julieartisans.com.

Ragazzis Flying Shuttle SEATTLE $–$$$$

Fiber arts and jewelry from a selection of area craftswomen; assorted textures, colors, droop and drape. Seattle is a city where one-of-a-kind style is appreciated, so this store has created a niche that serves with splendid drama.

BEST BETS   Bracelets of beads imprinted with quotes from famous people; will take custom orders, $28.

WEB TIPS   See much of the product and enroll for the newsletter. You cannot buy online.

WHERE TO BUY   1 store: 607 First Ave., Pioneer Sq., Seattle ☎ **206/343-9762.** Mon–Sat 10:30am–5:30pm; call for Sun hours. AE, MC, V. www.ragazzisflyingshuttle.com.

Venetia Studium ITALIAN $$$$–$$$$$

Wrinkles and crinkles and itsy-bitsy pleats of perfection for clothes, home style, accessories and history. Newly made fashion created in the image of Mauriano Fortuny. See p. 62 for full listing.

Chapter Five

Women's Shoes & Accessories

*A*s any smart shopper knows, it's not about the clothes on your back—it's more about the shoes on your feet or the watch on your wrist.

I used to work in Beverly Hills. Believe me, you could be wearing jeans and a torn T-shirt, but if you had the right shoes, handbag or wristwatch, you were golden and were treated with respect. Is that what Aretha was talking about?

Ask a salesperson at any luxury brand how they choose which perspective customers to fawn over and the answer is simple—by the quality of the handbag being toted around. You aren't what you eat. You are what's on your wrist. And if you carry a fake, it better be a darn good one if you want any r-e-s-p-e-c-t.

Accessories are about giving you freedom and choices. For many, the choice is to be comfortable. For others, the choice is to have the choice. I have shoes for comfort and I have shoes for public appearances. The modern woman is most likely to invest in accessories to give her the flexibility of looks and lifestyles that she craves. The best accessories are the ones that allow you to do that without growing old.

> I did not have 3,000 pairs of shoes; I had 1,060.
> —Imelda Marcos

This chapter is about women's accessories; those created for men or children are in their respective chapters in order to simplify this chapter.

In most cases, firms that make one kind of accessory also make another—Barry Kieselstein-Cord started out as the king of the statement belt, but also now makes sunglasses and handbags. Bottega Veneta makes clothes. Chanel makes everything. Life is a cabaret.

Belts, Eyeglasses & Sunglasses

Jackie O was no one without her shades; Audrey Hepburn was more Holly Golightly with hers on. Elton John and Dame Edna would barely be recognizable without their specs. Kris Kringle always wears wire-frames—can you even imagine Santa in horn rims? And various intellectuals from T. S. Eliot to Truman Capote are known for their words and their glasses frames. Pierre Cardin and Yves Saint Laurent are always pictured in eyeglasses, although perhaps they share the same pair. Anna Wintour is trying to get away from her ubiquitous shades, but The Devil will always wear Prada. Prada sunglasses begin at $100 at the outlet store.

1800contacts.com 🖱 VALUE

If you wear contact lenses, you'll love this resource. Acuvue and other leading brands are always discounted; rebates are offered on almost every brand. You'll need to register your prescription with the site (you can fax it in), then order new lenses as needed. They're the world's largest contact lens distributor and have over 20,000,000 lenses in stock. You'll save 20% to 25% off opticians' prices and they'll beat any other online price by 2%.

Alain Mikli FRENCH $$$$

Alain Mikli is French for *oohlala*. The king of Parisian eyeglasses stylists has shops all over the world and even serves up fashion in his Paris HQ. The stores tend to be tiny jewel box types with the frames displayed in various

Alain Mikli sunglasses.

cases and units as if they were pastries.

I once bought a pair of Mikli sunglasses at TJMaxx for $35—no one else in that Norwalk, CT, store had any idea what a score it was.

BEST BETS   You're going to get the latest in plastics, metals, shapes, scientific breakthroughs and color combinations. This is not for the shy—or the budget minded. Frames range $515 to $545 for eyeglasses, $495 for sunglasses.

WEB TIPS   You cannot buy online. If you go to www.eyeglasses. com you can only pick from a handful of Mikli styles but prices are lower, about $380 to $420 for the frames.

WHERE TO BUY   25 stores worldwide. **FLAGSHIP**   74 rue Saints Pères, Paris 7e. ☎ **01/45-49-40-00.** Mon–Sat 10am–7pm. All major credit cards. Métro: Solferino. U.S. 2 stores in Manhattan. 575 Madison Ave. (57th St). ☎ **212/751-6085.** Mon–Fri 9:30am–6:30pm; Sat 10am–6pm. 986 Madison Ave. (77th St). ☎ **212/472-6085.** Mon–Wed, Fri 10am–6:30pm; Thurs 11am–7pm; Sun noon–5pm. AE, MC, V. www.mikli.com.

Barry Kieselstein-Cord USA $$$$–$$$$$

The iconic belts are still important but there are other accessories such as sunglasses and handbags, trimmed with the signature critters. Handbags (price depends on the hide) cost about $7,000 while sunglasses are about $500. You can get glasses frames in the $500 to $900 price range.

The belts and buckles are most often sold separately and still sold by size—thickness (width) not length. Expect to pay about $1,500 for a buckle and another $600 to $800 for the belt strip. Used merchandise is sold on eBay.

BEST BETS   BKC also makes jewelry—some with precious stones, although for my money some of his best stuff is in silver and replicates his famous critters in bangles, necklaces and more. Give me the Herman toad earrings any day ($345).

WEB TIPS   You can view the collection online but cannot buy.

WHERE TO BUY   6 stores; also in luxe boutiques and Bergdorf-Goodman, NYC. **FLAGSHIP**   1058 Madison Ave. (at 80th), NYC. ☎ **888/BKC-7009** or 212/744-1041. Mon–Sat 10am–6pm. Mon–Sat 10am–5:30pm. Subway: 77th St. AE, MC, V. Also in Zurich, St. Moritz, Moscow, Munich and Jakarta. www.kieselstein-cord.com.

Beijing Eye Mart (Ming Jin Yuan) BEIJING

[VALUE] $–$$$

Many visitors to Beijing plan a visit to the famous weekend Dirt Market; few know that around the corner is the daily Eyeglasses Market—although it's actually a market building of showrooms (very civilized). There are almost 100 shops and each stocks thousands of pairs of glasses, from $8 to $80. You can bargain a little, especially on frames. If you have your prescription, you can have glasses made up in about an hour—although beware that complicated lenses may take hours or days.

All the glasses I had made here were checked out by my doctor in the U.S. and were given the thumbs up.

BEST BETS   Designer sunglasses frames for $20.

WHERE TO BUY   1 store. No. 43 Huaweibeili, north of Panjiayuan, Beijing. ☎ **8610/8773-0786.**

New Fei Optical Supply Ltd. HONG KONG

[VALUE] $–$$$$

Hong Kong is the largest exporter of lenses and frames in Asia and the second largest in the world after Italy. A trip to either of these destinations will save you money and make your heart go pitty-pat.

Because this Hong Kong showroom is right inside a factory block, the space is industrial. Hundreds of pairs of glasses hang on the walls; more are in boxes and bins. You can sit at a table in front of a mirror and try on frames all day. Qualified doctors are on hand to check your prescription or give you a new one. Iced tea and fruit drinks are served (free). Everybody parties. Avoid weekends if possible, since the place is jammed.

The genius behind the source is named Alice—she's the one with the bleach blonde and very spiky hair and yep, glasses. She has an artist's eye and will help you pick new frames. I trust her; she's brought me into designers I never would have tried. She'll also give me technical tips such as the fact that the frames I chose would distort my vision because of the curvature.

BEST BETS   There are designer big names (all but Chanel) as well as major brand licenses. I've bought Calvin Klein, Etro, Prada, Benetton and plain old no-brand—designer frames cost more but are still affordable.

WHERE TO BUY   1 store. Lucky Horse Industrial Bldg., 64 Tong Mi Rd., 12th floor, Hong Kong. ☎ **852/2398-2088.** Mon–Sat 9am–9pm; Sun 10am–7pm. MC, V. Call for shuttle bus pickup from Prince Edward MTA stop or from your hotel. No website.

Oliver Peoples USA $$$$

Hooray for Hollywood and the power of the Peoples. This brand began in a small way selling vintage frames and then retro looks and is now sold in 45 different countries and worn by countless celebs. Even Jack Nicholson, always seen in sunglasses, sports Oliver Peoples.

Oliver Peoples is not a person but a brand that has expanded to manufacture and license other names such as Prada and Paul Smith. They also make and distribute the limited-edition Elton John glasses frames which are to benefit John's AIDS foundation.

BEST BETS   I'm crazy for the frame name Aero, which is a metal spec selling for $400. Plastic frames begin in the high $200s and go to the mid-$300s. Metal frames begin at $340 and go up to about $400.

WEB TIPS   Very good site allows you to see the models and also get a feel for Larry Leight, the creator, and for the star quality of the glasses and those who wear them.

WHERE TO BUY 5 stores in LA, NYC, South Coast Plaza, and Tokyo; in glasses boutiques worldwide, including MyOptics. **FLAGSHIP** 8642 W. Sunset Blvd. (Sunset Strip), LA. ☎ **310/ 657-2553.** Mon–Fri 10am–7pm; Sat 10am–6pm; Sun noon–6pm. AE, DISC, MC, V. www.oliverpeoples.com.

Ottica Urbani VENICE $$$

This frame maker is known specifically for a heavy frame that makes a fashion statement; very Italian, very chic.

BEST BETS While smaller and less visible frames are the fashion rage right now, this house continues to specialize in owl-round T. S. Eliot/Harry Potter styles in colored but transparent resin with a selection of two dozen different colors. You'll pay $100 to $150 for the frames without prescription.

World Traveler

Several other Venetian shops specialize in fashion specs. You can stroll Venice and find great buys or drive the Veneto for outlet stores. Expect to get lost if you drive—it's not worth it for one pair, but if you're game, look up locations on www.factoryoutletsitaly.com.

WEB TIPS You can choose between English or Italian and see the basic styles but you cannot see the whole range of styles nor can you order.

WHERE TO BUY 1 store: San Marco, 1280, Venice, Italy. ☎ **3941/522- 4140.** Mon–Sat 9:30am–12:30pm, 3:30–7pm. MC, V. www. otticaurbani.it.

Allyn Scura USA $$–$$$

Vintage frames with a large selection from 1950s and 1960s— although beware that as a frame dries with age, it might not be flexible enough to take new lenses. Also note that certain styles can take certain prescriptions but not others.

BEST BETS Carrie Donovan glasses are the hot new look; cat eyes are passé, you know.

WEB TIPS Allyn doesn't have a retail shop, but you can order online or try the frames at numerous weekend shows.

WHERE TO BUY Hillsborough Antiques Show and other shows in California. Or contact him by mail or phone. 206 W. 4th St., Suite 305, Santa Ana, CA 92701. ☎ **800/393-7482,** 714/648- 0465. MC, V. www.alynnscura.com.

Gloves

Gloves are bought by the length and are calculated by the number of buttons that could be aligned, although the buttons themselves are not actually on the gloves. The shortest, wrist-length glove is a 7-button, whereas a 9-button comes up a tad more and is considered more chic. The 16-button is nice, especially if it is unlined and can be squished toward the wrist. The 22-button glove is only worn for white tie events and comes only in white, although you will find fabric gloves in various colors, materials and even metallic hues created in the 22-button length for shock value.

Leather gloves have to be judged by the quality of the hide because the gloves must have enough give in them to bend with the hand and be supple enough to allow the fingers to do their work. And just so you know I am on top of it, Chanel makes gloves out of very subtle and supple lambskin; since they cost about $5,000, I've decided not to mention it again.

Carpincho BUENOS AIRES, ARGENTINA $–$$

Argentinean beef produces a lot more than great steaks—the fabulous gloves at Carpincho are no bull. (Sorry.) Actually *carpincho* is the local name for the capybara, a scruffy little animal that makes, uh, perfect gloves. Various hides are tanned and dyed here to make gloves for men and women.

BEST BET   The colors are lyrical; gloves begin at $25.

WEB TIPS   The site is slow but beautiful. You can listen to tango music while you wait for the links to load. There are no prices and no online orders. Try eBay or Google "carpincho capybara," though you're not guaranteed the quality of the Carpincho brand.

WHERE TO BUY   1 store: Esmeralda 775; Retiro, Buenos Aires. ☎ 5411/4322-9919. Noon–8pm. AE, MC, V. www.carpincho net.ar.

Georgina von Etzdorf LONDON $$–$$$

If you are coming just for the gloves, call ahead to see if they have any. Georgina von Etzdorf makes artistic accessories, often hand painted, some one of a kind. This is wearable art by a famous English eccentric who has incredibly gorgeous and inventive designs in all accessories' formats.

BEST BETS   I have bought gloves that were so unique in their mix of color and patterns that anyone with an eye would stop you in the street to demand a look, a touch or a kiss. They were patterned velvet.

WEB TIPS   The website is a one-page flyer. There's no links to merchandise or prices; however, you can log on and sign up for the newsletter.

WHERE TO BUY   1 store: 4 Ellis St. (off Sloane St.), London SW1. ☎ 207/259-9715. Daily 11am–7pm. AE, MC, V. Tube: Knightsbridge. www.gve.co.uk.

Huis A. Boon ANTWERP $$$$

For over 120 years, Huis A. Boon has been the leading glove maker in this Belgian town of impeccable chic. There's pigskin and lambskin. There's driving gloves and lace mittens. And, of course, you'll find traditional styles in all sizes.

BEST BETS   Over 10,000 pairs of gloves in all hues from neutral to bright. Prices range from $100 to $200.

WHERE TO BUY   1 store: Lombardenvest 2/4–2000 Antwerp. ☎ 32-3/232-3387. Daily 10am–7pm. MC, V.

Madova FLORENCE VALUE $–$$

Whether you are looking for a long, white, classical pair of 22-button kidskin gloves for your coming-out or a pair of driving gloves, Madova has it—and more. There are gloves created for function (golf, driving, riding), for weather (cashmere lined) and for fashion—although the gloves tend to come more in fashion colors than in fashion styles. The styles themselves tend to be classics.

BEST BETS   Prices are low to mid-range, making the choices seem more like bits of candy to be consumed in multiples; you may find a pair of gloves for as low as $30 and will have many choices for less than $50.

WEB TIPS   If you order online, the gloves begin around $60 a pair. The website is clear and direct about currency conversions, shipping charges and duties. There is a separate color chart that is a pleasure to use. *Note:* Some parts of the information are confusing—I clicked on gloves that were noted to be 2 to 3 inches long. Excuse me?

WHERE TO BUY   1 store: via Guicciardini, 1r, Florence. ☎ 3955/239-6526. Nov–Apr 9:30am–7pm; closed Sun and Mon. Mar–Oct 9:30am–7pm; closed Mon. MC, V. www.madova.com.

Pickett BRITISH $$–$$$

Pickett specializes in just a few items and does each very well—pashminas/scarves/shawls, small leather goods and gloves. Each store is small and crammed with an Ali Baba–cave plethora of merchandise. Much of it can be color coordinated so that some of the customers for gloves actually come in to match them to their other accessories. Not only are the women's gloves made of highest quality leather, but they come in a wide variety of colors and sizes. Women with hard-to-fit hands will be delighted with the selection.

BEST BETS   The colors range from very obvious brights and jewel tones to odd-duck fashion shades such as a teal that would make Martha Stewart weep with joy. *Avoid:* Matching gloves, handbag and pashmina sets.

WEB TIPS   Excellent website allows you to shop online but warns you that for international shipping they must contact you with prices and you are responsible for duties on arrival of the goods.

WHERE TO BUY   3 stores in London. **FLAGSHIP**   32–3 and 41 Burlington Arcade, London, W1. ☎ **207/493-8939.** Mon–Fri 9am–6pm; Sat 10am–6pm. AE, MC, V. Tube: Piccadilly Circus. www.pickett.co.uk.

Sermoneta ITALIAN $$–$$$

This Italian brand has always had a gloved hand on the pulse of tourists. First they opened shops in Italy in touristy areas (such as the Spanish Steps in Rome); then they began international expansion. Their gloves are fashionable and more fashion forward than classical, but are not in the wildly creative category.

I bought a pair of gloves here after I arrived in Rome with the realization that I had forgotten to visit the Firenze shop. Since this brand has stores in all major Italian cities, it's a great insurance policy. Rome is actually the flagship store and was recently renovated.

BEST BETS   The gloves are displayed on racks that makes selection a breeze. Prices are competitive with Madova (see above), beginning around $40 for unlined gloves.

WEB TIPS   You can order online; the website is easy to use. The bad news: shipping to the U.S. costs about $35, as much as another pair of gloves. Also note that prices are listed in euros, so you will have to compute the rate of exchange.

WHERE TO BUY   6 stores, including Rome, Vienna, New York. **FLAGSHIP**   Piazza di Spagna 61, Rome. ☎ **3906/679-1960.** Mon–Sat 9am–9pm; Sun 9am–8pm. Metro: Spagna. NYC: 609 Madison Ave. at 58th St. ☎ **212/319-5946.** Mon–Sat 10am–7pm; Sun noon–5pm. AE, DISC, MC, V. Subway: Fifth Ave. www.sermonetagloves.com.

Hair Accessories

Alexandre de Paris FRENCH $$–$$$

There are bows, Alice bands, chignon makers and nets, clips and pins and many more items as well as a line of hair jewels and creations for brides. That was the good news. The bad news is that you are asked to pay upwards of $100 for the most simple of accessories.

BEST BETS   The winter velvets; prices start at $100.

WEB TIPS   If you have any self-respect, don't even try to go online. It's confusing and once you get to the proper website, nothing is for sale anyway and all you can see are designs for five barrettes. Try eBay.

WHERE TO BUY   8 stores in Paris; department stores such as Galeries Lafayette; 1 store NYC. **FLAGSHIP**   235 rue St. Honore, Paris 1er. Métro: Tuileries. ☎ **331/4261-4134.** Mon–Sat 10:30am–7pm. NYC: 971 Madison Ave. (at 76th St). ☎ **212/717-2122.** Mon–Sat 10am–6pm. MC, V. Subway: 77th St. www.jovy-alexandredeparis.com.

Evita Peroni DANISH VALUE $

When I first discovered this brand name, in a department store in Paris, I thought it was a joke or a play on the name Eva Peron. In truth, this is a Danish designer who makes a very wide range of hair accessories, always the latest mode and some are even trendsetting. There are hair bands, barrettes, ponytail ornaments, fancy bobby pins, combs and flowers. Expect to pay less than $10 for any one item in the line.

This brand has over 300 outlets in 30 countries worldwide, but none are in the U.S. They're big on demonstration—the stores have areas where customers can sit on high bar stools in front of mirrors and be styled by the staff. Or watch one of the plasma screens featuring the latest collection.

BEST BETS   High fashion at low prices. There is some jewelry in the line—forget it. Stick with hair items, $6–$12.

WEB TIPS   The website is good, but I couldn't figure out how to turn off the music—and you can't order online.

WHERE TO BUY   300 outlets in 30 countries (none in U.S.); department stores in Europe & Asia. Freestanding stores in Hong Kong, Bangkok and UAE. www.evitaperoni.com.

V.V. Rouleaux BRITISH $–$$

Scarlet ribbons for her hair? Perhaps so. This store does not sell hair accessories but they do sell materials so you can use them as you wish. There is no section of this book called Modern Miracles of Retail or even Wonderlands, so I made an executive decision. *Voilà*.

They sell adornments and trims for sewing, for crafts, for embellishing the worlds of fashion and design. There are some ready-made items here as well as artificial flowers and assorted feathers. There are ribbons and beads and ruffles and myriad supplies that can create a world of whimsy and the best of hair accessories.

The Marlyebone High Street store closed (that real estate had to be worth a fortune!) but thankfully a new store on nearby Marlyebone Lane opens as we go to press. Film at 11.

BEST BUYS   Ribbons, buttons and bows, starting at $2.

WHERE TO BUY   2 stores in London, also Glasgow, Newcastle. **FLAGSHIP**   54 Sloane Sq. ☎ **020/7730-3125.** Mon–Tues, Thurs–Sat 9:30am–6pm; Wed 10:30am–6pm. MC, V. Tube: Sloane Sq. www.vvrouleaux.com.

Handbags

The handbag of the moment is a slippery thing to define. Such a handbag is often called the It Bag; in any season there are probably a handful of It Bags and many wannabes, contenders for the title. Beyond the must-have of the season, there are certain classics—this can be a class act, such as an Hermès Birkin bag. (Not a Kelly, mind you, a Birkin.) It can be a no name, no price vintage handbag of extraordinary art and whimsy. It can be anything or many things but probably it costs more than you paid for your first car. Actually, a Birkin bag costs more than I paid for my current car, and it's a Volvo.

The bag needn't match the shoes (please, don't attempt to match the shoes) or cost $10,000. It does have to scream "power." And it should be real, or such a high-class, well-made lookalike, that the power of the visual statement is not tarnished. I saw a Liz Claiborne bag at Marshall's yesterday for $16 that met all the criteria of an It bag. I sometimes carry a bag I bought in a flea market in Comfort, Texas for $22—it's a vintage job from the sixties that tells the world I make trends and don't follow them.

The handbag is what you make of It.

BASIC BAGS

Anthony Luciano NYC $$$$–$$$$$

This handbag designer creates one-of-a-kind magic for Bergdorf's and Neiman's, bags of the take-your-breath-away category mostly bought by collectors and women of high style. You can actually shop his atelier in Manhattan for an out-of-body experience. In these days when you wonder where the value is in a $3,000 sac, you just might want to fly to NYC and go directly to the designer's office where you will get a 25% to 30% discount off regular retail prices.

BEST BETS   The designer does custom work but is truly famous for clutches on frames. A small clutch of printed linen with leather appliqué flowers and a contrast patent leather dangly bob costs about $1,200. A smaller patent leather piece on an antique Bakelite frame is $750.

WEB TIPS   The biannual sales are announced online.

WHERE TO BUY   Neiman Marcus, Bergdorf Goodman or directly from the designer, by appointment only. 347 W. 36th St., 14F, NYC. ☎ 212/563-2223. MC, V, or personal check with ID. www.anthonyluciano.com.

Ashneil HONG KONG ⸢VALUE⸣ $$$–$$$$

World's Best   I am not certain if it's the treasure hunt aspect of shopping in this store, or the bounty of the goods, but shopping in Ashneil is one of life's best pleasures. The shop is no larger than a walk-in closet; it is located in a dumpy mall in Kowloon but the space is piled with sumptuous handbags and you begin to drool shortly after you walk in.

Prices are in the $200 to $350 range per handbag; I have described this as a value resource because the bags sold here are more or less identical to big brand handbags that sell for $1,000 and more.

They are not exact copies; they are not fakes. They are not illegal—which is part of the charm of shopping here. The bags have merely been inspired by the world's most expensive names in design. I cannot say the quality is the same as in my years and years of shopping here; I have had a few misadventures in bags that came apart. On the

Buyer Beware

I have been shopping here for two dozen years and love these bags. However, readers have sent me letters about bags that have broken or not worn well. The firm stands behind its product and will repair.

other hand, I have often fooled experts in retail and frankly, I don't want to spend more than $300 on a handbag.

Ashneil does a lot of its business via trunk shows around the U.S.—you receive a flyer with the dates and then show up to order. Prices are the same as in Hong Kong. Sign up for the mailing list online.

BEST BETS The bag of the moment usually costs about $300. Shipping is from HK to the U.S. for a flat $25 fee.

WEB TIPS The website features many, but not all of the designs. They do not accept online orders, but you can call the North Carolina offices to order.

WHERE TO BUY 1 store: Far East Mansions, 5–6 Middle Rd., Shop 114, Tsim Sha Tsui, Kowloon, Hong Kong. ☎ **852/2366-0509** or **852/2722-0173,** or 336/725-7570 for special orders in U.S. Mon–Sat 10:30am–7pm. AE, MC, V. MTR: TST. www.ashneil.com.

Bottega Veneta ITALIAN $$$$–$$$$$

Bottega Veneta was an Italian handbag maker with a distinct enough style to advertise that their goods were for those whose own initials were enough. They actually had a logo that was a butterfly print. Then they invented woven leather and the rest is handbag history.

While the firm has never taken on a logo-encrusted look, they have grown to all sorts of leather goods and now clothing. Bottega's greatest contribution to the "it" bag legend has been their woven leather bags, which are still considered their signature look. These days, their bags usually cost over $2,000. When made with rare hides, they cost more (natch).

BEST BETS For those who don't mind an out-of-season bag, there is an outlet store outside of Florence, Italy, see p. 432. For those to whom money is no object, the woven leather bags of the moment, which cost about $2,000, are so stunning you could weep. You'll weep less during the sales.

WEB TIPS There is a stunning website that offers very easy online ordering—even on sale. Best yet, a BV bag ages well because it's almost as classical as an Hermès bag. Choose with care and you will use yours for many, many years. Hell, it could even pay for itself.

WHERE TO BUY 44 stores worldwide. **FLAGSHIP** Via Montenapoleone 5, Milan. ☎ **02/7602-4495.** Mon–Sat 10am–7pm. AE, MC, V. NYC: 699 Fifth Ave. ☎ **212/371-5511.** Mon–Wed, Fri 10am–6:30pm; Thurs 10am–7:30pm; Sat 10am–5pm. Subway: Fifth Ave. AE, DISC, MC, V. www.bottegaveneta.com.

Fendi ITALIAN $$$–$$$$$

Shockingly consistent, this Italian firm offers up a new must-have bag every year and often each season.

BEST BETS   The environment of the stores works with the cutting-edge chic of the accessories themselves. An elaborate handbag may cost $4,000 but a visit to stare at it is free. Don't miss the Rome flagship.

Buyer Beware

Fendi.com is the most annoying website I have ever attempted to use in my life. Good luck to you and yours. Try Yoox.com.

WHERE TO BUY   100+ stores worldwide. **FLAGSHIP**   Largo Goldoni 420 (at the junction of via dei Condotti and via del Corso), Rome. ☎ **06/696-661.** Mon–Sat 10am–7:30pm; Sun 10am–7pm. AE, MC, V. NYC: 677 Fifth Ave. ☎ **800/336-3469,** 212/759-4646. Mon–Sat 10am–7pm; Sun noon–6pm. AE, DISC, MC, V. Subway: E, V Fifth Ave. www.fendi.com.

Hermès FRENCH $$$$–$$$$$

World's Best   The move from saddles into handbags was a natural. After that, things get unnatural, like the way women clamor for these things. Even at these astronomical prices, it's hard to get a bag. And get this little factoid: Though the product costs 20% more in Beijing, shoppers go there to find a bag that might be sold out elsewhere in the world.

Yes, you can put your name on a waiting list, or you can create your own waiting list—any style bag can be made to measure in your choice of hides. But don't get carried away with your creativity—the Hermès honchos have to approve your choice, as you are keeping to the firm's image.

Prices vary with size. Size, by the way is in the metric system and you should know which size you want—but the answer is 40cm. You can get a simple Birkin for about $7,500 whereas it's $16,000 for an ostrich Kelly. Like I said, we don't even want Kelly bags—way too stiff. See listing on p. 46.

BEST BETS   The flagship store is like walking in a dream; especially stop by next time you're in Paris to see the new addition—the store has just doubled its space to offer even more luxury.

WEB TIPS   Charm is personified on this website, which opens with a ballerina dancing on a gift box and continues with adorable sketches and solid info. You can shop online.

WHERE TO BUY   200+ stores worldwide; all major cities. **FLAGSHIP**   24, rue St. Honore, Paris 8e. ☎ **331/4017-4717.** Mon–Sat

Faking It

There are more than $500 billion worth of counterfeit goods sold annually—some of those are prescription drugs, some are airplane parts and some are designer handbags.

With handbag prices as high as they are, it's tempting to consider a fake which leads to the question of what a fake is, anyway. Technically speaking, without a reproduction of the logo, the item might be an "inspiration" but it's not a fake. It is not illegal to be inspired by Hermès, or Chanel or Tod's . . . it's just illegal to defraud the public.

I don't suggest you snitch, but to demonstrate how high the stakes have become, *Harper's Bazaar* now provides a Web address that allows you to provide information on where fakes are being sold (iaccsleuth@iacc.org). I guess they haven't been to China lately.

To spot a fake, first check the hardware—this is usually the biggest giveaway. Then look at the stitching. If it's uneven or there are stray ends—it's probably a fake. Luxury goods are meticulously made.

If there is a logo, check to see if it's meant to copy the real logo or if it cheats the real logo; I've seen many an F for Fendi that was really an F and L combination in the Fendi style. This isn't illegal, although it is an attempt to fool the eye.

You must know the real thing fairly well to get a grip on a fake—the proportions of the handle, the elements in the design, the colors in which it was made, and so on.

Warning: Never buy a handbag on the Internet without knowing where it comes from—a large number of bags are fakes.

10am–7pm. AE, MC, V. Métro: Concorde. NYC: 691 Madison Ave. ☎ 212/751-3181 or 800/441-4488. www.Hermès.com.

CULT

World's Best *Chanel* FRENCH $$$$$

Not only does everyone want a Chanel handbag, but it is considered the entry-level aspiration bag. The first bag on most wish lists may very well be the most classic of the collection, the 2.55 (launched in February 1955)—this is the quilted bag with the leather laced chain shoulder strap. On a personal note, if you are in the market for a 2.55, be sure to pick one with an outside pocket because it's ideal for boarding passes when you travel.

Bags: All Around The Mulberry Bush

Napoleon said that Britain was a land of shopkeepers; others have noted that the English Eccentric is a classic in design philosophy. Nowhere is this more clear than in the number of wacky and wonderful handbag makers that originate in London and now do a very big business.

Anya Hindmarch (www.anyahindmarch.com; 30 stores in London, NYC, and more) offers a very ladylike group of bags for the modern lady who lunches—usually affixed with a tiny signature bow. Prices start at around $1,000 for a leather shoulder bag. I got a very nice coin purse in plastic as a freebie when I bought a magazine from a London newsagent. But wait, I haven't mentioned the $10,000 for the small croc bag or the average of $2,000 for an everyday bag. The "Be a Bag" program features your photo—or your kids, dog and the like—on a bag.

The creative, inventive, slightly wacky and very English Eccentric **LuLu Guinness,** 394 Bleecker St., NYC (☎ **212/367-2120;** www.luluguinness.com) has a new couture line of clothes as well. The small bags start at $1,200 but average price is closer to $4,000— rare skins and more old-fashioned ladylike in style than her bucket of roses bags and novelty items that first made her a star.

For the last several years, the venerable UK quality goods line **Mulberry** (www.mulberry.com) has had a major "It" bag carried by those in the know. To use their newfound status properly, Mulberry has just opened their first U.S. store in Greenwich Village. Their most popular bags are large enough to stash everything in except horse and rider. Fakes abound around the world.

Coco herself created the original bag but the incarnations into street chic are pure Karl. The bag comes in a variety of leathers, textures, fabrics and pop culture materials. I think the terry cloth one was among the most inventive, but the terry did pill and snag. Never mind.

Chanel bags are among the most copied in the world and make up a large portion of the faux market as well. Even the ID cards that come inside all genuine bags can be copied. Chanel makes the point of saying there is no such thing as a Chanel-style handbag. It's a Chanel handbag or it isn't.

Although the bags are expensive, they may pay for themselves in long wear. Choose a pebble leather because it lasts longer than lambskin. An oddball color may work better than black as it will go with everything.

BEST BETS If you are on a budget, try to buy a bag on sale (I got one for $500 at the half-price sale in Paris a few years ago) or at a resale store (I paid $800 for another bag at a French depot vente). I'd avoid buying online at auction because of the number of fakes on the market. An entry-level 2.55 usually costs about $1,000 but the average Chanel bag is closer to $2,000 when bought new.

Chanel lambskin classic handbag.

WEB TIPS You cannot buy from Chanel.com but you can get the bags from various sites such as eBay. The problem with used and vintage bags is that you can't tell online if they are fakes or not.

WHERE TO BUY 100+ Chanel stores worldwide. **FLAGSHIP** 31 rue Cambon, Paris 1er. ☎ **331/4286-2600.** Mon–Sat 10am–7pm. AE, MC, V. Métro: Madeleine. Also NYC, Beverly Hills, Vienna, Hong Kong, Beijing and more. www.chanel.com.

Harl Taylor NASSAU, BAHAMAS $$$$

Whether you style yourself after the various celebrity clients or just like summer chic, this little-known designer is *le dernier cri* of summer woven bags in the islands, in Florida and in international resort communities. The bags sell for $265 to $585. Trust me, the one you want is over $500. They are sold in Bergdorf-Goodman in New York as well as at various Florida stores. The brand is well known among the Palm Beach ladies with blond hair.

BEST BETS This is the most stunning summer bag you may own, even if it is expensive. These bags might become collectibles, as Mr. Taylor passed away in late 2007.

WHERE TO BUY 1 store: Festival Walk, Prince George Wharf, Nassau, Bahamas. ☎ **242/323-2710.** AE, MC, V. www.harl taylor.com.

Jamin Puech FRENCH/USA $$$$

These bags were first created in the U.S. by a Frenchwoman–Frenchman design team that went on to open stores in France. The bags are often one-of-a-kind and define whimsy.

BEST BETS Multi-material, raffia, fabric combos with many elements merged into small pieces of art ($500 and up).

WEB TIPS You can't buy online; only accredited resellers can see the collection.

WHERE TO BUY In Paris: 43 rue de la Madame, Paris 6e. ☎ 331/4548-1485. Mon–Fri 10am–7pm; Sat noon–7pm. AE, MC, V. Métro: St. Sulpice. NYC: 247 Elizabeth St. ☎ 212/431-5200. Noon–7pm. AE, MC,V. www.jamin-puech.com.

LLBean.com 🖱 USA VALUE $–$$

Few bags are more classical than the canvas boat bag made by L.L.Bean. And yes, dear ones, it's the only bag that Manolo Blahnik will carry. He favors the ones with the zip top. (The bag comes with and without top zip.)

I can understand his point about not ruining a classic, but when I get into this website and see all the options, I can't decide if I want colors, stripes, customized colors, preppy, the one with the zinnia or the one with the heart, my initials or my first name—and is it a security risk to walk around India with a tote bag with my name on it? Should I have someone else's name? Do I want large or extra large? I know I want long straps—it's all so much torture and such fun! The bag I want ends up being about $50 after I've changed it around to fit my needs and schemes and put my name on it.

BEST BETS Manolo says go with natural with navy trim.

WEB TIPS If you have an L.L.Bean Visa card, you get free monogramming. It takes about 2 weeks to get your order. Sometimes they are sold out of the most with-it colors, such as cocoa brown.

Loewe SPANISH VALUE $$$$$

This is the Hermès of Spain, same quality but lower name recognition and lower prices. The firm was founded in 1846 and has a string of fashionable boutiques on the most fashionable shopping street of any given town. Their logo, not known to that many Americans, is formed by making a square out of four script L's for Loewe, which is pronounced Lou-eh-vay. There are stores in every major city in Spain as well as in most Euro and Asian capital cities. Expect to pay $1,000 for a handbag, or more, but you won't see yourself with every Tom, Dick and Gucci.

BEST BETS Get a look at The Amazona, a bag made for businesswomen to hold all their gear. It comes in a velvet edition that is to faint for.

WEB TIPS I had trouble with the website; couldn't open most of the links.

WHERE TO BUY 100 stores worldwide. **FLAGSHIP** Passeig de Gracia 35, Barcelona. ☎ **3493/216-0400.** Mon–Fri 10am–8:30pm; Sat 10am–2:30pm. AE, MC, V. www.loewe.com.

Valextra ITALIAN $$$$

Valextra is one of the world's leading luggage and briefcase makers. They also make a very well-constructed handbag and are famous for stiff, heavy leather. Their bags are always sleek and chic, but are not in the IT category. They whisper not only of power but of the cult standing reflected in the knowledge that this is a bag few women know about.

BEST BETS Valextra does not make a soft, squishy bag nor is there anything flimsy about the construction. The firm stands for construction—think of it as the stiff of dreams. These are the handbags that last for 20 years and keep on ticking. You'll pay over $500 for the Flybook computer case.

WEB TIPS A lovely, useless website without prices or buying instructions. Try Yoox.com.

WHERE TO BUY 2 stores in Milan. Also Saks in NYC; Barneys in NYC and Dallas; Harrods in London, Tokyo, Hong Kong, Rome airport, more. **FLAGSHIP** via Manzoni 3, Milan. ☎ **3902/9978-6000.** Mon–Sat 10am–7pm. Metro: Bablia. www.valextra.it.

DRESSY

Judith Leiber USA $$$$–$$$$$

Judith Leiber became famous for a look, not her initials or her logo. In the course of her tenure as the queen of evening bags, she was known for several looks—from the animal-shaped and rhinestone-studded *minauderie* to the lizard clutch inset with semi-precious stones. The height of her fame was during the 1980s, but the work is still popular, in both vintage and new forms. In fact, the work is updated enough to stay hot—just take a look at the pave rhinestone evening bag that comes custom made with your initials in it—a very big item in Hollywood and Vegas circles.

Judith Leiber "Asscher crystal bag."

   Leiber also makes wallets ($1,000 and up), belts ($1,000 and up) and sunglasses ($700 and up).

BEST BET A bag with a strap rather than one of the bibelots that rest in the palm of the hand.

WEB TIPS The website's as easy to love as the bags; you can even order online.

WHERE TO BUY   Department & specialty stores. 4 stores world-wide. **FLAGSHIP**   680 Madison Ave. at 61st St., NYC. ☎ **212/223-2999.** Mon–Sat 10am–6pm. AE, MC, V. Subway: Hunter College. www.judithleiber.com.

Let's Do Lunch   USA $$$$

The creator of these bags has been a chef, so it makes sense that she turned her eye to the classic lunchbox shape. Let's Do Lunch is a series of handbags, many of which are custom made for the owner. They all begin with a lacquered box shape and then take on various charms and hardware to make them unique. The inside of the bag is finished in silk, and it comes in its own silk pouch. Bags cost $500 to $700 depending on the customized work. They work for day—if you can make do with a small bag—and are great for evening.

BEST BETS   Their most remarkable bag is very simple, with a tiny vase on the outside; you place a live or silk flower into the vase.

WEB TIPS   You cannot shop online but you can get an excellent understanding of the bag, the colors, the look and some of the custom designs that have been made.

WHERE TO BUY   Write or call Let's Do Lunch, 1840 S. Gaffey Street Suite 535 (office), San Pedro, CA 90731. ☎ **310/377-2078.** www.goldeneggboutique.com.

LouLou de la Falaise   PARIS $$–$$$$$

See listing on p. 51.

Swarovski   AUSTRIAN $$$$–$$$$$

This maker of crystals so real that they look like diamonds uses its own products and some fairy dust to create other-worldly evening bags, jewelry and accessories with prices ranging from $1,100 to $4,600.

The Madison Avenue store in New York is still considered the flagship, but don't miss the newly renovated shop at Rockefeller Center; it's the largest store and carries the complete Swarovski line.

BEST BETS   Evening bags that would make Cinderella weep with joy and put the Rhinestone Cowboy to shame.

WEB TIPS   The website is quick and easy, but the online catalog is limited in selection. Still, you'll get a good overview of the line.

WHERE TO BUY   200+ stores worldwide. **FLAGSHIP**   7 rue Royale, Paris, 8e. Mon–Sat 10am–7pm. AE, MC, V. Métro: Concorde.

NYC: 625 Madison Ave. ☎ **800/426-3088,** 212/308-1710. Mon–
Fri 10am–7pm; Sat 10am–6pm; Sun noon–5pm. AE, DISC, MC,
V. Subway: Hunter College. 30 Rockefeller Plaza. ☎ **212/
332-4304.** Mon–Sat 10am–7pm; Sun 11am–6pm. Subway: Fifth
Ave. www.daniel.swarovski.com.

Venetia Studium ITALIAN $$$$

Little handbags—perfect for evening—are among the to-
drool-over accessories made by this firm that follows in the
footsteps of Mariano Fortuny, the king of pleats. The bags are
silk or velvet, with a dropped center anchored with a Murano
bead and a wrist-length handle or drawstring. See listing on
p. 62.

Hosiery & Socks

If it's not the time of year when you apply your fake tan, then
it must be time to check your legwear to make sure you have
the fashion and technological trends in socks, knee-highs,
tights and pantyhose. Some brands claim their pantyhose will
massage or moisturize, even energize your legs. Then there's
footies that just cover the bunions to keep your sandals from
rubbing. Someday I'll show you my Chinese toe-slings (wrap
sockettes that protect the sides of your feet while leaving your
toes free to wiggle).

Defeet USA $

An old-fashioned knitting machine turned modern has created
new age socks—and other sports gear—including socks which
are padded and treated for bacteria and ones for extreme
sports.

As a marriage between art and science, the socks (which
can be customized) come in exciting designs of hot colors or
imprinted with things like pigeons, starfish, love birds.

BEST BETS   Sport socks, price $5 and up.

WHERE TO BUY   You can shop online; from the sale categories
you may find socks for as little as $5. The average price is $15
to $20. www.defeet.com.

Fogal SWISS $–$$

I used to believe in dime-store pantyhose, but they ran all the
time. And sometimes they didn't fit properly. When I invested
in Fogal, my life changed—I like their fashion tights in great
colors. A lighter denier hose may still run or snag, but there

are heavy enough tights to make your legs svelte and never snag . . . or sag.

BEST BETS   My secret way to afford this brand is to go in and ask for the sale bin, which is usually hidden in a corner year-round. There you'll find all sorts of things at very low prices. I once bought a pair of beige cashmere tights in London for £10 ($20). Prices on normal pantyhose begin around $10 a pair but go way up quickly.

WHERE TO BUY   25 stores worldwide. **FLAGSHIP**   Bahnhofstrasse 38 Zurich. ☎ **41/1-211-45-15.** Daily 9am–6pm. AE, MC, V. NYC: 515 Madison Ave., at 53rd. ☎ **212/355-3254.** Mon–Sat 10am–7pm. AE, DISC, MC, V. www.fogal.com.

Spanx   USA $$

The modern woman thinks pantyline is a major sin and therefore wears a product like Spanx which doesn't run, has tummy control, shapes the body and, of course, eliminates cellulite. These are body shaping tights, about $25 a pair, in five fashion shades, sizes A–E. There's also maternity and plus sizes as well as a range of lingerie. I like the hosiery bra since it has no wires ($34).

BEST BETS   Cheaper than liposuction.

WHERE TO BUY   Sold through department stores such as Nordstrom. www.spanx.com.

Tabio   ENGLISH/JAPANESE $

You may be attracted to these socks when you stumble upon them in a UK department store, but you really need to find one of the boutiques so you can enjoy being dizzy with delight. Don't miss the lace footies for sandals, men's, women's, leggings, tights, socks and sockettes, beginning around $15 a pair. Men's socks are usually $20 a pair.

WEB TIPS   If you don't use the British site, you will get the home page, which is in Japanese. You may order online but only for delivery in the UK.

WHERE TO BUY   Distribution in department stores worldwide; some freestanding stores. **FLAGSHIP**   94 Kings Rd., London SW3. ☎ **4420/7591-1960.** Daily 10am–6pm. MC, V. www. Tabio.co.uk.

Wolford   AUSTRIAN $$$

This is technically a bodywear firm, not just a hosiery source—they have bodysuits, underwear, bathing suits and even a line by Philippe Starck. You'll pay well over $100 for a T-shirt or bodysuit.

BEST BETS   The new Kenzo line is very exciting although possibly for the younger fashionista who enjoys wearing vines of flowers on her legs.

WEB TIPS   The website is pretty useless unless you want to shop online. The underwear is gorgeous; don't drool on your keyboard.

WHERE TO BUY   Department stores worldwide; 12 freestanding stores including Austria, NYC and London. www.wolford.com.

Jewelry

The need to adorn and decorate is ancient; nothing is more fun than visiting museum shows and galleries that display jewelry made centuries ago. Well, maybe shopping for your own jewelry is just as much fun.

To me, one of the most exciting things about this category of goods is that an item need not be expensive in order to be effective. One of my best necklaces was made by my son in the first grade. The variety of materials makes this an endless quest. I'm just trying to grow another hand so I can have more room for a few more rings . . . and things.

ETHNIC & TRIBAL

Ilias Lalaounis   GREEK $$$$–$$$$$

You fancy yourself Helen of Troy, Jackie O or maybe Maria Callas. Maybe you just like timeless classics, preferably in 18 or even 22kt gold. Then shop here. Lalaounis began his jewelry business right after World War II by making chains, but soon began to study historical pieces and reproduce them in fine gold. You can go to Greece for anything from Hellenic to Byzantine designs or shop any of the worldwide boutiques from 4th-generation designer Ilias Lalalounis. There's also stores in cruise ports.

BEST BETS   Etruscan anything in 22kt gold with a few gemstones sprinkled in; antique coin/ruby earrings, $2,500.

WEB TIPS   You'll find good representation of his jewelry on the site but can't order online. Try eBay.

WHERE TO BUY   Ilias Lalaounis Jewelry Museum, Karyatidon and Kallisperi sts., Athens. ☎ **30/210-9221044.** Mon, Thurs, Fri–Sat 9am–4pm; Wed 9am–9pm; Sun 11am–4pm; closed Tues. **FLAGSHIP**   6 Panepistimou, Athens. ☎ **30210/361-1371.**

Other cities include Paris, Geneva, Zurich, NYC, Hong Kong and London. www.lalaounis-jewelrymuseum.gr or lalounis.com.

Maria Oiticica BRAZILIAN $–$$$$

Originally an editor of *Elle* magazine in Brazil, Maria began creating her own jewelry made from vegetation found in the rain forests of Brazil and around the Amazon—some are dried and strung together, others are dried and then dyed with ancient natural dyes. The look is fun and funky and very chic.

BEST BETS   Necklaces made from oddball vegetation grown along the Amazon then dried and hand dyed. Prices begin around $55 and go up to several hundred dollars for an elabo-rate necklace of unusual bits.

WEB TIPS   Great photos; to order product, email tururi@tururi.com.br.

WHERE TO BUY   2 stores in Rio. Rua Barao de Jaguaripe 176/101 terreo (at the corner of Maria Quiteria St.), Ipanema. ☎ 5521/2522-2447. Mon–Fri 10am–7pm; Sat 10am–2pm. AE, MC, V. Rua Lauro Muller 116/3 piso-quiosque—Shopping Rio Sul. ☎ 5521/2522-2447. Daily 10am–10pm. AE, MC, V. www.mariaoiticica.com.br.

FUN, FAB OR FAUX

Antonio Bernardo RIO DE JANEIRO $$$$

This contemporary designer in Ipanema has a fabulous show-room and a variety of modern pieces.

BEST BETS   A charm bracelet called Best Wishes. This is not your mother's charm bracelet. It's a thin leather strap on which teeny weeny, extra small—and flat—18kt gold beads are strung. You choose the beads with the messages you want to impart. There are about 50 different charms, most impossible to read without a magnifying glass. I spent $125 and got the bracelet and five charms (love, diet, infinity, peace, sex). You can buy more charms by mail order.

WEB TIPS   The store wants buyers to contact them directly; there is no mention of the Best Wishes bracelet or the charms online.

WHERE TO BUY   1 store: rua Garcia D'Avila 121, Ipanema, Rio de Janeiro. ☎ 5521/2512-7204. Daily 11am–8pm. MC, V. www.antoniobernardo.com.br.

Carlo Zini MILAN $$$$

Every now and then you walk into
a store and are transported to
another dimension—something
like the Twilight Zone. This
tiny closet of a store—which
actually has more rooms to the
side—sells some handbags
(around $250) and some cos-
tume jewelry that is funny,
sublime, sophisticated and worthy of the Duchess of Windsor
on speed in Palm Beach (starting at $100).

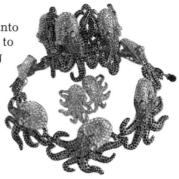

Carlo Zini octopus bracelet and earrings.

BEST BETS   The multi-colored faceted stone octopus pieces.

WHERE TO BUY   1 store: Ripa Ticinese 63, Milan. ☎ **3902/5811-
4505.** Daily noon–8pm. MC, V. carlozini@libero.it. No website.

Erwin Pearl USA (VALUE) $–$$$

Actually I don't like these guys for their pearls, real or fake or
whatever. But beam me up for the everyday category of earrings—gold plated over silver—great for travel.

BEST BETS   They make the world's best huggies, which are
reversible, and cost a reasonable sum—from $65 to $150.

WEB TIPS   There are great photos on the website and it's easy
to order. The site's quick to load and a breeze.

WHERE TO BUY   40 stores worldwide. **FLAGSHIP**   697 Madison
Ave., NYC. ☎ **212/753-3155,** 800/ERWIN PEARL. Mon–Sat
10am–7pm; Sun noon–6pm. AE, DISC, MC, V. www.erwin
pearl.com.

Fabrice FRENCH $$–$$$$$

Mostly vintage jewelry that is spectacular, breathtaking, talk
of the town, hit of the party kind of fabulous. **Warning:** Sometimes they have the real thing. I was stunned to fall in love
with a $10,000 gold snake necklace—hey, I was only kidding
and wanted it for, uh, maybe $1,500. Ooops.

BEST BETS   Large and extravagant brooches are the specialty.
Very collectible; expect to pay $300 to $400. Resin flowers
begin at around $150.

WEB TIPS   You can actually buy online, although to really use
the site well, you should speak French.

WHERE TO BUY   Some department and specialty stores such as Bergdorf Goodman in NYC. **FLAGSHIP**   33 rue Bonaparte, Paris 6e. ☎ **331/4326-5795.** Daily 11:30am–7pm. AE, MC, V. Métro: St. Germain des Pres. Also in U.S.: 1714 N. Wells St., Chicago. www.bijouxfabrice.com.

Francoise Montague PARIS $$–$$$

This store is in a courtyard right off the rue St. Honore not far from the famous Colette store. It's a small boutique packed with glittery glitz and enamel and resin and sparkle aplenty in the $100 range for a pair of earrings. A wonderful source made better by the fact that it's hidden.

BEST BETS   Most of the merchandise is under $100. I loaded up on glitzy earrings.

WHERE TO BUY   1 store: 231 rue St. Honore, Paris 1er. ☎ **331/4260-8016.** Mon–Sat 10am–7pm. MC, V. Métro: Tuileries. No website.

Kenneth Jay Lane (KJL) USA $$–$$$$

There is no more famous name in American costume jewelry—KJL, as he is called—He's simply the prince of glitz, the master. He's published books; there have been exhibits of his work. Every celebrity and woman of style has worn his work, including the late Princess Diana. KJL is synonymous for fake with style. He's copied from David Webb and all the big names. Pieces are signed with a tiny KJL and range from $50 on up, depending on the workmanship and the jewels.

BEST BETS   The pieces that would cost $30,000 if they were real cost but $300 because they are KJL.

WEB TIPS   You can buy vintage KJL on eBay. There is a website but it requires that you log in with an account that keeps your credit card information—this just to open the pages. No thank you, I'll just head over to Saks.

WHERE TO BUY   Department stores worldwide. www.kennethjaylane.net.

Laila Rowe USA ⟨VALUE⟩ $

This chain has stores that are small and packed with accessories—mostly jewelry—with an ethnic fashion twist to it and low, low everyday prices. This is not teeny-bopper land. Per the recent trends as we go to press, there's plenty of wood, fake jade, rhinestone brooches. The firm is nothing if not trendy. Everything is arranged in color groups; there are four or five different palettes per season. Note that the stores are not all alike and are uneven, so keep shopping at several until you realize I am a genius.

BEST BETS This is the stuff that looks like it was featured in a fashion magazine with price tags as if featured in the dime store. Pieces begin at $10.

WEB TIPS Easy to shop online.

WHERE TO BUY Freestanding stores: 13 in NYC, 11 others worldwide. **FLAGSHIP** 1031 Third Ave. at 61st St. ☎ 212/980-5535. Mon–Sat 10am–8pm; Sun 11am–7pm. AE, DISC, MC, V. Subway: 4, 5, 6, N, R or W to Lexington Ave. www.lailarowe.com.

Mariko USA VALUE $$$–$$$$

The best earrings of my life came from this store. Be aware that they do sell real jewelry, so if the price makes you sigh "Ouch," then you are into the good stuff. The faux and fabulous costs about $125 to $150 for a pair of earrings.

There's also brooches, chokers and enough to make Coco Chanel's eyes pop out. The store is a virtual Ali Baba treasure trove of treasures, some real, some inspirations inspired by the best names in the world. There are also silk flowers, some handbags (mostly for evening) and assorted small fashion items, but the jewelry is the way to go. There are 18kt gold earrings too, in the $650 to $800 price range. I vote for the Verdura-like earrings in the $455 area.

BEST BETS Look for the somewhat funky. In other words, not copies of your average big names—instead, think Vedura, Elizabeth Gage, and names like that. I'll take the scampi brooch for $1,600, thank you.

WEB TIPS While you can buy on this site, it doesn't do the store or the merchandise justice and you might think I am crazy for loving this place.

WHERE TO BUY 2 stores. **FLAGSHIP** 998 Madison Ave., at 77th St. ☎ 212/472-1176. Mon–Sat 10am–6pm. AE, DISC, MC, V. Subway: 6 to 77th St. Also in Palm Beach: 329 Worth Ave. Mon–Sat 10am–6pm. www.marikopalmbeach.com.

Michaela Frey AUSTRIAN $$$$

I first fell in love with enamel bangle bracelets thanks to an advertising campaign by Hermès, which is famous for this style. Years later I discovered that the bracelets are made in Vienna by Frey Wille; the firm that showcases the work of Michaela Frey and her designers and students as inspired by museum and art collections.

BEST BETS   Bangle bracelets; about $600 for a large enamel bangle bracelet.

WEB TIPS   Click on "request" to get prices and purchasing information.

WHERE TO BUY   Some specialty jewelry stores worldwide; also freestanding stores. **FLAGSHIP**   Gumpendorferstrasse 81, Vienna. ☎ **431/599-2545.** Mon–Fri 9am–6pm; Sat 9am–noon. AE, MC, V. Other cities include Paris, London, NYC. www. michaelafrey.com.

Overstockjeweler.com USA

With all the knockoffs on the web, this site offers good-quality, accurate copies of designs from Tiffany, David Yurman, Harry Winston and more. Most designs are set in sterling silver, but there's also some fab buys in 14kt gold. You can browse by price range or designer. I just ordered a pair of Tiffany-inspired diamond CZ earrings set in sterling silver for $30. They have a toll-free customer service line (☎ **800/586-0020**) if you need help. Call Mon through Fri 9am to 6pm EST. Best for "Tiffany" and "David Yurman" inspired replicas.

PRECIOUS & SEMI-PRECIOUS

Elizabeth Gage BRITISH $$$$$

I have always dreamed that my next engagement ring would be a subdued and sophisticated little number from Elizabeth Gage, queen of the baroque who works with pearls, old coins, intaglio, precious and semi-precious stones and her flexible and brilliant brain to create one-of-a-kind masterpieces. She does brooches, earrings and rings.

BEST BET   The store fixes their own attractive exchange rate for U.S. customers at $1.75 to the GB pound. That's a deal!

WHERE TO BUY   Specialty stores. Trunk shows. One of a kind. **FLAGSHIP**   18 Albemarle St., London W1. ☎ **4420/7823–0100.** AE, MC, V. Tube: Green Park or Bond St. www.Elizabeth-Gage.com.

Elizabeth Locke USA $$$$$

Calling this the poor man's Elizabeth Gage isn't fair, but I sometimes think of it that way—one of the best of her trademarks is the gold hoop necklace to which you attach a drop or charm. Her hammered gold has a slight Lalaounis look to it; the other Elizabeth also does scarabs, old coins, semi-precious stones and a funky rich girl look.

Hongqiao Market (The Pearl Market), Beijing

I just can't help it. Every day I spend in Beijing I come up with another reason to visit the **Hongqiao Market** (say "Hong-Jow"; or Pearl Market), Tian Tan East Road, east of the Temple of Heaven (☎ 86-010/6713-3354). This is partly because they sell more than pearls here—there's luggage, makeup, gifts, leather goods, fake everything and two floors of jewelry. Most of the pearls are made with glass or crushed bits of nacre, so they are not serious, but that's okay. I'd be reluctant to buy serious pearls here. (They are sold; I'm just chicken.)

The top three floors of this market consist of stores, showrooms, stalls, beads and beads and more beads. Vendors will string the pearls for you or work with you to string together a combination of pearls and beads to make your own creation. I've paid $250 for a double strand of Nishi pearls and $25 for a single strand of fake pearls. It's all in the wrist.

Bring cash and bargain like crazy. Some of the high-end jewelers on the top floors will take credit cards, but you'll get a better deal by paying cash. Hours are daily 8:30am to 7pm. Credit cards vary with dealers; you'll get better prices if you negotiate with cash.

BEST BETS   Multi mega-strand collars of cabochon stones are a good place to begin, about $7,000. There's much for less and don't make the earrings too matchy-matchy.

WEB TIPS   I don't want to sound greedy, but I'd sell my son, my dog and my laptop for the brooch on the homepage.

WHERE TO BUY   The Other Elizabeth, 17 E. Main St., Boyce, VA. ☎ 540/837-3088. Sat and Sun noon–5pm. 968 Madison Ave., NYC. ☎ 212/744-7878. Mon–Sat 10am–6pm. AE, DISC, MC, V. Subway: 77th St. www.elizabethlocke.com.

Mish NYC $$$$$

Mish is his first name; he makes collectable pieces with precious and semi-precious stones, from $2,000. He serves the hidden wealth of Park Avenue and like Liza or Goldie or Gwyneth, needs no introduction save his one name. His work is often colorful and very alive—sparkly not just with jewels but with energy.

BEST BETS   One look at his multi-multi-strand peridot choker with clasp inset with semi-precious stones and you know what important jewelry looks like these days. If only the Duchess of Windsor was alive.

WHERE TO BUY   1 store: 131 E. 70th St, NYC. ☎ **212/734-3500.** Mon–Fri 10am–6pm; Sat 11am–6pm. AE, MC, V. Subway: 68th St. www.mishnewyork.com.

Gem Palace INDIAN $$$$$

Think about it: a pink tourmaline necklace with Indian enamel medallions, diamonds, South Sea pearls and gold, all for only $43,250. Actually, the great thing about Gem Palace is that a large part of the merchandise is affordable. Many of the styles are slightly ethnic and all are the rage right now.

The main store is rather large in the New City portion of Jaipur—it's white stucco with pink stenciled designs out front.

The shocking tip is that in India, you are expected to bargain—even in this drop-dead fancy store.

World Traveler

The small shops in the Oberoi hotels are more fun than the Palace because they're not as intense and overwhelming. At the small shops in the hotel lobbies you can actually browse, whereas at the main palace, you sit, you are sold to, you negotiate, and so on.

Gem Palace earrings from the Byzantine collection.

BEST BETS   Hoop earrings with dangling tiny tourmalines for $600 are actually a bargain.

WEB TIPS   The site seems like a historical text and has much information but no romancing the stones.

WHERE TO BUY 10 stores throughout India. **FLAGSHIP** Mirza Ismail Rd., Jaipur. ☎ **91-141/374-175.** Also 49 E. 74th St., NYC. ☎ **212/481-2123.** By appointment only. AE, MC, V. www.gempalacejaipur.com.

H. Stern BRAZILIAN $$$–$$$$$

World's Best

Much of what I know about jewelry was taught to me by the late Hans Stern. Stern just passed away; his sons now run the business. Indeed, the business has changed in order to attract younger customers and even has some name designer lines now, such as Diane von Furstenburg.

While there are stores all over the world, the one to visit is the main store in Rio with its museum and factories.

Next door to the large show-rooms and educational venue is the outlet store called H. Stern Off Price. I didn't find any bargains there, although the staff told me the merchandise was a season old and therefore 30% off.

BEST BETS Jewelry with a rainbow of colored stones from Brazil; I paid about $1,000 for a pair of gold and gem-encrusted earrings.

WHERE TO BUY 100 stores, in NYC, Paris, Sao Paulo, more. **FLAGSHIP** rua Garcia d'Avila, Rio. ☎ **55-21/2259-7442.** NYC: 645 Fifth Ave. at 52nd St. ☎ **800/747-8376,** 212/688-0300. AE, DISC, MC, V. Subway: E or V to Fifth Ave. www.hstern.net.

Judith Ripka USA $$$$

Sign me up for a few ropes from the Bahama Mama collection of beads and pearls and pave and swag ($3,000 and up).

WEB TIPS You'll be directed from the Judith Ripka website to Neiman Marcus to order online.

WHERE TO BUY 10 stores worldwide. **FLAGSHIP** 777 Madison Ave., NYC. ☎ **800/JRJEWEL,** 212/517-8200. Mon–Sat 10am–6pm. AE, DISC, MC, V. www.judithripka.com.

Tiffany & Co. USA $$$$–$$$$$

Among other things, they sell pearls. Expect to pay over $200,000 for an opera-length (35-in) South Sea pearl strand. And then there's New York state tax on top of that. They do have a booklet on how to buy pearls.

See listing on p. 61.

Tony Duquette USA $$$$–$$$$$

Tony Duquette has died, but he lives in my memory because I interviewed him for *People* magazine many decades ago. He also lives on in the jewelry he created and as a brand, still ticking and now designed by Hutton Wilkinson. His pieces are big, bold, unique, made of various materials, whimsical, outrageous and a little bit inspired by Vedura but a lot inspired by nature. Breathtakingly imaginative.

BEST BETS A brooch in the Diana Vreeland, Nancy Cunard school of design.

WEB TIPS Enormous site with exhibits, examples of the work, biographical info—almost as amazing as the man.

WHERE TO BUY   Bergdorf Goodman, NYC. Stanley Korshak, Dallas. Geary's in Beverly Hills. www.tonyduquette.com.

Lotus Arts de Vivre THAI $$$$$

Very creative, slightly outrageous jewelry similar in concept to pieces by Verdura. Choose from necklaces, bangles, rings, brooches or handbags made from Thai straw baskets and finished off with fine jewels. The boutiques—there are a handful of them dotted around the world—are pieces of jewelry in themselves; entering one is like walking into a dream. Cushions are left on the floor; each one showcases a choker of precious stones.

BEST BETS   There's coral napkin rings and treasures worthy of Ali Baba. Many of the works are innovative, such as the flex rings, about $3,000 in diamonds, sapphires or pearls. There are many pieces of blackamoor jewelry; some seashell and diamond pieces—I'll take those squid earrings, thank you. Hmm, are they octopi?

WEB TIPS   You cannot order online but you can see the collection. Just make sure you are stable in your office chair, because the splendor will keep you spinning. As these things go, the prices in Asia are fair.

WHERE TO BUY   12 stores worldwide, including Bangkok. NYC: 725 Park Ave. ☎ **212/327-9217.** AE, MC, V. Subway: M to 68th St. www.lotussartsdevivre.com.

Verdura ITALIAN/USA $$$$$

Okay, close your eyes and picture Diana Vreeland. What do you see? The hair? The nose? The bracelets? The bracelets are cuffs from Verdura, who also made the ones worn by Coco Chanel. Verdura was founded by the Duke Fulco di Verdura who designed in the heyday of the 1930s, right before World War II broke out. The firm relocated to New York in 1939, just as Hitler invaded Poland. Verdura has since passed on, but his creations live on.

BEST BETS   Your bracelet will be fitted specifically to your wrist. Prices for a cuff start at $12,000, and they'll do custom designs.

WEB TIPS   Site allows you to order a catalog but not shop—there's a lot of company history and good shots of the collection. This is for dreamers.

WHERE TO BUY   1 atelier: 745 Fifth Ave. at 57th St., 12th Floor, NYC. ☎ **212/758-3388.** By appointment. AE, MC, V. www.verdura.com.

VINTAGE JEWLERY

A la Vielle Russie NYC/RUSSIAN $$$$$

Maybe there aren't too many Imperial Easter Eggs hanging around for sale, but there are smaller pieces of Fabergé that come on the market. A la Vielle Russie is the leading expert in Russian antique jewelry and fine art. Begun in Kiev in 1851, the business was forced to relocate. You must ring to enter, but they are very, very nice here. ALVR shows at four important antiques fairs each year; check the website for dates and locations.

BEST BETS Fabergé anything.

WEB TIPS The site is easy and friendly—not as stiff looking as the store at all. They provide zoomability on each piece, with full description, and then you request the price.

WHERE TO BUY 1 store: 781 Fifth Ave. at 59th St., NYC. ☎ 212/752-1727. Mon–Fri 10am–5:30pm; Sat 11am–4pm. AE, MC, V. Subway: Q, N, R, W to Fifth Ave. www.alvr.com.

Martin Katz USA $$$$$

Although Katz made his name in vintage jewelry, he also sells important contemporary jewelry. You already know this, however, because you've been nominated for an Oscar and your stylist has sent you over for a look-see with the understanding that you may buy or borrow.

BEST BETS Winning an Oscar and keeping the bling to celebrate.

WEB TIPS The website's slow; I think they want you to linger and look. No online orders.

WHERE TO BUY FLAGSHIP 9540 Brighton Way, Beverly Hills. ☎ 310/276-7200. NYC: ☎ 212/957-8295. www.martinkatz.com.

Fred Leighton USA $$$$$

You are a star. Maybe a movie star, maybe a mogul star, maybe just a woman with an aura. You, or your beloved, knows that you must have only the world's best estate and antique jewelry, so you shop at Fred Leighton. Leighton's commitment is to pieces that are old and beautiful—he does not discriminate or specialize in one period or another. He carries watches, pearls and everything from the big names in signed pieces to Golden Age of India and Court Jewels of the 19th century.

WEB TIPS   The website's dark and you must click carefully to open the pages. Skip the intro.

WHERE TO BUY   FLAGSHIP   773 Madison Ave., NYC. ☎ 212/288-1872. Also at Bellagio Hotel in Las Vegas. ☎ 702/693-7050. www.fredleighton.com.

Shoes

I have shoes for walking, I have shoes for standing, I have shoes for walking the dog at 3am, I have shoes for the beach. I have shoes for travel, I have shoes for bad weather, I have shoes for dressing up, I have shoes for seducing men, I have shoes for doing TV interviews, I have shoes for public appearances, I have boots and booties, too. And those are just the black shoes.

You are laughing because you understand.

What are the best shoes in the world? The pair that doesn't hurt. We buy shoes the way we buy lipstick. They please us. They represent hope and joy and possibility. It doesn't matter if you are having a fat day or a bad hair day. It doesn't matter how old you are. We buy shoes because we all know that a woman is more defined by her accessories than her clothing, that a pair of shoes can change your life. Just ask Cinderella.

BASIC SHOES

Bob Ellis USA $$$–$$$$

There is no Bob Ellis; the store is owned by the Kalinsky family which has a second Bob Ellis store in Charlotte. If the name rings a bell, the famed Jeffrey of New York and Atlanta is one of the owner's sons.

BEST BETS   They will ship you a ton of shoes to try, and then you send back the ones that aren't right.

WEB TIPS   The site is well organized and gives you a direct line to call if you have questions. The list of designers and selection of shoes is staggering.

WHERE TO BUY   FLAGSHIP   332 King St., Charleston, SC. ☎ 843/722-2515. Mon–Sat 9am–6pm. Also 4400 Sharon Rd., Charlotte, NC. ☎ 704/366-6686. Mon–Sat 10am–7pm; Sun 1–6pm. AE, DISC, MC, V. www.bobellisshoes.com.

E&J Designer Shoe Outlet USA VALUE $$–$$$$

Discount source for designer shoes, see p. 476.

WHERE TO BUY   8666 E. Shea Blvd., Scottsdale, AZ. ☎ **480/607-0170.** Mon–Fri 10am–8pm; Sat 9:30am–7pm; Sun 11am–5pm. AE, DISC, MC, V. No website.

Ferragamo ITALIAN $$$$

Italian immigrant Salvatore Ferragamo actually got his big break in Hollywood and even today the shoes are made in American sizes, not European. But the business has gone back to Italy where it has become more of an empire with hotels, an entire private village and a show-stopping museum in Florence. There's clothes, men's ties, scarves, leather goods and, of course, shoes for men and women. The Audrey flat is a ballet slipper with strap, named for Audrey Hepburn.

BEST BETS   Prices are no better in Italy than in the U.S.; in fact, you do better to wait for sales in the U.S. unless you hit the Ferragamo outlet in Italy. I bought a pair of men's mocs for $175 at the outlet; this is about half price.

WHERE TO BUY   225 stores, in Florence, NYC, London, Rome, Paris, more. **FLAGSHIP**   via Tornabuoni 14r Florence. ☎ **3955/292-123.** Tues–Sat 10am–7pm; Mon 2–7pm. AE, MC, V. NYC: 655 Fifth Ave. ☎ **212/759-3822.** Mon–Wed 10am–6pm; Thurs 10am–8pm; Fri and Sat 10am–7pm; Sun noon–6pm. Subway: 6 to 51st St. Outlet store at The Mall, Leccio, Italy, outside Florence: via Europa 8, Leccio, Reggello. ☎ **3955/865-7775.** www.ferragamo.com.

Hu's WASHINGTON, D.C. $$$$

Hu's is one of the most unusual shoe stores I have ever been to because the selection is from designers and brands that you rarely see anywhere in the world (certainly not in the U.S.). Who knew that Sonia Rykiel made shoes?

BEST BETS   Knowing that your feet will be shod with unusual masterpieces.

WEB TIPS   You can sign up for their newsletter online but can't order.

WHERE TO BUY   1 store: 3005 M St., Washington, D.C. ☎ **202/342-0202.** Mon–Sat 11am–8pm; Sun noon–5pm. AE, DISC, MC, V. www.hushoes.com.

Marmi USA $$$–$$$$

They only sell a few brands, but they have a lot of sizes and a lot of customer services, so that this small business makes a big impact—especially on fans of the Van Eli line of shoes, which is nice but not outrageously expensive.

BEST BETS The catalog allows you to do all the shopping you need in your own home. There's also a good fidelity program. Shoes are usually under $100.

WEB TIPS In-store sales are also noted and available online.

WHERE TO BUY 30 stores in U.S. **FLAGSHIP** 519 Madison Ave., NYC. ☎ **212/751-3100.** Mon–Wed, Fri 10am–7pm; Thurs 10am–8pm; Sat 10am–6pm; Sun noon–5pm. AE, DISC, MC, V. www.marmishoes.com.

Payless USA ⟨VALUE⟩ $

I love Payless because they make a great-looking shoe for not much money and let's face it, for some fashion trends, you don't need the shoe to last any longer than a season. They also carry large sizes, so I love them. I admit that some shoes don't have enough construction in them to support my feet for miles and miles of walking.

BEST BETS I love a $20 pair of shoes from this enormous chain. During sales, they offer half off the second pair.

WEB TIPS It's easy to order online, and shipping's two bucks a pair.

WHERE TO BUY 200+ stores in the U.S. Go online for the one nearest you. ☎ **877/474-6379** for customer service. www.payless.com.

Piperlime.com ⌂ USA

Gap, Inc.'s new shoe website offers more than 100 high-end brands and lists fashion tips from invited guest editors. Prices range from full retail to steep discount. A recent search found Taryn Rose boots at the $595 full price (ouch), but styles by Kenneth Cole were 30% to 40% off.

There's plenty of choices in hard-to-fit sizes and good inventory for men and children, too. This is a lets-watch-and-see-what-happens site.

Shoetrader.com ⌂ USA ⟨VALUE⟩ $–$$$

This online women's shoe store offers a broad selection of sizes, from 4 to 14, widths Narrow to WWWW. They offer some trendy formal styles, but emphasis is on comfort. Brands include EasySpirit, Naturalizer, Hush Puppies and New Balance. You'll get free shipping and free returns.

BEST BUYS Hard-to-fit sizes.

Zappos.com 🖱 USA VALUE $–$$$$

With their aggressive advertising campaign, this firm seeks to turn their name into a verb, as in, "Did you Zappos today?"

BEST BETS   For basic brands, for shoes you already know about, this site is a winner. Many sizes; fair prices.

CASUAL, FLAT & SENSIBLE SHOES

Aerosoles USA VALUE $$–$$$

These just may be the best shoes in the world if you combine comfort with price and throw in the range of styles from classic to somewhat fashionable, from heels to flats to boots. Aerosoles owe their fame to the flexibility of the sole and the fact that all shoes are soft, with cushioned footbeds. Most shoes and boots retail for under $100 a pair. There's also a range of sizes with some styles going up to women's size 12.

About the outlets: The price for a pair of shoes is the same as in stores—unless you hit a sale (usually second pair at half price).

WHERE TO BUY   250+ stores in the US. www.aerosoles.com.

Camper SPANISH $$$

Spanish brand that is equally known for the architectural design of their boutiques as for their fashion-forward and comfortable shoes for men and women. They even do their own version of the ballet flat. Shoes begin around $100 but most often cost closer to $150. There are outlet stores in Europe.

WEB TIPS   Note that some styles run a bit small (or at least their 44 is more like a 42).

WHERE TO BUY   50+ stores in 32 countries, in Barcelona, London, Paris, NYC, more; European outlet malls. **FLAGSHIP** Muntaner, 248 Barcelona. ☎ **902/364-598.** Mon–Sat 10am–9pm. MC, V. www.camper.com.

Masai Barefoot Technology SWISS $$$$

Masai specializes in walking, running, sports shoes and sandals, even clogs that change the way you stand and therefore the way you walk, to the benefit of your body and your posture. They also make sports training more effective and help to improve coordination and circulation. Expect to pay about $250 a pair.

WEB TIPS   www.swissmasaius.com.

Romax SEATTLE $$$$

This isn't the real estate firm Remax but a two-store master-piece of walking and comfort shoes for men and women with U.S. and European brands—many of the shoes are stylish enough so that you don't feel like your granny. Best store of its kind I have ever shopped. They will special-order for you.

WEB TIPS   The website is a horrible hodgepodge of links.

WHERE TO BUY   2 stores. **FLAGSHIP**   123 Pike St., Seattle ☎ **206/389-8677.** Mon–Sat 10am–7pm. AE, MC, V. www.romaxshoes.com.

Taryn Rose USA $$$$

Created by a doctor, an orthopedic surgeon no less, these shoes were originally meant to be high-end walking shoes for the kind of women who shop at Neiman Marcus. In fact, it was Neiman's that launched this brand.

The brand has grown, has its own stores and now has heels and even dressy shoes, although the forte is still the flat. The shoes are very expensive, beginning at $400 and going upward. It's hard to find them at discount sources, although every now and then you can luck out (try E&J Shoe in Scottsdale; see p. 476).

WEB TIPS   The website will link you to a retail store to place an online order.

WHERE TO BUY   5 stores, in NYC, Las Vegas, Beverly Hills, San Jose, Seoul; Neiman Marcus. **FLAGSHIP**   681 Madison Ave., NYC. ☎ **212/753-3939.** Mon–Sat 10am–6pm; Thurs 10am–7pm; Sun noon–5pm. www.tarynrose.com.

Toms USA/ARGENTINIAN VALUE $$

You've heard of Tod's (p. 153); well this is Toms—no relation. Toms shoes are the brainchild of Blake Mycoskie who was inspired by espadrilles he spotted in Argentina. The fashion flats are made in Argentina and a portion of the profits goes back to the village where they are made.

BEST BETS   Stripe Toms ($38).

WEB TIPS   You can buy online or find the nearest store anywhere in the world.

WHERE TO BUY   Sold in boutiques such as Scoop (New York) and American Rag (LA). www.tomsshoes.com.

"F**K ME" SHOES

Christian Louboutin EGYPTIAN/FRENCH $$$$

You've heard the expression: You've gotta have a gimmick? Let me tell you, I am an expert on spotting gimmicks, and I have seen few better than this. M. Louboutin makes a lovely, very chic, very sophisticated shoe— and sends each shoe he makes out to the public with a bright, shining, red sole. Who sees the sole of your shoes? I'll tell you. Next time you watch a late-night talk show, watch the leggy actresses cross their legs and reveal the secret of the Louboutin bottom. Shoes begin at $400. M. Louboutin made shoes for Chanel and YSL before going out on his own in the tiny and pic-turesque Passage Vero-Dodat, near the Louvre.

Christian Louboutin "Architek Noir."

BEST BETS   The instant status-y message written on your sole.

WEB TIPS   They call this the site for "luxury red sole shoes." The site shows a lot but sells zip. Try Bob Ellis (p. 142).

WHERE TO BUY   19 rue Jean-Jacques Rousseau, Paris 1er. ☎ 331/4236-0531. Tues–Sat 11am–7pm. MC, V. Métro: Les Halles. NYC: 941 Madison Ave. ☎ 212/396-1884. Mon–Sat 10am–6pm; Thurs 7pm. AE, MC, V. www.christianlouboutin.fr.

Jimmy Choo BRITISH $$$$

For all the tea in China, or all the pairs of shoes hidden under my bed, I cannot really tell you the difference between Manolo and Choo. Manolo fits me and makes a chic low heel; I never even think that Jimmy Choo makes anything practical at all. In fact, I think the success of the brand has to do with the successful marketing by company founder and president Tamara Mellon, who sells a strappy, breathless kind of shoe.

Don't get me wrong, the shoes are stunning. I don't wear them because I am already 6 feet tall and have little occasion to wear a 4-inch, catch-me-if-you-can sandal. But that's just me.

BEST BETS   Shoes that set the world spinning. You'll pay $400 to $600 for some sensational shoes.

WEB TIPS   Not all designs are available to order from the online boutique.

En Pointe

Ballet flats are the perfect flat, although they rarely have much support in them. Still, they are chic, come in a variety of materials and remain a classic no matter what other shoe styles come and go. The only thing you have to worry about is wearing them out.

At one season or another, almost every designer and large manufacturer has made a few ballet flats, even Chanel. Prices on ballet flats run the gamut from very inexpensive to well over $300, mostly depending on the brand.

French Sole

Princess Diana loved this shoe store, at 6 Ellis St., W1 London (☎ 207/730-3771; www.frenchsole.com), the maker of ballet flats in a zillion colors and skins and patterns and creative options. You'll pay about $100 to $150 for a pair.

London Sole

Yeah, yeah, I know, it is confusing. I see London, I see France and all that. This is yet another source for ballet flats, also from a British designer—Jane Winkworth. Her shoes are cute, chic, funny or funky.

London Sole shoes are more expensive than French Sole shoes, and they have more variations (especially if you are into toe cleavage). There are several stores in the U.S. If you are into celebrity spottings, hang out at the Santa Monica store, 1331 Montana Ave. (☎ 310/255-0937; www.londonsole.com), where many a star has been seen shopping.

PrettyBallerinas.com

They don't have a store but this is the best online source for ballet flats. And they have big shoes—up to size 42 (my size)! About 100 styles, all handmade and priced around $100 but going up to $150, which is more or less the going price for this genre. Shipping is 20€ ($25) to the U.S., with free shipping on exchanges. Expect delivery in 7 to 10 days. www.prettybalerinas.com.

WHERE TO BUY   60 stores worldwide. **FLAGSHIP**   32 Sloane St., London SW1. ☎ 207/823-1051. Tube: Knightsbridge. Mon–Sat 10am–6pm. AE, MC, V. www.jimmychoo.com.

Manolo Blahnik SPANISH/BRITISH $$$$–$$$$$

It didn't take *Sex & the City* to get me to love Manolo—oh no, it's the fact that he makes a size 11. I'm easy—give me a gorgeous shoe that has a chance of fitting me, add a princess heel (lower the better), and I am yours forever. My suede Manolos are about the only dressy heels I can wear for more than a half hour. I understand that the suede has molded to my feet, but what's wrong with that? Next year, I am having some custom made. Prices for shoes are in the $500 to $2,000 range, but I am told mine will come in on the low end of the scale.

Blahnik is Spanish but considers Sicily his summer home; his sister runs the shop in London so this is a very hands-on family business. His shoes are so artistic that photos of them have just been made into an art book, *Blahnik by Boman*. He is the master of the shoes you wish you could have designed. His fantasies are better than anyone else's.

BEST BETS   They announce the sale well in advance. The sales are in late January and late July, and prices go down as the sale progresses. Toward the end, they are practically giving away the $500 shoes (for $150).

WEB TIPS   Don't be fooled—M. Blahnik does not write the Manolo shoe blog.

WHERE TO BUY   Department and specialty stores. **U.S. FLAGSHIP** 31 W. 54th St., NYC. Mon–Fri 10:30am–6pm; Sat 10:30am–5:30pm. AE, DISC, MC, V. Subway: 57th St. www.manolo blahnik.com.

Rene Caovilla ITALIAN $$$$–$$$$$

While I used to relate a "F**k Me" shoe to the height of the heel, the truth is that Rene Caovilla makes the same shoe in three heights with variations that affect the proportion, so the concept is still there.

BEST BETS   These are not only dress-up shoes, they are the most extravagantly crafted, often bejeweled contraptions that have been created since Cinderella went to the ball. Expect to pay at least $500 but more likely $600 or even $700 for a pair. But at that price, you do get two shoes.

WEB TIPS   Site is bi-lingual, but you cannot shop online.

WHERE TO BUY   6 stores in Milan, Dubai, Tokyo, Paris, Palm Beach. **FLAGSHIP**   via Bagutta 28, Milan. Mon 4–7pm; Tues–Sat 10am–7pm. AE, MC, V. www.renecaovilla.com.

SNEAKERS

Flight Club USA $$$–$$$$

You don't have to be Japanese to love sneakers or to have a secret source for resale items that are hot or gonna be hot,

Will Drive for Shoes

At least once a year I go to the city of **Romans, France,** which is south of Lyon. I am not checking out Roman ruins—oh no. This is a shopper's field trip. Romans is the shoe capital of France and maybe the world. I have big, hard-to-fit feet, so I may not even be going for myself—I might just be out to look or visit the nearby outlet mall. There's no harm in looking, right?

In reality, Romans is one of two divided towns straddling a river—sort of like Buda and Pest. The town across the river from Romans is named Bourg-en-Presse. Tanneries need water to flush away all the chemicals they use; factories need rivers to barge their goods to market. There are independent shoe outlets on both sides of the river.

I enter town by leaving the A7 highway at exit 13 (when heading south from Paris) and following signs to Romans. Note that the exits on this stretch of highway do not match up, so if you are coming from the south headed toward Paris, you follow the exit for Romans which is exit 15. Go figure.

First up as you approach town is **Robert Clergerie,** on the very tiny rue Pierre Curie; then return to the main street (50m from where you are at Clergerie) and follow signs for center ville. Curve through town and stop at **Marques Avenue** a mid-size factory outlet village. Note that if you are coming from Clergerie, you will have to pass the outlet and go to the round-about then circle back to get to the entrance of the outlet mall.

Once finished there, proceed to the next roundabout (you can only turn right coming out of the outlet lot) and circle around to be in position to go across the river. Once on the other bank, almost immediately turn left when you see the golden arches of McDonalds. Park in the strip center alongside McDo for the **Charles Jourdan** factory store, a brand now liquidated by the French government.

From there you may want to visit the **Shoe Museum,** or Museum International de la Chaussure, located in a former convent nearby, at rue Bistour, Romans (☎ **334/7505-5181;** www.ville-romans.com). The museum has over 13,000 items depicting 4,000 years of shoe-wearing. Open May, June and September Tuesday to Saturday 10am to 6pm; July and August Monday to Saturday 10am to 6pm. Note that the Shoe Museum is actually back on the Romans side of town, but I took you shopping and to McDo first and then sent you backward.

Exit town by following signs for A7. The road will wind and curve and go on for a while, then feed into the N7 before you hit the A7.

Is it worth the trouble? That depends on what size shoe you wear, the luck of the draw, the dollar-euro exchange rate and your patience. There were shoes at Charles Jourdan for 15€ ($20) when I looked a few days ago. They have to fit and you have to want them. I am thrilled with the no-name raffia sandals I bought for 50€ ($65). They aren't even my size and I still love them.

especially to collectors. Not that sneaker-ness is a guy thing, but the place is crawling with men—well, guys.

Note that this is a shop for experts who speak in tongues (and I don't mean shoe tongues). There is a language all of its own and a way of knowing what's cool and what just isn't. There are over a thousand pairs of shoes for sale here; some are gently worn and most are limited editions. The shoes are in excellent condition—there's none of that "Eeeek, I could get athlete's foot" sensation.

Obviously not all shoes come in all sizes. There's an entire wall of just Air Jordans. (Hey, just do it.) Prices range from $200 to $2,000 and while Air Jordan is the big ticket, there are various other mainstream brands as well as some of the lesser-known brands; even the Japanese T-shirt line Bathing Ape (p. 229) has shoes sold here.

WHERE TO BUY 2 stores. NYC: 254 Greene St., between 8th St. and Waverly Place. ☎ **212/505-2330.** Daily noon–7pm. AE, MC, V. LA: 503 N. Fairfax Ave., between Beverly and Melrose. ☎ **323/782-8616.** Mon–Sat 12:30–7pm; Sun 12:30–6pm. www.vintagekicks.com.

Onitsuka Tiger JAPANESE $$$$

This is a cult brand of sneakers first worn in the sixties and now very retro-chic, with arched leather beams in assorted colors dancing across a white body shoe.

WHERE TO BUY FLAGSHIP Shop 3025, Level B, Westfield Bondi Junction Mall, Sydney. ☎ **02/9389-8488.** Mon–Sat 10am–6pm. www.onitsukatiger.com.au.

Patta AMSTERDAM $$$–$$$$$

Not far from the Dam and within the central shopping district you'll find a typical Dutch storefront with a huge green sign pointing the way. The ground floor belongs to a hip streetwear firm called Ben G but upstairs (on what Europeans call the first floor and Americans call the second floor) is one of the great sneaker stores of the world.

BEST BETS They carry all the cool brands of shoes that you've never heard of, T's and clothing.

WHERE TO BUY Nieuwezijds Voorburgwal 142, Amsterdam. ☎ **3120/528-5994.** CB, MC, V. Mon, Tues, Wed, Fri, Sat noon–7pm; Thurs noon–9pm; Sun noon–6pm. www.patta.nl.

Mita Sneakers TOKYO $$–$$$$$

The most famous of the sneaker shops in the Ueno district of Tokyo is Mita, which sells the limited editions and the hard-to-find stuff at high prices. Hey, this is Tokyo. Cult stuff.

BEST BETS   If you need some leopard print Nikes, this is for you. Also collectible AF1's and New Balance.

WEB TIPS   It's in Japanese. *Sayonara.*

WHERE TO BUY   1 store: 4f Arrieyoko Center Bldg., 4-7-8 Ueno, Taito-ku, Tokyo. ☎ **813/3832-8346.** www.mita.co.jp.

Undefeated USA $$–$$$$

This is one of the most exciting stores in America and a lesson on what retail should be. The architecture is cool and inviting, a fountain runs through the store and into the courtyard, an electronic billboard sits on the roof beating out the vibe of the moment and the merchandise is hot—sneakers from all over the world. Merch is collectible.

BEST BETS   Custom Nikes made in agreement with Louis Vuitton and Gucci.

WHERE TO BUY   3 stores in Los Angeles, 1 in Las Vegas. 112 S. LaBrea. ☎ **323/937-6077.** Mon–Sat 10am–7pm; Sun 10am–6pm. AE, DISC, MC, V. www.undftd.com.

WALKING/DRIVING/STOMPING

Luchesse TEXAN $$$$–$$$$$

The most famous cowboy boots in Texas . . . and Hollywood, since Luchesse made boots for John Wayne and other cowboy movie stars. Pre-made boots cost about $450, but a pair of seriously arty custom-made boots can easily cost $6,000. A pair made for Johnny Cash recently sold at Sotheby's for over $10,000.

Sam Luchesse is most famous for the set of boots he made representing each state in the union, complete with flower, state seal and state icons all appliquéd on the boots. These often travel in a museum show.

When you have your boots made, you choose the skins as well as how elaborate you want the body, then the type of heel—for walking, for riding, or for dancing. (These boots were made for strutting.)

WHERE TO BUY   Western stores. www.luchesse.com.

Mephisto FRENCH $$$$

Traditionally speaking, Mephisto shoes have been ugly but sensible. In the past few years, they have spruced up the line a bit—but this is the shoe for the person who knows that comfort and support are far more important than fashion or style.

BEST BETS   There's walking shoes, sports shoes, city shoes, sandals and more, for about $150 a pair.

WEB TIPS   You cannot buy online.

WHERE TO BUY   600+ stores worldwide, with international distribution through their own stores, other shoe stores and department stores. www.mephisto.com.

Pataugas FRENCH $$$–$$$$

Sporty ballerinas made for walking; fisherman sandals with gold lamé; men's, women's and children's shoes that are soft on the feet but daring in design and the use of contrasting fabrics and textures such as canvas, silk, rubber and webbing.

BEST BETS   These are affordable ($85–$150) and exactly the kind of shoe you want to find when you are on the road—different and yet exciting.

WEB TIPS   In French; click *points de vente* for where to buy.

WHERE TO BUY   3 stores in France. 53 rue du Four, Paris 6e. ☎ **331/5363-0035.** 211 rue Saint Honore, Paris 1er. ☎ **331/4455-3007.** Also 15 passage Agard, Aix en Provence. ☎ **334/4254-2549.** www.pataugas.fr.

Tod's ITALIAN $$$$–$$$$$

Tod's puts some 133 rubber pebbles down there and has created an entirely new category of flat—the car shoe—which is copied all over the world. The moc comes in a variety of colors and some style modifications, so you always need new pairs to keep up with the Joneses. Note that the shoes run big so they recommend one half-size smaller than you normally take, especially with suede.

BEST BETS   A pair of Tod's will cost you over $300; I have bought most of my pairs at Century 21 in New York for $99 a pair. Always aim for an oddball color.

WEB TIPS   Must choose English USA or English International.

WHERE TO BUY   27 stores; in NYC, Vegas, Beverly Hills, Chicago, Honolulu, Tokyo, Moscow, Paris, more. **FLAGSHIP**   Via della Spiga 22, Milan. ☎ **3902/7600-2423.** Mon–Sat 10am–7pm. NYC: Madison Ave. at 60th St. ☎ **212/644-5945.** www.tods. com.

Suzhou Cobblers SHANGHAI $$–$$$$

The world's most elegant embroidered shoes (for men and women) are stitched up with bok choy, goldfish, flowers and

more. Brightly colored silk embroidery goes onto contrasting satin shoes that come with low heels or in flats. Shoes cost $50 to $75; tote bags—which are not embroidered like the shoes—cost $65.

The store is the size of my closet in Texas; the location is right off the famed Bund, around the corner from all the action and glam hotels.

Suzhou Cobblers Chinese shoes with orange strap.

BEST BETS   This is one of the best stores in the world. They will custom-make shoes; they will embroider your initials, they will embroider anything you want. Orders begin at $75.

WEB TIP   You can order online but prices are much lower in Shanghai.

WHERE TO BUY   1 store: 17 Fuzhou Rd., Room 101, Shanghai. ☎ **8621/6321-7087.** Daily 10am–6:30pm. MC, V. www.suzhou-cobblers.com.

Small Leather Goods & Totes

I am still trying to find the perfect wallet. The one that is the right size is the same one that doesn't fasten and opens up in my handbag. The one that fastens weighs a ton. My Judith Leiber has lost a gemstone. My yellow plastic job from some supermarket in Italy—the best wallet of my life—is all marked up with pen smootz and filthy seams. I cannot afford Goyard. I persevere. To keep my handbag from becoming too heavy, I also carry a tote bag. To keep my tote bag from becoming too heavy (that laptop weighs a ton) I also schlep a roll-y roll-y when I travel. And then there's the dog tote. Some day I'll just break down and get a team of donkeys with some deep-fitted panniers.

Aspinal BRITISH $$–$$$$

Small leather goods, travel wallets, passport cases, luggage tags—all in covetable colors of leather that are so sensational you may not mind paying $200 for the travel collection (a collection of three items: passport case, travel wallet and luggage tag). Passport cases come in several colors and with the imprint of a variety of countries on the cover. The firm also makes albums, portfolios, pens, wallets and various other accessories for men and women. Their leather range is large and even includes leather jewelry boxes.

BEST BETS   The passport covers ($70) are delectable.

WEB TIPS   Shipping to the U.S. or Canada is via DHL and costs about $22. Since they have no store, you can order online or by phone.

WHERE TO BUY   Online or by phone: UK ☎ **0808/144-3302,** or 888/325-3302 toll free in the U.S. www.aspinaloflondon.com.

Goyard FRENCH $$$$–$$$$$

Proving that fashion is ephemeral, style is forever, marketing is king and Paris knows everything, the 100+ year old firm of Goyard—of cult status since before Louis Vuitton—now has the It tote and wallet of the in-set jet-set. Goyard has always had a signature print on their impregnated canvas; it's something of a stylized Y.

In the late 1990s, the Signoles family bought the firm and promptly took this quality, cult, little-known luggage and small leather goods firm into the new century by simply changing the color combinations and adding some stripes, monograms and

Buyer Beware

This brand is now sold in every fakes market from New York to China—and the fakes are horrible.

stencils. The results are the hottest thing in Paris, maybe the planet. Just watch out for the fakes, which really cheapen the brand.

Tote bags start at $800; handbags are in the $2,400 range—then you add on the extra for personalization, and so forth.

Insider's tip: There's a shorter waiting list at the Bergdorf Goodman store than in Paris.

BEST BETS   When I rob a bank, I get to buy it all. The wallet ($600) is very nice because it's large—good for euro bills. Don't forget the luggage ($1,000 and up, up, up). The dog leashes come in solid leather, not the house monogram. Drat. But wait, you can get a travel kit of folding chow dish and water dish encased in the monogram for only $600.

WEB TIPS   The site is easy to use and the images are clear but you cannot shop online.

WHERE TO BUY   2 stores; in Barneys and Bergdorf's in the U.S. **FLAGSHIP**   233 rue Saint Honoré, Paris, 1er. Métro: Tuileries. Mon 2–7pm; Tues–Sat 11am–7pm. ☎ **331/4260-5704.** San Francisco: 345 Powell St., Union Sq. ☎ **415/398-1110.** Mon–Sat 10am–6pm; Sun noon–5pm. AE, MC, V. www.goyard.com.

Hervé Chapelier FRENCH $$–$$$$

This is a cult object, an object of desire as well as a status item to the preppy and BCBG crowd. Chapelier makes flat nylon tote bags with bucket bottoms, in all sizes, many color combinations, often with leather handles or trim. Sturdy and classic must-have. For some reason beyond my grasp, they also sell cashmere sweaters. The sweater is your call. Trust me on your need for a tote from the source.

BEST BETS   The weekender is without doubt the best buy you'll make. Prices range from $100 to $250 depending on size.

WEB TIPS   You can shop online and arrange delivery to the E.U., the U.S. and those parts of Scandinavia in the E.U.

WHERE TO BUY   6 stores in Paris; some department and specialty stores. **FLAGSHIP**   390 rue Saint Honore, Paris 1er. ☎ **01/42-96-38-04.** Métro: Concorde. Mon-–Sat 10am–7pm. AE, MC, V. www.hervechapelier.com.

Lodis.com ⌐ USA/SPANISH

Lodis was created by Loewe of Spain and designer Dan Segat. (Lo + DS = Lodis.) They make high quality leather goods in styles similar to Hermès at a fraction of the price.

BEST BUYS   Check out the faux-crocodile leather piece that doubles as wallet and evening clutch ($115).

Shanghai Tang CHINESE $$–$$$

World's Best   This lifestyle store makes handbags, totes and small leather goods including an excellent passport case that is wide and has a full wraparound zip—hard to find in a passport case—for $150. See p. 57.

Sherpa USA $$–$$$$

Although Sherpa is primarily a dog-goods source, they do make travel gear and totes. I bought the best tote of my life at Tuesday Morning (p. 313) for $25 because it had wheels. I thought I had bought a dog tote with wheels but when I got home I discovered my mistake and was delighted to have a way to schlep my laptop. I just got lucky in terms of the price.

WHERE TO BUY   Most pet supply stores in the U.S. ☎ 800/743-7723 or 973/625-5900. www.sherpapet.com.

Smythson BRITISH $$–$$$$

With a royal warrant and a worldwide rep for their luxury goods, Smythson easily branched from paper goods to leather desk accessories to small leather goods and then even to handbags. No problem.

BEST BETS   A passport case made from imprinted calf that looks like croc (read: not real croc) costs $510.

WEB TIPS   You can shop online and in the currency of your choice; wide selection of items available.

WHERE TO BUY   FLAGSHIP   40 New Bond S., London W1. ☎ 4420/7629-8558. Mon–Wed, Fri 9:30am–6pm; Thurs 10am–7pm; Sat 10am–6pm. Tube: Bond St. NYC: 4 W. 57th St. ☎ 212/265-4573. Mon–Wed, Fri–Sat 10am–6pm; Thurs 10am–7pm. AE, MC, V. Subway: 57th St. www.smythson.com.

Un Jour Un Sac PARIS $$$$

This is a brilliant concept and, if you can afford it, a way to be more with-it than anyone you know. This small store right near the Elysees Palace in Paris, a step off the famed Faubourg St. Honoré, sells tote bodies and straps—you buy them separately and then you mix and match. This exercise is not inexpensive; it pays to spend a little more and get *detaxe* than to buy the least expensive item and not qualify for *detaxe*. That means your entry price is about $100 for the *sac* (main tote) and $100 for the *poignee* (straps)—but prices go way up from there. It's not unreasonable to pay $600 for several parts that can be interchanged. Extra straps become a great gift for anyone who uses this system.

The *sac* comes in various sizes in leather, canvas, and assorted plastics and fabrics. Straps come in a variety of materials and lengths. With six you get wonton.

BEST BETS   Mix-and-match items beginning at $200. Oprah loves 'em.

WEB TIPS   Site is in French. You need Macro Media Player.

WHERE TO BUY   1 store: 6 rue Saussies, Paris, 8e. ☎ **331/ 4265-0033.** Métro: Champs Elysees Clemenceau. Mon 2–6pm; Tues–Sat 11am–7pm. MC, V. www.unjourunsac.com.

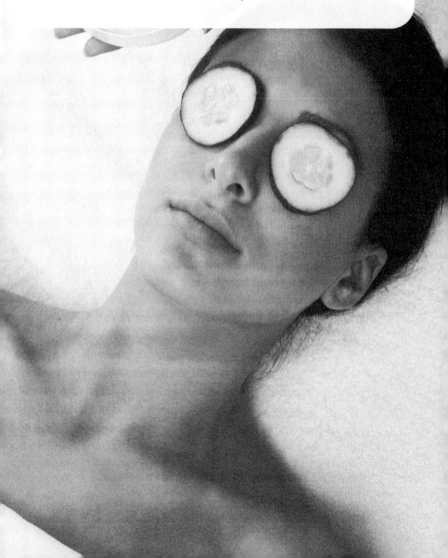

Chapter Six

Beauty

*I*f you think that beauty is only skin deep, you're not very into the business world. Beauty is billions of dollars, pounds, euros, yen and yuan deep. And that's just on the surface.

In France, it's not even called the beauty business any more. It's all about *bien être,* well-being. Maybe that comes from the fact that there's more and more doubts about if creams, lotions or potions actually do anything to you physically; we can only vouch for the psychological benefits, for our own personal well-being.

So what we have is a sociological factor and a cultural revolution the likes of which Chairman Mao could never imagine. Pharmaceutical companies produce makeup and beauty treatments, designers produce makeup and beauty treatments, dermatologists produce beauty treatments and sometimes makeup and most importantly, many of these products come from the same factories.

I sell hope in a jar.
—Helena Rubenstein

Many years ago, when I learned that couture loses money for the design houses each year, I questioned why couture still existed. This question was met with total disdain from insiders. Couture, and big design houses, exist for the money to be made from the fragrance . . . and the beauty products.

Spritz me again, you fool.

Aromatherapy

What you smell can influence your health and your mood. While aromatherapy is not considered a science, the use of plants, flowers and herbs for medicinal purposes is thousands of years old.

Bach Flower Essences PARIS/GERMAN $–$$

Roll over Beethoven; I'm talkin' flower power and aromatherapy, not music from that other guy. This is Dr. Edward Bach, an Englishman, who counts many celebs among his clients and has one very famous product—Rescue Remedy—and many oils and essences and treatments that you can mix yourself into your own version of Love Potion no 9.

🖱 Online Beauty

Beautyhabit.com
Specializing in hard-to-find and cult brands. There is a brick-and-mortar store at 2991 E. Thousand Oaks Blvd., Thousand Oaks, CA. (☎ 805/496-1011). The website is easy to use. I was impressed that they have Carthusia, a really esoteric perfume brand from Capri. Free shipping on orders of $100 or more.

Beautystore.com
This is a fabulous website, a very complete source for professional beauty brands. That's the good news. The bad news is that they are expensive. I buy Wella gel hair color at Sally's for $4.70 a tube; it is $6.50 on this site. If you want a more complete selection than what Sally's carries, or you don't have the chance to get these products for less money, you might want to spend some time exploring this site.

Note the flat rate of $5 for shipping on all U.S. orders.

Drugstore.com
Much like a giant drugstore, this Web-only site offers the expected health, beauty and well-being products but has a department store–like breadth with diet products, pet goods, contraceptives and sex toys, contact lenses, jewelry, gifts and so on. I don't find the site graphically pleasing, but hey, who cares?

Sephora.com
Let's stop arguing over how to pronounce this source (I say SEPH-a-rah but most seem to say Se-PHOR-ah). Pronunciation isn't important, but selection is. Not only will you find all your favorite brands here, including Sephora's own makeup, they'll throw in three free samples of your choice with every online order. If you can't make it to a Sephora retailer, this is almost as good. Check out the list of most popular items and their new product launches.

Skinstore.com
I think this is the best of the online sources because they carry a ton of brands, many of them hard to find. They have a policy whereby with certain items and/or brands you can "stock up and save," which gives you a price break on multiples.

There are some 38 different floral essences, each with properties to aid health or elicit cures homeopathically. They are usually sold in small bottles with eye-droppers, the idea being that a little dab will do ya.

BEST BETS Rescue Remedy (or "Urgences"), often used for jet lag, is made of 5 key ingredients: impatiens, Star of Bethlehem, clematia, cherry plum, and rock rose. This product is meant to be used during times of greatest stress and can be put directly onto the tongue or consumed in a glass of warm water. It is also available in spray form or cream. A travel-size bottle costs about $12. *Note:* This product is often used for pets, too.

WEB TIPS   Excellent website which allows you to buy online or simply learn more about Dr. Bach and his formulations. There are links to each of the ingredients and their properties.

WHERE TO BUY   1 store; drug stores, health stores, some department stores. Le Fleurs de Bach, 11 blvd. Port-Royal, Paris, 13e. ☎ **331/4707-3888.** Mon–Sat 10:30am–2pm and 3–7pm. MC, V. Métro: Port Royal. www.bachfloweressences.com.

Decléor FRENCH $$–$$$

This French line treats everything with flower or herbal infused oils. Wrinkles? A little oil of rose will do the trick. As goop goes, this stuff is expensive. Since a little dab will do you, it actually can amortize out even though the 100ml size bottle of product will cost around $50. If you don't want to dab it on yourself, perhaps you need one of the Decléor Spas—try the Sofitel hotel in Paris or in LA.

BEST BETS   Aromessence Circularome (rub it in to get maximum benefits), about $40.

WEB TIPS   Website is in French but guides you to U.S. offices in Darien, CT. ☎ **888/414-4471.**

WHERE TO BUY   Department stores around the world, fancy pharmacies in Europe and some spas. www.decleor.fr.

Durance FRENCH $–$$

World's Best

The firm makes candles, soaps, creams, bath products and aromatherapy—all are natural and made with French fruits, flowers and herbs. The best place to find product in Paris is their store near the place de la Madeline; there is also a store in Marseille. The brand is fairly well distributed throughout Provence, even in TTs (tourist traps).

BEST BETS   The lavender hand cream is thick and deeply infused with lavender. It costs $25 but is the best hand cream you will ever buy.

World Traveler

There's a factory store alongside the factory in Provence; the discount is only about 10%, so the savings might not be worth the gas. On the other hand, Grignan is one of the most adorable villages in France—this is in the *Drome Provencale, departement 26.* See www.tourisme-paysdegrignan.com.

WEB TIPS Click on English or French language. Although you can shop online, shipping is only in France.

WHERE TO BUY Specialty stores throughout France. **FLAGSHIP** 24 rue Vignon, Paris, 9e. ☎ **331/47-42-04-10.** Mon–Sat 10:30am–4pm and 4:30–7pm. MC, V. Métro: Madeleine. Factory store: route Montelimar, ZA Dagasse, Grignan. Mon 2–6pm; Tues–Sat 10am–12:30pm and 2–6pm; July and Aug, daily 10am–7pm. www.durance.fr.

Kiss My Face USA VALUE $

So there I was, all those years ago, shivering and sweating my way through a fever, unable to concentrate on the magazines I was leafing through, wanting my Mommy (still dead), aching all over. In walks the husband with a bottle of something called Kiss My Face Cold & Flu Bath. How could you not love a product with a name like that?

This brand has changed a bit recently, with new packaging and over 200 products, including those for shaving and skin care.

BEST BETS Cold & Flu is a clear goop, something like liquid Vicks with a strong smell of eucalyptus and rosemary that will

Kiss My Face "Cold & Flu Bath."

cure anything. At $8 for a large bottle, this is the best gift you can give anyone or buy for yourself. In fact, this is one of the best products in the world.

WHERE TO BUY Whole Foods, health food stores, some drug and grocery stores. ☎ **800/262-KISS.** www.kissmyface.com.

Bath Mavens

Rubba dub dub, three men in a tub? I don't think so; there wouldn't be room for me, them and all my bath products. Baths have come a long way since my childhood—they are considered sensuous, they are considered a spa activity, a couples sport, a treatment method. In France, you can even buy products that when poured into your bath water will help you lose weight. Decléor makes one. Could I make this up? Actually, it didn't work for me so I haven't listed it here but Decléor is a good brand; see p. 162.

Note, if you aren't a bath person, many of these firms make products that work as shower gel.

The Best Spa Treatments of My Life

Best Overall Spa Experience: I spent four days at **Caudalie Wine Spa,** at Chemin de Smith Haut Lafitte, Martillac-Bordeaux, France (☎ 335/5783-1122; www.caudalie.com), and when I wasn't soaking in wine barrels or being pounded with cabernet sauvignon, I could use as much of the products in the dressing rooms as I wanted. I was quickly addicted. I love the Gommage Crushed Cabernet ($42) and the Vino Perfect Serum ($60); buy at Neiman Marcus or Sephora, or order online.

Best Spa Treatment: For the **"Celebrate the Seasons"** treatment at the Four Seasons Resort Aviara, 7100 Four Seasons Point, Carlsbad, CA (☎ 760/603-6800; www.fourseasons.com), four different earth elements were massaged into my body and hair to restore me to total balance. I was wrapped, scrubbed, massaged and soothed for 80 minutes ($200). View spa menus and book online, or purchase products by **La Natura** (www.lanatura.com).

Best Jet-Lag Spa Treatment After Long Haul: The **Peninsula Hotel Hong Kong,** Salisbury Road, Kowloon (☎ 86852/2920-2888; www.hongkong.peninsula.com), has opened **E-spa** in a space that is so soothing you melt into your treatment or just lounge on a terry bed and sip tea and stare at China. Prices begin at $100. **Note:** I have just tested the E-spa at the Peninsula Bangkok and found it lavish and dreamy but not the same earth shattering, emotional experience as in Hong Kong.

Best Mud Products: The Napa area is famous for its wine and, yup, its mud. Retire to the 16-acre **Indian Springs,** 1712 Lincoln Avenue, Calistoga, CA (☎ 707/942-4913; www.indianspringscalistoga.com), and get the mud treatments ($75). This is one of the few spas in the area that uses real and proper product. You can also buy products online, $8.50 for 5oz of "pure ash" or $19 for 8.7oz of "volcanic mud mask." The robes (terry on the inside, seersucker on the outside; $86) are also among the best robes you may ever slip into. Rates for property bungalows are $185 to $550.

Best Water Massage: When the **Watermark Hotel,** 212 W. Crockett St., San Antonio, TX (☎ 210/223-8500; www.watermark hotel.com), right in my hometown, was named among the best spas in the U.S., I began to stutter and shake because I knew nothing, zip, about them. I found out: After the 90-minute Rain Massage—one of the best of my life—I slithered out, still smelling of lavender and coffee. I also swoon for the avocado and lime scalp and body treatment. Book far in advance.

Jo Malone BRITISH $$$$

World's Best

Jo Malone has created about a dozen different scents. They come in a variety of beauty and bath products as well as directly in fragrance. One of the nicest items in the range is a sampler kit of all the scents; this costs about $150 and makes a great gift for the woman who has everything. On the other hand, I gave this gift to a woman in Beverly Hills who has everything. Unfortunately, she had never heard of the brand and did not understand what a generous or luxurious gift I had offered.

The line is carried in Neiman Marcus stores; there is a freestanding flagship in the U.S. in Manhattan with expansion being planned throughout major U.S. cities. **Best trick**: Hotel amenities are made for the Mandarin Oriental in London; tip the housekeeper to bring you extras.

World Traveler

Here's one of the few good buys you'll find in the UK. Jo Malone is about 30% less expensive there, even with a bad rate of exchange.

BEST BETS   Lime & Basil anything, beginning around $72.

WEB TIPS   You can buy directly online but prices are in sterling; you do better to buy from Saks or Neiman. Prices are in U.S. dollars and are higher than in sterling, but you don't have the shipping problem.

WHERE TO BUY   Some international department stores such as Bon Marche in Paris, la Rinascente in Milan; 23 freestanding stores worldwide. **FLAGSHIP**   150 Sloane St., SW1, London. ☎ 207/730-2885. NYC: 949 Broadway at Fifth Ave., Flatiron Building. ☎ 212/673-2220. Mon–Sat 10am–8pm; Sun noon–6pm. AE, DISC, MC, V. Subway: N or R to 23rd St. www.jomalone.com.

LUSH BRITISH $

With a strong understanding of trade dress, each LUSH store is set up like a deli—freshly made beauty products are sold from a fridge or on crushed ice, as if dispensed from a salad bar. Home made soaps come in loaves and wheels and are cut as if they were cheese. The distinctive aroma of the store is enough to send an asthmatic into convulsions.

BEST BETS   I always return to the cinnamon and spice scent of Red Rooster soap, my favorite product. The best gimmick of them all is called a "bath bomb" or "bath ball" (*bomb* not as popular a word as it once was)—it's a giant Alka-Seltzer for the bath and comes in various shades and flavors ($4).

World Traveler

In the U.S., the product comes from Canada in accordance with FDA laws, so you're not getting the original recipe. In a few countries, local ingredients are used and specific products are developed—especially in Italian LUSH stores.

WEB TIPS   Click on any of 31 flags for language translations. The site is a lot like the products—hot and fun and bubbly.

WHERE TO BUY   400+ stores, in London, NYC, Santa Monica, San Francisco, Scottsdale, Aspen, Miami, and more. **FLAGSHIP**   123 Kings Rd., London SW3. ☎ 207/ 376-8348. Mon–Sat 10am–7pm. AE, MC, V. Tube: Sloane Sq. 65 other stores in the UK. NYC: 1293 Broadway (at 34th St.). ☎ 212/564-9120. Mon–Sat 9am–10pm; Sun 10am–8pm. Subway: Herald Square. www.lush.com.

Original Source BRITISH   VALUE $

World's Best   This is a British brand that has no distribution in the U.S., which is a terrible shame verging on the criminal. How can anyone live without Tea Tree & Mint shower gel, I ask you?

The shower gel is great for shaving the legs (has a nice tingle to it) and is especially splendid for a cooling shower after sporting activities or on hot and humid days. If you live through summer without air-conditioning, you can't go any further in life without Tea Tree & Mint shower gel. Cost is about $4 for a large bottle. Often, when I am looking for a great gift for the person who has everything, I give a selection of three or four different scents. There are shampoos, hair conditioners, deodorants, bath gels, bath foams, body mousse and lotions in the range.

BEST BETS   Tea Tree & Mint anything, without question, about $4 a bottle. The lavender Tea Tree is very, very nice; lemon is good and fresh—great for guys.

WEB TIPS   You can sign on and get a free sample, but only if you live in the UK or have a UK mailing address.

WHERE TO BUY   You can buy yours at Boots, SuperDrug and Tesco in the UK. www.originalsource.co.uk.

Beauty Departments & Supermarkets

When the world was flat, you went to department stores for premium makeup brands and drug stores for low-cost brands. (You also stole a Tangee lipstick from the drugstore as a coming-of-age ritual, but that is another subject entirely.) In those days, retail was about serving the needs of the customers.

Salt of the Earth, Part 1

So there I am, prowling the shops of St. Wolfgang, Austria, which may not be on your radar screen (big mistake), and the stores are cute in a Heidi sort of way until I walk into this salt store and almost fall over in stunned disbelief. This is what retail is all about! This is something I have never seen before! Completely devoted to one product, **Benediktiner Salzkontor,** Pilgerstrasse A-5360, St. Wolfgang (☎ **43061/382-8270**), is a rustic little boutique which sells salt products mostly for health and beauty, although there are also eating varieties. The bath salts (about $6)—with 84 different natural elements in crystals the size of the Ritz—all come with instructions, which you should pay attention to; if you do it properly, the boiling water is hot enough to release the minerals inside the salts and you'll never need krypton. See www.frommers.com/destinations/st wolfgang for more on St. Wolfgang.

I discovered **Hervy Gilles Sel Naturel de Guerande (☎ 3302/ 4015-5969;** no website) at a small fair in Paris and have been going back twice a year to buy more salts. This is magic in a bottle. He makes three different flavors—Lavender for sleep, Eucalyptus for breathing and Arnica for pain. After the salted bath, you are advised to rest in a prone position for 20 minutes. Buy directly from his booth every Sunday at the Bio Marche on Blvd. Raspail, Paris 6e, from 9am to 1pm (only 9€, or $15, for a big tub of the stuff).

Kneipp (www.kneipp.de; say "Neep"), created in 1891, has often saved me from jet lag. After a long-haul flight, I bathe with the travel-size Rosemary gel ($4.50 for about 3 baths) or bath tablet (7 for $22). The bath salts come in Spruce, Lavender, Melissa and more ($18 for about 10 baths). This is one of those lines that costs less in Europe than in the U.S. Order online or buy at Bath and Body Works and other beauty shops.

For more "Salt of the Earth" (the edible kind), see p. 392.

Now it's about show business, and department stores are fighting their wars for customers with unique specialty makeup brands. In Europe this means U.S. brands; in the U.S. it means Asian or European brands.

Boyd's NYC $–$$$

Attention Boyd's fans, we've got the update; and out of loyalty to what Boyd's used to be, I list it here although I have not been able to do a personal inspection before we go to press.

Okay, history and background: Boyd's was a European-style drugstore and beauty mart right smack on Madison

Avenue in the middle of everything. The store did well, gave up the Mad mad mad world and opened two stores, one on Third Avenue and one on the West Side of Manhattan. Then something went wrong; those stores closed.

Now Boyd's has a showroom—open to the public—for wholesale and retail orders, and yes, you can go in just to browse.

BEST BETS   The store has been famous for its hard-to-find European brands, although I always loved it because of the hair accessories.

WHERE TO BUY   1 store: 385 Fifth Avenue at 36th St., Suite 808, NYC. ☎ **917/217-9245.** Mon–Sat 9am–6pm. AE, DISC, MC, V. Subway: 42nd St. www.boydsnyc.com.

Beauty Monop   PARIS $

Not to let Sephora take all the glory or all the floor space, the French dime store Monoprix has reversed the concept and come up with a winner. The first of their beauty-only store is in Montmartre and serves a hip residential customer as well as tourists who are wandering around near Sacre Coeur.

Divided into seven zones and selling some 3,500 different items, the store has products for men and women with an area of new and novel items right up front.

BEST BETS   Tons of Bourjois (p. 173) and other low- to mid-priced brands; check out Nacara—a Canadian line for multi-ethnic skin.

WEB TIPS   You cannot buy online; the information is in French on the corporate Galeries Lafayette site—Galeries owns Monoprix.

WHERE TO BUY   1 store: 28 rue des Abbesses, Paris, 18e. ☎ **331/ 4252-8961.** Mon–Sat 10am–8pm. CB, MC, V. Métro: Abbesses. www.groupegl.com.

Brownes & Co. Apothecary   MIAMI $–$$

This large shop carries every brand you can think of and plenty you've never heard of.

BEST BETS   Because the store is located right in the thick of the Miami Beach shopping, strolling and dining experience, you can even go out for dinner, wander around and end up shopping here. Now that's a perfect evening.

WEB TIPS   Shop online by category of goods or by brand. There are many hard-to-find brands.

WHERE TO BUY   1 store: 841 Lincoln Rd., Miami Beach, FL. ☎ **888- BROWNES.** Mon–Fri 9:30am–9pm; Sat and Sun 9:30am–10pm. AE, DISC, MC, V. www.brownesbeauty.com.

Printemps FRENCH $–$$$$

This is a little confusing, so pay attention. The flagship Printemps department store in Paris is composed of three buildings. The one called Printemps Maison (home) is the one that features the beauty department. Go figure.

Beauty takes up the entire ground floor plus a mezzanine and is the largest in continental Europe. It is also among the more interesting partly because of the array of brands and partly because the French mix up designer beauty brands with pharmacy brands with hair treatments and skin care and spas and nails and various known and unknown brands of color cosmetics.

BEST BETS   Don't miss the mezzanine. Shoppers can get a discount card at the welcome desk or online for savings and additional savings if you qualify for *detaxe.*

WEB TIPS   Excellent site, in English and very tourist forward— you can even print out a discount card for a 10% discount on purchases in the store, including beauty and perfume brands. Shipping only within France.

WHERE TO BUY   20 blvd. Haussmann, Paris, 9e. ☎ **331/4282-5000.** Mon–Sat 9:30am–7pm; Thurs 9:30am–10pm. AE, MC, V. Métro: Havre Caumartin. www.printemps.com.

Selfridge's BRITISH $–$$$$

The flagship of this store in London is the mother of all beauty departments, possibly the largest in the world. There are no surprises here—only high prices due to the currently weak U.S. dollar. If price is not an object and you are looking to wade through more product than you can imagine exists, this is your mecca.

BEST BETS   Finding brands you've never heard of.

WEB TIPS   When you click on a brand, you are connected to its website for buying.

WHERE TO BUY   FLAGSHIP   400 Oxford St., London W1. ☎ **4420/7318-3730.** AE, MC, V. Mon–Wed 8am–8pm; Thurs 9am–9pm; Fri and Sat 8am–8pm; Sun noon–6pm. Tube: Bond St. www.selfridges.com.

Sephora FRENCH $–$$$

In France, we say "Seph-a-rah." In the U.S., we say "Se-For-ah." I say tomato you say tomah-to—it's all the same when you're having a shopping moment, believe me.

Although Sephora is now a global brand owned by a luxury conglomerate, the best is in the Champs Elysées flagship, which is a supermarket of beauty products conveniently laid out on one floor with wide aisles, easy-to-use signage and adorable salesgirls in cute little uniforms. Of course, some of the U.S. stores are extraordinary too. Been to Vegas lately? Now that's entertainment!

Conceptually, one of the best things about Sephora is that all stores are not exactly alike and the product mix does reflect the destination. Even within any given destination, the product mix will reflect the postal code or the profile of the shoppers in that neighborhood.

BEST BETS   The pharmaceutical lines and the hair care lines are plentiful; the house brands of color cosmetics and bath products offer excellent value.

WHERE TO BUY   560 stores worldwide. **FLAGSHIP**   74 Champs Elysées, Paris, 8e. ☎ **331/5393-2250.** Daily 10am–midnight. Metro: F.D. Roosevelt. NYC: 1500 Broadway. ☎ **212/944-6789.** Daily 10am–midnight. AE, MC, V. Subway: Times Sq. Other cities include: San Francisco, Dallas, Chicago, Monte Carlo, Rome. www.sephora.com.

SpaceNK Apothecary   BRITISH $$–$$$$

This is a boutique more than a supermarket, but they specialize in cult brands—many of them American and French—for the UK market. But just when you thought you had it figured out—they go and open in New York. Perhaps there's one coming to a theatre near you.

The company strives to discover new talent, so you may find something new here. For UK shoppers, of course. The new-ness has often been American brands, which cost more in the UK than the U.S., so this isn't necessarily a store for U.S. residents to frequent while in London. On the other hand, they are constantly adding and changing and also have a variety of French brands. There's a new spa, SpaNK, 127 Westbourne Grove (☎ **4420/7727-8002**).

BEST BETS   The selection of unique brands. I'm in love with the seaweed bath crystals but at $36 for a container, I am not seriously in love.

WEB TIPS   Unless you have just robbed the Bank of England, you do not want to shop in BPS. A bottle of Phyto shampoo costs $23 because of the dollar/pound exchange rate. (The same shampoo costs $13 in France.)

WHERE TO BUY   60 stores in London, NYC, more. **FLAGSHIP**   307 Brompton Rd., London SW3. ☎ **4420/7589-8250.** Mon–Sat

10am–6pm; Thurs 10am–7pm; Sun noon–5pm. AE, CB, MC, V. Tube: South Kensington. www.spacenk.co.uk.

Ulta USA $–$$$

Whooooaaaa, Nelly! as they say in old-fashioned movies. Ulta is a Sephora manqué that has so much more to offer—a professional salon, professional hair color goods, serious hair care equipment, videos and DVDs for diet and health and a mix of both dime store brands and cult makeup and care brands.

The store I visited was enormous and left me breathless. You can join their club and get coupons for discounts on future purchases. This was one of the inspection highs of my entire career. It's possible I just caught a good store. Salon services are low-key and moderately priced—you choose between a "designer" ($40) and a "master" ($50).

Buyer Beware

A recent issue of *Consumer Reports* gave the website very low marks, saying prices were high and shipping prices were outrageous.

BEST BETS   The mix of low-end with high-end and perfume on top of that.

WEB TIPS   Free shipping on orders of $50 or more.

WHERE TO BUY   Stores in 36 states; most often located in malls or strip malls. www.ulta.com.

Beauty Supply Stores

Beauty supply stores are for the trade, for professionals who know what they are doing, so to shop in one is heady entry into a secret world for which we may not know the password. On the other hand, this is a growing category of regular retail, so many sell trade and consumer goods. Anyone can shop.

Larchmont Beauty Supply LOS ANGELES $–$$

The husband-and-wife team who run this place are very friendly and knowledgeable—I often take advice. Professional hair products and colors are also sold; there is a full-service salon in the rear.

BEST BETS   The amount of interesting product is overwhelming; there are a lot of hard-to-find brands here.

WEB TIPS   The website doesn't begin to give you a feel for the store; it just lists product brands and services and suggests you call.

WHERE TO BUY 1 store: 208 N. Larchmont Blvd., Los Angeles, CA. ☎ **323/461-0162.** Mon–Sat 8:30am–8pm; Sun 11am–6pm. MC, V. www.larchmontbeauty.com.

Ricky's USA (VALUE) $

Ricky's creates its own house line of products and sells wigs, hair accessories and just about anything else that's fun, funky and unusual, including body glitter in every color imaginable. This is a must-stop for Halloween products.

BEST BETS   The range of merchandise makes this more like a beauty candy store and they do have professional brands.

WEB TIPS   For a few months before Halloween, you can also shop at www.ricksyhalloween.com.

WHERE TO BUY   15 stores in New York, 2 in Florida. **FLAGSHIP** 509 Fifth Ave., near 42nd St., NYC. ☎ **212/949-7230.** Mon–Fri 9am–8pm; Sat 10am–7pm; Sun 11am–7pm. AE, DISC, MC, V. Subway: B, D, F or V to 42nd St./Bryant Park. www.rickys-nyc.com.

Color Cosmetics & Cult Brands

Color cosmetics have only a handful of different stories:

- price;
- scientific breakthroughs;
- palette

In the long run, I'm not sure that there is a lot of difference between the Lancôme makeup I buy at the duty-free in Paris and the L'Oréal I buy in the U.S. drugstore—both come from the same factories. So in the end, this gets to be a matter of gimmicks . . . and the above three factors.

Avon USA (VALUE) $–$$

Best known for good quality products at sensible prices and a representative who came into your home and showed you what you needed and how to use it, Avon also has some break-through products that set the industry standard.

BEST BETS   Those who like to test anti-aging treatments should dabble with Anew Alternative, which tests very well with magazine editors and retails for an affordable price, $32 for 1.7 oz.

WHERE TO BUY   To find the representative nearest you, call the toll-free number, ☎ **800/FOR AVON.** In Canada, call 800/265-2866 or go to www.Avon.ca.

Armani ITALIAN/FRENCH $$–$$$

The line was originally developed by the British makeup artist Pat McGrath, who has another line now, BTW. It is made by Lancôme, so that you can argue that the same products are available for less in the Lancôme or L'Oréal label. Skin care has just been added to the line.

BEST BETS   Their pearlized, light reflecting foundation makes me feel that I look 5 years younger. With makeup, perception is everything. It's worth the $50.

WEB TIPS   The trick here is to shop at www.giorgioarmanibeauty-usa.com, not the regular Armani site. If you "join" by registering your name on their database, you qualify for free shipping.

WHERE TO BUY   The line is sold in some department stores in the U.S. and Europe, at some Sephora stores and at large Armani stores.

By Terry FRENCH $$$$

By Terry is an astonishing line—it is unbelievably expensive with a very status-oriented cult following. On the other hand, I can see the temptation. While the line is carried in Barneys in the U.S., I shop for it in Paris where you get a custom-pack made up for your needs from the existing ready-to-wear makeup, or you get a custom blend. The custom blend can cost up to $500 for a bottle of liquid foundation. Why, you ask, would anyone pay this? Well, it has to do with how the makeup refracts light, which of course makes you look better.

   If I were a player, I would open my handbag frequently and retrieve a By Terry compact with which to powder my nose.

BEST BETS   There is a ready-to-wear line; prices begin at $125.

WEB TIPS   The site is geared to the UK. For U.S. orders try www.shopstyle.com or www.barneys.com.

WHERE TO BUY   Stores in Paris and Moscow; Saks, Sephora, other department stores worldwide. **FLAGSHIP**   36 Passage Vero-Dodat, Paris, 1er. ☎ **331/4476-0076.** Mon 2–7pm; Tues–Sat 10:30am–7pm. MC, V. Métro: Louvre. www.byterry.com.

Bourjois FRENCH ⌐VALUE⌐ $

World's Best   You've heard of Chanel, sure, but Bourjois? Smart shoppers the world over, pay attention. Bourjois is the name of the company that owns the Chanel brand of makeup and perfume; it makes a lower priced line of makeup under the Bourjois name—at the same factories where Chanel is manufactured.

This doesn't mean that the lines are identical, but if you can't afford Chanel and want to give this line a whirl, you may be pleased with the investment (about 50% less expensive than Chanel).

BEST BETS   For starters: Many, many shades of eye shadow are sold in big containers, which last forever, for $11. The nail polishes and lipsticks are also good. Women in France discuss the mascara ($14) as if in prayer.

WHERE TO BUY   All major department stores; some Sephora and Ulta stores in U.S.; Monoprix in France; Boots in the UK. www.bourjoisusa.com.

Chanel FRENCH $–$$

World's Best   I often confess that I belong to a cult—I love just about everything Chanel. Chanel makeup is, yes, bought by people who want the glamour and the status, but is, bottom line, a very good product. I discovered it when I worked on the set of the TV show *Dallas*. Victoria Principal was allergic to stage makeup, so the makeup artist switched to Chanel. Victoria looked so good on-camera that soon everyone was using Chanel. Because I know the Bourjois trick (above), it's sometimes hard to pay the steep prices for this brand—but often I think I'm worth it.

BEST BETS   I invariably splurge on the eyeliner pencils, the concealer, the foundation and the nail polish.

WEB TIPS   Click on "beauty & fragrance"; note that the cult fragrances are not sold online. If you join the Insiders Club you get notification by e-mail of new products and events.

WHERE TO BUY   Chanel boutiques, department stores and duty-free stores worldwide. I buy duty free (and save 10%) at Catherine in Paris (p. 411); they ship to the U.S.

MAC USA/CANADIAN [VALUE] $

World's Best   Yeah, I agree that it's a little bit hard to call MAC a cult brand since there's now a store in every big mall in America, but when this was a Canadian line—back before Estée Lauder bought it—this was a makeup artists' cult brand that became popular because the colors are good; they last a long time.

MAC makes an excellent concealer and assortment of textures in moisturizers to help even out and smooth skin. This is really the only makeup brand you need in the world.

BEST BETS   You can buy a very nice eye shadow for $14. This is the most affordable designer makeup made.

WEB TIPS   Try www.maccosmetics.ca for Canada, www.maccosmetics.de for Germany and so on.

Asian, Black & Hispanic Skin Products

For women of color, there are more and more brands of makeup geared to the variations in skin tone. **Mary Kay** Cosmetics (www.marykay.com) sells most of their product to black women and has developed its line accordingly.

Cover Girl (www.covergirl.com) has expanded to cover (excuse the pun) Hispanic, Asian and black skin tones. They have recently launched the Queen line—Queen Latifah is the spokeswoman—with shades from "sand" to "ebony."

Lancôme (www.lancome.com) and its younger sister brand **l'Oréal** (www.loreal.com) each have a line of "true match" foundations to match any skin tone. My girlfriend Janelle, who is Chinese, uses **Chanel** (www.chanel.com) and has no trouble finding a match.

Fashion Flair (www.fashionflair.com) is the most famous of the traditional makeup brands in the U.S. for black skin—it is also sold in most department stores around the world. This brand offers a three-way container with three shades of cream base that allows you to mix the exact tone you need.

Nacara (www.nacara.ca) is a Canadian line that caters to multi-ethnic skin; **Maria B** (www.mariab.com) has zebra packaging and gears its line of color cosmetics to Latina women—the website is attractive and appealing.

A chain of hair salons in Paris and 'burbs caters to ethnic hair: **Kanellia**, with its flagship right on the Champs Elysees, 66 av. Champs Elysees, Paris, 8e (☎ **331/4256-0257**).

Perhaps the best line—although my testing doesn't count for much—has been created by super-model Iman whose **Iman** line (www.i-iman.com) has 16 different shades of foundation, geared first to black skin but also to other ethnic blends. I have used the color stick to work on my cheekbones. The line is distributed by Proctor & Gamble and is available in Target and Wal-Mart stores as well as at international department stores.

WHERE TO BUY Department stores, some specialty stores and duty-frees; 36 freestanding stores worldwide. NYC: 148 Columbus Ave. ☎ **212/769-0725.** Also in London, Milan, Aix–en-Provence, and others. www.maccosmetics.com.

World's Best

Makeup Forever FRENCH $–$$

This is another of those professional brands that has crossed over from obscurity—in this case it's more due to exposure. This line could/should be known as the French equivalent of MAC. This is not only a true professional brand, but aside from fashion shows and stage work, they also create special effects with makeup for cinema, such as wounds. Various training sessions for wannabe makeup artists include a 30-hour program; contact the main office.

BEST BETS   The cream concealer in a tube ($23) is, without a doubt, the best I have ever used.

WEB TIPS   You cannot shop online but there is a ton of information, including what tools and products to use to achieve certain looks.

WHERE TO BUY   1 store; also department and specialty stores; Sephora. 5 rue la Boetie, Paris, 8e. ☎ **331/5305-9330.** Mon–Sat 10am–7pm. AE, MC, V. Métro: St. Augustin. www.makeup forever.com.

Mary Kay   USA   VALUE $–$$

Okay, no comments about the late Mary Kay Ash who founded this company and turned out to be somewhat controversial; surely you saw the movie. No comments about her sales incentive reward of a pink Cadillac (which is a pink Toyota in Japan). This firm is amazing—they took a good look at its demographics, saw that a large number of the customers were women of color and expanded their range accordingly. This firm now sells in 33 countries besides the U.S. and adjusts color shades to the local market's needs.

Because they have no retail outlets—Mary Kay is sold by their team of 1.6 million consultants—prices are considerably lower than those of other major brands. Foundation costs $14; mascara costs $15 and blush is $10.

BEST BETS   Makeup for women of color.

WEB TIPS   Try their Virtual Makeover whereby you choose a model with your skin tone, watch as she is made up, then buy from the products used.

WHERE TO BUY   Buy online or through your local rep. www.marykay.com.

Nars   FRENCH/USA $$–$$$

World's Best

Although the makeup artist behind this line is French, this is an American brand which concentrates on color.

BEST BETS   The most famous item in the range is the stick called The Multiple, meant to have, duh, multiple uses. Other firms have since copied this format, but I haven't found one as good. The stick costs $36 in the U.S., plus tax. The price is slightly higher in Europe but tax is included.

WHERE TO BUY   Available at Sephora and all major department stores in the U.S., at Space NK in the UK, and at Colette in Paris. www.narscosmetics.com.

World's Best — *Shu Uemura* JAPANESE $–$$$

Shu Uemura was the grandfather of makeup artists, the one to whom all artists today owe a debt of thanks. He is famous not only for color and the quality of his products but for introducing to retail an enormous testing bar.

This Japanese line is carried in some department and specialty stores, so you needn't make a pilgrimage to one of the boutiques—but it is great fun. This brand has more shades of cosmetics than just about any other line in the world, and there are many pieces of equipment as well. It's Shu who brought back eyelashes and has even introduced Eye Lash Bars in some department stores.

You'll also find a range of skin care products. Excellent, but pricey.

BEST BETS   The color selection for products is dazzling; the testing bars in all stores are the best of any brand.

WHERE TO BUY   Department stores worldwide as well as freestanding stores. 4 U.S. locations. NYC: 121 Greene St., between Prince and Houston sts. ☎ **212/979-5500.** Mon–Sat 11am–8pm; Sun noon–6pm. AE, DISC, MC, V. Subway: R or W to Prince St., C or E to Spring St. Other locations include Milan, Paris, Tokyo. www.shuuemura-usa.com.

T. Le Clerc FRENCH $–$$

First, a stupid story with a life lesson (maybe): A makeup artist once asked me to bring him back some of this brand's powder when I returned from Paris. He called it Le Clerk. To be polite, yet to correct his French, I said, "Oh yes, Le Cler, that is a great line."

He got very hoity-toity and told me the correct pronunciation was Le Clerk and he should know, he was a professional makeup artist and this was a professional brand.

I saw no reason to explain further. But you can trust me on this.

The brand, whose powder is known as the best in the world, has closed its Paris shop and is concentrating on department store distribution in addition to research and development. The latest launch is a complete line of face and beauty treatments.

BEST BETS   There is loose powder and pressed powder. Shades include greens and yellows to correct skin tone. The translucent powder ($75, large box) is made of angel wings.

WHERE TO BUY   Department and specialty stores and some pharmacies in Europe. www.t-leclerc.com.

Valerie BEVERLY HILLS, CA $$–$$$$

After training with Joe Blasco, one of the most famous professional makeup artists in Hollywood, Valerie went out on her own in 1984. Her current salon is in the flats of Beverly Hills, 1 block from Rodeo Drive. She has a large celebrity following and is also the makeup provider of choice for numerous films and TV shows.

BEST BETS   One of Valerie's specialties is a pre-wedding preview, not days before the wedding but weeks or months so you can know where you are going with your look and how to get there.

WHERE TO BUY   1 store: 460 N. Canon Dr., Beverly Hills. ☎ **310/ 274-7348.** AE, MC, V. www.valeriebeverlyhills.com.

Doctors' Brands

Dr. Hauschka GERMAN $–$$

World's Best Dr. Hauschka was a German chemist way ahead of his time when it came to using holistic and therapeutic products. His philosophy was to combine ancient wisdom on beauty and healing with modern chemistry to create products that could make a difference.

The line includes a wide number of fruit- and floral-based products. I swear by the rose oil, while Nora Ephron writes about the lemon bath oil in her memoir *I Feel Bad About My Neck.* Products cost from $18 to $55; the color cosmetics are a newer addition to the line. I sometimes use the foundation because it's light and fresh and comes in a flat plastic bottle that makes it easy to pack.

BEST BETS   The oil-based products—try the rose oil for skin. It smells great while hydrating skin.

WHERE TO BUY   Whole Foods, Sephora; other health and beauty stores worldwide. www.drhauschka.com.

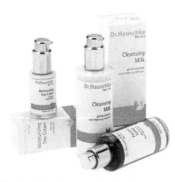

Dr. Hauschka cleansers and moisturizers.

RéVive USA $$$$

I have only tested this product from the free samples handed out at Neiman Marcus but was very impressed. The line was created by Dr. Gregory Bays Brown, a plastic surgeon. The stuff is expensive, although I guess it costs a lot less than a trip to a plastic surgeon. The Intensité Volumizing Serum costs $600 for an ounce.

BEST BETS   The cellular repair eye cream that I love costs $180 for 2 oz. The *intensité crème lustre* is $375—for 2 oz. I also like the eye renewal cream that you use twice a day, $95 for ½ oz.

WEB TIPS   You can shop online but when you click to buy you are linked to Bergdorf's or Neimans.

WHERE TO BUY   Neiman Marcus; or call corporate offices for phone orders. ☎ **888/704-3440.** Also sold at Joyce in Hong Kong, Sogo in Taipei and SpaceNK in the UK. www.revive skincare.com.

Rodan + Fields USA $$–$$$

Talk about the new American woman! These two ladies (Dr. Rodan and Dr. Fields) are medical doctors trained at Stanford. They are as gorgeous as movie stars and this line is a no-nonsense group of treatments for a variety of skin types or problems (sensitive skin, anti-aging, blemished skin and so on). The packaging is clean white with a bright color; the color indicates which treatment line you have in hand. The price range depends on the line; anti-age is the most expensive. Moisturizers range from $40 to $90; anti-age cleanser is $35.

BEST BETS   Anti-aging products.

WEB TIPS   You can shop online, but if you go to www.skinstore. com you'll note a "stock up and save" program for the line. This line has excellent printed materials at the point of sale but I found Nordstrom very stingy on handing out samples.

WHERE TO BUY   Available in department stores such as Nordstrom. www.rodanandfields.com.

Face Creams & Moisturizers

Amore Pacific KOREAN $$$$

Amore Pacific uses green tea, red ginseng and bamboo to make a full range of skin care. Products cost in the $200 to $300 range, but a small amount goes a long way.

Amore Pacific "Time Response" cream.

BEST BETS   Time Response Renewal Cream has six patents so you won't find this in the big vat in the sky (p. 181).

WEB TIPS   Website pop-ups and hassles took so long I needed new anti-aging products before I discovered you can only buy online by linking to Bergdorf or Neimans.

WHERE TO BUY   Neiman Marcus & Bergdorf Goodman in the U.S. All Korean department stores. Spa in NYC: 114 Spring St. ☎ **877/55-AMORE.** Mon–Sat 11am–7pm. AE, MC, V. Subway: Prince St. www.amorepacific.com.

Garnier Nutritioniste FRENCH VALUE $

Garnier is a French firm, a dime store brand that is a division of L'Oréal. They moved into the U.S. with hair color and were so successful with a youngish market that they developed three different levels for their skin care line, with three different price points—all value oriented: $6, $13 and $15. The anti-aging creams are the most expensive and are made with vitamin A, Omega 3 and Omega 6 as well as rice proteins—which gives them a nice texture and good slide. These are good products at a good price.

BEST BETS   Ultra Lift for anti-aging, $15.

WEB TIPS   You cannot buy online. If you cannot get the site to come up in English, go to www.garnier.ca.

WHERE TO BUY   Grocery stores and drugstores in the U.S. and France. www.garnier.com.

June Jacobs USA $$$

World's Best   This is a full range of spa products, but I use the moisturizers often because they are a good size for travel—and the products are just plain yummy. They smell great because of the large helping of natural fruits and veggies infused into the line.

BEST BETS   Protective Moisturizer is the one I use most, $58 for the tube. I also like the night cream, $58.

WEB TIPS   I love this website because aside from all the text, there's something called Express Shop which is just a giant ordering form. This form is longer than the list I left for Santa last year, but it is comprehensive and easy to use. Prices are clearly marked. I wish every website had this feature.

WHERE TO BUY   Some spas. Online at www.junejacobs.com as well as on numerous other online beauty sites.

Price Check: Beauty Creams

Any cynic in the beauty business will be happy to share a giggle with you over what's called **"The Big Vat in the Sky Theory."** By this un-scientific but marketing-savvy theory, all skin cream (maybe all makeup) is the same and comes from one big vat in the sky where it is doled out and squeezed into various bottles and tubes with different labels and different price tags.

That's not to say that you are being cheated—after all, perceived value is important. But it does prove that you can buy a perfectly great product for less than a glam one. Very often I shake my head and wonder how different some of these products really are. Consider the following lists.

Most expensive beauty products:
Sisley Sisleya Daily Line Reducer, $380
La Prarie Skin Caviar Luxe Cream, $580
ReVive Instité Volumizing Serum, $600
LAB21 DNA based skin cream, $750
Kanebo Sensai Premier Cream, $1,320
Crème de la Mer "The Essence," $2,100

My personal favorites:
Sisleya Global Anti-Age, $200 in Paris/$350 in U.S.
Dermatologica Super Rich Repair, $75
Galenic, $40 in French pharmacies
Dove ProAge, $15

World's Best *Sisley* FRENCH $$$–$$$$

While this entire line is excellent, and they make very good color cosmetics, the subject now is face cream; and Sisley makes a wide range of creams, all great. My favorite—which I actually think is worth the high price—is Sisleya Global Anti Age, but there are a variety of creams from light to very rich. All Sisley products are made of natural ingredients and smell like a small piece of heaven. The cucumber moisturizer is nice and light for day wear in summer.

BEST BETS   I don't care what it costs, I have to have the Sisleya selection. Note that in France, this brand is half the price as in the U.S., which counts when you are talking about a $300 skin cream. I buy my Sisley skin care discounted at Catherine, a duty-free in Paris (p. 411).

WEB TIPS   If you go to Evecare.com they offer a 20% discount.

WHERE TO BUY Department stores, Sephora stores and some duty-frees. www.sisley.fr.

Zelens BRITISH $$$$

I found this tip in a magazine and had to go to Selfridge's in London to test it—as expensive creams go, this is middle of the road at about $250 for the day cream and $300 for the night cream. The basic ingredient is Fullerene C60, which soaks up free radicals. Another of those doctor lines, this one was created by Dr. Marko Lens who studied at Harvard in the U.S. and Oxford in the UK. He considers himself English and the brand is usually sold in BPS, which is one of the reasons it's so expensive.

WEB TIPS You can shop online but prices are in sterling, ouch!

WHERE TO BUY Selfridge's Oxford St., London W1. ☎ 44-870/837-7377. Tube: Marble Arch or Bond St. Also NKSpace stores in UK and U.S. NYC: 99 Greene St. ☎ 212/941-4200. Mon–Sat 11am–7pm. AE, MC, V. Subway: Prince. Also sold in Italy, Spain, Taiwan, Japan and other locations. www.zelens.com.

Feminine Products

I'm sure you can get all sorts of things by mail order, but I blush to think. These are all over-the-counter.

Fleur d'Elle GERMAN/FRENCH $

The name means Her Flower, and the product comes from a division of Nivea called Nivea Intimate. Essentially this is just a little foil package of wipes, but I am in love with the French expressions that go with it. It is meant to be used to wisk away *le parfum d'amour.* If you can't translate that or figure it out, you are under 21 and this is X-rated. The product has no soap, no alcohol and is simply a chamomile wipe for external use.

BEST BET The package of 20 wipes costs $4.

WEB TIPS There's no mention of any of this sort of thing on the Nivea website, trust me.

WHERE TO BUY French grocery stores, pharmacies and so on.

Oh! DUTCH $

This natural cream is for external use only and is meant to intensify orgasms. It's made of green tea, aloe vera and other natural

Facial Sprays

Facial sprays began as a cosmetic and beauty aid when Evian introduced their spritz as a makeup fixative in the seventies. While the idea got a lot of press—and many makeup mavens insisted you could affix your makeup with a quick spritz of mineral water—the trend didn't really take root as a cult practice until the turn of the 21st century, when homeopathic brands began to announce you could spray yourself with well-being.

Similar in concept to aromatherapy, the idea here is that a spray of just the right herbs can protect skin, restore health or revive your spirit. Aromatherapy brands often sell spray-on-the-pillow sleep aids. Facial sprays carry forth the concept one step closer to home.

Jurlique Rosewater Spray.

The Australian firm **Jurlique** (p. 188) markets several different sprays, including for travel and one made of rose water. I have found the rose water so exceptional that I even pay $45 for it, and consider it a travel necessity. I spent a fortune on this product until I discovered the same thing for sale in Mexico at any grocery store for $3, called **Wettsy**, Aqua de Roses, hecho en mexico, Laboratorie Wetts, Colonia Granjas Modernas, 07460 Mexico DF (☎ **800/557-2800**).

I have suffered from extremely dry eyes all of my life. Since this wasn't a condition that interested many people, my inability to wear contact lens was chalked up to lack of effort. Nowadays dry eye syndrome is so common there are all sorts of tears, drops, stimulants and ointments to help. The best one I have ever tested, however, is a facial spray for the eyes called **Nature's Tears EyeMist®** (☎ 800/ FOR-MIST; www.naturestears.com).

products with some mint that accounts for the tingle. This is known as a sensual health cream, in case you were wondering. Insider's tip (excuse the expression)—do not confuse this product with "Oh What a Night Cream" which is a facial moisturizer.

BEST BETS   A little dab'll do ya.

WHERE TO BUY   Henri Bendel, Victoria's Secret Beauty stores in the US. www.ohcream.com.

SweetSpot USA $

I love this line because it's smart, chic and well packaged. I also lean on it psychologically so that I never need to panic. Feminine panic can be so cruel. The line sells "intimate grooming products." There's wash products, clean up wipes, a very nice travel kit for overnight dates, and more.

I have lived in France for 7 years and have seen various intimate products on the shelves, but this is a first for the U.S. Sweet Spot isn't a sex toy; the items in the range are pH balanced for feminine health and well-being. Most unusual item in the line: Hormone Harmony, a scent to use during your period. Most of the products cost $12.

BEST BETS   The on-the-go wipe package of three wipes is $2.50 and perfect for long-haul flights.

WEB TIPS   In this pink and very girly website, there's a box to click called "tell a girlfriend," which I think is fabulous. Girls do talk about these things, you know. Buy three of anything online and get a 10% discount.

WHERE TO BUY   www.sweetspotlabs.com.

Five & Dime

Any beauty editor will be happy to tell you that you can find perfectly good products in the drugstore, the dime store or the big box store out yonder. All fashion magazines share ad pages and editorial information about premium makeup and mass market makeup. Who knows what real difference there is in any of these brands? See the Big Vat theory on p. 181.

Aveeno USA VALUE $

This line is really a pharmaceutical line of treatments with an emphasis on natural ingredients. I sometimes call it the poor man's Aveda, but that's mostly because of the similarity of the names, not the products. In truth, this began life as a bath line developed in conjunction with the Mayo Clinic at the end of World War II. I first learned about it because my younger sister (a natural redhead) had eczema and had to bathe in their oatmeal treatment.

The firm has branched out of the tub and was acquired in 1999 by Johnson & Johnson. They have blossomed into a skin care firm with fair prices and excellent quality.

BEST BUY   I've gone bonkers for their Positively Ageless Serum, just introduced at $18. I swear this is as good as a similar product I pay $45 for—I use this on the airplane to fight dryness on board.

WEB TIPS   Coupons available.

WHERE TO BUY   Available at Walgreens, Target, CVS, Ulta, Duane Reade and Drugstore.com. www.aveeno.com.

Boots No. 7 BRITISH ◦VALUE $–$$

First there's the droll British sense of humor. Chanel has No. 5, so Boots decided to take No. 7. Get it? They also use similar packaging to Chanel. The line has color and some treatment and is, of course, sold in Boots chemist shops. It's such a good line that it has spawned a younger sister, No. 17—which is a teeny-bopper line of makeup.

BEST BETS   This line has good products overall. I like the mascara and the cream foundation. The skin cream, Protect & Perfect ($32) is actually a serum and is the brightest star to come from the UK since Mary Poppins.

WEB TIPS   Also at www.target.com, www.amazon.com.

WHERE TO BUY   No. 7 products are now available in the U.S. at select Target stores, Target.com and CVS pharmacies as well as a variety of international venues including airports. www.boots.com.

Dove USA ◦VALUE $

Let's talk briefly about the soap which came onto the market when I was a girl and revolutionized bath time. Now that cream bar comes in half a dozen varieties, including rose or cucumber. But it doesn't stop there.

   In recent years Dove has expanded its soap empire to shampoo and hair care and personal care. (I like the deo a lot.) Then they launched a few skin treatments, all very low key.

BEST BETS   **ProAge,** a total skin care treatment line at mass-market prices. Packaged in plum and sold in grocery stores and drug stores, the line retails for $10 to $15 per item. I have become totally addicted to many items in the line, including their oil-cream (which is a body cream) and the cream cleanser.

WEB TIPS   You cannot buy online, but you can sign up for a free sample.

WHERE TO BUY   Grocery stores and drugstores; www.dove.com.

Nivea GERMAN ◦VALUE $

Nivea hand cream has long been a well-known stable in the U.S. as well as around the world. In the last 2 decades the line has moved way past cream in a travel tin and into health and beauty care and even color cosmetics and has been among the first to reach out to the mass market. International shoppers will note that the same products are not available all over the world.

BEST BETS   Spray Corps Hydrant, a dry oil spray I buy in France for $8, that you spray on after the shower but is not greasy or sticky and does not stain the clothes.

WEB TIPS   The body spray that I adore is nowhere to be found on the website. You can't shop online anyway, but the entire site has very poor selection in terms of body care.

WHERE TO BUY   Drug stores, parapharmacies and supermarkets worldwide. www.nivea.com.

Vaseline Intensive Care USA VALUE $

I actually worked on the launch of this product; you could tell it was going to be a monster by the rate at which it was stolen from the office. Back in those days, Vaseline Intensive Care was a simple but excellent product that took the world by the hands and made life better. In the intervening years, as brand extensions have become so important in marketing, VIC has come up with such a confusing array of variations on the original product that I am dizzy and annoyed.

BEST BETS   Original.

WEB TIPS   Try unilever.com or Vaseline.com or, better yet, one of the sites like drugstore.com.

WHERE TO BUY   Grocery and drugstores. www.vaseline.com.

Green & Organic Beauty

Aesop AUSTRALIAN $$-$$$

Your first tip-off that this is a good line is that the products come in brown glass bottles to better protect the natural ingredients inside. The only products I have seen in plastic containers are the ones made as hotel amenities, but maybe plastic is coming—certainly it is easier for travel.

This line is made of plants and essential oils with a pharmaceutical type of label and package to impress you with the botanical pedigree. It's called an alternative beauty system for men and women.

BEST BETS   I travel with Rind Aromatique Body Balm ($30), made from grapefruit, orange peel and lemon rind.

WEB TIPS   You can only buy directly from the firm online if you live in Australia or New Zealand.

WHERE TO BUY   17 stores worldwide. **FLAGSHIP**   72a Oxford St., Paddington, Sydney, Australia. ☎ **612/9358-3382.** Daily 10am–10pm. MC, V. Also 20 rue Bonaparte, Paris, 6e. ☎ **331/4441-0219.** Métro: St. Germain des Pres. www.aesop.net.au.

Aubrey Organics USA VALUE $

Natural beauties and Hollywood stars have begun to go nuts for this 100% natural line even though the line was one of the first hippies in the world and is now 40 years old. There are only a few color cosmetic products. The line fills out with hair and skin care items yet the ingredients remain pure. These are the people who not only invented green, but led the movement to print ingredients on health and beauty products. They have also pioneered the use of a variety of fruit and healthful extracts for beauty treatments.

BEST BETS   Skin tone color costs $6; complexion spray mist is $7.25 and lip color costs $6.95.

WEB TIPS   Not only can you shop online, but some UK and Japanese international orders can be filled from the U.S.

WHERE TO BUY   4,500 organic and health food store points of sale worldwide. www.aubrey-organics.com.

Aveda USA $–$$

One of the first important green lifestyle hair care brands, Aveda has found a place on the world stage for its aromatherapy and treatments, and serves both professional and consumer branches of the industry. Stores fall into several different flavors: concept stores, lifestyle salons, experience centers, destination spas and institutes. (Some cities have several.)

BEST BETS   This company makes hair and beauty treatments, make-up, soap, candles, aromatherapy and even tea. They have won numerous environmental awards, which would mean little if the products weren't as good as they are.

WEB TIPS   This is an excellent and easy-to-use site; click on "Almost Gone" for a shot at near-discontinued products.

World Traveler

Because this firm is from Minneapolis, hotels in the Twin Cities often use Aveda amenities. There's your chance to stock up on travel sizes. If you visit Minneapolis (company headquarters), be sure to book into the training center.

WHERE TO BUY   Some grocery stores and drugstores in the U.S. Freestanding stores in 22 countries worldwide. **FLAGSHIP**   Gavidae Common, 555 Nicollet Mall, Minneapolis. ☎ **612/376-7900.** Mon–Fri 10am–7pm; Sat 10am–6pm. AE, MC, V. Corporate HQ has training school with low-cost treatments: 400 Central Ave. SE. ☎ 612/378-7401. www.aveda.com.

Jurlique AUSTRALIAN $–$$$

All those cosmetic companies racing to be more organic than thou will have to do a lot of work to catch up to Jurlique: The company's herb farms in South Australia are not only biodynamic—harvested by hand, following the cycles of the moon—they annually hire orchestras to play in the fields . . . *for the herbs.* It sounds extreme, but their overall obssessiveness seems to pay off. This is one of the most reliable product lines available for sensitive skin. They make gentle cleansers, creams, mists and oils infused with fresh lavender, calendula, arnica and more.

World Traveler

You can see the meticulous farming upclose at the **Jurlique Herb Farm** in Australia (☎ 618/8391-7400), about 30 minutes outside Adelaide. One-hour tours are Tuesdays and Thursdays at 2pm and Saturdays at 10pm. Products and herb-filled lunches are available.

BEST BETS The Daily Exfoliating Cream with crushed almonds and oats ($25) and Herbal Recovery Gel ($67) are indeed worthy of Mendelssohn.

WHERE TO BUY 50 stores and 1,000+ spas and shops worldwide; Whole Foods. **U.S. FLAGSHIP** 477 Madison Ave., NYC. ☎ **212/752-1980.** Mon–Thurs 10am–8pm; Fri 10am–7pm; Sat 10am–6pm; Sun noon–5pm. AE, MC, V. www.jurlique.com. —*SB*

Pangea Organics USA $

This brand is from Colorado, which makes it sound healthy right there. Their products are made without petroleum, sulfates, detergents or synthetic preservatives. The brand is very down home with a wide range of body care, face creams and bathing products.

BEST BETS Indian Lemongrass with Rosemary shower gel, $11; wide range of lavender-based products.

WHERE TO BUY Health food stores and specialty markets; Whole Foods; Wild Oats; World Market. www.pangeaorganics.com.

Hair Products

A few years ago, if you asked me about the best shampoo or hair care products in the world, I would be singing the praises of the Michaeljohn line of lavender shampoo. Alas, Michaeljohn salon no longer makes or authorizes products. Which is to say that whatever I talk about now could be out of business by next year. Just don't wash that man right outta your hair.

Christophe Robin FRENCH $$

The most famous colorist in Paris has his own line of hair care products, including ones that come in travel sizes. This is not a fly by the frizz of your pants wannabe line, it's been available for almost 10 years. It's just a well-kept secret. Some salons around the world sell the products, but they are hard to find. And, yes, in case you were wondering, Catherine Deneuve has her hair colored by M. Robin and uses the products.

BEST BETS   Christophe is one of the gurus of hair color so you pick his products if your hair has been fried by chemicals and needs tender loving care.

WHERE TO BUY   Sold in Paris at Au Printemps, Colette and Sephora. Salon: 7 Mont Thabor, Paris, 1er. ☎ **331/4260-9915.** Mon–Fri 10am–7pm by appointment only. Métro: Tuileries. No website.

John Masters Organics USA $

Awarded best new organic products when launched a few years ago; shampoos and hair treatments cost $15 to $20. There's also a range of skin care—4 ounces of cream cleanser costs $19. Mr. Masters has a salon in SoHo; his products have become so popular that they are sold in 20 countries worldwide.

BEST BETS   I vote for Evening Primrose shampoo for dry hair, $16.

WEB TIPS   This site is an amazing lesson in marketing—from page one you like the man and his products. It becomes an emotional issue. Extensive product info is available.

WHERE TO BUY   Salon: 77 Sullivan St., NYC. ☎ **212/343-9590.** Mon–Fri 11am–7pm; Sat 10am–6pm. Subway: Spring St. www. johnmasters.com.

Kerastase FRENCH $–$$

So my old friend Barbara Cady and I are walking down the street in Paris, looking in store windows, as is our wont. "Wait here!" Barbara screams, ditches me and dashes into a tiny hair salon. She emerges a few minutes later with a big bag, a big grin and a triumphant howl. "Do you know how much this stuff costs in the U.S.?" she demands.

Although this brand has existed since the mid-sixties, it has now reached cult status all over the world because of the advanced technology poured into these hair care products. The packaging is color coded so that you know which special-ties the product has been formulated to cure. I buy the orange stuff, which I think is the most popular.

BEST BETS   I am addicted to the Bain Oleo-Relax shampoo (orange package) which I only buy when feeling flush, since it's about $25 a bottle in the U.S. It has a very smooth glide to it that feels like it's coating my damaged hair.

WEB TIPS   Try www.luxuryparlor.com, www.beautika.com for about 35% off, or www.fredsegalbeauty.com.

WHERE TO BUY   Beauty salons in Europe ($18); salons and specialty stores in the U.S. ($25–$32).

Leonor Greyl FRENCH $–$$

This is a cult brand in France, not that well known there and certainly not well known outside of France. It is a botanical line that adds vitamins into its treatments and specializes in hair and scalp problems. People with oily hair swear by the line, although there are treatments for all kinds of hair.

BEST BETS   *Serum de Soie Sublimateur* is the hot ticket right now, $35. I also use this on cuticles.

WEB TIPS   A portion of the site allows you to self-diagnose your hair and scalp problems and find the cure before Marcus Welby gets there.

WHERE TO BUY   French department stores and pharmacies; or online in the U.S. at www.spaskin.com or www.BeautyBridge.com. Products cost less in France. www.leonorgreyl.com.

Phyto FRENCH $–$$

Mon dieu, this is an empire to know and appreciate—the firm owns only three companies, but all of them are fantastic and are listed separately in this book—Phytotherapie for hair, Lierac for beauty and Caron for perfume.

So the subject now is Phytotherapie—a large range of botanic products sold in color-coded packages so you can easily choose what you need. Treatment is beyond compare, but it is usually packaged in glass, which makes it heavy for travel and fragile and difficult in the shower where one slip could spell disaster. The glass protects the integrity of the ingredients. *Note:* Some products come in tubes, which are easy for travel.

They have recently opened their own spa/salon in Manhattan. *Note:* The salon does not do cuts or color, but they do treatment and also use their Lierac brand for skin care (p. 194).

BEST BETS   Phyto makes the best hairspray in the world in a little red plastic spritzer, $13.

WHERE TO BUY   Sephora stores and various online beauty stores. It costs less if bought in France where you can find it at Monoprix. U.S. Salon: Phyto Universe, 715 Lexington Ave. at

58th St. ☎ **212/308-0270.** Subway N,R,W, 4, 5, 6 to 59th St. www.phyto.com.

Rusk USA VALUE $

This is a professional brand with a friendly price and sweet-smelling ingredients that do the job for me.

BEST BETS   I like the grapefruit shampoo for colored hair and the ginger conditioner. I have splurged on some of the treatment and styling products when I can get them at my hairdresser but they are in the $18 to $22 range, which I find hefty. I am more comfortable with a bottle of shampoo that costs about $10.

WEB TIPS   The website is meant for professionals. Try drugstore.com or http://shopping.yahoo.com.

WHERE TO BUY   Beauty First stores in U.S., professional salons, some off-pricers and some Target stores. www.rusk1.com.

Maternity Care

Once I heard that a hotel group was marketing "Babymoon"—the last getaway weekend before the baby arrives—I knew that marketing had reached a new, uh, plateau. There are now several lines of treatment to help ease women down the pregnancy road. **Secret:** I have used many of these products and they worked just fine on me.

World's Best *Basq skincare* USA $–$$$
While Basq was created as a maternity and post baby spa and skin care line, what I like about it is that Basq makers like to consider any body-changing events—especially weight loss—as a time to celebrate the skin with aromacology and essential oils. There is a very good spa kit for $56 that includes everything you need to feel good about yourself and your body—body polish, body oil, foot relief and eye gel.

BEST BETS   I use the foot relief product when I travel, as it really helps with the swelling. Belly Oil is $36.

WEB TIPS   Free shipping on all gift sets.

WHERE TO BUY   Neiman Marcus stores; also sold on QVC. www.basqnyc.com.

Belli Oil USA $$–$$$$

This is more of a medical line geared toward treating the dermatological aspects of pregnancy; it was created by a physician. The line treats everything from swelling, stretching and itchy skin to any other unexpected skin changes.

BEST BETS I admit that I use this product on my hands and cuticles and find it wonderfully rich. At $26 for a 1.7 oz bottle, I keep my nails in excellent shape. This is perhaps one of my insider's tips—any product safe enough for pregnant women and recommended by OB-GYN doctors is going to be just fine for you whether you are pregnant or not.

Elasticity Belly Oil by Belli.

WHERE TO BUY Some doctors sell this line; otherwise shop online. www.bellicosmetics.com.

MamaMio BRITISH $–$$

This line was begun in the UK but now has U.S. offices to meet the, uh, boom. And the bloom. The products are made of essential oils specifically chosen for sensitive noses. The products are meant to make the skin more elastic so that as it stretches it does so with ease . . . and can bounce back after the baby's birth. The line is made up of items such as Tummy Toner ($65) and Stretch Mark Minimiser ($65).

BEST BETS There's a kit for after-pregnancy skin care that makes a great shower gift.

WHERE TO BUY Sephora stores; Flight 001 stores in the U.S. www.mamamio.com.

Pharmaceuticals

It's no secret that most makeup and beauty treatments are made by pharmaceutical labs under contract to the big names or their holding companies. Pharmaceutical firms often make color cosmetics (don't miss Lierac), but are most known for their treatments. These are high-end brands that are not sold in dime stores or big box/mass market stores.

Cupra ITALIAN $

Mass market brand especially geared to extremely dry skin and made from bee's wax. This is how you mind your own, Burt's and the Italian's all at the same time.

BEST BETS There's a cream for extremely dry skin that I use and find to be one of the best in the world, about $5. The hand cream, in a travel-worthy tube, costs $1.45 and is called Cera di Cupra. This product line has been created by Dottore (doctor) Ciccarelli, who is probably related to Madonna.

WEB TIPS   The site is in Italian, and you cannot buy. Look for these products when you are out and about in Italy.

WHERE TO BUY   Grocery stores and drugstores in Italy. www.ciccarelli.it.

Eucerin USA $

This is a basic lesson from my Mom and from my friend Arnie Klein, one of the most famous dermatologists in Beverly Hills. Here goes: Eucerin is a good basic moisturizer. I buy it by the tub and use it all over my body. I don't happen to use it on my face, but I am sure you can do so happily.

BEST BETS   There are several other products in the range created for sensitive skin, very dry skin and so forth. With prices in the $4 to $6 range, you might want to start here.

WEB TIPS   The site lists websites where you can buy products online. Among them is www.oprah.com.

WHERE TO BUY   Available in drugstores in the U.S. www.EucerinUS.com.

Galenic FRENCH $–$$

Effective hydrating skin creams for those who don't need designer brands or high prices. Gel is more lightweight than a cream and is especially good in summer.

BEST BET   Rose-scented hydrating cream for every day, about $40.

WEB TIPS   The site is in French; click on your shipping destination for other languages.

WHERE TO BUY   French pharmacies.

Kinerase FRENCH/USA $–$$

Skin care and treatment for blemished or aging skin from a very serious pharmaceutical company based in California and from Valeant Pharmaceuticals in France. This is a very full range of products with creams, cleansers, masks, goops, supplements and travel kits. Prices are generally high, but there is something no-nonsense about this line that tells me it's a value. The line is made with extract from blue anemone flowers, which is what makes it different from other brands (and therefore not from the Vat in the Sky; p. 181).

BEST BETS   Intensive Kinetin Skin Cream ($129). This is a very thick cream that I use mostly before, during and after long-haul travel.

WEB TIPS You may find some of the line at a discount of 10% to 30% at www.drugstore.com.

WHERE TO BUY Pharmacies in Europe. ☎ **800/321-4576.** www. kinerase.com.

Lierac FRENCH [VALUE] $–$$

Little known outside of France, this pharmaceutical line has excellent skin care products. The prices are for real people, and the line keeps expanding so that if you find a well-stocked store you will be shocked at the number of stock-keeping items ranging from skin care to sun care to color cosmetics.

BEST BETS Their lightweight foundation tint is the best I have ever used. It's called Aqua-D+ and comes in a tube ($32).

WEB TIPS You cannot buy online, but you can click on *offre du mois* to see available promotions.

WHERE TO BUY French pharmacies, Monoprix and Parashop stores; excellent distribution in Europe; Phyto Universe salon in Manhattan (p. 190). www.lierac.net.

Nuxe FRENCH $–$$$

OK, so I'll start with the secret info—the woman who began this line is sisters with Terry de Gunzberg, who also has a line of makeup and skincare (By Terry, see p. 173). Good skin is genetic, so maybe good makeup is, too.

Nuxe is a dime store brand—well, a pharmacy and para-pharmacie brand to be exact—that has excellent treatment products, many of which are innovative. They were using chocolate in skin cream before anyone else; they began the trend in gold flecked body oil. The line is made from natural foods, flowers and scents; comes in simple plastic or glass packages that keep costs down and is considered a cult favorite in France. There is a spa in Paris.

BEST BETS The gold-flecked body oil is a summer must-have, $30 per bottle. One bottle lasts me the whole summer. The Nuxuriance skin cream has won prizes from French maga-zines and cosmetics associations.

WEB TIPS The site is in French. You cannot shop online; how-ever, the site tells you the code to use to request that your pharmacist order the items you want.

WHERE TO BUY Sephora, French department stores and phar-macies. Spa: Nuxe 32, 32 rue Montorgueil, Paris, 1er. ☎ **331/ 5580-7140.** Mon–Fri 9am–9pm; Sat 9am–7:30pm. MC, V. Métro: Chatelet. www.nuxe.com.

Santa Maria Novella Farmaceutica ITALIAN $–$$

Okay, so this isn't technically a pharmaceutical, but if you figure that before there were pharmacies there were convents and nuns with healing hands, then you can appreciate this firm, which makes soap and skin care. This is the oldest *farmacia* in the world, started in the Dominican monastery in Florence in 1221. The shopping bag states that the house has existed as it is now since 1612.

They now have a few stores dotted around the world and some small amount of international distribution, but the thing to do is go to the main store, in a medieval chapel in Florence. It's so beautiful and sublime that you will melt . . . and buy everything in sight. While you will spend time on the products, the tour and the gardens, don't forget to look at the ceilings. If Michelangelo opened a boutique, this is what it would look like.

BEST BETS   One of my favorite products is called Weekend Soap. It's a small but long bar of soap that breaks into three equal parts marked Friday, Saturday, Sunday ($15). The product list (available in English) looks like the menu from your favorite restaurant.

WHERE TO BUY   25+ stores in 24 cities, including NYC, LA, Rome, Milan, Kyoto, Tokyo, Barcelona, more. **FLAGSHIP**   Via della Scala 16r, Florence. ☎ **39-055/216-276.** Mon–Sat 9:30am–7:30pm; Sun 10:30am–6:30pm. MC, V. www.sm novella.it.

Problem & Sensitive Skin Treatments

Dermablend USA

This is a product for someone with a serious problem, although I have worked with it as an attempt to re-shape my face for photography. The people who use this product need it because they have something they want to cover, be it a tattoo or a skin condition.

BEST BETS   There's concealer for men and women and various other products too. Foundation costs $25; loose setting powder costs $19; concealer is $18.

WHERE TO BUY   Dermablend is also sold internationally in department stores and through dermatologists and plastic surgeons. www.dermablend.com.

Dermalogica USA/UK $$–$$$

I learned about this line when its products were in the travel kit provided by my airline on a long-haul trip to Asia a few years ago. The brand is a tad hard to find at retail but is worth the search—it falls into the middle ground price wise but the high ground quality wise. I think these treatments are as good as any of the big name, fancy and overpriced brands I have used. The line was developed by the International Dermal Institute, which kinda makes me giggle—I have no way of knowing if this is a serious medical concern or a business put together to sound very officious.

BEST BETS   I continually buy the hydrating products, $40 to $50.

WHERE TO BUY   Beauty supply and specialty stores; assorted websites. www.dermalogica.com.

Kiehl's USA $–$$

This is the story of the little pharmacy that could. Opening its doors in 1851, Kiehl's is still dishing out old-fashioned and very pure treatments, lotions and potions. Since being bought up by a monster conglomerate, the chain has expanded the product range so there are some fashion items (lip gloss, tinted moisturizer) and more hip products than what was *au courante* 150 years ago.

BEST BETS   Kiehl's makes good shampoo and conditioner; I like the papaya and pineapple facial scrub ($25) for every now and then.

WHERE TO BUY   Sephora, some department stores, Colette in Paris and freestanding stores worldwide. **FLAGSHIP**   109 Third Ave., NYC. ☎ 212/677-3171. Mon–Sat 10am–8pm; Sun noon–6pm. AE, DISC, MC, V. Subway: L, First Ave. Other locations include San Francisco. www.kiehls.com.

Malin + Goetz USA $–$$

If even Kiehl's (above) irritates your skin, try this brand. Matthew Malin left Kiehl's in 2001 and wanted products more suitable for his sensitive skin. With Andrew Goetz, he created a line that is indeed gentle yet

(MALIN+GOETZ)
apothecary and lab.
NATURAL INGREDIENTS. PERFORMANCE TECHNOLOGY.
ADVANCED SKIN CARE AND PARFUMS.
new york.

more effective and better smelling than most sensitive-friendly brands. In a marked departure from Kiehl's, you'll find a select line of products meant for all skin types; so there's only 1 moisturizer, not 15. Goetz hails from Vitra design firm, which accounts for the utilitarian-chic packaging and the enamel-white, Corian-decked boutique in Chelsea.

BEST BETS   The peppermint hair shampoo ($20) has an invigo-rating smell and tingle. All the products look striking in your bathroom, which does count for something. The shop's dogs are minor neighborhood celebrities.

WEB TIPS   Free shipping on orders over $75.

WHERE TO BUY   2 stores in NYC and LA; in 20+ countries worldwide; in Barneys, Flight 001, select hotels and spas, more. **FLAGSHIP**   177 Seventh Ave., NYC. ☎ **212/727-3777.** Mon–Fri 11am–8pm; Sat noon–8pm; Sun noon–6pm. AE, MC, V. www.malinandgoetz.com. —*SB*

Mario Badescu NYC/ROMANIAN $–$$

This line was created in 1967 by a Romanian cosmetic chemist working in New York's Upper East Side and offers effective, luxurious treatments for acne, rosacea, sensitive skin and more. There's a lengthy celebrity client list; this may be the only thing Lil' Kim and Gwyneth Paltrow have in common.

BEST BETS   If you have problematic skin, there are lots of pro-tective creams and soothing night treatments ($15 to $40). I like the Control Cream for sensitive skin ($15). Drying Lotion ($17)—also known as the pink stuff—is a legendary acne spot treatment. Almond & Honey Scrub is $15.

WEB TIPS   Click on "consulting" and fill out a short question-naire to get their product recommendations.

WHERE TO BUY   1 store; 300+ beauty stores worldwide; Nord-strom in U.S., Harvey Nichols in UK. 320 E. 52nd St., NYC. ☎ **212/223-3728.** Fri–Tues 8:30am–6pm; Wed–Thurs 8:30am–8:30pm. AE, MC, V. www.mariobadescu.com. —*SB*

Soap
....

Claus Porto PORTUGUESE $

This soap has the most beautiful packaging in the world. It is even more unusual because its regular shape is oval and each bar weighs a whopping 12.5 ounces.

BEST BET   The price tag of $14 begins to make sense when you see how big the product is. You can get bars in other sizes, but the hefty one is most impressive, especially as a gift item.

WHERE TO BUY   To buy in the U.S. go to www.lafcony.com. Sometimes available at TJMaxx for $7. No store, no website.

Sabon ISRAELI $

This chain of stores reminds me of a fancy version of LUSH, although the stores are much more sophisticated and the fact that there aren't that many of them makes the merchandise even more special. When you walk into a shop, aside from the overwhelming smell of fruity clean, you see heaps and rows of packages and bars and loaves of soaps and products. It makes you want to rush home immediately to bathe, wondering if perhaps Lady MacBeth would have washed even more frequently if she had this option. All soaps are made from natural ingredients. They smell great.

BEST BETS   There's a lot of creativity in the line, so that you can find unique gift items at good prices, such as soap on a rope, which is like a kebab of little soap pieces ($11); and shaved soap that goes into organza baggies ($4). They have a very good men's skin care line; the after-shave balm ($30) is a favorite at my home.

WEB TIPS   You can shop online, but they do not ship to international destinations or P.O. boxes.

WHERE TO BUY   12 stores in U.S. **FLAGSHIP**   93 Spring St., SoHo, NYC. ☎ 212/925-0742. Subway: Spring St. Other stores in Boston, Chicago, San Francisco, Toronto. www.sabonnyc.com.

La Companie de Provence (LCDP) FRENCH $

This is one of those businesses where the package becomes part of the icon, so you get not only a quality gem but something that is known for its look. As most soap historians know, soap as we know it today was invented in Marseille. This brand began in Marseille, has a shop there and is now expanding with a spiffy shop in Paris on a street coincidentally bathed in soap stores.

The original items in the line are big hunks of square olive oil soap and liquid olive oil soap in a pump container. Now various other natural scents are added including my favorite, *temps de cerise*. They make a very good hand cream in a tube; the body lotion comes in a pump bottle like the liquid soap.

BEST BETS   One of the best things about the firm is that they make a huge range of products in 1-ounce travel sizes. You can also buy these online.

WEB TIPS   Online prices in the U.S. are fair, but about 30% higher than in France. Fig bubble bath is $23, body lotion

$33—these are large pump containers. Liquid soap is $21 online and $15 in Paris.

WHERE TO BUY   Department and specialty stores. **FLAGSHIP**   16 rue Vignon, Paris, 9e. ☎ **331/4268-0160.** CB, MC, V. Métro: Madeleine. www.lcdpmarseille.com.

Marius Fabre FRENCH $

Superchef Alain Ducasse got me hooked on this brand, a very small, very local Provençale brand that has been in business since 1900. You can even go to the factory on a tour and shop in their store. The packaging is lovely and the price is good.

BEST BETS   The 100-gram size is great for travel, $3; I always go for lavender. I also like the liquid soap in rose.

WEB TIPS   The site is in English and in French. You cannot shop online but you can arrange your tour online.

WHERE TO BUY   Street markets and tourist stores in France. Some pharmacies. ☎ **334/9053-8275** for points of sale in France. Factory: 148 av. Paul Bourret, Salon-de-Provence, France (near Avignon). www.marius-fabre.fr.

Tanning

St. Tropez Tanning System BRITISH $$–$$$

St. Tropez tinted self-tanning lotion.

I botched so many self-tanning projects that my late husband asked me to pledge I'd never try again. I waited until he had been dead for several years before I dared to test St. Tropez Tanning system, partly because of my pledge to him but also because of the price. I paid about $100 for this three-step regimen. In reality, you only need Step 3, the tan itself. Instead of asking your skin to turn a color due to a chemical reaction, this product is more like makeup. It goes on mud colored and makes you look tanned. I layer on a bit every day. This is the most remarkable, extraordinary product, and I hope it can help everyone break the color barrier.

BEST BETS   Part 3 of the kit, which is the tanning gel itself, $45.

WEB TIPS   You can buy online at www.drugstore.com, www. beauty.com or www.amazon.co.uk.

WHERE TO BUY   Boots in the UK, some Sephora stores worldwide. www.st-tropez.co.uk.

Chapter Seven

Menswear & More

*T*his is a slightly indiscreet but (I think) yummy story about my late husband. When he was 13, in the mid-1950s when none of us were as sophisticated as today's kids, he went to Saks Fifth Avenue to be fitted for his bar mitzvah suit. During the fitting, the tailor asked, "How do you dress?"

"Preppy," Mike answered simply.

Yeah, yeah, I get it, but in those days there might not have been other styles of dress for a guy, while today there are many—from Rock & Roll to Elegant Peacock to British or European to Conservative to Casual. There could be many more answers to the question besides Right or Left.

When I worked at *GQ*, about 30 years ago, it was believed that most men's clothing was bought by women. A few years later, Art Cooper came in and revolutionized men's fashion and what a men's magazine could and should be. Now we see brands not only marketing directly to men, but to various segments in the market, be it gay, straight, middle-aged ("Do you have E.D.?"), sports-oriented, surfer and so on. There's *Teen Vogue* for young women as well as *Cosmo Girl* and a few others for girls. Pretty soon I expect there will be *Teen Guy* to accompany *Men's Vogue*.

This chapter includes most aspects of men's fashion so that it can be a simple, single section for use by men or women. Such topics as skin care and shaving products for men are covered in this chapter; clothes for boys are in Chapter Eight: "Babies, Kids, Teens & Tweens."

> *Clothes make the man.*
> —Mark Twain

Accessories & Gear

Bamford & Sons BRITISH $$$–$$$$$

Bamford is a veddy proper English provider of clothes for gentlemen and boys, but they have a particularly lush and luxurious accessories line and green policy toward home gear and clothing. They even have an organic cafe within the store, so you could call this a lifestyle store. But if you are looking for just the right gift for just the right guy, you can't do better than the travel cases, hot water bottle covered in cashmere, suede neck pillow or kaftan-for-the-plane package that folds into nothing. The store on Sloane Square shows the firms' intent to become a bigger name in luxury.

BEST BETS   Customized iPods cost about $1,000.

WEB TIPS   The store hosts customer evenings and specialty events that you can sign up for online.

WHERE TO BUY   FLAGSHIP   31 Sloane Sq., London SW1. ☎ **4420/ 7589-8729.** Mon–Sat 10am–6pm; Wed 10am–7pm; Sun noon–5pm. AE, MC, V. Tube: Sloane Sq. www.bamford.co.uk.

Brella Bar NYC $$–$$$$

This Manhattan boutique sells the accessories that never go out of style—handmade umbrellas, brollies and walking sticks from around the world, including designs from Pierre Vaux, Flann Lippincott and Francesco Maglia. Featuring handmade wooden handles and silk canopies, the umbrellas are priced between $100 and $500, which is indeed what you need to pay for the Rolls-Royce of anti-raindrops. You'll also find antique umbrellas and vintage parasols dating from the early 1900s through the sixties.

BEST BETS   The old-fashioned, traditional, black, big top at $395; just don't lose it.

WEB TIPS   Excellent site with brollies for men, women and unisex; you can shop online. There's even a category for rare and vintage as well as beach and also parasols.

WHERE TO BUY   1 store: 1043 Third Ave., between 61st and 62nd sts., NYC. ☎ **212/813-9530.** Mon–Sat 11am–7pm; Sun noon–6pm. AE, DISC, MC, V. Subway: 59th St./Lexington Ave. www.brellabar.com.

Brightfeet USA $$

Maybe he wants you barefoot and pregnant. You want him in comfy bedroom slippers equipped with guiding lights in the toes. Sensors switch 'em on, so you don't have to remember to turn your feet on or off.

BEST BETS   This is obviously one of the best gifts in the world for the guy who has everything or who gets up in the middle of the night and trips over his clothes.

WEB TIPS   You can order online.

WHERE TO BUY   Distribution is spotty through gift, novelty and department stores. It's easiest to go online. www.brightfeet slippers.com.

Buck X-tract USA $$

Called a multi-tool—and every guy (and gal) should carry one except that they are illegal on planes and through security gates these days. This isn't the only manufacturer of these items, so look around. Buck knives and tool units usually can be opened with one hand and solve more problems than a Swiss Army Knife. The firm that makes them is over 100 years old and is famous for a variety of knives with folding and fixed blades. They also do custom work and collaborate with collectors.

BEST BETS   The X-tract costs $50.

WHERE TO BUY   Hunting, fishing, camping and work-related specialty stores. www.buckknives.com.

Jack Spade NYC $$–$$$$

There is no Jack Spade; he is not Kate Spade's husband, although Jack Spade is a division of the Kate Spade accessories empire. Created by Kate and her husband, Andy (this will be on the final exam), Jack Spade has a core philosophy of com-bining utilitarian modes with simple design. The firm is best known for its totes, gym bags, travel bags and messenger bags. A locker bag will cost $300 while a flight kit is $85.

Jack Spade messenger bag.

BEST BETS   Aside from the bottom-line basics, the line has a sense of humor that carries into the products—you can buy a slingshot ($40) or a leather case for your Ping-Pong paddle ($65). The range is a balance of paper goods and books, curiosities, toys and the essentials of guy wear—gloves, sunglasses, small leather goods and so on.

WEB TIPS   The website is easy to use and allows you to shop online; regular FedEx rates apply.

WHERE TO BUY   1 store. Also at Apple stores, Flight 001, Bloom-ingdale's, Barneys, Nordstrom and international department stores. 56 Greene St., NYC. ☎ **212/625-1820.** AE, DISC, MC, V. Mon–Sat 11am–7pm; Sun noon–6pm. Subway: C, E at Spring. www.jackspade.com.

Jim Thompson THAI $–$$

For great gifts for men, visit the flagship store with the wide selection of ties and pocket squares and an extraordinary range of accessories in silk—printed or twill. The tie travel

Tie One On

Almost all men's clothing and luxury brands make ties. **Ralph Lauren** (p. 49) got his start in the tie business. Sometimes, the tie has a distinguishing look to it that becomes part of its status—an **Hermès** (p. 122) tie for $158 is usually recognizable in a blink. In case you didn't recognize the tie, note that today's young turks now wear theirs backwards so the label faces out.

Other distinct ties: **Paul Smith,** always colorful and bad-boy (p. 221) for $130. **Ferragamo** (p. 244) ties, $145, are similar to Hermès, with small, tight patterns, though still different. **Burberry** (p. 224) makes their classic checkered-pattern tie for $130. The French firm **Façonnable** (p. 219) sells silk ties for $90. **Favourbrook** (www.favourbrook.com) also sells silk ties for $90; with a business suit, one of these would make a powerful statement. You can buy very nice silk ties for $7 in markets in Italy.

There is a whole business in novelty ties, especially around holidays; **Josh Bach** (www.joshbach.com) makes sophisticated ties— considering we are talking novelty ties. The tie with all the signatures from the Declaration of Independence is perfect, as is the price, $45. He also makes a tie of math formulas and a *Space Invaders* tie.

You'll find many of the ties above discounted at **www.tiedeals. com**, which buys ties in Italy and passes on the savings. They sell Burberry ties for $77 (normally $175), Ted Baker for $59 (normally $95) and Fendi for $53 (normally $135). You pay $6.99 for shipping from San Diego. **BlueFly.com** also sells discounted ties; designer brands run $30 to $125, and shipping is $7.95.

cases and Dopp kits are downright memorable—the silk pouches are finished with leather and, when appropriate, plastic lined. Prices are by size but range from $25 to $45.

For the full story on Jim Thompson, see p. 48.

J.M. Weston FRENCH $$$$–$$$$$

In case you are wondering, the J.M. stands for Jean-Marie. This is an elite shoemaker to the richly and famously shod, making shoes off the rack or bespoken in quality hides with prices in the $300 to $5,000 range. Weston has turned their talents with leather into a widening business with some accessories that are simple yet expressive in telling the world you have arrived. All accessories (card cases, wallets and the like) come in a variety of hides. There are also belts with assorted buckles. Note that there is a logo on each piece, but it's an italicized letter O taken from the format of the house logo.

BEST BETS   The briefcase, Mr. Bond.

WEB TIPS   Accessories are not even shown online.

WHERE TO BUY   27 stores, including NYC, Beverly Hills, Chicago, Greenwich, San Francisco; department stores such as Saks. NYC: 812 Madison Ave. ☎ **212/535-2100.** Mon–Sat 10am–7pm. Subway: Hunter College. Paris: 114 av. des Champs Elysees, 8e. ☎ **331/4562-2647.** Mon–Sat 10am–8pm. AE, MC, V. Métro: F.D. Roosevelt. www.j-mweston.com.

G. Lorenzi MILAN $$–$$$$

Inspector Gadget could call this home: It's a specialty store that sells knives and small tools for grooming as well as for the home—masterful and exquisitely made products that you'd expect Leonardo da Vinci invented.

This kind of store is unusual for the dress-up designer street where it is located, but is not uncommon for Italy; most small towns have a store like this that has no comparable retail position in the U.S. There are also various shaving instruments and brushes. This is one of those stores where you want to touch everything and buy gifts for all the men in your life. There are about 20,000 different items for sale.

Note that I am writing about G. Lorenzi, but there is an incredibly similar store in Milan in the upscale residential area of Magenta. It was started in the 1920s by his brother, Olimpio, and is therefore O. Lorenzi.

BEST BETS   The long fire-starter wand is chic and so much better looking than the plastic butane job you buy at the local hardware store. This will set you back about $50. Many men like the combs, shaving gear and specialty scissors—there are 20 different kinds of scissors for sale.

WEB TIPS   To get to the right site, you must know which store you want and which brother you are patronizing. Once you get to G. Lorenzi, note that you cannot view the collection of products, and they have no catalog—so you can order by phone, but it is difficult. Your best bet in the U.S. is Bergdorf Goodman (p. 40).

WHERE TO BUY 1 store. Also at Bergdorf Goodman. 9 via Monte Napoleone, Milan. ☎ **3902/7602-2848.** www.glorenzi.it. AE, MC, V. Mon 3–7:30pm; Tues–Fri 9am–1pm and 3–7:30pm; Sat 9:30am–1pm and 3–7:30pm. Metro: Monte Napoleone. O. Lorenzi store: 1 Corso Magenta. ☎ 39/02-869-2997. www. o-lorenzi.com.

Oakley USA $$–$$$$

The difference between a birdie and a bogey can come right down to the sunglasses you wear on the golf course. Golf pros love the polarized lens/lightweight frame combo of Oakley's, and give rave reviews to the Oakley M Frame which has interchangeable lenses to suit varied light conditions. This model has the option of popping in a reddish tint lens for partly cloudy skies, or an amber hue for bright sun, and the frame's distortion minimizing shape provides clear vision over the whole surface of the lens. The glasses are $150, with additional lenses running $40–$70.

BEST BETS   Oakley also makes the Thump ($229–$299), the world's first digital audio eyewear—sunglasses with built in MP3, capable of storing up to 120 songs. Also look at the Razrwire B ($225)—combining Oakley's optics with Motorola technology equals a wearable cell-phone link.

WEB TIPS   You can view all on the website, but you cannot order online. All models are available at Oakley stores and optical retailers.

WHERE TO BUY   60 Stores worldwide. Discontinued models available at Oakley Vault locations. Check website for nearest store. www.oakley.com.

Persol ITALIAN $$$–$$$$

Persol sunglasses were originally made for pilots and sports drivers but have since captured the attention of Hollywood— they were a favorite of Steve McQueen and were featured in the last two James Bond films.

BEST BETS   The company is best known for sports model frames and was the first to perfect the flexible stem.

WEB TIPS   A store locator is provided once you input what country you want to shop in. You cannot shop online.

Persol prices range from $120 to $230, depending on style.

WHERE TO BUY   Available through retailers worldwide. You can sometimes find them in a duty-free. www.persol.com.

Ray Bans USA $$$–$$$$

The two most popular and best-selling styles of sunglasses in history were created by Ray Bans. The Wayfarer is a classic style which has been featured in movies such as *Risky Business* and *The Blues Brothers.* And who can forget Tom Cruise's shades in *Top Gun?* He was wearing the Aviator. Both classic styles are still best-sellers, retailing at slightly over $100. Ray Bans that cost $10 are fake.

BEST BETS   You can get Ray Bans that will hold a prescription lens.

WEB TIPS   First select the country where you want to shop, then find "store locator" in tiny type at the bottom left.

WHERE TO BUY   Available at www.SunglassHut.com and other retailers worldwide; some duty-free stores. www.ray-ban.com.

Swaine Adeney Brigg LONDON $$$–$$$$

This 200+ year old firm makes the iconic Brit Brolly that you think of when you close your eyes and imagine a rainy day in London Town. They are handmade by master craftspeople and, contrary to popular myth, do come in other shades besides black. There's also selection in the handles, in little plaques that can be engraved, in size and so on. Along with brollies, this firm makes a full range of proper accessories for gentlemen such as briefcases and small leather goods, and even luggage. There's also clothes, tailoring services, hats and the essential equestrian needs, my dear fellow. Oh yes, and don't forget the canes and/or walking sticks, croquet mallets and grooming kits. Prices are so stiff upper lip that they aren't even printed in the catalog.

BEST BETS   No proper gentleman would buy anything besides black; do consider the black plaited leather handle and specify the height of the umbrella when you order so you can lean on it out on a shoot, old chap.

WEB TIPS   You can order online.

WHERE TO BUY   1 store: 54 St. James, London, SW1. ☎ 4420/ 7409-7277. Tube: Piccadilly Circus. Daily 9am–6pm. AE, MC, V. www.swaineadeney.co.uk.

Action, Sporting & Team Wear

I can't possibly list every major active-sportswear chain and brand in the world or even the ones I find the best because best today is old-hat tomorrow—this is a field that is very much related to novelty and technology.

If you need to make a quick purchase, try a branch of the chain **Sports Authority;** also note that the various athletic-shoe companies have snazzy shops, such as **Niketown.** Most of the Activewear listings in Chapter Four: "Women's Clothing" also sell men's gear. See p. 65.

Adidas GERMAN $–$$$$

This German athletic brand is back in style—it even got Stella McCartney to design a line (p. 66). The New York store will knock your socks off; it's not as large as Niketown, but the store is sleek and black and minimalist and functional all at once. What has made this brand so popular with young men is the retro edge that borders on kitsch and camp. There's also excellent color combinations in shoes, clothes and gear.

BEST BETS   If you are planning a trip to Paris, don't miss the new Adidas store on the Champs Elysees. Otherwise, wander in your chosen store and marvel at the colors and sleek designs, and the sneakers you can't live without.

WHERE TO BUY   6,000+ stores worldwide, half in China alone. **FLAGSHIP**   8 av. des Champs Elysees, Paris, 8e. ☎ **331/5659-3280.** Mon–Thurs 10am–8pm; Fri–Sat 10am–10pm. AE, MC, V. Métro: Clemenceau-Champs Elysees. NYC: 610 Broadway, at Houston St. ☎ **212/529-0081.** Mon–Sat 10am–8pm; Sun 11am–7pm. AE, DISC, MC, V. Subway: B, D, F, R to Broadway/Lafayette. www.adidas.com.

Beretta ITALIAN $$–$$$$

This firm is over 400 years old and has stores in major shopping capitals all over the world as well as distribution through some specialty stores. The brand is best known for their firearms, but it has fashion and field clothes and accessories. They wholesale worldwide but also have their own stores, called Beretta Gallery.

BEST BETS   Since I don't like guns, I have to go with the clothes, which are stunning and offer an understated look at perfect country living. Gloves cost $70 whereas a gamekeeper's jacket is $130, a relative bargain. A leather-covered 4-oz flask is $95. This brand has a lot of status associated with its name and is an insider's source.

WEB TIPS   The online store is for the U.S. market only. You cannot buy guns online. Go to berettausa.com to shop.

WHERE TO BUY   Specialty stores and 7 Beretta Gallery stores worldwide, in Milan, NYC, Paris, Buenos Aires, more. **FLAGSHIP** 5 via Durini, Milan. ☎ **3902/7602-8325.** NYC: 718 Madison Ave. ☎ **212/319-3235.** Mon–Sat 10am–6pm. AE, MC, V. www. beretta.com or www.berettausa.com.

Cabela's USA $–$$$

Enormous, but I mean monster-sized, big-box store, naming themselves the world's foremost outfitter for fishing, hunting and outdoor gear. I'd say this is L.L.Bean on steroids but without fashion finesse. Yes, there are clothing items but they tend to be more functional than fashionable, as if the wearer/shopper might be offended if he or she looked too cute. There are active/action clothes, training clothes, outback/territory clothes and so on. You can be ready for field, stream or bush. And don't forget to take along your portable dry toilet. While this is mostly a "guy source," there are plenty of items for women; performance has no gender.

BEST BETS   The catalog; some one million go out each season to all 50 states and some 120 different countries.

WEB TIPS   You can shop online, book a trip online and even apply for a fidelity Visa card online.

WHERE TO BUY   37 stores. **FLAGSHIP**   115 Cabela Dr., Sidney, NE. ☎ **308/254-7889.** U.S. toll-free: 800/237-4444. International line: 308/234-5555 (Spanish and French operators available). www.cabelas.com.

NBA USA $–$$$$

There are two types of NBA stores—the regular store, of which there is only one (NYC) and then their newer concept called **NBA City.** City stores are super-stores with cafes, interactive equipment, retail sales and a lot of promotions and community-oriented programs.

I think the Manhattan store, right there on Fifth Avenue with all the big fashion names, is one of the best stores in the world because of the focus and fun they bring to the shopper. This is entertainment with a sideline of shopping.

Insider's tip: Kids can book a birthday party in the Fifth Avenue store. Ask your hometown store if this is allowed, too.

The NBA City stores consider themselves an entertainment site—they have huge restaurants and some retail. The food choices are all-American and come with names your children will think are clever—Miami Heat Dogs, and so on. If you go online you can often find a coupon for $5 off a meal of $25 or more.

WEB TIPS   The NBA website is more fan oriented and is difficult to use for shopping or even retail information, but if you go to NBAShop.com you can do some retail therapy.

WHERE TO BUY   3 stores. **FLAGSHIP**   666 Fifth Ave. ☎ **212/515-6221.** Mon–Sat 10am–7pm; Sun 11am–6pm; weekdays in summer the store stays open until 8pm. AE, DISC, MC, V. Subway: Rockefeller Center or Fifth Ave. stops. www.nba.com. NBA City stores: Orlando and Minneapolis.

NFL.com USA $$–$$$$$

Teams have their own stores that sell their logo merchandise, but the NFL website allows you to shop all teams for a wide variety of merchandise, including custom-made jerseys—yes, with your name. Custom jerseys start at $89 and go up to about $300. Regular jerseys are less.

BEST BETS   My favorite is the pet jersey for $30, which for some reason does not come in small—it's just medium, large and extra large. Does the NFL think a miniature dachshund doesn't care about football?

WEB TIPS   The website is easy to use. There are promotions, deals on shipping and coupons.

WHERE TO BUY   Online only. www.nfl.com.

Nike USA $$–$$$$

World's
Best

Perhaps the best example of retail as theatre and advertisement for branding in modern history, Nike is a way of life. Even their advert tag—just do it—has become an internationally known slogan.

Their stores are all big and bold; often called Niketown, they represent the fact that it takes a brand to make a village. Note that while the brand—and the stores—are called Nike, in two syllables in the U.S., in many parts of the world this is simply Nike, rhymes with Mike. The Champs Elysees store is called Nike Paris, not Niketown or Ville du Nike. Likewise there's Nike Bologna, Nike Milan and so forth.

The stores feature product as art; product as trophy and plenty of space to view, to try and to try on the mainstay of the business—the shoes. The logo, an artistic check mark, permeates the designs. Technology and function go together to provide cutting-edge fashions and footwear. Nike keeps its edge with technology; they work with athletes as well as fashion houses. One of the newest launches is a men's shoe in conjunction with Cole Haan.

There are a number of outlet stores all over the world. In fact, there are far more Nike outlets than there are Niketown stores in the U.S. alone.

BEST BETS   Techno advancements in science and design always provide a hot must-have—such as shoes that carry your iPod while you run. Just do it.

WEB TIPS   You can order customized gear online through the Nike ID program.

WHERE TO BUY   15 Niketown stores in US. 90 factory stores in US. **FLAGSHIP**   6 E. 57th St., NYC. ☎ **212/891-6453.** Customer service ☎ **800/806-6453.** Mon–Sat 10am–8pm; Sun 11am–7pm. AE, DISC, MC, V. International branches: London, Paris, Berlin and others. www.niketown.com, www.nike.com.

Orvis USA $–$$$$

Outfitters for sports and country lifestyle with expertise in fishing; also does safari and hunting but is famous for their dog beds. While there are stores dotted around the U.S. and UK (and outlets too), a large business is done online and by catalog. The firm is 150 years old and works to personalize its business. The flagship stores are called Destination Stores; they are fairly large and serve to represent the entire lifestyle. Each has its own Fishing Director whom you can consult.

BEST BETS   Orvis sells the most popular dog bed in the U.S., $125. Yes, dogs are welcome in all stores.

WEB TIPS   Free shipping if you have an Orvis Visa card. You get $10 off on orders of $100 or more on the day you sign up for the Visa card.

WHERE TO BUY   38 stores in the U.S. Locations include 7012 E. Greenway Pkwy., Scottsdale, AZ. ☎ **480/905-1400.** Mon–Sat 10am–7pm; Thurs 10am–8pm; Sun noon–6pm. DISC, MC, V. Other cities include San Francisco, Denver, Atlanta, Boston, Raleigh, NYC. www.orvis.com.

Paragon NYC $–$$$$

If you consider Manhattan the height of sophistication and the Union Square area as the mecca for foodies, you are in for a treat when you visit Paragon, a department store of stuff. There's equipment, gear, matches, designer clothes, sleeping bags; tennis, anyone? You name it, it's here. Yes, even bathing caps. To paraphrase Stephen Sondheim, Does anyone still wear a bathing cap?

BEST BETS   This is a four-story department store of stuff—for athlete and for extreme actionman but also for kids with backpacks for school and for all needs functional. There are some 50,000 items for sale in the store.

WEB TIPS   The site has 30,000 items for sale.

WHERE TO BUY   1 store: 867 Broadway, NYC. ☎ **212/255-8036.** Mon–Sat 10am–8pm; Sun 11:30am–7pm. All major credit cards. Subway: 4, 5, 6, L, N,Q, R, W, 14th St., Union Sq. www.paragonsports.com.

Pearl Izumi USA $$–$$$$

Pearl Izumi has been leading the pack in producing cycling gear for over 50 years and is now branching out into other sport categories, including cross-country skiing, triathlon and running. They're known for their well-priced athletic footwear (under $125) and also make high-tech performance clothing. Comfort and fit are what put this line of gear ahead of the competition.

WEB TIPS   Log on to the website to find a local source.

WHERE TO BUY   The products are sold through retailers worldwide, including REI. www.pearlizumi.com.

James Purdey & Sons Ltd. LONDON $$–$$$$$

The Front and Back Rooms are where you'll shop for gifts, accessories and clothing. Guns and rifles are located in the Gun Room (duh). The Long Room at the rear of the building houses a collection of historic Purdey guns dating from 1816 to 1880; this room is still where many of the world's most distinguished people come to be measured for their new guns.

BEST BETS   Like a bespoke suit, Purdey guns are crafted to fit the shooter; prices start at about $90,000 for a side-by-side game gun and go up to the hundreds of thousands for other custom models. If you don't want to wait 10 to 12 months to have one made, new guns are sold in this tony Mayfair shop.

WEB TIPS   The site advises that you call the store directly for mail service. It is against the law to ship/bring guns into the U.S. without proper paperwork.

WHERE TO BUY   1 store: 57–58 S. Audley St., London. ☎ **4420/ 7499-1801.** Mon–Fri 9:30am–5:30pm; Sat 10am–5pm. AE, MC, V. Tube: Bond St. or Marble Arch. www.purdey.co.uk.

REI USA $–$$$$

Gear for all sports and events, even adventures and classes to sign up for and in-store events for the whole family. You can have your bike's tires inflated in the store, test sporting equipment, get expert advice and partake of an entire lifestyle. The architecture of the flagship is so striking it belongs in a book about modern architecture.

BEST BETS   Family gear—good stuff for all sports and even things like sport utility stroller ($300) or a doggy backpack ($50 and up). Merchandise comes from all major makes; there are extended sizes in some ranges of clothing.

WEB TIPS   Not only can you shop online, but if you sign up to subscribe to the newsletter, you'll get a coupon for 15% off your first purchase. There is a store locator online as well as information about the outlets and "The Garage."

Vilebrequin FRENCH $$$$

Vilebrequin "Moorea" bathing suit with stamps pattern.

The celebrity swimwear of choice, these trunks have been spotted on Jack Nicholson, Hugh Grant, Brad Pitt, Paul Newman, George Clooney . . . the list goes on and on. Originally made in St-Tropez out of quick-drying sail canvas, Vilebrequin swim trunks have become a sun worshippers' staple on the French Riviera (where they were created, along with the bikini) and in chic European resorts. The trunks last a lifetime and feature a patented waterproof wallet, guaranteed to keep your money dry. That's a good thing, as you'll need plenty to keep Vilebrequins in stock; they sell for $165 to $185. Infant sizes run $90 and go up to $115 for boys' size 14.

BEST BETS   Although there are hundreds of prints, they are all similar enough in styling to provide instant brand recognition. You can count on the usual beach themes such as fish, flowers and parrots, but I flip for the French pastry print.

WEB TIPS   For current patterns and styles, visit the website; you can also order online from the U.S. only. You can buy on Yoox.com.

Cashmere

The $99 cashmere sweater you can find at any U.S. discount store is not the same quality as the £179 ($360) cashmere sweater you'll see on sale at N.Peal or one of England's other icon sweater dealers. Any cashmere that has been produced in Scotland will cost more than a cashmere from the Far East, and the difference between a $200 sweater and a $500 sweater is invariably the quality of the cashmere itself and the way it has been processed. See p. 74 for more on cashmere as well as p. 75 for how to shop the Cashmere Trail in Scotland.

Brunello Cucinelli ITALIAN $$$$$

Cucinelli is called both the King of Cashmere and the Franciscan of Cashmere. The Franciscan part is related to the almost religious and very philosophical ideas behind this firm. One look at the website and you'll get goosebumps. This is a small firm, maybe the best and most expensive of the Italian cashmeres. Cucinelli himself travels to Mongolia and meets with his goat herders; he takes only the best cashmere fibers (from the throat of the goat, which will be the title of my next book).

The inspiration for this line—some 25 years ago—was the fact that fellow Italian Luciano Benetton was flooding the world with inexpensive and very colorful sweaters.

BEST BETS   Cucinelli decided to take color to cashmere as Benetton did to cotton. Sweaters start around $1,000 although there are T-shirts and other items for less.

WEB TIPS   You cannot buy on the official site, although there are other ways to buy online. The site is one of the most beautiful you will ever see. Do not let the Italian designation throw you; just click on English. The site is very slow because it has many pictures and many quotes from Socrates. I went onto the Italian discount clothing website Yoox.com and found a stunning camisole for $114.

WHERE TO BUY   Sold in U.S. specialty stores. Bergdorf Goodman and Saks. www.brunellocucinelli.it, www.yoox.com.

Franck Namani FRENCH $$–$$$$$

No brand epitomizes the rich casual Euro look more than this small brand, which sells aristos their country and weekend clothes. The store is famous for its cashmeres in which sweaters often come in yummy ice-cream colors.

BEST BETS   Look "with it" in a cashmere hoodie with zip front. You'll pay $300 to $500 for the privilege.

WHERE TO BUY   3 stores in Paris. Also Brussels and Geneva. **FLAGSHIP**   2 rue de Castiglione, 1er. ☎ **331/49-27-05-53.** Mon–Sat 10am–7pm. Metro: Concorde.

N. Peal BRITISH $$$$

Don't overlook the cashmere accessory items; the striped socks for £29 ($58) are to die for, as is the iPod cover (£7.50/$15).

BEST BETS   Classic cable knit cashmere in ice-cream colors, along with gift accessories, are unique.

See listing on p. 77.

Casual & Smart Casual

Club Monaco CANADIAN $$–$$$$

There's actually clothes for men, women and children as well as cosmetics and lifestyle designs. But for a metroman, this is one of the best clothing sources in the world—a way to look hip at an affordable price.

BEST BETS   I think the most defining thing I can tell you about this store is that all their cotton dress shirts have a stretch element—this customer cares about fit. (Stretch cotton shirts cost about $79.)

WEB TIPS   You must click on "mens" to get anywhere with menswear. Prices are in U.S. dollars.

WHERE TO BUY   80 stores worldwide. 38 stores in U.S. **U.S. FLAG-SHIP**   6 W. 57th St., NYC.   ☎ **212/459-9863.** Mon–Sat 10am–9pm; Sun 11am–7pm. AE, DISC, MC, V. Subway: 57th St./Fifth Ave. Other locations include Beverly Hills, Seattle, Dallas, Philadelphia. www.clubmonaco.com.

Cordings LONDON $$$$

Ever wonder where Ralph Lauren got his ideas when he first started out? From basic English country clothes lines such as Cordings, that's where. Now owned by none other than Eric Clapton, the firm has items such as corduroy trousers in a style that hasn't changed in decades, yet they come in amazing rainbow hues. There's everything English you can imagine, from tweeds to waxed jackets. The store was begun in 1839 and is exactly that old chap's resource you are searching for (outside a Ralph Lauren outlet).

BEST BETS   Stick with the traditional stuff, such as corduroy trousers for $180. They come with a three-button fly which makes them worth the difference.

WEB TIPS   Yes, you can shop online; delivery charges are $10 for the UK, $40 for the E.U. and $70 for the U.S. Ouch.

WHERE TO BUY   1 store: 16 Piccadilly, London, W1. ☎ **44-20/7734-90830.** Mon–Wed, Fri 9:30am–6:30pm; Thurs 10am–7pm; Sat 10am–6pm. AE, MC, V. Tube: Green Park or Piccadilly. www.cordings.co.uk.

C.P. Company ITALIAN $$$–$$$$

This Italian brand has given up most of its retail stores to concentrate on manufacturing the kind of casual clothes that look like a million bucks. Prices do not require millionaire cus-tomers, but can be steep. The look is a little bit rugged but the fabrication is top-quality Italian cottons, wools and linens. The line is for the man who hates labels and logos and wants chic but high-performance clothing. The customer considers him-self a no B.S. kind of guy.

BEST BETS   CP makes the kind of clothes that at first glance are average and on further inspection are extraordinary—it in the materials and the details, both of which hinge on the latest technology.

WEB TIPS   You cannot buy online, and while the site is nice, there's not much in terms of solid info on the clothes, the prices or anything other than philosophy.

WHERE TO BUY   Nordstrom stores in the U.S. **FLAGSHIP**   12 Corso Venezia, Milan. ☎ **3902/7600-1409.** Mon 3–7pm; Tues–Sat 10am–7pm. CB, MC, V. Other stores in Rome, Palermo, London, Tokyo and Prague. www.cpcompany.com.

Etro Man   ITALIAN $$$$

Flamboyant and witty clothes that are so unusual they don't come anywhere near macho and might very well fit some women. But then again, there's the Etro Su Misura made-to-measure line of suits which is classical on the outside but may have interesting linings or details inside the suit, just to give

you that inner twinge of a giggle.

BEST BETS   The styles are so unusual and out there—especially in the more casual clothes—that they are time-less.

WEB TIPS   You can book an appointment for a made-to-measure fitting online.

WHERE TO BUY   20+ stores worldwide, in Verona, Venice, Florence, Rome, Paris, Berlin, Munich, London, Moscow, Beverly Hills, Las Vegas, Tokyo, more; sold in Neiman Marcus, Saks, Barneys, more in the U.S.; outlets in Wood-bury Commons, Milan and Serravale Scriva. **FLAGSHIP**

An outfit from the Etro Fall 2007 collection.

via Montenapoleone 5, Milan. ☎ **3902/7600-5049.** Mon–Sat 10am–7pm. AE, MC, V. For direct line to Etro Su Misure, call ☎ **3902/7639-4216.** NYC: 720 Madison Ave. ☎ 212/317-9096. www.etro.com.

Hugo Boss GERMAN $$–$$$$

Ja, Hugo Boss makes suits and is an outfitter of almost all things male, with a female line as well. I think they are outstanding in the smart casual field. They also have a very good fit, which is part of their success. There are three lines which make clothes for men and women and one line for men only.

There is a less expensive leisure line, Boss Orange, which combines unusual materials with vibrant color. The Boss Green collection offers functional sportswear aimed at the athletic and fashion conscious, while the Hugo brand is unconventional and avant-garde fashion defined by attitude, not age group.

BEST BETS   Sports jackets at $200 seem like a bargain considering quality and fit.

WEB TIPS   Extensive site but you cannot shop. You can sign up for the newsletter.

WHERE TO BUY   Department stores including Macy's, in many airports. 550 freestanding stores worldwide. 31 stores in US. **FLAGSHIP**   Konigstrasse 54, Stuttgart, Germany. **U.S. FLAGSHIP** 717 Fifth Ave., NYC. ☎ **212/485-1800.** Mon–Sat 10am–7pm; Sun noon–5pm. Other cities include Seattle, Boston, Dallas, San Francisco. www.hugoboss.com.

Tommy Bahama USA $$–$$$$

World's Best   Total lifestyle brand that makes the transition from just-for-vacations to regular weekend wear and even business clothing for casual or dress-down days.

I personally think it's the solids that make this line great, but they push their prints, even on the bed linen, so this is the place to buy banana-leaf printed sheets. The solids come in a nice soft, almost Armani-esque color palette, so you are buying classics you can wear for a long time.

Stores are done up in island style with dark woods and plantation fans. Some of the stores have a cafe inside.

BEST BETS   A lot of the styles have Hawaiian and island-style prints, but the best parts of the line are the solid color shirts, often made in silk, that are casual and dressy at the same time. They cost about $65 each.

WEB TIPS   The website isn't visually exciting but will give you a quick click or two to check out the goods. No online shopping.

WHERE TO BUY   80 stores worldwide. There are stores in Canada and Dubai as well as throughout the U.S. **U.S. FLAGSHIP** Kierland Commons, Scottsdale, AZ.   ☎ **480/607-3388.** Mon–Sat 10am–9pm; Sun noon–6pm. AE, MC, V. Corporate ☎ **888/868-6888.** www.tommybahama.com.

Men's Concept Stores

Brooks Brothers   USA $–$$$$$

Although Brooks Brothers has changed corporate hands a few times in the last decade or so, the store has changed enough to hold its own and keep its place in men's fashion history. This is one of the oldest businesses in America and is a wonderful story in not only survival, but triumph. And yes, since you asked, Abraham Lincoln was assassinated while wearing a Brooks Brothers garment (bespoke).

Yes, they do make a boxy cut suit and offer great clothes for the man with a typical American body (in other words, big) but wait, now they do tailored and skinny as well. The firm can outfit a man from cradle to grave and makes all aspects of clothing; it is a lifestyle brand. Brooks also makes custom suits and has just initiated a system whereby you can choose the elements of your dress shirts online and customize them yourself. For something totally new, they have added a line by Thom Browne who does fitted jackets with short trousers.

BEST BETS   The logo of the golden fleece is not as obvious as a polo player but adds a layer of "in-the-know" to any garment.

WEB TIPS   You can custom-order your shirts online.

WHERE TO BUY   170 stores in U.S.; 70 others worldwide. **FLAG-SHIP** 666 Fifth Ave., NYC.   ☎ **212/261-9440.** Mon–Fri 10am–8pm; Sat 10am–7pm; Sun 11am–7pm. AE, DISC, MC, V. Subway: E, V at Fifth Ave./53rd St. Also in Paris, Cernobbio (Italy), and more. www.brooksbrothers.com.

Comme des Garçons   JAPANESE $$$$–$$$$$

World's Best   If you ever wondered how a guy can wear ripped jeans or clothes with raw seams and still look cool, you have only to thank Rei Kawakubo and the team at Comme des Garçons that, despite the name, does women's as well as men's lines. The clothes take fibers that aren't often used in clothing, distress them, bring in a comfort factor and create news on the catwalk and in the stores, bringing streetwear to a new dimension—often for a steep price.

BEST BETS   There's a sub-line by Junya Watanabe. The synthetic "anti-perfumes" (with notes like burning rubber and dry-cleaning steam) range from wearable to amusing.

WEB TIPS   Find locations of guerrilla or "pop-up" stores online. They are often in exotic locations such as Krakow or Beirut.

WHERE TO BUY   12+ stores in Tokyo, New York, Paris's place Vendôme, London's Dover Street Market; dozens of "guerilla" stores that open for less than a year. **FLAGSHIP**   5-3 Minami-Aoyama, Tokyo.   ☎ **03/5774-7800.** Daily 11am–8pm. www.guerilla-store.com.

Façonnable   FRENCH $–$$$

If you lived in France and were named Albert Goldberg, you'd come up with another name for your company too. Façonnable is often considered hard to pronounce by Americans—it's Fashion-ab-lay. Voilà. The image of the firm is slightly different in France from the rest of the world because the French consider this an iconic brand.

Façonnable has freestanding stores all over the world. The U.S. stores are a joint venture with Nordstrom, which also has exclusive rights to the line in their stores.

BEST BETS   Although the company offers a full range of all fashions—and also has some womenswear—they excel at men's casual clothing. There are suits and dress-up fashions, but get a look at the sweaters and shirts and the range of resort colors that no one else makes. Silk ties are $90 and a classic shirt runs $145.

WEB TIPS   In the U.S. you can buy through nordstroms.com.

WHERE TO BUY   14 stores worldwide. **FLAGSHIP**   7–9 rue Paradis, Nice, France.   ☎ **334/9387-8880.** Mon–Fri 10am–1pm, 2–7pm; Sat 10am–7pm. **U.S. FLAGSHIP**   636 Fifth Ave., Rockefeller Center, NYC.   ☎ **212/319-0111.** Mon–Fri 10am–8pm; Sat 10am–7pm; Sun noon–6pm. AE, DISC, MC, V. Subway: Rockefeller Center. www.faconnable.com.

Jeffrey   USA $$$$–$$$$$

This lifestyle store sells a total look for women and for men, each piece bought to continue the Jeffrey myth and propel the look of cool edginess possibly by the women who shop here or the couples who come in tandem while exploring the Meat Packing District. For men, Jeffrey has fashion, shoes, accessories and some toiletries. See p. 47.

Joe Bananas SYDNEY $$$$

Joe himself is quite a character, but his look is even more memorable—he is able to do chic within the confines of hand-loomed and native-crafted textiles and come away with an important look that is in no way touristy or costumey. He has many celebrity clients, he claims, which is fitting because his look is rather rock-and-roll. Jackets begin at $1,000. There's off the rack or bespoke; nubby, loopy, texturized and linenified.

BEST BETS   The one-of-a-kind, handwoven fabrics that make nubby, chic, have-to-have-it sports jackets that are worth any price.

WEB TIPS   Be careful when entering the Web address. Joe bananas.com will link you to a restaurant in Hong Kong.

WHERE TO BUY   1 store: Queen Victoria Building, no. 45, 455 George St., Sydney, Australia. ☎ **612/926-42733.** Mon–Wed, Fri–Sat 9am–6pm; Thurs 9am–8pm; Sun 11am–5pm. AE, MC, V. www.joebananas.com.au.

Joseph Abboud USA $$$–$$$$$

Joseph Abboud is the man who would be king, but for some reason he has never gotten the break that elevates him from cult status to Ralph Lauren level. Various stores and collections have put him in and out of business, yet his talent and sophisticated taste level ensure that he's always got product out there for loyal customers who can't get enough of the suits, ties, casual clothes and lifestyle home style that are subtle and always chic. There's also women's clothing.

BEST BETS   Texture and fabric play a big part of the story, as does the use of neutral tones that give the clothes the ability to wear season after season. Abboud does suits and office wardrobe, casual clothes and jackets and trousers that can mix and match so you can put together your own suit, your own way. Expect to pay about $400 for a jacket and $200 for the trousers. Sizes range from S to XXL in merchandise that is not specifically sized.

WEB TIPS   Brings up assorted links to the various licensees.

WHERE TO BUY   Nordstrom, Saks, Macy's and Bloomingdale's. www.josephabboud.com.

Loro Piana ITALIAN $$–$$$$$

Loro Piana makes their own fabrics and offers cut-and-sewn fashion in everything from shawls and scarves to men's suits. There's even shoes and accessories. It's sort of a rugged outdoorsy look. There's also women's wear and home style;

country clothes, weekend gear and accessories and all the dress-up a guy would ever need. This is as much a lifestyle as anything else. Think Hotel Villa d'Este in Lake Como and you've got the whole picture of the brand and the customer.

BEST BETS I bought a feather-light cashmere scarf for a man who rides a Harley—it cost $150 at the outlet (which I found pricey but too delish to leave behind). Imagine my shock at discovering the same item for $450 in stores in the U.S. That's worth the trip to Italy right there.

See p. 76.

Paul Smith BRITISH $$–$$$$$

No one epitomizes the English Eccentric better than Sir Paul Smith, who gained his title in providing an international face to a very British aspect of design and lifestyle. Although primarily a menswear designer, Smith does women's clothes as well as accessories and home style. He is currently known for a series of colored stripes that are something of a signature look, almost an identity logo.

Men's suits may be traditional with one bizarre twist; casual clothing may be truly bizarre. Prints—often large and loud—are paramount; a Paul Smith tie can be instantly recognized by the knowing onlooker. For the rock star, or the man who likes to flaunt his individuality, this line offers a complete wardrobe and a way of life.

There are some outlet stores in the UK as well as an outlet shop in the heart of London where ties sell for a mere £25 ($50). Average prices are £65 ($130) for ties, shirts, suits.

BEST BETS Stripey casual shoes in the Smith logo pattern, $300.

WHERE TO BUY 15 stores worldwide. **FLAGSHIP** 122 Kensington Park Rd., London W11. ☎ **207/727-3553.** Mon–Fri 10am–6pm; Sat 10am–6:30pm. AE, MC, V. Tube: Notting Hill Gate. **U.S. FLAGSHIP** 104 Fifth Ave., NYC. ☎ **212/627-9770.** Other cities include Milan, Paris, Tokyo. www.paulsmith. co.uk.

Department Stores for Men

Barneys Men's Store USA $–$$$$$

Barneys left its downtown roots and now dominates the world of men in black. It's a way of life as well as a good store for men of all sizes and shapes.

BEST BETS   Menswear is sold in all Barneys stores and outlets, but the flagship store in Manhattan actually stands as a separate department store of men's merchandise with an enormous range of product and sizes, especially good for hard-to-fit sizes. Standing adjoined and adjacent to the women's store, the men's store must be accessed on the first, second, fourth or sixth floor of the main store or through the 60th St. back door.

WEB TIPS   Click on "mens" and you can shop online, if you call that shopping. For such a fabulous store, this is not an exciting website nor does it have much selection.

WHERE TO BUY   8 stores in the U.S. **FLAGSHIP**   660 Madison Ave. (at 61st St.), NYC. ☎ **212/826-8900.** Mon–Fri 10am–8pm; Sat 10am–7pm; Sun 11am–6pm. AE, MC, V. Other locations include Beverly Hills. www.barneys.com.

BHV Homme PARIS $$–$$$$$

This department store takes up five floors, has an eco twist and the usual man candy—barber, spa and so on. All brands and looks are carried, organized by brand. The model for the store was undoubtedly the Galeries Lafayette men's store on blvd. Haussmann, with further inspiration by D*G Uomo in Milan, but this store is more moderne, more up-to-date and more young in its fashion perception. There's also a cafe, a barber, a tailor for alterations, an optician and my fave—wedding registry for guys. France allows same-sex unions via a civil ceremony called a PAC. Straight and gay men are invited to register their wedding preferences. Note this is not the BHV department store, but a new store, behind it.

BEST BETS   Eat your heart out, Tom Ford.

WEB TIPS   This is one of the best websites out there, especially from a French firm. Among the many features that I've never seen before, you can click to get a route map by car, bus or bike from your hotel or home directly to the store. *Vive la France.*

WHERE TO BUY   1 store: 36 rue de la Verrerie, Paris, 4e. Mon–Sat 10am–8pm; Wed and Fri 10am–9pm. Métro: Hotel de Ville. www.BHVHomme.fr.

Dunhill BRITISH $$–$$$$$

This is the gentleman's men's department store, run very much as a private club—although anyone can enter, of course. Even women. This is the shop for the man who has everything, likes everything (or can't stand to shop), is social, wants to drop in at "his" store to fulfill his needs for suits, accessories and smokes. If he has a Harley bent to him, he also appreciates the moto-trends.

Walking into the Jermyn Street store is something like walking into a magazine layout for guys: Airplanes hang from the ceiling; motorcycles harrrrumph near the ties. The motorcycles can be traced directly to Nick Ashley (yeah, son of) who began on Ledbury Grove with moto fashions and has had such impact on British testosterone that he has helped Dunhill find its place in this century.

BEST BETS   The upstairs walk-in humidor room filled with cigars.

WEB TIPS   You can shop online; select a country where you will take delivery—prices are displayed in local currency.

WHERE TO BUY   FLAGSHIP   48 Jermyn St., London W1. ☎ **44-20/ 7290-8600.** Mon–Fri 9:30am–6pm; Sat 10am–6pm. Tube: Green Park, Piccadilly. NYC: 711 Fifth Ave. at 54th St. ☎ **212/ 753-9292.** Mon–Sat 10am–6:30pm, Thurs 7pm; Sun noon–5pm. Subway: E, V at Fifth Ave./53rd St. AE, DISC, MC, V. www. dunhill.com.

Men's Store Bergdorf Goodman NYC $$–$$$$$

The store, located across the street from Bergdorf's regular store, is quiet and regal with mostly classical clothes from all the international big brands. Mortal shoppers may not even recognize some of the brand names, since they are esoteric luxury brands, often imported from Italy.

Don't miss Cafe 745, which is a hidden gem and usually not crowded—even during lunch hour.

BEST BETS   Gucci G-print trainers with Velcro closure tabs, $385.

WEB TIPS   Go to the BG site and click on "men"; the pictures are impressive and the models are very pretty. And that's in the guys' section.

WHERE TO BUY   1 store: 745 Fifth Ave., NYC. ☎ **800/558-1855.** Mon–Fri 10am–8pm; Sat 10am–7pm; Sun noon–6pm. AE. Subway: Fifth Ave. www.bergdorfgoodman.com.

Paul Stuart USA $–$$$$$

Knowing this store, shopping it and even depending on it as your main source says that you are a fashion insider with money to spend and style to demonstrate. When you enter the store, it may at first glance look like a yawn, but that just proves that good taste never shouts. The store sells everything you need for business, travel, weekends and even dress-down days; there's a small women's department. There is a made-to-measure division of the firm; you can also be notified when big-name design firms visit from foreign destinations.

BEST BETS   This is a store that has soul and is worth selling yours for the privilege.

WEB TIPS   Colors are bright and snappy; there's some 29 choices of goods to click on.

WHERE TO BUY   4 stores, in NYC, Chicago, Tokyo, Seoul. **FLAG-SHIP**   Madison Ave. at 45th St., NYC. ☎ **212/682-0320.** Mon–Fri 8am–6:30pm; Thurs until 7pm; Sat 9am–6pm; Sun noon–5pm. Subway: 42nd St. Grand Central. www.paulstuart. com.

Saks Fifth Avenue Mens USA $–$$$$$

The flagship store has the very best men's department but some Saks cities actually have freestanding men's stores. Saks carries all the big-name brands, has visits by international tailors who will do a bespoke garment and carries a range of boys' and young men's sizes too. For many, this is special-event headquarters for teen boys.

WEB TIPS   Click on "Men's Store"; this is an excellent site with good pictures and tons of merchandise; there is a designer sale section online. Note that when you click on "Find a Store" there's no specific mention of the Saks Mens freestanding stores, of which there are a few.

WHERE TO BUY   100+ Saks stores and Off Fifth outlets. Use the website to find the store nearest you. **FLAGSHIP**   611 Fifth Ave. at 49th St., NYC. ☎ **877/551-7257.** Mon–Fri 10am–8pm, Sat 10am–7pm; Sun noon-5pm. AE, DISC, MC, V. Subway: Rockefeller Center. Other cities include Chicago, San Francisco, Bal Harbour. www.saks.com.

Designer Menswear

Burberry BRITISH $$–$$$$$

In keeping with its new image, Burberry has begun to take over the world. Certainly they knocked us all on our socks, which are now Burberry plaid. We all say "bravo" to Rosemary Bravo and her team that made this old-fashioned icon and maker of raincoats into the must-have brand of the turn of the 21st century.

The brand represents great design as well as hot retail design. A few years ago, it was the new flagship on New Bond in London; now there's Scotch House in Knightsbridge, and a new flagship seems to be popping up in every major city in the world. All stores feature everything known to man (or woman) that could possibly be made in plaid, including accessories for your dog. I happen to think the lavender braces (that's Brit-speak for suspenders) in the trad plaid are incredibly chic and well priced at £75 ($150).

Along with all this myth making, a new customer has come into the fold, or the plaid if you will. Teens—male and female—consider this a status, must-have brand.

Also note that many old-fashioned Burberry styles—especially in traditional rain gear—are available in vintage stores and flea markets.

BEST BETS   The classic check tie is $130.

WEB TIPS   You can shop online in either the UK or the U.S.; prices will come up in U.S. dollars if you click on "U.S." Promotions often offer free shipping on orders of $175 or more.

WHERE TO BUY   100+ stores worldwide; in 18 U.S. states; some department stores, vintage stores. **FLAGSHIP**   21–23 New Bond St., London W1. ☎ **4420/7839-5222.** Mon–Fri 9:30am–7pm; Sat 9:30–6pm; Sun noon–6pm. AE, MC, V. Tube: Bond Street. NYC: 9 E. 57th St. ☎ 212/407-7100. Factory outlet: 29-53 Chatham Place, London E9 (Hackney). ☎ 4420/8985-3344. Tube: Bethnal Green. Mon–Fri 11am–6pm; Sat 11am–5pm. AE, MC, V. www.burberry.com.

Calvin Klein USA $$–$$$$

I mourn Zack Carr, the designer who did the old Calvin Klein line of womenswear; I mourn the old Calvin Klein the way it was when it represented American fashion on the cutting edge, and yet I applaud the fact that the line is far from dead: Thank you Philips Van Heusen for leaving me a little something. The menswear is still sleek and hot. But I say that with a sigh since when I go online, all I find are links to underwear.

BEST BETS   The suits are slim and well priced at $275 and up.

WEB TIPS   You'll do better at macys.com.

WHERE TO BUY   40+ stores in NYC, Beijing, Milan, Dubai, more; department stores in the U.S., including Macy's, Nordstrom, Bloomingdale's, Bon Ton, Lord & Taylor, more. 654 Madison Ave., NYC. ☎ **212/292-9000.** Mon–Sat 10am–6pm; Sun noon–6pm. AE, MC, V.

Dior Homme FRENCH $$–$$$$$

Hedi Slimane, the designer who brought Dior Homme into the news, came to the new, improved Dior shortly after John Galliano breathed new life into the brand and brought it back from the dead. Slimane is so good he even makes Karl Lagerfeld's clothes. He is the shy toast of Paris; the kingmaker who dresses the man who would be king. He's also just left Dior Homme, so watch this space.

But the house is determined to be trendy. Known for a thin and dark silhouette in dress and casual clothes, Hedi (not Heidi, thank you) made sure the Dior line was considered the cutting edge, the line that leads the way into the future of menswear.

There are a number of freestanding Dior Homme stores around the world; invariably they are designed to be as top drawer and modern as the master's clothes; most are fitted out with new-fangled technology. Often the store is worth visiting just to grasp the cutting edge of cool.

BEST BETS   The cut of the clothes, if you are thin enough to wear them.

WEB TIPS   There is no menswear represented on the Dior Web page. However, there's usually tons of eBay listings for used pieces from the line.

WHERE TO BUY   Stores worldwide. **FLAGSHIP**   30 av. Montaigne, Paris 8e. ☎ **331/4073-5301.** Mon–Sat 10am–7pm. AE, MC, V. Métro: Franklin Roosevelt. **U.S. FLAGSHIP**   17 E. 57th St., NYC. ☎ **212/421-6009.** Mon–Sat 10am–7pm; Sun noon–6pm. AE, DISC, MC, V. Subway: Fifth Ave. www.diorhomme.com.

Jil Sander GERMAN $$$$–$$$$$

This design house has had a troubled past—in recent years they were part of the Prada family and now they are not. In the rebirth, the firm has come on especially strong with very hip menswear. It's all in the cut and the very simple lines. They tried out a shop on London's Savile Row, but that didn't work out. Now they sell the menswear from their own boutiques to the thin and the rich. See p. 457.

John Varvatos USA $$$$–$$$$$

I recently saw an ad for the shoes Varvatos designs for Converse—the model wears a T-shirt that says 'Who the hell is John Varvatos?' So I'll tell you—he used to be the designer for Ralph Lauren's menswear. If that isn't enough to know, take a look at the casualwear, the look, the suits and the accessories that are coming into the mainstream.

WHERE TO BUY   5 stores, in NYC, LA, West Hampton, Las Vegas, more; Barneys, Bloomingdale's, Saks, Bergdorf, more worldwide. **FLAGSHIP**   122 Spring St., NYC. ☎ **212/965-0700.** Mon–Sat 11am–7pm; Sun noon–6pm. AE, MC, V. Subway: N, R at Prince St. www.johnvarvatos.com.

Prada ITALIAN $$–$$$$$

I think we have to do this as a good news/bad news listing. The good news is that there are several outlets around the world and you can get a more than good deal on suits, casual clothes, shoes and accessories. The bad news is that you can pay up to $30,000 for a totally custom-made suit.

To get the Prada look clearly in mind, think of a slim black suit worn with a black T-shirt and never chunky black trainers. Perhaps a nylon messenger bag over the shoulder. Clothes for activewear depend on technology and new fabrics. Casual clothes are a tailored version of streetwear. You wear this line because you can.

BEST BETS   The shoes are affordable and comfortable and are made with a self-distinguishing red tab in the rear of the sole so that those in the know can know.

WEB TIPS   The website is very women's fashion–oriented. You'll do better to find Prada's menswear on other sites, such as Bluefly.com.

WHERE TO BUY   Stores worldwide. Outlet stores called Space. **FLAGSHIP**   Outlet in Prada factory in Montevarchio.

Discount & Deals

See Chapter Eleven: "Bargains & Alternative Retail" for more on discount shopping in this book; the stores listed below specialize in men's clothing at discount. They may carry women's clothing also, but they have excellent menswear at excellent savings. None of these are hit-or-miss sources.

Depot-Vente 17e PARIS $–$$$

Go downstairs for the men's things, although some items are featured in the vitrines. This is one of the few resale stores anywhere in the world that specializes in classic designer menswear at reasonable prices. See listing on p. 433.

Harry Rothman NYC $–$$$$$

This is more or less an old-fashioned department store with plenty of customer service (yes, personal shoppers) and all the big brands you can imagine. The only difference is that prices are 20% off regular retail. There are departments for dress up and dress casual as well as boys and boys' ceremonial (bar mitzvahs, communions) and, of course, weddings and formal events. Harry died recently, but his grandson has run this business in a very hands-on fashion.

BEST BETS   A fashion guy can pull you together totally.

WEB TIPS   You can sign up for advance notification of sales online.

WHERE TO BUY   1 store: 200 Park Ave. S., at 17th St. ☎ **212/777-7400.** Mon–Wed and Fri 10am–7pm; Thurs 10am–8pm; Sat 9:30am–6pm; Sun noon–6pm. AE, DISC, MC, V. Subway: Union Sq. www.rothmansny.com. There is a suburban store in Scarsdale, NY.

Filene's Basement USA $–$$$$

Filene's Basement, like all true discount sources, is a matter of how lucky you get and what size you happen to be. Nonetheless, they have incredible merchandise at very good prices; the flagship Boston store especially has an automatic markdown deal that will knock your already discounted socks right off. The price tag on each item is marked with the date it hits the selling floor; the longer an item remains unsold, the greater the discount—beginning at 25% off, then 50%, then 75%. Any merchandise not sold is given to charity.

WEB TIPS   Sign up for notification of the Big Suit Events. See listing on p. 428.

Syms USA $–$$$$

This is more lifestyle store or department store or an icon to smart shoppers—Syms specializes in men's needs but also sells other things. They also have a very unique markdown system wherein the longer a garment stays in the store, the lower the price. Check the codes on the back of the tag. Also ask about their Dividends promotions when things are marked down even more.

BEST BETS   The Manhattan flagship is four floors of fashion, including all aspects of a man's life from U.S. and Euro designers as well as big-name makers. There's underwear to outerwear and, of course, tuxedos, shoes, fragrance and even cuff links. The store might not be the greatest on New Age and street fashion but there is plenty that is cutting edge. Expect discounts of up to 50% off regular retail; there are over 200 designer names on the racks.

WEB TIPS   You cannot shop online but you can apply for a fidelity credit card online. The card gives you 5% off on each purchase.

WHERE TO BUY   Stores in 14 states. **FLAGSHIP**   400 Park Ave., NYC. ☎ **212/317-8200.** Mon–Fri 8am–7:30pm; Sat 10am–6:30pm; Sun noon–5:30pm. AE, DISC, MC, V. Other cities include Washington, D.C.; Dallas, TX. www.syms.com.

Dress Down & Mass Market

A Bathing Ape JAPANESE $$–$$$

Okay, I'm going to pretend you don't know that much about this brand and need to know, first off, that it is often called—by insider's—Bape. There, don't you feel better now?

A Bathing Ape began life as a T-shirt firm—shirts created by an artist known as Nigo were sold in the street near the Harajuku metro station in Tokyo—this is where all the cool stores are located.

The Bape empire includes a cafe, a hair salon and stores all over Japan. There's also the Bapy line, for Bape customers looking for lower-cost goods. Nigo was fascinated with the movies in the *Planet of the Apes* series and that's what got him going. Before you could even learn how to pronounce Harajuku, Nigo was famous and had real stores all over the world and line extensions and multiple businesses—even going into business with a hip-hop artist to launch Billionaire Boys.

Buyer Beware

Prices vary enormously from shop to shop. Bape-only stores have the best prices; stores that include A Bathing Ape in their mix are often forced to charge more for the same goods.

BEST BETS   Aside from being a decent graphic artist, Nigo is a serious student of retail and marketing. Many of his creations are limited editions, so they have become collectible. He has aligned himself with the art scene, has an art gallery and then places his stores—and galleries—in hard-to-find locations in hip 'hoods to add to their cachet. It's unlikely you would ever find a Bape store just because you were walking down the street. You have to *know*.

WEB TIPS   My computer actually asked me if I wanted to read Japanese before the site uploaded itself (in Japanese).

WHERE TO BUY   Urban streetwear boutiques, online and eBay. 20 Bape Stores worldwide. **FLAGSHIP**   Tokyo. **U.S. FLAGSHIP** SoHo, 91 Greene St., NYC. ☎ **212/925-0222.** Mon–Sat noon–7pm; Sun noon–6pm. MC, V. www.Bape.com.

TopMan BRITISH $$–$$$$

You'll find decent tailoring and casualwear at London's Top-Man at highly affordable prices. Of course, a suit from TopMan priced from £95 ($190) to £120 ($240) can't compare to a bespoke Savile Row number, but the store nonetheless provides young men on a budget the opportunity to look good without blowing their credit card limits on clothing.

BEST BETS   Casual, trendy clothes, like shirts for weekend wear at $40.

WEB TIPS   You can shop online although it's not anything like being in one of the stores.

WHERE TO BUY   TopMan is the men's division of Top Shop. There are some freestanding TopMan stores but the flagship is the one to experience—located within the flagship Top Shop at Oxford Circus, 214 Oxford St., London W1. ☎ **44-20/7636-7700.** AE, MC, V. Tube: Oxford Circus. 15 stores in London. Also stores in Tokyo, Dublin and Moscow. www.topman.co.uk.

Ethnic Dress, Work Clothes & Cowboys

If everyone loves a man in uniform, consider the power that uniforms give the wearer. The uniform becomes a costume when worn out of context or when worn to evoke a stereotypical reaction. I was just driving by a Texas construction site and, I swear, saw the bossman making his site inspection. He was wearing jeans, cowboy boots, a cowboy hat and a Drizabone.

Carhartt USA $$–$$$$

Taking American work and ranch clothes to their furthest extreme possible parlays them into the world of the chic, which is where the Carhartt brand has landed, especially in Europe. Known for rugged looks and trucker hats, bib overalls and fireproof clothing, Carhartt has been making work clothes since 1889 and sells everything a guy could want, from thermal underwear to outward bound.

BEST BETS   The macho subtext is emphasized with corporate sponsorships, as is the distribution of the line, often sold in hardware stores. Hee-Haw.

Carhartt menswear.

WEB TIPS   The website it easy to navigate; you can order directly from Carhartt, or be directed to an online retailer.

WHERE TO BUY   Stores in U.S. and 10 E.U. countries. www. carhartt.com.

Dickies TEXAN $$–$$$

Fort Worth–based maker of work clothes made with industrial strength to withstand rugged work and much washing. This brand has been a leading name since 1922.

BEST BETS   Now sold at Target.

WEB TIPS   You can shop online, although prices only come up with you click on an item to enlarge it.

WHERE TO BUY   Target stores in the U.S. www.target.com, www.dickies.com.

Drizabone AUSTRALIAN $$$$

The shearling-style jacket worn by the Marlboro Man is a generic, but the raincoat worn by an Aussie sheep herder or rancher can only be a Drizabone. As in slang for Dry As A Bone. Similar to a driving coat popular in the early 20th century and somewhat like the raincoat that can be worn by a horseback rider, the Drizabone was indeed meant to keep both rider and saddle dry. Now that it's become iconic, the raincoat has bred a shorter version and even dog versions. (Could I make this up?) In fact, there's all sorts of line extensions, including some bush gear and a Wallabies Rugby kit.

BEST BETS   Hands-down—the raincoat duster is what we all want. While the Drizabone is sold all over Australia, it can be bought throughout the world and directly online. The classic Riding Coat is $170.

WEB TIPS   Yep, there's a bone on the home page. Then you go to online link to retailers.

WHERE TO BUY   Mail order; men's and department stores. Tourist stores in Oz. www.drizabone.com.au.

F.M. Allen NYC $$$$

Safari outfitter (yes, even Clark Gable was outfitted here) is located in a tiny uptown Manhattan store where you buy clothes and gear and things the gentleman will need when he goes to ground, such as the right Dunhill flask. The store is new, the brand is old and the look is classic. There's bush luggage; there's trips and safaris to book; there's mood and adventure and millions of miles of bloody Africa.

BEST BETS   Gentlemen's sporting antiques.

WHERE TO BUY   1 store: 962 Madison Ave., NYC. ☎ 212/737-4374. Mon–Sat 10am–6pm; Sun noon–5pm. AE, MC, V. www.fmallen.com.

Kinloch Anderson SCOTTISH $$–$$$$

Balmoral or bust. With three royal warrants and all the plaid you can muster, this 150-year-old kiltmaker is THE place to find the sporran of your dreams.

BEST BETS   The store itself is right on the docks, which means it's really in Leith—which is an adorable neighborhood for browsing and sitting at a cafe when you are shopped out. The store sells everything you and your clan may need. Look past the touristy stuff if you are serious about a kilt.

WEB TIPS   It's easy to order a custom kilt on the website; just enter you choice of tartan (over 800 available) and measurements; the price will be $600 and you can expect delivery in 6 to 8 weeks.

WHERE TO BUY   Commercial St. and Dock St., Leith (Edinburgh), Scotland. ☎ 44-0131/555-1390. Mon–Sat 9am–6pm. AE, MC, V. www.kinlochanderson.com.

Maverick Fine Western Wear TEXAN $–$$$$

Maverick is a great spot to "belly up" and enjoy a cold beer at the in-store bar; it's also one of the best places to shop for top-of-the-line western gear. They carry a wide variety of western lifestyle products, including clothing, boots, hats and some housewares.

BEST BETS   In addition to selling leading brands such as Stetson (hats $150–$270) and Lucchese (boots $250–$1,200), they manufacture their own custom hats, boots and accessories.

WEB TIPS   If you can't make it to Fort Worth, you can easily order online. The website is quick with clear graphics.

WHERE TO BUY   1 store: 100 E. Exchange Ave., Ft. Worth, TX. ☎ **800/282-1315.** Mon–Thurs 10am–6pm; Fri and Sat 10am–10pm; Sun 11am–6pm. AE, DISC, MC, V. www.maverick westernwear.com.

Pinto Ranch TEXAN $$–$$$$

This Houston store is for the rhinestone cowboy in everyone, although the George Bush family has been shopping here for generations. Mama don't let your sons grow up to be presidents. The store is sort of an open warehouse that looks like a lodge with trees on the roofline. There's very upmarket brands for men and for women.

BEST BETS   Saddles begin at $3,000; dusters $180; python boots $1,500; belt buckles from the world's leading silversmiths in a variety of prices ranging from, typically, $275 to $650.

WEB TIPS   The website provides the direct extensions for the various departments.

WHERE TO BUY   One-of-a-kind store: 1717 Post Oak Blvd., Houston. ☎ **800/393-8001** or 713/333-7900. Mon–Fri 10am–6:30pm; Sat 10am–6pm; Sun noon–5pm. AE, DISC, MC, V. www.pinto ranch.com.

R.M. Williams AUSTRALIAN $–$$$$$

This is the firm that helped win the West—western Australia. While they're best known for their stockman's riding boots, they also make leather belts, wallets, backpack and other accessories. Gear for the outback is sold here, but much of it works in a casual lifestyle around the world or even for cowboys.

Don't miss: belt buckles encrusted with indigenous gemstones.

BEST BETS   Extraordinary range of sizes, especially for big men, as in really, really, *very* big men.

WEB TIPS   Enter by clicking on the bucking bronc. There is an e-shop but prices are in AU dollars. You have to register to buy and go through a lot, and then you don't know if they will ship.

WHERE TO BUY   24 stores in Australia; 4 worldwide. **FLAGSHIP** 389 George St., Sydney. ☎ **612/9262-2228. U.S. FLAGSHIP**   46 E. 59th St., NYC. ☎ **212/308-1808.** Daily 10am–7pm. AE, MC, V. Subway: Fifth Ave./59th St. www.rmwilliams.com.au.

Haberdashers

There are a few old-fashioned specialty stores left that serve only to outfit the gentleman. These are often cradle-to-grave stores with excellent customer service and multi-generational perspective so they are an extension of the family for some shoppers. You turn yourself over to them, knowing you will never be embarrassed in public.

Claude Bonucci FRENCH $$$$–$$$$$

Originally from a family of Italian tailors and with headquarters in Nice (which was part of Italy until the end of the 19th century), Bonucci has made his name dressing many of the stars who frequent the Film Festival in Cannes, where he also has a shop in the Sofitel Cannes Hotel. He can do a traditional black tuxedo, *mais oui,* but he can also do jazzy prints, resort sunny shades and metallic threads.

Bonucci does a fabulous bespoke suit or tuxedo but also has some stock off the peg. His cut is European with a higher, tighter armhole than is customary in an American tuxedo and a slimmer line in the torso. His jackets are created to make men look taller and thinner. He will do custom work and book special hours during festivals such as FIF in Cannes.

Buyer Beware

Avoid Elton John look-alikes; there's a fine line between Resort Chic and Rocket Man.

BEST BETS   Garments are made in France with highest-quality Italian fabrics. Prices begin at $350. The hand tailoring shows the world that you care about the look, which is Italian and Riviera resorty all at the same time.

WEB TIPS   Website under construction.

WHERE TO BUY   FLAGSHIP   10 rue Massenet, Nice. ☎ **334/9387-4887.** Tues–Sat 11am–7pm. MC, V. Also in Cannes: 50 La Croisette. Mon–Sat 11am–7pm. www.claudebonucci.fr.

Furest SPANISH $$$–$$$$$

One of Barcelona's most famous men's clothing stores, founded in 1898, Furest has been supplying the Spanish royals with clothing since the turn of the 20th century. This is one-stop shopping for suits, shirts, socks, knickers, pajamas, coats, shoes, ties and accessories.

BEST BETS   Along with their own distinctive brand, they stock lines from international designers as well as look-alike lines for those on a budget.

WEB TIPS   You cannot shop online. All you get are nice pictures and names of brands.

WHERE TO BUY   9 stores in Barcelona. **FLAGSHIP**   Passeig de Garcia, 12–14 Barcelona. ☎ **34-93/301-2000.** Mon–Sat 10am–7pm. AE, MC, V. Métro: Catalunya.

Rolo   SAN FRANCISCO $$–$$$$

Silly you, it is Rolo not Polo we're talking about. Rolo's three San Francisco stores have been important to the local scene for bringing cutting-edge fashion into the mainstream community. You've got everything from your big Italian brands to Paper Denim & Cloth jeans to men's skincare. There are also clothes for women. The store at 1301 Howard St. is an outlet where unsold merchandise is marked down.

BEST BETS   One of the most amazing list of brands ever seen at an indie, yes Band of Outsiders. Does that tell you everything you need to know? If they don't have what you want or need, ask their personal shopper to find it for you.

WEB TIPS   You cannot shop online.

WHERE TO BUY   3 stores in San Francisco: Rolo Castro, 2351 Market St., between Castro and Noe sts. ☎ **415/431-4545.** Rolo Soma, 1235 Howard St., between Eighth and Ninth sts. ☎ **415/355-1122.** Rolo Garage outlet: 1301 Howard St., at Ninth. ☎ **415/861-2097.** Mon–Sat 11am–7:30pm; Sun 11:30am–6:30pm. AE, DISC, MC, V. www.rolo.com.

Wilkes-Bashford   SAN FRANCISCO $$–$$$$$

Back in the days of Wilkes Bashford himself, he brought designers to San Francisco and proved there was a market for big names, expensive clothes and chic and elegance. Today, the store has men's and women's clothing, a baby line and a home-style department that carries the likes of Pratesi sheets. Everything is edited to a fare-thee-well and refined to meet the needs of the local population.

BEST BETS   It's hard to find a men's department that has Kiton from Naples made to measure, Luciano Barbera cashmeres, D&G, Yohji and Issey Miyake all under one roof. Furthermore, every sales associate is a fashion consultant who will coordinate your entire look.

WHERE TO BUY　1 store: 375 Sutter St., between Stockton and Grant, San Francisco, CA. ☎ **415/986-4380.** Mon–Sat 10am–6pm; Thurs 10am–8pm. AE, DISC, MC, V. www.wilkes bashford.com.

Outerwear

Barbour BRITISH $$$–$$$$

With three royal warrants and scads of copycat brands, this is the most British of brands and an important staple in the wardrobe because of the weather and the lifestyle.

BEST BETS　A waxed coat, for those not in the know, is treated for the ultimate in weather proofing. Helen Mirren wore the Beaufort, one of Barbour's classic wax jackets, in *The Queen.* The wax jackets are manufactured by hand and cannot be washed, only dry cleaned at an authorized Barbour facility (all in the UK).

WEB TIPS　The various promotions and in-store events in the UK and U.S. are announced online. There are even invitations to bring in your jacket for a free re-waxing.

WHERE TO BUY　Department stores, outdoor and hunting stores. 8 stores in the UK. **FLAGSHIP**　123 Sydney St. (off Kings Rd.), London SW3. ☎ **4420/7626-2924.** Tube: Sloane Sq. www.barbour.com.

North Face USA $$–$$$$

This is a strange case of a retail store that ended up as a manufacturer because they wanted to control the quality of the product they were selling and wanted to provide product that didn't exist in the wholesale markets they were working. They offer the most technically advanced products on the market to accomplished climbers, mountaineers, snowsport athletes and explorers.

World Traveler

Note that most North Face branded goods sold in China are fake.

BEST BETS　Much of the gear has been cited by experts as the best in the field.

WEB TIPS   After you read about the Cioher windstopper jacket and its awards and accolades, it's pretty upsetting to discover this is not one of the models sold on the website.

WHERE TO BUY   13 stores in the U.S. **FLAGSHIP**   180 Post St., San Francisco, CA. ☎ **415/433-3223.** Mon–Sat 10am–8pm; Sun 11am–6pm. AE, DISC, MC, V. Also NYC, Chicago and more. www.thenorthface.com.

Shirts & Pajamas

Don't laugh; most custom shirt makers also make pajamas, and many also make boxer shorts. Just stop by Turnbull & Asser in London to see the shorts Prince Charles wears. And his jammies. While the real guy may claim to sleep in the buff or shop at Gap, the truth is there's more than Nick & Nora out there, especially if you are willing to spend $500 for pajamas. Stop laughing. If you want to spend that amount per shirt, that, too, can be arranged.

Ascot Chang CHINESE $$$$

Ascot Chang is a famous institution in Hong Kong and, indeed, around the world. He is one of the world's best-known and best-loved shirt makers. Now he's come to New York (well, his son has) to open a more conveniently located shop for those who know how comfortable a custom shirt can be. Prices are higher than in Hong Kong, but not unreasonable—you'll pay about $150 for a custom shirt.

BEST BETS   The shop also has ready-made shirts, as well as made-to-measure; you can choose from about 2,000 fabrics. There are also suits, suspenders, ties, tennis togs and the usual apparel for a well-dressed gent.

WEB TIPS   If you can't make it to one of the stores to be measured for a bespoke shirt, you can go online to access the special-order catalog. You'll be able to create a virtually custom-made shirt from the convenience of your computer. The website instructions will walk you through the links, from choosing fabric, collar and cuffs, to taking precise measurements. This is as close to a bespoke shirt as you can get without a visit to a tailor. The shirts begin at about $110 and go on up to over $300 depending on fabric.

WHERE TO BUY   9 stores worldwide. U.S. **FLAGSHIP**   110 Central Park South, NYC. ☎ **212/759-3333.** Mon–Sat 10am–7pm. AE,

DISC, MC, V. Subway: Columbus Circle. Also Beverly Hills. www.ascotchang.com.

Charvet PARIS $$$$

Founded in 1838, this men's shirt maker across the street from the Ritz Hotel also makes ready to wear, pajamas, bathrobes and dressing gowns. Still, this is a shirt maker extraordinaire. There are over 100 different shades of blue shirtings on the shelves . . . and 400 of white.

Their clients include most of the famous gentlemen of France and many of the world, including John F. Kennedy and Gary Cooper. And yes, you may need to be president with a trust fund to buy the shirts—they cost almost $500 each . . . and you usually have to start with an order of three. The store also sells ties (they are famous for their bow ties), pajamas, robes and pocket squares.

BEST BETS   The men who shop here.

WHERE TO BUY   Charvet events held at Saks in U.S. 1 store: place Vendome, Paris, 1er. ☎ 331/4260-3070. Mon 2–7pm; Tues–Sat 10am–7pm. AE, MC, V. Métro: Opera or Pyramides.

Emma Willis LONDON $$$–$$$$

Men's shirts made by a woman, and all bespoke, using Swiss or Italian cottons and made with French seams, hand-finished gussets, cross-stitched fastened buttons and hand-embroidered monograms, of course.

The gimmick is in the va-va-va-voom: All the saleswomen are, uh, women. And they do the fittings. Emma and her team come to New York twice a year; you can get on the mailing list to be notified of the next visit. Shirts are in the $300 to $400 range. Yes, that's each.

BEST BETS   The one-of-a-kind service: Your shirt fabric is researched and then retired so no one else has the same shirt. In this age of customized wares and VIP service, you can't beat this firm.

WEB TIPS   Click on "Bridegroom" for wedding choices for groom and ushers.

WHERE TO BUY   1 store: 66 Jermyn Street, SW1, London. ☎ 4420/7930-9980. Mon–Sat 10am–6pm. AE, MC, V. Tube: Green Park/Piccadilly. www.emmawillis.com.

Hilditch & Key BRITISH $$$–$$$$

You won't find better quality for the money anywhere than from this London Mayfair shirt maker. Prices begin at $150

Price Check: Men's Designer Shirts

These days, it can cost an arm and a leg to give someone the shirt off your back:

- Alexander McQueen = $410 for cotton pique (www.alexander mcqueen.com).
- Calvin Klein Collection = $320 for Euro-style shirt in the U.S. See p. 225.
- Dolce & Gabbana = $375 for sleek fit and ultra-fine fabric (www.dolcegabbana.com).
- Domenico Vacca = $475 for an impeccable, wide-collared shirt. See www.domenicovacca.com.
- Duncan Quinn = $275 for a dandy British mobster look in colorful stripes. Tommy gun sold separately. See www. duncanquinn.com.
- Etro = $300 for a shirt fit for wild and crazy guys from Candy-land. See p. 216.
- Jil Sander = $315 for a shirt that's soft and stiff, sleek and chic. See p. 457.
- Paul Smith shirt = $250 for colors, prints and stripes for non-shy types. See p. 221.
- Ralph Lauren Black Label = $250 for a white as pure as a WASP. See p. 49.
- Tom Ford = $350 for Italian cotton (www.tomford.com).
- Zegna = $285 for Italian-milled beauties that speak of money and a Ferrari. See p. 253.

and go up depending on fabric and a full selection is available to order online. If you decide to go the bespoke route, you'll of course have style and fabric options; in addition, they will hand-embroider your initials on the cuff and engrave your monogram on the buttons. Hilditch and Key's clientele ranges from crowned heads of Europe to diplomats, government ministers and leaders of the arts, entertainment and business world. Yes, they make Karl Lagerfeld's shirts.

BEST BETS   Twice a year they visit the U.S. The average shirt is $200.

WEB TIPS   You can shop online.

WHERE TO BUY   4 stores worldwide. 3 in London, 1 in Paris. **FLAGSHIP**   37 Jermyn St., London. ☎ **4420/7734-4707.** Also at 73 Jermyn St., London. ☎ **4420/7930-5336.** Daily 9am–6pm. AE, MC, V. Tube: Green Park/Piccadilly. www.hilditchand key.com.

Ike Behar   USA $$$$

I first discovered the brand at an N-M outlet and later found out that Ralph Lauren was ahead of me in the discovery—he merged Ike's business into Polo in the 1970s. As all history buffs remember, Ralph Lauren began in the tie business. When he needed shirts to show off his ties, he went to Ike.

Now Ike sells a lot of shirts and ties, especially at Nordstrom and Neiman. The Cuban-born Behar also outfits movie stars, sells at Barneys and is considered an insider's source because of craftsmanship and quality. The shirts are made with single needle stitching, 18 to 22 stitches per inch, and are made in America. There is a bespoke program.

BEST BETS   Note the ceramic buttons, said to be unbreakable. The Sea Island cotton shirts are very soft on those with sensitive skin; price is $159.

WEB TIPS   The website is not only updated daily but bears the date, which is comforting since many Web pages are years old.

WHERE TO BUY   Neiman Marcus, Nordstrom and Saks. Customer service: ☎ **800/637-3013.** www.ikebehar.com.

Jhane Barnes   USA $$$–$$$$

Jhane's (say Jane) colorful and brightly colored shirts (called fancies in the trade) are what made her famous, although she also designs a home-style line. She creates her own fabrics and then manufactures the shirts combining several processes for each one. For example, one shirt might be yarn dyed and then printed; another yarn dyed and printed and then have a fancy yarn woven in and clipped. The creativity in the color and design is what makes this line unique.

BEST BETS   Not-so-plain Jhane is best known for her fancy fabrics, but she gives equal attention to manufacturing detail, right down to making a perfect pocket. All designs are limited editions, and after each group is produced, the design is retired.

WEB TIPS   There are large photos of the complete line on her website, and you can place orders online. A long-sleeve classic-style shirt in silk and cotton is about $165.

WHERE TO BUY   Department stores including Saks, Nordstrom and Neiman Marcus. www.jhanebarnes.com.

John Smedley   BRITISH $$$–$$$$

Knit specialists, Smedley whips up Sea Island cotton into the best beloved polo shirt in the world. Long before there were polo shirts, the firm began business in 1784 by spinning cotton. In recent history, the firm has teamed with guest designers to do something creative; check out the Vivienne Westwood underwear.

The London store is very tiny and not too exciting visually, but there's more stock downstairs.

BEST BETS   Sea Island cotton knits; expect to pay £127 ($250) for a polo shirt.

WEB TIPS   You can get a list of stockists near you from the site.

WHERE TO BUY   Department stores worldwide such as Le Bon Marche and Printemps in Paris. 8 stores worldwide. **FLAGSHIP** 24 Brook St., London, W1. ☎ **207/495-2222.** Mon–Sat 10am–6pm; Thurs 10am–7pm. AE, MC, V. Tube: Bond St. Also in Tokyo. www.john-smedley.com.

Loretta Caponi FLORENCE $$$$

This is a froufrou store for fine linens, bed, nighties, under-wear and baby items. They also make traditional custom pajamas for men and women in linen or silk for about $500 a pair. You get the monogram thrown in for that price. Sting shops here.

BEST BETS   The sleep shirts are so chic that even James Bond would consider wearing one; cotton costs $350 and linen, $420.

WEB TIPS   You cannot shop online but can see photos of the wide range of luxury merchandise.

WHERE TO BUY   1 store: 4r piazza degli Antinori, Florence. ☎ **39-055/213-668.** Also in Rome and Milan.

Frank Rostron MANCHESTER $$$–$$$$

Frank Rostron is a bespoke shirt maker from Manchester, England, who has become famous for making London/Jermyn Street quality shirts for half the price. Of course, real estate in Manchester is probably half what he'd pay for space on Jermyn Street. Also note that the fabric mills of the UK have always been in the Manchester area and that many immigrants entered the UK through Liverpool, making this the perfect destination for skilled workers from foreign shores and the best fabrics off the bolt.

Rostron's shirts are typically chosen for style, subtle lines and superior quality. He uses only the best two-fold cotton poplins for his shirts. Seams are sewn with twin needle stitching for added strength; the sleeves and the two-piece collars are soft, with slots for removable bones. At the back there is a shoulder yoke, typically used by bespoke shirt makers in order to adjust the height of each shoulder separately.

BEST BETS   You don't need to book a trip to Manchester to be fitted; Rostron personally travels to the U.S. at least 6 times a year and will arrange to meet you at home, at work, during the day or in the evening—always at your convenience.

WEB TIPS   You can also order online, by selecting fabric and style details; of course, a shirt ordered from the website won't fit like a bespoke design. *Note:* Shirts cost $200 to $250 each for bespoke; $150 to $180 if ordered online.

WHERE TO BUY   1 store: 39 Princess St., Manchester, UK. Mon–Sat 9am–6pm. AE, MC, V. To arrange a fitting, call ☎ **44161/236-5379,** or write frank@frankrostron.com.

Turnbull & Asser BRITISH $$$$

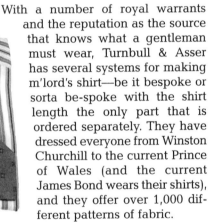

With a number of royal warrants and the reputation as the source that knows what a gentleman must wear, Turnbull & Asser has several systems for making m'lord's shirt—be it bespoke or sorta be-spoke with the shirt length the only part that is ordered separately. They have dressed everyone from Winston Churchill to the current Prince of Wales (and the current James Bond wears their shirts), and they offer over 1,000 different patterns of fabric.

Turnbull & Asser shirt and tie.

WEB TIPS   You can browse the goods online, but you'll need to visit a shop to pick up one of these finely made shirts. The site has a nice layout but there's not much information on pricing and sizes.

WHERE TO BUY   6 stores worldwide. **FLAGSHIP**   71 Jermyn St., SW1 London. ☎ **207/808-3000.** Daily 9am–6pm. Also in New York: 42 E. 57th St. ☎ **212/752-5700.** Mon-Fri 10am–6:30; Sat 9:30am–6pm. Subway: Fifth Ave/57th St. Also 9633 Brighton Way, Beverly Hills. ☎ **310/550-7600.** AE, MC, V. www.turnbull andasser.com.

Shoes & Boots

Allen-Edmonds USA $$$$

This footwear firm provides an Italian look with a mostly made-in-the-U.S. shoe. The brand is actually from Wisconsin, which was once among the shoemaking capitals in the U.S., along with Massachusetts.

BEST BETS   The brand makes an excellent dress shoe that looks like money. They also do casual but you come here for the shoes to go with your bespoke tailored suits.

WEB TIPS   The brand has a wide range of sizes and widths. You can go online to see which styles are made in your size, although you cannot shop online.

WHERE TO BUY   55 stores in the U.S., including 551 Madison Ave., NYC. ☎ **212/308-8305.** 36 Newbury St., Boston, MA; 541 N. Michigan Ave., Chicago, IL. ☎ **312/755-9306.** Outlet store Serravale Scriva, Serravale, Italy. ☎ **39014/360-1776.** www.allenedmonds.com.

Berluti FRENCH/ITALIAN $$$–$$$$$

This Italian bookmaker since 1845 actually has the flagship store in Paris and does ready-to-wear and bespoke lines of shoes and boots—for a price ($1,000 and up). They created the elongated loafer made famous by Andy Warhol—the line is always very thin and sleek.

BEST BETS   The most gorgeous men's shoes in the world. Hmmm, well, among them.

WEB TIPS   The website is done with illustrations—some of it is a tad oblique. Click on the red telephone to get store addresses.

WHERE TO BUY   15 stores in 8 countries. **FLAGSHIP**   26 rue Marbeuf, Paris 8e. ☎ **331/5393-9797.** Métro: Franklin Roosevelt. **U.S. FLAGSHIP**   971 Madison Ave. ☎ **212/439-6400.** Mon–Sat 10am–6pm; Thurs 10am–7pm. AE, MC, V. Subway: Hunter College. Other cities include Hong Kong, Seoul, Moscow, London, Milan and Dubai. www.berluti.com.

Bluefly.com USA $$$$

Website for men's and women's fashion has excellent shoe section for men. Each shoe is pictured along with the Bluefly price and the regular retail. Discounts run 25% to 30%.

BEST BETS   Gucci horsebit loafers marked down from $515 to $370; Hermès dress oxford from $1,025 to $738.

WEB TIPS   You can sign up to be notified of sales.

WHERE TO BUY   Online only.

Cesare Paciotti ITALIAN $$$$

A well-made, top-of-the-line shoe with some street styling; sort of hip shoes with pointy toes and fine leathers and buckles on the side—West Side Story meets lotsa money and class.

BEST BETS   Only $575 for a sleek dress shoe.

WEB TIPS   E-shopping only in the US.

WHERE TO BUY   Stores worldwide. 2 stores in the U.S. 9528 Brighton Way, Beverly Hills, CA. ☎ **310/273-3220.** 833 Madison Ave., NYC. ☎ **212/452-1222.** Also in Italy, Paris, Moscow, Istanbul. www.cesarepaciotti.it.

Cole Haan USA/ITALY $$$$

Well-made, fairly fashionable shoes at fair prices. That's not to say they give away shoes; dress-up oxfords are $425 if you don't get them on sale. The shoes are made in Italy.

BEST BETS   You will pay $200 to $250 regular price and much less if you hit a sale.

WEB TIPS   You can buy online—the search begins when you input your size so you don't waste time with shoes you love that are sold out.

WHERE TO BUY   Stores in 22 states in the U.S. and Canada. Factory outlets in 16 states, including Shops at Columbus Circle, 10 Columbus Circle, NYC. ☎ **212/823-9420.** Mon–Sat 10am–9pm; Sun 11am–7pm. 260 N. Rodeo Dr., Beverly Hills. ☎ **310/859-7622.** Mon–Sat 10am–7pm; Sun 11am–6pm. www.colehaan.com.

Ferragamo ITALIAN $$$$

Stunning shoes for dress up and casual, although the casual shoes have an extra bit of pizzazz that makes them sharp—such as burgundy suede loafers with silver-bit hardware ($385). Sizes are in American even if the shoes are made in Italy.

BEST BETS   The suede slip-on mocs I bought at the La Vallée Village/Val d'Europe outlet for $150 (p. 432).

Gucci ITALIAN $$$$

Perhaps the most famous men's loafer in the world, also known to be fashionable only when worn without socks.

BEST BETS   It's the classic loafer with horsebit hardware, about $350 in solid suede. There are also kitschy shoes in Gucci canvas print, such as espadrilles for $300.

WEB TIPS   You can buy online; click away from all the fragrance stuff until you find "shoes."

WHERE TO BUY   35 stores worldwide. **FLAGSHIP**   Tournabuoni, Florence. ☎ **3955/264-5432.** Outlet: The Mall, via Europa 8, Leccio (outside Florence). www.gucci.com.

John Lobb BRITISH $$$$

Ready-to-wear or made-to-measure shoes. Very structured in style.

BEST BETS   Very old money and prices.

WHERE TO BUY   **U.S. FLAGSHIP**   680 Madison Ave., NYC. ☎ **212/888-9797.** Also in the UK, Japan and France. www.johnlobb. com.

Onitsuka Tiger JAPANESE $$–$$$$

Begun in 1949 as a local brand of sports shoe, by the 1960s this brand gained international cult status and is now distributed in the U.S. through Asics. The shoes are so identified with cutting-edge cool that most know The Bride wore these shoes in both of the *Kill Bill* movies.

BEST BETS   Collector's editions.

WEB TIPS   You cannot buy online from the home site, but you can download wallpaper or find a nearby retailer.

WHERE TO BUY   4 stores in London, Paris, Sydney, Tokyo; Urban Outfitters and other specialty stores. **FLAGSHIP**   15 Newburgh St., London. ☎ **4420/7287-7480.** Tube: Oxford Circus. www. onitsukatiger.com.

Prada ITALIAN $$$$

Prada makes trainers and comfort shoes in a variety of comfort and hip styles, appealing to the metroman who knows it's okay to have a rubber sole. There's a red stripe inset into the heel that runs through the bottom of the shoe, to make sure everyone knows you've laid down a heap of cash for this brand and are wearing the genuine article.

BEST BETS   If you can go $400 for a sneaker and $500 for a dress shoe, you'll get comfort, good engineering and a lot of style.

See full listing on p. 227.

Rbk USA $$–$$$$

This is a division of Reebok which appeals to more cutting-edge customers who are possibly doing more extreme sports.

BEST BETS   Skateboarding shoes.

WHERE TO BUY   Reebok stores (www.reebok.com) and outlets as well as specialty stores. www.rbk.com.

Tod's ITALIAN $$$$

Iconic driving shoe known for the "pimples" on the soles that give grip to the shoe—they make men's and women's shoes as well as handbags; trainers are offered up in their lower-cost line, Hogan.

BEST BETS   The iconic driving shoe in an oddball color that goes with everything and displays your personality, $325. I can be wearing khakis from Wal-Mart, a big white linen shirt from China and my bright green Tod's and feel as chic as any super model.

See listing on p. 153.

Vans USA $$

Concept cool shoe for skateboarders, trekkers, men, women and kids from high school up who give up their clunky Nikes to go for printed canvas or less clunky trainers.

BEST BETS   Printed canvas slip-ons, $37 to $50.

WEB TIPS   Too goth for a grown-up. You can shop online.

WHERE TO BUY   Department and specialty stores. www.vans.com.

Zappos.com 🖱 USA

See p. 145.

Skin Care & Shaving

Ten years ago, with a blush and a giggle, there was discussion of beauty aides and skin care items for men. Now the shelves are laden with hundreds of products as men come out of the closet and open the medicine cabinet. Now there's mass market brands (Nivea, L'Oreal Men), upscale women's brands that are branching out for men (Shiseido), as well as mens-only brands (see below).

For many more brands, see Chapter Six: "Beauty," as some lines are unisex. (Anything can be unisex, really, if you ignore the packaging and sometimes the scent.) See especially: Aesop (p. 186), Dermalogica (p. 196), Dr. Hauschka (p. 178), Jurlique (p. 188), Kiehl's (p. 196), Malin + Goetz (p. 196) and Mario Badescu (p. 197).

Anthony Logistics USA $

With clean, clear, open and bright packages, this men's line has products for skin, hair, body, sports, face, including anti-age, anti-acne, and more. A popular brand in the New York Chelsea scene for years, it's now available at Sephora. This is a very wide line, impressive in coverage, packaging (sufficiently macho) and price. Most items are $14 to $30.

BEST BETS   Try the gentle shaving products, alcohol-free toners, acne products and gently exfoliating algae facial cleanser.

WHERE TO BUY   Sephora stores in U.S. and Europe. Anthony. com or anthonyeurope.com.

Czech & Speak LONDON $$–$$$$

Old-fashiony and moderne all at once, selling men's shaving and skin care and aromatherapies and colognes—the signature scent is No. 88 cologne—they also do bathrooms and kitchens.

WEB TIPS   You can shop online. This is not a good site and I spend my time on it wondering if the girl in the bathtub is dead and whodunit.

WHERE TO BUY   1 store: 39 c Jermyn St., London SW1. ☎ **44-20/7439-0216.** Mon–Fri 9:30am–6pm; Sat 10am–5pm. Tube: Piccadilly Circus. www. czechspeake.com.

Elemis BRITISH $–$$$

Not so many years ago, Elemis was a brand made specifically for cruise ship spas—it smelled good but wasn't quite taken seriously. A lot of marketing bucks have brought the line off the boat, into its own London day spa and now onto the shelves of upmarket department stores such as Harvey Nicks in London. The products reflect the influence of travel and exotic ingredients gathered from around the world.

BEST BETS   There is a range for men including an Energising Skin Scrub ($26). An excellent Fitness Treatment line includes Musclease Active Body Concentrate ($61). A 10-piece travel kit is $140.

Elemis "Musclease Active Body Concentrate."

Steve Goes on a Shaving Spree

An *Onion* headline from 2004 read "Gillette CEO: 'F**k Everything, We're Doing Five Blades.'" Not only did this satire come to pass (in 2005), it represented everything wrong with the American shaving industry at the time. Thankfully, more options are turning up in the States, beyond the 5-bladers and foaming gels that smell like underarm deodorant. I tried both domestic and international products in an attempt to find the World's Best. I'm a picky tester; my skin reacts to most irritants, so if it worked for me it'll probably work for you (or your man).

Best Wet Shavers: I'm a big fan of the industry trend toward old-fashioned wet shaving. It involves a badger brush, pre-shave oil, lathering shave cream and after-shave. The brush preps your skin for a closer shave, and you'll ultimately save money since a very "little dab will do ya"; a tub of soap or cream should last several months. You'll feel like a British dandy for a few minutes a day.

Top honor in this category goes to—a bit of a dark horse—**Nancy Boy,** 347 Hayes St. (☎ **888/746-2629;** www.nancyboy. com), a boutique in San Francisco that uses over 150 natural plant extracts for a superior shave without irritation. The Signature Shave Cream ($16) lathers well and bowled me over daily with the strong scent of fresh peppermint, lavender and rosemary. The unscented pre-oil ($19) and Replenishing After Shave Gel with cucumber oil ($17) kept my face smooth and bump-free. I've waited for a brand like this ever since I first cut myself with a Bic a dozen years ago.

Otherwise, the Brits are still the leaders of the field. I hate to lump them together but you'll get bloody good results (er, minus the blood) with any of these brands: **D.R. Harris** (www.drharris.co.uk), **Taylors of Old Bond Street** (www.tayloroldbondst.co.uk), **Truefitt & Hill** (www.truefittandhill.com) and **Trumpers** (www.trumpers.com)—all available in high-end apothecaries and online. These glycerin-based creams (averaging £10/$20) generally smell fantastic, lather like champs, and are surprisingly okay for sensitive skin—though long term, I did best with the Unscented and Lavender lines, or Taylor's Avacado (£7/$14). You might also try **The Gentleman's Refinery** (www.thegr.com), a line found in Las Vegas barber shops. Started by a former Truefitt & Hill master barber, it updates the British

WEB TIPS   You can get four free product samples with every online purchase. For U.S. orders you'll be directed to www.timetospa.com.

WHERE TO BUY   Department stores, spas, on board some ships, in Elemis day spa. **FLAGSHIP**   2-3 Lancashire Court, London W1.

shaver with all natural, paraben-free, alcohol-free products. All these brands have slick packaging and make fine gifts.

The most affordable way to ease into wet shaving may be with a start-up kit that includes the badger-hair brush. **The Art of Shaving** (www.theartofshaving.com) has a kit with a travel-sized brush for $38; separately, larger brushes start at $50. Their Unscented line is one of my most reliable, though you can also get Lemon, Sandalwood or Lavender. Their pre-shave oil is thicker than most (with castor oil), but it's effective and didn't cause breakouts. Despite the name, **eShave,** 211 E. 43rd St., NYC (☎ **800/947-4283;** www.eshave.com), has nothing to do with online shaving; it offers silky smooth latherers ($20) infused with White Tea, Cucumber or Almond (for dry skin), and more, and has a nice array of modern brushes and razors, including a "melted" nickel-plated one inspired by Dali ($84). The starter kit with brush is only $35.

Best Brushless Shavers: This method doesn't make economic sense to me; non-lathering creams only last a few weeks, not months. Still, I know people who swear by brushless shavers. Best might be **Zirh**'s (p. 250) thick, non-lathering cream ($20). Also, their slick, thin, pre-shave oil ($16) and after-shave ($30) were the best I tried. **Malin + Goetz** (p. 196) makes a soothing brushless cream ($22) that supposedly doesn't need any pre- or after-shavers (though I wound up using additional products).

Web Sources: Talk with the shave geeks at the **www.shavemyface.com** message boards, and you'll realize my recommendations are just the tip of the shorn iceberg. This is truly an amazing resource for products and techniques, plus a few vaguely fetishistic user-created video demonstrations. To become a better label reader, try **www.cosmeticcop.com**'s Ingredient Dictionary, where you'll learn that sodium *laureth* sulfate is much gentler than sodium *lauryl* sulfate, and other tips. For decent shipping fees on various creams (including British products), try **www.emsplace.com** and **www.classicshaving.com**. For online razor orders, try **www.blademail.com**. For antique Gillette double-edge razors from the 1950s—before Gillette went number crazy—you'll pay $30 to $150 on **www.ebay.com**. — *Stephen Bassman*

☎ **4420/7499-4995.** Mon–Thurs 9am–9pm; Fri–Sat 9am–8pm; Sun 10am–6pm. MC, V. Tube: Bond Street. www.elemis.com.

Shiseido Men JAPANESE $–$$

This line is extremely sophisticated and appeals to a man who already knows he wants high-quality skin care. The packaging is very sleek. This is a little more expensive than other brands for men and is meant to attract the upmarket guy who knows that his wife is spending a fortune on face cream and that Shiseido is one of the best brands in the world.

BEST BETS The products cost from about $30 to $60 per item. There are some 15 different products in the range. The firm's motto is "Power your skin," which I guess is meant to inject a little macho into the concept.

WEB TIPS Sold online at the Shiseido site but also at various other sites, such as amazon.com. What I love about the Amazon site is that underneath the description of the cream or gel and its price is a list of books about Japan that you may be interested in reading. www.shiseido.com.

Skeen PARIS $–$$

Men with sensitive skin, you are officially *au courant*. This French boutique is not only geared exclusively to men, it features all natural products, all fragrance free to minimize irritation. You'll find creams, peels and shavers that actively treat, soothe, combat wrinkles and even fight hair loss.

BEST BETS The Revitalizing Self-Tanning Fluid (€30/$42) is the tanner for people who hate tanners. It gives skin more of a healthy glow than a tan.

WEB TIPS Unfortunately, shipping fees to the U.S. can be steep ($25 and up). Buy this one on your next trip to Paris.

WHERE TO BUY 1 store. 21 rue des Archives, Paris 1e. ☎ **331/4276-0407**. Mon–Sat 10am–7pm. AE, MC, V. Metro: Hôtel de Ville. www.skeen.fr. —*SB*

Zirh USA $–$$

I am certain that the Three Kings brought gifts to Bethlehem that included zirh, which happens to be pronounced to rhyme with sir. (Go figure.) This popular shave line is part of Shiseido U.S. See above.

BEST BETS A travel kit costs $45, which is a very good price for a high-caliber line. The non-foaming shave cream is $20; foaming is $17.

WEB TIPS You can shop online.

WHERE TO BUY Sephora stores. ☎ **800/295-8877.** www.zirh.com.

Suits

....

There are three kinds of suits most readily available to the man who wants a traditional business suit—off the peg, bespoke and customized. Often, a firm does two—maybe three—of these formats.

Off the peg: Ready-made suits sold by chest measurement and often available in one of three sleeve lengths, S for short and L for long. There is no delineation for normal, although it is spoken of as "regular." Alternations may be needed according to body type.

Customized: Your basic off–the-peg suit which has been modified from one fitting. Sometimes "customized" is dressed up as "made-to-measure," which is wrong. It's not bespoke but parts of the garment are made to measure.

Bespoke: Suits made from scratch to customer's measurements and choices. Three fittings usually required, sometimes more. The proper bespoke suit takes into consideration how a man moves so the suit moves with him and also takes body shape faults to task by masking them; the tailor spends 50 to 60 hours making a bespoke suit. A bespoke suit is a serious investment, in both time and money. When done properly, the suit will last for many years and you'll look like a million bucks.

Before you authorize the first cut, take the time to discuss all aspects of the process with your tailor:

- **Make sure you're really getting a custom-made suit;** ask about a personal pattern. Bespoke clothing is created without a pre-existing pattern, as opposed to made-to-measure which alters a pattern to fit the customer. Some tailors will take your measurements, and then create a suit using a standard pattern that has been modified to fit your specifics. It will probably be a great suit, but it won't be bespoke.

- **Ask about the tailor's technique.** Along with the cut, fabric and trimmings, you should be concerned with who's actually sewing the garment. Some make a firmer coat with more stitches per inch, creating a sharper image and less fullness; you may prefer easier stitching for a more relaxed look.

- **Find out which parts of the suit will be machine sewn** (the outer seams on the jacket and pants) and which will be done by hand (the buttonholes). Confirm that your coat has a floating canvas (a lightweight fabric lining the front for body), and ask to see it at the fitting. If a fused canvas is used, your jacket will be glued together and won't last.

- **Request horn buttons,** not plastic.

If you're not completely satisfied with the fit, speak up. A good tailor would rather remake the jacket than have an unsatisfied customer.

ON & OFF THE PEG

Barneys USA $$$$–$$$$$

Barneys essentials have already been delineated in this book. Yet men in need of some tailoring should know that twice a year the store hosts a Made to Measure Month in which a large number of manufacturers send reps who will make or adjust specifically for the customer. There are shirts, shoes and clothing makers in this international stew of the very best. Call direct: ☎ **212/826-8900,** ext. 2548.

Armani ITALIAN $$$$–$$$$$

World's Best   Giorgio Armani began his career as the window dresser for the Milanese department store La Rinascente and began designing with a men's line. He is the man who created the unstructured jacket and is responsible for most of men's fashion—especially what is accepted as cool and not classical—for the last 40-odd years. Today's man can buy off the peg or made to measure. Handmade-to-measure service is offered at all Armani boutiques worldwide. Even classical suits are not too stiff, which allows them to move.

If you want to shop any of the outlets, you can not only get a break on prices but you can possibly buy some sample or runway pieces, which are marked TU (one size in Italian). At an outlet store, an unstructured blazer sample costs about $150; an off-the-rack suit will cost $500 to $800. See p. 79.

Brioni ITALIAN $$$$–$$$$$

Brioni is a name synonymous with men's style and elegance. James Bond (Pierce Brosnan) wears Brioni suits; see below. One of the most famous of the Italian tailors, Brioni is known for a specific, much-copied cut that is wide in the shoulder and fitted in the torso. In recent years the firm has expanded with a women's ready-to-wear line; they do custom work for both men and women.

There are stores—and stores that sell the brand—all over the world, but the Milan shop is the temple for service, and Rome is the original flagship. The factories are in Penne.

BEST BETS   Bond, James Bond. It's about the suit.

WEB TIPS   Easy-to-use website; I'll take the smiling guy on the home page. Actually, is that a guy?

WHERE TO BUY   Stores worldwide. **FLAGSHIP**   via Barberini 79, Rome. ☎ **3906/484-577.** Other cities include New York, Las Vegas, Beverly Hills, Prague and Madrid. www.brioni.it.

Brooks Brothers USA

See p. 218.

Ermenegildo Zegna ITALIAN $$$$$

Even if you can't pronounce it (say "Zenya"), you can shop here, knowing the northern Italian line—which began by making its own wools—is superior to most other lines. And despite being Italian, Zegna has a wide range of sizes that fit most bodies, including the larger frame of a typical American body.

Zegna does classical suits but also casual wear and outerwear. They also sell their wools off the bolt so that you can buy the fabric and take it to your own tailor. Indeed, the quality of the fabrics in the weave, fiber, patterns and color are so chic that Zegna tells you everything you want to know about Mr. Right.

WEB TIPS   You can shop online in the U.S. only.

WHERE TO BUY   27 points of sale in U.S.; stores worldwide; discount oulets in U.S.; factory store in Biella, in the hills near Switzerland between Turin and Como. **FLAGSHIP** Montenapoleone 27E, Milan. ☎ **3902/7600-6437.** Toll-free U.S. ☎ **888/880-3462.** www.zegna.com.

Hickey Freeman USA $$$$–$$$$$

Hickey Freeman has been in business for over 100 years making ready-to-wear suits that compare favorably with custom tailoring; all of their suits are made with the same expertise and materials usually associated with bespoke tailors. The textiles come from the finest mills in Italy and Great Britain. Hickey Freeman's experienced tailors handcraft the shoulders and reinforce the critical parts for comfort and durability.

BEST BETS   The suits have a slightly fuller classical cut through the body for comfort, no dramatic lines or heavy shoulder pads. Both the jacket and pants are bamberg lined. The buttonholes are hand sewn with silk thread for flexibility, and all buttons are made from the horns of water buffalo and mother-of-pearl shell.

WHERE TO BUY   5 stores and assorted department and specialty stores. **FLAGSHIP**   111 Broadway, NYC. ☎ **212/233-2363.** Also

666 Fifth Ave. ☎ 212/586-6481. Mon–Fri 8:30am–6pm; Sat 11am–5pm. AE, MC,V. Also in San Francisco and Chicago. www.hickeyfreeman.com.

Ralph Lauren USA $$$$$

World's Best I probably should have just dedicated this book to Ralph. He is possibly the most important lifestyle designer of our time and his menswear is sublime. Purple label suits $4,000 to $6,500. Black label wool suit about $1,500. See p. 49.

Zara SPANISH VALUE $$–$$$

Zara may not have the caché of the other brands in this category, but I know a prominent Los Angeles business owner who secretly swears by their elegant, affordable suits (some under $400). He laughs when associates ask him, "You're wearing Armani, right?" though he doesn't always dissuade them. —*SB*
See listing on p. 297.

HONG KONG TAILORS

A-man Hing Cheong Co. Ltd. HONG KONG $$$$$

Known to all simply as Amen, this tailor has been the go-to guy for the British population in downtown and business districts of Hong Kong since the fleet arrived. Well, since 1898 to be exact. They do one of the best bespoke suits in town and will also make shirts.

BEST BETS Expect to pay about $1,200 for a super 200 suit.

WHERE TO BUY 1 store: Mandarin Oriental Hotel, 5 Connaught Rd., Central, HKG. ☎ **852/2522-3336.** Mon–Sat 9am–9pm. AE, MC, V. MTS: Central. No website.

W.W.Chan & Sons Tailor, Ltd CHINESE $$$$–$$$$$

It's probably fair to say that W.W.Chan made my late husband's clothes for 10 years, and has made my son's suits—from bar mitzvah to graduation to wedding. This is about fit and quality and a bit about price as the Savile Row quality comes at Hong Kong prices. Smart shoppers note that suits from this same tailor in Shanghai are 20% less due to a crazy tax structure.
Chan's business suits range from $650 to $1,200; he also makes shirts.

BEST BETS Custom-made suit coordinated with shirt and tie. Your choice of European fit, Asian fit or American fit.

WEB TIPS Website tells you everything you need to know about getting an appointment in Hong Kong or Shanghai and provides the travel sked for stateside visits.

WHERE TO BUY Hong Kong: A2, 2F Burlington House, 94 Nathan Rd., Kowloon. ☎ **852/2366-9738, 852/2366-2634.** Also 129-A02 Maoming Nan Lu, at Huai Hai Zhong Lu, Shanghai. ☎ **86-21/5404-1469.** Daily 10am–10pm. AE, MC, V. www.wwchan.com.

ITALIAN & NEAPOLITAN TAILORS

Brioni See listing on p. 252.

Caraceni MILAN $$$$$

This is a little confusing, so here goes. This famous firm was founded in Rome in 1913. They made suits for the great actors of the 1930s to 1950s such as Tyrone Power, Gary Cooper and Cary Grant, and also for royal families of blue blood and industry (Gianni Agnelli, Aristotle Onasis). After that it gets murky—many members of the family, all with the same last name, splintered off but claimed to be the real dude while one of the student tailors actually bought the brand in 1998. Today's business is anchored in Milan.

BEST BETS Suits range from $4,500 to $18,000.

WHERE TO BUY via Palestro 24 at Corso Venezia, Milan. ☎ **3902/778-811.** Metro: San Babila.

Kiton ITALIAN $$$$$

One of the most exclusive tailors in the world, Kiton (say Key-tone) can make you a suit in 25 hours or in 50 hours—the price difference will only be about $20,000. The brand was created north of Naples after World War II by Ciro Paone, who guards the quality so rigidly that he runs his own tailor school to make sure he's always got properly trained worker bees. The company only makes about 20,000 suits a year, and the average suit costs $5 to $15,000, but the K-50, the house specialty, costs $30 to $50,000.

BEST BETS If the suit fits, wear it.

WEB TIPS Click on "inglese" to get the information in English.

WHERE TO BUY 8 stores in NYC, more; Neiman Marcus, Bergdorf-Goodman, Louis Boston and Wilkes Bashford in San Francisco. **FLAGSHIP** 4 E. 54th St., NYC. ☎ **212/486-5250.** Subway: Fifth Ave. AE, MC, V. www.kiton.it.

Zegna Su Misura ITALIAN $$$$$

450 different exclusive fabrics, shirts and suits, even shoes and leather goods/accessories.

Shoes take 6 weeks—fitting is at Zegna boutique or road show; 4 weeks for the suit. See full listing on p. 253.

SAVILE ROW & LONDON TAILORS

Gieves & Hawkes LONDON $$$$$

Gieves & Hawkes specializes in modern classics, traditional British tailoring and bespoke formal wear. They also cater to and welcome children. A casual line is called, appropriately enough, "Gieves." (Say Jeeves.) Good thing, since a bespoke suit starts at $5,000. Since this is a trad British firm, there is also a horse and rider division that makes breeches to measure.

BEST BETS   There are two branches to this firm—Gieves offers off-the-peg service and has less expensive product. Bespoke suits range from $3,500 to $11,000.

WHERE TO BUY   22 stores in the UK. **FLAGSHIP**   1 Savile Row. ☎ 207/434-2001. Mon–Thurs 9:30am–6:30pm; Fri 9am–6pm; Sat 10am–6pm. Tube: Green Park. www.gievesandhawkes.com.

Henry Poole LONDON $$$$$

In 1860, Henry Poole made a short "smoking jacket" for the Prince of Wales to wear to informal dinner parties at Sandringham, the royal retreat. Subsequently, Mr. James Potter of Tuxedo, NY, was invited to spend a weekend with the prince at Sandringham. He was also advised that he could have a dinner jacket made by the prince's tailors, Henry Poole & Co.

Upon returning to the States, Mr. Potter proudly wore his new jacket to the Tuxedo Park Club and his fellow members

soon started having copies made for themselves; they adopted these jackets as their informal uniform for club "stag" dinners. As a result, the dinner/smoking jacket became known as a Tuxedo or Tux.

BEST BETS   Henry Poole will outfit you in an exquisite two- or three-piece suit for about $5,400 to $6,000.

WHERE TO BUY   1 store: 15 Savile Row, London. ☎ 020/7734-5985. Tube: Green Park. www.henrypoole.com.

A tuxedo from Henry Poole.

Huntsman LONDON $$$$$

Among the most expensive of the Savile Row bespoke tailors, with starting prices over $6,000, but with a very specific fit and customer—look for the fitted waist and for tight, narrow, high armholes. Huntsman also makes riding and hunting clothes as well as a line for Alexander McQueen, who has a line of bespoke suits sold from his shop on Old Bond.

BEST BETS   They also make casual clothes and coats; this beats the made-to-measure price of $4,500 to $11,500.

WHERE TO BUY   11 Savile Row, London. ☎ **4420/7734-7441.** Mon–Fri 9am–5:30pm; Sat 10am–5pm. Tube: Green Park. www.h-huntsman.com.

Richard James LONDON $$$$–$$$$$

If you think the British look has never changed or that all tailors have stiff upper lips, then you haven't heard how Richard James changed menswear or about his collars stiff enough to allow men to go without ties and still look crisp.

BEST BETS   Hugh Grant is the poster boy for the look.

WHERE TO BUY   1 store: 29 Savile Row, London. ☎ **4420/7434-0605.** www.richardjames.co.uk.

Douglas Hayward LONDON $$$$$

If you have money for a good suit but don't want to go $6,000 or more, fret not. This is one of the most famous of the non–Savile Row British tailors, a man who had Peter Sellers and Michael Caine as clients when he went out on his own and then brought in Roger Moore and James Bond after Moore relocated to France as a tax exile and his regular tailor would not fly to France for fittings.

BEST BETS   This tailor handles celebs, proffers a casual atmosphere and makes a great-looking suit for $4,000. Since he is not on Savile Row, he can offer these bargain prices.

WHERE TO BUY   1 store: 95 Mount St., London. ☎ **4420/7499-5574.** Tube: Bond Street.

U.S. TAILORS

Georges de Paris Custom Tailor WASHINGTON, D.C./ FRENCH $$$$$

Known as the tailor of the presidents, Georges works right around the corner from the White House and has made suits for the inaugurations of the past seven presidents. He also continues with bespoke business for local politicians and even for emergencies—he once had to stitch up a white-tie ensemble in fewer than 24 hours for a Kennedy honors recipient who didn't know he needed white tie get-up.

BEST BETS   Dark suits—Georges says presidents always wear dark suits because they exude power.

WHERE TO BUY   1 store: 650 14th St. NW, Washington, D.C. ☎ **202/737-2134;** Metro: Metro Center. AE, MC, V. No website.

William Fiorvanti NYC $$$$

The man who invented the Power Suit in the U.S. and originally made it for *The Man in the Gray Flannel Suit* starting in the late 1950s.

BEST BETS   Suits begin at $4,250.

WHERE TO BUY   1 store: 45 W. 57th St., NYC. ☎ **212/355-1540.**

Vintage

Vintage clothing has never been more chic, thanks to a steady stream of celebrities who wear vintage. Teens wear vintage jeans, models wear vintage slips, fashion editors wear vintage Pucci. Robin Williams got his start in comedy shopping at thrift shops like Aardvark in Hollywood; see below. Vintage is so chic that Tiffany Dubin has become a New York celebrity (she's the founding director of Sotheby's fashion department) and vintage has become an auction staple.

Aardvark's Odd Ark USA $–$$$

Made famous 30-some years ago when Robin Williams admitted that he bought his clothes—and Mork's—at Aardvark's, this Los Angeles store also has a branch in San Francisco. It's considered the granny of the vintage look, although insiders consider it too expensive and touristy.

WHERE TO BUY   7579 Melrose Ave., Los Angeles, CA. ☎ **323/655-6769**. Mon–Thurs noon–8pm; Fri–Sat 11am–9pm; Sun noon–7pm. 1501 Haight St. at Ashbury, San Francisco, CA. ☎ **415/621-3141.** Mon–Thurs noon–8pm; Fri–sat 11am–9pm; Sun noon–7pm. AE, MC, V. No website.

Bentleys LONDON $$$–$$$$$

Bentleys is not a traditional British antiques shop. They specialize in top-quality vintage luggage and accessories; in fact, it's one of the best places in the world to find vintage Louis Vuitton trunks. Cigar-related items and walking sticks are also well represented.

WEB TIPS Be very careful when you log on to the website, as the address Bentleys*of*london.com will link you to a high-class escort service.

WHERE TO BUY 1 store: 204 Walton St., London. ☎ **4420/7584-7770.** Mon–Sat 10am–6pm. AE, MC, V. Tube: Knightsbridge, Sloane Sq. www.bentleyslondon.com.

Bodega BOSTON $$$–$$$$$

This store looks like any other "stock up on Tide or bananas" bodega or 7–Eleven until you get to the vintage clothing in the rear.

BEST BETS Considered the best store for sneakers in the area, priced from $80 to $2,000.

WHERE TO BUY 1 store: 6 Clearway St., Boston. ☎ **617/421-1550.**

Retro Man LONDON $–$$$

This men's store has an enormous diversity of discount designer denim. (Try saying that 10 times fast.) It features a large selection of denim pants and jackets (the Tennessee Tuxedo) with huge names to match: Evisu, G-Star, Edwin, Paul Smith, Helmut Lang, Armani Jeans and Levi's Engineered, to name a few. The store is right on your way to Portobello Market but unlike Portobello is also open during the week (when it's less crowded).

BEST BETS All are expensive, but there are serious bargains to be had if you're willing to be a relentless tag-checker. Most jeans are under $140, and I saw some Evisus for $80, about 75% off regular retail!

WHERE TO BUY 1 store: 30–34 Pembridge Rd., London NW11. ☎ **4484/5644-1442.** MC, V. Tube: Notting Hill Gate. No website.

Rokit BRITISH $–$$$

Rokit is like a vintage-shopping conglomerate or almost-high-street multiple. It has quite a stronghold on the local vintage scene and thus is able to raise prices pretty high. I saw a dirty pair of used Nikes selling for $250.

This store is popular with a younger crowd, and they occasionally rent out the space for style magazine parties and rock shows.

WHERE TO BUY   3 locations in London. 101 & 107 Brick Lane. ☎ 4420/7375-3864. Tube: Shoreditch. Also at Camden High St. ☎ 44-20/7267-3046. Tube: Camdentown. And at 42 Shelton St., Covent Garden. ☎ 44-20/7836-6547. Tube: Covent Garden. All stores daily 11am–8pm. MC, V. www.rokit.co.uk.

Chapter Eight

Babies, Kids, Teens & Tweens

*M*y son, born in 1980, was part of a baby boom known as Generation Y. Before Generation Y there was Generation X—let's say Madonna represents that age group. Both of these groups are now child-bearing and with that comes a whole new world in terms of kids and merchandise.

I'm looking at a generation of baby girls named Madison and MacKenzie for whom "sneakers" cost hundreds of dollars; diaper bags cost thousands of dollars. There are designer blue jeans for toddlers; 10 year olds who write to Santa to send them Juicy Couture.

Designer clothes worn by children are like snowsuits worn by adults. Few can carry it off successfully.
—Fran Lebowitz

Big name designers, of course, are in on it. But you are finding big time and important statements being made from the least likely of places—such as Belgium. And who among us has not been intrigued by reports from parts of Tokyo where teenage street fashion is staggeringly strange and actually makes the news?

Part of all this is related to the fact that more and more families have only one child. There's more disposable income to lavish on the child; more focus on high-end goods and personality-trait clothing. Indeed, how can you deny the sociological importance of a line named Finger in the Nose?

Please note, this chapter's organization is somewhat different from the organization in other chapters in this book. The listings are done in chronological order; that is, beginning with infants and moving through the ages of man—er, child.

Carried Away

Wherever thou goes, I goest—so says the Bible and today's young things. There are more and more social and environmental reasons to keep your child next to your body as much of the day as possible, so there are more and more products to accomplish this end.

Babybjorn SWEDISH $$–$$$

This popular carrier continues to win rave reviews from new parents who agree it's the best choice for transporting newborns. It provides safe and snug support for the smallest baby as she rests against your chest. When her neck is strong enough to support her head, the head rest can be folded down and your baby can be carried facing outward.

BEST BET   Best for tiny babies as the front carrying design can be awkward as the child grows. The original Babybjorn carrier retails for $70.

WEB TIPS   There's a link on the website to find a store, but don't waste your time, as the only Web listing in the U.S. is a distribution center in Ohio. You'll find detailed product information on the site but can't order online.

WHERE TO BUY   Specialty and department stores worldwide such as Macy's and Babies "R" Us. www.babybjorn.com.

Bebes en Vadrouille PARIS $$$–$$$$

In addition to clothing, Bebes en Vadrouille carries a selection of baby carriers from all over the world, many of which involve wrapping the baby in a huge sari-like garment, then tying it around your waist; this is sort of a papoose sling like device that is both secure and comforting to the infant.

BEST BETS   The soft wraparound baby carriers in fab colors; most of these are in the $100 range.

WEB TIPS   The website is in French; however, if you don't read the language, it's easy to search the site as the links are obvious.

WHERE TO BUY   1 store. 47, blvd. Henri-IV, Paris, 4e. ☎ **331/ 4887-1968.** Tues–Fri 11am–2pm, 3–7pm; Sat 10am–1pm, 2–7pm. AE, MC, V. Métro: Bastille. www.bbenv.com.

Bugaboo USA $$$$$

The stroller of choice by Hollywood moms, the Bugaboo is one of the most popular and versatile strollers on the market. To celebrate Mother's Day, Ellen Degeneres recently gave one to each of the moms-to-be in her studio audience.

Whether two-wheeling at the beach, four-wheeling on a hiking trail or just strolling through the park, each ride is as smooth as the next. With a unique suspension system, the entire seat in these strollers reclines, not just the back as in most strollers. In the Frog model, an adjustable handle bar works so that you can face the baby, or with a flip of the bar, face him outward to see the sights.

Bugaboo Bee stroller.

The Frog can also be used as a basinet, and with the sun canopy, mosquito net and rain cover, rest assured that he's well protected.

BEST BETS   The Frog is the original; the Bee is newer and more compact. Prices start at $750, and sales are rare.

WEB TIPS   Go online to get product information and a list of retailers. No orders from the website.

WHERE TO BUY   Children's specialty and department stores including Neiman Marcus (www.neimanmarcus.com) and Nordstrom (www.nordstrom.com).

Maclaren by Philippe Starck FRENCH/USA $$$$$

The lightweight and ultra-portable Starck stroller features a sleek continuous aluminum frame line, giving it a clean sophisticated look. Suitable for babies from 6 months through toddlers, it's available in stain resistant and water repellent fabrics in dreamy colors like yellow, orange and purple.

BEST BETS   Low on maintenance but high on quality and style, the lightweight design is remarkably compact. Retailing at $300, it features one-hand folding and a five-point harness system.

WEB TIPS   Enter Philippe Starck in the Web "search" boxes to find the strollers.

WHERE TO BUY   www.BabyUniverse.com and www.TinyRide. com. AE, MC, V.

Portamee USA $$$$$

This hands-free, sling-type carrier is designed with comfort as the first priority—for both parent and baby—and is suitable for infants from 5 months (or as soon as they can hold their heads up) to over 30 pounds. Designed by an on-the-go working parent, the Portamee is very chic (it comes in either a brown/pink or brown/blue combination) and provides lumbar support for Mom's back. Along with flexible orthopedic support bars, it features built-in slots for cellphones, diapers and baby bottles. Best of all, the Portamee rests on your side, providing eye contact between you and your baby. The whole thing folds into a matching tote when not in use.

BEST BETS   Of the carriers on the market, this one puts the least stress on your back. It's also one of the most expensive, retailing for $198.

WEB TIPS   A Web link shows you construction details and how to use the carrier.

WHERE TO BUY   www.Portamee.com. MC, V.

Phil & Teds e3 NEW ZEALAND $$$$$

This two-in-one stroller from New Zealand's Phil & Teds Most Excellent Buggy Company is a great choice for carrying two children at the same time. Most double strollers are big and bulky, with either a side-by-side or one-behind-the-other configuration. The e3 accommodates a second child, still on the same "footprint" as the single stroller. A double-decker design makes the concept work (there's a flat surface for a newborn, with an added seat for an older sibling), and the whole thing folds up quickly for easy transport. This all-terrain stroller/double buggy comes in seven colors and will accommodate two children up to age 4.

BEST BUYS The beauty of this stroller is the double-decker design, so you should buy both parts together. The e3 single stroller is $349; the doubles kit second seat is $89.

WEB TIPS From the Regal and Lager webpage, follow the links to Phil & Teds, then click on e3.

WHERE TO BUY Web only. www.regallager.com. AE, DISC, MC, V.

Silver Cross BRITISH $$$$$

Often referred to as the Bentley for babies, a Silver Cross pram announces to the world that not only has your little one arrived, but that she has arrived in style. The buggy is a long-time favorite of royalty (Princes William and Harry both rode in one) and Hollywood's It moms—Brooke Shields, Catherine Zeta-Jones, Sarah Jessica Parker and Elizabeth Hurley all used it.

The prams come in two styles—the Balmoral and the Kensington. The Balmoral sets the standard by which all baby buggies are judged. Each steel-bodied pram rides atop a hand-sprung chassis cushioned with leather straps and hand-spoked wheels. It's available in either shiny midnight navy, or onyx black.

The Kensington offers more flexibility with a detachable body and fully folding chassis. The wheels on this model are detachable for transport; however, it takes some time to take apart and reassemble.

BEST BETS Both prams are over the top fab. If you need to transport it in your Porsche SUV, the Kensington is the one you want ($2,700), or if you'll only walk from your house to the park, you'll probably choose the Balmoral ($3,000).

WEB TIPS   You can have a look-see online at www.silvercross.co.uk, but can't order from the website.

WHERE TO BUY   Children's retail stores worldwide. Also at Harrod's 87–135 Brompton Rd., Knightsbridge SW3 London. ☎ 4420/7730-1234. Mon–Sat 10am–8pm; Sun noon–6pm. AE, DISC, MC, V. Tube: Knightsbridge. www.harrods.com.

Snugli USA $$–$$$$

World's Best   This carrier is another good bet for newborns. It's a front-riding model with head support for tiny babies, and converts to a facing outward position as the baby grows and can hold his head up.

The Snuggli is available in several fabrics and styles; denim is the most likely choice.

BEST BETS   Prices range from $20 for a soft fabric carrier to $100 for a structured frame model. At $20, the Comfort Vent carrier is well priced and has button-close side vents to keep you and the baby cool in hot weather.

WEB TIPS   If you want to buy online, go to either www.toysrus.com or www.target.com.

WHERE TO BUY   Children's specialty and department stores worldwide, including Babies "R" Us (www.toysrus.com) and Target (www.target.com).

Designer Diaper Bags

First there was the It handbag, then there was the It dog carrier. For the It girl, there's no choice but to get into the It diaper bag as she becomes an It Mom. Since this is a fashion statement but the baby is not a fashion accessory, it is hard to know what to do. After all, the famous Birkin bag was designed by Hermès for Jane Birkin who needed a bag big enough to stash baby gear when her daughter Charlotte was born.

Diaperbags.com USA $$–$$$$

World's Best   One-stop shopping for all sorts of diaper bags, designer and non (though nothing from the really big names). Still, this Web-only store has diaper bags for Dads; diaper bags in messenger-bag style, in tote bag or sling bag; in stroller holder styles, back-packs and more.

BEST BETS   I am blown away by the number of styles on offer, the good prices (items are discounted) and the bags you want whether you have a baby or not. A camo diaper bag? A diaper bag with a speaker set into it that attaches to your MP3 player? Prices range from $39 to $200 depending on brands, bells and whistles. Baby not included.

WEB TIPS The site is organized by brand, by price, by style; there's mark-downs, sales, specials and free shipping incentives.

Juicy Couture USA $$$$$

Available in pink, blue or black, the Juicy baby bag is a large nylon tote trimmed in leather. It has a waterproof lining and comes with changing mat, bib and binkie. How juicy is your baby? See listing on p. 292.

Mia Bossi USA $$$$$

Mia Bossi's couture diaper bags look more like designer hand-bags than diaper totes; the bags are handmade from the finest Italian fabric and skins, finished with metal hardware and adjustable soft leather straps. They have zip-out liners which can be replaced with computer inserts when the time is right (for you or the kids).

BEST BETS All the styles are great; it's a matter of personal preference. The top of the line Audrey in Italian Barolo leather with snakeskin trim doubles as a purse or briefcase with an optional computer insert ($1,200).

WEB TIPS You can order online with free standard shipping, or ship your bag overnight for $45. They'll send to international destinations for $75; all can be purchased through PayPal or with a credit card.

WHERE TO BUY Children's and maternity shops across the U.S. Bloomingdale's and Takashimaya in New York. 693 Fifth Ave. ☎ 212/350-0100. Mon–Sat 10am–7pm; Sun noon–5pm. AE, MC, V. Subway: E, V, at Fifth Ave. www.miabossi.com.

Louis Vuitton FRENCH $$$$$

First it's the dog carrier, now it's the diaper bag! Oh those Frenchies.

If you're a Louis Vuitton fan, you'll love the Monogram Mini Lin diaper bag featuring the LV logo. (After a couple of years of toting baby gear, it will make a great travel bag.) The tote features an adjustable strap and comes with a separate diaper mat and removable pocket.

BEST BETS It's available for $1,870 in pink, blue or black, but darling, who wants a black diaper bag?

WHERE TO BUY   200+ stores worldwide. **FLAGSHIP**   101 Avenue des Champs-Elysées, Paris 8e. ☎ **331/4549-6230.** Mon–Sat 10am–8pm. MC, V. Metro: George V. www.louisvuitton.com, www.eluxury.com.

Burberry BRITISH $$$$$

There are several baby bag styles in the Burberry line—all have shoulder straps and feature Burberry's signature novacheck pattern. You may want to buy the matching Burberry Folding Stroller to keep your little guy outfitted in signature style.

BEST BETS   Go for one of the larger totes; the smaller ones are very cute but won't hold many diapers. . . . The bags run from $299 to $495; the matching stroller is $695.

WEB TIPS   Enter "diaper bag" in the search box of the website. The diaper bags are only available on Burberry's U.S. website.

WHERE TO BUY   www.burberryusaonline.com. AE, DISC, MC, V.

Kate Spade USA $$$$$

Kate Spade was the first designer to jump on the baby bag band wagon over 20 years ago and her popular practical styles have stood the test of time. There are several designs available in a variety of colors.

WHERE TO BUY   25+ stores worldwide. **FLAGSHIP**   454 Broome St. NYC. ☎ **212-274-1991.** Mon–Sat 11am–7pm; Sun 12–6pm. AE, MC, V. Subway: C, E to Spring. www.katespade.com.

Layette & Infantswear

Absorba FRENCH $$–$$$$

Absorba, a premium French line, is known for exquisite detailing including hand embroidery, superlative fabrics and up-to-the-minute designs; this is top-of-the-line baby couture at reasonable prices and one of the most sought-after names in infant wear.

BEST BETS   You can't go wrong with everyday basics; a set of two *bébé* onesies is a reasonable $20.

WEB TIPS   Don't log on to www.absorba.com, a site offering reuseable incontinence products. Try the adorable Oliebollen. com or Mychildclothing.com.

WHERE TO BUY   Department and specialty stores worldwide. www.absorba.net.

Carter's for Baby Dior USA $-$$

Buying this line is somewhat tricky because Baby Dior is a license of the Carter's babywear division and is sold in the U.S. in department stores, not Dior stores. However, there is another Baby Dior line sold in France as part of the Christian Dior empire. Note that the John Galliano–designed and inspired items are not part of the Carter's line, so if you are looking for a little something outrageous, you may have to call Paris.

BEST BETS   Most Carter's outlet stores also sell the Baby Dior line, which is not very couture-y but does make a nice gift, about $20 for a onesie.

WEB TIPS   Good luck. Even the Carter's site doesn't know how to buy the line.

WHERE TO BUY   Department & specialty stores in the U.S. only.

Hanna Anderson USA/SWEDISH

Great colors, high-quality cotton, often a good choice when you do not know the sex of the baby, as anyone small looks good in yellow and orange striped onesies. See listing on p. 272.

Kissy Kissy USA $$-$$$$$

This premium layette line uses only the softest Pima cotton to make hand-me-down quality basics. Special attention is paid to the smallest details; hand embroideries and traditional designs. All baby gowns are either lined or come with a matching slip, and all sets include a bonnet. Accessories include booties, bibs, caps and blankets.

BEST BETS   The mix-and-match sets are the best, with many options available—an infant baby boy's nautical romper is $46; the matching knit cap is $22.

WEB TIPS   You'll be required to register online to order from the website. Be careful when logging on—kissykissy.com will give you advice on your love life; you want kissykissyonline.com.

WHERE TO BUY   Children's specialty and U.S. department stores such as Nordstrom and Saks Fifth Avenue. www.kissykissy online.com.

Mamas & Papas BRITISH $-$$$$

This chain of designer nursery stores throughout the UK and Republic of Ireland offers everything new parents need from the time the baby's born until he's ready for preschool. There's a complete selection of nursery furniture and baby gear including carriers and accessories, toys, layette items and even potty chairs.

BEST BETS   One-stop shopping for all baby needs. Best bets in clothing include itty-bitty blue jeans for baby boys ($24) and a good selection of dresses for girls in the $40 to $60 range.

WEB TIPS   All prices are in British pounds on the website; remember to convert to dollars before ordering.

WHERE TO BUY   30+ stores throughout the UK and Ireland, one in Dubai. **FLAGSHIP**   256–258 Regent St., London W1. ☎ **44870/ 830-7700.** Mon–Wed 10am–8pm; Thurs 10am–9pm; Fri 10am–8pm; Sat 9am–8pm; Sun noon–6pm. AE, MC, V. Tube: Oxford Circus. www.mamasandpapas.com.

Children's Clothing

I spent much of my childhood wearing hand-me-downs. Today's kids wear designer clothing, even if it comes from Target. The days of the smocked party dress made by dozens of nuns is long gone; now little girls have clothes like Mom's by her favorite designers. Just what is Dakota Fanning doing in Marc Jacobs clothes, I ask you?

Agatha Ruiz de la Prada SPANISH $$$–$$$$

There's also a wide variety of children's accessories, including rain boots and umbrellas, backpacks and bags, bath soaps and toys and desk accessories—all in the same vibrant palette.

WHERE TO BUY   12+ boutiques worldwide. **FLAGSHIP**   Marqués de Riscal 8, Madrid. ☎ **3491/319-0501.** MC, V. www.agatha ruizdelaprada.com.

Bonpoint FRENCH $$–$$$$$

Oohlala, this is the leading status symbol for French mothers. Although the line held on to classic styles for a very long time, it has since moved into fashion, so that whatever trend Mom is wearing—or the fashion magazines are now featuring—can also be found in kids' sizes. Prices are not low; style is sublime, subtle and simply charming—especially for little girls. (Thank heaven for little girls.) Bonpoint has a new concept store, with museum-like showcases and a children's play area. Don't think play area as you know it; this is a French chateau from the turn of the 19th century. Honest.

BEST BETS   Mini-me versions of drop-dead chic, with most dresses in the $250 range.

WEB TIPS   I tried several times and couldn't open any links on the website.

WHERE TO BUY   18 stores in Paris, 55 worldwide. **FLAGSHIP**   15 Rue Royale, Paris, 8e. ☎ **331/4742-5263.** Mon 2–7pm; Tues–Sat 10am–7pm. AE, MC, V. Métro: Concorde. NYC: 1269 Madison Ave., at 91st St. ☎ **212/722-7720.** Mon–Sat 10am–6pm; closed Sun. AE, MC, V. Subway: 86th St. Outlet: Bonpoint Fin de Series. 42 rue de l'Universite, Paris 7e. ☎ **331/4548-0545.** Tues–Sat 11am–7pm. AE, MC, V. Métro: Solferino. www.bonpoint.fr.

Caramel LONDON $$–$$$$

What would the British economy have done if Madonna hadn't moved to town and/or married an Englishman? Now the Material Girl is always on the prowl for funky fashions and has turned many a minor resource into a landmark.

Most of the things in this store were designed by the Greek owner, who was disheartened by kids who wore only frills or Gap togs. Her house collection is called Caramel Baby & Child.

BEST BETS   Unique clothing in the "splurge" category. Madonna bought young Rocco a pair of cashmere trousers for just over $100. Oy.

WEB TIPS   If you plan to ship to the U.S., you must first e-mail them for shipping information.

WHERE TO BUY   1 store. 291 Brompton Rd., SW3 London. ☎ **4420/7589-7001.** Mon–Sat 10am–6pm; Sun 10am–5pm. AE, MC, V. Tube: S. Kensington. www.caramel-shop.co.uk.

Crewcuts by J.Crew USA $$–$$$

J.Crew now offers the same lines of preppy clothing for children ages 2 to 10 that their parents have worn for years. A few of the larger brick-and-mortar stores carry the children's line (also available at www.jcrew.com/crewcuts_home.jhtml).

Gap Kids & babyGap USA $–$$$

While the Gap seems to be continually redefining itself with merchandise for teens and adults, the children's store remains a reliable source for chic, practical and well-priced clothing.

BEST BETS   The newborn layette items are a good buy for the money (a 3-pak of onesies for $18), and there's a good selection of Slim and Plus sizes for older children.

WEB TIPS   Order carefully; although returns and exchanges are free, it can take up to 3 weeks to process the transactions.

WHERE TO BUY   Over 3,000 Gap stores worldwide. All listed online. www.gap.com. AE, DISC, MC, V.

Du Pareil au Meme   FRENCH $$–$$$

I consider Du Pareil au Meme (written DPAM sometimes) the best of the mass-market kiddie boutiques, and I curse the fact that my niece has grown up and no longer wears kids' clothes. Most of the line is casual and in strong colors; prices are very affordable. There are stores in every shopping district in Paris.

BEST BETS   Girls' denim jackets are under $30; skirts are $18 to $22; jackets for boys are under $25.

WEB TIPS   Click the flag in the upper-right-hand corner of the home page for the English link. Online prices are the same as in the shops; however, you'll find good sale items on the website. DPAM ships overseas.

WHERE TO BUY   Over 200 stores worldwide. **FLAGSHIP**   15 rue Mathurins, Paris, 8e. ☎ **331/4266-9380.** Mon–Sat 10am–7pm. AE, MC, V. Métro: Madeleine. www.dupareilaumeme.fr.

Hanna Anderson   USA/SWEDISH $$–$$$$

This is a wonderful source for high-quality pure-cotton butter-soft clothing in contemporary colors, all in comfy shapes that aren't too tight or too grown-up.

Along with producing great clothes, Hanna Anderson is deeply ingrained in giving back to the community. A portion of every Hanna purchase goes to support children in need through the HannaHelps Program. The company awards yearly grants to hundreds of schools and non-profit groups serving children across the U. S. It's also environmentally friendly, using organically grown cotton.

Hanna Anderson boys explorer toggle coat.

BEST BETS   Great online sales. I found baby onesies normally priced between $35 and $40 on sale for $18, and a good selection of clothing for older children at 30% off.

WEB TIPS   You may need glasses to see the photos.

WHERE TO BUY   12 stores in the U.S. **FLAGSHIP**   327 NW 10th Ave., Portland, OR. ☎ **503/321-5275.** Mon–Fri 10am–6pm; Sat 10am–5pm; Sun noon–5pm. 258 W. Market (Mall of America), Bloomington, MN. ☎ **952/854-9598.** Mon–Sat 10am–9:30pm. 8687 N. Central Expwy. (NorthPark Center), Dallas, TX. ☎ 214/369-2700. Mon–Sat 10am–9pm; Sun noon–6. AE, DISC, MC, V. www.hannaanderson.com.

I Pinco Pallino MILAN $$–$$$$

Attention rich grandmothers and hotel heiresses. I have never seen more cute clothes in my life. Silver and rhinestone ballet slippers, layers of gauze worn with T-shirts, layette for rock stars. There are two different stores: one for layette and the other for small kids. There's also an outlet near Florence.

BEST BETS   Shoes at $170 a pair, but oh what shoes. The I'm-ready-for-my-close-up rock-star kids look is worth every penny of the $800 if you've got it.

WEB TIPS   Mamma mia!

WHERE TO BUY   Via Spiga 6 and Via Borgosspesso 25 (these addresses are 100m apart), Milan. ☎ **3902/781-931.** Mon 3–7pm; Tues–Sat 10am–7pm. AE, MC, V. Metro: Montenapoleone. There is an outlet store outside of Florence at The Mall (p. 432). www.ipincopallino.it.

Ness & Chloe USA/TURKISH $$–$$$

Ness & Chloe is an organic line of infant and toddler clothing, all designed for comfort and mobility. The apparel is made from organic cotton, which means that toxic pesticides are eliminated at every step of the cotton-growing process, resulting in less impact on the environment and health of the growers and consumers. In addition, the clothing is manufactured in small European plants, ensuring that there is never any child labor involved in making the products.

BEST BETS   The toddler line is the best, with subtle ruffled styles for girls and patch pocket designs for boys. Most pieces are in the $30 to $50 range.

WEB TIPS   If you can get through the annoying baaaaahing sheep in the intro, ordering from the website is easy.

WHERE TO BUY   Upscale children's shops in the U.S. and all Nordstrom children's departments. AE, MC, V. www.nordstrom.com. www.organic4kids.com.

Oilily DUTCH $$–$$$$

This chain has stores all over the world and prices that break my heart because I am so attracted to the clothes, the colors and the look: happy splashy designs, bright mixed patterns and all the celebration a garment can take. There's a women's line along with some accessories in addition to the children's clothing. Why won't our kids be kids forever just so we can dress them up? This is the line for the mom or child who wants hot colors and look-at-me clothes; not for the shy.

BEST BETS   The complete outfits, dresses with matching cardigan sweaters for example, make Oilily a best bet. The little girls' dresses begin at about $50 and sizes run small.

WEB TIPS   The website is slow; you can't order online. However, if you're patient, you can view about half of the collection on the website.

WHERE TO BUY   70 stores worldwide. **FLAGSHIP**   P. C. Hooft-straat 131-133, Amsterdam. ☎ **3120/672-3361.** Mon 1–6pm; Tues, Wed, Fri, Sat 10am–6pm; Thurs 10am–9pm; Sun noon–5pm. AE, MC, V. Tram no. 2 to van Baerlestraat. NYC: 820 Madison Ave., between 68th and 69th sts. ☎ **212/772-8686.** Mon–Sat 10am–6pm; Sun noon–5pm. Subway: 6 to E. 77th St. 465 W. Broadway. ☎ **212/871-0201.** Mon–Sat 10am–6pm; Sun noon–5pm. Subway: Houston St. 9520 Brighton Way, Beverly Hills, CA. ☎ **310/859-9145.** Mon–Sat 10am–6pm; Sun noon–5pm. South Coast Plaza, Orange County California. ☎ **714/432-7505.** Mon–Fri 10am–9pm, Sat 10am–8pm; Sun 11am–6:30 pm. AE, MC, V. www.oililyusa.com.

OshKosh B'Gosh   USA $–$$$

This maker of clothing for tots has been popular in the U.S. for a long time, and almost has cult status in continental Europe. Now a division of Carter's, OshKosh still sells trademark children's bib overalls along with jeans, pants, T-shirts and swimsuits. This is icon-wear for little ones. There are lines for infants, toddlers and children up to size 14.

BEST BUYS   Corduroy bib overalls; most are priced under $25.

WEB TIPS   Log on to the website to locate the nearest outlet; there are no online sales. There's an application on the website for your child to become a model.

WHERE TO BUY   OshKosh stores and outlets, major department stores worldwide such as Nordstrom and Macy's, and children's specialty stores. OshKosh **FLAGSHIP**   586 Fifth Ave., near 48th St., NYC. ☎ **212/827-0098.** Mon–Fri 10am–7pm; Sat 10am–6pm; Sun noon–6pm. AE, DISC, MC, V. Subway: B, D, F, or V to Rockefeller Center. www.oshkoshbgosh.com.

This Little Piggy Wears Cotton   USA $–$$$

The Little Piggy brings the best of European and American made merchandise together for newborns to age 14, featuring comfortable 100% cotton (duh) clothing in whimsical designs. The apparel combines comfort, style, and nostalgia with a big dose of humor to bring out the kid in everyone. If you're looking for a unique baby gift (and if the parents have a sense of humor), check out the baby toupees and wigs. Favorites include the "Donald," "Lil Kim" (long pink curls) and the "Bob," mellow dreads for the rasta-inspired babe.

BEST BETS Personalized denim jackets are *très chic* ($98) and the long john set ($40) comes in adorable prints. Those toupees? $30.

WEB TIPS The graphics are LARGE and clear which makes ordering a snap for those of us over age 50.

WHERE TO BUY 8 stores in California and Arizona. **FLAGSHIP** 311 Paseo Nuevo, Santa Barbara, CA. ☎ **805/564-6982.** Mon–Fri 10am–9pm; Sat 10am–8pm; Sun 11am–6pm. Stanford Shopping Center, Palo Alto, CA. ☎ **650/853-7002.** Mon–Fri 10am–9pm; Sat 10am–7pm; Sun 11am–6pm. 929 Newport Center Dr. (Fashion Island), Newport Beach, CA. ☎ **949/718-0533.** Mon–Fri 10am–9pm; Sat 10am–7pm; Sun 11am–6pm. AE, DISC, MC, V. www.littlepiggy.com.

Mass Market Kidswear

You don't need to spend a fortune to get cute baby clothes, especially these days when mass market retailers are making an effort to get designers to do inexpensive lines for them and everyone loves to create baby clothes. The lines may not come with big names attached, but still may be adorable . . . and fairly priced.

Babies R Us USA $

This division of Toys "R" Us carries everything in the world you would need, making one-stop shopping not only easy but easier than getting pregnant. In striving to serve all families, there are information services and toys/equipment for less-abled children.

BEST BETS The store carries clothes and supplies and equipment and diapers and yes, breast pumps. They also have a fair selection of pale yellow clothing for the person who does not know the sex of the newborn.

WEB TIPS Site does everything but cry at night.

WHERE TO BUY 250+ stores in U.S. AE, DISC, MC, V. www. babiesrus.com.

Target USA $

When my girlfriend Jill returned from Africa with her newly adopted daughter, she asked me where to go for a total wardrobe. I sent her to Target. Target isn't the least expensive resource, but the clothes are sturdy enough for play and priced fairly enough to be able to buy a wardrobe. Mostly importantly, everything you need is here, even shoes—so one-stop shopping is easy. The styling is a blend of classics (yawn) and hot fashion like the big kids are wearing.

BEST BETS   Cowboy boots for girls, in pink ($9).

WEB TIPS   You can shop online.

WHERE TO BUY   1,500 stores in the U.S. AE, DISC, MC, V. www.target.com.

Monoprix FRENCH VALUE $

World's Best   This is basically the French national "dime store" and I write about it a lot (p. 53). Their kids' clothing is sublime, usually below $25 an item, and across the board offers smart shopping for infants, little boys and girls.

Designer Mini-moms & Kids

It's not like I didn't warn you. Even Karl Lagerfeld did a line for teens through H&M. When he starts doing Chanel baby clothes is the day I retire. Don't mind me if I sound like Fran Lebowitz on this subject, but I can't help but notice that many of the same designers who make a kiddie line also offer pet couture.

Armani Junior ITALIAN $–$$$$

Making Armani a cradle-to-grave choice, the designer actually has layette in soft colors (but just pink, blue or cream—not the usual Armani palette) and an entire range of clothes for kids up to age 6.

BEST BETS   Clothes begin at $145.

WEB TIPS   The website has many adorable photos but no information save store addresses and press contacts. However, various other listings from any search engine will offer you ways to buy new and used clothes from the line.

WHERE TO BUY   Armani Junior stores in Dubai, Hong Kong, Shanghai, Mexico City, Kuwait City; and in department stores such as Harrods in London. **FLAGSHIP**   10 via Montenapoleone, Milan. ☎ **3902/783-196.** Mon–Sat 10am–7pm. Metro: Montenapoleone. www.armanijunior.com.

Baby Dior FRENCH $–$$$$

World's Best

John Galliano has played a large role in bringing the Baby Dior line into the world of too hip for my diapers. There's Dior baby bling (p. 269), baby accessories (such as baby bottles and sunglasses), as well as infant and toddlerwear. When M. Dior offered the world the New Look he had no idea it would come to this.

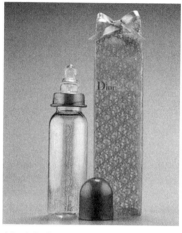

A bottle by Baby Dior.

BEST BETS   "My Dior" girl's T-shirt, $145; designer teddy bears are also cute, $125 and up. Keep either in mint condition to preserve value; never wash by machine.

WEB TIPS   The Dior site does not mention the baby line; however, any Google search will give you plenty of ops to see and buy. EBay.fr (the French version) has Dior duds on sale regularly; a recent search revealed an "overall jogging" on offer for $13.

WHERE TO BUY   Baby Dior, 30 av. Montaigne, Paris, 8e. ☎ **331/5367-6665.** Mon–Sat 10am–7pm. AE, MC, V. Métro: Alma-Marceau. Baby Dior outlet store, 27 rue Charles Sanglier, 45000 Orleans, France. www.dior.com.

Burberry BRITISH $$–$$$$$

You'll find the same plaids and raincoats for kids as in the adult collections. The line is conservative, adorable and veddy, veddy British. See listing on p. 268.

BEST BETS   The children's trench coat, from $300. You can also buy Burberry Baby Touch cologne (without alcohol) for $38.

WEB TIPS   Click on "childrenswear" to find clothing, accessories and fragrance.

WHERE TO BUY   Select Burberry stores carry the children's collections. www.burberry.com.

Snips & Snails: Just for Boys

Having a son was not the non-fashion statement I suspected it would be. From cutie-pie dinosaur layette to his first leather jacket, size 6, my son proved that guys can be fun. I am not really certain what happened to my little boy; somehow he got to be 6'4" and married, but he remains a living lesson to me in what is cool for guys.

Bonpoint Boy Boutique PARIS $$–$$$$

This branch of Bonpoint is for boys only.

WHERE TO BUY   86, rue de l'Universite, Paris. ☎ **331/4551-1768.** Mon–Sat 11am–7pm. AE, MC, V. Metro: Solferino. www.bonpoint.fr. See listing on p. 270.

Brooks Brothers USA $$–$$$$$

The same classic ultra-conservative styles that Dad loves are available for Chip and Trip as well; the boys' clothing line is available in most Brooks Brothers stores and online. Not all of the retail stores carry the boys' line, but it's usually available in the outlets. Brooks specializes in suits for boys for special events. See listing on p. 218.

Hickey Freeman USA $$–$$$$$

Like father, like son. So of course there's a Hickey Freeman collection for boys that makes them look like little men. It includes suits, tuxedos, sport coats, trousers, dress shirts and ties. See listing on p. 253.

Ralph Lauren USA $$–$$$$$

World's Best Ralph Lauren's country club–ready clothing for boys is available in sizes newborn through 20; you can find the complete collection at the Ralph Lauren Boys Store in New York, as well as select Ralph Lauren stores in the U.S. See listing on p. 49.

Shoes

Gotta be Buster Browns? Forget it. Today's kids are so into their shoes that you can read newspaper articles or watch TV shows about gangsters who kill kids for their must-have shoes.

Even for kids who wear uniforms to school, very often the footwear is the most important part of their fashion statement. For the moms who buy the shoes, sometimes the small, adorable and frivolous shoes are the most fun because they

Aaron Shops London's Brick Lane

London has been swinging like a pendulum for decades—this is the home of trends and street fashion. There are plenty of cool stores—especially for teens and tweens. As you're prowling the Brick Lane area, don't miss the following shops and stops.

If you're here on a Sunday, you'll likely head first to the **Old Truman Brewery**, 91–95 Brick Lane, E1 (Tube: Shoreditch or Liverpool St.), an 11-acre historic site that houses all kinds of vendors, including a few worthwhile vintage dealers in the alley. The highlights include **eatmyhandbagbitch**, for mid-century modern design; **Public Beware Co**., for trendy clothes and shoes; and **Junky Styling,** which recycles old clothes into hip new fashions. Junky is by far my favorite; its classic Mr. T prints are priceless, but it was the custom-made neckties that won me over—these old thrift-store finds are sliced up and stuffed with packs of rolling papers, or glued with plastic cigarette butts, and come complete with the anti-smoking label ripped off a pack of smokes.

After you finish browsing the Old Truman Brewery, you might as well make a whole Sunday of it and find Cheshire Road, off Brick Lane, and then go to the nearby **Spitalfields Market,** which is pretty good for vintage clothes and new designers. If you find the markets a bust, the other stores in the area will more than make up for it.

The Laden Showroom, 103 Brick Lane, E1, is an amazing place. It features separate booths by different indie designers such as Red Mutha, Your Majesty, Charles of London and many more. Some of the booths have cheesy stuff, but many clothes feature one-of-a-kind cut-ups, sew-ons and paint-and-marker additions. A little pricey, but well worth it. Supposedly, tabloid darlings Pete Doherty and Victoria Beckham have been spotted here.

Rokit, 101 and 107 Brick Lane, E1, is like a vintage-shopping conglomerate or almost-high-street multiple. Aside from this string of stores right on Brick Lane, it has a location on Camden High Street, as well as a newish one in Covent Garden. Rokit has quite a stranglehold on the local vintage scene—and thus is able to raise prices pretty high. I saw a dirty pair of used Nikes selling for £125 ($231). On Brick Lane, note that there are two separate Rokit stores here, with the Laden Showroom sandwiched in between them.

Mendoza, 158 Brick Lane, E1, has a terrific selection of vintage clothes and modern styles. Among its best items are painted trucker hat one-offs and rare Nike Dunks. But the ultimate prize of my visit was to be found lying helplessly on the £10 ($19) rack: a red-and-white baseball tee sporting the slogan, "Born to Shop," with a dollar sign for an S. —*Aaron James* represent a look or a splurge you might not make in an adult size. Are there "now" designer shoes for kids? You betcha; Weejuns are so retro, but Hush Puppies are cool, dawg.

Harry's Shoes for Kids NYC $$–$$$$$

This New York Upper West Side shoe shop can be a madhouse, but local parents are happy to brave the weekend and after-school crowds to shop for the best kids' shoes in town.

Harry's carries a comprehensive selection of footwear for boys and girls from traditionally styled prestige brands like Aster and Primigi to trendier designs from Puma, Ugg and Crocs. They carry a wide variety of styles, from flip flops to dress shoes, along with New York's most extensive selection of Ecco's for kids.

Harry's expert fitters will make sure little feet are comfortable, at least for a couple months, until it's time for a new pair.

BEST BETS   Eccos for kids. All Ecco styles are available. Prices range from $54 for children's sandals to $110 for boots.

WEB TIPS   Harry's has one website for both their adult and children's styles, so after logging on, click on "children's," then search by style or manufacturer.

WHERE TO BUY   1 store. 2315 Broadway, between 83rd and 84th Sts, NYC. ☎ **212/874-2034.** Mon and Thurs 10am–7:45pm; Tues, Wed, Fri and Sat 10am–6:45pm; Sun 11am–6pm. AE, MC, V. Subway: 1, 9, W. 86th St. www.harrys-shoes.com.

Primigi ITALIAN $$–$$$

From first walkers to young teens, Primigi is one of Italy's favorite children's footwear lines. They combine modern technology with Italian craftsmanship to create some of the most chic and comfortable styles available for children. A new collection, made with Gore-Tex, will keep little feet dry and blister-free—perfect for serious play.

BEST BETS   The Gore-Tex waterproof sneakers are $90; sandals begin at $65.

WEB TIPS   Check various websites to find the best prices. Piperlime (a division of Gap) and Zappos both offer free shipping and free returns.

WHERE TO BUY   Nordstrom in the U.S. www.zappos.com. www. piperlime.com. www.primigi.com.

ShooShoos SOUTH AFRICAN $–$$

These whimsical infant shoes are made from the softest 100% Nappa leather with all cotton thread and linings. They're safe for early walkers, featuring non-toxic dyes, elasticized ankle straps (no laces to trip over), and non-skid soles. Styles range from Mary Janes to faux sneakers—all in hip colors.

ShooShoos giraffe suede shoes.

BEST BETS   The styles with appliqués—dragons, flowers, planes and faux polka-dot Mary Janes. My neighbor, an American Airlines pilot, bought ShooShoos with an airplane appliqué ($23) for his son. Prices range from $17 to $23.

WEB TIPS   This is one of the easiest sites I've used. Everything is clear and quick, and they don't waste space with useless links.

WHERE TO BUY   Mothercare stores (550 worldwide), children's retail and specialty stores. AE, MC, V. www.shooshoosusa.com.

Tod's ITALIAN $$$–$$$$

Same idea as Gucci for kids. They sell baby shoes and kids' versions of their most popular styles. See listing on p. 153.

Toys, Books & Skills

Architecture Kids Store SCOTTSDALE, AZ $$$$

When I was a kid, it was a treat to go to friends' houses where there was a treehouse or playhouse in the backyard. In most cases, these were homemade numbers, quickly assembled by Dad over a summer weekend.

Well, kid houses have come a long way, and the ones designed by Architecture Kids are fancier than most family homes. They take a child's quest for a playhouse, mix in the parents' wish for something chic, add an adventure story or fantasy and create something unlike anything else on the block, or possibly in the state.

The creative designs include windmills, pirate ships and tree lofts. Each structure is first rate—crafted entirely by hand from maple and Douglas fir. Features include reading lofts, wallpaper panels, operable windows, decorative trims and mouldings, secret hideaways, upholstered pillows and cushions, bay windows and decorative lighting. Each house is custom built. —*SRL*

BEST BETS   Any custom design—I love the pirate's ship; however, it runs $40,000 to $50,000 installed.

WEB TIPS   The website is easy to use once you click past the music in the intro.

WHERE TO BUY   1 store. Scottsdale Fashion Sq., Scottsdale Rd. at Camelback, Scottsdale, AZ. ☎ **480/874-0112.** Mon–Sat 10am–9pm; Sun 11am–6pm. AE, MC, V. www.architecture kids.com.

American Girl Place USA $–$$$$$

These shopping and entertainment destinations are home to the American Girl Collection of dolls. In addition to the boutiques selling dolls (you can have one made to look just like your daughter), accessories and outfits for both girls and dolls, there are theaters featuring two musical revues starring

those American Girls (one for preschoolers, one for older girls); there's the American Girl Café where brunch, lunch, afternoon tea and dinner are served; there's a photo studio where you can have an *American Girl Magazine* cover made featuring you and your doll; and of course, there's the concierge who will plan a perfect birthday party complete with invitations, matching thank-you notes, a meal in the cafe and goody bag for each party guest.

American Girl "Bitty Twins" dolls.

Insider's tip: Many hotels have special promotions for mom, daughter and doll—there's a bed for the doll, special turn-down service and assorted tie-ins.

BEST BETS   Dolls start at $87 and go on up, way up. Expect to pay $18 to $22 for a meal in the cafe, $15 to $28 for Musical Revues. And don't forget to have your doll's hair styled in the American Girl Salon for $24.

WEB TIPS   If you go online, you can get dates to the once-a-year charity event seconds sale, see p. 437.

WHERE TO BUY   111 E. Chicago Ave., Chicago. ☎ **312/943-9400.** Mon–Wed 10am–7pm; Thurs 10am–9pm; Fri–Sat 9am–9:30pm; Sun 9am–7pm. 609 Fifth Ave. at 49th St., NYC. ☎ **212/371-2220.** Mon–Thurs 10am–7pm; Fri 10am–9pm; Sat 9am–9pm; Sun 9am–7pm. Subway: E, V, to 5th Ave. 189 The Grove Dr., Los Angeles, CA. ☎ **323/602-5900.** Mon–Fri 10am–9pm; Sat

9am–9pm; Sun 9am–7pm. AE, DISC, MC, V. www.american girl.com.

Au Nain Bleu FRENCH $–$$$$$

At the age of 170, Au Nain Bleu (blue gnome) is obviously doing something right. The oldest toy store in the world, they stock traditional games, jigsaw puzzles, dolls, musical instruments and a great selection of stuffed animals. You'll also find decorative room accessories. And for the politically correct, a *nain* in French isn't a Little Person, it's the garden-style plaster gnome that is the store mascot.

BEST BETS   The dolls and accessories including prams and furnishings. Most are over $100.

WEB TIPS   The website is completely useless, unless you're looking for the shop address or phone number. No merchandise, no online shopping, no clue as to the magic of the store.

WHERE TO BUY   5, Blvd. Malesherbes, Paris, 8e. ☎ **331/4265-2000.** Mon–Sat 11am–7pm. AE, MC, V. Métro: Madeleine. www.aunainbleu.com.

Childcrafter USA $$

Here's a unique gift idea that will entertain and educate for months on end. You provide the child's age, gender and special interests, and this Craft of the Month Club will deliver appropriate kits such as soap making, needlepoint and specialty painting. All are great indoor activities.

When you sign up, request a survey to be sent with the first shipment; the kids can then choose the projects they want delivered.

BEST BETS   You get a lot for your money; an annual subscription is $90; 3- and 6-month programs are also available. In addition to the crafts, check out their "diaper" cakes ($30–$42); made from Pampers in several combinations, these make great shower gifts.

WEB TIPS   There are many parenting resources listed; click "links."

WHERE TO BUY   Customer Service ☎ **888/458-4363.** www. childcrafter.com.

Hamley's LONDON $–$$$

Whether or not you have children, know any children or even like children, Hamley's deserves attention. This London icon is a veritable theater of retail. And if you're looking for that unusual toy not readily available in the U.S., then Hamley's is a must. The gift shop on the street level is the best (and easiest) place I know of to buy gifts for all your friends and neighbors.

If your child collects dolls, you'll have a tough time making a decision here. For the collectors in your family, there's a huge array of Britains, the small metal British Regiment Guard soldiers. Puzzles and brain teasers can be good gifts for older children or adults; they make nice little travel rewards for train journeys or transatlantic flights.

If you begin to feel dizzy by the selection, you'll be relieved to find a snack bar in the basement. The prices, however, will not make you dizzy (American toys are more expensive), and Corgi toys are a bargain.

BEST BETS   "Hamley's own" signature toys; a pushcart baby walker full of building blocks is $60, as is a 4-in-1 baby doll pram set including pram frame, carry cot, changing pad and brollie.

WEB TIPS   The website offers a small percentage of what's available in the store—you need to visit in person, if possible.

WHERE TO BUY   1 store. 188–196 Regent St., London W1. ☎ **44870/333-2455.** Mon–Fri 10am–8pm; Sat 9am–8pm; Sun noon–6pm. Tube: Oxford Circus or Piccadilly Circus. In addition to the flagship store on Regent St., there are smaller branches at the London airports (4 at Heathrow and 1 at Stansted), so you can pick up something for the kids on your way home. AE, MC, V. www.hamleys.com.

FAO Schwarz   USA $–$$$$$

The most famous toy store in America has scaled down enormously but still has two stores and a large plush footprint. You can still jump on the floor mat piano, just as Tom Hanks did in *Big*.

BEST BETS   The large selection of items at all prices. There's wild and crazy and stupidly expensive, but also many items under $25. Inquire about a slumber party in the store.

WEB TIPS   You can shop online and even order a couture tutu. At certain times of the year there are promos for free shipping on orders of $75 or more.

WHERE TO BUY   2 stores in NYC, Las Vegas. **FLAGSHIP**   767 Fifth Ave. at 58th St., NYC. ☎ **212/644-9400** or 800/426-8697. Mon–Wed 10am–7pm; Thurs–Sat 10am–8pm; Sun 11am–6pm. AE, DISC, MC, V. Subway: Fifth Ave. www.fao.com.

Kiddyland TOKYO $–$$$$

If you think all stores named Kiddytown or Kiddyland are alike, you've never been to Tokyo, where this store is so large, so crammed with stuff and so downright jaw-dropping amazing that you could never recover from shopping here. First off, this is not a toy store like Toys "R" Us so if you have preconceived notions, erase them. This is a store for kids and adults, it is six floors tall and it sells mostly plastics and then games. It has every fad item imaginable—I happen to be big on Japanese hamsters myself but there are still plenty of Pretty Kitty fans. Boys will like all the warrior kinds of card games.

BEST BETS   You can play with the toys; the store is next door to Chanel and very close to Oriental Bazaar (p. 56).

WEB TIPS   It's in Japanese but if you write/index after the address you can get it in English.

WHERE TO BUY   1 store: 6-1-9 Jinguame, Shibuya, Tokyo. ☎ 813/3409-3431. Daily 10am–9pm; closed 3rd Tues of every month. AE, MC, V. JTR: Omotesando. www.kiddyland.co.jp.

Kidbuilt.com 🖰 USA $$–$$$

Dads, here's a chance to spend quality time with your junior builder. You'll find kits to build simple furniture ranging from rocking chairs to toys chests, and it's all easy to assemble.

BEST BETS   Great projects for father/son bonding. Prices are under $100 for most items.

WEB TIPS   Each item is shown with detailed assembly instructions so you know what's involved before ordering.

Speedydog.com 🖰 USA $–$$$

Inspire your little genius with one of over 90 science-project-type items found on this site. You can choose from basic ant farms ($10–$25), mini greenhouses ($30) and even a frog metamorphosis kit ($30). These are great gifts for budding scientists.

BEST BETS   The ant farm is a bargain at $10. It comes with instructions for assembly and a coupon to order the ants. You'll want to order them in fair weather (Apr–Oct) to ensure safe delivery. Who wants frozen ants?

WEB TIPS   This site could entertain a 10 year old for weeks.

The Toy Market BEIJING $–$$

This building is located through an alley and alongside the Pearl Market in Beijing. It offers floors and floors of fake toys made in the style of the big brands, such as wannabe Legos and so on. When you finish laughing, you'll have a ball. Remember to bargain! Begin by offering less than half the asking price.

BEST BETS Kites cost about $7 each; big name miniature sports cars cost about $10 each (Ferrari anyone?); and joke gifts, such as snapping gum paks, cost $1.

WHERE TO BUY 1 store. Hong Qiao, Beijing. No nearby Metro.

Under Two Flags LONDON $$–$$$$

By the time toy soldiers became popular in America (during World War II), children in Great Britain were celebrating the 50th anniversary of William Britain & Co. Britain went into the toy soldier business in 1893, creating a set of the Life Guards to honor Queen Victoria's forthcoming Diamond Jubilee in 1897.

Many Britain sets (including the first) are available in London at Under Two Flags, on colorful St. Christopher's Place near Wigmore Street, just a stone's throw from Oxford Street and Selfridges.

The store also offers inexpensive lead soldiers for do-it-yourself painters, a selection of military books, magazine and prints; bronzes, porcelains and curios, such as a chess set made of toy soldiers.

World Traveler

For more toys in London, try the **TinTin Shop** near Covent Garden, 34 Floral St. (☎ 207/836-1131) for all things TinTin. Introduce the kids to TinTin before the Spielberg movie opens in 2009. Shop online at www.thetintinshop.uk.com, www.tintinologist.org, or www.store.tintin.com.

BEST BETS Collectible toy soldiers, of course. A set of six Zulu warriors is $120.

WEB TIPS You can choose by product or by price on the site and all items are sent insured.

WHERE TO BUY 1 store. 4 St. Christopher's Place, W1 London. ☎ 207/935-6934. Tues–Sat 10:30am–5pm. AE, M, V. Tube: Bond Street.

Teens & Tweens

With kids growing up as quickly as they do, with designer clothing as expensive as it is and with Baby Boomers realizing they are still teens at heart, it's hard to know who wears teen and tween fashion these days or even know who it is created for.

Designers often do lower-priced lines in order to lure customers to the brand to which they hope the customer will trade up when he has more money. On the other hand, the line between what's appropriate for a kid and an adult is getting very blurry. Before actress Dakota Fanning was even a teenager, she was the muse for the **Marc by Marc Jacobs** line. Barbara Walters recently admitted on camera that one of her favorite stores is **H&M.**

One of the main characters in the movie *In Her Shoes* finds her calling as a fashion consultant. Her first client doesn't want "Juicy written across my butt."

Those who are into Juicy are a strong financial presence. *Vogue* and *Cosmo* each have magazines geared for the teen market although *Elle* just dropped theirs. Target has a special service to provide trend info to teens: Now you can text them for fashion updates. Trends begin with teens who have a look of their own and create many of the looks of tomorrow.

American Apparel USA ⸢VALUE⸣ $–$$$

See listing on p. 93.

American Rag Cie JAPANESE $–$$$–$$$$

This brand has a Japanese and a U.S. branch—it's a stable in the LA culture of used and vintage clothing and cool teens. The clothes are a mix of new, used, new made from used and other stuff thrown in, including CD's. Some call it an insiders Urban Outfitters meets Barneys. This line—the clothing portion—has distribution through Macy's.

BEST BETS   Droopy/chic styles for girls; think Mary Kate and Ashley. A navasana indie style cotton dress, perfect with leggings, is $253.

WEB TIPS   The website appears to be in English, but when you click on the links, you'll see only Japanese. There's a link for online shopping, but it's slow to open and again, in Japanese. Just go to Macy's.

WHERE TO BUY   9 stores worldwide; also at Macy's. **FLAGSHIP** 2F, 3-37-1 Shinjuku. ☎ **813/5366-5425.** Daily 11am–10pm. Train: Shinjuku. Los Angeles: 150 S. LaBrea. ☎ **323/935-3154.** Mon–Sat 10am–9pm; Sun noon–7pm. AE, DISC, MC, V. www. americanragcie.co.jp.

Baby Phat USA $–$$$

You have to be impressed with this $200-million empire of clothing for girls, juniors, plus sizes, lingerie and everything else that Kimora Lee Simmons developed from the merger of hip-hop with teeny-bopper fashion. You can shop online.

BEST BETS   The lingerie is good quality, sexy and well priced: a floral appliqué bra and thong are priced at $26 and $10. There's a great selection of jeans in many styles; ankle-length skinny jeans are $59.

WEB TIPS   If you don't want to shop from the website, store locations are shown online but there are no hours or phone numbers listed.

WHERE TO BUY   FLAGSHIP   129 Prince St., NYC. ☎ **212/533-7428.** Mon–Sat 11am–7pm; Sun noon–6pm. AE, DISC, MC, V. Subway: N, R. W, at Prince St. Other locations online. www.babyphat.com.

Charlotte Russe USA ⟨VALUE⟩ $–$$$

This is a great, low-cost line for teens and tweens and I have only one warning for those over 20 who want to shop here—shop in moderation because if you wear too much of this stuff at one time, you turn into a troll. The clothing is very young and very inexpensive—it's amazing how on target they are with the latest hot looks at very low prices.

BEST BETS   What's hot this week may be out of style by next. . . . But oh, those prices . . . I couldn't find anything over $30 and lots of cute tops and shorts are in the $15 range.

WEB TIPS   Log on to "editor picks" to see what's featured in current top fashion magazines. You can create a "wish list" to send to parents or friends, but can't order online.

WHERE TO BUY   300 stores worldwide. 210 E. Magnolia Blvd., Burbank, CA. ☎ **818/566-1395.** Mon–Fri 10am–9pm; Sat 10am–8pm; Sun 11am–7pm. 19501 Biscayne Blvd. (Aventura Mall), Aventura, FL. ☎ **305/935-4141.** Mon–Sat 10am–9:30pm; Sun noon–8pm. AE, DISC, MC, V. All locations are listed on the website. www.charlotte-russe.com.

Custo SPANISH $$$–$$$$$

One of the most innovative lines in T-shirtland, this Spanish brand has expanded to be a little more average, but still packs a lot of creativity into a shirt. The signature shirts are illustrated with graphic faces or forms and hot colors which may be appliqués or pieced together from various patterns.

BEST BETS   The T's are unique at $78 to $150 and run small. Jackets are in the $250 range.

WEB TIPS   Online shopping is hit or miss; a lot of the inventory on the website is either sold out or limited (1 or 2 available).

WHERE TO BUY   31 stores worldwide. NYC: 47 Broome St. ☎ **212/274-9700.** Mon–Sat 11am–7pm; Sun noon–6. AE, DISC, MC, V. Other stores in Los Angeles, CA; Dallas, TX; Chicago, IL; Boca.

Etam, Cité de la Femme PARIS VALUE $–$$$

Etam is a gigantic chain—don't confuse the Paris flagship (Cité de la Femme) with the zillions of little Etams all over Europe. There is only one City of Women, and it's on rue de Rivoli in Paris.

Etam bought one of the landmark buildings from the late department store Samaritaine and turned it into a five-floor department store with an entire lifestyle worthy of design, including a cafe, hair salon, spa and beauty department. The Tammy clothing line was created specifically for hip 9 to 15 year olds. The cafe is quite good and offers a wonderful view of Paris rooftops, as well as a chance to sip "perfumed" (flavored) iced tea—try rose, the hottest (coolest) taste in town.

BEST BETS   Trendy T's under $12.

WEB TIPS   French, Spanish or Italian; there's no English version.

WHERE TO BUY   1 store. 73 rue de Rivoli, Paris 1er. ☎ **331/4476-7373.** Mon–Sat 11am–7pm. AE, M, V. Métro: Pont Neuf. www. etam.com.

Forever 21 USA VALUE $–$$$$

The poor man's H&M, Forever 21 is a teenaged girl's dream. The look is hot, the price tag is low and even the style of the stores is interesting—many of the stores are located in landmark buildings. Depending on the location of the store, it may attract a more upmarket shopper than just teenagers. The merchandise is more directly derivative of designer brands—almost flat out knockoffs of brands such as Marc Jacobs and Diane Von Furstenberg.

There are no designer tie-ins, no secondary lines—just lines of shoppers grabbing up the merchandise; ka$ching. Note that they have outlet stores too.

BEST BETS   Super designer copies at cheapie prices. A great dress for $25? Why not! Will it fall apart in the wash? Who cares? Earrings for $3.80—why do I have David Yurman? And the store in Pasadena? Way amazing!

WEB TIPS   Online sales are great; you'll find $25 shirts for under $10 and belts for under $5.

WHERE TO BUY   360 stores in the U.S.; 30 new stores open every year; you can shop online. **FLAGSHIP**   1 Powell St., San Francisco, CA. ☎ **415/984-0380.** Mon–Sat 10am–9pm; Sun noon–6pm. BART: Montgomery Street. NYC: 50 W. 34th St. ☎ **212/564-2346.** Mon–Fri 9am–9:30pm; Sat 10am–9:30pm; Sun 11am–8pm. Subway: 34th St., Herald Sq. www.forever21.com.

Freitag SWISS $$–$$$$

The name of this store comes from the owners' names, not the day of the week. They are two brothers who built their store out of shipping containers—it is a sight to see, even if you look at the site.

Their cult messenger bags are made out of recycled parts and bits, all industrial and yet ecologically sound. Almost 2,000 different bags are on hand.

BEST BETS   You can design your own bag, choosing size, fabric and so on. Wallets, $50; bags from $100 to $200.

WEB TIPS   I had trouble opening the shopping link on the website. My spyware blocked my ability to buy.

WHERE TO BUY   3 stores worldwide. **FLAGSHIP**   17 Geroldstrasse, Zurich. ☎ **4143/366-9520.** Mon–Sat 11am–6pm. Other stores in Hamburg and Davos. www.freitag.ch.

H&M SWEDISH VALUE $–$$$$

It's Hennes and Mauritz, if that ever comes up on a trivia quiz. Now then, let me catch my breath. Also please read the listing about TopShop because conceptually the two brands are very similar. H&M is the granddaddy of hot fashion, cool chic and disposable gotta-have-it style. People of all ages and sizes shop here; you don't have to be 20 (but it helps, especially on a Saturday).

There are stores in most international capitals (24 countries and growing); expansion throughout the U.S. is still continuing. The store logo is a slashy red H&M in big script which is bold and attention getting, something like the clothes. Whatever is shown on the runways and the catwalks comes here in a dumbed-down format and price. By street fashion rules H&M is king.

Among the news flashes here are limited-edition designer lines by the likes of Stella McCartney and Karl Lagerfeld, and a new high-priced line, COS—which debuts in London. Most items cost less than $100.

BEST BETS   My best buy was a knee-length down coat with shawl collar and zip/snap closure for $35. I chose taupe, but it was also available in black. Of course, inventory changes on a daily basis.

WEB TIPS   The opening page of the website will direct you to a podcast featuring the merchandise or to a store in your area; you can see what's available but can't order online. All links are slow.

WHERE TO BUY   1,300 stores worldwide. **FLAGSHIP**   22 Hamngatan, Stockholm. ☎ **4608/5246-3530.** Mon–Fri 10am–7pm; Sat 10am–6pm; Sun noon–5pm. AE, MC, V. NYC: 640 Fifth Ave. at 51st St. ☎ **212/489-0390.** Mon–Sat 10am–9pm; Sun 11am–8pm. AE, DISC, MC, V. Subway: E or F train to Fifth Ave. www.hm.com.

Harajuku Lovers   USA $$–$$$

If you've never heard of the Japanese neighborhood of Harajuku, then this listing probably isn't for you. Meant to be as cool as this part of Tokyo, the line has clothes for women, kids and babies as well as shoes, home style, diaper bags and even stationery. Their goal is to set trends. Some of the line is designed by Gwen Stefani. The clothes are inexpensive and quickly jump into the next big trend—this is where flower printed thermals started. You'll pay about $28 for one.

Harajuku Lovers puffy city vest.

BEST BETS   The print T's are adorable but expensive at $37 to $48.

WEB TIP   You must download Adobe Flash Player to get into the website and even they may not gain entrance. If successful, the online store has a size chart link, no doubt because this clothing runs very small.

WHERE TO BUY   Specialty and department stores worldwide including Macy's. www.harajukulovers.com.

Hollister USA $$–$$$

This brand is a division of Abercrombie and is meant to be younger and a little less expensive with a beachy, surf's up, Aussie, laid-back attitude. The women's division is called "Betty's" and guys are called "Dudes." You enter (usually from a mall) as if entering a beach shack; everything inside is theme dressed and includes jeans, T-shirts, hoodies, bathing suits and so on. This is atmospheric show biz selling at its best.

BEST BETS Bikini tops and bottoms are sold separately (under $50 for a set), and most T's are under $20.

WEB TIPS Check for online sales. A striped hoodie costs $40 whereas a hoodie on sale costs $30.

WHERE TO BUY 400+ stores in the U.S.; 47 in California alone. 865 Market St., San Francisco, CA. ☎ **415/227-4883.** Mon–Sat 9:30am–9pm; Sun 10am–7pm. BART: Powell St. LA: 10800 W. Pico Blvd. ☎ **310/474-0674.** Mon–Thurs 10am–9pm; Fri and Sat 10am–8pm; Sun 11am–6pm. AE, DISC, M, V. www.hollister co.com.

Juicy Couture USA $$–$$$$$

This began as a teeny-bopper line, crossed over to moms of teens and has crossed age barriers again since little kids now crave the line that revolutionized the sweat suit, but actually makes adorable handbags and totes.

Each piece combines at least two colors for a jazzy take on cuddle fashion—lavender and yellow suddenly work on more than an Easter egg. The logo and crown emblem dance across most designs; the bottom of the track suit says JUICY. Indeed.

But wait, our teen advisor Katie Martell says they are now doing some normal clothes that are very chic.

BEST BETS Prices have become outrageous (handbags begin at $225 but may go to $400–$900), yet this line with its soft colors and comfort zone of easy-to-wear non-fashion has created fashion. A doggy T-shirt is $30.

WEB TIPS When you click "shop now" on the website, you'll be directed to Neiman Marcus's site. Try Nordstrom.com as well for a good selection.

WHERE TO BUY Stores: 18 in US; also Tokyo; Nordstrom, Neiman Marcus, more. **FLAGSHIP** The Forum at Caesar's, 3600 Las Vegas Blvd. S., Las Vegas, NV. ☎ **702/365-5600.** Sun–Thurs 10am–11pm; Fri and Sat 10am–midnight. Orange County, CA: 401 Newport Center Dr. (Fashion Island). ☎ **949/718-0593.** Mon–Fri 10am–9pm; Sat 10am–7pm; Sun 11am–6pm. Atlanta: 3500 Peachtree Rd. (Phipps Plaza). ☎ **404/467-1871.**

Mon–Sat 10am–9pm; Sun noon–5:30pm. AE, DISC, M, V. www.
juicycouture.com.

Kitson   USA $$–$$$$

These trendy shops on the edge of Beverly Hills are part of the
celebrity scene where trendsetters go to get outfitted. Many of
the latest fashions come from Japan. This is where you might
expect to find bowling shoes edged with pink maribou. There
are four shops: Kitson, Kitson Men, Kitson Kids and Kitson
Studio.

BEST BETS   If you can't visit the shops, check out the Kitson
brand merchandise online. I can't decide which of the sneakers to order; all are $60 to $70.

WEB TIPS   This has to be the world's fastest website; it took me
less than 3 minutes to order six items.

WHERE TO BUY   4 stores in Los Angeles. Kitson, 115 S. Robertson Blvd. ☎ 310/859-2652; Kitson Studio, 144 N. Robertson
Blvd. ☎ 310/360-0051; Kitson Kids, 108 S. Robertson Blvd.
☎ 310/246-3829; and Kitson Men, 146 N. Robertson Blvd.
☎ 310/358-9550. Mon–Fri 10am–7:30pm, Sat 9am–7:30pm,
Sun 11am–6pm. AE, DISC, MC, V. www.shopkitson.com.

Le Shop   PARIS $$–$$$

Don't let this Paris address frighten you—it's easy to find and
worth seeing, possibly right after you check into your hotel.
The store is huge, has loud music blaring at all hours and hosts
quite the teen scene. The clothing is cutting edge; this is where
you'll find what's coming up next, as well as the crowd that
wears it. Plenty of giveaways for clubs and concerts as well.
This is one of the most important stores in French fashion.

BEST BETS   Affordable French street fashion and American
vintage.

WHERE TO BUY   1 store. 3 rue d'Argout, Paris, 2e. ☎ 331/4026-
3507. Mon 1–7pm; Tues–Sat 11am–7pm. MC, V. Métro: Etienne Marcel.

Lisa Kline   USA $$$$–$$$$$

Trend making and trend breaking must-see store on the edge
of Beverly Hills. It's near Kitson, which adds to the cachet.

BEST BETS   Hundreds of designer selections in stock; prices are
the same as at Neiman or Saks. Vince cashmeres run $320 to
$360.

WEB TIPS   The "shop by brand" link is helpful, as are the sections on "what's new" and "what's hot."

WHERE TO BUY 136 S. Robertson Blvd. ☎ **310/246-0907.** Mon–Sat 11am–7pm; Sun noon–6pm. AE, DISC, MC, V. www. lisakline.com.

Miss Selfridge LONDON (VALUE) $–$$$

I could go on at length about this London store. And really, you haven't shopped London until you've seen these clothes. There's a Miss Selfridge in the main Selfridges department store on Oxford Street, and there are also numerous freestanding Miss Selfridge branches all over London.

The brand specialty is the young, kicky look at inexpensive prices—this is a find for teens or those who want to dabble in a trendy look without spending too much money. A recent face-lift has brought in London design duo Odie and Amanda, creating their own line for the store, as well as the Miss Vintage line, tapping into the obsession with the previously worn.

BEST BETS The latest looks for teens on a budget. Dresses are $32 to $40; trousers are $50 to $80. They offer a standard 10% student discount (sometimes 20%); you must show a student ID and register.

WEB TIPS You won't find an easier shopping website; the bad news, Miss Selfridge will only ship to the UK.

WHERE TO BUY Stores in London; Selfridges department stores; separate (equally great) line at TopShop (p. 296). 36 Great Castle St., London. Mon–Fri 9:30am–5:30pm; Sat 9am–6pm; Sun 11am–5pm. AE, M, V. Additional locations throughout London and UK. ☎ **4420/7927-0214.** www.miss selfridge.co.uk.

Petite Bateau FRENCH $$–$$$

The T-shirt is part of the teen's uniform; those teens who can afford to have the best fit wear Petite Bateau, which is very pricey in the U.S., but one of the few bargains left in France.

BEST BETS Available in over 15 colors, the T-shirts range from $30 to $70.

WEB TIPS Special online site for buying baby and kids' sizes, which hopefully tweens and teens don't need.

WHERE TO BUY Over 100 stores worldwide. **FLAGSHIP** 116 Champs Elysees, Paris, 8e. Mon–Sat 11am–7pm. AE, MC, V. Métro: F.D. Roosevelt. NYC: 1094 Madison Ave. ☎ **212/988-8884.** Mon–Fri 10am–7pm; Sat 10am–6pm; Sun 11am–5pm. AE, DISC, MC, V. Subway: 6 at 86th St. www.petitbateau.com.

Primark BRITISH VALUE $–$$$

You need not be a teenager to be amused or amazed by this source, where you can buy inexpensive fashion, basics and some modish items at throwaway prices. The opening of the London flagship store was a riot; yeah, really. Young fashion-istas lined up hours in advance and there was madness as the doors opened. It was rumored that everything would sell for £1 on opening day, but that wasn't the case. Still, there's not much for sale in the store for over $20 and most items are ten bucks or less. The wait for a fitting room or cashier can be up to 30 minutes, so go early and grab fast to beat the crowds.

BEST BETS   Affordable teen fashion; this is the home of the $12 T-shirt.

WEB TIPS   The website's good for finding store locations; I couldn't find any merchandise and you can't order online.

WHERE TO BUY   166 stores in the UK, Ireland, 2 stores in Spain; London. **FLAGSHIP**   499–517 Oxford St. ☎ **208/748-7119.** Mon–Fri 9am–9pm; Sat 9am–8pm; Sun noon–6pm. AE, MC, V. Tube: Bond St. www.primark.co.uk.

Sun Arcade HONG KONG $–$$

This small mall is underground, as is the fashion—which is mostly Japanese. Sizes are small, but the clothes are so fab-ulous that creativity freaks will be drooling. The crowds are also fun. The location is perfect.

BEST BETS   Tiny teens will love the clothes and prices; lots under $10. Large or curvy figures need not apply.

WHERE TO BUY   78 Canton Rd., Kowloon. MTR: TST.

Timbuk2 USA $$$$

This is the firm that makes the IT bag for the urban yuppie teen (whose got about $200) for the best messenger bag in the world. The firm also makes yoga bags, duffels, market totes and more—but it's the printed one-panel messenger bag that is the required accessory of the moment. One of the reasons for the high price, aside from the quality and the status factor, is the labor costs—the bags are handmade in San Francisco.

BEST BETS   The messenger bag. Duh. $200 and up.

WEB TIPS   Click "Bag Builder" to design your own bag.

WHERE TO BUY   506 Hayes St., San Francisco. ☎ **415/252-9860.** Mon–Sat 11am–7pm; Sun noon–6pm. AE, M, V. BART: Civic Center. Retailers including Barnes & Noble. www.timbuk2. com.

TopShop BRITISH [VALUE] $$–$$$$

World's Best

Oh me! Oh my! My heart is beating faster, my mouth is dry. This is the most overwhelming, exciting, amazing store in London, maybe the world. I am speaking about the flagship store at Oxford Circus, not any of the branch stores.

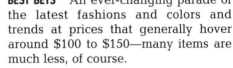

Now then, this is a multi-floor department store of affordable, young style. I can't say low-cost because with sterling as dear as it is now, from the American perspective, some of this stuff is more expensive than you want it to be.

There's everything from a penny candy shop to wig stand to jewelry, shoes, flip flops, bags, knickers (they sell 30 pairs a minute!) and so much more you could go mad with desire.

BEST BETS An ever-changing parade of the latest fashions and colors and trends at prices that generally hover around $100 to $150—many items are much less, of course.

TopShop silk sailor dress.

WEB TIPS Check the numbers carefully when ordering from overseas—prices are in GBP so you'll need to double that number to convert to U.S. dollars. Standard shipping to the U.S. is $20.

World Traveler

The Oxford Circus TopShop has a new Blow Dry Bar—pick from six hair styles for $40. No appointments, no waiting.

WHERE TO BUY Over 300 stores worldwide. **FLAGSHIP** 36–38 Great Castle St., at the corner of Oxford and Regent sts., London W1. ☎ **207/636-7700.** Mon–Sat 10am–6pm,; Sun 11am–5pm. AE, MC, V. Tube: Oxford Circus. 30 Howard St., NYC. ☎ **212/219-2688.** Mon–Sat 11am–8pm; Sun noon–7pm. AE, DISC, MC, V. Subway: Canal Street. www.topshop.co.uk.

Uniqlo JAPANESE [VALUE] $–$$

This is a Japanese fashion supermarket, with stores around the world; it's something like Gap with simple and classic must-haves, such as T-shirts in good colors and other basics.

BEST BETS Low, low prices. You'll find jeans in the $40 range and sweaters for $30.

WEB TIPS   Use the UK website to get this in English.

WHERE TO BUY   84–86 Regent Street, London, W1. ☎ **4420/ 7434-9688.** Mon–Sat 10am–8pm; Sun noon–6pm. MC, V. Tube: Picadilly Circus. NYC: 546 Broadway. ☎ **212/221-9037.** Mon–Sat 10am–9pm; Sun 11am–8pm. AE, M, V. Subway: A, C, E at Duarte Sq. www.uniqlo.co.uk.

Urban Outfitters USA $$–$$$

This mecca for teens features boho-chic styles at modest prices, making it a strong source for teens and tweens. There are lots of ethnic fashions and trendsetting styles here. Katie loves this one. See listing on p. 62.

Zara SPANISH $$–$$$

Zara is a Spanish brand with stores in major cities all over the world. A relative newcomer in the U.S., Zara makes well-priced, chic, fashionable clothes for teens and young men and women. Without being silly or cheap, it copycats the latest jacket shape or skirt silhouette or whatever fashion gimmick is cutting edge so that you can look on-the-minute, fashion-wise, but not go broke along the way.

BEST BETS $70 per piece for women's clothing, tops $40.

WEB TIPS   You can view the collection online but can't order from the site. Click on the "trends" link to see what's new.

WHERE TO BUY   2,700 stores in 60 countries. NYC: 580 Broadway. ☎ **212/343-1725.** Mon–Wed, Fri–Sat 11am–8pm; Thurs 11am–9pm; Sun noon–6pm. AE, MC, V. Subway: N, R, at Prince St. Centro Comercial ABC de Serrano, Madrid. ☎ **349/ 1576-6334.** Mon–Sat 10am–9pm; closed Sun. AE, M, V. www. zara.com.

Chapter Nine

Home Style & Tabletop

The public has decided that each person is entitled to live in the cute, or the minimalist, or the country French—with a big-screen television, of course, and possibly a gourmet bowl of snacks and a George Foreman grill. Many have even decided they are entitled to snuggle down into a bed that is as plush as any bed in a luxury hotel. Apparel sales are down and home environment becomes more and more important—be it at the low end (IKEA is booming) or the high end. (Sales of luxury mattresses are up 37%.)

Kitchen equipment is bought indiscriminately by people who come into department stores for men's underwear.

—Julia Child

Maybe it's because the world is a hard cruel place out there, but people want home to be as sweet as can be. They shop at fancy grocery stores. Take cooking lessons or buy ready-made gourmet to eat at home. They eat dinner in bed. They read and watch the telly at the same time, and talk on the phone too. This is a multi-tasking society. Outside the bedroom suite, they want a spa or a bathroom that competes with a hotel for luxury.

In fact, if you're trying to sell your house you already know that the way to move it is to enhance the kitchen and the bathrooms. Those are the priorities to today's consumer.

And so, to bed—perchance to dream but maybe to shop.

Beds

In the last 10 years, beds have gone from ho-hum to razzmatazz—they are bigger (most new beds bought in America are queen size), they are thicker, they are more varied in options (pillowtop, anyone?) and they are considered worth every penny paid. Only 3% of bed shoppers are willing to pay more than $2,000 for their new bed but get this: That number is rising by 1% each year. This interest in beds is said to be related to Baby Boomers who have the bread . . . and the backache.

The bed itself has to be differentiated from the bed frame (actually called the bedstead) and the bed dress (see p. 305 for bed linens). Beds (mattress and box spring) come in three basic formats: innerspring—the traditional bed we all most likely grew up with; the adjustable bed—once considered a hospital bed and only for sick people but now a feature in luxury sleep; and memory foam—a new-fangled device that comes to us via NASA. Sales of luxury beds are up almost 40% as consumers become more and more willing to part with serious money for a good bed. Most handmade beds come with a warranty for 20 years, so shoppers feel that prices are amortized. In most cases, the choices in a luxury bed mattress are related to science and technology, which are then reflected in the price.

While major brand beds come with wonderful mattresses and box springs, the prices for an important bed are not low— expect to pay $1,000 to $5,000 for a mass-produced big-maker queen-size bed. Note that the average big-brand bedding firm makes over 500,000 beds a year. Handmade beds often come from companies that make fewer than 5,000 beds a year. You can do the math and decide if it's worth it. After all, you spend 30% of your life in bed.

Hästens SWEDISH $$$$$

This Swedish bedding firm makes all beds by hand and uses all natural materials. They've been in business since 1852 and hold a royal warrant as bed makers to the king of Sweden. All beds are guaranteed for 25 years.

The first to eliminate foam rubber, latex and modern products from the modern bed, Hästens's mattresses are filled with horsehair, a natural substance that is light and airy, providing a cushion so that the body seems to float.

There are three types of beds made: adjustable (like a hospital bed, it goes up and down); a two-part mattress and a three-part mattress. The Hästens 2000T has individually fitted springs and is considered one of the best beds in the world; it is sold at ABC Carpet & Home (p. 36).

People considering a move into a bed such as this are encouraged to check

Hästens Vividus bed.

into a hotel that features the Hästens beds—a chart of hotels is provided on the website. (In the U.S., try the Peninsula Hotel in Chicago.) See the box, "Sarah & the Hästens" below.

BEST BETS   Tippy-top of the line is a bed named Vividus, considered the world's most exclusive bed. Custom built for its owner, the Vividus takes 150 to 160 man hours to create; a king size costs $59,750. Prices for other Hästens beds begin at $4,750; there's lots to choose from under $10,000. And no, the mattress doesn't come with the money hidden under it.

Sarah & the Hästens

I had a journalist's dream assignment—I was to travel to Chicago to stay at the Peninsula Hotel and test the Hästens bed. I couldn't wait to nod off in luxury.

Call me a princess on a pea, but this wasn't the bed of my dreams. My preference is more plush than firm and this mattress was just, shall we say, rigid—even with the horse hair–filled top. I tossed and turned, squirmed and twisted, tried to bounce around. I switched sides and finally pulled the sheets off the bottom of the bed to make sure I was on top of a Hästens. Sure enough, it was the real thing.

Curious about all this, I did some research and discovered that the mattress I slept on was the "Excelsior." It's a "Firm" model made for hotels and retails for $12,350. The 2000T, a "Medium" mattress, retails for $22,950. If you're considering buying either of these beds, you can check into the Peninsula, test a bed, then buy it at the Hästens store in Chicago. It's located at 430 Wells St., ☎ **312/527-5337.** They will deduct your Peninsula room rate from the invoice. You can also make bed-testing arrangements at Hästens stores. Go to www.hastens.com.—*Sarah Lahey*

WEB TIPS The website has good photos and information about the beds; of course, you'll want to try one before buying. The site has a list of hotels where you can check in for a test night.

WHERE TO BUY 40+ stores in over 25 countries; ABC Home & Carpet in NYC. ☎ **866/50-HASTENS.** www.hastens.com.

Dux SWEDISH $$$$$

Several of the top bed makers in the world are Swedish, including Dux, which makes the Duxiana bed. Perhaps the best-known luxury bed in Europe, it was named world's best bed by *Wallpaper Magazine* in 2005. There are 35 Duxiana bed stores in the U.S., including several in Manhattan. The stores are unique in that they feature a Sleep Chamber where you can go in, turn down the lights and actually get into bed for a 15-minute snooze to test the product under ideal circumstances.

BEST BETS The Dux 8888 model is considered the top of the line and the must-have accessory by aging Baby Boomers. Queen-size beds begin around $6,500; kings cost about $10,000.

WEB TIPS Considering that many of the customers are aging Baby Boomers, the print in the site is way too small. You can't order online, but log on to research the beds and locate the nearest Dux store.

WHERE TO BUY   FLAGSHIP   NYC: 235 E. 58th St. at Second Ave. ☎ **212/755-2600.** Corporate ☎ **877/389-2337.** Mon–Sat 10am– 7pm; Sun noon–5pm. AE, DISC, MC, V. www.duxbed.com.

McRoskey SAN FRANCISCO $$$$$

If you think Fisherman's Wharf is the most exciting sight in San Francisco, you aren't a bed maven who knows that since 1899 McRoskey has been hand-making what has become an internationally famous mattress. This is an icon of San Francisco retail and a leading factor in top-drawer bedding in America.

McRoskey beds are handmade; their claim to fame is their steel springs. You can buy from standard sizes or order customized beds; a specialty business customizes mattresses for antique bed frames.

BEST BETS   They are known for special sizes and special needs; they make a mattress for rollaway beds and a pet mattress with cover by furniture and accessory designer Jonathon Adler (comes in four sizes). You can get an adjustable bed or choose from one of four styles of mattress in terms of firmness. A queen mattress set will run about $3,500.

WEB TIPS   You must order the catalog from the website.

WHERE TO BUY   FLAGSHIP   1687 Market St. at Gough, San Francisco, CA. ☎ **415/861-4532.** Mon–Sat 10am–6pm; Sun noon–5pm. AE, DISC, MC, V. www.mcroskey.com.

Phyllis Morris LOS ANGELES $$$$$

Sonny & Cher introduced me to Phyllis Morris after I saw their bedroom and flipped out over their amazing bed frame. I ended up writing a story for *People* magazine about the woman who for over 50 years has created handmade furniture of theatrical proportions and has furnished many of the celebrity beds in LA and the world. Kenny Rogers was just photographed in a magazine spread in one of Phyllis's beds; this is the leading source for a statement bed frame.

The showroom—which is open to the trade and the public— is in the LA design district with 15,000 square feet of space. If you can't get to LA, order a catalog on DVD to see some of the merchandise.

BEST BETS   The preferred styles are historical—be they The Grand Venetian ($35,000 without mattress) or the DeMedici Bed (Kenny's bed, $22,000)—but you can also get a contemporary bed or have a bed made according to your own designs or

My Night on the Sofitel MyBED

Sarah had the assignment to sleep in a Hästens bed in a Peninsula Hotel and thought she had the, uh, dream job. I got to test MyBED, SLEEP BY SOFITEL.

Before I even jumped into the bed, I was in love with it because it was high, well dressed and looked like the kind of nest you might never want to leave. Toffee (my dog) and I both fell to the challenge, sinking into a feather bed. Perhaps this is what a cloud feels like. Even in June the bed was cool and comforting. I prayed for rain and/or snow just to test it; I cursed myself for never trying a feather bed on my own.

The Sofitel mattress ($1,100 for the mattress and box spring) is covered with a feather bed ($260 for a queen), then made up with linen ($275/queen set) and covered with a feather duvet ($280/queen). All materials in MyBED are natural; they come with their own tag telling you all about it in French and in English. You can also buy the elements online at www.soboutique.com.

modified from a photo you've seen. All beds are made locally in workrooms in the LA area.

WEB TIPS   The website does not do justice to this product. although it does tease you enough to know that something special this way comes. I clicked on the link to order a catalog—it's $250, which will be deducted from the price of the bed when you order. If you think that means that customers are high-rollers, you're right.

WHERE TO BUY   FLAGSHIP   655 N. Robertson Blvd., W. Hollywood, CA. ☎ 310/289-6868. Mon–Fri 9am–5:30pm. Also in Moscow and Dubai. AE, DISC, MC, V. www.phyllismorris.com.

Tempur-Pedic USA $$$$$

World's Best   The best bed I ever slept in during my entire life to date was a Tempur-Pedic bed. Unfortunately, it was a one-night stand, but I have never gotten over the sensation or the memory of the event. I sank into a hug—not a bed—and never wanted to leave.

Tempur-Pedic is the leading brand in the memory foam business; it is a Swedish brand, but beds are available internationally. They offer a "90-night" in-home trial period—if you're not happy with the bed, they'll pick it up at no charge.

Memory foam is heat sensitive so that it molds itself around the body lying in the bed. The inner workings of the bed

Bringing Home the Hotel Bed

In the brave new world of hotel marketing, somewhere toward the end of the 20th century, luxury hotels began to use deep, plush, extra comfy, high-quality beds, while bragging about it. War broke out.

Soon the kinds of beds, the sheets and the sleeping experience were touted as far superior to those at home and even further superior to the those at the hotel across the street. Hotels began one-upping each other: Westin announced its Heavenly Bed, a 10-layer ensemble of custom-made 13-inch Simmons mattresses, pillowtops, and 300-count linens; then Hilton introduced the Serenity Bed, a Serta-made plush-top mattress with luxury Anichini linens—and both were outdone by the 14.7-inch cotton-stuffed mattress and ultra-plush pillowtop at the Four Seasons Hotel & Resorts.

The good news is that the hotel bed-and-bath battle has come full circle and landed in your bedroom, and you can now purchase hotel bedding online. Buy **Westin's** queen mattress and box spring for $1,250, or get the complete souped-up bed package for about $2,990 at www.westin-hotelsathome.com or at www.nordstrom.com. **Hilton** charges $1,250 for a queen mattress and box spring, or pay about $3,600 to make it fully feathered and shammed; go to www.hiltontohome.com. The **W Hotel** runs www.thewstore.com, and queens start at $1,100, or about $2,000 with extras; you can also buy just sheet sets for under $200. Buy **Sofitel's** SO Bed at www.soboutique.com for about $1,100 for a queen and $2,400 fully loaded. To buy a **Four Seasons Hotel** bed, you'll need to log on to www.fourseasons.com and find the nearest hotel to place an order. A queen-size mattress and box spring set runs about $3,000, plus about $200 in shipping fees. Surprisingly, they flake out a bit when it comes to the full package—you can pay about $700 to add flat sheets, pillows and the duvet, but they don't sell a down comforter or even a fitted sheet.

Instead, you might contact some of the hotels' linen suppliers directly. Italian linen maker **Frette** (p. 308) provides linens for the Ritz Paris and the Savoy in London; their Hotel Bed collection runs about $420 for a queen sheet set. **Pratesi** (p. 311), another Italian luxury brand, provides linens for the St. Regis and Plaza Athenee hotels. Queen sets run $1,200 to $3,000. (A trip to the Woodbury Common outlet may be in order; see p. 433.) **Anichini** (p. 306), an American brand with an Italian name, sends their sheets to Hilton and many swanky hotels in Las Vegas, with queen sets from $350 to $1,200.

function as a firm mattress but the bed feels soft and comfy—you sink into it and forget about the real world beyond.

BEST BETS   The price on this luxury product is less than $2,000 for a queen-size bed—making it one of the best values in the world.

WEB TIPS   I had big problems opening links on this site; in fact, when I tried to search the U.S. page, my computer was closed down.

WHERE TO BUY   Corporate ☎ **888/811-5053.** www.tempur pedic.com.

Vi-Spring BRITISH $$$$$

This is a UK firm with strong international reputation and distribution. Founded in 1901, this company was the first to create the individual pocket spring system in mattresses. The innovation was so strong that this was the luxury brand of the early 20th century—they supplied beds to luxury hotels and oceangoing ships and yes, even the *Titanic.* They have also supplied beds to the royal family.

There are four degrees of beds in this line which determine firmness; there is also a couture line.

BEST BETS   Each bed is custom made. Prices range from $9,500 to over $17,000 for a queen set. Please note, Queen is not included.

WEB TIPS   There's lots of good information on this site about how to choose a bed, custom mattresses and the best styles for your body weight.

WHERE TO BUY   For a U.S. store that sells the line, call ☎ **877/589-6288.** www.vispring.com.

Bed Linen

Now that the new American Dream is to dream in a bed of layered sheets and pillows and duvets and spreads and throws, information about thread count in sheets is bandied about as if the shopper knows what it means. Bed talk is totally different from pillow talk. Unfortunately, there's a whole lot of marketing going on these days.

The shopper now thinks the higher the thread count, the better the quality. In reality, thread count does not matter as much as the quality of the cotton itself and how the cotton is treated. There is also a legal trick in ascertaining thread count, so that by counting the warp and the weft (both sides of a weave), the thread count can appear to be very high. It's not unusual to see sheets boasting a thread count of 1,000 or higher as if this explained all the mysteries of the world.

In reality, the body cannot really tell the difference between 300 count and 500 count, let alone 1,000 or more. Do not let thread count unduly influence your purchases.

The body can feel the texture of the cotton (or the cotton-poly), the treatments applied to the fiber and whether in fact the sheets are the old-fashioned kind, made of linen. Real linen and vintage linen require such extreme care that it is seldom used in the home or even a hotel—although one of the reasons I keep going back to stay at the Dorchester Hotel in London is the quality of the pure linen sheets. (See the "Bringing Home the Hotel Bed" box on p. 304.)

Anichini USA $$–$$$$$

Despite the Italian-sounding name, this is an American firm with roots in New England. The brand makes one of the fanciest and highest-quality sheets in the U.S. For the most part, the sheets have a Euro-elegant design flair and are solids with or without texture, embroidery or stitching details (such as scalloped edges).

Besides sheets, the company makes all bed linens, throws, down and pajamas.

Every now and then I spot some of their merchandise at Tuesday Morning (www.tuesdaymorning.com), a chain of off-price stores dotted around the U.S.

BEST BETS   The hotel embroidered sheets are classics. Price-wise, we're looking at tags that reflect the quality, $350 to $1,200 for a queen sheet set.

WEB TIPS   The website is an online catalog with complete information on all the products.

WHERE TO BUY   FLAGSHIP   645 N. Roberson, LA. ☎ **310/657-4292.** Mon–Sat 10am–6pm, Sun noon–6pm. AE, DISC, MC, V. At ABC Carpet & Home (p. 36). Outlet store: Manchester, VT, at 424A Depot St. ☎ **802/355-1200.** Mon–Sat 10am–6pm; Sun 10am–5pm. AE, MC, V. www.anichini.com.

Dwell USA $$$

This is a difficult line to buy because there are so many home-style references to the name Dwell, including an excellent home-style magazine. The line of bed linens—not related to the magazine—is known for its 1950s retro-cum-Japanese geo-finesse prints that appeal to a younger generation of people who want a less traditional bed.

On the other hand, Dwell does more than beds and even does baby design. The design sensibility—including color combinations like brown and turq or brown and orange—and the lack of cutesie-pie (even the florals are un-cute) makes the geometrics a standout for today's 20-something. This is the brave new bed, although there is also DwellTable, and so forth. I wouldn't be surprised if someday soon we see DwellStores.

BEST BETS   Get the sheet sets ($250 for queen). They only sell complete sets; no Cal king sizes.

WEB TIPS   To get a better view of the patterns, click on "catalog" and browse the pages before placing an online order.

WHERE TO BUY   Distributed through department stores and design shops such as Nordstrom and Bloomingdale's. www.dwellshop.com.

Eileen Fisher for Garnet Hill USA $$–$$$$

Fisher brings the same sensibility to her bed collection, which is even more exciting because heretofore this kind of design was too expensive to make it into the average cocoon. The look is devoted to a layering of neutral tones (check out names like sand, bone and parchment) with various textures, something you might expect from Calvin Klein or Armani Casa but instead you can now find for under $100 a sheet. That might strike you as high, but for this look and this quality it's somewhat of a deal. While it's not hard to find beige sheets in any number of sources, what makes this look individual is the use of nubby fabrics, cable knits, quilting and fabric mixtures–such as cotton and linen together—piled onto the bed in fashionable layers. The line is exclusive to Garnet Hill and is not sold in Eileen Fisher stores.

BEST BETS   The seamless silk comforter is about $600 in the king-sized version, but is certain to bring on visions of (beige) sugar plums.

WEB TIPS   Click on "Bedding and Home" to find the linens. There are often "online only" special deals.

WHERE TO BUY   Phone orders. ☎ **800/870-3513.** www.garnet hill.com.

Elegant Linens PARK CITY, UT $–$$$$$

It's not often that I go wild for a store in the middle of nowhere (excuse me, Mr. Redford) that has no bargains, but yup, here I am in a very touristy city, just drooling onto my chest and happy to tell you that this store has an excellent collection of hard-to-find sheets and features brands that even I have not heard of. This is your basic store painted the color of a barn, geared to the tourist traffic storefront, right on Main Street. The Cute is everywhere.

There's some emphasis on sophisticated bedtime looks, with many masculine styles—such as chocolate brown Matouk Italian sheets that are trimmed and monogrammed in white. Peel me a kiss, baby! There's also farmer chic, calico chic, rustic and ranch looks. Prices range anywhere from $60 to $900 a sheet.

They provide excellent service; do special orders, special sizes and custom work; and they'll even provide washing instructions on how to keep those chocolate brown sheets from fading.

Aside from beds, there's table linen, goods for the baby and any other household need (cast iron bedstead? no problem!) that they can supply for you. Sundance obviously needs a Bed Festival after the Film Festival.

WEB TIPS   The "Touch and Feel" program allows you to order up to four pillow cases or shams for an in-home test run. You keep them for 2 weeks and pay no outbound shipping charges. Since it's difficult to determine color and quality from a computer screen, this is a good way to compare the merchandise. Catalogs are available on request.

WHERE TO BUY   1 store: 509 Main St., Park City, UT. ☎ **435/658-2771** or 800/735-5541. www.elegantlinenspc.com. AE, DISC, MC, V. Daily 10am–6pm.

Frette ITALIAN $$$–$$$$$

This Italian line has maximized its look by going minimal and providing stark and simple lines in neutrals or what are often considered masculine shades. They stock various luxury hotels and have an international chain of stores that sell all manner of bedwear including pajamas and robes and lounge clothing. Some of the neutral and textured bed ensembles make me think of this line as the rich man's Eileen Fisher bed.

BEST BETS   The silk jacquard throws are pure luxe, which they should be at $1,800. But wait, they're often on sale online for around $1,000.

WEB TIPS   Prices are around $1,250 for a king sheet set, but save 50% to 70% by ordering online at discount sites such as overstock.com.

Lille: The French Linen Factory Trail

Just as Americans like to make jokes about Pittsburgh and its industrial heritage, the French make jokes about **Lille,** a northern industrial city that at one time was home to the French cotton mills. The most famous brand of French luxury linens is **Porthault** (www.dporthault. fr), made about an hour outside of Lille. They have a factory store on the premises, at 19 rue Robespierre, Rieux en Cambrésis (☎ **33327/822-233**). If you're driving from Paris, this outlet is midway between Paris and Lille; then, the various villages between the Porthault factory and downtown Lille are dotted with factory stores selling all the major French linen brands at discount prices. Choose **Kenzo,** 52 Rue Grande Chaussée (☎ **33320/517-879;** www. kenzo.com); **Yves Delorme**, 20 Rue Nationale (☎ **33320/129-085;** www.yvesdelorme.com); **Descamps**, 40 Rue Grande Chaussée (☎ **33328/040-191;** www.descamps.com); and more; and you'll find several of these brands at the **McArthurGlen Outlet Center** in the town of Roubaix, 44 Mail de Lannoy (☎ **33328/333-610;** www. mcarthurglen.fr). This is an American-style outlet store and the stuff of legends; the best linen outlet here is **Sous-Signe.** Visit www.lille tourism.com.

WHERE TO BUY FLAGSHIP Via Montenapoleone, 21, Milan. ☎ **390/278-3950.** Mon–Sat 11am–7pm. AE, DISC, MC, V. NYC: 799 Madison Ave., between 67th and 68th sts. ☎ **212/988-5221.** Mon–Fri 10am–6pm; Sat 10am–5pm. AE, DISC, MC, V. Subway: 68th St. Outlet: Woodbury Common, NYC. ☎ **845/928-4866.** www.frette.com.

Matouk USA $$–$$$$

Matouk is an American-made line dating back to 1927. The family firm makes fine linens for Neiman Marcus and The Horchow Collection (www.horchow.com) and is sold in 23 states in the U.S. as one of the country's leading brands of deluxe sheets, towels and even your basic $300 pair of pajamas.

WHERE TO BUY Linen stores in U.S. and Canada. www. matouk.com.

Nancy Koltes at Home USA $$–$$$$

The store is like the website—it doesn't do justice to the product. The sheets are to die for—luxe fabrics in rich jewel tones with subtle patterns that make you feel you are back a few centuries in Venice . . . but that they just did the laundry.

All patterns and colors are on display for order if not in stock. Go to the Mill Valley store for the bed linens and possibly some pajamas; ignore the rest. They just opened and hopefully will refine their look. The store has no focus; the bed linen is what you came for.

Here's some interesting news: On a recon visit to **Linens 'N Things,** I found some of the Nancy Koltes line. I bought a queen duvet cover with two shams for $99 in the Venetia set.

BEST BETS   Duvets run $500 to $600 for a full/queen.

WEB TIPS   You can easily order online and there's free shipping on orders over $40.

WHERE TO BUY   2 stores: Strawberry Shopping Center, 800 Redwood Hwy no. 211, Mill Valley, CA. ☎ **415/924-5811.** Mon–Sat 10am–7pm; Sun 11am–6pm. AE, MC, V. Also at 31 Spring St, NYC. ☎ **212/219-2271.** Mon–Sat 11am–7pm; Sun noon–6pm. AE, MC, V. Subway: Spring St. www.nancykoltes.com.

Olatz NYC $$$–$$$$$

Olatz is the wife of the artist/director Julian Schnabel (Olatz is her first name) and her eponymous and newish store is in the West Village, which sells bed linens made in Portugal. To win the hearts, minds and credit cards of the young women with serious money, these are not just sheets, they are bed linens which are decadently embroidered, scalloped, laced or draped in color borders to beat the band. There are some sheets that are so exquisite that you know immediately, innately, that, to paraphrase George Kaufman, this is what Marie Antoinette would have bought if she had money.

BEST BETS   The 100% linen sheets start at $1,135 for a queen. That's per sheet, not per set.

WEB TIPS   The website's rather limited in scope; it is lovely to look at but doesn't do much.

WHERE TO BUY   1 store: 43 Clarkson St., NYC. ☎ **212/255-8627.** Mon–Fri 10:30am–6:30pm; closed weekends. AE, DISC, MC, V. Subway: Houston St. www.olatz.com.

Porthault FRENCH $$$$$

World's Best   While this firm is called Porthault, for your research purposes, you need to know the proper name is D. Porthault. Now then, the most famous name in luxury French linen, this brand is pronounced "port-HO" and has nothing to do with portholes or ships for that matter.

Porthault is a century-old deluxe purveyor of cotton and voile sheets, nowadays straddling the centuries with both old and modern styles. The firm's signature is a stark white ground with a scattering of floral bouquets, shamrocks, hearts and/or ribbons in what many characterize as "old lady prints." Others can readily identify the brand by these prints and recognize them as the finest linens, towels, tabletop and robes.

While Porthault will custom-make anything you want, traditionally the firm offers the top sheet and two shams as their set. They do not regularly do a bottom fitted sheet with all sets—sometimes you find them but most often you special-order it. My personal trick has been to combine my Porthault linens with a hard white fitted sheet from Target or a discounter. This helps amortize the $1,000 you will pay for the top sheet and matching shams.

Shop Talk

Barbara Walters reportedly uses gifts of Porthault linens to woo her celebrity interview "gets."

The biggest drawback to buying or giving Porthault is that you have to know what it is to appreciate it. Fewer and fewer young Americans know the brand or recognize the traditional prints (or care). I gave a Porthault baby bib ($25 in Paris 15 years ago) to my sister at her baby shower and was met with total silence before she fell into a bored "Thanks, sis." Another drawback—while the sheets do last forever, if well cared for, they should be professionally laundered. The voile sheets are extremely, extremely fragile.

BEST BETS One of the best buys in the Lille outlet is the selection of baby pillowcases which can be teamed with a travel pillow to make a stunning gift in the $15 range. A baby pillow and sham costs $160 in the Manhattan Porthault store.

WEB TIPS It's a one-page listing of the Porthault stores. Let's face it, the old French aristocracy and retail world doesn't quite get the whole Internet thing. Call the New York store for assistance in English.

WHERE TO BUY 3 stores, in Dallas, NYC, and Paris. **FLAGSHIP** 50 av. de Montaigne, Paris, 8e. ☎ **331/4720-7525.** www. dporthault.fr. AE, MC, V. Mon–Sat 10am–6pm. Métro: Alma Marceau. NYC: 470 Park Ave. ☎ **212/688-1660.** AE, DISC, MC, V. Mon–Sat 10am–6pm. Subway: 4, 5, 6 at 59th St.

Pratesi ITALIAN $$$$

World's Best I was friends with Athos Pratesi until the day he died; I continue to consider myself part of this large Italian family that has been running their bed linen and textile business for four generations. In fact, before I tell you about the product, I'll

Indian Bed Quilts

As a girl, I always wanted to be an Indian Princess. As a Shopping Goddess, I buy much of my bed linen in or from India. Indian cotton is finely combed and very soft; the many hand blocks exhibit gorgeous colorations.

There is a direct historical connection between these Indian bed covers and what the French call a *boutis* (say boo-tee), which is often made from the *tissues indiennes*. Nowadays, a French *boutis* is most likely made in India or China and sold on market day in any village for $100 to $250. Older examples were handmade in France and are extremely collectable. See www.michelbiehn.com for **Michel Biehn,** one of the most famous dealers in Provence.

Although I collect French *boutis*, they're just for show and are far too fragile to use or to launder. I prefer new stuff, machine-made and washable, for personal use. My favorite bed quilts have been from **April Cornell** (www.aprilcornell.com), a Canadian designer who once had a retail empire in Canada and the U.S. but has cut back enormously now. Cornell operates a website as we go to press, but seems to be offering closeouts; bed quilts are about $100.

Check out **Anokhi** (www.anokhi.com), which I buy while in India; see p. 460. Anokhi as well as other similar brands of Indian quilts are sold in Paris at **Simrane** (www.simrane.com).

In Solana Beach, California (near San Diego) I found **Amba,** 355 N. Hwy. 101 (☎ **858/259-2622;** www.amba.com), which is an art gallery that often features artwork and textiles from India.

Amazon.com is another surprisingly good source (or not so surprisingly; see "The Amazon.com Rule of Shopping" on p. 13). I found a block-printed, vegetable-dyed cotton bedspread from **ShalinIndia** (www.shalinIndia.com) for $36. Granted, the spread wasn't a quilt or *boutis*, but was it ever so gorgeous—and a lot easier to bring home this way than on a 16-hour flight.

share a visual image with you: I once became seriously ill in the factory in Pistoia, Italy. I passed out; an ambulance was called. When I came to, I was in the bed in the outlet window—the only bed in the factory. For just one moment, I thought I had died and gone to heaven.

Pratesi is a very small linens firm with headquarters in the textile hills slightly north of Florence and just south of Prato. The family says with pride that most European royalty, as well as the Pope, sleeps on their sheets. I can vouch not only for the sleeping, but the washing. I have washed them regularly at home and seen them thrive over 25 years—no fading, no tears, no loose threads.

Most members of the family work on the team—Dede, Athos's widow, does a lot of the designing. Sheets come in solids, prints (flowers are big, although the style is different from the Porthault signature) and there are masculine styles and colors. In embroidered styles, the firm does a Greek key motif that is among their best known. There is also a baby linen line as well as bath and beach.

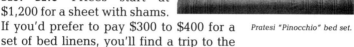

Pratesi "Pinocchio" bed set.

BEST BETS Prices start at $1,200 for a sheet with shams. If you'd prefer to pay $300 to $400 for a set of bed linens, you'll find a trip to the factory store at Woodbury Common in New York worthwhile.

WEB TIPS View patterns online, though you can't order through the website. Call the nearest location to order directly. Woodbury Common ships products as well, and here's a tip: They have no outlet catalog or outlet website, but they claim they sell all patterns a season or two behind the retail stores; items on the website now should be at the outlet in 6 months or so. Woodbury Common charges $15 for shipments of $250 or more, plus tax. Also try www.overstock.com for discounts.

WHERE TO BUY 31 stores, in Milan, New York, Paris, San Francisco, Chicago, more. **FLAGSHIP** 829 Madison Ave. at 69th St., NYC. ☎ 212/288-2315. AE, MC, V. Mon–Sat 10am–6pm. Subway: 6 at 68th St. Milan: Via Verdi 6. ☎ 392-8058-3058. Woodbury Common outlet: 498 Red Apple Ct., Central Valley, NY. ☎ 845/928-4810. AE, DISC, MC, V. Pistoia, Italy factory: Via Montalbano 41. ☎ 390573/526-462. AE, MC, V. www.pratesi.com.

Sferra ITALIAN/USA $$$–$$$$

This is a source for sheets with thread count over 1,000, woven in Italian mills from Egyptian cotton. Formerly based in Venice, the company is now based in Edison, New Jersey.

For ensembles made with lace, it takes over 4 months to put together a set which sells for about $15,000—they can make only about five sets like this per year. The firm is 120 years old and sells table linens also.

BEST BETS I have found closeouts at **Tuesday Morning** (www.tuesdaymorning.com) in the $199-a-sheet price range.

WEB TIPS   Click on "understanding thread count" for a lesson on yarn quality, construction and finishing. There's also good information on linen care.

WHERE TO BUY   Telephone orders: ☎ **800/336-1891.** www.sferra linens.com.

ThomasLeeltd.com ⌐ VALUE $$$

These sheets are the creation of a duo with 50 years of combined experience (as presidents) at leading linen manufacturers Westpoint Pepperel and Dan River. Made of 100% Pima cotton grown in the southwestern U.S., the sheets have a subtle natural sheen and are not treated, as are most "sateens" on the market. With a 500 thread count, they go from washer/dryer to bed and stay crisp yet soft.

The sheets are available in three solid colors—white, ivory and blue; they're made in limited sizes (queen and king) but will soon be offered in Cal king.

BEST BETS   The sheets are not for sale in retail outlets, so the price is half what you'd pay for comparable linens, if you could find them. King and queen sets are less than $200.

WEB TIPS   There's usually an online sale; and UPS ground shipping's free. Free fabric swatches available.

WHERE TO BUY   ☎ **877/866-5331.** www.thomasleeltd.com.

Megastores

Bed Bath and Beyond USA $–$$$

Bed Bath and Beyond is beyond all doubt the ultimate homestyle department store with enough range of product at reasonable prices that you feel no need to seek out off-price or discount sources. BBB has it all.

Some stores have cafes. Big city stores tend to be more compact than suburban stores; often they are below ground or in space that may be less expensive given the high cost of real estate in that market. In fact, the arrival of BBB in Manhattan has to be considered a watershed moment for retail in a city that never had big box stores. BBB actually changed the way Manhattanites began to shop.

BEST BETS   I find these stores to be very well organized. In a space the size of a football field, it's easy to find what you want without wasting a lot of time walking around. Of course, walking around is half the fun.

WEB TIPS Beyond the amazing amount of stock in the stores, there's an entire community online—subscribe to the magazine, find clearance items, learn about ClubMom (www.club mom.com). You can register for your wedding or shower.

WHERE TO BUY Over 800 in the U.S.; log on to the website to quickly find the closest one. www.bedbathandbeyond.com.

Frontgate USA $–$$$$

This catalog resource specializes in the big stuff—outdoor and yard furnishings, large pieces of furniture, gadgets and decorative gimmicks that you might not find in your normal browsing of Wal-Mart. While perhaps you don't want to decorate the whole house from here, this is a convenient way to shop for a fix.

BEST BETS Every gift-giving holiday I swear I will order the Therma Top Massage Table ($499).

WEB TIPS The entire catalog is online and you can shop just as easily as with the catalog.

WHERE TO BUY Catalog. ☎ **800/626-6488.** www.frontgate.com.

HomeGoods USA ⬡VALUE $–$$$

This is a growing chain of big box off-pricers that is a home-style only division of TJX, the friendly folks who bring us Marshall's and TJMaxx. Essentially, this store is devoted to the same goods you find in our favorite off-price stores—with the same departments greatly expanded. The average size of the stores is 27,000 square feet; prices are advertised as 20% to 60% less than regular retail. They are very big on seasonal merchandise.

Buyer Beware
The company has had some problems with credit card identity theft, so charge with caution.

You'll find bed and bath, home spa and treatment, tabletop, holiday decorations, dishes, cookware, picture frames, mirrors, some tote bags and then—get this—furniture. They do not deliver. Make friends with someone who has a truck.

This is something of a start-up for TJX; they have similar stores called Maxx'n'More. The ones I visited were in California, but a girlfriend found one in Maryland.

BEST BETS Chic for less.

WEB TIPS You can browse the website for ideas, but you'll need to visit a store to buy.

WHERE TO BUY 250+ stores in U.S. ☎ **800/614-HOME.** AE, MC, V. www.homegoods.com.

Clean Living

Cleaning Ideas TEXAN $

I hired a professional cleaning team to get my house in order; they treated the house with the utmost respect but seemed to have little left over for me. I am the Rodney Dangerfield of housewives, I guess. With great disdain, I was asked why I hadn't been shopping at Cleaning Ideas. I was given a list of products to buy and a website so I could find the store nearest to me.

The small stores are packed with products and tools. I bought a somewhat expensive scent distribution system that I did not think was worth the money (or any money), but all of the cleaning products I bought (under $10 each) are first rate. Some of them have heavy duty chemicals in them, the equal of which is not sold in grocery stores or normal cleaning products. They have a catalog and a magazine with tips in it, such as how to strip floors, and so on. And yes, they teach you how to read chemistry labels and when to go with a high PH in a cleaner! Amazing stuff. They will ship everywhere in the U.S. *Insider's tip:* Open a franchise.

BEST BETS   One of the products my cleaning team swore I had to have is named Out Most (under $10), which seems to clean anything and everything.

WEB TIPS   Log on to the website and print out the coupon to save 10% in any store. Unfortunately, you can't order online and prices are not listed.

WHERE TO BUY   4 stores in San Antonio. **FLAGSHIP**   1338 SW Military, San Antonio, TX. ☎ **210/927-5612.** Mon–Sat 9am–5pm. AE, MC, V. Exec offices: 1023 Morales St. ☎ **210/227-916.** www.cleaningideas.com.

Method USA $

Their motto is simply "People Against Dirty"—I want the T-shirt! The products are approved by the EPA—all-purpose cleaners, soap, hand and body products, air care, floor care, $3 to $25.

All products are biodegradable, non-toxic and made from natural materials like soy, coconut and palm oils. They don't use animal testing and all packaging is recyclable.

BEST BETS   The lemon ginger non-toxic floor cleaner, 25 ounces for $6.

WEB TIPS   Click on "Quick Shop," then choose a category.

WHERE TO BUY   Supermarkets and Target. www.methodhome. com.

Mrs. Meyer's Clean Days USA $

Begun in the early 1990s, this company makes soap, wipes and pet products. The aromatherapeutic household cleaners come in fragrances such as Geranium, Lemon Verbena and Lavender, which is my fave.

BEST BETS   The liquid Hand Soap ($5) in Lavender. You can buy a case pack (six products) for the price of five. If your pet has sensitive skin like my dog Toffee does, try the Oatmeal Pet Shampoo ($8); the Pet Wipes ($6) are also helpful.

Buyer Beware

Some shoppers confuse this brand with the older Dr. Bonner's line.

WEB TIPS   Sign up for e-mail postings (you can always cancel later) and get an e-coupon for $5 off any order of $25 or more.

WHERE TO BUY   3,500 grocery, bio, health food and hardware stores in the U.S. ☎ **877/865-1508.** www.mrsmeyers.com.

Containers & Storage Systems

World's Best *Container Store* USA $–$$$$

Shopping at the Container Store is like going to the supermarket when you're hungry; you'll want to grab every- thing on the shelves. The stores are organized by lifestyle sections—kitchen, closet, office, garage, laundry, travel and more. The sales staff (wearing blue aprons) will help you solve any storage problem; they'll pull products from various sections to create a custom solution to your organizational woes. The stores average over 25,000 square feet and are stocked with more than 10,000 products to help you save space and time.

BEST BETS   I shop here for holiday wrap and ribbons, along with cute stocking stuffers under $10 such as desk accessories. The Hanging Valet, a travel bag with layered plastic pockets ($30), and various Nalgene bottles ($1.50–$4.50) keep me sane when traveling.

WEB TIPS   The Web catalog is well organized by category, just like the store. While you'll find all the goods online, it's not nearly as much fun as shopping in person. Shipping can be expensive—up to 15% of the total on orders over $200. If you live in Manhattan, shop online or in person and have all of your purchases delivered the same day for a flat fee of $25.

WHERE TO BUY   39 stores in U.S. ☎ **800/733-3532.** AE, DISC, MC, V. www.containerstore.com.

 Tupperware USA $–$$

In the old days, Tupperware was only sold by a Tupperware hostess at a Tupperware party. Now they have stores, are distributed at Target and can easily be enjoyed the world over. Tupperware is expensive, partly because it's very innovative and also because the quality is so high.

BEST BETS   They're famous for their containers, be it the simple fridge-size containers for leftovers to a specially built cupcake holder. A set of three storage containers retails for $33.

WEB TIPS   Shop online by category, collection or price. You can also sign up to hostess a party—either online or in your home. By hostessing online, your party is active for 2 weeks and your guests receive e-mail invitations.

WHERE TO BUY   ☎ **888/TUPWARE.** www.tupperware.com.

Department Store Home Style

For a full list of the best department stores, see Chapter Three: "Lifestyle & Department Stores."

Lafayette Maison FRENCH $–$$$$

In the ongoing effort to reinvent itself, the French department store Galleries Lafayette bought department store–sized space across the street from their flagship Paris store and opened Lafayette Maison, a home-style store with its own cafes, gallery space and four floors of everything for the home. This is not your *maman's* Galeries.

BEST BETS   You can use the 10% tourist discount card for home-style items (even furniture) at this store. Get yours upon presentation of your passport at the Mogador entrance of the flagship Galleries Lafayette.

WEB TIPS   While the website is very nice, available in many languages and provides information about the store, it is not particularly interactive. There is no shopping. You can print out a map of Lafayette Maison to see where everything is located and you can peruse an alphabetical list of all the brands carried in the home store.

WHERE TO BUY   FLAGSHIP   40 blvd. Haussmann, Paris, 9e. ☎ **331/4282-8027.** 9:30am–7:30pm except Thurs, when open until 9pm; closed Sun. AE, DISC, MC, V. Métro: Chausee d'Antin or Havre Caumartin. www.galerieslafayette.fr.

Peter Jones BRITISH $$–$$$

This is an old-fashioned British department store that unfortunately, a few years ago, decided to enter the 21st century. Thankfully, they have not totally ruined their bed linen department, although it is more subdued than in the old days and mostly features solid colors in sheets and duvet covers.

Forget this store as a regular department store; do come for the home style, the bed linen and the wonderful location—directly on Sloane Square. Note that across the street there are other excellent home-style sources such as **General Trading Company** (www.generaltradingcompany.co.uk) and **The White Company** (www.thewhitecompany.com). The store stands at the beginning of the King's Road; there's much more shopping–and home style—down the ensuing blocks.

BEST BETS   You come here for the color selection. Indeed, there are six shades of green sheets; none of them resemble hospital green and all of them would make Giorgio Armani proud. Colors are sophisticated, subtle and simple—which isn't always easy to find. There's also a wide selection of duvet covers, which can be difficult to find in the U.S.

Prices are not really that high, especially considering that you are shopping in sterling—the house brands run $50 to $200 for duvet cover, pillowcases $15 to $20.

If you're looking for designer upholstery fabrics, check out the sales—end bolts are often marked down 75%.

WEB TIPS   Now then, the website is fine, but since they don't ship to the U.S., it will do you little good if you plan to order.

WHERE TO BUY   FLAGSHIP   Sloane Sq., London SW3. ☎ **207/ 730-3435.** Mon–Sat 9:30am–7pm; Sun 11am–5pm. All major credit cards accepted. Tube: Sloane Sq. www.peterjones.co.uk.

Design Icons

Armani Casa ITALIAN $$–$$$$$

Don't let the name Armani or the inference that Giorgio Armani is expensive scare you off this firm—the line and the concept are evolving, and in short order there will be hundreds of these stores around the world. Think of it as Pottery Barn for snobs. They now make their own furniture and offer everything you might need for the look—very simple, clean and Zen.

BEST BETS I like the Vietnam-style dishes that are made with matte or crackle finishes, beginning at $50.

WEB TIPS Artistically interesting site—all in black and white—in which sketches turn into real life furniture; it's very hard to turn off the music.

WHERE TO BUY 80 stores worldwide. **FLAGSHIP** via Manzoni 37, Milan. ☎ **3902/7231-8630.** Métro: Montenapoleone. Other cities include Paris, New York (SoHo), Athens, Antwerp and my personal favorite: Armani Casa Altamy (Kazakhstan). www.aramnicasa.com.

The Conran Shop BRITISH $-$$$$

Terence Conran is my hero: He loves shopping and eating. He's also incredibly creative in both arenas and has a nice little side business in his Conran Shops that he began after giving up his Habitat stores. The Conran shops are mass market with a difference—very sophisticated with a specific style agenda.

BEST BETS Variety of good-looking and sleek lifestyle items, everything from furniture to luggage to gift cards—all chosen with a design perspective.

WEB TIPS Excellent website; you can shop online.

WHERE TO BUY 8 stores in Japan, UK, France and U.S. **FLAGSHIP** Michelin House, 81 Fulham Rd., London SW3. ☎ **4420/7589-7401.** Mon, Tues, Fri 10am–6pm; Wed 10am–7pm; Sat 10am–6:30pm; Sun noon–6pm. AE, MC, V. NYC: Bridgemarket, 407 E. 59th St. ☎ **866/755-9079.** Mon–Fri 11am–8pm; Sat 10am–7pm; Sun noon–6pm. AE, DISC, MC, V. Subway: 4, 5, 6 at 59th St. www.conran.com.

Moss NYC $-$$$$

Modernism comes alive with a gift, gadget, design, lifestyle store. The museum-worthy accessories are a treat to see, but not necessarily best buys. Prices are very expensive; we're talking $5,000 and up for the likes of Venini glassware and Nymphenburg Porcelain (p. 349). Perhaps you are thinking of a $12,000 egg-shaped bathtub? Of course you are!

WEB TIPS Click on "DailyNew" to see the featured item, either a new addition to their stock or often a Moss classic. The products are photographed on a white background, which makes it easy to see detail.

WHERE TO BUY   1 store: 146 Greene St., NYC. ☎ **866/888-6677** and 212/204-7100. Mon–Sat 11am–7pm; Sun noon–6pm. AE, DISC, MC, V. Subway: Prince St. www.mossonline.com.

Solo SOLANA BEACH, CA $–$$$

This store is one of the most important in a group of stores in a district called Cedros Design District (p. 326), which is outside of San Diego in Solana Beach. Located inside a warehouse once used for boat building, the open space reminds me of ABC Carpet in Manhattan and HDButtercup in LA, conceptually and visually, although size wise, the store is much smaller.

Solo features a string of selling spaces set up as vignettes representing various vendors and artists all selling what we might call clutter-chic. This is a mix of antiques, handcrafts, stacks of books, unique and individual paper goods and more books. The loft space makes it easy to see everything; you will want to touch everything as well. This store falls into the category of stores I would have created if I had my own store.

BEST BETS   The store is a hodgepodge of delight. I bought a novelty notepad for $7; there were milagros for $25 that tempted me.

WEB TIPS   You'll find lists of designers and products represented, but no online catalog.

WHERE TO BUY   1 store: 309 S. Cedros Ave., Solana Beach, CA. ☎ **858/794-9016.** Mon–Sat 10am–6pm; Sun 11am–5pm. AE, DISC, MC, V. www.solocedros.com.

Takashimaya New York JAPANESE $–$$$$

This large Japanese department store chain has a tiny department store in Manhattan that is technically a specialty store. But who cares about technicalities when there's this much style to be absorbed? Don't miss a chance to eat in the cafe in the basement because the dishes are divine. The home-style merchandise in this store has a Zen feel but is by no means Japanese—there's goods from as far-flung places as France and Tibet.

The store also has a floral department at the entryway and several floors of selling space with clothes and accessories, bed style, dishes, food gifts and more. This is the kind of store that you can treat as a museum and just wander, absorbing the art and gaining ideas.

BEST BETS   Prices can be astronomical, but there are some simple items—such as a serving dish from Tibet—in the $25 to $50 range. These make extraordinary gifts because they are stylish and beautifully wrapped by the store in unique packaging.

WHERE TO BUY   NYC: 693 Fifth Ave., at 54th St. ☎ **212/350-0100.** Mon–Sat 10am–7pm; Sun noon–5pm. AE, DISC, MC, V. Subway: E or V to Fifth Ave., 53rd St. www.ny-takashimaya. com.

Crafts & Fabrics

Crafts, handwork and even sewing are all expressions from our souls, true forms of communication. For do-it-yourselfers, who want to decorate or make home improvements, there are stores like Home Depot and Lowe's that have everything you need and will teach you how to do it. But if you want to make a scrapbook, buy couture fabrics by the yard or make a stitch in time, I have some great sources.

Archivers USA $–$$

This is a small supermarket of crafty everything, especially built for scrapbookers—it's fancy, it's well displayed, it's well priced, it's heaven.

The small chain calls itself a specialist in "photo memories" but they are far more than that. In many ways, this is a store about old-fashioned community. You come together, instead of at the Town Hall, at the store where you can shop, use the photo stations, take a class, use the workroom, enroll your kids for lessons and check out the newest tools and imaging technology.

BEST BETS   There's a workroom you can use for free.

WEB TIPS   This is a good site but when I see Christmas info in June I am not sure if they are ahead of the season or in need of an update.

WHERE TO BUY   41 stores in the U.S. **FLAGSHIP**   Mall of America, 3F E., Bloomington, MN. ☎ **952/858-8292.** Mon–Sat 9:30am–9:30pm; Sun 11am–7pm. AE, DISC, MC, V. www. archiversonline.com.

B&J Fabrics NYC $–$$$$

Years ago, Martha Stewart taught me about this Manhattan fabric store that has traditionally catered to design students in New York City. They have since moved to a second floor of almost warehouselike space in one of the Garment District's most famous design buildings. Fabric is sold off the bolt and ranges from cheapie Halloween prints to the most extravagant of designer yardage.

BEST BETS   The staff is extremely helpful. They work with designers and students all the time and will go to the end of the bolt for you.

WEB TIPS   The website is mostly useless but there are instructions on how to order samples.

WHERE TO BUY   1 store: 525 Seventh Ave. (2F), between 37th and 39th sts., NYC. ☎ **212/354-8150.** DISC, MC, V. Mon–Fri 8am–5:45pm; Sat 9am–4:45pm. Subway: 1, 2, 3 at 34th St. www.bandjfabrics.com.

Britex SAN FRANCISCO $–$$

This store fills a town house right off Union Square and sells all sorts of fabrics, including Chinese silks at Chinatown prices, raw silks for home style and designer yardage. There's fashion fabrics, novelty cottons and polymers, craft fabrics (small crafts department with dyes, and so on) and fabrics for home decor and for brides.

BEST BETS   The remnants on the fourth floor offer good value; the colors all neatly stacked on the shelves of every floor and the bolts of colors are visual poetry.

WEB TIPS   The colors on the website alone are enough to make you want to take up stitchery. Each floor of the store is outlined online, which saves the wait for the elevator when you actually get to the store to explore—it's good to know where you want to go before you get there.

WHERE TO BUY   1 store: 146 Geary St., San Francisco, CA. ☎ **415/392-2910.** AE, DISC, M, V. Mon–Sat 10am–6pm; Sun noon–5pm. www.britexfabrics.com.

Crea FRENCH $–$$

Because merchandise is priced in euros, it may be more expensive than you would like—but this store is a mini-department store of creativity and products for crafters and those with a do-it-yourself talent. Unlike U.S. big box stores, this is a snazzy and intimate boutique with a backdrop of black walls. It has many levels showing off artistic displays of merchandise. Demonstrations are in french, but at least you can watch and see how to do the project.

World Traveler

In Paris, Crea is 2 short blocks from the department store **Bon Marché** (22, rue Sevres; ☎ 800/461-933) and is at the end of one of Paris's best streets for bargain shopping and kids' clothing. Also note the **Nitya** off-price store at no. 9 and the gemlike **Hotel Placide** at no. 3.

BEST BETS   Selection of colors and materials you haven't seen back in the U.S.; therefore you don't care what they cost.

WEB TIPS   The site is in French, but you can bounce around and see a lot just to get an idea.

WHERE TO BUY   14 stores in France, including Paris. **FLAGSHIP** 55 rue St-Placide, Paris, 6e. ☎ **331/5363-6000.** Mon–Sat 10am–7pm. MC, V. Métro: St-Placide. www.crea.tn.fr.

Ehrman Tapestry BRITISH $$–$$$

In Britspeak, tapestry is the word for needlepoint—this store is a branch of the Ehrman wool empire and sells kits and supplies including ones by all the big names in the business, including Kaffe Fassett.

Insider's tip: You can buy completed tapestries—some of them even made up into pillows or whatever—for sale on eBay. You can also shop online.

BEST BETS   Did someone say Kaffe Fassett?

WEB TIPS   The website is really a search engine, which will lead you to Neiman Marcus, eBay and so on.

WHERE TO BUY   Kits are sold in knitting and needle specialty stores in the U.S. or by mail. There are no stores. U.S. offices ☎ **888/826-8600;** UK offices **44-01226/733-366.** www.ehrman tapestry.com.

Hobby Lobby USA [VALUE] $–$$

I think this is the best of the big box crafts stores partly because it has everything it should—craft supplies, fabric by the yard, framing department, artificial flowers—but also because it has things you don't expect: tabletop, gift items and smalls. They even have some large pieces of furniture.

The store has an aggressive promotional rotation; wait for whatever you want to go on sale and then load up. When there's a 50% sale you will be smiling for a week.

BEST BETS   I buy plastic flowers by the armload during the sales so I can fill the antique wheelbarrow in front of my house with a seasonal selection.

WEB TIPS   The online affiliate for Hobby Lobby is named Crafts Etc. and they offer some 30,000 items for sale at the website—however, they do not offer the same sales and promotions you find in Hobby Lobby stores.

WHERE TO BUY   300+ stores in 30 states. Mon–Sat 9am–7pm. www.hobbylobby.com.

Dreyfus FRENCH $–$$$

This is actually in the Marché St. Pierre on the far side of Montmartre in Paris—an area filled with fabric stores including the rather large—five-story—**Dreyfus** which sells everything from inexpensive cottons to couture collection tissues extraordinaire.

BEST BETS   If you don't have the patience to shop from store to store or up and down the area, head directly to Dreyfus.

WHERE TO BUY   2 rue Charles Nodier, Paris 18e. ☎ **331/4606-9225.** Tues–Sat 10:30am–6:30pm. CB, MC, V. Place St. Pierre, Paris, 18e. Métro: Anvers. No website.

Nantucket Looms USA $$$$

See listing on p. 55.

Sennelier PARIS $–$$$

Centuries-old (since 1887 to be exact) French resource for serious artists and painters. They sold supplies to the great names whose works are now displayed across the river in the, uh, Louvre. Crawling with history and the smell of cadmium white.

BEST BETS   Papers and wash for watercolors; the psychological kick of knowing Picasso shopped here. A wooden paintbox with palette begins at $100. It was M. Sennelier who invented the pastel crayon; there's now more than 500 shades available—these can make a great gift for the artistically enabled.

WHERE TO BUY   1 store: 3 quai de Voltaire, Paris 7e. ☎ **331/4260-7215.** Métro: rue du Bac or Palais Royal (then walk across bridge to left bank). AE, DC, MC, V. Mon 2–6:30pm; Tues–Sat 10am–12:45pm and 2–6:30pm. www.magasinsennelier.com.

Tender Buttons USA $–$$$$

It's a closet, a museum, a place of worship—all of these and more because of the caliber of buttons for sale.

WHERE TO BUY   2 stores: 143 E. 62nd St., NYC ☎ **212/758-7004.** Mon–Fri 10am–5:30pm; Sat 10am–5pm. AE, MC, V. Subway: N, R. W at 59th St. 946 N. Rush St., Chicago, IL. ☎ **312/337-7033.**

Tokyu Hands JAPANESE $–$$$

World's Best

This is not just a crafts store—it's a department store of everything, including craft items, stationery, office supplies, gadgets and things you could never imagine. They call themselves a Creative Life Store but do not confuse this with what

U.S. Design Districts

Cedros Design District (San Diego)
From San Diego, head north on Highway 101 to Solana Beach, where a strip of shopping heaven has been named the Cedros Design District in honor of the street where the stores stand side by side for a 3-block stretch. There are almost 100 stores, some with street fronts, some off driveways and behind others. Stores sell clothing, gifts and, of course, home style. The best of the bunch is Solo (p. 321), but you can park the car and simply prowl the 100 to 300 blocks of S. Cedros Ave. www.cedrosdesigndistrict.com.

Design District (Miami)
The Miami Design District is an 18-square-block area north of downtown Miami which has been renovated in Art Deco style. It's home to 20-some art galleries and over 40 showrooms, all open to the public. On the second Saturday of every month, the district sponsors a block party, Art + Design Night. Free valet parking is available on NE 2nd Avenue between 39th and 40th streets. www.miamidesigndistrict.net.

LuxeHome at the Chicago Merchandise Mart
Home of the world's first and largest design center (open to the trade only), the Chicago Merchandise Mart also features Luxe-Home, located on the first floor of the building, 222 Merchandise Mart Plaza. Here, you'll find more than 30 high-end boutique showrooms stretching through 100,000 square feet of space. All are open to the public and showcase the best in kitchen, bath and home building products available in one place.

Designer showrooms include Ann Sacks, Christopher Peacock Cabinetry, Poggenpohl, Waterworks, Kohler and many more. The showrooms have designers on staff or you can contact the concierge at The Design Resource Center (☎ 312/527-7939) for recommendations. If you're not working with a designer, I recommend a preliminary visit to see what's available; while there, set up appointments to return and meet with showrooms' design staff. www.luxehome.com.

American knows as a lifestyle or concept store because those are fashion creatures. This is what L.L.Bean would open if they had a hardware, crafts and office supply store. There are over 100 kinds of hangers in the closets department. This is one of the best stores in the world, so you owe it to yourself to simply wander through every level. There are several stores in Tokyo; the flagship should be your main goal.

WHERE TO BUY   17 stores in Japan, 4 in Taiwan. **FLAGSHIP**   12-18 Udagawacko, Shibuya, Tokyo. ☎ **813/5489-5111.** Daily 10am–8pm; closed the 2nd and 4th Mon of each month. AE, MC, V. JTR: Shibuya. www.tokyuhands.co.jp.

V.V. Rouleaux BRITISH $–$$

This is not really a crafts store (they sell ribbon and trimmings) but there are so many items that a craftsperson might want, and the stores are all worth swooning over from a visual context, that I list the store here as a reminder. See p. 119.

Furniture

It's impossible to list the best furniture stores and sources in the world, so these are some of the best with an emphasis on the quality of style and price, hopefully with a shopping experience or adventure thrown in.

For those who prefer to shop for furniture online (hey, some people do it) there are some specific furniture listings in Chapter Three: "Lifestyle & Department Stores." Also check out Chapter Eleven: "Bargains & Alternative Retail," for information on factory stores and outlets, warehouses, antiques barns, auctions, flea markets and so on. All the stores listed below will arrange shipping.

1stdibs.com

This unique site allows you to search for and negotiate prices on antique furnishings and accessories from all over the world. All pieces are listed by individual dealers (you can search by item or location) and you'll negotiate the sale directly with them. This is a popular source for the design trade, so inventory moves fast. If you want 1st dibs to handle a transaction for you, they'll negotiate the best price, arrange payment on your behalf and get shipping quotes; the charge is 20% for this service. These are high-end antiques, all fairly priced. Inventory is available from 20 countries and discounts are available to the trade.

BEST BUYS   Designer furnishings at trade prices.

Brandon USA $$–$$$$$

This is a discount source for furniture, accessories, art, rugs and some tabletop. There are about 20 stores dotted across the U.S.—because they sell closeouts, returns, orphans and what not, the merchandise can be different in each store. The idea is that big name furniture is sold at a fraction of the suggested retail price—some comes from show houses, photo shoots or clients who changed their minds. Brandon's has a strange price code system, so make sure you have the key before you begin to browse. The Scottsdale store is in an airpark, so ask for a map.

BEST BETS   As long as I live, I'll never get over that twiglike bar unit for $450.

WEB TIPS   You'll get an idea of what the stores are like from the online photos; however, there are no brands listed and there's no online catalog.

WHERE TO BUY   1 store in Europe (Amsterdam); 18 others across the U.S. in cities including Scottsdale, Denver, St. Louis, Houston, more. www.brandonhomefurnishings.com.

David Linley BRITISH VALUE $$$$–$$$$$

For anyone who has spent the last half century locked in a turret of Daddy's castle, David Linley is the son of Princess Margaret and Anthony Armstrong-Jones. He is the only member of the current royal family to exhibit both talent and business sense; his work is not only spectacular but exceedingly collectable—therefore the value icon above. Linley does a lot of custom commissions and mostly makes what is called "important" furniture—usually board room tables or executive desks. However, his shop does sell smalls and he is known for his decorative boxes.

BEST BETS   The boxes. Look for hidden drawers and secret spaces; look for a hidden sense of humor in each piece. Prices begin at £76 ($156).

WEB TIPS   You can order small accessories from the website. Shipping to the U.S. will be quoted after your order is placed; they will wait for your approval before shipping.

WHERE TO BUY   2 stores in London. 46 Albermarle St., London W1. ☎ 4420/7290-1410. Mon–Thurs 10am–6pm; Fri and Sat 10am–5pm. Also at 60 Pimlico Rd., London SW3. ☎ 4420/7730-7300. Mon–Wed 10am–6pm; Thurs 10am–7pm; Fri 10am–5pm and Sat 11am–6pm. AE, MC, V. www.davidlinley.com.

Forgotten Shanghai SAN FRANCISCO $$$$$

Retail store adjacent to assorted wholesale sources in the San Francisco design district and created as a small Chinese house with mostly large pieces of furniture but some pillows and accessories.

BEST BETS   The giant lanterns that Sarah and I bought to turn into end-tables are pretty fabulous but the truth is, someday I am going to buy one of the large armoires and ship it to my latest home. Prices are higher than I'd pay in Shanghai, about $2,000 for the armoire I dream of, but then I don't have to pay to ship from China.

Forgotten Shanghai "Shanxi elmwood large cabinet."

WEB TIPS   Inventory is shown online, but the photos aren't great. You really must visit this store to see the quality of the furniture.

WHERE TO BUY   1 store: 245 Kansas St., San Francisco, CA. ☎ **415/701-7707.** Mon–Fri 9am–5pm; Sat 10am–5pm. AE, MC, V.

Great Stuff by Paul FREDERICK, MD $$–$$$

52,000 square feet of stuff, a lot of it furniture in a warehouse setting.

BEST BETS   If you can't find anything to love in 50,000 square feet jam-packed with stuff, you were not born to shop.

WEB TIPS   You'll find good online bargains by clicking on "great deals." Also check out "just off the boat" for new arrivals. Unfortunately, some items listed for sale come without photos.

WHERE TO BUY   1 store: 257 Sixth St. at East St., Frederick, MD. ☎ **301/631-5340.** Mon–Sat 10am–6pm; Sun 11am–5pm. AE, MC, V. www.greatstuffbypaul.com.

Hu & Hu SHANGHAI $$$–$$$$

Oh my, oh me, oh oh oh—if I sound speechless that's how mute I become when I enter Hu & Hu in Shanghai. Located outside of town, so you will have to make a special trip—it's well worth the effort if you are a serious shopper.

Note that this one is not only the best, but the owner and staff speak perfect English. The owner MaryBelle speaks perfect English because she grew up in America. I promise you will love her and love doing business with her because there are no communications problems, she follows through when she says she will and she explains everything to you up front (such as shipping).

The store consists of several warehouses with rows and rows of Chinese rustic furniture. Lots of chests, armoires, mirrors, tables and some wedding trunks and smaller pieces too. There are some gift items. Much of the furniture has been refinished or brought back from the dead—some pieces (out in rear warehouse) are more natural. You will need a taxi to get here; ask the taxi to wait for you. Taxis are very inexpensive in Shanghai so take your time shopping. And yes, the bathrooms are very clean here.

If you don't see what you want, they will e-mail you photos of new pieces when they arrive. Prices are competitive when you add in the shipping and you should still come out better than if you bought the same items through a dealer.

BEST BETS   I've bought 400-year-old ancestor paintings for $600; Chinese medicine cabinets (restored) are about $1,200. Even if you ship, you save money.

WEB TIPS   There's lots of store information on the website, but unfortunately no photos of the furniture. Inventory moves quickly, so maybe they don't have time to keep it updated.

WHERE TO BUY   1 store: Cao Bao Lu Alley 1885 no. 8, Shanghai. ☎ 8621/3431-1212. Daily 9am–6pm. AE, MC, V. www.hu-hu. com.

Italydesign.com   VALUE $$$–$$$$$

This is the Web's "virtual store" for Design Centro Italia, located in Emeryville, California. They stock residential and commercial furniture from Italian manufacturers including Knoll and Le Corbusier; all are available for purchase online at discount prices. Most items are in stock, but custom orders can take up to 10 weeks. Shipping can be expensive, so ask for a quote before ordering. These designs are timeless and rarely available at these discount prices (which are better than those you'll find from each brand's manufacturer).

Newel NYC $$$$$

What's old again is Newel again: that's what the ads say. This store is more like a museum of the odd, one-off, unusual, unique and sensational—all are antiques: the exact kind of place you go when you must have something no one else has, when you need a wow piece or are looking for conversation-stopping furnishings. You'll find everything from a simple yet very stunning desk to chairs carved in mysterious ways and dancing with figurines. You can rent.

BEST BET   Stock changes so quickly that you can't focus on any one thing—you're looking at furniture and pieces for the person who wants something different and is willing to pay for it.

WEB TIPS   They have an online tutorial to guide you through the site. Click on the category of interest on the bottom of the home page, then "tutorial for detailed instructions."

WHERE TO BUY   1 store: 425 E. 53rd St., NYC. ☎ **212/758-1970.** Mon–Fri 8:30am–5pm; Sat by appointment. AE, DISC, MC, V. www.newel.com.

Old Plank Road WESTMONT, IL $$$–$$$$$

Chicago may be like New York that works, but its suburbs have some amazing retail ops that are like nowhere else. This store is 25 miles outside of Chicago and is one of those somewhat enormous showroom places (37,000 sq. ft.) with antiques, home style, garden, painted and unpainted furniture, including a division that sells painted rustic-style French furniture. They also do restoration for you.

BEST BETS   Prices are moderate—reproduction armoires are around $2,000 while the real deal is $5,000 to $6,000.

WEB TIPS   The website is complete and makes viewing stock very easy but you cannot buy online.

WHERE TO BUY   1 store: 331 E. Ogden Ave., Westmont, IL. ☎ **630/887-1995.** Tues–Sat 10am–5am; Sun noon–5pm. www.oldplank.com.

The Painted Lady CHICAGO $$–$$$$

This Wicker Park boutique will inspire you to rethink, refurbish, repaint, reinvent and redo all of the furniture you inherited from your in-laws. That's exactly what the owners do, bringing charm, personality and a new coat of paint to old treasures found at flea markets and tag sales. On my last visit, I saw a large 1940s dresser which had been prepped, painted and transformed into a changing table for a lucky newborn. A queen four-poster bed was awaiting its final coat of gloss, and I tried to figure out how that adorable bedside table would fit into the overhead bin on my flight home.

Along with hand-painted vintage dressers, chests and beds, this shabby chic shop features vintage-inspired glassware, chandeliers, mirrors and much more.

BEST BETS   The refurbished furniture. Most items are priced under $500; chandeliers run $300 to $400.

WEB TIPS   Inventory is one of a kind and moves fast so you can't order online, buy you'll be inspired by the website.

WHERE TO BUY   1 store: 2128 N. Damen Ave., between Webster and Shakespeare, Chicago. IL. ☎ **773/489-9145.** Tues–Sat 11am–6pm; Sun noon–5pm. AE, MC, V. www.thepaintedlady chicago.com. —*SRL*

Shabby Chic USA $$$$

Upholstered furniture was about as chic as your grandmother's blue hair until Shabby Chic came into being in Santa Monica in 1989. The brand is now written as "Rachel Ashwell Shabby Chic" after being knocked off consistently when Mrs. Ashwell changed the way the world spins. Now she's on TV, writes books, makes baby furniture and sits on top of a stylistic empire that is cozy yet fresh.

Begun as another cutie-pie store, this one combining slip-cover looks with flea-market finds, the brand soon graduated to such an important place in contemporary design that they design and produce their own new furniture to look old, although it is oversized and super stuffed. The slipcovers come in a variety of price ranges.

BEST BETS   The upholstered pieces. Prices are dear; $3,500 for a settee. Sold in their stores and as a brand at other stores; trade discounts and sold in D&D showrooms.

WEB TIPS   The website is nice to look at but does not offer sales or shipping, and in fact does little that is helpful except list the addresses of the six stores.

WHERE TO BUY   FLAGSHIP   83 Wooster St., SoHo, NYC. ☎ **212/ 274-9842.** Mon–Sat 10am–7pm; Sun noon–6pm. AE, MC, V. Subway: Canal St. www.shabbychic.com.

Tobacco Barn ASHEVILLE, TN $–$$$$$

If you are driving across the Smokies, you will know this is as important a landmark as Pigeon Forge and Biltmore Estate. If you love shopping as I do, you may find it more important.

This former tobacco barn (hence the name) has been turned into an antiques store cum flea market that for the last 10 years has been voted the best in the area. Prices are so low that dealers come from all over the U.S. (and yes, there is a trade discount.) You can go online and find bloggers who report to decorating college dorm rooms and homes from a visit here. This is a local shrine to furniture shopping.

This is destination shopping at its best—there are motels nearby or you can go upscale by staying on property at the famed Biltmore Estates (www.biltmore.com) 1 mile away or at the Grove Park Inn & Spa (www.groveparkinn.com).

BEST BETS   Although smalls and gifts are sold, the big stuff is what really moves—architectural salvage priced from $8 to $3,000. Bedsteads range from Mission to Victorian with prices from $150 to $1,000; armoires begin around $125 with simple cedar and go up to $3,600 for a triple English import. There's even vintage clothing.

WHERE TO BUY   75 Swannanoa River Rd.; Asheville, TN. ☎ 828/252-7291. Mon–Thurs 10am–6pm; Fri–Sat 9am–6pm; Sun 1–6pm. Dec 23–Feb, weekends only (answer machine will announce winter hours). MC, V. No website.

Via Diva   SAN RAFAEL, CA $$–$$$$$

This warehouse store, packed with Asian furniture, is difficult to find as it's located in an industrial area in San Rafael, CA, just north of San Francisco. However, it's well worth the search, as you'll discover one of the Bay Area's best sources for furniture and accessories from China, India, Thailand and Indonesia. With low overhead and a middle-of-nowhere location, Via Diva offers merchandise priced 30% to 50% lower than comparable goods in San Francisco. They stock both antiques and reproductions, with conditions ranging from "very distressed" to pristine.

Don't expect to see a fancy store—this is a crowded warehouse with furniture stacked ceiling high. As you enter Via Diva's front room, you'll see a large display of antique pieces; keep walking, there's lots more in the back. You'll find antiques on the first floor including armoires, apothecary cabinets, tables, chests and benches. Continue upstairs to see more tables, chairs, mirrors and accessories, most of which are reproductions.

BEST BETS   There's a very good selection of old hand-painted chests and cabinets priced $200 to $2,000 and up, depending on size and age. The ticket prices can be flexible; depending on how long a piece has been on the floor, a lower offer may be accepted. Trade discounts are also available.

WEB TIPS   The website shows some examples of stock, but there's a high inventory turnover, so you really must visit in person.

WHERE TO BUY   1 store: 516 Irwin St., San Rafael, CA. ☎ 415/257-8881. Daily 10am–6pm. AE, DISC, MC, V. www.viadiva.com.

Furniture Festivals

For a very thorough and international list of furniture festivals, visit **www.penrose-press.com** and click on "furniture." One of my favorites is the International Home Furnishings Market, held twice a year (generally April and October) in High Point, NC. It stretches out over 12 *million* square feet of shopping in almost 200 buildings—it totally takes over this honky-tonk town not far from Greensboro–Winston Salem. This market is for the trade only; you need credentials to shop it and to buy. See www.high pointmarket.org.

Wow & Zen CHICAGO $$–$$$$

I took one look at the window display and walked right into this mecca for antique Asian furnishings and artifacts. Most of the furniture is 100 to 200 years old, as are the cultural artifacts and decorative accessories. The items, which are stacked floor to ceiling and line the center of the shop, tend to be clean-lined utilitarian pieces that can be creatively adapted for use in Western homes. I loved the sets of Burmese and Chinese marionettes priced from $245 to $256 each; and a large colorful temple cabinet from Tibet was a steal at $1,750. There was a huge bamboo armoire, circa 1800, which could house my winter wardrobe; other storage units were suitable for both clothing and video equipment. I found a good selection of low chests, Bantam Buddha cabinets, rice farmer stools and rustic grain baskets that could be used for seating or storage.

With low prices, inventory moves fast, so if you see it and want it, buy it as it probably won't be there tomorrow.

BEST BETS   The armoires and chests, all under $1,800.

WHERE TO BUY   1 store: 1912 N. Damen Ave., Chicago, IL. ☎ **773/269-2600.** Tues and Wed noon–6pm; Thurs and Fri noon–8pm; Sat 11am–6pm; Sun 11am–5pm. AE, DISC, MC, V. —*SRL*

Hardware & Fixtures

Berings TEXAN $–$$$

It's a bird, it's a plane, it's a superstore. No, wait: It has a bird (the store's mascot is a macaw named Hacksaw); it's on a plain—in Houston, Texas—and by George, it is an amazing store.

Berings is part upmarket Home Depot, part General Store for the New Age and part darn good store, despite its loss of focus in the expansion years. Berings claims to be a hardware store. They are a hardware store like Gucci is a handbag store. The two-part store just a mile from Houston's Galleria mall in the Post Oak section of town sells just about everything— much of it is imported and expensive. Yet the store survives, and thrives, in this age of the big box store because it has the class to sell the best quality and the best selection of quality items for the house—be it furniture pulls or Laura Ashley paint. (Home Depot does not carry Laura Ashley paint.)

They also sell Texas boot pulls (helps you remove your boots), thousand-dollar reproduction Chinoiserie coffee tables, Emile Henry French cooking crockery and retro tricycles for the under-6 set. Here and there you spot a surprise—a gourmet foods department, imported hand-painted faience.

The second part of the store lies in a perpendicular position in the parking lot, a freestanding shop that includes children's clothes and toys, garden supplies, gift wrap, paper goods and home decor you might expect to find in the kind of homes regularly pictured in *Architectural Digest*.

BEST BETS   The diverse selection and fair prices.

WEB TIPS   This is one-stop shopping for foul weather preparedness—order everything you need for the next hurricane, tornado or earthquake by clicking on "Prepare for hurricane season." There's batteries, generators, weather radios and much more.

WHERE TO BUY   1 store: 6102 Westheimer, Houston, TX. ☎ **713/785-6400.** Mon–Fri 8am–6pm; Sat 8:30am–6pm; Sun 11am–6pm. 3900 Bissonet, Houston, TX. ☎ **713/665-0500.** Mon–Sat 8:30am–6:30pm; Sun 11am–6pm. AE, DISC, MC, V. www.berings.com.

Bazar de L'Hotel de Ville (BHV) PARIS $-$$$$

If you think this is a funny name for a store, you can call it BHV (say beh-ahsh-veh), or remember that the full name of the store will tell you just where it is—across from the Hotel de Ville in Paris. The store is famous for its do-it-yourself attitude and housewares. You owe it to yourself to go to the basement (SS) level; if you're at all interested in household gadgets or interior design, you will go nuts.

The upper floors are ordinary enough, and even the basement level can be ordinary (I assure you–I'm not sending you to

Paris to buy a lawn mower), but there are little nooks and crannies that will delight the most creative shoppers among you. I buy brass lock pieces and string them on necklaces for gifts.

Personally, I think BHV should get rid of fashion entirely and just do home style, but what do I know?

BEST BETS   You certainly don't come here to buy clothes or accessories, although they are sold. Instead, concentrate on the crafts and art department; excellent office papers, folders and paper goods; and the adorable Café Brico in the Basement.

WEB TIPS   While the website is extensive, colorful and fun to use, it is in French and you can't shop from it anyway.

WHERE TO BUY   1 store: 52–56 rue de Rivoli, 1er, Paris. ☎ **331/ 4274-9000.** Mon–Sat 9:30am–6:30pm, and until 10pm on Wed. AE, MC, V. Métro: Hotel de Ville. www.bhv.fr.

Charles Street Hardware BOSTON $–$$$

This small, deep and very packed hardware store is right in the heart of Boston's Beacon Hill district, on tony Charles Street. Surrounded by cuter-than-thou retail, this store is practical and useful but also has a New England accent to it that speaks of Federal-style architecture, wood floors and old china plates hung on the wall. If geography defines who we are, this store is very New England and serves the needs of the community and those who restore old houses.

BEST BETS   They have the best selection of sizes of wire plate/ tray hangers that I have ever seen.

WEB TIPS   The website links you to ACE Hardware; order online and pick up at your local ACE. Free shipping.

WHERE TO BUY   1 store: 54–56 Charles St., Boston. ☎ **617/ 367-9046.** Mon, Thurs 6am–7pm; Tues, Wed, Fri 8am–7pm; Sat 8:30am–6pm; Sun noon–5pm. AE, DISC, MC, V. www. charlesstsupply.com.

Gracious Home NYC $–$$$$

Oh my gracious, how to even classify this store—a department store? A dream? A cultural phenom? Well, it began as a hardware store and became all of the above. Their motto claims that they are a store for extraordinary lives, which is why Gracious Home is a cultural icon—surviving in Manhattan means you have an extraordinary life, so this store has been able to make life easier for the stressed and pressured and therefore has built its fortune on the basis of service.

The store sells just about everything except food and clothes; they will get you just about everything, except food and clothes. There are several Manhattan locations and they differ not only in how they present their merchandise but in who shops there, which makes the moods of the stores different.

Essentially, Gracious Home is a hardware/home-style store that sells everything from allergy relief to vacuum cleaners. There are over 200,000 products in stock—each product is chosen either to fill a need in the high-rise lifestyle peculiar to New York City or to represent chic merchandise perhaps not found elsewhere. I bought a set of dishes in a small store in Paris which I have never seen anywhere in the world except at Gracious Home. That's the kind of lines they specialize in selling. Prices are not cut-rate but to someone living with alligators in the sewers beneath Manhattan, price is meaningless.

BEST BETS   Inventory and customer service.

WEB TIPS   All brands are represented on the website, so you'll get an idea of what's available in the stores. While you can order online, go to the store if possible; they'll deliver your purchase, assemble it and return for repairs, if need be.

WHERE TO BUY   FLAGSHIP   1220 Third Ave., at 70th St., NYC. ☎ 212/517-6300. Mon–Fri 8am–8pm; Sat 9am–7pm; Sun 10am–7pm. AE, DISC, MC, V. Subway: 68th St. www.gracioushome.com.

Guerin Inc. NYC $$$

You are, perhaps, Marie-Antoinette and you are building a little playhouse in the backyard so you need very specific hardware to co-ordinate with the look of your palace. The local artisans and craftspeople are busy at their bellows, so where can you turn? Well, Guerin could be the place.

BEST BETS   This is the place for distinctive fittings that can't be found in "big box" stores. Designs are intricate and expensive; we're talking thousands of dollars for a complete doorknob and lock set.

WEB TIPS   The photos on the website are small and difficult to see, even when enlarged. No online orders.

WHERE TO BUY   1 store: 21–23 Jane St. between Greenwich and Eighth Ave., NYC. ☎ 212/243-5270. Mon–Fri 9am–5:30pm; closed Sat and Sun. $25 for catalog. AE, DISC, MC, V. Subway: 14th St. www.peguerin.com.

Liz's Antique Hardware LOS ANGELES $–$$$

The name says it all. Note this is part of a strip of vintage furniture and clothing stores south of Sunset. This is one of those you'll-be-dizzy-from-it-all, overwhelming experiences. Most of the goods are repro, but it's more fun than a trip for ice cream.

BEST BETS   Fixtures and fittings, repro, beginning at 99 cents.

WEB TIPS   There's a Web link to eBay where the store often holds auctions—a great source of bargains. Of course, you'll need to register on eBay first.

WHERE TO BUY   1 store: 453 LaBrea Ave., LA. ☎ **323/939-4403.** Mon–Sat 10am–6pm; closed Sun. AE, MC, V. www.lahardware. com.

Home Scent

Back in the old days, before "home ambiance" was a buzz-word, when I had my house up for sale, I would bake an apple pie when the house was being shown by a broker. The scent filled the house and I hope added thousands of dollars to the selling price.

Since then, candles, sprays, gels, sand, rocks and various diffusers have become a big business. While I keep a fancy spritz spray in the bathrooms of my home, the point is not to cover up oh-so-human odors but to fill your house with a mood-enhancing scent. See Chapter Six: "Beauty" for more on aromatherapy, which often ties into home scents.

Agraria SAN FRANCISCO $–$$

This firm makes potpourri, burning sticks, fragrance sheets, sprays, spa and bath products, candles (doesn't everyone?) and offers a medley of exotic blends. I stick to the original scent, Bitter Orange, and use the burning sticks—40 come in a box for $26. Scents range from Riveria Pear to Lavender & Rosemary with a handful of choices in between.

Agraria "Bitter Orange" potpourri.

BEST BETS   My idea of heaven is to splurge on the bath salts. A 32-ounce box costs $28.

WEB TIPS   Too bad you can't sniff online. At least you can order, with free shipping on orders of $100 or more.

WHERE TO BUY   You can buy online or at Gump's in San Francisco (p. 44). www.agrariahome.com.

Diptyque FRENCH $–$$

First, a warning: If you are not familiar with the store, you may take a look at the Paris address and think you know where the store is. It isn't. This particular number is in the 5e, closer to St. Michel and not in the thick of St. Germain de Près. That said, let's get more specific about what this brand is, not where it is located, because you can frequently buy the soaps, candles and sprays in department stores around the world.

Diptyque is one of those small brands that has acquired cult status by creating their own scents, which vary from fig (a best seller) to burning wood (a personal favorite). Also note that the product is significantly less expensive in France than in the U.S., even with a bad rate of exchange—making this a great gift for the person who has everything.

BEST BETS   The candles, about $40 in France and $60 in the U.S.

WEB TIPS   Various beauty websites sell the products in the U.S. You cannot buy from the store's site.

WHERE TO BUY   4 stores in Paris, London, Boston, San Francisco; department and specialty stores worldwide. **FLAGSHIP** 34 blvd. St. Germain, Paris 5e. Tues–Sat 11am–7pm. MC, V. Métro: St. Michel. www.diptyqueparis.com.

Esteban FRENCH $

Although the French are known for their noses (ahem), they are known for perfumes for the body, not the home. Enter Esteban, the most famous maker of home fragrance in Paris, who takes home scent to a new low, all the way to the carpet with perfumed vacuum cleaner powder. This designer has a few stores of his own but has better distribution throughout Europe within department stores. The brand sells all sorts of mediums for conveying home scent, from sprays, candles and powders to incense sticks, rocks, gels and little doodads that you put on the hangers in your closets (they make great gifts). There are a variety of collections for masculine or feminine scents or seasonal scents or scents that come attached to memories, such as summer at the beach.

BEST BETS   There are scented "rocks" that look like sea glass. You can refresh the fragrance by buying additional oils.

WEB TIPS   The site is in (your choice) French or English; you cannot shop but you can see the products and get a good feel for the line. To buy in the U.S., try www.fourseasonsproducts. com (☎ 800/555-8082), which carries the full line and ships from Florida.

WHERE TO BUY   Several stores in France; perfume and specialty shops worldwide. **FLAGSHIP**   49 rue de Rennes, Paris, 6e. ☎ 331/4549-0939. Mon noon–7pm; Tues–Fri 11am–7pm; Sat 10am–7pm. MC, V. Métro: St. Germain des Pres. www.esteban.fr.

Incense of the West ALBUQUERQUE, NM $

My father loved incense cones in the years before people used them to disguise the smell of pot. So I grew up with a family favorite—piñon—which can only be bought in Santa Fe or Albuquerque. The product is available in any tourist trap between Albuquerque and Santa Fe. I always stop at **Jackalope** on my way into Santa Fe and load up.

BEST BETS   The cones smell of pine, juniper and mesquite and represent all that is sexy and dreamy about high sierra winter. You'll pay about $4 for a box of 40 cones.

WEB TIPS   Click on "fragrances" and buy the piñon; ignore the other scents, especially that seven-scent package.

WHERE TO BUY   Incienso de Santa Fe, 320 Headingly NW, Albuquerque, NM. ☎ 505/345-0701. Mon–Fri 9am–6pm. AE, MC, V. www.inscents.com.

Kenneth Turner BRITISH $$–$$$

A florist who has branched out (ha ha) into home scent and now body care has a range of scents, although it's the original one that I think is the best. It is creatively named "original"— a blend of cinnamon and spice. I don't even mind when the dog farts if I can spray this stuff around the house.

   I buy at the outlet in Oxfordshire, UK. The brand is carried by most UK department stores and Brown Thomas in Ireland. Turner also has books published on flower arranging and has his most complete representation in Harrod's in Knightsbridge.

BEST BETS   You will pay $30 for a spray bottle of home scent.

WEB TIPS   Everything's available online, but shipping to the U.S. could cost as much as your goods.

WHERE TO BUY   Kenneth Turner outlets: Bicester Village, 50 Pingle Dr., Oxfordshire, UK. ☎ 441/869-320-998. Mon–Wed, Sun 10am–6pm; Thurs and Fri 10am–7pm; Sat 9:30am–7pm. AE, MC, V. Kildare Village, Junction 11, M7 Motorway, Kildare, Ireland. ☎ 353/45-520-501. Mon, Wed, Sat 10am–6pm; Thurs 10am–8pm; Fri 10am–7pm; Sun 11am–6pm. MC, V. www.kennethturner.com.

Lampes Berger FRENCH $$$

Historians may tell you that the telephone or the computer are the most important inventions of modern times. I could vote for the Lampe Berger. The lamp device is a small, genie-like bottle that was invented 100 years ago. Choose from hundreds of shapes and designs—it eliminates odors in a room through a catalysis system. It doesn't spritz a nice scent to mask the cat pee; it ionizes the air with a new scent. You burn a liquid scent—there's about two dozen scents available.

BEST BETS The lampes retail for $20 to $250 and you'll pay $30 for a 16.9-ounce bottle of oil. A 1-liter bottle provides 40 hours of scent.

WEB TIPS Check out the lampe designs on the website. You'll need to visit a retailer to purchase the system.

WHERE TO BUY Sold in the U.S. in fancy drug and retail stores. Call the corporate number, ☎ 800/321-0020 for a retailer near you. www.lampeberger.com.

> **Buyer Beware**
>
> It is illegal to bring these scents in your luggage from France, or from anywhere else. Sarah was paged at the New Orleans airport and had to return to the check-in counter to throw away 2 bottles of oil, as it was illegal to transport them in her luggage.

Slatkin & Co. USA $$$$

Perhaps you know this firm through Elton John who sells these candles to raise money for AIDS research. Maybe you know it through chichi magazines you've been reading at the doctor's office. Or perhaps you are into the Kabbalah collection through your friend Madonna. No matter.

You can go directly to the firm and pay $75,000 to have your own custom scent made. If you think that's a tad over the top, but you do fancy yourself as a creative consumer, there's a home fragrance CD player you might want to try. This is the best-selling home fragrance line in the U.S.

BEST BETS If you are into candles, this is one of the best candles for the home (I'm in for fig). It costs $38, and can be ordered through Neiman Marcus.

WEB TIPS If you want to order online, you'll be directed to Neiman Marcus's website.

WHERE TO BUY Retailers and department stores throughout the U.S. including Neiman Marcus. www.slatkin.com.

Kitchen & Cookware

Broadway Panhandler NYC $–$$$

Begun in 1939 as a supplier of cookware and cutlery to the U.S. military, Broadway Panhandler made a dent in the culture in the 1970s by selling restaurant size and quality cookware to the public. This was the beginning of the food revolution in the U.S.—having good-quality cookware was a new kind of status symbol.

Today Broadway Panhandler is one of the leading suppliers of major brands of cookwares; they have all the big brands from the U.S. and from Europe. In the store—this a new address— they have a demo kitchen and sponsor various events and book signings. Better yet, the staff here is not only friendly but possesses an expertise that is hard to find elsewhere, so they will guide you to the right equipment for your personal lifestyle.

BEST BETS The service. A similar knife may cost $38 or $60— the staff will guide you to the right one for your cooking and hands-on style.

WEB TIPS You can shop by phone or online but the human touch is so important here that I advise you to move away from online sales if you can. UPS shipping within the continental US.

WHERE TO BUY 1 store: 65 E. 8th St., NYC. ☎ **866/266-5927,** 212/966-3434. Mon–Sat 11am–7pm; Sun 11am–6pm. AE, DISC, MC, V. Subway: 8th St./NYU. www.broadwaypanhandler.com.

A.Simon PARIS $–$$$$

A major supplier of kitchen and cooking supplies for over 100 years, this store is conveniently located down the street from the Forum des Halles mall. You can buy everything from dishes to menus here; touch everything in the wonderland of gadgets and goodies.

BEST BETS I buy white paper doilies by the gross—many sizes and shapes not available in the U.S.—at fair prices.

WHERE TO BUY 1 store: 48 rue Montmartre, 2e, Paris. ☎ **331/ 4233-7165.** Mon 1:30–6:30pm; Tues–Sat 9am–6:30pm. AE, MC, V. Métro: Etienne Marcel or Les Halles. www.simon-a.com.

Le Creuset FRENCH $$–$$$

World's Best

Proving that what we cook and what we cook it in is cultural, note that I moved to New York in 1969, when the gourmet cooking revolution was just beginning in the home. Although my mother used Revere pots and pans as was the mode for her generation, to prove that I knew far more than she did, I immediately bought the starter set of Le Creuset cast iron cookware, which in those days only came in a disgusting orange color called "flame." The seven-piece (five pots plus two lids) set could be bought on sale for $99 and demonstrated your serious commitment to the very best in cookwares.

Le Creuset cast-iron round French oven.

Today Le Creuset comes in almost a dozen colors (including black) and it's hard to find a single piece that costs less than $99. It's heavy and it's not as fashionable as it once was although it is still considered one of the best brands in the world because of the way it cooks.

Originally created in 1925 from a single old-fashioned French cast-iron stew pot, the line is a favorite of those who like heavy enameled cookware. It can be difficult to clean but its heft makes it ideal for long-cooking items.

Bargain shoppers may find individual pieces in off-price stores in the U.S. or even the firm's factory outlet stores, located in all prominent outlet malls.

BEST BETS   One of the most interesting inventions of the line is the Dofeu Oven ($269) which allows water to nestle into the top to keep roasts from drying out.

WEB TIPS   Although the website appears to let you order online, in fact it just gives you the websites of various retailers who sell the brand. Go for one that doesn't charge shipping since this stuff weighs a ton.

WHERE TO BUY   40 outlets in the U.S; department and cooking stores worldwide. ☎ **803/943-4308** for corporate assistance. www.lecreuset.com.

Sur la Table USA $–$$$

While Sur la Table has an excellent website and you can shop online or by catalog, nothing in the world can replace a visit to a real live store—especially if you are new to this brand, especially if you go into one of the larger stores. The brand began on the small side in the Pike Place Market in Seattle. There's still a store there, but it is not reflective of the current style and importance of the brand.

Sur la Table takes the best of international brands—and this includes Asian as well as European brands, especially on the West Coast of the U.S.—and mixes them with the best cook

Cookware: Paris When It Sizzles

As any Frenchman will happily tell you, the French invented cooking. So it makes sense that some of the best stores for cookwares, utensils and the arts de la cuisine are in Paris. Note that most of these stores are located on the rue Montmartre (which is NOT in Montmartre) alongside what used to be Les Halles Market (now a shopping mall). There are three or four other good stores on the same rue Montmartre; if your back is to A.Simon walk toward the River Seine.

A.Simon

Old-time visitors to Paris and its food preparation stores may be dismayed to note that the old A.Simon of years of shopping pleasure has been turned into a trendy jeans store. Nonetheless, the store has re-located across the street and the new location, 48 rue Montmartre, 2e (☎ **0142/337-165;** www.simon-a.com) has the same mix of tabletop, cooking, professional supplies and novelties that will make your heart sing. While you may not want to lug back the cooking pots or the dishes, the little French details that can dress up a table, make a party or even decorate a theme party are a pleasure to touch. Prices for many smalls are under 10€ ($1.30). If you bake for the Feast of the Three Kings (Epiphany, which features a cake with a "bean" baked inside it), you can buy from an assortment of *feves* here.

The store ships internationally. They have been specialists in arts de la table et de la cuisine since 1884, which makes them a relative newcomer to the trade with their fellow icons in the 'hood. While they are helpful in the store, I'd plan to speak some French.

E. Dehillerin

Since 1820 this cookwares and utensils specialist, at 18–20 rue Coquillere, 1er (☎ **0142/365-313;** www.e-dehillerin.fr), has been considered one of the best in the world. Of the stores listed here, this one is the most romantic looking from the outside and is very traditional in what they sell and how they sell it. The aisles inside the store are narrow; the merch is piled up on baker's racks—as in the other nearby shops—but the traditional storefront itself and the window displays are fancy and welcoming.

M.O.R.A.

This resource, at 13 rue Montmartre, 1er (☎ **0145/081-924**), is more for utensils than tabletop and is the most professional of the group. You are welcome to shop here but may feel excluded if you're not a chef. But consider the fact that the store carries Wilton (p. 345) and feel right at home. Established in 1814, the firm has over 5,000 items in stock to serve restaurants, kitchen, pastry and bread-making needs. They are also big on professional knives, although it's hard to get those past security these days.

books, cooking demonstrations, linens, foodstuffs and food trends so that the mélange is heart stopping and eye popping.

I find that the goods sold by this store are on the expensive side but when I am in one of the stores, I don't care because I want to be part of the culture. I want the Laguiole Cheese Knife set for $40, the daffodil-yellow Beehive mixing bowl set for $40 and the Dragonfly napkin rings for $20.

BEST BETS   You'll find the entire line of Le Creuset cookware along with other top brands, all at retail prices.

WEB TIPS   Sur la Table publishes a monthly catalog which can be seen online or ordered online. There's also a lot of information online, from recipes to promotions to the ability to shop. When I am shopping online, I am bored and quickly find the merchandise overpriced. Pomegranate glaze for $20? You've got to be kidding!

WHERE TO SHOP   Original store: Pike's Place Market, Seattle, WA. ☎ 206/448-2244. **FLAGSHIP**   90 Central Way, Kirkland, WA. ☎ 425/827-1311. Mon–Fri 9:30am–7pm; Sat 9:30am–6pm; Sun 11am–5pm. AE, DISC, MC, V. www.surlatable.com.

Wilton USA $

As the mother of a child who grew up in a very competitive social environment, I discovered Wilton when I began to strive to have my birthday parties and bake sale goods stand out from the crowd's. I even considered a trip to the suburbs of Chicago to attend Wilton's Cake College.

In no time at all I became famous for my unusual chocolate cake, which was oft-requested at parties and events. The truth to my cake is embarrassing: It was a simple Duncan Hines cake mix baked in a Wilton pan that was a size no one else had—a professional round that made a large wafer of a cake that was well respected in my circle. Wilton offers the best professional baking gear for the home chef who does not want to become Pierre Herme.

It's more than 20 years since I fretted over Beverly Hills birthday parties. Wilton is a better-known brand and their cooking school and specialty classes have expanded enormously. There are now 125 different courses. If you can't make it to Cake College, no reason to sing the chorus of MacArthur Park, just order the books and/or videos. Regular prices vary from $2 for a lollipop mold to $13 for a 3-D rubber duckie pan.

BEST BET   For those shoppers who are addicted to this brand, or just love a big shopping fete, once a year Wilton has a tent sale at their headquarters in Woodbridge, Illinois (a suburb of

Chicago). Get the dates and all needed information online and be sure to reserve your hotel in advance. This is a competitive sale and you surely don't want to miss out on a $5 Smurf cake pan. Tent sale address: 2240 W. 75th St., Woodbridge, IL.

WEB TIPS   The firm offers online shopping, but only ships within the U.S. For Canadian shoppers, you must get the name of a Canadian distributor.

WHERE TO BUY   U.S. craft stores. www.wilton.com.

Table Linen

Indigo Seas   USA $–$$$$

Tablecloths from the fifties and all sorts of fun, silly, artistic, colorful and yummy stuff.

BEST BETS   The mix of Porthault linens and baby pillow cases with antique kitsch tabletop and beachy funky style in prices from $35 to $250. A visual feast.

WHERE TO BUY   123 N. Robertson Blvd., Los Angeles, CA. ☎ 310/550-8758. Mon–Fri 10am–6pm. AE, MC, V.

Le Jacquard Francais   FRENCH $$$$

As the name implies, this firm uses only the Jacquard loom to stitch in the designs of French lifestyle. Most patterns are two or three colors, Also sold in most French department stores, although the store has a large selection and an easy way to view the full cloth on a pole.

BEST BET   The table linens are available in many sizes, rich colors and patterns. Prices begin in the $20 range for small items and go way up for large tablecloths.

WEB TIPS   You'll find plenty of photos with product information on the website, but there's no online shopping available.

WHERE TO BUY   12 rue Chevalier de St. George, Paris 1er. ☎ 331/4297-4049. Mon–Sat 10am–7pm. MC, V. Métro: Madeleine. www.le-jacquard-francais.fr.

Lisa Corti   ITALIAN $$–$$$$

There is no one who dines at my table who does not appreciate the Lisa Corti linens set before them; no gift of Lisa Corti has met with less than enthusiastic tears of joy. Corti's linens are sold through Saks Fifth Avenue in the U.S., but her stores in Italy—which sell the whole range—are a delight to the soul and a colorful reminder that you can design with brights and still be sophisticated.

Lisa Corti prints.

There's some clothing, but it can make you look like you're wearing the, uh, table. I have several pieces and love them, but wear them with care in resort environments. The bed quilts and table linens are the masterpieces, as is the overall look of color gone wild and finished with rosebuds. You'll pay about $90 for a small tablecloth and $250 for a bed quilt. The dresses cost about $150.

BEST BETS   The large tablecloths in a swirl of bright colors and leopard spots, about $100 in Italy and $150 at Saks in the U.S.

WEB TIPS   The website is in English and Italian and gives you an immediate grasp of the look and philosophy. You cannot buy online.

WHERE TO BUY   Sold in Saks and through Saks Home catalog; 3 stores in Italy, assorted boutiques worldwide. **FLAGSHIP**   Via Conchetta 6, Milan. ☎ **39-2/58100031.** Other stores: via de Bardi 58, at the Ponte Vecchio, Florence. ☎ **39-055/2645600.** Via di Pallacorda 14, Rome. ☎ **39-06/68193216.** Sun–Sat 10am–2 pm, 3–7pm; closed Mon. www.lisacorti.com.

Tabletop

I've rarely met a set of dishes I didn't like or want to own. When I returned to the U.S. last year, I did an everyday set of rooster dishes mixed from various sets and patterns and pieces collected at Target and my off-price favorites and ended up with a dressy set of stoneware from Wedgwood to mix with the Heath and Armani Casa stonewares I had begun to collect before leaving France.

Astier de Villatte PARIS $$$

Rustic dishes with a raw edge, tabletop, serving pieces of all shapes, old-fashioned white wares and then a mix of items that come and go—gifts, sweaters, gloves, brooches, and more.

BEST BETS   Expect to pay $150 for a serving dish.

WEB TIPS   This is one of the most creative websites I've seen. Begin by clicking on the crystal ball on the home page, and then on "catalogue." To see dish details, click on the stack of dishes on the dining table. You can't order online, but you'll have lots of fun playing with the graphics.

WHERE TO BUY   2 stores: 99 rue du Bac, Paris, 7e. ☎ 331/4222-8159. Métro: rue du Bac. 173 rue Saint-Honore, Paris, 1er. ☎ 331/4260-7413. Métro: Palais Royal. Mon–Sat 10am–7pm. www.astierdevillatte.com.

blås&knåda STOCKHOLM $$$$

You don't have to walk far in Stockholm to find a store that sells glass; this is a gallery known for ceramics and for glasswares that are art forms but still useable in real life.

BEST BETS   Look at the paint can glasses made by Nilla Eneroth, beginning at $135 each.

WHERE TO BUY   1 store: Hornsgatan 26, Stockholm. ☎ 46/8642-7767. Tues–Fri 11am–6pm; Sat 11am–4pm; Sun noon–4pm. AE, MC, V. Subway: Sodermalm. www.blasknada.com.

Diners En Ville FRENCH $$$-$$$$

Have you ever been stopped in your tracks by the windows of a store that stunned you and then beckoned you inside? Such is this case with this small, two-room store on the Left Bank of Paris. Heavenly tabletop and all the pieces put together for you so you can Frenchify your *arts de table* and make Martha Stewart turn bleu, blanc and rouge with delight.

BEST BETS   Tablecloths from the best French makers in sophisticated colors with as many screens as an Hermès scarf, $200 to $400.

WHERE TO BUY   2 stores, in Paris and Lyon. 89 rue du Bac, Paris. ☎ 331/4222-7833. Mon–Sat 11am–7pm. AE, MC, V. Métro: rue du Bac. No website.

Heath SAUSALITO, CA $-$$$

Artist, ceramist and entrepreneur Edith Heath has passed on, but her tabletop and tile business remains—a tribute to Bay Area craftsmanship and an icon for those of the Russell Wright and 1950s matte-finish school of thought. The wares are often two tone—inside one shade and outside a contrasting or complementary shade. There is a slightly Zen feeling to the work. Prices are moderate at regular retail: A salad or serving bowl is $120; a teapot is $65; a dinner plate is $35.

BEST BETS   The good news: there's a small factory store on the premises in Sausalito and while you have to get lucky or be flexible, you will find that prices are about half of regular retail.

WEB TIPS   Factory store inventory is listed online, and there's a "quick ship" link under online shopping.

WHERE TO BUY   1 store: 400 Gate Five Rd., Sausalito, CA. ☎ 415/332-3722. Daily 10am–5pm. www.heathceramics.com.

Laguiole FRENCH $$–$$$

Laguiole (say lie-oul) is a city in southwestern France that is famous for its knives; think Limoges is to china as Laguiole is to knives. Except Limoges is fancy and Laguiole is known for the style of the handle and the quality of the cutting blade. Many, many firms make a Laguiole knife, although many are sold as if Laguiole was the brand name.

BEST BETS   The price for a set of six steak knives is $500.

WEB TIPS   The website makes ordering easy—it features large print, clear photos and quick links to all merchandise.

WHERE TO BUY   U.S. distribution is through a New Jersey firm that may make the knife in China, not France. Never mind. Also carried in all E.U. department stores and many small shops; all over southwestern France and in the town of Laguiole. www.laguiole.com.

Nymphenburg Porcelain GERMAN $$$$

Produced in a baroque palace factory near Munich, Nymphenburg porcelain is one of the most elegant, intricate and expensive lines in the world. The production process involves aging the porcelain mixture for up to 2 years, firing it at temperatures as high as 2,500 degrees and adorning each piece with the Bavarian coat of arms.

Known for their lifelike porcelain animals, the firm also produces tableware and accessories. Choices range from simple platters with brightly colored borders to place settings with images of Bavarian castles (or your castle) wrapped in antique brushed gold.

A lot goes into making Nymphenburg's animal figures which may justify the over-the-top prices; a hand-painted near life-size peacock statue will set you back over $23,000. For those on a more modest budget, a porcelain keychain costs $36.

BEST BETS   American designer Ted Muehling's contemporary collection features butterflies and insects, each hand painted and unique. Expect to pay upwards of $350 for one of his dessert/fruit plates.

WEB TIPS   The website is good for viewing the designs. There are no prices listed and you can't order online. If you're interested in buying, contact the Chicago showroom.

WHERE TO BUY   Nymphenburg Store, Odeonsplatz 1, Munich. ☎ **98938/849-949.** Mon–Fri 10am–6:30pm; Sat 10am–4pm. AE, MC, V. Nymphenburg USA by appointment only. 470 N. Milwaukee Ave., Chicago, IL. ☎ **312/421-3500.** Moss, 146 Green St., NYC. ☎ **866/888-6677.** Mon–Sat 11am–7pm; Sun noon–6pm. AE, MC, V. Also at Gump's, San Francisco; J. F. Chen, Los Angeles; and Bergdorf Goodman, NYC. www. nymphenburgusa.com. —*SRL*

Reidel AUSTRIAN $–$$$$

Famous not only for their stemware as "the" wineglass to be holding, but also champions of the stemless wineglass. Reidel was created 250 years ago in Bohemia when Bohemia was a place name—it is now in Austria but is actually a part of the world that has changed hands due to wars and politics. It was this glassmaker who determined that different wines required different shapes of glassware to be best enjoyed. Today they sell a large number of different shapes for everything from sparkling wine to after-dinner drinks.

BEST BETS   The glassware is relatively affordable so you might as well spring for the best. Usually sold in pairs of two, you can get stemless wineglasses for white wine for $16.

WEB TIPS   Site is packed with information and links and connections to stores and dealers. It even allows you to sign up for a factory tour in Austria and provides a map to the factory store.

WHERE TO BUY   Williams Sonoma in the U.S. A-5212 Schneegattern, Austria. ☎ **43/077-45-2307.** Mon–Fri 9am–5pm; Sat 9am–noon. MC, V. You can also find the wares on sale on various websites, including www.wineenthusiast.com and www. riedel.com.

Replacements, Ltd. GREENSBORO, NC $–$$$$

Walking into Replacements Ltd., is like going to Disneyland for dishes. The world's largest inventory of dishes rests here with a mere 2% showcased in the showroom. There's a tour every half hour, a lounge, restrooms, and free information to take away. There's even a stack of pens and fridge magnets. The help is enormously friendly and helpful. In the back is a small clearance corner; it's a heart-stopping destination.

The store sells more than dishes. They have china, crystal and silver as well as tabletop, Christmas ornaments and gift items. There's logo merchandise and silver polish, napkin rings and porcelain animals, even a free identification service and an entire research staff that can help you find the name and/or make of a pattern. There's everything except a cafe or a Starbucks.

BEST BETS   I fell in love with a 🛍 **Wedgwood** pattern called "Rattan" and paid full retail ($18 each) for four buttercup yellow plates because the soup bowls were on sale for $8.

WEB TIPS   This is the ultimate guide for china and tableware. You can add to your service, search for new patterns or register a wish list so they can contact you when goods become available.

WHERE TO BUY   1 store: Exit 132 off Interstate 85/40 between Burlington and Greensboro, NC. ☎ **900-REPLACE.** Daily 9:30am–6pm. www.replacements.com.

TableArt LOS ANGELES $$–$$$$

This is a small, seemingly simple store that you probably walk (or drive) by all the time. You have to go inside and study the wares to realize there are few stores more perfect than this for a wide selection of international tabletop.

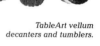

BEST BETS   Check out the unusual accessories, such as napkin rings with Swarovski crystals, resembling huge Cartier interlocking wedding rings; a set of four sells for $107.

TableArt vellum decanters and tumblers.

WEB TIPS   Search for patterns online or create an online registry. You can also purchase gift cards from the Web store.

WHERE TO BUY   1 store: 7977 Melrose Ave., LA. ☎ **323/653-8278.** Mon–Sat 10am–6pm; Sun (Dec only) noon–6pm. AE, MC, V. www.tartontheweb.com.

Thomas Goode & Co. LONDON $$$$

Thomas Goode is a veddy, veddy fancy tabletop shop in the heart of London's posh Mayfair district. They've been in business since 1827, 10 years before Queen Victoria began her reign. Since then, they've designed and sold bespoke fine-bone china, as well as china, crystal and silver from other high-end manufacturers such as Daum, Puiforcat and Baccarat. They also carry a good selection of Herend animal figurines. Don't miss the linen section, where you'll find hand-embroidered Belgian, Irish and Italian tablecloths, placemats and napkins.

It's a treat to stroll through this store, which is comprised of a series of parlors, each more elegant than the previous. There's also a museum room displaying exquisite china patterns used by the world's royal families.

BEST BETS   The variety and selection contribute to the magic of this shop. On my last visit, I wanted to buy some guest soaps in a beautiful gift box.

WEB TIPS   The website's every bit as fancy as the store, but not nearly as much fun as a personal visit. Don't miss this store when you visit London.

WHERE TO BUY   1 store: 19 S. Audley, London, W1. ☎ 207/499-2823. Mon–Sat 10am–6pm. AE, MC, V. No nearby tube. www.thomasgoode.co.uk.

Carocim FRENCH $$–$$$$

You can order a catalog, you can buy this brand in design shops all over the world (especially in France) or you can go to the showroom. While tile is a difficult souvenir to bring home, you might find it worthwhile once you learn about French cement tiles, which have a matte finish and are imprinted with geometrics or designs.

Cement tiles were popular in Europe in the mid-1800s and into the 20th century; any old middle-class building in Paris (especially residential) has a cement tile floor at least at the entry. The tiles could not be retrieved whole, so the old ones are mostly lost. Carocim makes new tiles in the old manner. Some of the patterns are reproductions of old favorites; others are new and some are even bold and bright.

WEB TIPS   Examples and suggested pattern layouts are featured online. If you can't make it to France, you can get some great ideas from this website.

Tiles in Delores de Hidalgo, Mexico

Rustic Mexican-style tiles can easily be found all over the Southwestern portions of the U.S. and successfully ordered online. But if you want the adventure of a lifetime, head to the village of **Delores de Hidalgo** outside San Miguel de Allende, where you can go to factories and buy tiles for about $25 per square meter. That's about 90 tiles, which is all you will be able to carry with you anyway. Use a rollerboard; do not check. Tiles are made of earthenware and will crack in extreme weather or break inside luggage. Go to www.internetsanmiguel.com.

WHERE TO BUY   FLAGSHIP   This French firm is located outside of Aix-en-Provence, 1515 route du Puy Sainte Reparade. ☎ **334/ 4292-2039.** Tues–Fri 2:30–6:30pm. MC, V. www.carocim.com.

Heath SAUSALITO, CA $$ - $$$$

See listing on p. 348.

Sant' Anna Tile Factory PORTUGUESE $–$$$$

Portuguese *azulejos,* hand-painted tiles, were used as ballast on the ships that left the port of Lisbon during the Age of Discovery. You can buy your own at many stores in Lisbon—in new or used condition. This tile factory sells faience of all sorts and tiles by the unit, or the fresco. The painting is very fine—in terms of the actual brush strokes—and may not be as rustic as some people like. They also use many colors, not just blue and white.

BEST BETS   The frescoes, which come in a variety of sizes, around $300 for a small one. Single tiles range in price from $9 to $14.

WHERE TO BUY   FLAGSHIP   95 rua do Alecrim, 95 Chiado, Lisbon. ☎ **351/342-2537.** Mon–Fri 9am–2pm; Sat 10am–2pm. No credit cards.

Solar PORTUGUESE $$–$$$$$

While these guys have a showroom in Manhattan and it's excellent, if in Lisbon do not miss the opportunity to stop at their mother store, in the Upper City in the midst of a row of antiques stores. They sell only antique tiles. It is a little dusty, but you will be pumping so much adrenaline that you won't care. The house specialty is antique blue-and-white tiles. They are sold individually, in groups and sometimes in frescoes.

BEST BETS   You can buy a 15th-century Ottoman tile mural for $20,000 or individual 1930s Art Deco tiles for about $40 each.

WHERE TO BUY   FLAGSHIP   Avenida Dom Pedro v, Biarro Alto, Lisbon. ☎ **21/346-55-22.** Hours vary; call ahead and then ring the bell for entry.

Tierra y Fuego SAN DIEGO $

Mexican tiles conveniently already across the border in San Diego/Chula Vista; little earthenware squares in the tradition we all know and love in the usual colors: blue, green, ochre and white in a million different combinations and styles with a rustic kind of glaze.

Patterns are either classical or modern, such as cubes that make the tiles jump in front of your eyes. The warehouse ships. A case of tiles equals 1 square meter, which most Americans do not know how to calculate—it's about 90 tiles. Often prices are lower if you buy by the case. The showroom is in an industrial park that is not easy to find. If you get to the Rio Grande, you went a little too far.

BEST BETS   Top quality, endless selection and great pricing. Tiles cost between $1 and $2 each.

WEB TIPS   Detailed instructions on the home page for placing orders, excellent graphics.

WHERE TO BUY   Showroom: 8785 Dead Stick Rd., San Diego, CA. ☎ **619/710-8885.** Mon–Fri 8am–3pm. AE, MC, V. www.tierrayfuego.com.

Tubs & Towels

Acquatonica by Franco Sargiani for Fantini Spa
ITALIAN $$$$$

Fantini is a family-run business toward the north of Italy (main office in Pella, in Piedmont); they contract various Italian designers to make kitchen and bathroom fixtures.

BEST BETS   Their most famous product is a bathtub named Acquatonica, designed by Franco Sargiani.

WEB TIPS   Search for products by designer or category. No prices are given and you can't order online.

WHERE TO BUY   www.fantini.it.

Edition 2 by Philippe Starck FRENCH $$$$$

While I have long been a personal fan of French architect turned designer/bad boy/cult hero Philippe Starck, I do not basically like modern or even moderne. Imagine my surprise when I did a hotel inspection some years ago and went starck raving bonkers for a freestanding, oval bath tub. I was told it was the newest from Philippe Starck and so I was instantly converted to someone who thinks the man's bathroom designs are among the best in the world.

Starck does various tubs; some are freestanding and others are drop-in style. Sir Norman Foster does a tub very similar to the Starck model I like so much, proving that even genius bathes. The Starck tub is very large—yes, large enough for two adults—and allows one to be submerged in water, which Starck himself considers to be the main pleasure of the bath in the first place.

Although Philippe Starck enjoys taking an everyday object and making it his, he is also involved in the latest technology in tub renewal—one of his models includes an exterior light switch that refracts light into the tub and makes the water appear to be colored—this is meant to soothe, energize or appropriately modify the mood.

I did try to price the Starck Edition 2 tub when I did my bathroom in San Antonio, Texas. I went to the fanciest bathroom supply wholesaler in town and asked if they could get me a Philippe Starck tub. "Who?" they asked.

BEST BETS $5,625 to $6,562 for the freestanding models.

WEB TIPS   Search for Hoesch Philippe Starck to find the tub.

WHERE TO BUY   To price and order, go to www.hoesch.de, the German maker of many of Starck's tubs. *Note:* the German word for bathtub is *badekar*. Also available at www.quality bath.com.

Kohler USA $$–$$$$

This plumbing design firm has been fashion forward but not over the top for many years and has just boldly stepped out of the bathroom to open their first retail store showcasing their hardware and plumbing products. Located in LuxeHome at the Chicago Merchandise Mart, the store is interactive—you can flush as many toilets as you like or even wash that man right outta your hair. Everything you need to renovate, create or merely replace in your bathroom is available in this chic and spacious 7,000-square-foot space. There's over 300 products on display, including tubs and sinks with running water. The displays are arranged by product, so it's easy to compare all the basins, tubs and fixtures without running from group to group.

The seven NKBA-trained sales associates have collectively consulted on over 1,000 bath and kitchen projects and will assist you with planning, purchasing and installation. Services run the gamut from a simple sink replacement to detailed planning for a complete renovation or add-on bath. They'll work with you individually or in tandem with your architect and designer.

BEST BETS   Great tubs and sinks for the price. Retail prices for tubs range from $300 to $1,200, pedestal sinks $500 to $1,500 and kitchen faucets begin at around $500. Pricing is 20% off retail to the public, with additional discounts available to the trade. Most fixtures and tiles are in stock; however, if you need to special order, the lead time is usually less than 3 weeks.

WEB TIPS   I find the website somewhat confusing. You must click through numerous links to find specific products, and then select them from room settings. However, you may get some design ideas while you search.

WHERE TO BUY   100 Merchandise Mart, Chicago, IL. ☎ **312/ 755-2510.** Mon–Fri 9am–5pm; Sat 10am–3pm. AE, MC, V. www.TheKohlerStore.com. —*SRL*

Water Monopoly BRITISH $$$–$$$$

British firm that restores antique tubs and also makes reproductions. Sometimes they do something a little wacky to an old tub—like paint it, insert portholes and so forth.

BEST BETS   The French copper tubs are *très chic,* also *très cher.* Plan to spend around $10,000.

WEB TIPS   There's limited information about the tubs on both websites. If you're a serious buyer, you'll want to call for an appointment to test your tub.

WHERE TO BUY   Available in the U.S. through Martin Lane. ☎ **310/274-1231.** www.watermonopoly.com or www.martin lanebaths.com.

Waterworks USA $$–$$$$$

As luxe as any to-the-trade-only showroom, Waterworks stores have that aura of designer talent that makes mere mortals feel they have come to bathe not in a new tub but the River Ganges of bathroom design. Using international sources,

Waterworks creates their own product and supplies all things bathing in order to make the bathroom a singular, visual statement. They sell wholesale and retail, with 40 stores dotted around the U.S. If you cannot get to a store, you can order or download the catalog and a separate price list.

The store provides everything you need for the bathroom, from apothecary (bathing products) to valves (shower valves). Everything is very good looking and sleek; products are regularly featured in home decor magazines—the brand is a favorite of editors at *O at Home*.

When it comes to tubs, there's everything from an old-fashioned copper-plated tub to freestanding and drop-in styles. Freestanding can come with or without claw feet; in fact there are retro styles as well as the most modern of fixtures.

BEST BETS   The bathtub selection can make you drool enough saliva to fill said tub. Tub prices range from $3,500 to $8,000.

WEB TIPS   Suggested retail prices are shown on the website; no online orders.

WHERE TO BUY   50 stores in US. **FLAGSHIP**   225 E. 57th St., NYC. ☎ **212/371-9266.** Mon–Fri 9am–6pm; Sat 11am–5pm. Subway: 59th St. AE, DISC, MC, V. www.waterworks.com.

Yard Goods

Cath Kidston BRITISH $–$$$

If you don't need a gimmick to succeed, you sure need a strong design perspective, which is what Cath Kidston brought the world when she began doing her own contempo version of 1950s kitchen prints in textiles and home style.

BEST BETS   This is one of the few sources for fashionable oilcloth ($40/meter). I love the birds, the strawberries, the roses; swatches are available.

WEB TIPS   Enter the Web name carefully. www.cathkidston. com.

WHERE TO BUY FLAGSHIP   Michelin House, 81 Fulham Rd., SW3 London. ☎ **4420/7589-7401.** Mon–Sat 10am–6pm; Sun noon–5pm. AE, MC, V; Tube: Parson's Green. NYC: Mulberry St., between Kenmare and Spring. ☎ **212/343-0223.** Mon–Sat 11am–7pm; Sun noon–6pm. AE, MC, V. Subway: Spring St.

Outlet in Bicester Village, Oxfordshire, see p. 431. www.cath kidston.co.uk.

Jim Thompson THAI $–$$$

Top-notch wholesale and retail silk from a company with a quirky backstory. See listing on p. 48.

Marimekko FINNISH $–$$$

This Finnish graphics textile designer has had ups and downs in fashion, being extremely well known in the pop-art sixties

A fabric swatch from Marimekko.

and then fading from view in the American scene although never dropping out of Europe. Known for the use of stripes, bold graphics and bright colors, the Marimekko line consists of yard goods as well as clothing, home style and accessories. There are outlet stores outside of Helsinki and on the grounds of the factories and workshops, as well as some six other outlet stores in Finland.

BEST BETS   Fanciful fabrics that work well with minimalist and retro styles.

WEB TIPS   The online catalog is a series of beautiful full-page photos; no Web orders.

WHERE TO BUY   25 stores in Finland, 1 in Sweden, 2 in U.S. (1 in South Beach, FL.) **FLAGSHIP**   31 Esplanade, Helsinki. Mon–Fri 10am–8pm; Sat 10am–3pm. AE, MC, V. Cambridge, MA: 350 Huron Ave. ☎ **617/354-2800.** Mon–Wed, Fri–Sat 10am–6pm; Thurs 10am–7pm. AE, MC, V. www.marimekko.com.

Silk Trading Co. USA $–$$$

This is one of my favorite chains in the world because they look and function like a design showroom with more fabric selections than you can begin to imagine, but they cater to the public. While the bulk of the floor space is devoted to bolts of fabric, there are ready-made drapes and some accessories whipped up in their fabrics (tote bags, pillows, and so on). There's also always a bargain corner.

They will come to your home, measure and do the work for you; or you can wander in and choose from an international bevy of fabrics. There are stores in every major U.S. market;

there's also a store within ABC Carpet in Manhattan. Prices are very close to wholesale since the yard goods come directly from the mills—expect to pay $50 to $75 a yard for interesting silk.

You can order from the website, but try to visit a store, if possible. The Web photos are small, which makes it difficult to visualize large panels.

BEST BETS   Drapery panels at about $100.

WEB TIPS   There's always an online sale underway, and shipping is free on orders over $500.

WHERE TO BUY   6 stores: Los Angeles, New York, San Francisco, Atlanta, Dallas, Greenwich, CT; also ABC stores (p. 36). **FLAGSHIP** 360 S. La Brea Ave., Los Angeles, CA. ☎ **800/854-0396** and **323/954-9280.** Mon–Fri 9am–6pm; Sat 9am–5pm. AE, DISC, MC, V. www.silktrading.com.

Chapter Ten

Cooking & Foodstuffs

*W*hen pizza first came to America it was called "pizza pie." The entire slogan was used, as if we didn't know a pizza from an apple pie. In those days, there was only one kind of Chinese food (shrimp with lobster sauce). Hunan and Szechuan were the sounds you made when you sneezed. Most had never heard of Thai food or Asian fusion—or even knew where Vietnam was, or what pho soup tasted like.

I don't need to tell you how different the world and the supermarket are now. Yes, the melting pot of immigration has sped us to discover new tastes, but so have travel and the media. These days, the best travel magazines are food-related magazines; our children grow up eating sushi and sashimi; there's a United Nations of choices in supermarkets and gourmet markets—which continue to do a huge business in exotic tastes. Americans have been starving for crunch and flavor and variety. They seek it everywhere and then discuss it—over dinner, of course.

Fine cooking is 10% talent and 90% ingredients.

—Alain Ducasse

Already most cookbooks come with a resource list to tell you where to find the ingredients needed. All you need do is go shopping before you step up to the plate.

Food Classes & Tours

It's not hard to find cookbook authors, restaurateurs or foodies who lead tours or know someone who gives classes in a villa in Italy or tours markets from their chateau in France. The classes below are the ones I can vouch for (I came, I saw, I cooked) and are geared for entry-level civilians.

Central Market Food Classes TEXAN $$–$$$

Central Market is the gourmet food division of the Texas supermarket chain HEB. They have their own food specialist and cooking class program, held in all of their stores dotted around Texas. Most classes sit 30 people and sell out quickly. Classes cost anywhere from $30 to $75 and usually last for 3 hours. You get a printout with recipes and lots to eat; also water, coffee and a notepad.

Often the classes are taught by visiting firemen who are on book tours with their latest cookbook. They sell the books and do signings before and/or after the class. I attended two different classes: one with Dorie Greenspan and one with George Geary. In both cases, the classes were driven by the charming personalities of the guests, so we all had a lot of fun.

This is the best series of classes because the firm produces each as if it were a mini-show business adventure. There's a lot of value, a lot to be learned and a very smooth experience to be shared. Don't miss kids' cooking camp.

WEB TIPS   You can get the list of classes online before the brochure gets to your mailbox.

WHERE TO BOOK   6 markets, throughout Texas. www.central market.com.

Chef's Holidays YOSEMITE NATIONAL PARK $$$$

The classes are just what they are named—well-known chefs are invited to "vacation" for a 3-day stint in the kitchens of the Ahwahnee Hotel in Yosemite National Park. As the guest you have cocktails, go to demos, have a lesson or two, do some tastings and attend a gala dinner. There are usually three chefs for each event and eight to ten different events offered during January and February of each year. One of the events is a promotion with *Food + Wine Magazine.*

There's actually no charge for the demos, so you can stay elsewhere and just drop in. Price depends on your hotel choice: If you stay at Ahwahnee, it's about $1,000 a person but if you stay at the Yosemite Lodge, it's half that.

WEB TIPS   The official websites are very confusing; I was much happier at www.fabuloustravel.com, which told me everything I needed to know.

WHERE TO BOOK   www.yosemitepark.com or www.national parkreservations.com.

Faith Willinger FLORENCE $$$$

An American living in Italy—famous for her articles in major U.S. food magazines as well as what is considered the best book in any language on Italian food resources—Faith also does one-day classes in Florence.

First thing, Faith teaches you how to use the espresso machine. One-day events cost $570. You can do a market tour for $285 with Faith's assistant, Jennifer.

WEB TIPS   Click on "market-to-table" for tour info.

WHERE TO BOOK   www.faithwillinger.com.

Four Seasons Hotel CHIANG MAI, THAILAND $$$

Although I went to Chiang Mai for the shopping, what turned out to be the hit of the trip was the cooking lesson that included a tour of the downtown food market and then lessons and preparation of six different dishes. What made the class extraordinary is that first you watched the chef do it, then you went to your own station and made it yourself. Better still, the dishes could easily be made back home and I stunned friends and family with my ability to Thai one on. The class lasts 6 hours and costs $200.

Note: I hear that the Mandarin Oriental Dhara Dhevi resort, also in Chiang Mai, has a similar class. Next trip I book that. You can also find similar cooking classes at other Four Seasons hotels, each tailored to the location.

WEB TIPS   After you book the resort and cooking lessons, book a spa, too.

WHERE TO BOOK   ☎ **6653/298-181.** www.fourseasons.com/chiangmai.

George Geary Classes & Tours USA $$–$$$$$

George Geary is technically a pastry chef, but frankly, I find him a stand-up cooking comic. He's a warm and funny guy who got his start as the pastry chef for Mickey Mouse and then left Disneyland to become a global guy, teaching glasses in over 100 different schools around the U.S. and leading tours to major U.S. cities and some European destinations. He has also opened a school in his home base area of Orange County, California. Here he teaches 3-hour classes that range from "World of Chocolates" ($55) to "Thanksgiving Dinner Sides" ($65) to "The Great Cupcake Caper" ($95), a hands-on course.

He also gives tours in cities such as L.A., Chicago and New Orleans; day tours ($150) have only six people so you get lots of attention. The weekend food trips ($600–$800) have about 45 people so they are less cozy but you get to eat a lot.

WEB TIPS   The site is nice but doesn't give the details I wanted—so I wrote him. You can, too. George sent me a personal e-mail the next day with answers.

WHERE TO BOOK   ☎ **951/277-2858.** george@georgegeary.com. www.georgegeary.com.

Food Shows & Festivals

Food shows are part party, part tasting and part shopping expedition. They invariably lead to the inspiration that creates a memorable meal. As for best of show, or a whole lot of food fun, there are local gimmick food festivals held all over the world,

A model dons a chocolate dress and guitar at Paris' Salon du Chocolat.

often for publicity, but maybe to add a little energy to an otherwise dull season. One of my favorites is the **Annual Cheese Rolling** in Stilton, UK (www.stilton.org).

In some cases, a show appears to be a professional event (for which you'll need an appropriate industry business card), but is actually a big bash for consumers. Such is the case with the **Chocolate Show** (www.salondu chocolat.fr) held in Paris each winter and in New York each November. You pay about $20 admission and then work your way around exhibits. You'll find lots of small quarter-sized samples plus larger samples and boxes to buy. Then consider **Eurochocolate** (www.euro chocolate.com), an Italian show, in Perugia (of course).

Also check out various food competitions that often feature events and sampling: Gilroy (California) has an infamous **Garlic Festival** (www.gilroygarlicfestival.com), while the **Pillsbury Bake-Off** (www.pillsburybakeoff.com) has become a national media event. Who hasn't dreamed of a trip to Munich for **Oktoberfest** (www.oktoberfest.de)?

Should you be more interested in wines than foodstuffs, the two leading (trade) wine events are **Vinitaly** in Verona, Italy, and **Wine Expo,** held every other year in Bordeaux, France. In the States, you'll find the **Nantucket Wine Festival** (www.nantucketwinefestival.com), and the **Aspen Food + Wine Classic** (www.foodandwine.com/promo/classic).

To find more international food and wine festivals, try **www. foodreference.com**, **www.localwineevents.com**, **www.official winery.com** (U.S. only), and Frommer's **http://events.frommers. com**.

Food & Farmers' Markets

Austin Farmers Market (AFM) TEXAN $

With Whole Foods at its flagship in Austin, it wasn't a far stretch to get a local farmers' market going, this adjacent to Whole Foods each Saturday and Wednesday year-round.

BEST BETS   Local farmers sell regional fare, fruits, veggies, honey, peppers, flowers from the Hill Country, artisanial breads and even fresh-made kolaches, as this part of Texas has a lot of German and Eastern European immigrants who have passed down recipes for generations.

WEB TIPS   No website for the market, but you are near the Four Seasons Austin and the concierge knows everything.

WHERE TO BUY   AFM at Whole Foods, Lamar at 6th St., Austin. Sat 9am–1pm; Wed 8:30am–1pm.

Borough Market LONDON $

It's a good market for tourists and even for children, and is walking distance from London Bridge, The Tower and other attractions. The market's motto is, "If we don't sell it, perhaps it's not worth eating."

BEST BETS   The market is in a part of town called Southwark (say Suttack) and features cooked and fresh foods and pro-duce, a few vendors who come over from France for the day, some wine merchants and even a few potters and publishers.

WEB TIPS   The weekly newsletter is online.

WHERE TO BUY   8 Southwark St., London SE1. ☎ 4420/7407-1002. Thurs 11am–5pm; Fri noon–6pm; Sat 9am–4pm. Tube: London Bridge. www.boroughmarket.org.uk.

Ferry Building Marketplace & Farmers' Market
SAN FRANCISCO $

First, you have to understand the historical relationship between San Francisco, its love affair with chefs and their inter-est in locally grown ingredients. The interior of the landmark

Sarah Goes to the Fancy Food Show

Every year, over 2,000 food manufacturers gather at the NASFT Fancy Food Show to present and promote new foods and beverages with hopes that they'll be snatched up by specialty food buyers. This is a trade show; you need food trade creds.

Here's the lowdown:

- Salt is big. I tasted salts from South America, Asia, Europe and the U.S. **Coastal Goods of Massachusetts** (www.coastalgoods.com) offers lavender, cucumber and mushroom flavored salts. **Hawaii Kai** (www.hawaiikaico.com) makes three grades, Gourmet, Pal Island Premium, with Soul of the Sea being top of the line. **Le Saunier de Camargue** (www.amazon.com) was promoting their sea salt from Provence; this was my favorite. **Saltworks of Seattle**'s (www.saltworks.us) display of cork-topped glass bottles filled with pastel salts caught my eye. The white, pink and black salts' intensity is dependent on mineral content.

- Teas are hot (and cold), and outnumbered coffees 4 to 1 at the show. **Republic of Tea**'s Luna (www.republicoftea.com) is being marketed to women, offering flavors such as lemon blueberry and vanilla macadamia, both vitamin enhanced. A "cleansing" brew from **Harney & Sons** (www.harney.com) is flavored with vanilla and grapefruit. At 5 calories per cup, try the chocolate-infused green tea from **Mighty Leaf** (www.mightyleaf.com)—it's perfect for dessert. My favorite was the Chinese jasmine tea from **Te Tea** (www.teteas.com), where an olive-size tea ball blooms into a visually striking fragrant flower in boiling water.

Ferry Building contains some food stalls, restaurants and stores selling food-related merchandise, such as a branch of **Sur La Table** (p. 343). While the indoor vendors and restaurants are open throughout the week, the place really pops on Saturdays with the outdoor market, chef tours, cooking classes and a circus of food-related events. Smaller markets are held on Tuesdays, Thursdays and Sundays, but you really want to visit on Saturday.

BEST BETS   In good weather, you'll start to think the five people you meet in heaven will all be farmers.

WEB TIPS   Check the website for chef appearances.

WHERE TO BUY   Ferry Building, San Francisco. ☎ 415/693-0996. Sat 8am–2pm. www.ferrybuildingmarketplace.com.

- Water is on the wave. There were enough water vendors to create a small flood. All waters are now enhanced with natural flavors, antioxidants and/or energy boosters. I tried **Hint**'s (www.drinkhint.com) cucumber water (yum) as well as the peppermint (yuck). **Essn** (www.drinkessn.com) is producing vitamin enhanced, lightly carbonated, all-natural fruit-flavored sodas; the Meyer lemon and pomegranate were winners. **Vignette-water** (www.winecountrysoda.com) is flavored with juice from wine grapes including pinot noir and cabernet, all sugar free.
- Chocolate is changing. The reinvention of chocolate had everyone buzzing. Like fine wines, chocolate varietals abound, all boasting neutraceuticals; chocolate is now health food, thank goodness. **Theo** (www.theochocolate.com) roasts certified organic cocoa beans from Venezuela, the Ivory Coast, Ecuador, Panama and Ghana, while **Dagoba** (www.dogoba chocolate.com) organic chocolates are enhanced with nutritional foods—Tibetan Goji berries and turmeric spice. The best was Monrovia's **Choctal** ice cream (www.choctal.com). Each pint is made with a different varietal bean. You can also buy regional chocolate ice cream from San Dominica, Indonesia and Costa Rica.

In its own category—the best ever: **collagen marshmallows** from Japan (www.eiwamm.co.jp). Yeah, each marshmallow contains 3,000mg of collagen; they're available in fruit flavors and claim to be better for your face than Botox. —*Sarah Lahey*

Greenmarket, Union Square NYC $

Vendors sell all kinds of fruits and veggies, cheeses, wines and ciders, and even flowers. It is simply heaven . . . although I'm not sure if heaven is this crowded on a Saturday.

BEST BETS   While the market is held Monday, Wednesday, Friday and Saturday year-round, it is a tad sparse in the winter months. Saturday is always the busiest day. There's not too much in the way of prepared foods, but there are baked goods and quiches.

WEB TIPS   There's lots of eco-tips on the website.

WHERE TO BUY Union Sq., NYC. Mon, Wed, Fri and Sat 8am–6pm. Broadway, between 14th and 17th sts. Subway: Union Sq. www.cenyc.org/greenmarket.

La Boqueria Mercat BARCELONA $

La Boqueria market is the largest and most touristy of Barcelona's food markets, offering the area's highest-quality produce—a visual feast that will leave you drooling. You'll find fresh seafood, tropical fruit, sausages and Serrano ham, cheeses, meats, dried nuts, breads and vegetables. Freshly squeezed juices are ready to drink in icy cups. There are several small bars where you can stop for a snack, beer or cup of coffee. The building itself is wrought iron and a historical landmark; located on the main tourist drag of Las Ramblas.

BEST BETS You can do all your shopping for gifts and your eating in one place.

WEB TIPS You can actually see each and every stand in the market on the website.

WHERE TO BUY La Boqueria Mercat, 100 Las Ramblas, Barcelona. ☎ **34933/027-260.** www.boqueria.info.

Dane County Market MADISON, WI $

The Dane County Farmers' Market is the largest producer-only farmers' market in the country; all products are Wisconsin-grown. Don your cheesehead now, please. In addition to the season's best bounty of vegetables and flowers, you'll find specialty products such as maple syrup, honey and candies.

BEST BETS Arts and crafts vendors are located in a side section; live music adds to the festivities.

WEB TIPS Seasonal specialties are listed online.

WHERE TO BUY County Courthouse Sq., Madison, WI. ☎ **608/455-1999.** May through October, Sat 6:30am–2pm; Wed 10am–2pm. The Winter Market's times and dates vary. www.madfarmmkt.org.

Marin County Farmers' Market SAN RAFAEL, CA $

The third largest farmers' market in the state, and this is the state once called the land of fruits and nuts. You will have the time of your life—especially when the weather is perfect. There's over 150 stands selling organic produce, prepared gourmet food to go, flowers and baked goods, with live entertainment on hand.

BEST BETS   There's an artisan section with up to 40 juried craftspeople on any given Sunday (with scaled-down version on Thursday mornings).

WEB TIPS   Chef demos and weekly specials are listed on the website.

WHERE TO BUY   Marin County Civic Center. From San Rafael, take North San Pedro exit off Highway 101 follow the signs east. ☎ **800/897-3276.** Sun and Thurs 8am–1pm. www.marin countyfarmersmarkets.org.

Pike Place Market SEATTLE $

Spread out over 9 acres, "The Market," as the Seattle locals affectionately say, is home to 200 year-round commercial businesses, 190 craftspeople and 120 farmers who rent table space by the day. It's also right downtown.

BEST BETS   As you shop for local produce and fresh flowers, you'll be entertained by street performers and able to stand in line for a look at the original Starbucks.

WEB TIPS   Click for food demos and auctions.

WHERE TO BUY   Pike Place/1st Ave., Seattle. Open 7 days a week. Closed Thanksgiving, Christmas, and New Year's Day. Mon–Sat 10am–6pm (some vendors open as early as 8); Sun 11am–5pm. No credit cards. www.pikeplacemarket.com.

Reading Terminal Market PHILADELPHIA $

There are more authentic Pennsylvania Dutch markets, but they aren't as convenient as this one in Philadelphia, right near all the tourist attractions and very easy for your children to see, smell and taste. This could be classified as family entertainment.

BEST BETS   I admit that this market has gotten a tad glitzy in the past 20 years; it is, alas, a TT (tourist trap). But there are still Amish vendors and there is still early morning, country-style breakfast to make you remember the good old days. The market first opened in 1893 and does have a lot of history behind it.

WEB TIPS   Check online for events including author appearances and food festivals.

WHERE TO BUY   51 N. 12th St. at Arch, Philadelphia. ☎ **215/ 922-2317.** Mon–Sat 8am–6pm; Sun 9am–4pm. www.reading terminalmarket.org.

Food Halls/Department Stores

David Jones SYDNEY $–$$

David Jones is the fanciest department store in Sydney; the food hall/grocery store is a little hard to find as you go into the basement, through a food court and then back into the store and its grocery—but the food court thing throws you for a few seconds. Press on because it's worth it.

This is a wonderful store with assorted cafes and food stations, cooked foods, fresh foods and zillions of spices culled from all over Australia. There are a lot of British imports, so you can stock up on old friends, and there's lot of new things to bring home and play with.

WHERE TO BUY   86–108 Castlereagh St., Sydney. ☎ **612/9266-5544.** Mon–Wed and Fri 9:30am–6pm; Thurs 9:30am–9pm; Sat 9am–6pm; Sun 10am–6pm. AE, MC, V. www.davidjones.com.au.

Fortnum & Mason LONDON $–$$

This 300-year-old firm just reopened after a $50-million refurb. While the upper floors have been transformed into a classy gift shop (you can find beautiful antique china), the food hall has been expanded into the basement, so there's now two floors of gourmet teas, sweets, jams, meats and fish, along with dishes-to-go prepared by on-site chefs. There's a new wine bar and fancy ice cream parlor. The famed Fountain restaurant has been revamped and expanded.

BEST BETS   Buy lemon or lime or orange curd, $8 a jar.

WHERE TO BUY   1 store: 181 Piccadilly, London W1. ☎ **44-20/7734-8040.** Mon–Sat 10am–6:30pm; Sun noon–6pm. Fountain Restaurant, Mon–Sat 8:30am–8pm. AE, MC, V. Tube: Piccadilly. www.fortnumandmason.com.

Harrods Food Halls LONDON $–$$$

I do not think Harrods is one of the best stores in the world, forgive me. I do think the best part of the store is the Food Hall, which is extraordinary. It is visually appealing and merchandised as a destination; there are a few restaurants and cafes attached directly to the food halls.

BEST BETS   The edible luxuries go on for rooms; the Stilton selection of cheese is in itself monumental and yes, it is legal to bring Stilton back into the U.S. or just about anywhere because it is aged so long.

WEB TIPS   You cannot do your grocery shopping online but you can order gift hampers, which are especially popular at Christmas, during The Season and for expats stationed abroad.

WHERE TO BUY   1 store: 87 Brompton Rd., London. Tube: Knightsbridge. www.harrods.com.

Lafayette Gourmet FRENCH $–$$

Lafayette Gourmet is a small chain of upmarket grocery stores dotted around France and usually adjacent to the parent store Galeries Lafayette. The flagship, as part of the flagship Galeries Lafayette store, is upstairs over Lafayette Homme, the department store's men's store.

> **World Traveler**
> Lafayette Gourmet has a small supermarket in CDG Airport for travelers looking for fine French foods to take home.

Shop or eat here; there are seven different eating stations distributed throughout the market. On Thursday evenings, singles are invited to shop here, pick up a purple shopping basket and therefore indicate to other single shoppers that they are available for chat . . . or more.

BEST BETS   The selection of gourmet products right in the thick of tourist land.

WEB TIPS   On the website, click on "Services" for more on Lafayette Gourmet.

WHERE TO BUY   Throughout France. **FLAGSHIP** Lafayette Gourmet, 40 blvd. Haussmann, Paris 9e. ☎ **331/4282-3456.** Mon–Wed, Fri–Sat 9:30am–7:30pm; Thurs 9:30am–9pm. AE, MC, V. Métro: Harve Caumartin. www.galerieslafayette.com.

L'Épicerie PARIS $–$$$

This may be the best department store supermarket in the world. It's very expensive, but you can consider it a museum. Every French gourmet specialty is sold here—breads, pastries, salts, fresh fruits and vegetables, meats and fish and cheese. Did someone say cheese? There is a cafe and a sandwich bar. I suggest you buy all your souvenirs of Paris here—you can get salt, fruit *sirops* and many goodies for not much money. Of course, there's also a wine and champagne department at which things are, uh, *cher.*

BEST BETS   At check out you have the choice between using plastic bags or buying your own carry-all and therefore saving the earth. I think their tote bag is very cute. It costs $12, but I feel ever so clever when I walk through an airport with it as my travel carry-on.

WEB TIPS   The website is in French. *C'est ça.*

WHERE TO BUY   24 Rue de Sèvres, Paris 7e. ☎ **331/4439-8100.**
Mon–Sat 8:30am–9pm. Métro: Sevres-Babylone. www.la
grandeepicerie.fr.

Paprika tins at the Budapest Central Market.

Central Market Hall

BUDAPEST $

Budapest's Central Market Hall (Központi Vásárcsarnok) is conveniently located right at the river's edge so that your cruise ship or barge may tie up alongside it. The market building is fairly large, comprised of two floors. The second floor is a mezzanine with tourist souvenirs for sale.

BEST BETS   The main floor is the market and the best place to buy local paprika of all kinds; prices begin at $3.

WHERE TO BUY   Bridgehead of Liberty Bridge, Pest, Fovam ter. ☎ **36/1-21-0052.** Tram nos. 2, 2A, 47, and 49. Bus no. 15. City and trolleybus no. 83, stop Fovam ter.

Stockmann's FINNISH $–$$

Stockmann's grocery store isn't a supermarket; it's an icon for anyone going in and out of Russia or for the homesick who are looking for traditional European and American tastes. This market is filled with the brands you can't find elsewhere as well as foods to cook and already prepared foods.

BEST BETS   Even if you just want a nice picnic while you are in town, this is a must-do stop—the department store is located in the thick of the tourist and main street shopping.

WEB TIPS   Only locals can order groceries online.

WHERE TO BUY   7 stores in Finland. Aleksanterinkatu 52B.
☎ **358-9-1212.** Mon–Fri 9am–9pm; Sat 9am–6pm; Sun noon–7pm. ☎ **358/9-121-3606.** www.stockmann.fi.

Tokyo Department Store Food Halls

Who knows the price of Tokyo roses when cantaloupes can cost $30? I know this because I often hang out in the grocery store and supermarket departments of the big-name Japanese department stores. Their food halls are filled with exotics so unusual to this island nation that they are considered status symbols. To bring a pricey melon as a house gift is the ultimate expression. Markets are usually in the lower level of department stores, or "depachika" ("depaato" = department store; "chika" = basement). They offer a heavy-duty testing and sampling program so many people like to visit these grocery stores at lunch time to try to make a meal of it. What's exotic here may be ho-hum to you or you may find something odd or delish—even collagen marshmallows. Major department stores include **Mitsukoshi,** 1-4-1 Nihombashi Muromachi (☎ **813/ 3241-3311**), **Matsuzakaya,** 6-10-1 Ginza (☎ **813/3572-1111**) and **Matsuya,** 3-6-1 Ginza (☎ **813/3567-1211**). For an extensive list of department stores throughout Japan, see Wikipedia (http://tinyurl.com/ynroz8).

A food hall in Tokyo's Ginza district.

Ostermalmshallen Market Hall STOCKHOLM $–$$

Ostermalm was up until recently a hidden district only visited by locals. It's not far from downtown Stockholm but not in the swim of things. It has become a trendy 'hood, visited by everyone and often mobbed with visitors off cruise ships who come in for the day and flock not only to the neighborhood (good H&M store), but to this late Victorian redbrick food hall where they have a lot more than herring for sale.

BEST BETS   The food hall is medium size so it's not overwhelming; it includes many vendors of local specialties—you can easily do a caviar tasting with the roe of various local fish (not sturgeon). There are also several cafes, so come for coffee or lunch. There are some already cooked foods so that you can do take-away for a picnic or a day trip. My regular haunt is **Lisa Elmqvist** for fresh seafood.

WHERE TO BUY   1 store: Ostermalmstorg, Stockholm. Metro: Ostermalmstorg. Mon–Fri 9:30am–6pm; Sat 9:30am–4pm.

Food & Grocery Stores

City Super HONG KONG $–$$

Combo gourmet grocery, prepared foods, country club and hanging-out store, which has branches in all the key locations in Hong Kong, usually inside big-name malls.

BEST BETS   The grocery store is really a general store with many gift items and a full beauty aids department. There's fresh foods, cooked meals, packaged goods from all over the world and yep, you can get bagels here.

WEB TIPS   Recipes often online.

WHERE TO BUY   Times Sq. Basement One, Hong Kong. ☎ 852/ 2506-2888. Fri–Sat 10:30am–11pm; Sun–Thurs 10:30am– 10pm. AE, MC, V. MTR: Causeway Bay. Also: Harbour City, Kowloon 7/7. Daily 10:30am–10pm. MTR: TST.

Dean & DeLuca USA $–$$

For the uninitiated, Dean & DeLuca is the dean of fancy food markets, the fanciest of the chic purveyors of things imported and sublime. Need I say it's expensive?

  In addition to the well-rounded selection of everything you might want to eat, to cook or to take to go, there's some cookware and a few cookbooks. I sometimes find the same foodstuffs in other markets for a lot less money, and I won't pay outrageous prices for the privilege of being chic. Nonetheless, it's a landmark, an icon and a statement in food and fashion.

BEST BETS   Look for European cookware, French jams and Serrano ham.

WHERE TO BUY   14 stores in the U.S. **FLAGSHIP**   560 Broadway, at Prince St., NYC. ☎ **212/226-6800.** Subway: R, W to Prince St. Daily 8am–8pm. AE, DISC, MC, V. www.deananddeluca.com.

E.A.T. NYC $–$$$

This store and restaurant is only part of the Eli Zabar magic. Eli, as all foodies know, is the youngest son of Louis Zabar, one of the founders of Zabar's on Manhattan's West Side. Eli owns the East Side. And some of France, but that's another story. There's also a gift/kids' store next door.

BEST BETS   E.A.T. has a gift shop next door which is filled with novelty items; the catering part of the business prepares gift baskets with combinations of food and little gift items. They have made a business from simple, good food that is beautifully displayed but is not too over the top or artsy fartsy. Unless you are talking about the prices, which are high. But then, New Yorkers are happy to pay for, well, style.

WEB TIPS   Click on E.A.T. for menus and gift ideas.

WHERE TO BUY   1064 Madison Ave. at 80th St., NYC. ☎ **212/772-0022.** Subway: 4, 5, 6 at 86th St. Daily 7am–10pm. Credit cards: AE, V. www.elismanhattan.com.

H-Mart USA/KOREAN $–$$

This mega mart differs from other Asian markets in that you can also buy other ethnic foods, including Latin and Eastern European. Serving the diverse communities that now make up the population of many U.S. cities and 'burbs, there are 17 locations throughout the eastern U.S. Some have food courts; all have a vast selection of everything from noodles to kimchi. There's spaghetti on one isle, tortillas on the next, with soup and ginger tea nearby. This is one-stop shopping for all nations. There's a good variety of items available on the website; after you register and fill out a short survey, you'll get a coupon for free shipping.

WEB TIPS   I had to download Korean characters in order to access this site, but once that was done, it was easy to order my ginger tea. The site is bilingual—Korean and English.

WHERE TO BUY   17 locations throughout the eastern U.S. **FLAGSHIP**   141–40 Northern Blvd., Flushing, NY. ☎ **718/358-0700.** Daily 24 hours. www.hmart.com.

Igourmet.com 🖰

Enormous online retailer founded in 1997 and providing an overwhelming amount of choice in a very well-organized site.

There's over 600 kinds of cheese and truly thousands of products. My only problem is that when I tested the olive oil section, I only knew two of the brands out of maybe a dozen. I'm not saying I know a lot about olive oil, but how can we judge anything if there are no known benchmarks? In this case, you probably just have to go with the one that has the papal seal, and have a little faith.

BEST BETS   There's fresh foods, there's pantry items, there's kosher, there's holiday, there's gift baskets, there's wine in various categories, there's everything—but there might not be brands that you know. They ship your order within the U.S. by FreshWave, a trademarked system that keeps food fresh for 48 hours.

WEB TIPS   This site is completely overwhelming. Allow plenty of time. Shipping obviously is related to weight, so it's hard to know if you are doubling the cost of your order with the shipping charges.

Peck MILAN $–$$$$

If northern Italy is a food lover's Paradise then Milan is the capital of heaven and this store is the most famous address in town. A store (since 1883), now with a restaurant and even a wine shop, Peck is located not too far from the Duomo, thus in the heart of the tourist area and also near La Scala.

BEST BETS   Buy picnic foods to take on the plane with you before you head to the airport.

WEB TIPS   The site can be switched into English; you can shop online and even send goods to the U.S. However, note that there are restrictions on chocolate related to the weather, and restrictions during the month of December related to the volume of holiday packages coming into the U.S.

WHERE TO BUY   1 store: via Spardi 9, Milan. ☎ **392/802-3161.** Mon 3–7:30pm; Tues–Sat 8:45–7:30pm. CB, MC, V. Metro: Duomo. www.peck.it.

Stew Leonard's USA $–$$

Unlike traditional grocery stores which carry up to 30,000 items, Stew Leonards stocks only 2,000, which means that you still have to do regular shopping elsewhere. The trade dress of the store is very particular—as you weave around the concourse, there's stacks of packs of foodstuffs. The original store was a dairy, so you watch the bottling process as you shop. There's a fresh bakery, there's good cold cuts and a deli; the fried chicken was a favorite of my son's when he was growing up. Mac and cheese, did I mention the mac and cheese?

BEST BETS   Okay, the reason you really go here is the animatronic cows that will thrill your kids. The market is laid out in a path from which you cannot deviate—along the way an entire barnyard of robotic animals brays and moos. You shop while the kids behave. Imagine that.

WEB TIPS   Click to find new arrivals and special events.

WHERE TO BUY   4 Stores in the U.S. **FLAGSHIP**   100 Westport Ave., Norwalk, CT. ☎ **203/847-7214.** Daily 8am–9pm AE, DISC, MC, V. Also in Danbury, CT, and Yonkers, NY. www.stewleonards.com.

Wegman's USA $–$$

Wegman's has been the most innovative market in the U.S. since its opening in 1915 to now. They have been the first to break through in many areas. The flagship store has a restaurant named Tastings at which diners interact with the chef. These are the guys who brought Pierre Herme' chocolates to the U.S.

BEST BETS   Most new stores fit into the mega market mold; most sell wine, have cooking classes and feature exclusive creations from famous chefs.

WEB TIPS   They support the community through online services such as quick and easy grocery and prescription renewals online.

WHERE TO BUY   72 stores in U.S. **FLAGSHIP**   3195 Monroe Ave., Pittsford (Rochester), NY. ☎ **585/586-6680.** Open 24/7. www.wegmans.com.

Whole Foods TEXAN $–$$

Organic and natural foods market that sells exotics as well as health and beauty aids, prepared foods, cookware, magazines as an alternative lifestyle gone chic. Sushi anyone? Soy milk, perhaps? A little Dr. Hauschka? Is it marketing or market?

BEST BETS   Excellent prepared foods; good place for hard-to-find brands and condiments you can't get at regular stores. The colors and the fresh items make you feel that you've gotten as close to a European market as America allows. This could be classified as a lifestyle store and indeed, for many it is a way of life.

WEB TIPS   The website has information about health, nutrition, organics, seafood allergies and of course, food.

WHERE TO BUY 188 stores in U.S., UK and Canada. **FLAGSHIP** Austin, TX. www.wholefoods.com.

Woodland's Market KENTFIELD, CA $-$$

Their chefs make over 50 entrees each day, including comfort foods (meatloaf, fried chicken, mac 'n' cheese) and gourmet selections varying from beef Wellington to grilled salmon.

BEST BETS Along with the deli selection of meats and cheeses, you'll find gourmet salads (including lobster), sushi, pizzas to bake at home, fresh pastas, soups and sandwiches to go. There's complete wine and cheese sections and a bakery offering homemade cakes, cookies and breads; their California sourdough is the best in the area.

WEB TIPS Click here for catering menus, wine tastings, new arrivals, health guidelines and much more.

WHERE TO BUY 1 store: 735 College Ave., Kentfield, CA. ☎ **415/ 457-8160.** Daily 7am–9pm. www.woodlandsmarket.com.

Trader Joe's USA $-$$

World's Best Begun in California as an alternative source for wine, bulk foods, gourmet items and organic foodstuffs, Trader Joe's has grown into what they term a culinary adventure. Because so many of their foods come from assorted international destinations, the store means to capture an international spirit inside a neighborhood grocery mart.

BEST BETS Salted soy beans, $3 a pack.

WEB TIPS Find the store nearest you online.

WHERE TO BUY 250 stores in the U.S. www.traderjoes.com.

Zabars NYC $-$$

This grocery store on the west side of Manhattan is as much an icon in New York as many of the more traditional sights. It existed way before there were foodies as a family business, part deli and part general store that even sold cookwares and small appliances.

BEST BETS Well, I'll go for the pumpkin coffee although you can argue that point.

WHERE TO BUY 1 store: 2245 Broadway, at 80th, NYC. ☎ **212/ 787-2000.** Mon–Fri 8am–7:30pm; Sat 8am–9pm; Sun 9am–6pm. AE, DISC, MC, V. Subway: 1 to 79th St. www.zabars.com.

Foodstuffs: A to Z

I'm not sure when dinner got to be my favorite subject, maybe shortly after lunch or snack. I like tea time, too. I could write a book of my favorite food stores, tastes, chefs and weight-loss techniques. Instead, here's a select list of sources I simply can't live without.

CANDY & CHOCOLATES

Angelina PARIS $

This Parisian tearoom is actually famous for its mont-blanc, but serves a hot chocolate that is famous because it's so thick and rich that the cutlery can stand upright. This tearoom is over a century old and is one of the places that is such an icon that tourists insist on visiting and yet locals still come.

BEST BETS   Angelina serves meals and desserts, tea time and hot beverages, and also has a takeout counter for desserts and chocolates. You can buy the hot chocolate mix for about $6 a bag. The chocolate macaroons are also world famous (about $3 each).

WHERE TO BUY   1 store: 225 rue du Rivoli, Paris 1er. ☎ **331/42-60-8200.** Mon–Fri 9:30am–6:30pm; Sat 9am–6pm. Métro: Tuilieres. AE, MC, V.

Bernachon LYON, FRANCE $

Bernachon is perhaps the most famous of the old-school French chocolatiers; his family shop makes pastry as well as chocolates and is most famous for a praline called a *pallet d'or* that has real gold flecks in it. You'll pay about $30 for a cake-confection but the French person you give it to will forever know that you are a well-educated foodie.

BEST BETS   Next door to the pastry shop there's a small cafe where you can get lunch or coffee and dessert.

WHERE TO BUY   1 store: 42 cours Franklin-Roosevelt, Lyon, France. ☎ **334/7824-3798.** Tues–Sat 8:30am–7pm; Sun 8am–5pm. Bernachon Passion tea salon at same location. ☎ **334/7852-2365.** www.bernachon.com.

La Maison du Chocolate FRENCH $$–$$$

The box looks like one from Hermès and the website is just as classy. The stores vary from some that are small and rather casual to some of flagship status that are very fancy. This is one of those status brands that says you care enough to buy the very best. A box of chocolates begins around $50 and escalates.

Besides traditional chocolate bonbons, the firm has chocolate milk and other chocolate products. The New York store takes fresh deliveries by air from France.

La Maison du Chocolat truffles.

BEST BETS   The holiday chocolates make great gifts.

WEB TIPS   You can enter your shopping budget before ordering online, which saves time and temptation.

WHERE TO BUY   25+ stores. Paris, Cannes, London, New York, Tokyo, more. 1018 Madison Ave., NYC. ☎ **212/ 744-7117.** Mon–Sat 10am–7pm. Sun noon–6pm. AE, MC V. Subway: 4, 5, 6 at 77th St. www.lamaisonduchocolat.com.

Edelweiss Kitchen USA $

When I first moved to Beverly Hills, in the mid-1970s, I heard tell of all sorts of show business urban legends. One that I never forgot was that people were invited to movie screenings in private homes, where they snacked on chocolate covered pretzels. At the time, I knew little about food and didn't understand that the combination of sweet and salty is one of the laws of gourmet food.

BEST BETS   This is the source for chocolate-covered pretzels of the rich and famous.

WHERE TO BUY   444 N. Canon Dr., Beverly Hills, CA. ☎ **888/ 615-8800.** No website.

Frango Mints USA $

So you know that Frango Mints are a signature of the Chicago department store Marshall Field's and you know that Marshall Field's is gone and has been turned into Macy's. And you turn to me for guidance. So rest assured, dear reader, I've got the scoop on this chocolate icon. The classical bonbon is a tiny square of chocolate mint but other flavors have been introduced to expand the brand, including a double chocolate and even a pink mint in honor of breast cancer awareness.

Godiva U.S. vs Godiva BRU

Godiva was the first gourmet chocolate brand to come to the U.S. and commercialize itself enough for people to recognize it as a brand. It immediately struck a status chord and was pronounced in the American fashion as in Lady Godiva's name. Godiva quickly meant luxury chocolate. At some point the U.S. branch of the firm was bought by Campbell's Soup, but the brand remained a status item not associated with soup. Still, the chocolate is mass manufactured.

The original Godiva (pronounced Go-deeva in Europe) is a Belgian brand and follows E.U. regulations on chocolate making and butter fat content—meaning the pralines taste quite different from their U.S. counterparts. This too is a status brand, although not an esoteric one—it's a commercial brand of premium chocs sold in department stores, airports and of course their own stores worldwide. In some stores they also sell ice cream and chocolate dip fruit.

If you've ever up for the Pepsi Challenge of chocolates, bring back a *ballotin* of Godiva from Brussels and do a blind tasting with some U.S. counterparts. Even if you can't tell the difference, it's a great way to appreciate science. Log on to www.godiva.com.

WHERE TO BUY   Frango mints are now sold at all Macy's stores and can be bought online. www.macys.com.

Fralinger's Salt Water Taffy ATLANTIC CITY $

World's Best

Be still my heart! There are all sorts of salt water taffy firms, mostly in beach communities around the world—but there's only one Fralinger's, The modern Fralinger's is actually a merge of two big beach snack names James and Fralinger—both make salt water taffy. There's also popcorn, chocolates, peanut brittle and assorted other treats.

BEST BETS   There is only one way to go: the mixed vanilla-chocolate box of taffy.

WEB TIPS   The site has e-commerce but it's not easy to use and less easy to get what you really want. They offer pre-packaged assortments, and while there are some 25 flavors to choose from, at no time can you signify you want black and white or lemon and lime or whatever you want. You're going to have to call them to get it right.

WHERE TO BUY   1325 Boardwalk, Atlantic City. ☎ 609/344-2529. www.fralingers.com.

Joël Durand FRENCH $

World's Best

Joël Durand is what's called a *maitre chocolatier*. He is a master in chocolates and in marketing—he works with a gimmick. His bonbons are small, flat squares with a contrast letter printed across the center. Each letter represents a different taste. He's very generous with samples, understanding that when your product is a little different from others, you have to get the public hooked. The first time I went to his shop, he handed me a printed legend and asked me what flavor I wanted to try. I became hooked on No. 13, which is now called "L" when he switched from numbers to letters of the alphabet.

World Traveler

Boulevard Victor Hugo in St. Remy is a great street for foodies. Close to Joël Durand, try **Huile de Monde** (no. 16) for olive oils, and save room for more chocolates and cookies at **Le Petit Duc** (no. 7).

BEST BETS   I am a fool for lavender (L). The combination of chocolate and lavender is a very Provençal taste. I also like Szechuan pepper (U) and rose petal (made fresh seasonally). The flavors are bold and original—some are made with dark chocolates, some with light. He also makes a few sauces and other treats.

WEB TIPS   You can see all 32 flavors online, or read the little chart enclosed with each box of chocolate. The site is in French and English, and you can order via FedEx. Shipping 1 kg (2.2 lbs) or less will cost you $24. An isothermal bag (for summer shipping) is an extra $4.

WHERE TO BUY   2 stores. In the U.S., only available at Paradou restaurant in New York. **FLAGSHIP**   3 blvd. Victor Hugo, St. Remy de Provence, France. ☎ **334/9092-3825.** Tues–Sat 9:30am–12:30pm and 2:30–7:30pm; Sun 10am–1pm and 2:30–6:30pm; Mon 9:30am–12:30pm and 2:30–6pm. MC, V. www.joel-durand-chocolatier.fr. Paradou Restaurant: 8 Little W. 12th St. ☎ **212/463-8345.** www.paradounyc.com.

Lamme's TEXAN $–$$

World's Best

It is not unusual for a local brand of chocolate or candy to be related to the cultural and emotional fabric of a given geographic area. Lamme's has been part of the local scene from peppermints kisses for Valentine's Day, which are red and white and came in a giant and very enviable box, to pecan chewies., with or without chocolate.

BEST BETS   Lamme's has been making chewy pralines since 1885. Thankfully they are very expensive so I cannot eat as many as I would like. You only get six for $11. A two-unit gift box is available, $5.

WEB TIPS   Order sugar-free chocs for diabetics, online.

WHERE TO BUY   78 stores, most in Texas malls and major Texas airports. Outlet: 3939 IH 35, San Marcos, TX. ☎ **512/396-1875.** www.lammes.com. Mon–Sat 10am–9pm; Sun 10am–7pm. DISC, MC, V.

Mymandm.com (personalized M&Ms) USA $

Custom-printed M&Ms can only be ordered online and take at least 2 weeks for delivery—so plan ahead. Your message can be two lines of 8 characters each. There is a minimum order of just under $50 but additional bags cost only $11 each. There are often holiday promotional codes that will get you a free bag.

Neuhaus BELGIAN $

Pronounce this "noy-house" to show you understand the European roots of this Belgian chocolate maker. Sold in a handful of freestanding boutiques in the U.S. and often through exclusive department stores such as Neiman Marcus, this brand is much more sophisticated than Godiva.

BEST BETS   I am hooked on one specific taste—Astrid—which is a hazelnut ganache. I will indeed pay $100 for a pound of this confection and consider myself lucky to get it. Of course, it costs much less if I buy in Brussels so I have been known to hop a train in Paris and head to the Grand Place where I can buy a 1 kilo box (over 2 pounds) for $60. I insist on a hand-created box of only Astrid, hand-plucked from the shelves—no pre-mixed box will suffice.

While Neuhaus chocolates can be found around the world and often in duty-free stores, the most common form of distribution is the pre-mixed gift box. You need a real Neuhaus store in order to select the Astrid praline. (Praline is the French word for a piece of candy; we're not talking New Orleans pralines here.)

WEB TIPS   Alas, poor Astrid, you cannot buy her online.

WHERE TO BUY   FLAGSHIP   Hotel Amigo, rue de l'Amigo 1–3, Brussels. ☎ **322/547-4747.** www.neuhaus.be.

Pierre Marcolini BELGIAN $

Perhaps the fanciest boutiques in the world of master chocolatiers belong to Pierre Marcolini, a Belgian who has gone
international. His tastes are extravagant, as are his packages
and his elegant stores—every detail is a little more fancy than
you were expecting, a little more haute couture than you
thought possible for a chocolate shop. You can shop online in
the U.S.; prices range for $18 to $225.

BEST BETS Marcolini is known for over 60 different types of
chocolates enveloped in a very thin couverture.

WEB TIPS Order online; pay $21 shipping for orders up to
$100.

WHERE TO BUY 10 stores worldwide, in NYC, Brussels, Paris,
Tokyo, Kuwait, more. **U.S. FLAGSHIP** 485 Park Ave. at 58th St.,
NYC. ☎ **212/755-5150** for store and orders. www.marcolini
chocolatier.com.

Sampaka SPANISH $

A small chain of beautiful shops mostly in Spain (but there's
one in Berlin). There's candies, desserts and coffee shops and
this is the "in" place to go for a coffee. Most stores are closed
in August.

BEST BETS They specialize in Spanish dark chocolate.

WEB TIPS Lots of information; no orders.

WHERE TO BUY **FLAGSHIP** Calle Orellana 4, Madrid. ☎ **91/
319-5840.** Mon–Sat 10am–9:30pm; Sun 11am–9:30pm. www.
cacaosampaka.com.

Scharffen Berger USA

Considered the best chocolate in the U.S., this San Francisco
Bay area maker has chocolate and couverture slabs. There are
bonbons and cocoa powder as well as chocolate bars. To
reserve a space on a free public tour of the factory, call 510/
981-4066 in advance. The tour includes a factory walk-
through, a lecture on how chocolate is made and a tasting.
Participants must be age 10 or older and wear closed-toe shoes.

BEST BETS This is the best domestic baking chocolate.

WEB TIPS Shop online for home baking supplies.

WHERE TO BUY 914 Heinz Ave., Berkeley, CA. ☎ **510/981-
4066.** www.scharffenberger.com.

See's USA $

It's about the suckers, dummy. But there are chocolates, too.

BEST BESTS   I like the lollipops; Sarah's fave is the key lime truffle. We both like the stores' free samples.

WEB TIPS   You can pick what goes in the box, an offer available in stores or through catalog; there's a sweet savings program for those who buy 50 lb. of choc a year. Stores are mostly in California. During holidays, the brand does pop-up stores in some parts of the country.

WHERE TO BUY   2 stores in San Francisco and LA; also CA airports; dozens of candy stores in U.S. **FLAGSHIP**   3423 S. La Cienega Blvd., Los Angeles. ☎ **800/347-7337.** www.sees.com.

Thornton's BRITISH $

Although Thornton's does make chocolates, for my calories, I don't care. I have two things to tell you about Thornton's.

1. Thornton's has a nice business in writing personal messages on their chocolates. They sell chocolate tablets which they will personalize (for free) while you wait and also do giant Easter eggs which can be personalized.

2. Thornton's makes toffee, and my dog Toffee is named after it. (He's the same color.) The toffee comes in about one dozen different flavors; I am addicted to "original."

BEST BETS   This is simply the best toffee in the world. You can buy it in some UK airports.

WEB TIPS   You can order online, but beware: Delivery charges to the U.S. are $40 to $60.

WHERE TO BUY   Close to 400 stores throughout the UK and Ireland. www.thorntons.co.uk.

zChocolat.com FRENCH 🖱 $$$–$$$$

This is a Web-only company that ships all over the world. The premium chocolates are always sent out in amazing containers—including real mahogany boxes and sometimes leather-bound book cases that you can have personally engraved. This firm is not a chocolate maker but a clever marketer of the work of four master *chocolatiers*, including one World Champion, Pascal Caffet. They all use 100% pure cocoa butter, with no preservatives, and flavors include everything from star anise to bourbon vanilla.

BEST BETS   Once again, my favorite is lavender. Most packages included a pre-selected assortment, though you can hand-pick each individual chocolate if you order the Explorer (29 pieces for $62) or Luna (61 pieces for $108) packages.

WEB TIPS You can get free shipping during the holiday season; otherwise there is express worldwide shipping, and they promise "pristine" delivery to the U.S. in 1 to 3 business days. They ship in insulated containers during the summer months.

COFFEE & TEA

Hag Kaffe GERMAN $

Having been told it was uncivilized to leave the dinner table without taking coffee or tea, but reluctant to put caffeine into my bloodstream at night or to drink chamomile tea, I discovered Hag.

BEST BETS It's the world's best decaf coffee. It is also the world's best instant coffee.

WEB TIPS Be careful in a search, you may end up with the e-mail address of a woman who calls herself Coffee Hag.

WHERE TO BUY Available in UK supermarkets; this German brand is harder to find in the U.S. No website.

Ineeka INDIAN $

Ineeka is an organic tea that comes in it's own filter system,

sort of like a tea bag with straps so that you brew it by the cup but get the flavors of loose tea as if made in a warmed pot by the Mad Hatter. Whatever difficulties you have figuring out how to secure the filter into your cup will be forgotten when you breathe in the aroma. This is natural tea, without additives or scented oils to enhance the perception of the flavor.

Ineeka Himalayan Green tea.

For those who just care about taste, you don't need to boost this cuppa with sugar, honey, lemon or cream.

BEST BETS Several different teas are available—black or green—familiar (Darjeeling) or exotic (Ma-chai).

WEB TIPS The website is a one-page photo and no info.

WHERE TO BUY The teas are available at Whole Foods markets. www.ineeka.com.

Mariage Freres FRENCH $–$$$

This tea is sold and served in Mariage Freres shops in Paris but is also sold on a wholesale basis all over the world. The candles are hard to find outside the tea salons.

BEST BETS   Any tea in the signature black tin ($18) makes a great hostess gift.

WEB TIPS   Click on the website for information; unfortunately, they don't ship to the U.S.

WHERE TO BUY   Some department stores have a boutique selling the brand of loose teas and some of the accessories but they do not serve hot tea. www.mariagefreres.com.

Starbucks USA $

It is totally beyond me why one of the highlights of my week is the one trip to Starbucks that I allow myself. No other coffee tastes the same to me, no matter how much chocolate syrup I pour into it. *Travel tip:* If you are traveling abroad and need to bring a business gift that represents the U.S. yet crosses cultural borders, bring some Starbucks coffee.

WEB TIPS   You can reload your Starbucks card online.

WHERE TO BUY   Everywhere. www.starbucks.com.

HAM & CHEESE

Agrinascente FIDENZA, ITALY $–$$

This particular cheese house is a virtual deli, just lacking the Zabar family and a few dill pickles and onion bagels. They have local wines, oils, vinegars and, of course, cheese. You can buy the cheese prepacked or ask them to cut it for you. The price is based on the age; the expensive stuff is the oldest and is not exported to the U.S. Speaking of which, to answer your next question: yes. Yes, it is legal to bring cheese into the U.S. if it has been aged more than 60 days.

BEST BETS   If you are attracted to this kind of shopping experience, I am going to assume that you are used to cheese that costs $20 a kilo and balsamic vinegar that costs $45 for a teeny, weeny bottle.

WEB TIPS   The site is in Italian, but it has a clear map and basic information that you can understand.

WHERE TO BUY   1 store: Via SM Campagna 22/b, Fidenza, IT. ☎ 05-24/522-334. Mon–Sat 10am–7pm; Sun 11am–3pm. www.agrinascente.it.

Artisanalcheese.com USA ⌐🖰 $$

Chef Terrance Brennen made his name and the fame of his first Manhattan restaurant through his deft cooking and his wonderful cheese board.

BEST BETS   There are over 300 cheeses on selection at the website as well as other gourmet foodstuffs and specialties. Reminder: $35 to $50 per pound is a common enough price for these delicacies.

WEB TIPS   During the month of July, you can celebrate Christmas with 20% off holiday gift certificates.

WHERE TO BUY   Web only, or call ☎ **877/797-1200.**

Barthelmy FRENCH $

And first, our daily French lesson: say, "Bar tell me." This is a very small, Left Bank Parisian cheese shop that I like to visit because it's homey and friendly and if you just know a few basics—like cow versus goat—and when you want to eat the cheese, they will send you off with an earth-shattering experience.

BEST BETS   They provide an education for free; especially good with chevre.

WEB TIPS   No website, although you can find plenty written about this shop by food bloggers and French government information sites.

WHERE TO BUY   1 shop. 51 rue du Grenelle, Paris 7e. ☎ **331/ 4222-8224.** Tues–Sat 7am–1pm and 3:30-7:30pm. CB, MC, V. Métro: rue du Bac.

DiBruno Bros PHILADELPHIA $–$$

This family-owned gourmet destination superstore has been around since the 1930s, providing one of the best selections of gourmet cheeses and specialty foods on the East Coast. The Philadelphia City Center shop has a 300-square-foot cheese *cave* where you'll find over 500 varieties of international cheese. Domestic brands from Wisconsin, California and Vermont are also available.

BEST BETS   If you're looking for any cheese in the world not in stock, they'll be happy to locate it and order it for you. In addition to cheese, there's olive oils, vinegars, pates, gourmet meats, smoked fish, caviar and so on.

WEB TIPS   The online catalog is easy to use. You can select by type of cheese or country of origin; each listing has suggestions for usage and wine pairing. I found one of the finest English Stiltons in the world—Colston Bassett Stilton—for $23/lb. and a French Chaumes for $18/lb. A house aged Vermont cheddar was available for $11/lb. Shipping charges are based on destination.

WHERE TO BUY   1 store: 930 S. 9th St. ☎ **215/922-2876.** Mon 9am–5pm; Tues–Sat 8am–6pm; Sun 8am–2pm. Also Rittenhouse Sq., 1730 Chestnut St. ☎ **215/665-9220.** Mon–Fri 9am–8pm; Sat 9am–7pm; Sun 9am–6pm. Coffee and Espresso Bar opens at 7am daily. MC, V. www.dibruno.com.

Murray's Cheese Shop NYC $$

A Greenwich Village institution, this small cheese shop has about 300 to 350 types of cheese from all over the world.

WEB TIPS   You can order complete dinner packs online.

WHERE TO BUY   1 store: 254 Bleecker St. ☎ **212/243-3289.** Mon–Sat 8am–8pm; Sun 9am–6pm. www.murrayscheese.com.

A selection of cheeses from Murray's.

Padow's USA $–$$

This family-owned-and-operated resource has been selling Smithfield and smoked hams since 1936. They also have a deli that sells local Virginia specialties (peanuts).

BEST BETS   Several different types of ham in assorted Southern traditional styles.

WEB TIPS   You can order online.

WHERE TO BUY   14 franchises in Virginia with expansion planned for Northern Virginia and the two Carolinas. **FLAGSHIP** 9864 W. Broad St., Circuit City Plaza, Glen Allen, VA (outside Richmond). ☎ **800/344-4267.** MC, V. www.padows.com.

Paxton & Whitfield BRITISH $$

Winston Churchill once said, "A gentleman only buys his cheese from Paxton & Whitfield." Lots of people must agree, as this shop's been thriving since 1797. Known primarily for their excellent variety of over 200 cheeses, they also carry specialty meats, pâtés and a limited selection of wines.

BEST BETS   French and English blue cheeses including Beaufort, Roquefort and Stilton. If you're a fan of soft cheeses, they carry the excellent Brie de Meaux as well as their own private-label Camembert.

WEB TIPS   The website's easy to use and you can order online, and they will ship overseas; charges vary according to what's ordered.

WHERE TO BUY　4 shops in the UK. **FLAGSHIP**　93 Jermyn St., London. ☎ **4420/7930-0259.** Mon–Sat 9:30am–5:30pm. AE, MC, V. www.paxtonandwhitfield.co.uk.

OILS, DRESSINGS & SAUCES

When I wander grocery store aisles in markets around the world, I am invariably drawn to sauces, dressings and oil. Oil is hard to bring back home, especially now that it has to be packed into your luggage for security purposes. (Use bubble wrap and discarded plastic bags; buy tins not glass bottles.) Even though the shelves of an U.S. supermarket are packed with choices, I find stronger flavors from international markets. Hell, I even like Portuguese olive oil better than what you get in the U.S. In fact, I love **Gallo** brand Portuguese olive oil and I know that to foodies, oil from Portugal is not considered the high end of the scale. Never mind, I know what I like.

Maille FRENCH $

Although this mustard maker hails from Dijon, the flagship shop is in Paris.

BEST BUYS　I love the fruit-flavored mustards.

WEB TIPS　There's a recipe listed with each mustard.

WHERE TO BUY　6, place de la Madeleine, Paris. ☎ **331/4015-0600.** Mon–Sat 10am–7pm. Métro: Madeleine. www.maille.com.

O & Co. FRENCH $–$$$

This French chain, begun by the people who created L'Occitane, specializes in olive products–everything from designer tapenade to olive oils from different parts of the Mediterranean. There's French, Spanish, Italian and even Greek oils. A small can of oil costs around $21; every now and then one is on special—there was a big sale on Serbian olive oil last time I was here, no joke. O & Co. has some American branches, but prices are much higher in the U.S.

BEST BETS　The French Grands Crus oils are expensive, but worth it ($40 and up).

WEB TIPS　Click on "Delicious Deals," their sale page.

> **World Traveler**
>
> The stores surrounding Maille and the place Madeleine are almost entirely food specialty shops, including **Maison de la Truffe, Fauchon** and **Hédiard.** One block over on rue Vignon is the **Maison de Miel,** the honey shop. And you are just a big block from **Galeries Lafayette** and the **Lafayette Gourmet** grocery store.

WHERE TO BUY   50 stores worldwide; 11 in the US. 28 rue de Buci, Paris. ☎ **01-44-07-15-43.** Mon–Sat 11am–7pm. AE, M, V. Métro: St-Germain-des-Pres. www.oliviersandco.com.

Aziliari FRENCH $$–$$$$

Packaging freaks will know and remember this product because it has the most gorgeous hot blue tin you have ever seen. The oil is as good as the packaging. There is some distribution throughout France, at the Nice airport and in some international gourmet stores, but the best place to buy is in their own shop at the edge of Old Nice. You'll pay $30 and upward, depending on the size, but *ooh la la.*

BEST BET   Another great gift . . . in a gorgeous blue tin. You can buy it at the Nice airport.

WHERE TO BUY   14 rue St-Francois-de-Paule, Old Nice. Mon–Sat 11am–7pm. AE, M, V.

Soy Vay USA $

Once upon a time, a nice Chinese girl offered a nice Jewish boy a taste of her homemade marinated beef sticks. "This could be the start of something big," mused the nice Jewish boy: SOY VAY! A sauce was born.

The original Chinese marinade is now called Hoisan Garlic Asian Glaze & Marinade. Soy Vay makes five different marinades, all from natural ingredients and preservative free. Along with the original sauce, try the Cha-Cha Chinese Chicken Salad Dressing and Very Very Teriyaki sauce.

BEST BETS   I like the original sauce best.

WEB TIPS   Quick and easy online catalog.

WHERE TO BUY   Safeway, Trader Joe's, other retailers. www.soy vay.com.

SALT

Blessac FRENCH $

I found this brand at Whole Foods and have never seen it in France. This is a product that will change the taste of anything and everything. The lavender-colored rock salt has bits of

Salt of the Earth, Part 2

We love it. We all crave it. Most of us think of it as simply that white granular stuff in the shaker on our kitchen table. Yes, it is that, but it's much more. This essential food element can be mined from deep inside the earth or taken from the sea. And it's available in a world of varieties.

Australia offers **Murray River Pink Salt** ($8 for 4 oz.; www.chef shop.com) that comes from the waters of the continents' largest rivers; it has mineral tang and a pale apricot color. With a mild flavor, these crystals melt quickly and evenly, making Murray River a best bet for finishing, roasting and baking.

From France, you might try **Le Tresor Fumee de Sel Chardonnay** ($20 for 7.4 oz.; www.gourmetsleuth.com). These pale beige crystals are smoked over retired Chardonnay-aging barrels. Denmark's **Viking-Smoked Sea Salt** ($24 for 4 oz.; www.salttraders.com) is a deep brown variety with wood-smoked flavor. India's **Kala Namak Black Salt** ($9 for 9.5 oz.; www.faeriesfinest.com) is pinkish black in color and has a sulfuric taste; it's used in Indian *chaat* snacks. From Peru, **Mountain Spring Pink Salt** ($15 for 6.5 oz.) is bold with intense salt flavor and hints of citrus.

Hawaii's **Red Alaea Salt** ($11 for 4 oz.; www.nirmalaskitchen. com) gets its color (anything from orange to dark burgundy) from the clay lining the tidal pools where it's harvested. Coarse, hearty, rose-hued **Himalania Pink Salt** ($12 for 12.8 oz.; www.ssaltworks.us) is taken from a 25-million-year-old Jurassic-era seabed in the Himalayas, and has been used to lower blood pressure and stimulate circulation. From Bali comes **Big Tree Farms Course Kechil** ($7 for 8.5 oz.). Crystals are panned on black-sand beaches from Indian Ocean seawater.

For more "Salt of the Earth" (the bathing kind), see p. 167.
—Sarah Lahey

dried lavender in it; I put it into a Lucite pepper mill; $4.99 a lb. There's also smoked salt and a "rainbow collection."

WHERE TO BUY   Order on amazon.com.

SNACK FOODS

World's Best *Garrett Popcorn* USA $

Like ants drawn to a picnic, people form long lines outside this kernel-size shop on Michigan Avenue. Yes, the caramel corn is heavenly and cheese corn decadent, but is it worth all the fuss? Absolutely. The aroma draws you in, the lines move quickly and you're soon in possession of one the best treats and bargains on the Magnificent Mile.

Using top quality ingredients, Garrett Popcorn is air-popped fresh (no fats or oils needed) right before your eyes from a privately grown blend of kernels. Selection is limited to Plain Popcorn, Buttery Popcorn, Cheese Corn and Caramel Crisp (which may be blended with cashews, macadamias or pecans).

BEST BETS   The Chicago Mix., at $4.45 to $13. Single-flavor bags are $2.35 to $14; tins are also available.

WEB TIPS   If you can't handle the crowds, order online. However, munching fresh from the popper is worth the wait.

WHERE TO BUY   FLAGSHIP   670 N. Michigan Ave. (at East Erie St). ☎ **312/944-2630.** Mon–Sat 9am–10pm; Sun 9am–9pm. NYC locations: 2 W. Jackson Blvd., 26 E. Randolph St., and 4 E. Madison St.; 1 Penn Plaza, 34th St. at Seventh Ave. ☎ **212/290-0044.** AE, DISC, M, V. www.garrettpopcorn.com.

Maui Potato Chips USA $

Maui Potato Chips (officially called The Original Maui Kitch'n Cook'd Potato Chips) are only available on the islands of Maui, Kauai and Oahu in Hawaii. There are lots of Maui *style* potato chips out there, but this is the real enchilada, or uh, potato.

Thicker than average potato chips, they're very light and crunchy. They have not been peeled before frying and are not oily to the touch. Lightly dusted with salt, the flavor is that of a perfectly prepared French fry.

WHERE TO BUY   If you can't make it to Hawaii, you can order by sending a check or money order (no credit cards accepted) to Maui Potato Chip, Inc., 295 Lalo Street, Maui, HI 96732, or call ☎ **808/877-3652.** The chips are available in 6 packages for $23. Each package contains a total of 7 oz., two separately wrapped bags inside one large cellophane package. The chips will arrive in excellent shape. No website.

SWEETS (NON CANDY)

Auntie Anne's USA $

Auntie Anne's pretzels are mixed, twisted and baked on-site at each location and come with a guarantee: if you don't like your selection, they'll give you another pretzel, free. They make traditional pretzels sprinkled with salt, but the sweet varieties are the best.

BEST BET My favorite is the Almond Pretzel with Caramel Dip: thank you, Mimi, for showing me the way.

WEB TIPS The pretzel mix is available online ($13).

WHERE TO BUY Over 900 locations worldwide. www.auntie annes.com.

Christine Ferber FRENCH $

Finding the best maker of French confiture is an impossible task, although this woman is known to foodies as one of the best. Her production is small and not very well distributed and concentrates more on hotels and fine restaurants, so you are more likely to taste her spreads at a hotel than a home.

WHERE TO BUY Made in Strasbourg, the line is sold at fine Paris grocery stores such as L'Epicerie, the Bon Marche department store.

Costco birthday cakes USA $

Costco, the shopping warehouse, carries more than big cases of paper towels and dog food; they make industrial-size sheet cakes which can be personalized for any occasion. They're big, and they're tasty.

These cakes are perfect for feeding an indiscriminate yet hungry group of young ball players or birthday celebrants. If size matters, this may be the best deal in town. You must be a Costco member to purchase. www.costco.com.

Frank Cooper BRITISH $

A famous name in British jams, this Oxford-shire maker has a store in Oxford and distribution through food halls and gourmet shops all over the UK. Most famous for his marmalade, Cooper also makes an excellent strawberry jam as well as several other flavors.

WHERE TO BUY Order online from www. englishteastore.com.

Frank Cooper's "Fine Cut Oxford Marmalade" from Oxfordshire.

Laduree FRENCH $–$$

While the Angelina tearoom in Paris (p. 379) may be more traditional, the staff at Laduree is more friendly and the macaroons are more beautiful (and varied). The original tearoom is on the rue Royale right off the place Concorde; new tearooms—with shops—have opened around Paris and in major international cities, such as London.

With a baroque interior of pale, water-green and packaging to match, the tearooms have branded their look and their color. (The packaging has been extended to a range of candles and home scent.)

BEST BETS   A box of treats presented in the pale green box means you care enough to bring the very best.

WEB TIPS   The site is available in English and is decorated with such rococo flourish that you get a real feel for the product just through looking. The best part: You can send a postcard (via e-mail) to anyone you want (or as many anyones as you want). The bad news: You cannot shop online.

WHERE TO BUY   FLAGSHIP   16 rue Royale, 8e Paris. ☎ 331/ **4260-2179.** Mon–Sat 8:30am–7pm; Sun 10am–7pm. Métro: Concorde or Madeleine. www.laduree.fr.

Pierre Hermé FRENCH $

The most famous pastry chef in France—maybe the world—has two shops in Paris where he sells pastries, some foodstuffs and candies. The shops themselves are designed just like jewelry stores; the pastries are the jewels on show. The bags are die-cuts—expensive and lush, just like the morsels you buy to eat.

BEST BUYS   Hermé makes a lemon cream tart that is very unusual and sublime; he is also famous for his salted butter caramel flavors. But then, he's famous for everything he creates. And yes, he too participates in the war of the macaroons.

WEB TIPS   Order from the website; it's in French.

WHERE TO BUY   2 stores in Paris, 4 in Tokyo, including New Otani Hotel. **FLAGSHIP**   72 rue Bonaparte, Paris 6e. ☎ **334/ 354-4777.** Tues–Sun 10am–7pm, until 7:30pm on Sat. 185 Rue de Vaugirard, Paris 15e. ☎ **33/4783-8996.** Tues–Wed 10am–7pm; Thurs–Sat 10am–7:30pm; Sun 10am–6pm. www.pierre herme.com.

Chapter Eleven

Bargains & Alternative Retail

*D*o you like to shop off the beaten path, to walk the extra mile to find a trading post right down yonder, to dream the impossible dream? Is that the same dream I have: fabulous merchandise at an everyday low price? You don't mind items in bins, boxes or just off-loaded from barges? Does a good flea market make you sweaty all over? If not sweaty all over, at least do you get itchy palms and/or dry mouth? How do you feel about yard sales? Yeah, I thought so. Me, too. I just love alternative retail, especially when it involves a bargain.

There are two contradictory mottos most Shopping Goddesses live by:

- You get what you pay for; and
- Why pay retail?

It is this paradox that drives us and makes us question the structure of the system we all work within. Not that we don't appreciate capitalism; we just like to be the one with the invitation to a sample sale in our fist. The conventional wisdom here is that you are welcome to the bargain if you are willing to work for it. Okay, the Shopping Goddess says, that's agreed. But what about brands that make merchandise for their outlets so that you think you are getting a deal when in fact you are getting *exactly* what you pay for?

It's a mystery.

There are businesses that raise the retail price so it can be marked down, to offer what is called "perceived value" in the trade. There are bins in China that have for less than $1 the same merchandise you are required to pay $10 for in a store in the U.S. . . . or more. There is the private label business and then there is vertical merchandising.

When I was about 22 years old, I went to work for a magazine called *Chain Store Age,* as the fashion editor. A new brand of pantyhose was being introduced by a major maker. It would be indiscreet to name names, I fear. I covered the story and became friendly with the brand manager who then taught me that this company made its own pantyhose; that the mills ran 24 hours a day, chugging out product. That this very same product was then packaged 10 different ways and sold under 10 different brand names.

Cloistered nuns placed an order for seven pairs of Miu Miu mules.

—Frederico Marchetto, Yoox.com

I rest my case.

Architectural Salvage Yards

Architectural salvage includes everything from structural details—from cornices to window sashes. For example, some suppliers specialize in barn siding or floorboards. You may find bathroom specialists who have a sideline in old tubs or just bathroom fixtures.

The best salvage yards are located close to the source, so if you want pieces of a French castle, you go to France, not Chicago. Duh. In some cases, the extent and quality of the architectural salvage is directly related to the heritage of the city and its fallen trophies. Chicago has some of the best salvage stores in the U.S., but it also has some of the most important architectural history in the U.S. Berkeley, California, is known for its architectural salvage partly because the real estate there used to cost less than in San Francisco, so warehouses and salvage lots could be developed. The Belle Epoque buildings of Cannes, in the South of France, were mostly destroyed in the 1960s because the cost of renovating them was too high—yet Cannes does not have an architectural salvage business. Go figure.

Purists must note that even the big, famous salvage sources—especially in the U.S.—may sell reproductions.

Adkins Antiques TEXAN $$–$$$$

Officially named Adkins Architectural Antiques & Treasures, the emphasis needs to be on treasures. Or heart-stopping fun. The main part of the "store" is a Victorian-style house (circa 1912, which is post-Victorian for those who keep track of these things) with overrun into a 20,000-sq-ft. warehouse. There's stuff everywhere; those who love clutter will go crazy on first approach. The specialty is decorative elements, which means there aren't many structural elements. There are repro items; they also do restorations and custom work. Best of all, the business operates on a wholesale, retail and rental basis. They speak many languages and will arrange shipping.

BEST BETS I use copper sinks as one of my measuring tools—theirs sell for $180 to $225, which is middle of the road. Chandeliers are $850 to $3,500, and their weathervanes are under $300.

WEB TIPS The website is easy to use; you can shop online—there are even online specials and sales. I don't think you can see the definition in the pieces that well online, but you can get a basic idea and let's face it, you pretty much know what a claw-foot tub looks like.

WHERE TO BUY   1 store: 3515 Fanin Rd., Houston, TX. ☎ **800/522-6547** or 713/522-6547. Mon–Sat 9:30am–5:30pm; Sun noon–5pm. MC, V. www.adkinsantiques.com.

Architectural Artifacts CHICAGO

$$–$$$

Argentinian carved door from Architectural Artifacts, Inc.

Considering how important the city of Chicago is in American architecture, it's no surprise that one of the best salvage companies in the U.S. is in the Windy City. This famous firm is so complete that it even has its own museum—a must-do for anyone (yes, kids and dogs are welcome.) While the stores sell all of the usual suspects in salvage, they are most famous for their doors and have instituted a new category—religious relics.

There's 80,000 square feet of selling space, making this one of the largest salvage stores in the U.S. In the atrium, there's gallery space and regular shows/events. You can also rent this space for a party . . . or a wedding. Talk about something old, something new, something borrowed and so on.

BEST BETS   You'll find the best quality and largest selection of fireplace mantels in the country here; they range in price from $1,000 to over $20,000.

WEB TIPS   Not only is this an excellent site, but it differs from other salvage sites and inspires your imagination. There's music and moderne touches, so if you think all salvage is about clutter—take a look and be surprised.

WHERE TO BUY   1 store: 4325 N. Ravenswood, Chicago, IL. ☎ **773/ 348-0622.** Daily 10am–5pm. MC, V. www.architecturalartifacts.com.

Nostalgia CHESHIRE, ENGLAND $–$$$$$

Tiles, tubs, fireplaces—Nostalgia specializes in British Victorian salvage, particularly those needs

World Traveler

The cities between Manchester and Leeds and Liverpool form a playground of salvage and antiques warehouse. Assuming you will be sending a container, and therefore controlling the shipping expenses, you'll find much in terms of architectural detail as well as furniture; remember that Leeds is the area for fireplaces.

8 Best Airports For Shopping

I've rarely met an airport I didn't like (once I make it through security and have a little mini-trolly rolling along ahead of me). Airport shopping is no longer just about duty-free but selection, entertainment and the chance to get a last crack at locally made merchandise and even handcrafts.

1. **Amsterdam: Schiphol International (AMS)**
   Here's your chance to buy tulip bulbs that have the proper government seals to export them into the U.S. www.schiphol.nl.

2. **Paris: Charles De Gaulle International (CDG), Terminal E**
   Although the firm Airports de Paris (www.adp.fr) has been consistently good over the years, it has only become among the best with the opening of the E terminal at CDG, where you'll find a Galeries Gourmet, luxury grocery store, makeup stores and designer boutiques. For the most part the other parts of CDG are unremarkable; if you're lucky you'll end up in E. www.paris-cdg.com.

3. **Copenhagen: Kastrup (CPH)**
   Feathers! Duvets! Furs! Chocolates filled with liquor! Cute little lanes of old timey storefronts make this a wonderful destination on your way home or elsewhere. www.cph.dk.

4. **United Arab Emirates: Dubai International (DIA)**
   For years I thought the whole schtick to Dubai was the airport—now I know better, but do note that this is a remarkable airport for shopping. Duty-free prices are excellent and promotions are manifold. www.dubaiairport.com.

the local clientele would have in restoring a home. There's enough to make you drool for a day; the problem becomes the combination of paying in sterling and needing to ship.

BEST BETS   The fireplaces, which start at $2,500 and top out over $35,000.

WEB TIPS   Great photos (several views of each piece) are featured on the website, along with dimensions and pricing.

WHERE TO BUY   1 store: Hollands Mill, 61 Shaw Rd., Stockport, Cheshire, UK. ☎ **44161/477-7706.** Tues–Fri 10am–6pm; Sat 10am–5pm; closed Sun and Mon. www.nostalgia-uk.com.

5. **London: Heathrow (LHR)**
   The airport sucks, but the stores are great. British Airport Authority (www.baa.co.uk) runs retail at Heathrow and has perhaps the best retail in any airport in the world. Terminals 4 and 5 are the newest and best; Terminal 3 is not as dramatic, but nonetheless offers very good shopping. In March 2008, Terminal 5 will have a 2-floor Harrod's. www.heathrowairport.com.

6. **Hong Kong: HK International, or Chep Lap Kok (HKG)**
   Not only was this airport designed by Sir Norman Foster, but it has so much retail that many stores have several branches. When I tell friends to meet up at Shanghai Tang after they clear security, they may well ask, "Which one?" There are multiple levels of shopping with a guarantee of main street pricing. Choose from the usual designers and news agents to local heroes such as Shanghai Tang and Amazing Grace. There are also traditional Chinese medicines and a chance to have a 15-minute Chinese massage. Make use of the free shopping carts (about half the size of a real luggage trolley). www.hongkongairport.com.

7. **Singapore: Changi International (SIN)**
   Good on the luxury brands (Cartier, Chloe, Prada, Tod's and more), but also excellent bookstores and even a Krispy Kreme. www.changiairport.com.

8. **Sydney: Kingsford Smith International (SYD)**
   Among the best selection of aboriginal art and designs of any store in Australia. www.sydneyairport.com.

ReBuilding Center PORTLAND $–$$$

This is the largest nonprofit salvage resource in the U.S., affiliated with Our United Villages as well as Habitat for Humanity. There's a 40,000-square-foot store of salvage plus a furniture store and an amazing website that helps you find what you need.

BEST BETS   Stock changes on an hourly basis.

WEB TIPS   You'll find lots of information about the store on their website, but not much on inventory.

WHERE TO BUY   1 store: 3625 N. Mississippi Ave, Portland, OR. ☎ **503/331-1877.** Mon–Sat 9am–6pm; Sun 10am–5pm. MC, V. www.rebuildingcenter.org.

⊕ Online Auctions: Sarah Does eBay

Every time I travel out of town for *Born to Shop*, I know to expect a surprise when I get home: My husband has been on eBay. My last two trips have prompted major purchases by him—a 1931 Ford Model A Coupe and a custom hot rod racing car, both won on eBay auctions. Parking in the driveway isn't so bad, except when it rains.

My eBay spending habits are more across the board; I'm always looking for a find. I know Suzy was impressed by my $12 Armani jacket; okay, with shipping the total was closer to $20. I've also bought French linens, kitchen gadgets, custom collars for Bentley and Toffee (my canine pals), out-of-print books and more. The only mishap involved antique porcelain shipped from England. When my platter arrived shattered, I contacted the seller, who helped file the insurance claim; and because I'd paid with PayPal, my money was refunded. It was a gorgeous platter; R.I.P.

A few rules and tips I've learned:

- Stay calm when bidding so you don't overspend or snatch up items without properly inspecting them—like that "antique English silver frame" that was made in China last year. It now rests on my book shelf next to my computer, as a reminder of my stupidity.
- The best time to shop and bid is late at night, especially on weekends. That's when lots of people are busy with other things, so there's less competition for bargains. Sellers are catching on, however, and listing items so they end during a busy time—like Sunday afternoon.

Catalogs

My favorite catalog story is about the child who was a peer of my son's. This young lady—aged 6—was asked to bring her favorite book to first grade for a class project. She brought the Tiffany catalog. You go, girl!

I am ignoring the fact that these days, many catalogs are reproduced online, come in CD format or are available for $2 as what the trade calls a "digital catalog." To me, shopping online is something you do to be efficient. Shopping by catalog is an emotional experience that cannot be replaced.

There are firms that provide catalogs to interested parties; call ☎ 800/547-0600 to reach Emporium of Catalogs. Some of their catalogs are free; others have a fee.

- Not all eBay sellers are geniuses. You'll find bargains by "searching" with misspelled keywords. For a vacuum, try *vacume, vaccum, vaccuum,* and the like. Since those incorrect spellings aren't accessed by the searches, you may have no competition for the product.
- Be friendly with the seller. After I bid on an unsuccessful auction (the "reserve" price wasn't met), I sent the seller an e-mail offering what I thought was a fair price and was successful. The seller remembered I had sent several queries and responded by saying my price was fair and he was happy to sell the item to me.
- My favorite trick is **Esnipe**.com. Esnipe places bids for you during the last few seconds of an auction. With Esnipe doing the bidding, your privacy and bids are hidden until the auction ends. Esnipe also allows you to enter multiple bids or withdraw a bid at any time, and it's easy to do. Just enter the e-Bay item number on the Esnipe Web page along with your maximum bid, and they'll do the rest. If you're outbid before the auction ends, you'll be notified by e-mail and asked if you want to enter a higher bid. If you change your mind, you can withdraw your bid up until 5 minutes before the auction ends, which you can't do by bidding directly on e-Bay. Of course, this service isn't free. For auction wins under $25, you'll pay $0.25, for wins between $25 and $1,000, you'll pay 1% of the winning bid and for wins over $1,000, the fee is a flat ten bucks. *—Sarah Lahey*

Things you should know about catalog shopping:

- Catalogs that charge often deduct the cost of the catalog from your first purchase. If they don't, reconsider.
- Catalogs should be free after you have purchased from the firm.
- Catalogs should have online support systems.
- Catalogs should (but sometimes don't) offer the same prices and same promotional deals. See that code on the front of the catalog—it's related usually to your zip code and may offer a discount (or may not when others do get the discount).
- Catalogs can be recycled by taking them to a retirement home.

Archie McPhee SEATTLE $–$$

My late sister introduced me to this catalog about 20 years ago. These days they have an online catalog, but the printed one is

The cover of Archie McPhee's Catalog 74.

much, much better and I urge you to sign up for one; they're free. You sign up online (see below). There is now a store, but basically this is a catalog business selling silly things. www.mcphee.com.

The Company Store USA

$–$$$$

So sue me; this is a boring choice. I can't help it. I don't find it boring. Vanilla ice cream isn't boring, is it? Their bed linens are usually colorful and energetic—different from what you see elsewhere and fairly priced, which means you usually don't mind paying the price, even if it's a little more than you wanted to pay. Charisma 420-thread count cotton sheets are individually priced under $75, and 500-count cotton sateen sets are under $125. There's a good selection in Cal king. www.thecompanystore.com.

Levenger USA $–$$$

I am bonkers for their pocket leather envelopes and the printed note cards and inserts. A set of 250 personalized note cards is $68 and the leather envelope to hold them is $20. www.levenger.com.

Lillian Vernon USA $–$$

Here it is—the secret of my best inexpensive wedding gift ever, brought to you directly from the pages of this catalog. If the bride is changing her name with her upcoming nuptials, you order a few dozen pencils engraved with her new name.

Indeed, this catalog specializes in products that can be personalized. Most of the merchandise is inexpensive; a lot of it is far from classy. But anyone with a good eye, or a good idea, will find this worth a prowl. www.lillianvernon.com.

L.L.Bean USA $–$$$$$

More than 50 catalogs are published each year; you can also shop online. All products come with a guarantee of satisfaction. While the catalog isn't really sexy, it's got a fundamental practicality that makes it work for everyone.

The best item sold? The canvas boat tote ($19–$39), which is one of the icons of the firm. It has been modernized to come in colors now, so get a look at the red one. And don't forget to have it monogrammed ($5 extra). www.llbean.com.

Charity Events

Do you shop red, green or pink? Green is a lifestyle—shopping with an ecological eye on environmentally sound products. Pink and Red, however, are organized merchandising methods meant to raise funds—and awareness—for breast cancer and AIDS prevention. You still pay the retail price but the retailer or the maker gives up a portion of the profits to an alternative party. Sweet charity!

Old Bags Luncheon USA VALUE $$$$

I love this. Who among us doesn't have some perfectly nice, hardly ever used handbags that are just sitting in the closet gathering moss? The idea here is to grab one of those bags and donate it to this cause. Then you buy a luncheon ticket ($300) and attend the silent auction for previously owned and donated bags. It's all on behalf of the Center for Family Service held in early April each year at The Breakers, Palm Beach. This event began in Palm Beach, but Old Bag fundraisers across the country are held throughout the year to benefit various charities. www.palmbeachpost.com.

7th on Sale Online USA $–$$$$$

The world's largest online sample sale is held once a year with proceeds distributed through the CFDA-Vogue initiative/NYC AIDS Fund. The sale usually runs for 1 month, from early November to early December, and features one-of-a-kind, impossible-to-find items for men, women, kids and home. The extensive array includes cashmere sweaters, shoes, handbags, and red-carpet dresses worn by celebrities.

The event kicks off with a 10-day auction of "fashion adventures" including vacations at designers' exotic private homes. "Shop til AIDS drops" is the motto. www.ebay.com/7thonsale.

QVC FFANY Shoes on Sale USA $$$–$$$$$

Held in NYC, this annual gala and television event is a 3-hour QVC footwear program in which 100,000 pairs of designer shoes are sold at half their retail price.

🖱 Coupon Coups

Sunday newspapers have been the main avenue of distribution for coupons in America, but the same cents-off (or dollars-off) notion is available online. You can either search for a "coupon" link on the seller's website (these are rare) or go to one of the coupon search sites for help. The best is **www.couponcabin.com** where you can find discounts to more than 700 online stores; when you find a coupon you want to use, just click on the provided link, shop at the site as you normally would, then enter the provided coupon code at checkout. If "coupon code" isn't available, you've probably already received the discount, but check to be sure. Other coupon options include **www.keycode.com**, which is well organized with easy-to-read print and directions. For referral to retailers, check out **www.currentcodes.com**. At **www.findsavings.com** you'll find rebates and freebies, and go to **www.slickdeals.net** where there's a message board with postings from members.

A word to the wise—sometimes the codes on these sites are outdated or invalid and you won't know until you check out.

During the month of October (Breast Cancer Awareness Month), QVC carries a "Shoe of the Day" segment each weekday until it sells out. All proceeds go to breast cancer research. www.bcrfcure.org.

Crafts Fairs

American Craft Show USA $–$$$$

This annual San Francisco event (well over 30 years popular) showcases more than 250 artisans and their latest designer jewelry, clothing, furniture, home decor and more. There's a special children's section, and guests can indulge in wine tastings from top area vineyards.

WHERE TO BUY Fort Mason Center, San Francisco, CA. Annually, Aug. www.craftcouncil.org.

Bazar del Sábado MEXICO CITY $–$$$

As the name indicates, this crafts market is only held on Saturdays. Sprawling across a plaza in the suburb of Angel—an upper-middle class residential area in Mexico City—this market begins in a mansion, weaves outside the house and into the park out front, sways under tents and dances into the streets beyond and even into a few stray buildings that by dint of location have been absorbed into the culture.

Prices may be a little higher than elsewhere, but you are paying for the ambiance and the clean bathrooms. Speaking of bathrooms, do stop into the men's room to see the papier-mâché sculptures.

The most expensive of the craft items are sold in the main mansion; there's art sold outdoors in the plaza and then a series of tents and alleys with average local crafts at prices you can bargain for. The high-end items include brass decorative items, jewelry, children's clothes and some souvenirs. The thrills of this market are related to the colors of the merchandise, the colors of the food sold by the vendors, the upmarket patrons and the local peddlers. There's cobblestones, there's stucco, there's hand-painted tiles.

No public transportation; take a taxi—about $10 from the Zona Rosa. Bring cash, although dealers inside the main house usually take bank cards (not American Express). Some will accept U.S. dollars. No website.

WHERE TO BUY   Bazar del Sabado, Plaza San Jacinto 11, Colonia San Angel Mexico City. Sat only 9am–6pm.

Crafts on Columbus NYC $–$$$$

Some might think that the perfect Sunday in Manhattan involves brunch and a trip to a museum. I'll take the brunch and a stroll to the Museum of Natural History and then forget the museum, opting instead for the vendors who line the sidewalks on Columbus Avenue for a twice-a-year fair—three weekends in October and three weekends in April or May.

Each vendor has his own little hut of white plastic tenting, so you—and the wares—are protected from the elements. The craftspeople are funky and their goods are funky but fabulous—and often expensive.

Some vendors take credit cards, most do not. They will take personal checks, if you are convincing in your demeanor.

WHERE TO BUY   W. 82nd St. and Columbus Ave., around the corner from the Museum of Natural History, NYC. For dates call ☎ 212/866-2239.

Crafts at Rhinebeck DUTCHESS COUNTY, NY $$–$$$$$

Though I always suspected I was born to shop, it's possible I didn't know for sure until the June day in 1976 when I set foot into the Duchess County Fairgrounds and attended the crafts show that would grow to be the largest in the world—and one of the best. Hell, it was one of the best the day it was born. There were almost 300 vendors then; now there are over 500.

And yes, this is a juried event—not any old weekend craft kid can get in.

The event earns some $5 million in the spread of 4 days and gets bigger and better, as if that were possible. The fair has four open-sided buildings, three tents and assorted stalls in the walkways; it serves buyers, gallery dudes, New York sophisticates and local hippies.

Shows are twice a year (June and Sept), although the June event is the biggie. Not much bargaining goes on, by the way, and wares are not inexpensive.

WHERE TO BUY   Tickets online or at Dutchess County Fairgrounds. ☎ **845/876-4001.** Admission $7. Sat 10am–6pm; Sun 10am–5pm. You can take a tour bus from Manhattan; call Shortline Tours. ☎ **914/876-2828.** www.dutchessfair.com.

One of a Kind Show & Sale   CHICAGO $$–$$$$

This is a once-a-year shopping event held at the Merchandise Mart in Chicago, usually the first weekend in December. Book hotel rooms way in advance; this is so hot people fly in from all over the country. The event kicks off on Thursday evening with a First Look event that is a benefit for Children's Memorial Hospital. Mere mortals can shop Friday to Sunday for a $10 ticket; $7 for seniors or students. It's held on the eighth floor with about 400 booths. Categories include painting, sculpture, glass, photography, furniture, jewelry and fiber art. All items are handmade, one at a time.

WHERE TO BUY   Chicago Merchandise Mart, 222 Merchandise Mart Plaza, 8th Floor. ☎ **800/677-6278.** www.merchandisemart. com.

Philadelphia Museum of Art Craft Show   PHILADEL-
PHIA $$–$$$$

Thousands of artists apply to exhibit at this popular show, but fewer than 200 are chosen, so that tells you how dynamic the contemporary crafts are. The exhibits range from jewelry to clothing to tabletop; prices range from reasonable (under $100) to "don't touch" (many $1,000s). The 4-day event includes a fancy preview party, corporate receptions, student exhibitions and on-site artist demonstrations. All crafts on display are available for purchase, and you can buy more through the silent auction, featuring items donated by participants. Tickets are $15 to $20; download a discount coupon from the website.

WHERE TO BUY   Pennsylvania Convention Center, Phildelphia. ☎ **215/684-7930.** Annually in November. www.pmacraftshow. org.

Santa Fe Indian Market SANTA FE $–$$$$$

Many southwestern venues have annual Native American markets, but the one in Santa Fe each August is the most famous. The entire month of August is packed with events in Santa Fe and the surrounding area, so you may want to go in early or stay late.

It's very hot in the area in August; the crowds are thick and the tourist business is almost overwhelming. Still, there's a lot of hustle and bustle in the galleries, on the blankets at the Governor's Palace and in the stalls and stands set up to create a marketplace. There are some 1,200 vendors from almost 100 different tribes—this is considered the largest pow-wow of the year; a great chance to meet with the artists themselves.

Make no mistake, the gallery people know the ins and outs and would scalp you to get an important piece; if you are a serious collector, you already know to set up appointments before you get there . . . or to have things put aside.

Make hotel reservations a year in advance; don't miss the food ops and the chance to dine on Native American cuisine in the fair's specialty booths. Blue corn pancakes? Indian fry bread? I'll be right there!

WHERE TO BUY   The area around Governor's Palace and in galleries throughout the Santa Fe area. Offices. 141 E. Palace Ave., Santa Fe, NM. ☎ **505/983-5220.** www.swaia.org.

Donation Centers

Emmahuis FRENCH   VALUE $–$$

This is a bit esoteric for tourists, but you just never know when you're going to need this resource and it is a doozy. Created by the late Father Pierre, this is the French version of Goodwill. Donations are taken in, homeless men are given shelter, they do the repairs as needed and the merchandise is sold to fund the project. Accordingly, there are Emmahuis stores all over France. I've only checked out one in Paris; it wasn't great and I swore off the Paris stores.

BEST BET   I regularly shop the store in Courthezon near Orange in my part of Provence. They have tons of furniture, an entire house filled with clothes, another with tabletop and a yard filled with bathroom supplies. I bought an armoire for $10, then paid $50 to have it delivered.

WHERE TO BUY   Stores all over France; city shops are much smaller than the expansive province shops. Favorite: Emmaüs Courthezon, 748 Chemin de la Papeterie, Quartier Segurets, Courthezon, France (Northern Vaucluse). ☎ **334/9070-6107.** Tues–Thurs 2–6pm; Sat 9am–noon and 2–6pm. www.emmaus.fr.

Goodwill USA VALUE $–$$$$

I'm not sure how it happened, but at some point shopping Salvation Army stores became déclassé and shopping Goodwill became socially acceptable. I speak not only for myself, but for other shoppers out there. We shopping snobs like Goodwill better than just about any other charity shop.

When I lived in Westport, CT—a wealthy community on Long Island Sound—I was a regular at Goodwill where I bought furniture and clothes. I'm still sorry I didn't buy that drum set ($400) for my son, but hey, what would the neighbors say? *Insider's tip:* Shop the good zip codes.

WHERE TO BUY   www.goodwill.org.

Duty-Free

Not all duty-free stores are located within airports. For the most part, I think that "duty-free" is a trick and rarely offers a great deal. But that is such an over-simplification that I am embarrassed. After all, I am the one who spent 2 years stalking a specific Hermès watch at duty-free stores all over the world and saw it go for anything between $1,500 and $1,200. (Bought it in Prague airport for $1,250.)

Most cruise ships have duty-free shops onboard; the stores are run by firms that specialize in duty-free and they guarantee their prices against those on shore or those elsewhere.

Note that many duty-free stores and associations now post their prices online. Try the British guide **www.dutyfreeshoppingindex.com** or **www.thedutyfreepriceguide.com** (an Australian firm).

Should all this seem like too much trouble, use the basics of retail logic—countries that normally impose high duties (such as Japan) offer no bargains in their duty-free shops.

My favorite duty-frees happen to be French:

Air France In-Flight Duty-Free FRENCH $–$$$

Although the euro is an awfully strong currency right now, one of the best ways to save on luxury goods is through the in-flight duty-free program on long-haul Air France flights. Best deals are on luxury brands. www.airfrance.com.

Catherine FRENCH $–$$$$

This duty-free source in Paris is not at the airport; in fact, it's in the high rent district of Paris's finest retail stores. The store sells handbags, small gift items (watches, scarves, Paris souvenirs), some beauty treatments, some major makeup brands and—most importantly—fragrance. Not only do they sell the major brands but they specialize in hard-to-find scents.

Prices tend to be less than at the duty-free stores in the airport because the discount is 20%, whereas airport duty-free is usually 13% less. There may be additional price breaks based on French retail price versus U.S. department store price. I buy Sisleya, a face cream by the French firm Sisley, that costs about $300 in U.S. stores, for about $210 at Catherine (160€). The euro price stays stable; the U.S. dollar price therefore fluctuates. Fax or call them for updates.

BEST BETS   The best deals overall are on Sisley beauty products, but Catherine also carries Lancome, Dior, La Prairie and ▣ **Yves Saint Laurent.** Chanel lipstick (the most requested at Catherine) sells for 18€ discount and 15€ detaxe. The Chanel foundation is 24€ ($34), versus a U.S. price of $45 (plus tax).

WHERE TO BUY   FLAGSHIP   7 rue de Castiglione, Paris, 1er. ☎ **01/ 4260-4817.** Fax 01/4261-0235. Métro: Concorde or Tuileries. Mon–Sat 10am–7pm. AE, MC, V. No website. Shipping is easily arranged by mail but may affect the cost/savings ratio.

DFS (Duty-Free Shoppers) USA/FRENCH $–$$$$

With stores in a variety of international airports, DFS superficially looks like just another duty-free face. What's extraordinary about this business is their non-airport freestanding stores that are mini-department stores selling luxury brands, local brands and souvenirs. They also specialize in multi-paks, offering a price break on items bundled together in groups of 3, 5 or more—cheaper by the dozen and all that. I shop in Hong Kong but there are in-town stores in many Asian cities. The stores are often called DFS Galleria.

WHERE TO BUY   25+ locations, in Hollywood, Sydney, Bali, Hong Kong, New Zealand; JFK International (Terminal 4), LA International (Tom Bradley Terminal), San Francisco International (Concourse A). Hollywood: 6801 Hollywood Blvd., CA. ☎ **323/960-4888,** or 800/244-5595.

Flea Markets

Annex Antiques/Hell's Kitchen Flea Market & Garage NYC

These are three different venues that have merged into one giant fun fair with shuttle bus service connecting the Chelsea portion with the Hell's Kitchen portion. Historically, this whole shebang used to be in Chelsea, but the outdoor flea market lost its parking lot venue to the real estate boom (they tore down Paradise and put up a parking lot) so now there are two areas and three parts to the adventure. At least they no longer charge a $1 admission fee.

The Garage is a building—well, it's a parking lot structure; the **West 25th Street Market** is a building of dealers; and **Hell's Kitchen** is an outdoor market. The markets are held on weekends; outdoors if open weather permits.

BEST BETS   The "in" New York thing is to go clubbing all night and then go to the flea markets at dawn.

WEB TIPS   Lotsa information on all markets.

WHERE TO BUY   Annex/Hell's Kitchen: 39th St. between 9th and 10th aves. Subway: A, C or E to Times Sq. The Garage: 112 W. 25th St., between 6th and 7th aves. W. 25th St. Market, 29–37 W. 25th St. ☎ **212/243-5342.** Markets open sunrise to sunset. www.annexantiques.com.

Berlin Flohmarkt BERLIN

There are over 100 flea markets in Berlin. About 20 of them are weekend markets that are really good. I go to Berlin just for the flea markets sometimes; bring bubble wrap and an empty suitcase.

The one that I find world class is named after its street location: **17 Juni** (Sat–Sun 11am–5pm; S-bah Tiergarten) right along the Tiergarten park and chockablock with what came out of grandma's attic after the Unification. There's also real and fake Soviet souvenirs and lotsa chunks of the, gasp, Berlin Wall. (All fake.) It is against the law to sell family photos or any souvenirs of either of the world wars, but you will find everything else. In the path leading to the actual flea market, there's a crafts market that is also great fun.

The Flohmarkt in Berlin.

BEST BETS If you want to get away from the tourists (or attempt to), there are several other good flea markets not far away that can fit into your weekend schedule:

- **Arkonapltaz** (alternative lifestyle Mitte crowd), U8 Bernauer Strasse. ☎ **786-9764.** Sun 10am–6pm. S-bahn: Mitte.
- **Heidestrasse Train Tracks** (in stalls under the tracks; mostly collectibles and teddy bears). Heidestrasse 10. Sat–Sun 10am–2pm. S-bahn: Tiergarten.
- **Museum Island** (very funky with lots of kitsch). Flohmarkt am Kupfergraben, Museum Island. Sat–Sun 9am–3pm. S-Bahn: Frederichstrasse.
- **Treptow.** *Note:* Treptow is a suburb on the River Spree, but you can get there on the S-bahn; there are few tourists here. The market is held inside a huge warehouse. This one is lots of fun and yes, most young people speak English. Marktander Arena in Treptow. Sat–Sun 8am–5pm. S-Bahn: Treptow.

La Braderie de Lille LILLE, FRANCE

Once upon a time, in medieval times, m'lord and lady accumulated some junk in their manse. They had servants back then in the day when servants knew how to be servants and so the good servants said, "Hey guys, why don't you sell this junk?"

Alas, it was considered *moche* (tacky) for the highborn to sell their used stuff. So they gave the servants permission to sell everything on 1 day a year. That day falls in early September and this medieval tradition continues today, only now it's one of the largest flea markets in the world, with over 10,000 vendors and 60 miles (100km) of selling space. Hotels in Lille must be booked a year in advance. However, you can do this as a day trip from Paris because there is TGV service every hour for the 1-hour train ride. Bring a rolling cart or suitcase with you, maybe the 40-mule team.

BEST BETS   Because the market is open 24/24, you can shop at odd hours to avoid the crowds.

WHERE TO BUY   Once a year event, throughout Lille, first weekend in September. www.mairie-lille.fr.

Brimfield Antique Shows MASSACHUSETTS

World's Best   This so-called dealer's-only show is held three times a year but because the weather can be iffy in May, the July show is considered the best. Shows last for 10 days in May, July and September, when in fact the event lasts 10 days and most shows last only 3 or 4. The whole of it, held in a one-street, tiny town in southern Massachusetts, is made up of many promoters who lease out fields and let vendors set up for days on end. The amount of stuff is totally mind-boggling. Motels sell out a year in advance; for some shows people get up at dawn and search for treasures by flashlight.

WHERE TO BUY   Three times a year in Brimfield, between Exits 8 and 9 of the Massachusetts Turnpike (Route 90). http://brimfieldshow.com.

Budapest Ecseri BUDAPEST

I consider this one of the world's greatest flea markets and dream of going back not only for the joys of the entire market but to specifically buy hand-painted Hungarian dishes, which speak to my soul more than Grandma Jessie's goulash.

Speaking of goulash, they even have a cafe here that serves home-style cooking. But I digress.

The flea market tends to be home style with a few Communist-era souvenirs thrown in and some religious relics. I bought a fabulous naïf Virgin Mary painted on glass from behind. But best of all: I collect painted bowls from the 1930s to 1950s that have big bold flowers on them and a name or slogan. Learning the difference between Ertzi (Elizabeth) and the words for "good luck" took years of training.

This market is outside of town; there is a bus but it takes forever and no one will speak English to help you. You can take a Cityrama tour from the Central Market, which you sign up for at your hotel. I simply splurge for a taxi and then arrange for the driver to return at a given time. I've never been stranded although I have been forced to leave before I wanted to.

While some of the vendors are here during the week, this market is best on Saturdays and good on Sunday mornings.

BEST BETS Hungarian folk art.

WHERE TO BUY Ecseri, 9th district Budapest. ☎ **1/348-3200.** Mon–Fri 8am–4pm; Sat 8am–3pm; Sun 8am–1pm. No credit cards.

Charnock Richard CHORLEY, ENGLAND

This is a professional flea market that is not going to be for everyone. Located outside Manchester, England, the indoor market goes on forever selling all sorts of junk each Sunday. Owned by the same people who have the Camelot theme park next door, this flea market draws a local crowd and is a must-do only for pickers. If you don't know what a picker is, this is not worth driving on the wrong side of the road.

Nearby in the town of Chorley (it shouldn't be a total waste), you'll want to catch whatever market you happen upon—there's market every day, be it regular market or antiques day or junkers day. The covered market is great fun; on Friday there is an outdoor market.

BEST BETS Affordable English antiques and bric-a-brac, junk, stuff and kitchen sinks.

WEB TIPS View a clear map on the website.

WHERE TO BUY Charnock Richard, Chorley, Lancashire. On the A49 between Preston and Wigan, old mill towns.

Chatou FRANCE

World's Best My motto is simply "Chatou, I love you." This food and antiques fair is held about an hour outside of Paris twice a year, usually March and September, but sometimes the spring event falls into April. Some 800 antiques vendors team up with several dozen food stands from various French provinces and build a small village with dirt streets; you simply walk up and down these *allees* and shop 'til you have to stop for oysters or wine or sausage or a ham sandwich.

Originally the site of a medieval pig fair, this is one of the best antiques shows in the greater Paris area because the prices are much, much lower than at Paris flea markets and few tourists know about the event. There is a modest admission fee paid at the door.

BEST BETS Most of the vendors come from outside of Paris and sell rustic wares. I bought a series of 12 Napoleonic black and white copper etched cheese plates for $150. There are items for as few as some euros; there's also some high-end dealers who are under rooftops to protect their more serious wares.

WHERE TO BUY   Foire Nationale a la Brocante Ile de Chatou & Chatou Pig Fair. ☎ **331/4770-8878.** Twice a year, daily 10am–7pm. Direct access via RER train, A1. www.sncao-syndicat.com.

Dirt Market BEIJING

Without doubt, the Beijing Dirt Market is one of the best flea markets in the world, although you must take it for granted that much of what is for sale is fake. Still, it's fun, it's colorful and the prices are good.

The Panjiayuan ("Dirt Market") in Beijing.

The marketsite has been cleaned up so the dirt ground—hence the name—is almost gone. It's not clean enough to eat here (only one place to eat, anyway) but the bathrooms won't shock you.

This market is divided into three portions—if you are at the entrance and facing into the market, to the farthest left—really over there where you can't see from where you are standing, vendors have blankets on the ground. These represent the tag sale guys, and your chance for your best buy.

The central part of the market is under a tin roof and flows by lanes, each lane devoted to a different kind of Chinese merchandise—ceramics, paintings, beads, Mao figurines, jade, embroideries and so forth.

To the right of where you are standing is a small village of lanes with tiny storefront hut jobs—in here there are more serious antiques dealers, some of them well known and selling good merchandise.

Insider's tip: You are around the corner from the eyeglasses mart (p. 112).

BEST BETS   The one-stop shopping nature of the event.

WHERE TO BUY   200 W. Panjiayuan, Third Ring Rd., Chaoyang District, Beijing. ☎ **6775-2405.** Sat–Sun 4:30am–3pm. Cash only.

Heart of Country USA

This show is held twice a year, in Nashville in the spring and Texas in the fall, always booked into Gaylords Opryland Hotel. The market is not huge, 100 to 150 dealers, but it specializes in American country and has an event formula that makes it a popular weekend away.

BEST BETS   Often there are lectures and parties that go with the market; visitors can buy a package that includes admission to everything.

WEB TIPS   Nearby hotels offer deals to attendees.

WHERE TO BUY   Nashville in spring; Grapevine, Texas in fall. Thursday preview party 6–10pm; Fri 10am–8pm; Sat 10am–5pm. www.heartofcountry.com.

Isle-sur-la-Sorgue FRANCE

Isle-sur-la-Sorgue, as the name implies, is an island town on the banks of the River Sorgue. The water wheels are an important part of the town's charm. But the flea markets are more important. They are arranged on a complicated schedule partly related to the village's place as a dealer's haven. This is how it works:

1. There are dozens of small villages of antiques dealers tucked away off the main street. They are open Friday to Monday only and prefer to deal with the trade. They are closed Tuesday to Thursday. I have friends with serious money who only want good stuff; they shop on Mondays with the dealers—no tourists, no crowds, no flea market, no bullshit.

2. On Sunday, the village also hosts market day as well as a flea market making this a holy zoo of shopping ops—without a chance to park after 11am.

Obviously, you want to go on a Sunday. My plan is to arrange my schedule so I can be there no later than 9:30am; this allows me to get parking and get to dealers who are just setting up. There is a parking lot attached to the Spar grocery store on the main street—they charge, which means most people prefer not to use it. (Yes!) Pay a few euros and be walking distance to everything.

During market hours, this can be an overwhelming part of town. The crowd pushing through the food and soap dealers is very intense by 10am. Also note, because a lot of the dealers are tucked out of view, you may miss a lot of what's going on unless you pay attention. I park my car, shop the dealers on the sidewalks at the end of the main street, buy my chicken and return to the car with my purchases.

Don't miss: **Michel Biehn's** house (7 av. des 4 Otages), right there on the main street (p. 52).

BEST BETS   Twice a year, Easter and Assumption (Aug 15), there are specialty market events with about 1,000 dealers in the fields behind the town. You can still park in the Spar parking lot—the fields abut it. If you attempt the August market, go very early, wear a hat and sunblock. It is a total madhouse and is so much fun you could faint. Or is that the heat? There are several shipping agents in town; the dealers who sell to you will help you co-ordinate.

WHERE TO BUY   The village of Isle-sur-la-Sorgue is located in the Vaucluse between Avignon and Carpentras. Antiques Market days are Sat–Mon. Flea market: Sun only. Food market: Sun only. No website.

Paddington Market SYDNEY

This market is different from most of the others in this section, but it incorporates a very nice day out in Sydney and should be part of your schedule there. This is a small market, more crafts and up-and-coming designer-oriented than fleas and junk . . . and very upmarket. Think soaps, vintage clothes, kids' clothing, handmade jewelry. There are 250 stalls here and many food booths.

World Traveler

Aside from the market on the main drag, shop the rest of Oxford Street for Aussie brands and global fashion types. On side streets check out galleries and cherished designers such as Colette Dinnigan (www.colettedinnigan.com.au).

Paddington Market is built around a schoolyard in the heart of the best shopping neighborhood in Sydney, Paddington. You want to schedule your trip to be in Sydney and without jet lag on a Saturday to take in the shopping glories of the whole area.

WHERE TO BUY   Paddington Elementary School, Oxford St., Sydney. Sat only 10am–4pm, and in summer months, until 5pm. Take bus no. 380 from Circular Quay. www.paddington markets.com.au.

Christmas Markets FRENCH/GERMAN

See listing on p. 463.

Portobello Road LONDON

It's crowded, it's touristy and these days it's downright expensive—but to me, it's not Saturday in London unless I spend a few quick hours prowling around Portobello Road Market. Since I'm mostly there for atmosphere and a few knickknacks, I don't go into the many market halls. I just walk through the middle of the street and look at antiques and souvenirs and sweaters and dishes and buy a hot jacket potato and keep on going under the railroad bridge and into the really junky yard sale part of the market and on up to Golborne Road, which is filled with Portuguese coffee shops and funky little stores . . . and much charm.

BEST BETS   Despite it all, you can still find some unique bargains or gift items selling at fair prices.

WHERE TO BUY   Portobello Road, London NW11. Sat only. Tube: Notting Hill Gate.

127 Corridor SOUTHERN USA

Once a year, in mid-August, this two-lane highway turns into the country's largest (or longest) flea market, stretching from Tennessee to Alabama. Now then, a few warnings—if you try the route any other time of the year, you will fall asleep driving as you'll be bored out of your mind. There is nothing, and I mean nothing, there. Don't ask me how I know this as well as I do.

If you go for the event, the traffic on much of the route is bumper to bumper, people park on lawns and jump out of cars that are stalled in traffic, and when motels are full, they go up to strangers' homes and ask to be taken in. This is a 450-mile flea market.

WHERE TO BUY   The market lasts for 9 days—it begins the Thursday before the third Sunday of the month and lasts through that week (so there's two weekends included). Start in Covington Kentucky and keep on goin'. ☎ **800/327-3945.** www.bargain-mall.com/127cor.

Scott Antique Markets ATLANTA

This one is big—real big: almost 2,500 booths. Held 10 months of the year (no show in Jan or Feb), this show is held the second weekend of every month and is the largest indoor show in the U.S.—with air conditioning. To get the exact dates, go online. The promoters also have shows in other cities. Once online, you may luck into a free admission coupon.

WHERE TO BUY   Expostion Center, 3650 Jonesboro Rd., Atlanta, GA. Fri–Sat 9am–6pm; Sun 10am–4pm. Entry fee $3 for the whole weekend. www.scottantiquemarket.com.

Paris: Queen of the Fleas

First there are French flea markets, a regular event and a blessed way to spend a Sunday in Paris. Next there are *brocante* shows, which are held as special events every few months—but on a regular basis.

Brocante, by the way, is the French word for junk; *brocante* and those who sell it are not antiquers—this is very strict in the French sense of things. Brocante is sold everywhere in France, but the regular Paris shows are spectacular events. The shows are usually advertised in the papers and announced in guides to weekly events. But you can also check with the best promoters: **Sadema,** 86 rue de Lille, 75007 Paris (☎ **01-40-62-95-95;** fax 01-40-62-95-96) and **Joel Garcia** (☎ **01-56-53-93-93**).

Note that Paris also has a series of venues called Antiques Villages, which include the **Village Suisse** (Métro: Bir Hakim), the **Village St. Paul** (Métro: St. Paul) and the famous **Antiquaires du Louvre**, across the street from the Louvre Museum (Métro: Louvre). These are usually open every weekend and serve as an always-there sort of staple for the *chineur*, or French bargain hunter.

The best regular Parisian flea market is **Puces de Vanves,** av. George Lafenestre, av. Marc Sangnier, and av. Maurice d'Ocagne, 14e. (Métro: Porte de Vanves; open Sat and Sun 9am–1pm.)

A mannequin enjoys a view of a Paris flea market.

Warrentown Antiques Week TEXAN

Forget about how tony the artists' colony of Marfa, Texas, has become—instead concentrate on tiny tot Warrentown and its twice-a-year (Apr and Oct) antiques market when hundreds of dealers come to town. This is the Texas version of Brimfield, with markets in a dozen little Texas dirt towns, halfway between San Antonio and Houston

There are various dealers inside several venues; check out Zapp Hall, which used to be a dance hall; www.zapphall.com. There's markets that last 3 to 4 days in certain towns; few markets go the whole time. Marburger Farm also has a market. You just won't believe the whole schtick.

BEST BETS   The scene: There is also a dance in one of the tents, called the Junk-O-Rama Prom and, of course, there's the Gospel Brunch. The show includes two weekends and the intervening week—obviously selection is best at the beginning and prices are cut by the last day.

WHERE TO BUY   Identify the towns you want to visit, then use either mapquest or a good roadmap. www.antiqueweekend.com.

"Gallery" Shops: Product As Art

Apple USA $$$$–$$$$$

An apple a day may keep the doctor away but a visit to the Apple store in your local mall or in any international destination will make you wonder why you are not already connected to the Apple World.

BEST BETS   You can test all the new merchandise or even send out personal e-mail for free. You don't have to buy anything to have a great time.

WEB TIPS   You can reserve your space at the Genius Bar online to get an appointment with one of their computer gurus.

Shop Talk

Parisian rumor: Is it true that Apple had a lease on the Champs Elysees but was not allowed to put in the kind of windows they wanted, and that Steve Jobs was so mad he has been boycotting France ever since?

WHERE TO BUY   160 stores in the U.S., 9 in the UK, 7 in Japan, 4 in Canada and other worldwide destinations. U.S. customer service ☎ 800/MY-APPLE. NYC: Apple Fifth Ave., 767 Fifth Ave. ☎ **212/336-1440.** Daily 24 hours. AE, DISC, MC, V. www.apple.com.

Gift Cards: 10 Rules of Saving Face Value

Gift cards are a difficult form of currency because so many people simply don't use them; Americans spend over $27 billion a year on gift cards and over $8 billion of that goes unused. People lose cards. People forget to use them. People disregard them as real gifts and no longer view them as a way to alleviate the slings and arrows of an expensive lifestyle.

To make it worse, some cards are tricky little dudes in that after you've made a purchase with a gift card, the leftover sum may not be allowed to roll over—so you forfeit money or are forced to spend more than you wanted. The average shopper spends 20% more than the face value of the card when he redeems it.

If you were given a gift card as a holiday gift, note that they are most often spent in the last week in December and in January and February. The rule of thumb is that if you haven't used it by March 1, you very likely will not use it—ever. How to avoid contributing to that wasted $8 billion:

1. Call the store and register the cards with the mothership; if the card is lost or stolen, you still have stored value.
2. Sort and combine your cards; always have them handy.
3. See if you can use any of the cards to pay off existing debt on a store credit card.

Microzine LONDON $$–$$$$

Magalog catalog online and a store-cum-gallery where you look at the merchandise and order it but do not take it home with you. They sell fashion, boy toys and books, and claim to sell everything the fastest. Much of the merchandise is limited editions and they sell out quickly.

BEST BETS   This is a great store for guys.

WEB TIPS   There's sale stuff on the site.

WHERE TO BUY   1 store: 1–2 Kingly Court, Carnaby St., London W1. ☎ **4420/7434-0909.** Tube: Oxford Circus or Picadilly. Mon–Sat 11am–7pm; Sun noon–6pm. Another store in Liverpool.

Renault PARIS $$$$$

While the face of the Champs Elysees in Paris is rapidly changing, the thoroughfare still hosts numerous car show-rooms. Each one is a type of entertainment destination; some are so hot that they have clubs or have hosted fashion shows.

4. Scope out what cards are left, and look online—it is easiest—to see if you really can use them or if you are willing to top them out if needed.

5. Re-gift or swap cards you really can't use. Craigslist is chock-full of people who want to trade a clothing store card for an electronic store card, or vice versa.

6. Buy something on sale, and let the value of the card earn you up to 50% more.

7. Build your gift closet with cards while sales are still in progress. Look to the whole year ahead and take a chart shopping with you—upcoming birthdays, weddings, graduations. Save your own cash and let the cards work for you.

8. Use the card as a psychological discount service—you love an item for $100. Would you love it more for $80? Then use the $20 gift card, pay the difference and consider it a triumph.

9. If all else fails, sell gift cards on eBay or Craigslist—though you'll have trouble selling at face value. The better bargain is to buy cards online (search for "gift cards" on Craigslist)—though be very cautious of frauds and beware of cards that allow the seller to wipe out your card online using the card number. See "10 Shopping Scams & How to Avoid Them" on p. 6.

10. Give it to a charity.

Many have their own cafes. I think Renault is the best of the bunch. Oh yes, you can actually buy a car here.

BEST BETS   The cafe which is set onto a catwalk above the autos.

WHERE TO BUY   53 Champs Elysees, Paris, 8e. ☎ **331/4853-7033.** Sun–Wed 10am–midnight; Thurs–Sat 10am–2am. AE, M, V. Métro: Franklin Roosevelt.

Sony Style JAPANESE $$$$–$$$$$

To showcase their latest and greatest and to give people a chance to actually play with the electronics gadgets, Sony has stores all over the world that allow customers to test drive the merch. You can buy a CD from Sony Music or a fancy TV or see gizmos that have not been fully launched in the mass market yet.

BEST BETS   The new merchandise testers.

WEB TIPS   You can shop online for hard and soft wares.

WHERE TO BUY 55 stores in the U.S. **FLAGSHIP** 550 Madison Ave., NYC. ☎ **212/833-8800.** Also Metreon flagship: 101 Fourth St., San Francisco. ☎ **415/369-6050.** Sony Style outlets in several outlet malls such as the Lake Elsinore Outlets in Los Angeles. ☎ **951/245-1155.** Also Camarillo, CA. ☎ **805/389-9592.**

Markets & Souks

Khan Al Khalili CAIRO

Forget the Casbah since we're in Cairo and while you are pretending to know what you are talking about, you refer to this market fondly as The Khan, although it could be The Con. The official name of this souk is Khan Al Khalili and it is one of the most vast and exciting souks in the world of soukdom. Never mind. Follow me and don't get lost. We stop for coffee.

Drink coffee to shop all day; this is the place to buy Egyptian cotton right off the bolt; this is the market where you'll be tempted to buy the nails of the devil, the sting of a snake, the wings of a dove or the penis of a crocodile. (Don't ask.) And that's just for starters.

Buy amber in the chunk; spices and oils, medicines and magic. Don't worry about the cigarette smoke. Just don't inhale. Being in the souk is far more than a shopping expedition—it's a cultural expedition into how society has worked for centuries. And remember, a lot of this stuff is fake or is now made in China, so buy for fun or be very serious when you go for the good stuff. For antique jewelry try **Al-Sokkaria Palace,** where "for you—you're such a pretty girl"—it's only twice the regular price.

Your hotel can book you a guide who will get a percentage of what you buy and steer you to his cousin's shop, but hey, that's part of the charm.

Some stores may be closed on Fridays for religious purposes; some on Sunday. There's enough here that it won't affect you too much.

BEST BETS The market is surrounded by other markets, so it's hard to tell where things begin and end. Goods are most often sold by category so there is a street of the goldsellers, and so on. Locals tend to shop in the northern part of the market where prices are said to be lower and tourists do not visit. *Insiders tip:* You will find locals and tourists alike at the **El-Fishawi** cafe which is the original Starbucks.

WHERE TO BUY In Cairo, extending south to Bab Zuwayla.

The Khan Al Khalili bazaar in Cairo.

Grand Bazaar ISTANBUL

The famous Grand Bazaar of Istanbul is a covered market divided into two markets: stalls laid out in a grid—mostly fake Polo T-shirts and souvenirs and tea—and a small city of antiques dealers. The gold brokers are mostly in a row at the far edge of the souk as you enter. The carpet dealers are everywhere. There are some 4,000 shops here and 250,000 shoppers Monday through Saturday.

This market is a short stroll from the Four Seasons Hotel, so when you've had enough haggling, you can walk here for a refreshing drink or coffee. *Tip:* The Spice Market is a totally separate market in a different part of Istanbul. The Grand Bazaar does not sell food or spices, although some dealers have a few assorted packs of tourist items.

BEST BETS   A carpet salesman here once taught me the secret of life: "The only way to not buy a carpet is to not go into the shop."

WHERE TO BUY   Kapali Carsi; tram to Carsacapi.

SOUK JERUSALEM

You can make the famous stations of the cross or you can shop in Old Jerusalem. Actually you can do some of both at the same time. Old Jerusalem is divided into four ethnic quarters but you can enter from the Jaffa Gate and simply head down the center on David Street and find yourself in the midst of the souk.

BEST BETS   The best time to shop—if you like market hustle and bustle (who doesn't?) is early Friday afternoon when locals are doing their shopping for Shabat.

WHERE TO BUY   Enter at the Jaffa Gate, Jerusalem Old City.

Jemma–a–Fnaa MARRAKESH

Something inside me jumps to life when I approach the souks of Marrakesh. Maybe I am worried about my handbag, but maybe I am just in heaven—surrounded by the colors, the people and the merchandise I love. And no thank you, I don't want to buy a carpet.

World Traveller

When you finish getting lost in Marrakesh, hop a carriage for **La Mamounia,** Avenue Bab Jdid (☎ **21224/388-600;** www.mamounia.com), one of the fanciest hotels in town, where you can sit in the garden and have mint tea.

Set into a series of streets and lanes off the Jemaa-al-Fnaa main square, this market is bursting with merchandise and people and probably gypsies, tramps and thieves. Does anybody really care? *Insider's tip:* It helps to speak French.

BEST BETS   The Street of the Dyers. Hold your nose, but it's gorgeous to look at.

WHERE TO BUY   Jemaa-al-Fnaa, the main square in Marrakesh.

Chatuchak BANGKOK

I have been to many a market and souk in my time. But I have never seen anything like this in my life. This market has 8,000 vendors and over 200,000 shoppers each weekend. It is only open on Saturdays and Sundays.

The structure of the market is very hard to discern because it is built in concentric circles. You can get a map and ask an expert—each section has a number, and stores or stalls actually know where they are. Shoppers will not. In fact, this market is so vast that I doubt I could even find my way back to a source once I was past it.

There's antiques, paper goods, artificial flowers, fake designer goods, toys, dishes—there is everything in the world and then things you could never think of. In between, there are food stalls.

BEST BETS   We found endless bargains, but the silk flowers were a steal at 25¢ to 50¢ per stem. The silk-bound diaries, finished off in metallic brocades for $5, made great gifts to take home.

I'd Walk a Mile for the Pushkar Camel Fair

My father once told a Masai warrior that my dowry could be paid in cattle. If perhaps you instead need to buy camels, you must head to northern India in time for the annual Camel Fair, although to be truthful, they also have cattle at the camel fair.

Even if you aren't buying on the hoof, you still might want to go since there's lots of market stalls and scads of shopping adventures to be had. Pushkar is not in the middle of nowhere; it is about an hour outside of Jaipur—a few hours from New Delhi. Hotels do book up in Jaipur any time it's not raining, so book ahead. See p. 459 for more on Jaipur.

The annual fair is held for 12 days each November (excellent weather); if you thought population issues in India were overwhelming, note that this village takes on several hundred thousand who come to pray, to trade and do business. The dates vary each year because they must coincide with the full moon. Bring your own tent. Rose petals can be bought at the fair.

So what's to buy, besides the obvious? And the rose petals? Well, the religious part of this event is a celebration of Lord Brahma so there's merchandise for everyday living in tent cities, there's special event merchandising and souvenirs, there's religious trinkets for pilgrims and more. See www.pushkar-camel-fair.com.

WHERE TO BUY   Chatuchak Weekend Market, Chatuchak Park, Bangkok. Skytrain: Mo Chit station.

Off-Pricers

Century 21 USA VALUE $$–$$$$

World's Best

Quick! The smelling salts! Get me the cattle prod—I want these other folks outta my way and now! I am dizzy, I am faint, I am hot onto it but very much wishing I was a size 6.

Century 21 is one of the best bargain resources in Manhattan and metro New York City. This is a mini-department store that sells heavy duty designer names and other stuff at good to great prices.

BEST BETS   Like all off-pricers, this is a matter of how you hit it and what size you wear. But I have found Tod's for $99, Gucci sunglasses for $50 and all sorts of other astounding buys.

WEB TIPS   You can click on a video tour of the store or even sign up for a Century 21 MasterCard which gives discounts and coupons.

WHERE TO BUY 4 stores in Manhattan, Brooklyn, Long Island, New Jersey. **FLAGSHIP**   22 Cortlandt St., NYC. ☎ **212/227-9092.** Mon–Fri 7:45am–8pm; Thurs–Fri until 8:30pm; Sat 10am–8pm; Sun 11am–7pm. AE, DISC, MC, V. Subway: R/W to Cortlandt St. www.c21stores.com.

Designer Shoe Warehouse USA ⸰VALUE $–$$$$

Designer Shoe Warehouse (DSW) is a national chain with at least one store in just about every major U.S. market. The large and open-style stores feature boxes of shoes stacked by style and size. There are shoes for men, women and children. Toward the rear of each store, there's racks with sale shoes. Shoes may be color-coded to indicate the discount.

There's an active merchandise program—you'll get a $25 gift certificate for your birthday if you join the birthday club (must be used within 10 days of your birthday and yes, you show your driver's license); you get a $25 gift certificate for every $250 you spend in the store.

Larger cities tend to get more designer brands—I have seen Pucci shoes in San Francisco but not in San Antonio.

BEST BETS   The sale racks in the rear, organized by size, where shoes cost half their discounted price. I find things there for $25 when I get lucky.

WEB TIPS   Sign up for DSW Rewards online or frequent-buyer program for shoeaholics.

WHERE TO BUY   250 stores in U.S. www.dswshoes.com.

E&J USA

See listing on p. 476.

Filene's Basement USA ⸰VALUE $–$$$$

There is Filene's Basement, the mothership that really is in the basement of Filene's (a normal department store); and then there are branch stores of Filene's Basement. I mention this because branch stores may or may not be good but the mothership is fabulous, simply fabulous.

A Boston institution for shoppers of many generations, this two-level bargain basement is a lifestyle experience—not only are things on racks, in bins and thrown to the winds but there is a date on each ticket and a chart hanging here and there on a wall or two which explains the automatic markdown system based on the date on this tag.

Insider's tip: if you think you will get a better deal on an item if you rip off the tag and present it to the counter as tag-less, think twice. All tag-less items go back on the floor at full price, so matter how far they have advanced on the markdown schedule.

BEST BETS   The Basement, as it is called, is famous for its bridal events (p. 72); it's the Men's Suits Events and its markdown policy that reduces the price on merchandise that hasn't sold quickly.

WEB TIPS   Special events including the famous bridal sale are listed on the website.

WHERE TO BUY   FLAGSHIP   497 Boylston St., Boston, MA. ☎ **617/ 424-5520.** Mon–Sat 9am–9pm; Sun 11am–7pm. AE, DISC, M, V. www.filenesbasement.com.

Jeremy's SAN FRANCISCO ⸢VALUE⸥ $–$$$$

Take me out to the ball park and on the way, can we please stop off at Jeremy's, a medium-size store with a big appetite for designer goods at almost giveaway prices? The best prices are on merchandise that is damaged—so don't freak, just remember what you learned in Home Ec class. I bought an Armani skirt here for $13 once.

BEST BETS   A few weeks ago I bought a man's Armani blazer for $99.

WHERE TO BUY   2 South Park, San Francisco, CA. ☎ **415/882-4929.** Also 2969 College Ave., Berkeley, CA. ☎ **510/849-0701.** www.jeremys.com.

Loehmann's USA ⸢VALUE⸥ $–$$$$

Loehmann's in the Bronx can be reached by public transportation, but it's a schlep. The Chelsea location (former site of Barneys men's store) is better. The slick space offers four floors of shopping for women's clothing and accessories and one floor for menswear. Although most suburban Loehmann's stores have the "good stuff" in the Back Room, this store is packed with deals.

BEST BETS   I have found some of my best deals on French designer merchandise from brands that most Americans are not familiar with.

WEB TIPS   You can sign up online to be notified when merchandise from your favorite designers arrives in the stores.

WHERE TO BUY   FLAGSHIP   Seventh Ave. at 16th St., NYC. ☎ **212/ 352-0856.** Mon–Sat 9am–9pm; Sun 11am–7pm. New West Side Loehmann's: 2101 Broadway, NYC. ☎ **212/882-9990.** Mon–Sat

9:30am–9:30pm; Sun 11am–7pm. 5740 Broadway, Riverdale, The Bronx. ☎ **718/543-6420.** Mon–Sat 10am–9pm; Sun 11am–6pm. AE, DISC, MC, V. www.loehmanns.com.

Moda di Andrea PARIS $$$–$$$$

World's Best

I wish I had a secret source as good as this one in every major city of the world. Andrea's is a small shoe store located directly behind Galeries Lafayette in Paris, so you are more than likely going to be in the neighborhood anyway. They sell men's, women's and children's shoes—mostly from Italian designers.

BEST BETS Prada, Tod's and other big-name designer shoes for half price. I paid $200 for a pair of linen and leather Hogan's.

WHERE TO BUY 79 rue des Victoires, Paris, 9e. ☎ **331/4874-4889.** Mon 2–7pm, Tues–Sat 11am–6pm; closed Jewish holidays. AE, MC, V. Métro: Chausee d'Antin. No website.

Syms USA $–$$$$

This source is actually better for men than for women; see listing on p. 228.

TJMaxx & Marshall's/HomeGoods USA $–$$$$

I have listed all of these stores together because they are owned by the same holding company and have much the same merchandise shuffled among their numerous stores. Please note that for reasons I cannot explain, TJMaxx in the UK is named TK Maxx.

Before we get all carried away with the name brands you can find here and the great deals (yes and yes), insiders know that many brands make goods for distribution in these off-price stores, just as they make goods for their factory outlets. Off-price is a huge business, so the bargain you are drooling over may not be worth any more than what you are about to pay for it. See p. 315 for more on the HomeGoods division.

BEST BETS Real life on a marked-down basis.

WHERE TO BUY 800+ stores in U.S. www.tjmaxx.com.

Il Salvagente MILAN ⌐VALUE⌐

World's Best

This looks like an apartment house in a residential neighborhood and you would have no indication to walk through the driveway, into the courtyard and into the store—a two-floor nirvana of men's and women's designer clothes and accessories sold for low prices.

BEST BETS   Most of the goods are from Italian designers. I recently spied an Armani jacket for $275.

WHERE TO BUY   1 store: via Fratelli Bronzetti 16, Milan. ☎ **392/7611-0328.** AE, M, V. www.ilsalvagente.it.

OUTLET MALLS

Bicester Village BRITISH

The best outlet mall in Continental Europe, Bicester Village (say Bista) is a little more than an hour from London and nestled into a world where British big names may just be affordable, even if you take into account the strength of sterling right now.

This is Value Retail's flagship property—they have several other excellent outlet malls all over Europe, including La Vallee, listed below. This mall is organized in the cutie-pie village style and has a very, very nice restaurant, Carducci's. The stores include the usual names in global big brand retailing as well as some very specifically British brands.

You can get here by train, but then you need a taxi or a shuttle to and from the station. If you take the train into Oxford (make a weekend out of it or an overnight jaunt), catch the shuttle bus in front of the department store Debenhams right on Magdalen, which is the main drag in Oxford.

BEST BETS   Don't miss Molton Brown for makeup and spa products at reduced prices; Cath Kidston—the fabric designer—has a lot of cute items for gifts that you won't find back home.

WEB TIPS   All directions are listed online.

WHERE TO BUY   50 Pringle Dr., Oxfordshire. ☎ **44-1869-323-200.** Mon–Sat 10am–6pm; Sun noon–5pm. MC, V. www.bicestervillage.com.

Gilman Outlet Strip BERKELEY, CA $–$$$$

This outlet mall is really a strip center, and not a very big one at that. Still, it's one of my all time favorites. It has maybe half a dozen outlets including **Travel Smith** and **Territory Ahead.** The anchor is **Smith & Hawken,** although I do not think it's worth the trip for Smith & Hawken. One of the best stores is a home design firm called Trove.

BEST BETS   There are so few stores that you can shop them all and not get exhausted or overwhelmed.

WHERE TO BUY   1310 Tenth St., Berkeley, CA.

La Vallée Village/Val d'Europe FRANCE

If you buy the argument that Disneyland is for kids, then you will find it refreshing to know that right outside of Disneyland Paris is a form of theme park for shopper's—a factory outlet mall.

Developed by one of the American firms that does outlet villages so well, this one is particularly charming because it is adjacent to a French commercial center, Val d'Europe (with hypermarche and cheap gas) and a nursery (flowers, not child care). You can get here by public transportation—it's about an hour outside Paris.

BEST BETS   Designers with stores here include many Euro big names such as Kenzo, Anne Fontaine, Ferragamo, Camper, Nitya, Wolford and Bodrum.

WHERE TO BUY   3 cours de la Garonne, Marne la Vallee. ☎ 331/ 60-42-35-00. Mon–Sat 10am–7am; Sun 11am–7pm. AE, MC, V. RER (train): Val d'Europe. www.lavalleevillage.com.

The Mall REGGELLO, ITALY

You have to be pretty confident to name your mall simply The Mall, but this may be the mall that ends all. It's more like a fancy strip center since it is not enclosed, or you could even call it a little village. Located about a half hour outside of Florence, this mall has outlets from a whole lot of very, very big names. Yeah, name stores such as Armani, Bottega Veneta, Gucci, Tod's, Hogans, La Perla, Fendi, Loro Piana and more. There is a cafe that is even wired for Wi-Fi. For the most part, goods are one-half off regular retail prices.

Some of these stores are not well stocked. You may be done at this mall in an hour and singing, "Is that all there is?'

BEST BETS   This is a fairly easy drive from Florence. However, you can take a tour bus here; ask at your hotel. There is also an official shuttle, $30 per person round-trip with a variety of times—ask at your hotel or check online.

WHERE TO BUY   2–8 via Europa, Reggello. ☎ 39-055/865-7033. Mon–Sat 10am–7pm; Sun noon–5pm. AE, MC, V. www.design management.it.

San Marcos TEXAN

Located half way between San Antonio and Austin, this mall area is composed of two different outlet centers and is one of many in the area. It is different from the competition, and all other outlet malls, in that part of it is a Venetian village (just like Las Vegas) and there is a gondola ride.

There's actually two outlet malls side by side—the Tanger property and then the Prime Outlets property. Between them, just about every big name in retail is represented, including many designer names that don't have that many outlets. Both malls are located on the frontage of highway I-35 at exit 200.

BEST BETS   There are 50 ways to leave your cash.

WHERE TO BUY   Exit 200, IH-35, San Marcos, TX. ☎ **512/396-7446.** Mon–Sat 9am–9pm; Sun 10am–7pm. www.tangeroutlet. com.

Woodbury Common CENTRAL VALLEY, NY

World's Best   The single best outlet mall in the world is Woodbury Common, which is also the largest (841,000 sq ft.) and the home of the only Chanel outlet store in the world. With well over 200 premium stores, this is the one by which all others must be measured. Let's see: Barneys, Celine, Loro Piano, Etro, Gucci, Ventilo, DVF, Frette, Pratesi and on and on.

There is a Gray Line bus tour that can get you there from Manhattan for about $40 round-trip, www.graylinenewyork. com, and a Shortline tour for $30, www.shortlinebus.com.

BEST BETS   Because this mall is totally daunting and there is so much there, you may want to spend the night nearby. Embassy Suites (www.embassysuites.com) has a Shop & Save program with coupons for the outlets.

WHERE TO BUY   Central Valley, NY. ☎ **845/928-4000.** www. premiumoutlets.com/woodburycommon.

Resale

Depot-Vente 17e PARIS

For my euros, this is the best depot vente in Paris and one of the best in the world—the reason is simple: This is a residential area that gets few tourists. While some ex-pats live nearby, the area is simply a classy French district where women of means turn in their slightly used garments—and some accessories—and you can get a good shot at affordable Chanel suits, fur coats, home style and even men's clothes and accessories—it is very rare for a French depot vente to carry good quality menswear.

The 17 in the address represents the 17th arrondissement of Paris (just across from the 8e); the shop is large by French standards and sells merchandise on a seasonal basis. There

⌐ **Online Bartering**

With little competition, barter websites are quickly growing in popularity and the practice is becoming a successful and profitable business. So far, online bartering is popular for media goods and books, as values are standardized and easy to assign.

Trades are made on a credit system, not between individuals. For every item shipped, the seller receives credit for another item in the network. Value is determined by the website.

Here's how it works: Log on to the website and sign up (membership is usually free). List the DVDs or books or CDs you have and the ones you want. When one of your disks or books is requested, print the postage-included mailer, follow instructions for mailing and send it off. Receive goods listed on your want list from other members and keep what you want or trade again. Typically, these sites charge about $1 per trade plus postage.

Bartering networks are becoming popular for media trades: DVDs (**www.Peerflix.com**), CDs (**www.LaLa.com**), video games (**www.GameSwap.com**) and books (**www.PaperbackSwap.com**).

On **www.craigslist.com**, click on "barter" in the "for sale" category, and items are listed by area. A recent lister offered a "very nice stereo system in exchange for a working washer/dryer."

On **www.intervac.com** (☎ 415/839-9670), you can save big bucks on your next vacation by trading homes. It's easy to find a swap; click on the country you want to visit, then scroll through the available properties. This company has been in business since 1953, which says it all.

are sales during the sale times and at the end of seasons; they do not know how to give you a detaxe refund.

Note: This shop is near where rue du Courcelles crosses blvd. du Courcelles; do not get the two mixed up. Rue du Courcelles (the street you want) runs north-south.

BEST BETS   Major big time hot-stuff designer brands in excellent condition; some home style, coats (fur and otherwise), accessories and even menswear. Prices are about half of what the items would cost if new.

WEB TIPS   The website is in French and does not sell merchandise but does give directions on how to get to the store. For tourists who may be out sightseeing, the store is not very far from the Champs Elysees at the Arch de Triomphe end, but this is a residential neighborhood without other tourist attractions.

WHERE TO BUY 109 rue du Courcelles, Paris, 17e. Mon–Sat 11am–7pm. MC, V. Métro: Courcelles. www.depotventedeparis.fr.

Encore NYC

Upstairs to two floors of gently used clothing, most of it a year old and from famous designers. The bulk of the clothes are sizes 6, 8 and 10, but you can get lucky in other sizes. The store claims that they do not take merchandise more than a year old, although I was buying up Adolfo suits (considered collectible at the time) way after Adolfo went out of business. There's some accessories.

Shop Talk

Encore became very hot several decades ago when it was leaked that Jackie O sold her clothes here.

BEST BETS The merchandise is said to be only 1 year old.

WHERE TO BUY 1 store: 1132 Madison Ave., NYC. ☎ **212/879-2850.** Mon, Wed, Fri 10:30am–6:30pm; Thurs 10:30am–7:30pm; Sat 10:30am–6pm; Sun noon–6pm. Closed July and Aug. www.encoreresale.com.

Reciproque PARIS

Although this is the mother of all resale shops in Paris and the most famous, I list it only because of its selection—I find the prices very, very high and I do not know any Frenchwomen who shop here now. They've all quit in disgust as the store has become more and more driven by foreign dollars and oil money. Still, you can't ignore this baby—or babies, since the store has several different freestanding shops strung along the rue de la Pompe in the 16th arrondissement.

The main shop is two levels, with shoes in the lower level in their own salon space. My last purchase here was a Pucci blouse (Christian Lacroix designed Pucci) for $250 which I thought was a fair enough price, so you just don't know what you are willing to pay, or what someone else is willing to pay.

A rack of dresses at Reciproque in Paris.

Other shops sell accessories (and luggage), menswear and home style/gift items, as in the bride's leftover wedding gifts or grandma's silver that is so old-fashioned no one even in a French family wanted it.

BEST BETS   You have never seen so much designer merchandise in your life.

WHERE TO BUY   Several stores. **FLAGSHIP**   88–101 rue de la Pompe, Paris. ☎ **331/4704-3028.** Mon–Sat 11am–7pm. M, V. Métro: Rue de la Pompe.www.reciproque.fr.

Sample Sales

When I go to heaven, every day there will be a sample sale and of course, in heaven, I will have the money to buy and the space to store all my great finds. Sample sales that are open to the public are a relatively new phenom, not much more than a decade old. Originally, samples were sold in-house or to the press. Now they are sold to an eager public who will go through boxes, plow through bins, fight over sizes, hide merchandise and stand in line for hours just for the privilege of doing all this.

In theory, anyone can go to a sample sale. You just have to know about them. In the U.S., most are in Manhattan and can be found through online sources or private informational subscriptions. In Paris, the best of the business is by invitation only—you must belong to a club that gets the invites; see Catherine Max, below.

Most well-organized sample sales take cash and credit cards. If you want to try on clothing, be prepared for little—or no—privacy.

Catherine Max PARIS

There is a Catherine Max; she is a young woman from a good family, as the French saying goes. In fact, her family has textile mills so she grew up knowing most of the big designers. This fact led her to establish the first sample sales in Paris, which are held through private invitations. You join Catherine Max for a year and get tickets in the mail. You may write ahead for a one-shot ticket or to get the show schedule. Catherine's husband is in the wine business so there are some wine events during the year.

Mostly these sales are held in one of two salons in the 16e; women stand in line for hours to get in. They are all very well dressed but fall into two categories—women who are shopping for themselves (and families), and women who live in the suburbs and who buy armloads to bring home and sell to their friends. You are issued or know to take a tote or plastic cart when you enter.

BEST BETS   Often prices are shockingly low, such as a box of six Baccarat cocktail glasses for $100. I bought a Christian Lacroix skirt for $50.

WEB TIP   You must register for the sales events on the (French) website.

WHERE TO BUY   Venue is printed on ticket. www.espacemax.com.

LazarMedia.com

Elyssa Lazar used to publish a monthly bulletin—*The S&B Report (Sales & Bargains)* that gave subscribers all the lowdown on upcoming sample sales in the New York metro area. She has taken it online; you can get a free sample and then subscribe.

WHERE TO BUY   Online only.

Warehouse Stores & Sales

ABC Carpet Warehouses NYC

I have good news and I have bad news. As you know, ABC Carpet & Home is a very chic and very expensive store. If you hope to do better on the price, and you have a car (possibly a truck) you may want to head to the Bronx to the outlet, where items are marked down 30% to 50%. That was the good news. Now the bad news: The prices may still be way too steep and if you have to ship or arrange delivery, you may not have saved anything.

Insider's tip: When they have sales or promotions in the warehouse, there is an online announcement.

See listing on p. 36.

American Girl Tent Sale MADISON, WI

Held as a benefit, this event is in Madison, Wisconsin, and is organized by the makers of American Girl dolls online. You get the dates online and reserve tickets online. Your ticket is for a specific time; you will only be allowed to enter at the time marked on your ticket. This is a charity event.

WEB TIPS   www.americangirl.com.

Barneys Warehouse Sale NYC

In your heart you know you are a Barneys customer but in your wallet, you know the truth. If that's the case, the Barneys warehouse sales may be just the ticket. Prices are not dirt cheap, but they can be affordable. They also go down as the sale progresses; be sure to read the handwritten signs and posters through the store as they provide clues to additional mark-downs.

WEB TIPS   The sale dates are announced online. See listing on p. 39.

Brandon USA ⊙VALUE

See listing on p. 327.

Frugal Fannie's WESTWOOD, MA $–$$$$

Located in a 60,000-square-foot warehouse outside Boston, Frugal Fannie's sells overruns from various big name makers of women's clothing—there's also jewelry and shoes. This business is about 25 years old and is considered a Boston institution; shoppers come from all over New England for the selection and the deals, although frankly, I didn't find the prices any lower here than at outlet stores. I like Jones New York and there was a very good selection.

   Part of the gimmick is that the store is only open on weekends or within a limited time frame, so be sure you know the hours before you head over there.

WHERE TO BUY   24 Wilson Way, Westwood, MA. ☎ **781/329-8990.** www.frugalfannies.com.

High Point Furniture Market HIGH POINT, NC ⊙VALUE
$$–$$$$

Oh my word, what can I say? If you go to the trade market, you may find amazing deals. If you go to the assorted warehouses and showrooms in the area surrounding High Point you may get a headache or a heartache. And then again, you may get a bargain, even with shipping. There's a lot of hype here and I would bet you can find the same things—at the same prices—closer to home. See "Furniture Festivals" on p. 334.

Tse Cashmere SANTA ANA, CA ⊙VALUE $$–$$$$

This event is usually held in an industrial park where Tse Cashmere has offices, so this is not a factory per se. I have been to the sale in Hong Kong where Tse just rented empty office space for a few days and unloaded cashmeres for men, women and children at 50% to 80% off regular retail. Samples

Chapter Twelve

The Best Shopping Destinations & Adventures

*M*any years ago, I sat outdoors at a small bistro table in a Parisian market with my girlfriend Carolyn Bloodworth, who is now Carolyn Logan. It was a mild April day, my birthday, in fact. Birthdays, it is a well-known fact, are meant to be spent at an excellent shopping venue. CB and I were taking a break from a few hours on the prowl at the semi-annual **Bastille Flea Market.** We had bought little, but the *foie gras* sandwiches and cold white wine were divine, the energy was strong enough to dance to and the sun was bright. I smiled with contentment and said to Carolyn, "It doesn't get much better than this." She nodded her agreement.

As I travel, I often find a place that serves as an entire experience that defines a whole—it's not one best store or one best thing, it's the entire experience. This place can be a city, a market, a street, a time of year— it's both ethereal and specific. You don't need a lot in terms of directions from me; you just need to know where to land and where to stay. I'm only wishing you a girlfriend as dear as Carolyn Bloodworth and a sky as blue as the one that day in Paris.

Anyone who lives within his means suffers from a lack of imagination.
—Oscar Wilde

Note that I simply don't have room to include all the destinations I love—and some (London, New York, Paris) I'm excluding because I've already written about them extensively in the *Born to Shop* books.

Amsterdam, NETHERLANDS

I find touristy canal boat rides sublime, especially at dusk. The museums are world-class (the Rijksmuseum equals fab gift shop). There's diamonds, bicycles, affordable food and everyone speaks English. But Amsterdam has more—the architecture ranges from medieval Hanseatic League–style row houses along the canals to converted warehouses and restored guesthouses to big brand, big name architects doing wild and crazy things to apartment houses, bridges and public buildings. Often museum curators and mavens in home style and design come from around the world to Amsterdam, just to see what's going on. Amsterdam is quietly on the cutting edge possibly emerging as the new London.

While we've grown up to associate the Dutch with wooden shoes, insiders know the work of **Jan Jansen**, Rokin 42 (☎ 3120/625-1350; www.ledermuseum.de/jansen), a shoe designer so innovative that he won a lawsuit against Giorgio Armani. His tiny shop right on the Spree will leave you breathless with the ways the man has joined uppers to lowers and added in some sole. Prices are about $150 to $175 per pair of shoes. If you prefer chocolate shoes, all tourist stores—including the ones alongside the Flower Market—sell a box of edible clogs for about $6. No tulips, just clogs.

The multi-ethnic population makes for a variety of stores and services you might not find at home—various hair procedures, colors of makeup, and gay products/services are readily available. And let's not forget the Indonesian influence in food and fabrics and all the places to eat *pannekoeken* (pancakes).

Amsterdam is a city of neighborhoods, more so because of the canals and the modern sprawl. I usually start at Muntplein where the pedestrian shopping street Kalverstraat begins. Almost immediately you're at **Hema,** 119 Kalverstraat (☎ 3120/422-8988; www.hema.nl), one of my favorite stores in the world, a two-story Target kind of general store with a small food and chocolates department.

Because I've never met a bath or soap store I could resist, I like to stop by **Rituals,** 73 Kalverstraat (☎ 3120/344-9220; www.rituals.com). This excellent mass market line of natural products for body and well-being, also sold at Hema, is not too expensive, with a men's line and a Haman Hot Scrub that is worth the $10 purchase price. There's mud, olive and Chinese inspired products.

Then hit the nearby **Christine Le Duc,** Spui 6 (☎ 3120/624-265; www.christinelerduc.com), a very, very fancy store with clothes, lingerie, DVDs, and sex toys. From this street, you have many choices—go to the red-light district, to the **Flower Market** (on Singel Canal between Koningsplein and Muntplein) or pop on a streetcar and head to the **9 Streets** (www.theninestreets.com) and the **Jordaan** shopping districts.

The 9 Streets are a series of, yep, nine little streets organized on a grid system along a canal; several famous hotels and a series of small unique shops are in this district. Some of the stores showcase big-name Dutch designers; many also have branches or outlets in Antwerp (p. 445). Wander up and down the streets looking for shoes, jewelry, vintage clothing and designer duds. You'll also find little specialty stores, like one that only carries items for the mouth (toothbrushes, toothpaste, teeth and so on). ***Note:*** Stores in this area usually open at 1pm on Monday, 11am other weekdays, and 10am on Saturdays. Stores are closed on Sundays.

For home design and a peek into new trends, seek stores such as **Droog,** 7 Staalstraat (☎ 3120/523-5059), which is not a drugstore at all, but a design collective; **Frozen Fountain,** 645 Prisengracht (☎ 3120-622-9375); **Pols Potten,** 39 KNSM-lann (☎ 3120/419-3541), which is on trendy KNSM Island (Eastern Docklands). Note that there's also a branch of Sissy Boy on the island as well as other hip stores. *Insider's tip:* This area has been developed from old warehouses and is the up-and-coming part of town for those in the know.

For more home-style and design ideas, **Cornelis Johannes,** Willemsparkweg 67 (☎ 3120/616-0184), has more of a lifestyle concept, with an ever-changing parade of goods for home and body. Real design freaks should visit **Alfons de Letter,** 410 Singel (☎ 3120/623-1853; www.alfonsdeleteer.nl), which makes house numbers and street signs; and **Bed Habits,** Reguliersdwarsstraat 57 (☎ 3120/625-4350; www.bedhabits.nl), for futons, mattresses, bed linens, robes and a Zen look adapted to small spaces. Eat your heart out, Hans Brinker.

The big brands are all lined up on Hoofstraat—not far from the Van Gogh Museum. Yes, you can find Armani and Hermès, but what you came for is something more original. Head instead to **Oilily,** 131-133 P.C. Hoofstraat (☎ 3120/672-3361; www.oilily-world.com), for women's and children's clothing and accessories. Oilily defines Dutch design—it's young, it's vibrant, it's a mixture of colors and patterns and it makes classics for each season—think of it as the Marimekko or Lilly Pulitzer of the Netherlands.

Don't miss **Spiegelkwartier,** a 2-block street that leads directly to the Rijksmuseum and is all dealers—some 70 high-end antiques shops are lined up in a row. The word translates into "Mirror District," which is a good handle for stores selling hard-core fine art and very serious antiques. There is nothing funky about this street or any of the wares sold here.

WHERE TO SLEEP
Amsterdam Hilton

The best hotel in town is The Amsterdam Hilton, which is not in the city center but some 2 miles away. Located on its own canal in an architecturally famous building from the sixties by SOM (Skidmore Owens Merrill), this is the hotel where John Lennon and Yoko Ono staged their Love-In—you can book that suite for about $650. The room comes with its own letterhead with a drawing of John and Yoko (by John).

While the hotel isn't in the downtown area, it's midpoint to various neighborhoods that can be reached by taxi or public transportation. Expect to pay $300 a night in high season; but check for various Hilton promos. Apollolaan 138. ☎ **3120/ 710-6000.** www.hiltons.com.

The Dylan

The chicest hotel in town is The Dylan, which was once known as Blake's—it's a must-see for those who love high design and cutting-edge style (don't miss the gold leaf walls). Originally built in 1772, the hotel and its bar are the hangout for visiting celebs. Each of the 41 rooms is unique. Rates begin at $600 per night. 384 Keizersgracht. ☎ **3120/530-2010.** www.tablethotels.com.

Shopper's Lunch

Check out the restaurant in **The Dylan Hotel** (see below). The restaurant menu is very unusual, featuring all sorts of fusion choices to demonstrate that you aren't in Kansas any more. Rates are about $50 per person if you dine with the chef.

Antwerp, BELGIUM

Every fashionista in the world knows about Antwerp, also known as Anvers, one of the must-do cities on the shopper's list of adventures. If you come for culture, note that **Rubenshuis** (Ruben's house) is located smack dab in the center of the best shopping in town.

To get the best of this shopping street, Schuttershofstraadt, start at no. 50, for **Chine Collection,** and keep going—don't miss **Delvaux**, the Hermès of Belgium with exclusive leather goods. Also find the usual luxury retail mega brands from **Gucci** to **Goyard, Nitya** to **Natan** at no. 5 (☎ **323/225-1772;** www.natan-fashion.com)—the kind of boutique that dresses ladies who lunch . . . and the Belgian royal family.

Away from the hoity-toity in the real-people part of the shopping district, my best find was **Cora Kemperman,** Schrijnwerkstraat 9 (☎ **323/231-2722;** www.corakemperman.nl), a Dutch designer with deconstructed clothes cut to fit, scoop, droop and flatter at very fair prices ($65–$175). She does tons of pieces in black and has stores throughout the Netherlands and Belgium.

The well-known Anvers Design6 designers' stores were tricky to suss out. I persevered in order to scope out the group of designers that fashion magazines have been saying are the

The 10 Commandments of International Gift Shopping

1. **Shop in local grocery stores**—not only for inexpensive gifts but for locally made items that bring home the flavor of the destination. In Paris, I buy Maille Provencale mustard; in Italy I buy Knorr instant mushroom risotto mix. Since I live in Texas, I buy (and give) mesquite flavored BBQ Sauce, Alamo coffee and so on.

2. **Don't buy expensive gifts abroad,** especially if it's an item you cannot return and if you're buying for good friends or family who know you well enough to reject the gift.

3. **Don't buy fake merchandise as a gift** unless you plan to acknowledge that it's fake and is a joke gift.

4. **Stock up on the best looking $10 items in the world.** If these items are crafts from a Third World country, they enter the U.S. duty free under the GSP (Generalized System of Preferences) laws.

5. **Shop with caution at the TT's (Tourist Traps).** Be careful to separate the junk from the good stuff. Picture how the item will look in real life out of the junk store context.

6. **For group gifts, look to foodstuffs.** If you're buying for a multitude of people—such as everyone at your office—avoid individual gifts and instead bring back food that can be shared (and those on diets can nibble or ignore). In a group food gift, it's the thought that counts.

7. **For individual gifts, avoid candy or fattening sweets—or booze.** Make exceptions for foodies, of course—but most people don't eat or drink the way they used to. In a personal food gift, it's the *calories* that count.

8. **Don't buy into the national craze** at a foreign destination and bring gifts back to the U.S. expecting them to be appreciated. No one cares about the soccer team, the scalloped seashell cockles worn by ancient pilgrims or the national flag made into a headscarf if they haven't been to that country. Saying "this is the latest thing" only works if it's from Paris.

9. **Novelty counts.** Despite the 8th Commandment, an item's uniqueness is far more important than its cost. Just make sure it's useful as well.

10. **Shop *before* you travel, too**—for friends on the road or to help you make new friends. Go online and plan ahead so the gift isn't daft. I like the customized M&Ms at www.mymms.com. Mine say BORN TO SHOP but they can say almost anything. THANK YOU works great.

most important in Europe, and I came away satisfied . . . and broke. **Walter Van Beirendonck,** 12 Sint-Antoniusstraat (☎ 323/213-2644), is one of the original six and incredibly creative—the glass garage door rises electronically when you enter the warehouse space to gawk at the art and clothes. **Ann Demeulemeester,** Verlatstraat 12 (☎ 323/216-0133), was easy to find, across the street from the contemporary art museum in an area without a lot of other shops. The museum is often written as MUHKA, by the way. **Veronique Branquinho,** no. 73 Nationalstraat (☎ 323/233-6616), is in the thick of the funky shopping area. In fact, **Nationalstraat** is all you need to know if you want to shop 'til you drop.

Nearby is the temple for proper worship of my design guru **Dries van Noten,** the world-famous funky couture artist who does beads and BoHo. The store itself is named **Het Modepaleis,** 16 Nationalstraat (☎ 323/470-2510); it's a cupcake of Old World manners; the racks are hung with embroidered, beaded and carefully crafted suits, skirts, dresses and blouses as works of art, fine enough to make me weep. Smattered throughout this area are also shoes and accessories, all right near the **Mode Museum,** Nationalstraat 28 (☎ 323/470-2770), also called MoMu.

If you prefer furniture to fashion, visit **Kloosterstraat,** a whole street with many blocks devoted to antiques shops, from high end to junky. It's walking distance from the cruise terminal or the fashion district, and prices are lower than in other big Euro cities. Stores here are usually open Saturdays and Sundays but closed on Mondays.

This is also a diamond town—check out the **Diamond Museum,** 19-23 Koningin Astridplein (☎ 323/202-4890; www.diamantmuseum.be); as well as the **Diamond Jewellers Association,** 22 Hoveniersstraat (☎ 323/222-0545; www.adja.be) to check on the rep of anyone. You can also walk the length of **Appelmanestraat** to get the idea—poke in at **Diamondland,** 33 Appelmanestraat) or **Katz's,** 19 Appelmanestraat—this is a very glam showroom with an owner who is tops in the trade. The other big-name jeweler/dealer is **Adelin,** 20/45 Steenhouwervest (☎ 323/231-9947), which has a lot of antique pieces. For a more down-market look, stroll **Pelikaanstraat.**

Shopper's Lunch

Don't miss Grand Café Horta, right at beginning of the shopping street and near Rembrandt's place, Hopland 2 (☎ 323/232-2815)—lunch will be about 15€.

WHERE TO STAY

Hilton Antwerp

Once again, a Hilton takes the cake. But this hotel is totally different from the Amsterdam hotel, and maybe different from most Hiltons you can think of. This Belle Epoque grande dame is right in the middle of the shopping district. And yes, it was once a department store. Fitting, eh? The hotel is everything you want and need, complete with a Metro stop and a super-market. Rooms are about $250 a night. Groenplaats. ☎ 323/204-1212. www.hilton.com.

De Witte Lelie

This is the fancy address of charming town houses connected into a stylish but small hotel where the fashion and money crowd likes to congregate. The name means The White Lilly. Rooms begin at $300. Keizerstraat 16. ☎ 323/226-1966.

Bangkok, THAILAND

Bangkok is so huge, and the shopping possibilities so endless, that you can only make this destination work by limiting yourself to a few venues, indulging in the famous spa scene and allowing your senses to open up to the exotic sights. The traffic is bad, but you can get many places either on the modern rail system (Sky Train), by boat or by *tuk-tuk* (pedicab, pronounced "took-took").

The must-do shopping is a delicious combination of snazzy modern mall and funky market. Many western-style malls are lined up in a row next to the **Grand Hyatt Erawan Hotel,** 494 Rajdamri Rd. (☎ 662/254-1234; www.bangkok.grand.hyatt.com). This is the center of the shopping universe. Warm up on those malls then head to the mother lode: **Siam Paragon,** 991/1 Rama 1 Rd. (☎ 662/610-9000; www.siamparagon.co.th), one of the largest malls in Asia and home to every name brand from the U.S. and Europe as well as one floor of local talent (4th floor). About 250 stores share space here as well as gourmet-food stores and restaurants. Several of the eateries are branches of the luxury hotels, such as The Oriental and The Pen. The lower level Food Court is astonishing. Get there on the Skytrain; the stop is Siam. Daily 10am to 10pm.

After this stop, simply take a tuk-tuk to **Jim Thompson's House,** 6 Soi Kasemsan 2 Rama 1 Rd. (☎ 662/216-7368), which is a museum with a small gift shop. Open daily 9am to

Stone Buddhas at Bangkok's Chatuchak Weekend Market.

5pm, the house is an architectural wonder made by combining six different historical teak structures in a traditional style that is elevated from the ground for flood season. This isn't the main store, but it is the main tourist site.

Thompson, an American who was probably a CIA operative who disappeared in 1967 and hasn't been heard from since, is an almost mythical figure in Asia. (He possibly left the building with Elvis.) He set up a silk-producing business and single-handedly revived the Thai silk industry—the fabrics and wares made from his fabrics are world famous.

The Thompson merchandise covers everything from accessories and ties made in signature prints to scarves, tote bags, stuffed animals (elephants are always popular), clothing, handbags, note cards and a wonderful line of bed linen and bed style. Almost every luxury hotel in town has a store branch, and often the selection of merchandise is different. ***Note:*** The main branch of **Jim Thompson,** 9 Surawong Rd. (☎ 662/632-8100; www.jimthompson.com), is worth the taxi ride. Another 2 blocks away is a **small outlet shop,** 149/4-6 Surawong Rd. (☎ 662/235-8930), which just sells fabric from the bolt. Another outlet is in Phuket, if you're going that way.

Shopper's Lunch

For the perfect shopper's lunch, hit the mall (Erawan Center) adjoining the Grand Hyatt Erawan (p. 448), where the **Erawan Cafe** specializes in Thai salads, about $12 each. Don't miss the Thai iced tea.

Jim Thompson silks are expensive, partly because of the advertising efforts behind the brand. You can get far better deals in markets, either the **Chatuchak Weekend Market** or the **Suan Lum Night Market** (near the Four Seasons Hotel in the thick of town but threatening to close in 2008 due to the high value of the real estate). At Chatuchak be prepared for 8,000 vendors, 250,000 visitors and temperatures that soar to 120 degrees. Chatuchak is open Saturday and Sunday only, from 8am to 6pm. Considering the heat and the crowds, it's wise to get here at 9am. Take the SkyTrain to Mochit and walk.

Spas are an important part of the culture—day spas are more for locals, but every hotel has its own spa to amp up the competition. If you're the do-it-yourself spa type, head to one of the outposts of **Boots,** the British chemist chain, which sells a wide range of Thai-made spa and well-being products. Otherwise, book into the **Grand Hyatt Erawan** (above)—or at least hit the spa since non-guests can sign up for treatments. Overlooking the river, **The Peninsula Bangkok** (below) has the brand new ESPA (☎ **662/861-2888**).

WHERE TO STAY
Conrad Hotel

Right next to the American Embassy, this hotel is not luxury class, but it also costs half the price—a bargain at $99 per night. You can get a promotional rate of $150 on a weekend package. All Seasons Place. 87 Wireless Rd. ☎ **662/690-9999.**

The Four Seasons Hotel

This resort is in the heart of town, within walking distance of shopping and right alongside the SkyTrain. The hotel has a pool, spa and an exotic breakfast buffet. I had various intricate business problems involving visas, international travel and television crews—the concierge solved everything brilliantly. The private courtyard is surrounded by restaurants and shops; you can now eat breakfast there. Rooms begin around $200. 155 Rajadamri Rd. ☎ **662/250-1000.**

Peninsula Bangkok

Truly the best nest in town if you don't mind being spoiled by service, restaurants, spa and pool, river barge shuttle boat and other amenities. This isn't a hotel; it's a destination unto itself. All rooms have river views. There's good stores and a famous chef. The breakfast is jaw-dropping. Rooms begin around $200. 333 Charoennakorn Rd. ☎ **662/861-2888.**

Barcelona, SPAIN

Shopping adventures in Barcelona include a) the outlet mall at La Roca Village; b) the many chocolate shops; c) the many shoe shops; and d) the home style, art and architecture. Just save time to eat!

Foodies will be impressed by **La Boqueria** (shown in photo below and on p. 368) on Plaça de la Boqueria, a fresh-food market where you can buy produce, ready-cooked foods, meals to go, ingredients for dinner—or sit down and actually eat a meal. Indeed, food shopping is a big part of being here; don't miss **Cacao Sampaka** (p. 384), which is not only the most famous chocolate shop in town, but is owned by Albert Adria, brother to three-star chef Ferran Adria whose El Bulli is between the outlet mall and the French border. The department store **El Corte Ingles** (www.elcorteingles.es), the Macy's of Spain, has an excellent supermarket in their basement.

WHERE TO SLEEP

Hotel Palace

This five-star palace was once the Ritz and was indeed built by Cesar Ritz. More importantly, it has a fabulous location, so you can walk almost everywhere or take the Metro. Renovated, but still replete with grandeur, the hotel has a magnificent winter garden where you can eat breakfast. Rates

Fresh produce at Barcelona's La Boqueria Market.

How To Be A Shipping Goddess

Shopping abroad doesn't stop at the purchase itself; one has to get everything home. Some of these rules sound like a lot of fuss over some heavy bags, but when you keep in mind 5kg (11 lbs.) can cost an extra $150 in airline's excess baggage fees, it all becomes worth it.

1. **Ask shopkeepers if they'll ship your purchases.** Even the Hall of Master Craftsmen in Tashkent, Uzbekistan offers FedEx services. Don't sign shipping papers until fees are finalized. If they don't ship, ask for "discounted" receipts for your purchases; you may save on airport fees.
2. **Send it by post office boat mail service.** Sure, it may take up to 6 months, but you'll save hundreds of dollars if you're shipping large furniture or carpets.
3. **Find a local cargo company.** They're often cheaper, can ship by boat and road or by air and usually have no box size limit. This includes the cargo divisions of major airlines.
4. **Ask a U.S. soldier to ship for you.** This one can be tricky, but overseas servicemen are generally a friendly group. They can ship to the U.S. from anywhere in the world using their A.P.O. (Army Post Office) service at U.S. domestic shipping rates—so it's worth the effort.
5. **Calculate excess baggage weight *before* you get to the airport.** It's worth asking a friend or the hotel for a scale. Economy class passengers are usually allowed two bags at 20kg

begin at $300. Member Leading Hotels of the World. Gran Via de les Corts Catalanes 668. ☎ **93/510-1130.** www.hotelpalace barcelona.com.

Casa Camper

Long known for the exciting design of their retail stores, Mallorca-based Camper shoe company recently opened their own boutique hotel, where rooms go for about $250 a night. Design is crisp, young, and trendy. Carrer Elisabets 11. ☎ **34-93/342-6280.** www.casacamper.com.

Buenos Aires, ARGENTINA

Don't cry for me, Argentina—I'm on a shopping tango where the dollar is strong, the hotels are grand and the food is

(44 lbs.) per bag. Look up weights and fees online, and switch airlines if necessary. For example, Finnair charged me $614 in baggage fees on a flight from Thailand to Moscow, and Aeroflot charged me only $44 dollars for the very same bags to fly from Moscow to Washington, D.C.

6. **Check airline websites for baggage fee vouchers.** Print out at your hotel. You may save 20% to 30%.

7. **Once at the airport, be nice to check-in workers.** If you're friendly before they weigh your bags, they sometimes waive or discount your fee.

8. **Stick "fragile" stickers all over your bags, even if they're not.** It won't guarantee their safety, but it will help. If nothing else you'll spot your bags faster on the carousel.

9. **Know where friends and associates are traveling.** I have a mini-network going for personal use; I asked my sister to bring me more perfume from my favorite Arabian perfume shop in Dubai; a friend brings me books from Berlin. In this case, shipping is free.

10. **Never give up.** You can get anything home. In Uzbekistan, land of limited vans and no such thing as "pick-up service," a woodcarver tied his intricately carved column to the roof of two taxis, which drove *very slowly* to a shipping port. It's all about being creative and not taking "no" for an answer. — *Kimberly Zenz*

fabulous. On top of that, if you are arriving from the United States, the jet lag is minimal.

Buenos Aires, or "BA" as it's known, is a large city with a variety of neighborhoods and many tango shows. In most cases, your hotel will arrange for tickets to performances and even for private tango lessons. To buy your own pair of tango shoes, the best place in town is **Bailarín Porteño,** Calle Suipacha 251 (☎ **5411/4390-4067**). For tango CDs, head to **Calle Florida,** the main downtown shopping street.

BA's shopping expedition leads from tango accessories to leather goods—where you find cows, you're sure to find handbags!—and assorted *pampas* merch—native items that you never knew existed until you learn a little about local customs. Bring on the *mate* spoons!

For those who haven't gotten past Starbucks, *mate* (mahtay) is a local beverage (now sold in U.S. grocery stores) that is technically a type of tea. If you order y*erba mate* you get the herbal version (no caffeine). It is most often imbibed with a specific kind of spoon-straw (called a *bomilla*), which can be bought in BA in ceramic or even sterling silver.

Silver is, in fact, everywhere. Argentina means "silver place": jewelry and also gaucho belts are made with antique silver coins and/or pieces of eight. Several famous silversmiths in town make table-top and serving utensils as well as jewelry. The best is **Juan Pallarols,** Defensa 1039, San Telmo (☎ **5411/4300-6555**). In fact, the whole San Telmo area has plenty of antiques shops and sources for silver. Don't miss the **San Telmo Antiques Fair** each Sunday at Plaza Dorrego. If you prefer contemporary jewelry set in silver, head to **Kallalith,** Av. Alvear 1883 local 14 (☎ **5411/4809-0905**) in Recoleta.

The best store for leather handbags is **Casa Lopez,** M.T. de Alvear 640, near Plaza San Martin (☎ **5411/4311-3044;** www.casalopez.com.ar), which makes handbags and leather goods in traditional heavy-duty styles. Prices are the most expensive in town but less than in Paris or London, and the products last forever. **Rossi & Caruso,** Posadas 1387 (☎ **5411/4811-1965**), is another excellent source, especially for saddles and luggage. For gloves, head to **Carpincho** (p. 115).

Shopper's Lunch

Cabaña Las Lilas, Avenida Alicia Moreau de Justo 516 (☎ 5411/4313-1336; www.laslilas.com) is perhaps the most famous of the traditional local steakhouses. They serve lunch and dinner.

WHERE TO STAY

Four Seasons Alvear

Located in the high-end residential district of La Recoleta, Four Seasons Hotel Alvear is the best in town because of its location, and its Old World style that sequesters you and cossets you in otherworldly luxury. All rooms are very large; rates begin at $400. Avenida Alvear 1891, Recoleta. ☎ **5411/4808-2100;** www.alvearpalace.com.

Park Hyatt

If you prefer modern hotels, then this is the other best in town—more for sleek chic and young money. It's also in Recoleta and near the Four Seasons. Rates $350 and up. Avenida Alvear 1661. ☎ **5411/5171-1234.**

Quick Take: Cape Town, South Africa

The good news is that Cape Town is directly south of continental Europe. The bad news is you can't get there from every EU gateway. London is often the best route, via British Airways or Virgin.

The main tourist and shopping district on the waterfront is **Victoria & Alfred,** also known as V&A (www.waterfront.cp.za). Malls, markets and freestanding stores are open until 9pm nightly. Don't miss **Trading Post** (www.atp.co.za) for everything from the famous Swazi candles to T-shirts to masks and, of course, local ceramics; the little grocery store **Pick 'n Pay;** and **Carrol Boyes** (www.carrol boyes.co.za), your HQ for home style, including her signature pewter. For more home style, **Carole Nevin** (www.carolenevin.co. za) has sophisticated, bold African prints. **Safari Club** (www.safari club.co.za) is a whole other world—chic clothes and skin gifts. **Exotics** sells very fancy, very expensive handbags from French and Italian firms, most of which are from local skins (such as ostrich). **Lorenzi** (www.lorenzi.co.za) has been in business for over 40 years, specializing in handbags, wallets, belts and so on.

The main shopping drag is Long Street; try the **African Market** at **Greenmarket Square,** at 80 Long St. Prices are half what they are in stores—but you must bargain with vendors as if you were fighting for Mr. Mandela's life. This area is a little seedy, so bring only what you need. Open Monday through Saturday 9am to 6pm. On Sunday, many sellers head to the **Greenpoint Market,** Somerset Road, which has hundreds of stands and is *huuuuuge.* Again, bargain, bargain, bargain.

There are many great antiques shops just off Greenmarket Square, including the must-see **Pan African Market,** 76 Long St., which isn't a market per se but an old building filled with shopping booths.

For hotels, try **Cape Grace,** West Quay at V&A (☎ 2721/410-7100; www.capegrace.com; $450 a night), which tops several "Best Hotels in the World" lists; **Table Bay Hotel,** Table Bay Quay 6 at V&A (☎ 2721/406-5000; $500 a night), the best-situated hotel in all of Africa; or the more moderately priced **Commodore Hotel,** V&A waterfront (☎ 2721/794-9050; $250 a night). —*Trude G. Boodt*

Chicago, ILLINOIS

—Sarah Lahey

My first shopping trip to Chicago wasn't really a shopping trip—at least, it wasn't meant to be. I was sixteen, and my high-school art teacher had arranged a 3-day museum field trip.

By day two, I was bored to tears so I persuaded my best friend Judy to cover for me while I took a detour to the prestigious Marshall Field's department store. I still remember the magic of that afternoon as I rode the elevators (serviced by smartly dressed attendants) from floor to floor, trying to figure out how to stretch my $20 travel allowance.

Unfortunately, the excitement was short-lived. Judy turned out to be a snitch and I was soon discovered and led back to the hotel by the ever-efficient chaperone, Mrs. Hensinger. Needless to say, my high school field trip days were over. Still, the taste of my first shopping adventure lead me forward. Besides, shopping is an art form—what was wrong with Mrs. Hennypenny, anyway?

While the original flagship **Marshall Field's building,** 111 N. State St. (☎ **312/781-1000;** www.macys.com), with its Tiffany-glass dome, still dominates State Street, once inside this mega-Macy's, you'll realize the soul and substance of Marshall Field's has disappeared.

Chicago's prime retail area moved north to Michigan Avenue from downtown. You can walk right out of your hotel onto the **Miracle Mile** for big city shopping at its best. This glossy strip of upscale shopping complexes and designer boutiques runs for, yeah, about a mile along North Michigan Avenue—from the Chicago River to the Drake Hotel at Walton Street.

Dubbed the "Mag Mile" by locals, Chicago's premier shopping destination is home to over 450 high-end stores including department stores like **Saks Fifth Avenue**, 700 N. Michigan Ave. (☎ **312/944-6500;** www.saks.com), and **Bloomingdales**, 900 N. Michigan Ave (☎ **312/440-4460;** www.bloomingdales.com). I think of the Magnificent Mile as "New York shopping" made clean and easy. And with popcorn.

Is it really all that magnificent? The answer is "yes" if you like big names, big shopping centers and large-scale retailers. Beginning at the southern "river" end, **Westfield North Bridge,** 520 N. Michigan Ave., is home to **Nordstrom (☎ 312/ 464-1515;** www.nordstrom.com), and **Sephora (☎ 312/494-9598;** www.sephora.com).

If you still have a few thousand bucks burning a hole in your Chanel wallet, you'll be right at home on **Oak Street,** between Michigan Avenue and Rush Street. Here, the most elite designer goods, including clothing, accessories and home furnishings, are showcased in classy boutiques—most of which are former brownstone homes. Look for big international names like **Prada,** 30 E. Oak (☎ **312/951-1113;** www.prada.com);

Hermès, 110 E. Oak (☎ **312/787-8175;** www.hermes.com); and **Jil Sander,** 48 E. Oak (☎ **312/335-0006;** www.jilsander.com).

For the best of Chicago's local shopping scene, take time to explore the adjacent neighborhoods of **Bucktown** and **Wicker Park.** About a 10-minute/$10-taxi ride from the Miracle Mile, this area on the city's near, northwestern side is a retailing mecca for youthful high-style designs, New-Age boutiques, vintage clothing shops and trendy home furnishings. Oprah loves it here.

A good place to begin exploring is at the corner of Damen and Milwaukee avenues. Walk south on Wicker Park's Milwaukee Avenue, taking in shops on both sides of the street, including **Jade,** 1557 N. Milwaukee Ave. (☎ **773/342-5233**), a contemporary women's boutique owned by a former fashion stylist. **Hejfina,** 1529 N. Milwaukee Ave. (☎ **773/772-0002;** www.hejfina.com), stocks men's and women's clothing from cutting-edge designers as well as furniture and architectural books.

Backtracking to Damen Avenue, walk north into Bucktown, where you'll find reasonably priced custom T-shirts at **T-Shirt Deli,** 1739 North Damen (☎ **773/276-6266;** www.tshirtdeli. com), and don't miss the fine Asian antiques at **Wow & Zen,** 1912 North Damen (☎ **773/269-2600**; www.wowandzen.com). Neighboring boutiques **P.45,** 1643 North Damen (☎ **773/862-4523;** www.p45.com), and **Helen Yi,** 1645 North Damen (☎ **773/252-3838**), feature lesser-known local designers who make ultra chic clothing for very, very thin women.

Continuing into North Bucktown, don't miss **Red Balloon Company,** 2060 North Damen (☎ **773/489-9800;** www. theredballoon.com), for children's toys, clothing, and gear; and **The Painted Lady,** 2128 North Damen (☎ **773/489-9145;** www.thepaintedladychicago.com), which features hand-painted antique furniture and vintage repro accessories.

Fox's, 2150 N. Halsted St., in Lincoln Park (☎ **773/281-0700**), is a not-so-well-kept secret source for chic and cheap women's designer apparel, all discounted 50% to 70%. **Lori's Designer Shoes,** 824 W. Armitage Ave. (☎ **773/281-5655;** www.lorisshoes.com), stocks the city's largest selection of American and European designer shoes, all at 10% to 30% off department store prices. Great bags, too; figure $300 and up.

WHERE TO STAY

The Drake Hotel

At the northern tip of the Miracle Mile, the palace-like Drake features a regal lobby and grand staircase, all befitting the numerous kings, queens and presidents who frequently stay here. I, too, was treated like royalty: The staff, doormen included, greeted me by name, and my simplest requests (a down pillow, afternoon ice) were attended to quickly. My "deluxe" room was spacious with 12-foot ceilings, traditional decor and a killer view of Lake Michigan and North Lake Shore Drive. Rates begin at $365. 140 E. Walton Place, Chicago. ☎ 312/787-2200. www.thedrakehotel.com.

The Peninsula Hotel Chicago

I couldn't wait to collapse in comfort into the Hästens bed I had requested in my room. That wasn't exactly the case (p. 301), but I still enjoyed the Peninsula's luxuries—such as a separate dressing room leading to the huge marble bathroom with walk-in shower, and a bedside computer to control the world (or at least the lights, TV, and window shades). The hotel's Miracle Mile location is perfect for shopping. Rates begin at $525. 108 E. Superior St. ☎ 312/337-2888. www.chicago.peninsula.com.

Chiang Mai, THAILAND

That shopping in this northern Thai resort village is the best in the world is one of the world's great hypes, so I am here to say the Emperor has no clothes. Go to Chiang Mai to stay at some of the finest resorts in the world—we're talking big time memories and major honeymoon considerations whether you pick the rustic tree-house style **Four Seasons,** Mae Rim-Samoeng Old Road (☎ 6653/298-181; www.fourseasons.com) overlooking rice paddies or the Disney-esque dreamland of **Dhari Dhevi Mandarin Oriental**'s incredibly divine village and shrine, Sankampaeng Road (☎ 6653/888-888; www.mandarinoriental.com).

Both of these resorts have free shuttle service into downtown Chiang Mai, where you will go to the Night Bazaar, where they sell local crafts, mulberry paper, ornate silver elephants, clothes, art and antiques—truly one of the world's best shopping experiences. Oh yes, they even have illegal DVD's (try to refrain). Beyond that, it's oh so touristy and the so-called factories in the assorted villages are major TT's. Stick to shopping on-property at the Mandarin Oriental, or head to Elephant Camp in Chiang Rai. Don't miss **Doi Tung** (www.doitung.org) in either Chiang—it's a lifestyle store/project that redirects former opium growers to create handmade goods and foods.

Quick Take: Houston, Texas

Houston has a very famous mall (www.galleriahouston.com) and a fairly decent factory-outlet scene, but the best shopping spree is a trip through the **Montrose District,** filled with antiques and thrift shops that specialize in home style. Head to Westheimer and Montrose streets. Check out **The Guild Shop,** 2009 Dunleavy at Welch (☎ **713/528-5095**) as well as **2nd Debut Resale,** 10968 Westheimer at Wilcrest (☎ **713/782-0300**), although this is farther west than the traditional boundaries of Montrose. The residential part of this 'hood is being revitalized while the shoppers clamor on board all weekend. Also check out the fabulous mystery bookstore, **Murder by the Book,** 2342 Bissonnet St. (☎ **713/524-8597**).

Jaipur, INDIA (with Delhi on the side)

First the bad news: Everything in India does not cost $5 or less, as I expected.

Now the good news. India has lots to buy:

- Those see-through chiffonlike embroidered blouses cost $3 each, if you bargain hard and buy a lot.
- The hand-blocked table linens—that cost hundreds of euros in France—cost $20 each in India. Napkins are $2 each.
- Jewelry is so gorgeous and so fairly priced that you may turn to diamonds and rust.

India can be a difficult trip; the good stuff is hidden, and you need serious connections and/or nerves of steel to find anything worthwhile. But if you're ready for the rough stuff, this could be the shopping adventure you've been looking for. I personally have yearned for the Far Pavilions of India for a long time (at least ever since I read the M.M. Kaye novel). That a lot of the clothes come in one-size-fits-all and have drawstrings only made the idea more attractive.

Recently, I began to obsess with what's called **The Golden Triangle** of India—the delta of Delhi, Agra and Jaipur. Granted, most of my interest was concentrated in Jaipur and its famous **Gem Palace** (p. 138). I imagined being part of all the photo essays I'd been seeing in magazines, of taking to heart Diana Vreeland's confession that pink is the navy blue of India. So *Born to Shop* Editorial Director Sarah Lahey and I spent our mileage awards on business-class tickets and

Jaipur's Silk Road Bazaar.

headed to Delhi, dreaming of endless $1 prairie skirts and $100 diamonds.

We had a day to get acclimated in Delhi—where we went crazy in the **Anokhi** store (see below) in **Santushti Village**, Race Course Rd. (☎ **91141/2688-3076**)—and then piled our empty suitcases into our chauffeur-driven Ford and headed for Jaipur. Despite the fact that Jaipur is a mere 160 miles from Delhi, the trip takes 5 hours. Camels, elephants and goats take up vehicular traffic lanes. Four wheels, four legs—hey, what's the difference? At the midpoint of the drive, the driver pulled into the tourist approved rest stop for clean bathrooms, snacks and, yep, shopping. We bought items there we never saw again and wished we'd bought more of. Who knew the shopping in Jaipur would be so difficult, that we'd never see this kind of crafts selection again for weeks, or that there are no $1 skirts anywhere in India.

Tip: All the luxury hotels in Jaipur are outside of the city center; transportation—even by taxi—is almost non-existent. The way to shop is with a car and driver, provided by your hotel, at the rate of $30 per half day and $60 for the full day. As it turns out, this is the best shopping investment you will make in India.

We ooohhed and aaahhhed over our chosen villa (**Le Royal Meridien**) and hailed our driver Babu to get us to the main markets, *en toute hâte*, as quickly as possible. Anyone who has ever seen an ad or series of photos of Jaipur has seen the building that represents the city center and main market. In pictures it is exotic and rosy pink and gorgeous and worth flying for 17 hours and driving for another 5. In person it is small, exotic, crumbling, filthy and touristy. The combination of aggressive beggars, aggressive vendors and very aggressive elephants (one spat on Sarah) sent us back to Babu after only an hour of shopping.

Anokhi Jaipur, 2 Talik Marg, C-Scheme (☎ **91141/222-9247;** www.anokhi.com), which we had already visited in Delhi, is the flagship store and the gem of Jaipur. Located in the New City, Anokhi is far better stocked than its counterpart in Delhi, selling hand-block printed textiles quilted into bedspreads, tote bags and handbag accessories, while other yardage is made into clothes, table linen and sleepwear. Quilted tote bags for $10 each were the best buys of the trip. We had lime and ginger drinks on the terrace, toasted our good luck and flagged down Babu.

Fabindia (say "Fab India"), C-69, Sarojini Marg (☎ **91141/ 511-5991**) claims to be a lifestyle store, although I am not impressed by their home style. Downstairs in the Jaipur store the huge selection includes clothing for men and women, both Western and Indian style. They had some sizes up to 46, which is unusual in India.

Soma, 5 Jacob Rd. (☎ **91141/222-2778;** www.somashop. com), is located in a fancy residential part of Jaipur; walk up the stairs at no. 5. They offer tablecloths beginning at $20 and napkins from $2.50 each—less than what you'd pay at home, much less than what you'd pay for *les tissues indiennes* in France, yet high if you were expecting bargains in India. The store is better stocked and more fun to shop than the branch in Delhi. Soma's hand-blocked prints are protected by copyright and are used in bed linens; clothes for men, women and children; and gift items and tabletop. Gandhi-style pajamas come in styles for men and women.

En route back to the hotel, Babu took us to **Silk Road Bazaar,** Cottage Industries Exposition, Sarai Bawri, Amer (☎ **91141/263-2444**), which I thought was going to be a TT (tourist trap) but turned out to be a very charming TT . . . well worth the stop and with some of the best-looking merchandise we'd seen all day. Some of the merch was not our style, but the clothing was good, the scarves and shawls were fabulous, the saris were sensational and the layout of the place (a villa and gardens turned into a store) was photo-worthy. As it happens, Amer City is not to be missed, even if your hotel isn't just down the road, as ours was. (However, take a pass on the Anokhi museum in Amer City—it isn't very good—and the gift shop/factory shop isn't worth the stop.)

Some of the best shopping in town was in the small shopping arcade attached to the **Oberoi Rajvilas,** Goner Road (☎ **91141/268-0101;** www.oberoihotels.com). Rajvilas has a small strip with a half dozen or more shops in a row. Prices seemed fairly reasonable, from the $100 paid for a giant paisley shawl—large enough to spruce up a chair in my living room—to the $259 asking price for a pair of gold and ruby earrings at the jewelry store a few doors down.

Inside the hotel itself are a few other stores, including one of the best hotel gift shops I have ever seen in my life, a branch of **Gem Palace** (see below), and also the spa to end all spas. If you use the bathroom, there are amenities to be snatched and devoured with delight.

If you have a good sense of humor, a figure that is more like an Indian man's than woman's, or you're shopping for an XY in your life, check out **Raja Sahab**, Raja Park (☎ **91141/262-3001**) a complete men's store that mixes contemporary fashions with traditional.

Gem Palace, M.I. Road (☎ **91141/237-4175**; www.gempalace jaipur.com), is one of Jaipur's shopping icons: a downtown (New City) white-stucco store painted with the pale pink outlines of the Far Pavilions and filled with jewelry (duh). The most upsetting thing about the jewelry is that most of it seems reasonably priced. Nonetheless, polite haggling should be done even in a store this fancy, where gold hoop earrings with cascades of tiny tourmalines were priced at a mere $836.

WHERE TO STAY

Hyatt Regency Delhi

This contemporary hotel, with a hint of Delhi's Red Fort in the tiered style of the building's façade, is otherwise totally modern, with contemporary luxuries such as artsy black-and-white photos, two floors of club rooms, a glorious breakfast buffet and a wonderful spa.

Halfway between the airport and center of town, the Hyatt's location means it is pretty simple to get anywhere; they also offer airport pickup service and can arrange for a car to take you into Jaipur. Bhikaiji Cama Place, Righ Road, New Delhi. ☎ **91141/2679-1234.** www.delhi.hyatt.com.

Upall's Orchid: An Ecotel Hotel

Although we chose this hotel because it is very close to the Delhi Airport, it turns out to be the poster child for the Green Movement in India and offers a luxe hotel in a park with emphasis on organic food and produce and non-toxic materials. Our lower level room was complete with garden view and cicadas. Free shuttle to airport. Member Leading Hotels of the World; rooms about $250. National Highway No. 8, New Delhi. ☎ **9111/4151-1515**. www.lhw.com.

The Kristkrindlesmarkt (Christmas Markets)

Christmas markets, which date back to medieval times, are all over Europe; most are delightful. The best of the markets, the ones you want to see, shop, smell and sip, are located in western Germany or eastern France, many in the Alsace region that has been both German and French throughout history. Because the towns are not enormously far apart, you can pick several and squeeze in a number of markets over a long weekend or a few days out. They are usually located in the town square, or the heart of the old quarter. They begin with the start of Advent (the end of November) and go until December 23 or 24th.

Weekends in the most popular markets are hell—if you define hell as throngs of other tourists. Although most markets open at 9 or 10am, the whole point is to go at dusk or any time after 4pm; the cold and the dark add to the atmosphere. Markets stay open usually until 9pm but may stay open later, especially on weekends.

Shopping and eating are equal sports: The foods are winter specialties meant to warm and comfort you: roasted chestnuts, apple strudel, potato pancakes, hot chocolate, fried potatoes, mulled wine, sausage on a stick—you get the idea. The buys are usually crafts and Christmas gear, such as nutcrackers and ornaments. A modest market will have about 100 booths; the

Berlin's Christmas Market at the Deutscher Dom.

big-time markets have a few hundred. I prefer smaller markets in historic towns with fewer booths and fewer tourists—to me it's not just the shopping, it's the magic. Alsace alone has over 35 markets. To market, to market to buy a fat gingerbread.

Las Vegas, NEVADA

It shouldn't take TV shows like *Las Vegas* and *CSI* to tell you that "Sin City" is hot—the shopper's grapevine has been beating the tom-toms for several years. The new Las Vegas has more than gambling and girls with g-strings strutting on the wings of an airplane. Las Vegas has more big-name chefs than any other American city, and the city prides itself as a shopping destination.

Shopper's Lunch

The hotels and malls are filled with restaurants and cafes that represent the world's best chefs. The best meals I had in Las Vegas were at Ducasse's **Mix**, 3950 Las Vegas Blvd S. (☎ 702/632-9500) and **Corsa Cucina** at The Wynn, where Chef Stephen Kalt left me floating on air (and meatballs).

Sephora alone is one of the largest and best stores in the country (several locations; www.sephora.com). **Juicy Couture**, 3500 Las Vegas Blvd. (☎ 702/365-5600), which now has several freestanding stores around the States, chose Las Vegas for its very first store. Most of the hotels have their own shopping—I don't mean gift shops for furry dice, condoms and mouthwash, but big-name designer stores, along with themed malls and palaces worthy of a good gawk.

The normal malls here are a bit of a bore, but the hotel shopping is amazing. The **Bellagio**, 3600 Las Vegas Blvd. S. (☎ 888/987-6667), and the **Wynn** (see below) have the Euro big names, but the mall at **Caesar's**, 3570 Las Vegas Blvd. S. (☎ 800/851-1703) is a great venue because of its theatrical take on hospitality, entertainment and retail. Indeed, most of the shopping and strolling pleasures in Las Vegas are related to hotels. The **Walgreen's** and **CVS** in the middle of the strip are both good for life's essentials, from postcards to bottled water and in-room snacks.

Those interested in brand might be intrigued by some of the single-brand stores—**M&M's** (another M&M's store is in Orlando), **Coke** and **Harley-Davidson** all have their own shops, often with cafes. Get your art fix at the **Metropolitan Museum** of Art gift shop in the **Miracle Mile Shops,** 3663 Las Vegas Blvd. South (☎ **888/800-8284;** www.miraclemileshopslv.com).

WHERE TO STAY

Wynn Las Vegas

I booked into the Wynn right after it opened, determined to experience it for myself. Months after my stay, I discovered I had booked into the *wrong* part of the hotel. Mere mortals stay in the regular part of the hotel, but the Mobil 5-Star and AAA 5-Diamond awards go to the Tower Suites, which operate as a separate boutique hotel. Who knew? Rooms begin at $300. 3232 S. Las Vegas Blvd. ☎ **702/770-7100.** www.wynnlasvegas.com.

The Potteries, ENGLAND

Just as the name implies, The Potteries is an area of England where pottery is made . . . and, joyfully, sold at a variety of factory stores and warehouses strung through the English countryside. Although British sterling is very high against the U.S. dollar, one of the few bargains left in the UK can be found in the heaps of fine-bone china and everyday earthenwares that fill area warehouses, off-pricers and factory stores. No dish junkie should miss this experience.

Located 1 hour (by train) from Manchester and some 3 hours from London, The Potteries are a cluster of small villages woven around **Stoke-on-Trent,** which is where the train drops you. Town is about a mile away.

From the train station you can either rent a car or take a shuttle bus that makes a loop to assorted factories and showrooms. You can even walk into lovely downtown Stoke and shop directly at the **Spode** factory, Church St. (☎ **441782/744-011;** www.spode.com) which is possibly the highlight of the trip anyway.

Spode has a museum of blue and white porcelain, a cafeteria and a large sales room. In August, right before the annual summer closing, tents are pitched on the property to house the gigantic sale that takes place. You literally stand under a white tent agog at stack and stacks of Spode dishes with scrawled price tags on them—£14, £2, £45 and so on. ***Note:*** As we go to press, there are rumors that the factory was not protected by law and has been sold to be demolished. Check before heading over there.

Because all factories are closed on the same schedule, sale dates are uniform throughout the area. During the vacation period, a showroom may or may not be open for tourists, but vendors will not be able to ship anything for you. Smart shoppers will avoid the closures and stick to the sales or the everyday shopping during weekdays. This is not really a weekend adventure because of crowds and lines.

Remember that fees for shipping and U.S. duty will double your costs, so make sure you are actually getting a bargain before you pounce. (I paid $10 per plate for a set of plates that were, at the time, selling at Tiffany & Co. for $100, so that even with shipping I was still triumphant.)

WHERE TO STAY

Haydon House Hotel

Basford is a suburb of Stoke, so you will need a car to get here. Request one of the "china rooms," not Chinese but named for and decorated with local pottery. The small three-star hotel is converted from a Victorian town house; you might call it a B&B, though they have a restaurant. Haydon House totals 30 rooms, some of which are suites, and you can even bring a small pet. You'll pay about $100 per night for two people in one room. 5–9 Haydon St., Basford. ☎ 441782/711-311. www.haydon/house/hotel.co.uk.

Moat House

If you prefer a standardized room and all that goes with it, the number one hotel in town is the four-star Moat House, just outside Stoke. This Best Western–owned hotel has 147 rooms that go for about $150 per night. The rooms have every amenity you can imagine, although Wi-Fi costs about $35 a day. The restaurant on the premises is fairly good. Festival Way, Etruria Hall. ☎ 441782/609-988. www.bestwestern.co.uk.

Prague, CZECH REPUBLIC

Shoppers go for the glass—be it tablewares or art glass. The local word for crystal is *glas,* which in most cases refers to what you or I would call "lead crystal." Only the famed Moser brand is actually glass since it has no lead in it. *Note:* With an average of 18% lead content, that vase you are hand-carrying back home may set off bells and whistles when it goes through security.

Since glass occupies most of the shelf space in stores in town, you have to cast a quick and discerning eye. The most common form of Bohemian glass is not currently in style (hasn't been since 1907), so you must look past it to colored glass—very chic

Moser, the best crystal in Prague.

these days—or contemporary pieces, many of which have been inspired by French crystal.

The best crystal in town is made by **Moser,** Na Príkope 12 (☎ **420353/449-455;** www.moser-glass.com) a top-notch luxe name in Europe and one of the best brands in the world (sold in the U.S. in stores like Neiman Marcus and Bergdorf Goodman). Expect to pay at least $100 a stem, although prices come down at the factory store (see below). Since it takes glass to make glass, factory seconds don't exist in this business, and stores have no need to stock imperfect pieces.

Start your prowl on the main shopping street—and compare prices at **Sklo Bohemia,** Na Prikope 17 (☎ **420569/477-111**) and **Celetna Crystal,** Celetna 15 (☎ **420222/324-022**). I usually buy in bulk at Sklo Bohemia. Since a complete set of 24 champagne flutes, and water and wine glasses for 12, cost slightly more than $200, I didn't mind paying for shipping. A few stores are staked out in the airport, in case you want to finish off your funds.

WHERE TO STAY

Four Seasons Prague

Totally rebuilt since the flood, this is the fanciest hotel in town, and it's right where you want to be—within walking distance to just about everything and across the street from the main concert hall. Some of the rooms have river views (mine had a view of the garbage dump); the restaurant is one of the best in town. Veleslavínova 2a/1098. ☎ **420221/427-000.** www.fourseasons. com/prague.

InterContinental Hotel

This hotel is neither glam nor gorgeous—in fact, it's pretty ugly from the outside. There's nothing wrong with it; it just happens to have been built in the 1970s and looks like it. Prices and location, however, are sublime. You're a block from the main square and a half block from Hermès. Namesti Curieovych 43/5. ☎ **420296/631-111.** www.icprague.com.

Rio de Jainero, BRAZIL

Take back your samba, hang up your tanga. It's time to shop. Gemstones are the main attraction here. Most of the world's colored stones come from Brazil, so you can find them sold in markets, fancy stores and even at the airport.

The most famous name in stones and jewelry is **H.Stern** (p. 138), with stores in all of the world capitals and a large headquarters in Ipanema. You can tour the museum and the work rooms before you settle down in a private booth to see the collection. There's even **H.Stern Off Price** next door, where out-of-season merchandise is sold at a 30% discount.

If quality and guarantees are important, buy only from H. Stern or **Amsterdam Sauer.** If you are into more funky stuff, go to the **Hippie Market,** Plaza General Osorio (Sun only, 9am–6pm) or the beachside **night market at Copacabana,** open 6 nights a week. (It's dark on Sun.) The market begins at 7pm but really gets hot around 10pm. You can find everything from polished gemstones to ropes of egg-sized semi-precious rocks. Expect to pay $40 for a choker of amethyst that sells for $1,500 in the U.S.

Prices vary with quality, but the value of street gems is hard to ascertain. Still, at $8 a carat for blue topaz, who cares? (**Shopper's Note:** I took two blue topazes to Hong Kong with me to have them made into earrings; that cost an additional $250 which I still thought was very fair.)

As Frank Sinatra once told us, they have a lot of coffee in Brazil. Thankfully, Starbucks has not yet arrived, and locals hang out at juice bars, not coffee shops. As many as three **juice bars** occupy any given city block in the tourist districts (like Copacabana and Ipanema) and high-end residential areas (such as Leblon). The drink of choice these days is *acaia* (say "ah-say-ow"), which comes from a plant in the Amazon that is freeze-dried and then shipped to Rio where it is served as a purple pulp, often mixed with honey. The concoction was discovered by surfers who found that the high-protein drink also provides long-lasting energy.

Indeed, beach culture permeates all walks of life, even beauty treatments since the Brazilian-style wax job was created to accommodate the itsy-bitsy-teeny-weeny yellow-polka-dot bikini. The Sofitel Copacabana—right on the beach at Copacabana—is surrounded by bathing suit and surf shops that fill the tiny streets behind the hotel. Queen of bikinis, however, is **Lenni,** which also sells clothes, shoes and accessories, even supplying big-name U.S. stores like Bergdorf's and Neiman Marcus. Most bathing suits in Brazil are sold in two parts, so you can buy the appropriate sizes, respectively, or take a miss on a top entirely, if that's your style.

Local designers do create more than board shorts and bathing suits. Brazil is famous for its high-quality shoes—although amazing flip-flops also sell cheaply everywhere in town. In home decor, 1960s style is having a resurgence, led by sleek pieces made of indigenous wood. The most collectible are by Sergio Rodrigues, who makes Brazil's equivalent of the Eames chair—this man is so famous he is referred to only by his first name. The Sergio version is made of rosewood (which is called jacaranda in Brazil) and is highly prized in its original form because rosewood is now endangered. Look for Sergio's designs at **Novo Design,** the store at the Museum of Modern Art. For more retro designs, visit the Lapa District, where various stores and warehouses in a row sell furniture and home style from the 1940s–60s.

WHERE TO STAY

Copacabana Palace

It is indeed a palace and it overlooks not only the sea, but a wonderful street market held every night except Sundays. With good restaurants, very snazzy clients and private access to the beach beyond, this is *"the"* address in Rio. Avenida Atlantica 1702. ☎ **5521/2548-7070.**

Design Hotel Portinari

This is also in Copacabana, 1 block away from the beach and deep in surfboard shop and bikini land. The architecturally oriented hotel has mostly apartments, which go for under $200 a night. Rua Francisco Sa 17. ☎ **5521/3288-8800.** www.hotel portinari.com.br.

San Diego, CALIFORNIA

San Diego has become one of America's most beloved destinations, a city that is serving locals and tourists alike as one of the most ideal places to live, to spend time and, naturally, to shop. The downtown is littered with high towers and condos. A cluster of North, East and South counties are filled with sights, shopping, old money, new money, many malls and very, very expensive real estate.

Just past Lindbergh Field (the airport), housing takes advantage of incredible views of the ocean. Prices are already outta sight, but the sunbirds keep on coming, along with a branch of the grocery store **Ralph's,** a major league ballpark, and renovated districts such as **Gaslamp** and **Little Italy.** All are filled with restaurants, bars, boutiques and, on weekends, hordes of visitors who take advantage of the perfect weather (average temp: 74 degrees and sunny) and the ability to stroll everywhere. A trolley also goes through the cutie-pie districts and stops just shy of the U.S.–Mexico border at TJ, as locals call Tijuana.

My best find downtown is the **Paul Mitchell School,** 410 A Street, on the trolley line (☎ **619/398-1590**), where students practice on real people at slashed prices: a cut and styling is priced depending on the experience of the operator, either $10 or $15. Highlights start at $35. Hours are Monday to Thursday 9:30am to 10pm; Friday and Saturday 9:30am to 5pm; closed Sunday. Appointments are needed.

Shopper's Lunch

Grab a bite at Horton Plaza or go for the serious power lunch at the Grant Hotel Grill Room. The smoked salt on the fresh home-made bread is worth the world.

Along the northern coast, aging beach communities have reinvented themselves. In **Ocean Beach,** about 15 minutes north of the airport, the entire main street—Newport Avenue—has been renovated and turned into an antiques district. The old-fashioned, 1950s-style movie theatre is now an antiques mall, and even the local Rite-Aid drug store sells ice cream cones. Surfers wander downtown with boards tucked under their arms while old ladies totter on their walkers. The 3-block stretch of stores offers nothing too hoity or toity but instead has shops and malls filled with stalls selling informal antiques and vintage clothing. Start with **Retro,** 4879 Newport Ave. (☎ **619/222-0220;** www.retro.com)—it isn't the best store in the world but is a good taste of the flavor of the row.

Carlsbad, CA: Five Spas & an Outlet Mall

So there we are at what I think is going to be a romantic getaway from the real world—a weekend booked at the **Four Seasons Aviara,** 7100 Four Seasons Point, north of San Diego (☎ **760/ 603-6801;** www.fourseasons.com). Since we don't play golf, I ask the concierge about destinations nearby. I am informed that the number one destination is the **Carlsbad Factory Outlet,** 5620 Paseo Del Norte #100 (☎ **760/804-9000;** www.premiumoutlets.com) stores followed by **Legoland,** One Legoland Dr. (☎ **760/ 918-5346;** www.legoland.com) and the **Carlsbad Flower Farms,** 5704 Paseo Del Norte (☎ **760/431-0352;** www.theflowerfields. com). Who knew?

We have Four Seasons spa treatments (p. 164), we dine in the hotel, we walk the property and find the bird sanctuary. And while driving around Carlsbad, I discover that the Carlsbad region is filled with spas and resorts, all revolving around golf, weather and their proximity to the outlet mall. **La Costa,** 2100 Costa Del Mar Rd. (☎ **760/438-9111;** www.lacosta.org), started the trend, now there's half a dozen. Then I learn that all the hot young retail is going into a string of beach communities (p. 470) nearby and that Carlsbad is the most stylish new destination in America. All because of an outlet mall. And they all lived happily ever after. See www. carlsbadca.org.

Farther north is **Solana Beach,** the heart of cutesy shopping and design. A 2- to 3-block stretch of Cedros Avenue will delight, but nothing captures the whole mood better than **Solo,** 309 S. Cedros Ave. (☎ **858/794-9016;** www.solocedros. com). A group of small vendors located in a former factory and crammed into a light-filled space spilling over with books, furniture, antiques, style, cards and a cozy feel of style and comfort, Solo could be one of my favorite stores in America.

WHERE TO STAY

Four Seasons Aviara

The famed Four Seasons brand has a resort hotel, a residence community, a spa, a golf course and an award-winning chef tucked into a bird sanctuary in the North Counties. Guests are most likely to check in for some pampering, a visit to the spas, a stroll in the gardens, and—their favorite day trip—a visit to the outlet mall in nearby Carlsbad. 7100 Four Seasons Point, Carlsbad, CA. ☎ **760/603-6800.** www.fourseasonshotel.com/ aviara.

U.S. Grant Hotel

Long the grande-dame hotel of San Diego, the U.S. Grant closed for a 2-year, $52-million renovation to turn it into the talk of the town once again. This is a shopper's dream, with a location across the street from Horton Plaza, a mall. The Starwood-run Luxury Collection hotel tends to be noisy but is cutting edge in both decor and culinary offerings. Spa treatments can be booked in your room. Rates begin at $249. 326 Broadway, San Diego. ☎ **619/238-1818.** www.luxurycollection.com/usgrant.

Westgate

Located directly next door to the U.S. Grant Hotel (above), the Westgate is such an opposite that it bears contrasting. This modern building hosts an old-world-style hotel, with French influence down to the decor. Rates begin at $299. Member Leading Hotels of the World (www.lhw.com). 226 Broadway ☎ **619/232-3121.**

Santa Fe, NEW MEXICO

Jet-set destinations have always been defined by the fact that they are not served by public transportation. Such is the case with Santa Fe, which welcomes only private craft to its tiny airport. Mere mortals must fly to Albuquerque and drive about an hour north to get to this artsy-fartsy destination of adobe style, turquoise jewelry, famous chefs and funky shopping. Whether you like art galleries, native crafts or BoHo fashions, you'll find it all—and more—in one of America's most unique cities.

Despite the fact that Santa Fe has weather extremes (very hot in summer, snow and cold in winter), it is a year-round destination and a winter dream when the smell of piñon burning wafts onto the streets for tourists visiting galleries, fashion stores, jewelers, artisans and museums. Opera season—in the summer—plays to sold-out crowds; a good weekend flea market is on the way to the opera, summers only. And don't forget the joys of Southwestern cuisine.

Shopping is divided into various neighborhoods: The Plaza, Canyon Road and Cerillos Road. Thankfully the few big brands that have arrived in town work with the local look— **Coldwater Creek** (www.coldwatercreek.com) and **CP Shades** (www.cpshades.com), for example. The Plaza—the heart of town—has a few tourist traps, some natives on blankets selling their crafts and several jewelry stores. Right on the Plaza, **Santa Fe Dry Goods,** 53 Old Santa Fe Trail (☎ **505/983-8142;** www.santafedrygoods.com) is a pretty bland name for a serious shop, but don't miss its designer local look, rendered in silks and laid-back droop, often from European designers.

The jewelry scene is over-the-top and very confusing. My last trip to Santa Fe followed 3 weeks in Asia, so I know for certain that much of the native-looking ropes of turquoise and coral actually come from China and may be man-made at that. You've got a wide range of choices though, from $15,000 "storywheel" necklaces at **Nancy Brown,** 111 Old Santa Fe Trail (www.nbstorywheels.com), to pawn-shop Navajo pieces sold from specialty dealers . . . with everything in between. I think the best in town is **Packards,** 61 Old Santa Fe Trail on The Plaza (☎ **800/648-7358;** daily 9:30am–6pm), which sells jewelry and local crafts—the important stuff. **Ortega's,** right across the street at 101 W, San Francisco St. (☎ **800/874-9297;** ortegas plaza@cybermesa.com), also sells a lot of jewelry.

To really get into the local style, waltz into **Origins,** 135 W San Francisco St. (☎ **505/988-2323**), a medium-sized store that is hung with velvets, flounces, silks and prairie skirts— some hippie clothes, some hats, some fabulous colors and a sense of well-being that comes only from comfy clothes with miraculous drape. **Dancing Ladies,** 233 Canyon Rd. (☎ **505/988-1100**), is one of the first stores along the best shopping street in town, Canyon Road. The store specializes in big shirts made in Thailand from Thai silks; they cost close to $200 a shirt. The painter's smock is simply to weep for. Even if you don't want a silk shirt, this is a good first stop on your journey of exploration.

Canyon Road is very long; you need good weather and good walking shoes to make a stroll of the whole thing. The street is crammed with galleries and bistros and a hum that lets you know a lot of money is being spent by out-of-towners who've come in for a spree. Like Aspen, Santa Fe is a retail market where people wear jeans and act like just-folks but have heaps of dough that they are glad to spend.

WHERE TO STAY

La Posada de Santa Fe Resort & Spa

If you want the best in town, go directly to La Posada, a resort in the heart of town, and a village unto itself complete with award-winning chef. Walk everywhere within the walls of the complex or in downtown Santa Fe, or hole up in your little bungalow with wood-burning fireplace. The spa offers serenity galore. Member Leading Hotels of the World. 330 East Palace Ave. ☎ **866/331-7625.** http://laposada.rockresorts.com.

Hilton Santa Fe

Every major motel chain has a stake in town on the long road (Cerillos Road) from the highway into downtown. I prefer to be in the center of town where you can walk everywhere, although this means paying more. If you're upgrading from Holiday Inn Express but still on a budget, check out the Hilton, on the edge of the downtown area. 100 Sandoval Street. ☎ **505/988-2811.** www.hilton.com.

Seattle, WASHINGTON

Maybe we knew about Seattle before Microsoft, Nintendo and Starbucks, but we sure didn't take it seriously. Now the city has overcome its gray and rainy weather to bloom into a center for foodies. Indeed, there's **Archie McPhee** in Ballard, 2428 NW Market St (www.mcphee.com); apple farmers in Yakima (www.ci.yakima.wa.us); and a whole lot of shopping going on downtown. Seattle has become so important that various new neighborhoods are popping up within the city and the burbs.

Shopper's Lunch

Shucker's, in the rear of the Fairmont Olympic Hotel, is near the shops and satisfies your need to have seafood while in town. There are 12 different kinds of oysters and more, including non-seafood.

Speaking of downtown: I actually went to Seattle specifically because I wanted to inspect the **Nordstrom** motherstore, 500 Pine St. That wasn't worth the airfare, and the **Nordstrom Rack** 2 blocks away, 1601 2nd Ave. # 100, is downright scruffy. This is one store whose reputation is larger than its boundaries.

But there were other delights in town, especially **Pike Place** (p. 369), the market right in the heart of town that sells foods, souvenirs, flowers and crafts, and anchors a small village with the original **Sur La Table** store (p. 343) and the original **Starbucks** (p. 387). I went religiously to **Pappardelle's** in the market to buy more types of gourmet pasta. You can even sign up for a food tour (www.savorseattletours.com) of the market.

There are two different ways to approach a weekend in Seattle: Stay in the city center and walk (or ferry) everywhere; or rent a car and get to retail in outer stretches and suburbs. The Fairmont Olympic Hotel (below) offered to get me a rental for a day that would be brought to the hotel and then taken away for me when I was done; for $39 this was the deal of the trip.

WHERE TO STAY

Fairmont Olympic Hotel

The fact that this grande-dame hotel has been an InterContinental and a Four Seasons before becoming the Fairmont reveals the secret that this is the only place to be, always the best hotel in town in the best location. Fairmont has added layers of customer service and two of the city's best restaurants. They also have a Shopper's Package with Nordstrom. All shopping is walking distance or in the hotel itself. 411 University St., Seattle, WA. ☎ **206/621-1700.** www.fairmonthotels.com.

Four Seasons Seattle

As we go to press, Four Seasons is finishing a tower with hotel and residences, much like their hotel in San Francisco. This one is located across the street from the Pike Market. www.four seasons.com/seattle.

Scottsdale, ARIZONA

Scottsdale is a miles-long but very thin community, making it unsuitable for walking. It could take you a year to learn your way around and then you'd have to start all over again because so many new places will have cropped up.

I've always said I hate malls, but I met several in Scottsdale that made me eat those words—most are man-made villages of shopping and dining opportunities, but some even come with condos attached, like the innovative **Kierland Commons,** 15054 N. Scottsdale Rd. (☎ **480/348-1577;** www.kierland commons.com). The stores here are the usual upmarket brands you'd expect, with a few refreshing faces that might not have yet opened in your hometown, such as **Lather** (www. lather.com), which sells bath and beauty products, and **Soma**

Shopper's Lunch

Zinc Bistro, 15034 N. Scottsdale Rd., Kierland Commons, Space 140 (☎ 480/603-0922), is a French-style bistro with real zinc bar (hence the name) and serves lunch or dinner to mall shoppers; don't miss the frites wrapped in newspaper.

(www.soma.com), a division of Chico's that sells underwear and pajamas. The totally artificial complex is a 38-acre main-street shopping schema that makes you feel you are in Pleasantville, never a mall.

The Scottsdale Waterfront is a development on a canal (hence the water in the desert). A bridge crosses over to **Scottsdale Fashion Square,** 7014 E. Camelback Rd. #590 (www.fashionsquare. com), a more traditional mall. A smaller plaza-style shopping area that's won local acclaim is **The Borgata,** 6166 N. Scottsdale Rd. (☎ 602/953-6311) with several nice stores, although frankly, I prefer **El Pedegral,** 34505 N. Scottsdale Rd. (☎ 480/488-1072;** www.elpedregal.com), which has an amphitheatre and a lot of mystical vibes—and some shopping. Not world-class shopping, but the atmosphere, especially at dusk and into the evening, is enough to give you goose bumps of delight.

Plenty of discount abides in this town of much money—from **Arizona Mills,** 5000 Arizona Mills Circle (☎ 480/491-7300; www.arizonamills.com), a large value-oriented mall in nearby Tempe, to the far-more-interesting **E&J Designer Shoe Outlet,** 16251 N. Scottsdale Rd. (☎ 480/609-6905**), which differentiates itself from DSW and the like by having name brands that are seldom discounted elsewhere. (I bought a pair of Taryn Rose shoes for $199, which is a 70% markdown from their regular price. They even fit.)

Old Town Scottsdale is a cute district of stores and TTs that's fun to browse. Check out **Saba,** 3965 N. Brown Ave. and 7254 Main St. (☎ 480/947-7664;** www.sabawesternwear.com), for western wear. These two stores are across the street from each other. For a more chic take on cowboy gear, check out the belt buckles at **Saddlebags,** with two locations: The Borgata (☎ 480/948-1221;** www.saddlebagsaz.com) and The Phoenician (☎ 480/423-0636).

Rhinestone cowboys can't miss **Barbwire,** 15425 N. Scottsdale Rd. no. 230 (☎ 480-443-9473;** www.barbwire.com), one of the best stores in America for rock–and-roll western wear for men and women. They stock some shoes, boots and just enough glitter to make you outshine Annie Oakley: The clothes are actually funky fun and not costumey. Barbwire has their own warehouse store, but the hours are spotty so call ahead. You're gonna want to shop at the warehouse because prices at the regular store are very high—I wanted a belt buckle: no belt, just the buckle, for $600. Embroidered western shirts are over $200.

If you prefer the Indians to the cowboys, pop into **Gilbert Ortega,** 3925 N. Scottsdale Rd. (not related to Ortega's in Santa Fe). Gilbert Ortega appears to be a TT but has some serious Native-American art and jewelry put away. (This is not related to Ortega's in Santa Fe.)

WHERE TO STAY

Four Seasons Troon

Troon is a northern suburb of Scottsdale, the location of a few golf courses and, more importantly, the hidden sanctuary of the Four Seasons Resort where guests live in their own casitas and overlook the rocks, the cactus or the village-like tiers of the property. Gold is nearby, and rock-climbing is right on the property; we just kept going from the restaurant to the spa and back again. The nights were very dark, the air had a chill; we had a fire in our kiva and pretty much thought we'd booked the honeymoon. 10600 East Crescent Moon Dr. ☎ **480/515-5700.** www.fourseasons.com/scottsdale.

Scottsdale Princess

What I like best about this hotel is the location and the sprawl—this isn't really a hotel, it's a city. You'd better be prepared to walk within the property, as the spa is on the far side of what's much like a college campus with landscaping, fountains and gorgeous views that take you completely out of the real world. 7575 East Princess Dr. ☎ **480/585-4848.** www.fairmont.com/scottsdale.

Smalands, SWEDEN

Serious shoppers may have never heard of Smaland (www.smaland-oland.com), but will learn to call it Smile-land when they discover the glass factories and the outlet stores of southern Sweden. This is where you go to buy both art glass and lead crystal from warehouses laid out across beautiful countryside. One of the parts of this small region of Smaland (get it?) is called the **Kingdom of Crystal** (www.glasriket.se), home to 15 glassworks. *Note:* Smaland is a district, not a town, so it's not hard to get to if you are on a cruise ship that comes to port in Kalmar or Vaxjo.

The area is filled with lakes and trees, making it perfect for the production of glass. To make glass you only need water, sand, ash and a very hot fire. Glassblowers were brought over from Venice in the 1500s; many of the existing factories have been around since the mid–18th century. When the small factories fell on bad times, they merged with the larger firms so that today **Orrefors-Kosta Boda** (www.orrefors.com and www.kostaboda.com) represents most of the glassmakers. A few indies are still left though. You are welcome to visit their studios and shop at their outlet stores. Most factory stores sell seconds as well as out-of-season merchandise (score on Christmas ornaments in July) and items from discontinued lines.

If you can get to only one factory store, head some 10 miles northwest of Nybro to the **Orrefors factory** (☎ **464/813-4195**), where you'll find a glass museum, a factory tour, a chance to blow your own glass and a gigantic store with very, very good prices. (I paid $30 for a large piece of signed art glass.) A vase may be $50, but you will have to pay to ship it or hand carry it home. Figure $50 more for shipping.

Sydney, AUSTRALIA

I am not waltzing with Matilda for several reasons. One is that I think Matilda is a 'roo. The other is that when I am in Sydney, I am deep into aboriginal art. Other things are available to buy of course—with some local hotshot designers, some fun markets, a fine fish market, and a strong spa and beauty scene—but I've gone native.

I remember Prince Charles swapping one of his water colors for the work of a local artist, but frankly, it wasn't until I arrived in Sydney that I was gobsmacked by the earth and sky tones, the squiggly lines, the dots and dashes of this naïf art form—and its similarities to other native styles, such as those in Mexico, Africa and France.

Aboriginal-style art is sold in all forms in all venues—you can buy head scarves, silk scarves, pot holders, postcards, placemats, note papers, tea towels, beach towels, tote bags, ties, posters and canvases. Part of the charm of the whole thing is that the artist's name and photo is usually attached to the back of the canvas.

Canvases by important artists are totally beyond my price range—reaching into five figures and beyond. I was able to buy some canvases for $250, small ones for $50 and little souvenir items such as hand-painted boxes for $25 to $36.

I bought many items from the **Museum of Sydney** gift shop, right across the street from the Intercontinental Hotel (below); and from a gallery alongside the Four Seasons Hotel, **Aboriginal Dreamtime,** Shop 8, 199 George St. (☎ 612/9241-2953; www.aboriginalfineartgallery.com.au). **Rainbow Serpent** (☎ 612/8577-5300; www.rainbowserpent.com.au) is an excellent store in the Sydney airport. I saw many unique items that I never found during 1 week of intense shopping in Sydney.

The best source in town for serious art and textiles is **Caspian Gallery,** 469 Oxford St., near the Paddington Market (☎ 612/9331-4260; Mon–Sun 11am–5pm). You can find some works by Clifford Possum for sale, but be prepared to pay thousands of dollars for them.

Markets are a big part of the local culture. The best known is the **Paddington Market,** held on Saturday mornings in the part of town of the same name. This is more of a crafts and young-designer market than a flea market. **Oxford Street,** home of the market and the main shopping street in Paddington, is chockablock with tiny stores, as are the side streets. This is the best of Sydney retail—just wander and enjoy. **The Rocks,** a district along the waterfront, also has a weekend street market—I find this one very slick, but worth a stroll through, especially if you are en route to the Park Hyatt hotel (see below). This market is open on Saturday and Sunday, while Paddington Market is only open on Saturdays.

Shopper's Lunch

For a chance to check out the Hyatt and the shopping nearby, try **Hyatt Burgers on the Rocks.**

While I'm not big on shopping malls, I love the Victorian-style **QVB** (Queen Victoria Building), 455 George St. (☎ 612/9264-9209), which has some chains but also many very good and unusual stores. Nearby is the **Strand Arcade,** 412 George St. (☎ 612/9232-4199; www.strandarcade.com.au), a similar enclosed mall of Victorian vintage that houses many of the big names of Aussie style and beauty.

Beauty brands seem to blossom Down Under. Few realize that Helena Rubinstein began her empire in Australia. Modern brands include the likes of **Jurlique** (p. 188). Check out the stores called **Spa Universe** (www.spauniverse.com.au), sort of the local version of Sephora with a strong mix of Aussie and international brands. **Napoleon Perdis** (www.napoleonperdis.com) is an Australian makeup artist working in Los Angeles but with his own line of makeup sold in a small group of his boutiques—and also in department stores. Once you're made up, then you can put another shrimp on the barbie.

WHERE TO STAY

The Four Seasons

Although it's located in a mid-60s-style high-rise that should be torn down and rethought, the hotel has a great location in the heart of everything, overlooks the famous Opera House and offers all of the traditional Four Seasons amenities including service, good eats and an excellent spa. 199 George St. ☎ 612/9238-0000. www.fourseasons.com/sydney.

Park Hyatt

This small, modern, low-slung property is the most dramatic hotel in town. It's where Nicole Kidman spent her honeymoon and where everyone else wants to chill out with some fine dining, great service and the privacy offered at the far end of The Rocks, directly on the water. **Iluka** is a Jurlique (p. 188) spa. Rooms from $500. 7 Hickson Rd., The Rocks. ☎ **612/9241-1234.** www.sydney.park.hyatt.com.

Blue

This is one of those very chic warehouse conversions that juts into the water and makes you feel at one with Australian style. The warehouse was a wool-sorting plant; now it houses the Blue hotel—a member of Leading Hotels of the World (www.lhw.com)—and several restaurants. The location is a tad odd, but you can get a taxi anywhere and are within walking distance of the New South Wales Museum. 6 Cowper Wharf, Woolloomooloo. ☎ **612/9331-9000.** www.tajhotels.com.

Intercontinental

One block from the famed Sydney Opera House and half a block from the Sydney Museum, this hotel is a modern high-rise with views of the harbor and opera house as well as a giant lounge on the rooftop with views clear across the world. 117 Macquarie St. ☎ **612/9253-9000**. www.sydney.intercontinental.com.

Tokyo, JAPAN

Friends in Hong Kong have been dashing to Tokyo for long weekends and raving about what a trendy new destination it has become. Shanghai, they say, is old news as a weekend getaway. Tokyo is the new Shanghai.

The yen and dollar hover close to parity, so it is pretty easy to break even. The excellent subway system is marked in English, so you can get around just fine on your own, even if you (like me) only know three words of Japanese, all learned from the TV mini-series *Shogun.*

Unless you can read Japanese, you'll just want to explore all the neighborhoods, taking in especially the architecture of the big-name designer boutiques, the Japanese designer flagship stores and the whole neighborhood of Harajuku, where street fashion rules. Obviously the main drag here is Jingumae. My first stop off the train is always **Daiso,** 1-19-24 Jingumae (☎ **813/5775-9642**) which is like Monoprix, Target, a dime store or the Dollar Store all rolled into one. You may want to start at **Tokyo Hipsters Club,** 6-16-23 Jingumae (☎ **813/5778-2081;** www.tokyohipstersclub.com), just to warm up.

Once you've settled into what's going on and no longer feel inordinately foreign, head to **La Foret,** 1-11-6 Jingumae, the most important department store for street fashion. Before you know it, you'll be whispering "Harajuku, mon amour."

WHERE TO STAY

Four Seasons Marunouchi

The Marunouchi is the newest of the two Four Seasons in Tokyo and the smallest in the chain with only 57 rooms. Service is so extreme that I was met at Narita and put on the train by the hotel's "Greeting Service." An hour later, a white-gloved bellboy was waiting for me on the platform at Tokyo Station and took me directly to the hotel, a block away. Pacific Century Place. ☎ **813/5222-7222.** www.fourseasons.com.

Conrad Tokyo

Conrad's Asian flagship is nestled into a high-rise in a business park overlooking Tokyo Bay. The rooms are the largest in any Tokyo hotel, though the hotel itself was created for locals as a total destination with several big-name restaurants and a spa. Treatments are Western with a slight Japanese twist; real gold leaf floats in the spa's Japanese soaking tub. The hotel toiletries are custom made by Shiseido. 1-9-1 Higashi-Shinbashi, Minato-Ku. ☎ **813/6388-8000.** www.conradhotels.com.

Peninsula

Keeping in the Peninsula tradition, this brand-new hotel is close to the landmark Imperial Hotel yet offers all sorts of new technology and old-fashioned Pen amenities. Prices begin at

$499. 1-8-1 Yurakucho, Chiyoda-ku. ☎ **813/6270-2888.** www. tokyo.peninsula.com.

Saigon & Hanoi, VIETNAM

Some 60% of the Americans visiting Vietnam get there via Hong Kong, so here is your guide to one of the most fun shopping destinations you will ever encounter. Bring U.S. dollars.

HANOI

The main shopping area is called the "District of the 36 Guilds" and consists of small streets and alleys full of shopping ops. This area is just north of Lake Hoan Kiem, locally referred to simply as "The Lake."

The streets are not laid out on a grid; I have spent much time being lost. Good luck finding someone who speaks English or even French. Still, Hanoi has quickly grasped the concepts of the glam slam and the good deal. It has stores that would do Paris, New York or Tokyo proud. The locally made merchandise is far more sophisticated than in Hong Kong and China; designer and brand business is just getting going. Obviously, you don't go to Vietnam to buy designer.

You'll find the best stores, but not necessarily the best prices, on **Nha Tho,** a short street in the heart of the shopping district, on the side of **Nha Chung,** a more mainstream shopping street. Nha Chung means "Church Street"; the street runs alongside St. Joseph's Cathedral. The good stores include **Song,** 5 and 7 Nha Tho (☎ 848/289-650); **Mosaique,** 22 Nha Tho (☎ 844/928-6181); **Kien Boutique,** 18 To Tich (☎ 844/928-6835); **Nguyen Freres,** 3 Phan Chu Trinh St. (☎ 844/933-1699); and **LaCasa,** 12 Nha Tho (☎ 844/828-9616).

HO CHI MINH CITY (SAIGON)

While it is written Ho Chi Minh City in newspapers and magazine articles, most people still use Saigon when they refer to the southern city and former capital of Vietnam.

Several of the best stores in Hanoi also have branches in Saigon. I don't think **Song** here is nearly as good as in Hanoi, but I could have hit it on a bad day—and Song in Hanoi has changed a lot lately. Saigon also has a branch of **Nguyen Freres,** 2 Dong Khoi St. (☎ 848/823-9459) one of the best furniture and home-style shops in Hanoi.

The main market building (this is an indoor market), **Ben Thanh Market**, is filled with stalls selling clothes, souvenirs, silk tops for $5, wigs, makeup and sunglasses (Ray Bans, $3). Illegal DVDs tend to be hidden but can be found. Entire rows are full of shoe and handbag dealers. The foodstuffs are to the rear and left—avoid the fish department perhaps.

The market—and most of the shopping—is on a grid of streets called **District One,** which may be written as D1 on maps. The main shopping streets are Dong Khoi, HaiBa Trug, Le Thank Ton and Le Loi. For those in a hurry, **Kong Khoi Street** has just about everything you might want, from silks to lacquer. For me, I'll take the string of shops on **Le Loi** that sell silk clothing just as good as the designer line Dosa—I'd swear they came from Bergdorf's. **Orchids**, 84-86 Le Loi St., is a good one to try.

WHERE TO STAY

Park Hyatt Saigon

This town has other hotels, but forget about them. If you can't get a room here, change your dates of travel or save your dong until you can spring for the best. The hotel is walking distance to everything, is drop-dead gorgeous, wonderful, heavenly and is a welcome respite from the motorcycles outside. The food is great; I suggest you eat here at least once a day. Every detail of the hotel is sublime, from the room decor to the jazzy little free map of the city they give you to the low-cost dry cleaning. (Send out all your clothes.) 2 Lam Son Sq. ☎ **848/ 824-1234.** www.saigon.park.hyatt.com.

Index by Store & Market

See also Index by Destination on p. 493.

Index by Destination

This index is not a complete directory of where to find the stores in this guide; some stores have hundreds of locations worldwide and would be difficult to catalog. Instead, these listings and page numbers refer to specific addresses in the text. Note that one-of-a-kind stores are italicized for emphasis, while chains and multiples are not.

Photo Credits

p 1: © Tom Craig/Alamy and Photodisc/Alamy; p 16: © D. Hurst/Alamy; p 34: © ABC Carpet & Home; p 37: © Anthropologie; p 38: © Asprey; p 45: © Gump's; p 46: © Hermés; p 51: © Liberty; p 58: © Shanghai Tang; p 59: © Takashimaya; p 64: © Blanc de Chine; p 67: © www.shopadidas.com; p 71: © Kleinfeld; p 73: © Flickr/corig123; p 76: © Loro Piana; p 81: © www.doverstreetmarket.com; p 88: © Cleo; p 92: © Venilo; p 98: © Isabella Oliver; p 107: © Jilli Blackwood; p 109: © Image Source Pink/Alamy; p 111: © www.AlainMikli.com; p 125: © Chanel; p 127: © Judith Leiber; p 133: © Paula Virgilio; p 138: © Gem Palace; p 147: © Louboutin; p 154: © www.suzhou-cobblers.com; p 159: © Comstock/Jupiter Images; p 163: © Kiss My Face; p 178: © Dr. Hauschka; p 180: © Amore Pacific; p 183: © Jurlique; p 192: © Belli; p 196: © Malin + Goetz; p 198: © Sabon; p 199: © St. Tropez; p 200: © Henry Poole; p 203: © Jack Spade; p 213: © Vilebrequin; p 216: © Etro; p 231: © Carhartt; p 242: © Turnbull & Asser; p 247: © Elemis; p 256: © Henry Poole; p 261: © Jupiter Images/Creatas/Alamy; p 263: © Bugaboo; p 272: © Hanna Anderson; p 277: © Dior; p 281: © Shoo Shoo; p 282: © American Girl; p 291: © Harajuku Lovers; p 296: © Top Shop; p 298: © Digital Vision/Alamy; p 300: © Hastens; p 313: © Pratesi; p 329: © Forgotten Shanghai; p 338: © Agraria; p 343: © Le Creuset; p 347: © Flickr/Rachel Best; p 351: © TableArt; p 358: © Marimekko; p 360: © Borough Market; p 364: © Stephane Cardinale/People Avenue/Corbis; p 372: © PCL/Alamy; p 373: © Peter Horree/Alamy; p 380: © La Maison du Chocolat; p 386: © Ineeka, Inc.; p 389: © Murray's Cheese Shop; p 391: © Soy Vay; p 394: © Online Stores, Inc.; p 396: © Picture Contact/Alamy; p 399: © Architectural Artifacts; p 404: © Archie McPhee; p 413: © Iain Masterton/Alamy; p 416: © Yadid Levy/Alamy; p 420: © Clive Limpkin/Alamy; p 425: © Pegaz/Alamy; p 435: © Michael Jenner/Alamy; p 441: © Gavin Hellier/Robert Harding World Imagery/Getty Images; p 449: © Asia-Pix/Alamy; p 451: © Art Kowalsky/Alamy; p 460: © Brent Winebrenner/Lonely Planet Images; p 463: © Juergen Henkelmann Photography/Alamy; p 467: © Adam Eastland/Alamy